Cases and Materials on
UK and EC Competition Law

First Edition

Kirsty Middleton
Lecturer in Law, University of Strathclyde

Barry Rodger
Professor of Law, University of Strathclyde

Angus MacCulloch
Lecturer in Law, University of Manchester

OXFORD
UNIVERSITY PRESS

OXFORD

UNIVERSITY PRESS

Great Clarendon Street, Oxford OX2 6DP

Oxford University Press is a department of the University of Oxford.
It furthers the University's objective of excellence in research, scholarship,
and education by publishing worldwide in

Oxford New York

Auckland Bangkok Buenos Aires Cape Town Chennai
Dar es Salaam Delhi Hong Kong Istanbul Karachi Kolkata
Kuala Lumpur Madrid Melbourne Mexico City Mumbai Nairobi
São Paulo Shanghai Taipei Tokyo Toronto

Oxford is a registered trade mark of Oxford University Press
in the UK and in certain other countries

Published in the United States
by Oxford University Press Inc., New York

A Blackstone Press book

British Library Cataloguing in Publication Data

Data available

Library of Congress Cataloging in Publication Data

Data available

ISBN 0 19 925927 5

1 3 5 7 9 10 8 6 4 2

Typeset in ITC Stone Serif, ITC Stone Sans and Congress Sans
by RefineCatch Limited, Bungay, Suffolk
Printed in Great Britain by
Antony Rowe Ltd, Chippenham, Wiltshire

OUTLINE CONTENTS

DETAILED CONTENTS

PREFACE

Competition law has gained new significance in the UK and the EC in recent years and is now well established as an undergraduate course. The subject is strongly oriented towards EC law and underpinned by economics, both difficult subjects for the law student. The intention of this text therefore is to equip students with a broad range of materials—case extracts, statutory extracts and relevant academic writings—to enable them to study and make sense of this fast-developing and often complex area of law. We have endeavoured to source extracts from a wide variety of primary and secondary materials, not easily located elsewhere. This is the first text of its kind to include UK as well as EC materials in recognition of the developing significance and impact of the domestic regime and the combination also reflects the fact that the Competition Act 1998 introduced EC jurisprudence to domestic competition law. The text will therefore appeal to undergraduate students studying the optional subject of competition law as part of their LLB or BA.

Although this is essentially a text on UK and EC competition law, reference is made to US antitrust where appropriate, given its increasing influence in a domestic and EC context. The new Enterprise Act 2002 also brings UK competition law closer to the US regime and hence, an appreciation of US antitrust is important.

A number of crucial changes have taken place in UK and EC competition law in the past few years, reinforcing the rapid pace of change in competition matters and making this text all the more relevant and topical. The timing of these developments however, made completion of this text a particularly difficult undertaking. The Commission's new enforcement regulation, Reg 1/2003, was passed on 26 November 2002 and will enter into force on 1 May 2004. The significance of this development cannot be understated and the new regulation marks the most important change in the Community's competition law process in over 40 years. The official version of the new regulation, which was finally made available in January 2003, is largely reproduced in Chapter 3. At a UK level, the enactment of the Enterprise Bill on 7 November 2002 further coincided with copy proofs. This important piece of legislation makes further substantive changes to the existing competition law regime in the UK and enhances the competition law enforcement process significantly. The competition element of the new Act will enter into force in spring 2003 and academics will appreciate the difficulties we faced in noting the institutional changes this Act introduces. Recent proposed changes to the EC Merger framework were also briefly noted, where possible. The new draft merger regulation, published on 10 December 2002, was not in a format that enabled inclusion, and with so many issues still to be decided, commentary at proof stage was kept to a minimum.

None of these most recent developments have, as yet, bedded in and consequently there was little point in considering them in isolation from the present framework. Although the Fair Trading Act 1973 will largely be repealed by the

Enterprise Act 2002, students need to appreciate the legal framework applicable to monopolies and mergers embodied in the earlier legislation to understand the rationale for the recent statute, and we consider this in Chapters 7 and 9 in some detail. The same considerations apply in respect of the new Community competition law enforcement regime and proposed merger reforms.

We owe a great deal to a number of people who assisted us in completing this task. First, thanks must go to Jeremy Stein and Alistair McQueen, formerly of Blackstone Press Limited for commissioning this project, and to all the staff at OUP who were involved in the smooth handover in November 2001, in particular Helen Adams and Barbara Laing for their good humour, patience and efficiency. We were also fortunate to have an excellent research assistant, Jonathan Galloway, whose efforts proved invaluable, particularly in the later stages. Finally, we would like to thank the anonymous referees for their supportive comments on earlier drafts and colleagues, past and present.

The law is presented to 31 July 2002 although we have taken into account the important developments noted above.

Kirsty Middleton
Barry J Rodger
Angus MacCulloch
Glasgow, November 2002

DEDICATION

For Patric and Riley
K.M.
For Susan, Kirsty and Euan
B.J.R.
For Lucy
A.M.

ACKNOWLEDGEMENTS

We are grateful to the following publishers and authors for granting us permission to use material for the book and especially those who took the time to personally respond.

Basic Books for Robert H. Bork, *The Antitrust Paradox: A Policy at War with Itself*, copyright © 1978 by Basic Books Inc. reprinted by permission of Basic Books, a member of Perseus Books, L.L.C.

Richard Hart of Hart Publishing, for G. Amato, *Antitrust and the Bounds of Power*, published by Hart Publishing, Oxford 1997 and Rodger, B.J., & MacCulloch, A. (eds) *The UK Competition Act 1998: A New Era for UK Competition Law*, Hart Publishing, Oxford, 2000.

Kluwer Law International for B.E. Hawk, 'System Failure: Vertical Restraints and EC Competition Law' (1995) 33 *CMLRev* 973 and Sinnaeve, A. & Slot, P.J. 'The New Regulation on State Aid Procedures' 36 (1999) 1153.

Greg Smith of Sweet and Maxwell and respective authors for extracts from European Competition Law Review articles.

Tony Mason of Manchester University Press for Wilks, S., *In the Public Interest, Competition Policy and the Monopolies and Mergers Commission, 1999*.

Brenda Sufrin, University of Bristol and Professor Richard Whish, Kings College, London for 'Article 85 and the Rule of Reason' in (1987) 7 YEL.

TABLE OF CASES

Where extracts from cases are reproduced the cases and relevant page numbers are shown in **bold**.

Alphabetical Table

Numerical Table

European Court of Justice

Courts of First Instance

TABLE OF STATUTES

Page numbers in **bold** indicate that the text is reproduced in full.

TABLE OF STATUTORY INSTRUMENTS

Page numbers in **bold** indicate that the text is reproduced in full.

TABLE OF UNITED STATES STATUTES

Page numbers in **bold** indicate that the text is reproduced in full.

TABLE OF EUROPEAN MATERIAL

Page numbers in **bold** indicate that the text is reproduced in full.

1

Competition law and policy

SECTION 1: **Introduction**

What is meant by competition? *The Oxford English Dictionary* defines competition as the 'striving of two or more for the same object'. In a commercial context, competition is defined as 'rivalry in the market'.

Willimsky, S., 'The Concept(s) of Competition'
[1997] 1 ECLR, p. 54

Competition is the principal regulator of commercial forces in a capitalist market, presuming that individual competitors' motivating force derives from the pursuit of self-interest. The struggle for superiority in the marketplace is defined by the objective to persuade consumers on grounds of quality and value to make a particular purchase.

. . .

Competition policy is deeply embedded in the way one views human nature and the role of society and the state. The liberal view of the state and man, driven by self-interest as the supreme motivating force, favoured a more classical model of competition. Posner, for example, clearly favoured the view of individuals as rational maximisers of wealth. To advocate a more regulatory and interventionist model would, according to this view, unnecessarily interfere with the proper quasi-Darwinist pursuit for superiority and the natural selection of the most efficient market participants. It is believed that only selection as expressed through consumer choice, would lead to an equilibrium of demand and supply and hence further the interests of society as a whole. Adam Smith's 'invisible hand' as opposed to the very visible hand of the state would, according to this view, lead to the best overall solution.

Marxist social theory and the way human nature is perceived leads to the diametrically opposed view of competition. It would necessarily lead to a system whereby political and economic strands of thought would inevitably be closely intertwined with the perception of man as only one part of a greater web of society. Of course, it has to be remembered that even the crudest capitalist systems present a framework with a number of highly complex social, economic and political strata. However, the underlying value base is freedom as opposed to actual social equality and social justice and this general principle forms the foundations of commercial activity, assuming that the commercial and political ends are not separable.

Is there a difference between competition and competition policy?

Doern, G.B., Chapter 2, 'Comparative Competition Policy: Boundaries and Levels of Political Analysis', in Doern, B., and Wilks, S., *Comparative Competition Policy: National Institutions in a Global Market*
1996, OUP, p. 7

Competition policy consists of those policies and actions of the state intended to prevent certain restraints of trade by private firms. Stated more positively, it is policy intended to promote rivalry among firms, buyers, and sellers through actions in areas of activity such as mergers, abuse of dominance, cartels, conspiracies in restraints of trade, misleading advertising, and related criminal and economic offences that are held to be anti-competitive.

. . .

Competition and competition policy are not the same thing. However, understanding the former is crucial, and it starts with economics and economists. Understanding the latter means one has to deal with politics, because it is states that make public policies, and political interests and institutions that determine their implementation in practice.

NOTE: Whish notes that 'the competitive process contains an inevitable paradox. Some competitors win. By being the most innovative, the most responsive to customers' wishes, and by producing goods or services in the most efficient way possible, one firm may succeed in seeing off its rivals. It would be strange, and indeed harmful, if that firm could then be condemned for being a monopolist'. Whish, R., *Competition Law*, 4th edn, p. 11. Do you agree? Does the elimination of rivalry have to be anti-competitive?

Bishop, S. and Walker, M., *The Economics of EC Competition Law, Concepts, Application and Measurement*
Sweet & Maxwell, Chapter 1, pp. 13–15

On an intuitive level, effective competition might be equated with the process of rivalry. Such a definition is intuitively appealing since rivalry is the means by which a competitively structured industry creates and confers its benefits. Moreover, competition law investigations often arise in those situations in which rivalry is eliminated, e.g. by merger or through a cartel agreement. But this definition of effective competition provides no benchmarks for how much rivalry is required for competition to be effective and invites the erroneous conclusion that the elimination of rivalry must always be deemed to be anti-competitive or restrictive of competition.

. . .

Rather than always being anti-competitive, reductions in rivalry may be pro-competitive in the sense that they increase consumer welfare.

Hence, such a definition of effective competition is entirely inappropriate for the purposes of competition law. It would make rivalry an end in itself, regardless of whether the elimination of some rivalry had any substantive negative effect on consumer welfare. One must recognise that all market economies require there to be some elimination of rivalry, since this is necessary to every integration or co-ordination of productive economic efforts and to the specialisation of effort. As Bork notes:

> No firm, no partnership, no corporation, no economic unit containing more than a single person could exist without the elimination of some kinds of rivalry between persons.

SECTION 2: **Perfect v workable competition**

Willimsky, S., 'The Concept(s) of Competition'
[1997] 1 ECLR p. 54

The basic ideological premise about human nature also has to be viewed in context with the objectives of competition. 'Perfect competition' is a goal in which economic resources are allocated between different goods and services in exactly those quantities which reflect consumer demand, reflected in the price consumers are prepared to pay for goods. This basic utopian ideal is, of course, very difficult to attain and some would even question whether it would be desirable to pursue in any case.

There are, for example, sectors which ought to be 'inefficient', be it for economic reasons (for example agriculture) or for reasons of safety, such as transport. Sometimes, for R&D purposes, for instance, experts in a particular field have to be granted 'time out' from the competitive race in order to develop new drugs, etc., in situations where the drive for efficiency would not allow for such an investment in terms of time and money.

Allocative efficiency is also a term which denotes the state of a market in which resources are allocated precisely in accordance with consumer demand. Pursuant to the neo-classical theory, it is presumed that under allocative efficiency, where competition is perfect, a producer will increase output to the point at which marginal cost and marginal revenue, the net addition to revenue of selling the last unit, coincide. Consequently, a reduction in his own output cannot affect the market price and so there would be no reason to limit it.

Productive efficiency is achieved when a producer is unable to sell above cost: if he did, he would lose customers. He would of course not sell below it, presuming that each producer wishes to maximise profits. If a producer were to charge above cost, other competitors would enter the market in the hope of undercutting the other competitors, charging below price and therefore acquiring a large market share. Eventually, the point will be reached where price and average cost of producing goods coincide, i.e. price would not rise above cost. The combined effect of allocative and productive efficiency is that society's wealth is maximised.

NOTE: Recognising that perfect competition is a 'basic utopian idea', some economists developed the theory of 'workable competition' which is regarded as a compromise approach. The theory of workable competition rests on the assumption that firms should strive to attain the most competitive structure possible and has been invoked on a number of occasions by the Commission and the European Court.

In Case 26/76 *Metro-SB-Grossmarkte GmbH & Co. KG* v *Commission* [1977] ECR 1875 the European Court held that:

> The requirement contained in Articles 3 and 85 of the EEC Treaty that competition shall not be distorted implies the existence on the market of workable competition, that is to say the degree of competition necessary to ensure the observance of the basic requirements and attainment of the objectives of the Treaty, in particular the creation of a single market achieving conditions similar to those of a domestic market.

FURTHER READING

Furse, M., 'The role of competition policy: a survey' [1996] ECLR 250.
Wood, D.P., 'The Role of Economics and Economists in Competition Cases' [1999] OECD Journal of Competition Law and Policy, Vol. 1/1.

NOTE: Mention must also be made of a more recent theory upon which competition law might be based, the theory of 'contestable competition' which emphasises the need for freedom to enter and leave a market without incurring costs. Such a market need not be perfectly competitive. The application of the theory has focused almost exclusively on deregulated industries e.g. air transport.

SECTION 3: Goals of competition

What are the policy objectives of competition? Should competition serve non-political goals? Should the state interfere to re-create a competitive structure? If so, to what extent? Giuliano Amato discusses some of these issues and the ideological tensions inherent in the competition process in his book, *Antitrust and the Bounds of Power*.

Amato, G., *Antitrust and the Bounds of Power*
Oxford, Hart Publishing, 1997, pp. 2–3

Antitrust law was, as we know, invented neither by the technicians of commercial law (though they became its first specialists) nor by economists themselves (though they supplied its most solid cultural background). It was instead desired by politicians and (in Europe) by scholars attentive to the pillars of the democratic systems, who saw it as an answer (if not indeed 'the' answer) to a crucial problem for democracy: the emergence from the company or firm, as an expression of the fundamental freedom of individuals, of the opposite phenomenon of private power; a power devoid of legitimation and dangerously capable of infringing not just economic freedom of other private individuals, but also the balance of public decisions exposed to its domineering strength.

On the basis of the principles of liberal democracy, the problem was twofold and constituted a real dilemma. Citizens have the right to have their freedoms acknowledged and to exercise them; but just because they are freedoms they must never become coercion, an imposition on others. Power in liberal democratic societies is, in the public sphere, recognized only in those who hold it legitimately on the basis of law, while, in the private sphere, it does not go beyond the limited prerogatives allotted within the firm to its owner. Beyond those limits, private power in a liberal democracy (by contrast with what has occurred, and continues to occur, in societies of other inspirations) is in principle seen to be abusive, and must be limited so that no-one can take decisions that produce effects on others without their assent being given. On the basis of the same principles, the power of government exists specifically to guarantee against the emergence of phenomena of that sort; that is, it exists to protect the freedoms of each against attacks and abuses of others. But this, which is its task, is also its limitation: abuses forbidden for individuals are not allowed for rulers either. Here, then, is the dilemma. How can private power be prevented from becoming a threat to the freedoms of others? But at the same time, how can power conferred on institutions for this purpose be prevented from itself enlarging to the point of destroying the very freedoms it ought to protect.

. . .

What is coming out again is, then, the crucial issue of the boundary and hence the risk to be run depending where it is set, the risk of 'too much' public power or, contrawise, 'too much' private power.

The dilemma, as we said at the outset, has its roots in the very principles of liberal democracy, affecting first and foremost the interpretations and translations they are given. It is however wrong to think that antitrust law, now free of the initial, improper burden of democratic efficiency, guided by events and the refined doctrines of economists to pay attention to economic efficiency alone, is now immunized against the dilemma and consequently running along such well-defined tracks as to be sheltered from the choices it requires. The error lies not so much in the intervening awareness of the separation between democratic efficiency, which is actually beyond the direct antitrust horizon, and economic efficiency. The error lies in accepting as the truth the one dimensional economic efficiency mentioned earlier. Why should only the restriction of output of a given product, such as to shift demand to second-choice products (to do which society is constrained to higher costs with poorer results), be economically inefficient? This certainly is inefficient, and an agreement or concentration leading to such a result should certainly be prohibited by antitrust law. But who says that 'consumer welfare', the pillar of this notion of efficiency, amounts solely to not having to shift to second choice goods, and is hence satisfied where one or a few satisfy the demand for existing products, without output restrictions? Someone has rightly noted that 'there is a strong tendency among economists to define welfare in terms of efficiency in doing accustomed things in an accustomed way'. But might not consumers regard as serving their welfare the diversity of sources of goods and services, the existence of diversified potential for innovation, as much room as possible for market dynamics that favour the new products not yet designed and ways of producing them not yet designed? Can it be said that all this has nothing to do with economic efficiency just because it shakes up the antitrust views of those economists who feel safer with one-dimensional efficiency? The truth is that there is no one single concept of economic efficiency: there are at least two, and their antitrust implications are in the main different.

NOTE: There are two dominant schools of antitrust thought, the Harvard and Chicago schools. The Chicago scholars believe that the fundamental goal of antitrust is, or ought to be, the pursuit of efficiency, or rather the maximisation of allocative efficiency. Certainly, this is a view which Robert Bork, an influential American economist and antitrust lawyer associated with the Chicago school, supports.

Bork, R.H., *The Antitrust Paradox: A Policy at War with Itself*
(Basic Books, 1978, reprinted with a new Introduction and Epilogue, 1993), pp. 90–1
[footnotes omitted]

Antitrust is about the effects of business behavior on consumers. An understanding of the relationship of that behavior to consumer well-being can be gained only through basic economic theory. The economic models involved are essential to all antitrust analysis, but they are simple and require no previous acquaintance with economics to be comprehended. Indeed, since we can hardly expect legislators, judges, and lawyers to be sophisticated economists as well, it is only the fact that the simple ideas of economics are powerful and entirely adequate to this field that makes it conceivable for the law to frame and implement useful policy.

Consumer welfare is greatest when society's economic resources are allocated so that consumers are able to satisfy their wants as fully as technological constraints permit. Consumer welfare, in this sense, is merely another term for the wealth of the nation. Antitrust thus has a built-in preference for material prosperity, but it has nothing to say about the ways prosperity is distributed or used. Those are matters for other laws. Consumer welfare, as the term is used in antitrust, has no sumptuary or ethical component, but permits consumers to define by their expression of wants in the marketplace what things they regard as wealth. Antitrust litigation is not a process for deciding who should be rich or poor, nor can it decide how much wealth should be expended to reduce pollution or undertake to mitigate the anguish of the cross-country skier at the desecration wrought by snowmobiles. It can only increase collective wealth by requiring that any lawful products, whether skis or snowmobiles, be produced and sold under conditions most favorable to consumers.

The role of the antitrust laws, then, lies at that stage of the economic process in which production and distribution of goods and services are organized in accordance with the scale of values that consumers choose by their relative willingness to purchase. The law's mission is to preserve, improve, and reinforce the powerful economic mechanisms that compel businesses to respond to consumers. 'From a social point of view,' as Frank H. Knight puts it, 'this process may be viewed under two aspects, (a) the assignment or *allocation* of the available productive forces and materials among the various lines of industry, and (b) the effective *coordination* of the various means of production in each industry into such groupings as will produce the greatest result.'

These two factors may conveniently be called *allocative efficiency* and *productive efficiency*. (When, for convenience, the word 'efficiency' alone is used, productive efficiency is meant.) These two types of efficiency make up the overall efficiency that determines the level of our society's wealth, or consumer welfare. The whole task of antitrust can be summed up as the effort to improve allocative efficiency without impairing productive efficiency so greatly as to produce either no gain or a net loss in consumer welfare. That task must be guided by basic economic analysis, otherwise the law acts blindly upon forces it does not understand and produces results it does not intend.

NOTE: The Chicago school of economists believe that in free markets consumer welfare is optimised, rendering state intervention unnecessary. Even monopolistic markets are acceptable to the Chicago economists and intervention is only required in extreme cases where new entrants are prohibited from the market. However, Bork's thesis, that economic efficiency is the sole pursuit of antitrust, has been criticised. See e.g. Fox, E.M., and Sullivan, L.A., 'Antitrust-Retrospective and Prospective: Where are we coming from? Where are we going?' (1987) 62 New York Univ. Law Review 936.

Rodger, B.J., 'The Oligopoly Problem and the Concept of Collective Dominance: EC Developments in the Light of US Trends in Antitrust Law and Policy'
Columbia Journal of European Law, Vol. 2, No 1, 1995/96, pp. 28–30 [footnotes omitted]

The 'Harvard School' of analysis had its origins in the 1930s and its work developed into the structure-conduct-performance paradigm within economics: 'Before anyone starts prescribing struc-tural changes to improve performance he had better have some clear and convincing notions about the way oligopolistic structure affects conduct'. Proponents of this paradigm sought to provide the link between the three elements. The economists would justify structurally de-concentrative remed-ies on an empirical basis, by analyzing each of the three aspects within an industry. The empirical associations thus discovered would reveal the appropriate ramifications for public policy. Though the paradigm has been fiercely criticized, it is still enlightening to view oligopoly antitrust policy through the perspective of the Harvard School: the history and traditions of US antitrust law form an essential backdrop to the continuing debate about its role and purposes. As Sullivan commented, 'American antitrust law is not only about "law" but also a socio-political statement about our society'.

During much of the early development of antitrust law, the political consensus reflected in the law was that high concentration lessened competition—a notion derived from a basically liberal vision of society. This mainstream antitrust tradition was eclectic and its political input was embraced and encapsulated by industrial organization economic theorists, the main link between the economic and the socio-political liberal goals being the skepticism that markets adequately control market power. This is one of Sullivan's main contentions, namely that 'behind the theorizing, a political ideology can often be identified'.

The Harvard, or Structuralist, School of industrial economics placed great emphasis on market structure as the root of market failure. In particular, it stressed that excessive concentration of market power resulted in undeservedly high profits. Parallel to the academic prominence the theory achieved in the 1960s and 1970s, the Warren Court appeared to adopt a similar broad-based appeal to social and political objections with concern for increasing concentration, particularly in dealing with horizontal mergers. An essential element in this mainstream tradition was its more open acknowledgment of political objectives, though in practice, as Sullivan highlights, this skeptical tradition is both pragmatic and seldom doctrinaire.

The basic features of the Chicago School of antitrust law and economic analysis were formulated by the work of Aaron Director in the 1950s, and developed by his students—Bowman, Bork, McGee and Telsen, among others. This tradition approaches antitrust problems through the 'lens of price theory': 'In their intellectual universe, antitrust is embodied in a reductionist paradigm; antitrust concerns the functioning of markets; microeconomics is the study of the functioning of markets; therefore antitrust is microeconomics'.

The Chicago School tends to focus on two 'truths'. The first is the advocacy of the efficient allocation of resources by the market: antitrust ought only to intervene in cases where not to do so would result in the inefficient allocation of resources. A preliminary criticism of this approach is that the Chicago School adopts static models as the basis of its efficiency principle. The main problem, however, lies in the second 'truth,' derived from the first: that 'Chicago beliefs are only compatible with the most minimal law'. Consequently the role of antitrust law and government intervention in the functioning of markets is greatly reduced. This is, perhaps, a logical consequence of the Chicago School's presumption of the efficiency of firms and the functioning of markets, but, as Fox observes, the latter is not a 'descriptive observation . . . [but] . . . simply argument supporting the normative claim that people (including firms) should be left free to act and that there is almost never a higher social interest.' Thus the aim of the Chicago School seems to be 'keeping government out' and always seeking the least disruptive way to correct market failures. Flynn concludes that behind the Chicago School lies 'a simplistic form of deductive reasoning reaffirming the theological postulates underlying the model without regard for the reality under investigation or the moral ends of the law in question and the moral consequences those ends dictate'. In any event, the instalment of President Reagan in 1980 (who promised to curtail government's role in business), resulted in the administration's adoption of the Chicago School approach, and as a result, government enforcement of antitrust came to an ebb. However, even during that period, the Supreme Court never fully embraced the concept that only efficiency mattered.

As observed above, the two starting points of specific analysis—structure and conduct—are inextricably linked. Though the theoretical differences in approach are important, it is largely a matter of emphasis, linked to wider perceptions of the kind of 'important social judgements that should be made'.

The rapprochement between the two approaches has been particularly noted by Larner and Meehan. They comment on the recent rise of a new school of industrial economics in response to the Chicago School, seeking to analyze the effect of strategic behavior on competition under certain circumstances. Although wary of overemphasizing the importance of concentration, they recognize the need for further research. The identification of market power is crucial, but it is no substitute for in-depth analysis of the market. Larner and Meehan find that the structural concept of competition is analytically and practically admirable as a policy norm because of its essential simplicity. But although structural analysis is an essential element, it is inadequate: they conclude that 'while behavior is now subject to closer scrutiny and analysis than in the structural view, concentration is still an early and important component in any competitive analysis'.

Rex Ahdar, 'Consumers' Redistribution of Income and the Purpose of Competition Law'

[2002] ECLR, 341–353

No one would deny that competition law is, broadly speaking, designed to advance the lot of consumers. Even Bork agrees: '[a]ntitrust is about the effects of business behaviour on consumers'. But, as we shall see, Bork's conception of consumers is strikingly at odds with the normal understanding. To understand the issues more fully it is helpful to invoke Oliver Williamson's trade-off model. This depicts the economic effects of a merger that results in both an increase in market power and cost savings (see diagram p. 8).

Based on certain strict assumptions (the merging firms are duopolists, the product is homogeneous, etc. Williamson's model sought to show that society may still be better off despite the

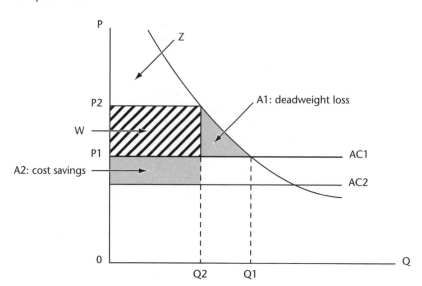

monopoly enhancement that transpires. Following the merger, the firm's market power has increased: the firm reduces its output from Q1 to Q2 and price rises from P1 to P2. The loss in allocative efficiency is represented by triangle A1 (the deadweight loss). This is the bad news. The good news is that the acquisition generates cost savings represented by the firm's level of average costs dropping, postmerger, from AC1 to AC2. The net allocative effect is ascertained by comparing the triangle (A1) with the rectangle (A2). Williamson demonstrated that a merger promising 'nontrivial economies—say greater than 2 per cent—will generally yield a net-efficiency gain'. Now there have been all sorts of qualifications and criticisms levied at this model which need not detain us here. What is of present concern is another effect of the increased market power. This is the income distribution effect (or wealth transfer).

The striped rectangle, W, immediately above rectangle A2, 'represents a loss of consumers' surplus (gain in monopoly profits) that the merger produces'. Income (or wealth) is transferred from consumers to producers, from the purchasers of the product to the owners of the company. Is this redistribution a concern of competition law? This issue has generated much debate, but before revisiting it, it is important to note that, generally speaking, vigorous competition policy operates to advance both efficiency and distributive goals simultaneously. Curtailing monopolies, oligopolies and cartels will generally enhance both aggregate social wealth and the consumers' share of that wealth. Kenneth Elzinga explains:

> Antitrust enforcement generally serves to help those at the low end of the income distribution range without decreasing efficiency. Antitrust achieves this double benefit when it promotes efficiency in resource allocation by preventing the cartelization or monopolization of a market shopped in by low-income buyers. The reason is straightforward: prices will be lower in the market so that for any given income, however low, a larger basket of goods and services can be purchased. Antitrust policy, therefore, need not concern itself directly with increasing the purchasing power of the poor because it accomplishes this indirectly when it prohibits cartels and monopolies in the single-minded pursuit of efficiency.

Actually, it is probably more accurate to say antitrust policy achieves the goals of superior economic performance (growth, innovation, efficiency) and 'equity' goals (greater income equality, dispersion of concentrated economic and political power, fostering business opportunity and so on) through the single-minded pursuit of competition.

Competition policy generally harmonises the goals of efficiency and egalitarian income distribution. There are occasions however, when, as Williamson's model demonstrates, an anti-competitive arrangement or merger may be beneficial in terms of net efficiency and yet result in a transfer of income from consumers to producers. There are two major responses to this phenomenon: first, ignore the redistribution, or, secondly, address it.

Ignore redistribution

The stance of Chicagoans, amongst others, is to ignore the transfer of wealth. If it is a concern at all, it is not a matter for competition law. Other arms of public policy are better suited to deal with the phenomenon. But what about consumers? Was not antitrust, according to Bork, 'about the effects of business behaviour on consumers'? Bork maintains that the sole goal of antitrust law is to forward 'consumer welfare'. How is consumer welfare advanced by customers paying higher prices in the form of monopoly profits that enrich the pockets of the corporate owners? The Chicagoan answer is that consumer welfare is really another name for allocative efficiency or total welfare:

Consumer welfare is greatest when society's economic resources are allocated so that consumers are able to satisfy their wants as fully as technological constraints permit. Consumer welfare, in this sense, is merely another term for the wealth of the nation. Antitrust thus has a built-in preference for material prosperity, but it has nothing to say about the ways prosperity is distributed or used.

To backtrack a little: total welfare comprises both consumer surplus (or welfare) and producer surplus. Defining consumer welfare as total welfare enables consumer welfare to be 'advanced' so long as producers gain—and even though consumers' lot is worsened. When monopoly occurs, a consumer surplus is expunged and becomes a producer surplus (monopoly profits) but this is fine since total welfare is still enhanced. Thus, the redistribution should be ignored.

In conventional neoclassical welfare economics the redistribution of income is, as Williamson puts it, 'a matter of indifference' and 'is treated as a wash'. Scherer affirms: '[i]n the standard analysis of efficiency, the redistribution is of no concern. It merely reflects a robbing of Peter (the consumer) to pay Paul (the producer), and since Paul may be more deserving than Peter, who knows whether society is worse off as a consequence?' This stance is sometimes reinforced by invoking Hume's law, 'that a dollar is a dollar'.

Hume's law means that if two persons are bidding at an auction for a seaside cottage and a poor homeless family is outbid by a wealthy family wishing to own a seaside weekender, the result is efficient. The house has been placed in the hands of those who offer the more dollar votes. The effect of Hume's law is to divorce consideration of the allocation of resources from consideration of the distribution of wealth (or income).

A sort of conjuring trick is involved here. Producers (the minority) are defined to be consumers whose welfare interests count equally, dollar for dollar, with those of consumers who are not producers (the majority). Bork brazenly glides over this.

Those who continue to buy after a monopoly is formed pay more for the same output, and that shifts income from them to the monopoly and its owners, who are also consumers. This is not a deadweight loss due to the restriction in output but merely a shift in income between two classes of consumers.

Consumers still benefit because producers are consumers too. Two supporting defences are sometimes advanced. First, submits Bork, some consumers are richer and more deserving than producers. Elzinga's example of artists who make handcraft porcelain might be what Bork had in mind. Would this justify price fixing by poorly renumerated producers? Antitrust law traditionally says 'no', indeed, a New Zealand decision refused to countenance price fixing by rural grape growers whose product would eventually be consumed by affluent, urban wine drinkers. Yet while there are some products manufactured by struggling producers and acquired by the rich, the vast majority of goods and services (electricity, bread, milk, petrol, dentistry) are not in this category. A second defence is similarly unconvincing. Some producers, being companies, are composed of numerous shareholders. In other words, some consumers may be producers. Again that is true but only for a minority of the population, and the more affluent section at that.

When the substantive merits of the wealth transfer are difficult to defend, the Chicagoan gambit is to stress the inappropriateness of entertaining the distributional question at all. Williamson acknowledged that the redistribution of income under monopoly produces 'social discontent'. Bork grudgingly conceded it may cause some but this was a matter for the legislature, not the courts, to address. The latter are simply the wrong institution to make 'these unstructured interpersonal comparisons'. The decision whether, to use Scherer's parlance, Peter is more deserving than Paul (or vice versa) is simply too subjective: '[t]here is no common denominator between these values, and there is no economics, no social science, no systematized knowledge of any sort that can provide criteria for making the trade-off decision'. Attempts to evaluate distributional matters is simply 'distracting' and to do it thoroughly would 'introduce horrendous complexities in which it is surely undesirable to mire the processes of antitrust'. Antitrust is better suited to the advancement of allocative efficiency leaving income distribution objectives to 'the province of taxation, expenditure, and transfer payment activities'. Dealing with distributional concerns in competition law is tantamount to 'tinkering and is apt to be unrewarding, because a massive reshaping of the system is really needed'.

Address redistribution
Let us return to the Chicagoan definition of consumer welfare as total welfare (or allocative efficiency). This is plainly wrong. Consumer welfare means 'consumer surplus'. Returning to Williamson's diagram, the consumer surplus prior to the merger was the entire area above AC1, (the triangle A1, the rectangle W, and Z, the white area above W). Following the merger, the consumer surplus has shrunk to Z alone—A1 is totally expunged, a deadweight social loss, and W redounds to the producer. Consumer surplus captures the notion that consumers receive more value from consuming a good than the money value they must pay to the seller. In less technical language it represents 'the direct and explicit economic benefits received by consumers of a particular product as measured by its price and quality'. It 'embraces what individual consumers are entitled to expect from a competitive economy'. Bork's redefinition of consumer welfare was counterintuitive and disingenuous, 'an Orwellian term of art that has little or nothing to do with the welfare of true consumers'!

The redistribution of income is said to be 'neutral'. This is a strange concept of neutrality for it means countenancing the betterment of a small, generally richer, collection of 'consumers' (corporate owners) at the expense of the multitude of less affluent consumers. How can a phenomenon (monopoly) which 'tends to tilt the income and wealth distributions toward greater inequality' be regarded with benign indifference? This link between monopoly and maldistribution of wealth and income is not pure speculation. There is some empirical evidence that indicates that monopoly power, past and present, has contributed significantly to the above average wealth of the most wealthy families.

The fact that antitrust law operates to advance a more equal distribution of income in society does not mean that competition law is the principal vehicle to secure some fair overall distribution of wealth. No one is arguing competition law is the major or a sufficient redistributive tool. Its contribution here is modest yet, nonetheless, it is still a contribution. Equitable redistribution is another of the many significant indirect benefits or by-products of a policy promoting effective competition.

Economists seem squeamish about the prospect of making value judgments. This seems to be part of a larger project to fashion their discipline into a value-free science. The futility of this venture has been well-exposed by others. Suffice to say economics has ineradicable normative premises that are necessarily political, ideological, and subjective. Fortunately, economists are spared the task of making decisions of a distributional nature as legislatures, including New Zealand's, are quite prepared to say one sector of society is more deserving than another. As Brodley comments: 'to hold that producers perform a civic duty when they systematically take from buyers the entire economic surplus is an Orwellian result that no democratic government could long sustain'. And so history has shown.

Robert Lande has argued convincingly that Congress's main goal in passing the Sherman Act was to protect ordinary consumers from the evils of monopoly:

Congress's primary aim was to enable consumers to purchase products at competitive prices. Artificially high prices were condemned not for causing allocative inefficiency but for 'unfairly' transforming consumers' wealth into monopoly profits. All purchasers, whether consumers or businesses, were given the right to purchase competitively priced goods.

The political reality is that when it comes to deciding whether consumers are more deserving than producers, the verdict is clear cut. Hume's law is nowhere to be found.

Chicagoans and other efficiency-only advocates seek to avoid subjectivity and awkward value judgments by excluding distributional questions from decision-making. Yet the notion of economic efficiency they posit as the sole objective of antitrust is itself a subjective, ideological choice imbued with an implicit value judgment.

If efficiency is judged under the Kaldor-Hicks or wealth maximisation criterion, the costs and benefits of a rule are valued according to the affected persons' willingness to pay (a hypothetical 'one-dollar, one-vote' referendum). If the beneficiaries of the rule could in theory compensate the losers for their losses and still came out ahead—in other words, if the total benefits exceed the total costs—the rule is efficiency-enhancing, even though the theoretical compensation sums are not paid to the losers. The last point is crucial, for it represents the losses incurred by ordinary consumers. Brian Easton explains: '[b]ut the compensation need not occur, so efficiency may increase but some consumers may be worse off, and there is no obvious, value free reason why this situation should be described as an improvement, without consideration of the distributional implications'. A notion of economic efficiency which ignores distributional effects (and the initial distribution of wealth) is hardly neutral in practice for it appears to encourage inequality in the distribution of income throughout society. It is neutral only if you believe helping the wealthy get wealthier is neutral.

NOTE: Note Amato's discussion of competition and the foundations of liberal democracy, see above. What other concerns should competition law protect?

Rodger, B.J., 'Competition Policy, Liberalism and Globalization: A European Perspective'

The Columbia Journal of European Law, Vol. 6, No 3, Fall 2000, pp. 303–304

In practice there are a number of different economic, social and political objectives which may form part of any particular competition policy. It is often the extent to which these other policies do and should play a role that causes the greatest debate, particularly on the basis that they cause tensions with the standards of the liberal rule of law. Some of these other policies have been termed 'extra-competition' policies or 'non-competition law proper' policies and it has often been suggested that competition law should not be concerned with them. This relates to the concern over the legal/political format of the rules and has consequences upon the method of enforcement of the competition rules. Competition law or policy has no fixed content and is dependent to a great extent upon the particular political and social emphases of the legal system in which it operates. It can therefore be justifiably stated that in applying the core economic thesis which informs competition law, any set of appropriate principles and policies may play a part in a coherent competition law system. Indeed, it has been recognized that the fundamental rationale for the introduction of a set of competition policies has been to promote the economy of a given country.

There are a variety of political objectives which may form part of competition policy, of which the following are examples. The prevention of the concentration of economic power is based on the idea that economic corporations should not become more powerful and influential than elected democratic governments. The dual objectives of the regulation of excessive profits and the more fair distribution of wealth are essentially derived from the neo-classical theory's concern with monopolies. The general idea has been fairly topical recently in the UK despite the advanced debate on incentives to new market entrants created by such excessive profits and the ongoing criticism that the redistribution of wealth should not be a concern of competition law. The protection of consumers is a key feature of most competition laws and is of particular and direct interest in the UK, where the link between consumer policy and competition policy is also highlighted in the UK by the existence of one official, the Director General of Fair Trading, who supervises both areas.

Regional policy may seem to be a strange component of competition policy but it can be understood given that competition law is part of an overall policy to promote and enhance a national, or other, economy. Thus, regional policy formed a clear part of UK competition policy under the Fair Trading Act 1973. Further, it constituted an overriding consideration in the analysis of a series of mergers which may have proven specifically detrimental to the Scottish economy and which were prohibited under this regional policy criterion. Regional policy is also important under Community law, specifically in relation to state aid, where financial assistance may be allowed for a deprived region of the Community.

The creation of unified markets is a political objective which is related to Community competition policy in particular. This is referred to as a policy of 'market integration' and is crucial to European competition policy. It is derived from the overall aim of integrating the markets of Member States to create a more united Europe. The concept of 'small is beautiful' seeks to foster smaller companies' ability to compete more directly with established powerful companies. One way that it can achieve this is by responding more leniently to forms of cooperation between smaller firms, which might involve the sharing of technology. The promotion of SMEs (Small and Medium-sized Enterprises) is a particular goal of the Community authorities as it is believed that such companies may start to compete across national frontiers and hence indirectly support the market integration policy.

SECTION 4: Competition problems

Whish, R., *Competition Law*
4th edn, Butterworths, p. 416

There have been and continue to be fierce debates about many issues in competition policy: for example the appropriate treatment of vertical agreements, 'abusive' pricing by dominant firms, refusals to supply, the inter-relationship of competition law and intellectual property rights and the standards for intervention against mergers. However, if competition policy is about one thing, it is surely about the condemnation of horizontal price fixing, market sharing and analogous practices: both on a moral and practical level, there is not a great deal of difference between price fixing and theft; US law has for many decades treated hard-core cartels as per se infringements of the Sherman Act and as criminal offences, punishable, inter alia by imprisonment.

NOTE: In recent years there has been a notable hardening of approach to hard-core cartels and several OECD countries (e.g. Ireland) now have provision for criminal sanctions. In July 2001, the UK set out proposals to follow in a DTI White Paper, *Productivity and Enterprise, A World Class Regime* July 2001. This was followed up by the publication of the Enterprise Bill in March 2000. The criminalisation of hard-core cartel activity in a UK context is considered in Chapter 4.

SECTION 5: Problem of oligopolistic markets

A particular difficulty for competition law is dealing with the complex economic problems of oligopoly. Oligopolistic markets illustrate the complex interplay between law and economics and demonstrate the limitations of using legal tools to address a market problem identified by economic theory. See generally Chapter 5.

Willimsky, S., 'The Concept(s) of Competition'

[1997] ECLR 54 at p. 56

Professor Whish argued that: the main argument against oligopoly is that the structural conditions of the market in which oligopolists operate are such that they will not compete on price and will have little incentive to compete in other ways; furthermore the theory of oligopolistic interdependence asserts that they will be able to earn supra competitive profits without entering into the type of collusive agreements generally proscribed by competition law.

An oligopolistic market is one which is characterised by the presence of a small number of a small number of key players in the market. A structure which is typical in oligopolistic markets is such that the group of oligopolists do not compete with each other on price or in other ways, although, of course, in some markets, competition is intense. The theory of oligopolistic interdependence sets out various reasons for the 'invisible bond' between the privileged few. Because of their inter-dependence, oligopolistic markets are very stable and subsist in a quasi-competition free vacuum. They are tied to one another in price, marketing and any other form of behaviour which would have an appreciable effect on the market. Unilateral actions would either force an oligopolist out of the circle or force the others to match. Parallel pricing strategies, therefore, are more the result of a heightened sense of awareness of each other's presence than necessarily evidence of a concerted practice or anti-competitive agreement.

Oligopolistic structures may only be combated by means of a structural attack on the particular market or a policy which would make parallel pricing unlawful per se. Galbraith stated that: 'The final problem of anti-trust policy . . . is its inability to make satisfactory contact with oligopoly' and it is argued that competition policy should focus more on oligopolies than on possible monopolies, which are much easier to destroy. Direct regulation of oligopolies may first of all not be possible in a free market and would be very cumbersome and bureaucratic.

FURTHER READING

Rodger, B.J., 'The Oligopoly Problem and the Concept of Collective Dominance: EC Developments in the Light of US Trends in Antitrust and Policy', Columbia Journal of European Law Vol. 2, No.1, 1995/96.

Niels, N., 'Collective Dominance: More than Just Oligopolistic Interdependence' [2001] ECLR 168.

[handwritten annotation: Oligopoly → is a market situation in which control over the supply of the commodity is held by a small no of producers]

SECTION 6: **US antitrust**

The starting point for competition laws may be traced to US antitrust. The Sherman Act 1890 is the earliest example of a competition law system and remains in force today. The Supreme Court in *US* v *Topco* (1972) described the antitrust laws as the 'Magna Carta of free enterprise' and compared them to the Bill of Rights. Section 1 of the Sherman Act states:

Every contract, combination in the form of trust or otherwise, or conspiracy, in restraint of trade or commerce among the several States, or with foreign nations, is hereby declared to be illegal. Every person who shall make any contract or engage in any combination or conspiracy hereby declared to be illegal shall be declared to be guilty of a felony.

Section 2 states:

Every person who shall monopolize, or attempt to monopolize, or combine or conspire with any other person or persons, to monopolize any part of the trade or commerce among several States, or with foreign nations, shall be deemed guilty of a felony.

The influence of US antitrust scholars on the development of competition laws throughout the world has been profound. See e.g. Bork above.

QUESTION

In 1970 Neale commented that 'There is evidence that the aims and scope of antitrust have changed a good deal since the passage of the Sherman Act, and may easily change some more in the future'. What are the goals of US antitrust? How have they changed since 1890? See e.g. the Harvard v Chicago debate outlined in excerpts from Ahdar, Bork and Rodger above.

FURTHER READING

Fox, E.M., and Sullivan, L.A., 'Antitrust-Retrospective and Prospective: Where are we coming from? Where are we going?' (1987) 62 New York Univ. Law Review 936.

SECTION 7: **EC competition law**

The creation of a single market has been the overriding aim of the Community since its inception and the commitment to free market principles is evident throughout the Treaties. The main objectives of the Community are articulated as follows:

Article 2 (as amended) states that:

The Community shall have as its task, by establishing a common market and an economic and monetary union and by implementing common policies or activities referred to in Articles 3 and 4, to promote throughout the Community a harmonious, balanced and sustainable development of economic activities, a high level of employment and of social protection, equality between men and women, sustainable and non-inflationary growth, a high degree of competitiveness and convergence of economic performance, a high level of protection and improvement of the quality of the environment, the raising of the standard of living and quality of life, and economic and social cohesion and solidarity among Member States.

Article 3 (as amended) lists the means necessary to achieve the goals in Article 2 and requires in para. (g) the institution of:

a system ensuring that competition in the common market is not distorted.

The Ninth Report on Competition Policy remains an authoritative view of the policy objectives of Community competition policy.

Commission Ninth Report on Competition Policy
(1980) pp. 9–12

The first fundamental objective is to keep the common market open and unified . . . There is . . . a continuing need—and this is the primary task of the Community's competition policy—to forestall and suppress restrictive or abusive practices of firms attempting to divide up the market again so as to apply artificial price differences or impose unfair terms on their consumers . . .

It is an established fact that competition carries within it the seeds of its own destruction. An excessive concentration of economic, financial and commercial power can produce such far-reaching structural changes that free competition is no longer able to fulfil its role as an effective regulator of economic activity. Consequently, the second fundamental objective of the Community's competition policy must be to ensure that at all stages of the common market's development there exists the right amount of competition in order for the Treaty's requirements to be met and its aims attained. The desire to maintain a competitive structure dictates the Commission's constant vigilance over abuses by dominant firms . . .

Thirdly, the competition system instituted by the Treaty requires that the conditions under which competition takes place remain subject to the principle of fairness in the market place [these principles are] . . .

First, equality of opportunity must be preserved for all commercial operators in the common market. A second aspect of the principle of fairness in the market place is the need to have regard to the great variety of situations in which firms carry on business . . . this factor makes it necessary to adapt the Community competition rules so as to pay special regard in particular to small and medium [size] firms that lack strength.

Finally, equity demands that the Commission's competition policy takes account of the legitimate interests of workers, users and consumers.

QUESTION

Korah has suggested that 'integration has been elevated by the Commission and the Court to a goal in itself, more important than efficiency'. Discuss.

Gerber, D., *Law and Competition in Twentieth Century Europe: Protecting Prometheus*
OUP, 1998, pp. 347–348

2. Integration and the goals of competition law

The goal of a unified market dominated the process of constructing the competition law system, because it was *the* central impetus for the 'new Europe'. As Barry Hawk has put it, 'Single market integration, and the elimination of restrictive practices which interfere with that integration, is the first principle of EEC antitrust law. . . .' This 'unification imperative' has shaped institutional structures and competences within the system, supplied much of its legitimacy, and generated the conceptual framework for the development and application of its substantive norms.

To begin to appreciate the centrality and force of this idea, one need only recall that economic co-operation was the last remaining hope for a co-operative Europe that would banish the specter of that continent's nationalist past. Attempts to move toward political union had been rejected, and the plans for a European Defense Community had been defeated. If there was to be a new Europe, it would have to be built on economic co-operation and integration.

In addition to this political goal of replacing conflict with co-operation, the Common Market was seen as serving a variety of economic goals. Above all, many viewed it as necessary for further economic improvement. European national markets were seen as too small to support significant economic growth. Moreover, an integrated market would allow European firms to acquire sufficient size to compete effectively on world markets, and consumers would benefit from a Europe-sized market with its concomitant economies of scale.

Many Europeans also saw economic integration as the only means of dealing with the combined economic and political power of the United States. These were the years of the Jean-Jacques Servan-Schreiber's famous *Défi Américain*, the 'American Challenge' to Europe, and an integrated market represented a means of regaining independence, power, and status *vis-à-vis* the country that had assumed world leadership in the wake of two world wars.

This does not mean that there was no interest in obtaining the generic benefits of competition. There was. Both the Commission and the Court referred at times to the potential benefits—lower prices, more rapid technological progress, etc.—anticipated as a result of improved competition. These references were imbedded, however, in a discourse and practice that was focused on economic integration. In particular, it is important to remember that socialist thought was still highly influential in many parts of Europe at this time, and thus there were political disincentives to associating competition law too closely with the protection of the competitive process as such.

Furthermore, there was little reason to distinguish between the two goals. They were related, and they reinforced each other. To the extent that competition law eliminated obstacles to the flow of goods, services, and capital across European borders, for example, it served the cause of unifying the market while simultaneously benefiting consumers by increasing the number of actual and potential competitors on European markets.

In the next extract Gerber asserts that market integration will not be the dominant concern in future years.

Gerber, D., *Law and Competition in Twentieth Century Europe: Protecting Prometheus*
OUP, 1998, pp. 388–389

This uncertainty is exacerbated by increasing demands for accommodation between competition law goals and other goals of the Community. Trade policy, social concerns and environmental claims, *inter alia*, demand to be reconciled with the objectives of competition law. Consequently, just as the keystone of the existing goal structure is being removed—and in part because of the imminence of that removal—lateral pressure on that structure from other values and policies is increasing, generating even further uncertainty about the roles of competition law.

One response has been to turn toward more 'generic' competition law goals—that is, generic benefits associated with protecting the process of competition. Such goals have lived in the shadow of the integration imperative since the foundational period, but they have been little explored in their own right, primarily because integrationist and generic goals have been intermingled, and there has been little reason to distinguish between them. This has led to the assumption that 'unbundling' these goals will change little, and to a lack of concern about the potential impact of eliminating integrationist goals. The assumption remains unexamined, however, shielded from examination not only by the natural resistance to changing one's conceptual framework, but also by the political risks of doing so.

Yet removal of the integration imperative necessarily alters competition law goal structures and the discourse associated with them. Without it, there will be increased pressure on DG IV's decision-makers to articulate other goals with far more care than in the past. Should market efficiency be the sole goal? If not, which other values should be served and how should they relate to each other—that is, what should be the new goal structure?

Do you agree?

A: Treaty provisions

The Community's rules on competition can be found in Articles 81–86 EC which apply to undertakings, private and public. Articles 81 and 82 EC in particular, are the cornerstones of Community competition policy. Articles 87–89 EC apply to state aid. Article 81 EC prohibits agreements, decisions or concerted practices, which have an anti-competitive object or effect, whereas Article 82 EC prohibits an abuse of a dominant position. These articles are not mutually exclusive and complement the free movement of goods provisions, Articles 18–25 EC and 28–30 EC.

As previously explained, the theory and practice of competition law is inextricably tied to economics. See e.g. the Chicago versus Harvard debate above. The following extracts explain the important role of economics in EC competition law although the authors' comments are not limited to EC law.

Faull J., and Nikpay A. (eds), *The EC Law of Competition*
OUP, 1999, paras 1.01–1.04

1.01 There is a growing awareness among competition policy makers of the importance of economics for their daily work. In the EU, admittedly with some delay compared to the US, it is now normal to discuss competition cases in terms of market power, entry barriers, sunk costs, etc and to evaluate cases according to their effects on the market. Competition policy is an economic policy concerned with economic structures, economic conduct, and economic effects. It is for this reason that in a book on competition law an introduction to the economics of competition cannot be omitted.

1.02 The growing acceptance and importance of economics in competition policy also raises the question of the usefulness of economics for devising competition rules and deciding on competition cases. A word of caution may be in place in this respect. Economic thinking and economic models have not proven to be perfect guides.

1.03 Economic theories and economic models are built on and around assumptions. These assumptions by definition do not cover (all) real world situations. In addition, when the assumptions are changed the outcomes of the models may look strikingly different, changing for example the price from a monopoly level to a competitive price level. It is for these reasons that economics may often not be able to give a clear and definite answer on what will happen in a market when companies merge, when a company imposes a vertical restriction, or when companies try to collude.

1.04 The best economics can do in general is offer a number of useful concepts and models, exclude certain outcomes, and provide relevant arguments. In other words, it helps to tell the most plausible story. It may be useful by helping to formulate rules, devise safe harbours, indicate under what conditions anti-competitive outcomes are very unlikely or rather likely. In individual cases it will be necessary to find first the concepts and the model that fit best the description of the actual market conditions of the case and then to proceed with the analysis of the actual or possible competition consequences.

FURTHER READING

Frazer T., 'Competition Policy after 1992: The Next Step' (1990) 53 MLR 609.

SECTION 8: **UK competition law**

The objectives of UK competition law are more difficult to discern. Section 84 of the Fair Trading Act 1973 articulates the criteria to be used in competition policy in the UK. The OFT and the DGFT are to consider 'all matters which appear to them to be relevant' and, in particular, the desirability of the merger for:

(a) maintaining and promoting effective competition;

(b) promoting the interests of consumers, purchasers, and other users of goods and services in respect of prices, quality, and variety of goods and services supplied;

(c) promoting, through competition, reduction of costs, development and use of new techniques and new products, and facilitating the entry of new competitors into existing markets;

(d) maintaining and promoting the balanced distribution of industry and employment;

(e) maintaining and promoting competitive activity in overseas markets.

It is not clear however, what the s. 84 'public interest' text encapsulates.

Trade and Industry Committee
HC 249 I, para. 20

. . . most importantly, a commonly cited difficulty with the [FTA] is the definition of the public interest. The DGFT defined the public interest as 'consumer well-being' but admitted that 'I do not think anybody could possibly pretend that they could sit down and do some sums and have an answer they can defend against all comers at the end of the day'. The Chairman of the MMC said that it was impossible to define the public interest in a general context, and the Minister simply referred to the criteria set out in the Act. These criteria, however, are extremely broad and lack an indication of priorities. As the Consumers' Association pointed out, 'with a little bit of creative analysis it is possible to define almost any industry situation as falling within one or other of those particular criteria'. Since the 'public interest' judgment lies at the heart of UK policy on monopolies, this ambiguity is a matter of concern.

NOTE: The 1984 Tebbit Guidelines are also significant as a general interpretation of criteria (a) and (b). The latest development in UK competition law, the Enterprise Bill 2002, proposes to replace the 'public interest' test with a new test, the 'substantial lessening of competition' (SLC) test. See Chapter 9. The UK framework for competition can be traced back to the World War II and has had many guises over the years. However, the Competition Act 1998 swept away much of the existing legal framework based on the Restrictive Trade Practices Act 1976 and brought domestic competition law in line with the Community model, namely Articles 81 and 82 EC. The Competition Act 1998 came into force on 1 March 2000 and brought with it the full force of Community law through the operation of s. 60, the so-called 'Euro-clause'. The Act does not define a number of key concepts, for example, 'undertaking', 'agreement' or 'concerted practice', and the national courts and competition authorities must look to the jurisprudence of the European Court and the decisional practice of the Commission for guidance. The Enterprise Bill proposes further significant changes to the current system, principally the introduction of criminal sanctions, based on US antitrust. See generally, Chapter 4.

2

UK enforcement

SECTION 1: Introduction

The framework for the enforcement of UK competition law has undergone a dramatic overhaul in recent years, and this is set to continue with the reforms to be introduced by the Enterprise Act. Until the enactment of the CA 1998, the enforcement structure under the principal legislation, the FTA 1973, was essentially tripartite, involving the DGFT, Competition Commission (previously the MMC) and the Secretary of State. UK competition law was essentially administrative in nature, lacking redress for private parties (with the exception of s. 35(2) of the RTPA 1976, and the possibility of judicial review of the administrative decision-making process), and ultimate decision making rested with a politician, the Secretary of State. The CA 1998 signalled the end of the tripartite structure of competition law enforcement in the UK.

Wilks, S., *In the Public Interest, Competition Policy and the Monopolies and Mergers Commission*
Manchester, MUP, 1999

Compared with the MMC the OFT is a mere stripling but, even so, it has survived rather successfully and was able to celebrate its twenty-fifth birthday in 1998, along with that of the tripartite structure of British competition authorities. In 1995 the DTI affirmed that 'the tripartite structure is designed to provide for effective action against damaging monopolies, and at the same time to provide checks and balances to the exercise of power by the authorities . . . The Government are content with this broad structure, which they believe has shown its worth over a period of more than 20 years'. The tripartite structure, with its checks and balances, has proved attractive enough to be retained for merger control and for some aspects of monopoly control. Under the 1998 Competition Act, however, the 'operational' aspects of the tripartite structure have been abolished. The prohibition will be operated by the DGFT who will become a more important, and a more controversial, figure. The 'structural' aspects of the tripartite system are, however, being retained and the system will continue to rely on co-operative relations between the OFT, the new Competition Commission and the DTI.

NOTE: There was debate during the 1990s, particularly following the influential House of Commons Trade and Industry Committee Report, 'UK Policy on Monopolies', 1995, suggesting the creation of a unitary authority by merging the OFT and MMC. See Wilks, above, particularly Chapter 9. This was ultimately rejected, but the tripartite scheme is effectively extinct. The Secretary of State has no real enforcement role under the CA 1998, and the Enterprise Bill will significantly curtail ministerial involvement in mergers and 'market investigations', which will replace the monopoly provisions under the FTA 1973.

A further key development in the enforcement of UK competition law has been the shift from a purely administrative system of enforcement to a 'hybrid' system, which also involves rights of redress to private parties through normal court processes. This was initiated in the CA 1998, and the availability of private rights of redress is to be enhanced by the Enterprise Bill.

SECTION 2: **Competition Act 1998**

The CA 1998 reformed UK substantive competition law but it also instituted a new enforcement framework in respect of the two prohibitions, based largely on the European model.

Wilks, S., *In the Public Interest, Competition Policy and the Monopolies and Mergers Commission*
Manchester, MUP, 1999

The Competition Act 1998
With an elegant accident of symmetry the Act comes exactly fifty years after the Monopolies and Restrictive Practices Act 1948. It is potentially a revolutionary piece of legislation which has considerable implications for the institutions of British capitalism. As explored in the concluding chapter, the 1948 Act catered to the voluntarism, the self-regulation and the accommodative arm's-length relationship between government and industry which permeated the political economy of the 1940s. The 1998 Act creates a more formal and legally objective framework for industry. It provides didactic guidance rather than the co-operative exploration which underlay its 1948 predecessor. The formal provisions of the Act are briefly reviewed in chapter 10.

Despite its European provenance, the new Act is a piece of British legislation although it builds in novel provisions to employ European jurisprudence. It is designed to dovetail with the European regime and doubtless many hope that this new, more effective, Act will increase the element of real subsidiarity. It represents something of a compromise, as can be seen if it is considered in the context of the debates reviewed above. In respect of the first debate it almost certainly represents a more active British competition policy, and one that stresses 'competition' as a principle rather than 'the public interest'. In respect of the second debate it adopts the European stance of prohibition and an effects doctrine, and does so for monopolies as well as restrictive practices. But the monopolies element is enacted with due caution and the mergers regime remains unaltered. In respect of the third debate the institutions have changed in their relationships with one another and in the abolition of one court and the creation of a new tribunal. These changes have been the product of wide consultation. The Government has pursued a neo-pluralist path of involvement of the policy network through a proliferation of Green and White Papers and by giving every indication of listening to the responses. There is nothing impetuous or dogmatic about this legislation. Government has sought advice, built consensus and moved with judicious caution. This is indicative of a neo-pluralist policy stance which seeks to build consensus but which also requires technical support. The Government was genuinely uncertain about the potential effects of new legislation and in true civil service style (and very unlike the sweeping Thatcherite policy initiatives) it enrolled the views and the advice of business, lawyers and other specialists. It is indicative of this caution that the new model has perhaps embraced the European certainties too emphatically. After years of being reproached as not being European enough, some lawyers are now suggesting that the Government has become too European. The European blueprint does indeed involve some major shifts in the regime of monopoly control. In order to evaluate the extent of change consider the following:

- the shift from agnostic investigation to prohibition
- the replacement of the 'public interest' test by an 'effect on competition' test
- the exclusion of the Secretary of State from the administrative process as regards actions and remedies
- the incorporation of the principles of European competition law jurisprudence into British administration
- hence the likely growth of legal involvement through defence, appeal and third-party action
- the empowerment of third parties through rights of appeal and the potential to pursue damages in the courts
- the imposition of substantial penalties.

NOTE: Along with the creation of a hybrid system of private and public enforcement, the DGFT adopted the central enforcement role, similar to the European Commission in relation to Articles 81 and 82 EC. Section 54, together with Sch. 10, provides for the concurrent exercise of the powers under the CA 1998 by the sectoral regulators, and for instance, DGOFTEL has undertaken a number of investigations already under the Act. See, for instance, OFTEL, The Application of the Competition Act in the Telecommunications Sector, OFT 417; and Prosser, T., 'Competition, Regulators and Public Services', Chapter 10 in Rodger, B.J., and MacCulloch, A. (eds), *The UK Competition Act: A New Era for UK Competition Law*, Hart Publishing, Oxford, 2000. Note that the DGFT's tasks are to be entrusted to the revamped 'OFT' following enactment of the Enterprise Bill.

A: DGFT/OFT

The CA 1998, in Chapter 3, amended the DGFT's role in two major respects—in relation to investigation and sanctions. First, following the criticisms in earlier reform proposals, see e.g. DTI Green Paper, 'Abuse of Market Power', Cm 2100, 1992; Chapter 2; second, the DGFT's powers of investigation were strengthened.

It should be noted that following the entry into force of the relevant provisions of the Enterprise Act (see below) the DGFT's functions are to be assumed by the OFT and references in this section to the DGFT are revised accordingly.

McNeil, I., 'Investigations under the Competition Act 1998', in Rodger, B.J., and MacCulloch, A. (eds), *The UK Competition Act: A New Era for UK Competition Law*
Oxford, Hart Publishing, 2000

Prior to the introduction of the Competition Act 1998 the framework of competition law in the United Kingdom did not give the competition authorities the extensive powers of investigation available to the European Commission and those national authorities whose competition law is based on the Community model. It is difficult to attribute this directly to the nature of the substantive provisions of competition law which have developed in the United Kingdom, but there were nevertheless several aspects of the framework which influenced the manner in which investigations were undertaken. First, the fragmentation of the substantive provisions of competition law between different statutes has resulted in separate provisions governing different types of investigation: the Fair Trading Act 1973, the Restrictive Trade Practices Act 1976 (RTPA 1976), and the Competition Act 1980 all have their own provisions relating to investigations. Secondly, the division of investigative functions between the Office of Fair Trading and the Monopolies and Mergers Commission resulted in an additional layer of complexity in the framing of powers of investigation. Thirdly, the use of the 'public interest' test, in section 84 of the 1973 Act, as the main criterion for distinguishing legitimate business conduct from anti-competitive behaviour, in the broad sense, has meant that the focus of an investigation differed from investigations under Community law which relate to prohibited behaviour. Fourthly, the absence of financial sanctions within the regime can arguably be seen to have limited the development of powers of investigation. Competition authorities in the United Kingdom, in contrast to most other national authorities in the Community, have not had to establish a link between an infringement and a financial penalty.

The absence of effective powers of investigation in the United Kingdom has generally been seen as a serious restriction on the ability of the competition authorities to enforce the law. Referring to cartels in the concrete industry, John Bridgeman, the Director General of Fair Trading, remarked in 1995:

> I feel that greater investigative powers would make our handling of such cases far easier. For that reason, I welcome the DTI's renewed commitment to reform, especially reform of the Restrictive Trade Practices Act. I look forward particularly to improvements such as an extension of my investigatory powers, both in pursuing secret cartels (where it is crucial) and in probing other possible abuses of market power (where our enquiries could be more focused and expeditious).

The 1998 Act aims to remedy these deficiencies and will bring UK competition law much closer to the Community model in terms of the process of investigation and the decision-making procedure which follows. The 1998 Act provides for more extensive powers of investigation for the Director General both in relation to the two new prohibitions contained in the 1998 Act and in relation to complex and scale monopoly investigations under the provisions of the 1973 Act.

The significance of the extension of investigatory powers is increased, as the extent to which the substantive rules of domestic competition law are being changed is not entirely clear. The nature and formulation of the rules has changed but, as recognised by the Trade and Industry Secretary, the identification of the particular conduct prohibited by the new rules, which was permitted under the old rules, is problematic. Viewed in this context, the primary purpose of the Act is arguably to allow for more effective enforcement action to be taken against obvious infringements. In other words, the real objective of the Act may not be to fine-tune the substantive rules of competition law but to provide effective means of taking action against those breaches of competition law which have in the past escaped enforcement action because of a lack of evidence and enforcement powers available to the competition authorities.

The key powers of investigation are contained in ss. 25 to 29 of the Act.

Competition Act 1998, [ss. 25–29]

Investigations

25. Director's power to investigate
The Director may conduct an investigation if there are reasonable grounds for suspecting—
    (a) that the Chapter I prohibition has been infringed; or
    (b) that the Chapter II prohibition has been infringed.

26. Powers when conducting investigations
    (1) For the purposes of an investigation under section 25, the Director may require any person to produce to him a specified document, or to provide him with specified information, which he considers relates to any matter relevant to the investigation.
    (2) The power conferred by subsection (1) is to be exercised by a notice in writing.
    (3) A notice under subsection (2) must indicate—
      (a) the subject matter and purpose of the investigation; and
      (b) the nature of the offences created by sections 42 to 44.

(4) In subsection (1) 'specified' means—
  (a) specified, or described, in the notice; or
  (b) falling within a category which is specified, or described, in the notice.

(5) The Director may also specify in the notice—
  (a) the time and place at which any document is to be produced or any information is to be provided;
  (b) the manner and form in which it is to be produced or provided.

(6) The power under this section to require a person to produce a document includes power—
  (a) if the document is produced—
    (i)   to take copies of it or extracts from it;
    (ii) to require him, or any person who is a present or past officer of his, or is or was at any time employed by him, to provide an explanation of the document;
  (b) if the document is not produced, to require him to state, to the best of his knowledge and belief, where it is.

27. Power to enter premises without a warrant

(1) Any officer of the Director who is authorised in writing by the Director to do so ('an investigating officer') may enter any premises in connection with an investigation under section 25.

(2) No investigating officer is to enter any premises in the exercise of his powers under this section unless he has given to the occupier of the premises a written notice which—
  (a) gives at least two working days' notice of the intended entry;
  (b) indicates the subject matter and purpose of the investigation; and
  (c) indicates the nature of the offences created by sections 42 to 44.

(3) Subsection (2) does not apply—
  (a) if the Director has a reasonable suspicion that the premises are, or have been, occupied by—
    (i)   a party to an agreement which he is investigating under section 25(a); or
    (ii) an undertaking the conduct of which he is investigating under section 25(b); or
  (b) if the investigating officer has taken all such steps as are reasonably practicable to give notice but has not been able to do so.

(4) In a case falling within subsection (3), the power of entry conferred by subsection (1) is to be exercised by the investigating officer on production of—
  (a) evidence of his authorisation; and
  (b) a document containing the information referred to in subsection (2)(b) and (c).

(5) An investigating officer entering any premises under this section may—
  (a) take with him such equipment as appears to him to be necessary;
  (b) require any person on the premises—
    (i)   to produce any document which he considers relates to any matter relevant to the investigation; and
    (ii) if the document is produced, to provide an explanation of it;
  (c) require any person to state, to the best of his knowledge and belief, where any such document is to be found;
  (d) take copies of, or extracts from, any document which is produced;
  (e) require any information which is held in a computer and is accessible from the premises and which the investigating officer considers relates to any matter relevant to the investigation, to be produced in a form—
    (i)   in which it can be taken away, and
    (ii) in which it is visible and legible.

28. Power to enter premises under a warrant

(1) On an application made by the Director to the court in accordance with rules of court, a judge may issue a warrant if he is satisfied that—

    (a) there are reasonable grounds for suspecting that there are on any premises documents—

        (i) the production of which has been required under section 26 or 27; and

        (ii) which have not been produced as required;

    (b) there are reasonable grounds for suspecting that—

        (i) there are on any premises documents which the Director has power under section 26 to require to be produced; and

        (ii) if the documents were required to be produced, they would not be produced but would be concealed, removed, tampered with or destroyed; or

    (c) an investigating officer has attempted to enter premises in the exercise of his powers under section 27 but has been unable to do so and that there are reasonable grounds for suspecting that there are on the premises documents the production of which could have been required under that section.

(2) A warrant under this section shall authorise a named officer of the Director, and any other of his officers whom he has authorised in writing to accompany the named officer—

    (a) to enter the premises specified in the warrant, using such force as is reasonably necessary for the purpose;

    (b) to search the premises and take copies of, or extracts from, any document appearing to be of a kind in respect of which the application under subsection (1) was granted ('the relevant kind');

    (c) to take possession of any documents appearing to be of the relevant kind if—

        (i) such action appears to be necessary for preserving the documents or preventing interference with them; or

        (ii) it is not reasonably practicable to take copies of the documents on the premises;

    (d) to take any other steps which appear to be necessary for the purpose mentioned in paragraph (c)(i);

    (e) to require any person to provide an explanation of any document appearing to be of the relevant kind or to state, to the best of his knowledge and belief, where it may be found;

    (f) to require any information which is held in a computer and is accessible from the premises and which the named officer considers relates to any matter relevant to the investigation, to be produced in a form—

        (i) in which it can be taken away, and

        (ii) in which it is visible and legible.

(3) If, in the case of a warrant under subsection (1)(b), the judge is satisfied that it is reasonable to suspect that there are also on the premises other documents relating to the investigation concerned, the warrant shall also authorise action mentioned in subsection (2) to be taken in relation to any such document.

(4) Any person entering premises by virtue of a warrant under this section may take with him such equipment as appears to him to be necessary.

(5) On leaving any premises which he has entered by virtue of a warrant under this section, the named officer must, if the premises are unoccupied or the occupier is temporarily absent, leave them as effectively secured as he found them.

(6) A warrant under this section continues in force until the end of the period of one month beginning with the day on which it is issued.

(7) Any document of which possession is taken under subsection (2)(c) may be retained for a period of three months.

29. Entry of premises under warrant: supplementary

(1) A warrant issued under section 28 must indicate—

(a) the subject matter and purpose of the investigation;

(b) the nature of the offences created by sections 42 to 44.

(2) The powers conferred by section 28 are to be exercised on production of a warrant issued under that section.

(3) If there is no one at the premises when the named officer proposes to execute such a warrant he must, before executing it—

(a) take such steps as are reasonable in all the circumstances to inform the occupier of the intended entry; and

(b) if the occupier is informed, afford him or his legal or other representative a reasonable opportunity to be present when the warrant is executed.

(4) If the named officer is unable to inform the occupier of the intended entry he must, when executing the warrant, leave a copy of it in a prominent place on the premises.

(5) In this section—

'named officer' means the officer named in the warrant; and

'occupier', in relation to any premises, means a person whom the named officer reasonably believes is the occupier of those premises.

NOTE: Section 26 allows the DGFT to require the production of a document or other specified relevant information, and ss. 27–29 extend to him the power to enter premises with or without a warrant.

McNeil, I., 'Investigations under the Competition Act 1998', in Rodger, B.J., and MacCulloch, A. (eds), *The UK Competition Act: A New Era for UK Competition Law*

Oxford, Hart Publishing, 2000

Entry to premises

The provisions of the 1998 Act providing for entry to premises by the Director General represent a significant expansion of the powers of investigation available under the previous regime, which made no provision for entry to premises. The 1998 Act provides for entry with a warrant issued by a court and in other circumstances without a warrant. The powers available to the investigator are more extensive where entry is with a warrant, but the powers available on entry without a warrant will be adequate in many cases to secure sufficient evidence of an infringement. The definition of premises in section 59 of the 1998 Act excludes domestic premises unless they are also used in connection with the affairs of an undertaking or documents relating to the affairs of an undertaking are kept there. This definition goes some way towards taking account of the provisions of Article 8 of the European Convention on Human Rights 1950 which provides for the right to respect for private and family life. However, the case law of the European Court of Human Rights does not provide quite such a categorical split between the private sphere in which Article 8 rights apply and the business or professional sphere in which they do not. For example in *Niemetz* v *Germany* the Court said that:

> to interpret the words 'private life' and 'home' as including certain professional or business activities or premises would be consonant with the essential objective and purpose of Article 8, namely to protect the individual against arbitrary interference by the public authorities.

In *Chappell* v *United Kingdom*, a case involving an Anton Pillar order directed against material in breach of copyright held by the applicant in premises used both for business and domestic purposes, the Court did not rely on the fact that the search was directed solely at business activities as a ground for excluding the application of Article 8 under the head of 'private life'. It may well therefore be the case that the category of premises defined by the 1998 Act as being open to inspection by the Director General may be too wide to comply with the European Convention and the Human Rights Act 1998.

Entry with a warrant

This power is designed to deal with three different situations. The first is where there are reasonable grounds for suspecting that there are on the premises documents which have been required to be produced which have not been produced. The second is where there is a suspicion that documents which could be required to be produced will be concealed, removed, tampered with or destroyed. The third is where an investigating officer has been unable to secure entry to premises without a warrant, where this is authorised by the 1998 Act. A warrant authorises the investigating officer to enter the premises using such force as is necessary, to search the premises and, if necessary for their preservation, to remove relevant documents. The investigator is also empowered to remove equipment, to require explanations of documents and to require the location of documents to be disclosed. The formulation of these powers is more specific than the parallel provision of Article 14 of Regulation 17/62 which does not expressly provide for a right to search for documents, although the European Court has interpreted it in such a manner. There is no wider power to ask questions not directly related to documents on the premises, such as questions relating to broader aspects of the investigation. As pointed out by the European Court, in dealing with this issue in the context of Community investigations, allowing investigators to compel answers to such questions would confuse the general power to require information with the more specific powers associated with on-site inspections.

Entry without a warrant

Where premises are occupied by a party to an agreement prohibited by Chapter I or an undertaking being investigated in relation to an infringement of the Chapter II prohibition, the Director General can enter premises without a warrant and without giving notice. This allows the Director General to engage in what are referred to in Community parlance as 'dawn raids'. In other circumstances, for instance, where the premises are occupied by a third party who has relevant information, the Director General can enter premises without a warrant provided that two days' notice, and the other requirements of the Act, are observed. In this respect the Director General's powers are more limited than those of the European Commission which is able to subject third parties to dawn raids as well as undertakings suspected of being a party to a contravention. Once on the premises, the investigating officer cannot undertake a search but has the right to require the production of relevant documents, take copies and require explanations of the documents. A similar power of entry without a warrant is available in the case of monopoly investigations under the 1973 Act.

   The power to enter premises without a warrant puts the Director General in a privileged position by comparison with other public agencies undertaking investigations. No such power is granted to the Financial Services Authority under the Financial Services and Markets Act: such a power was proposed in the first draft of the Bill but was withdrawn following opposition during parliamentary scrutiny. Entry to premises without a warrant is not available to the Department of Trade and Industry when undertaking a company investigation, nor to the Serious Fraud Office when undertaking an investigation into serious fraud. All these agencies may be involved in the investigation of activity which constitutes a criminal offence, but none has powers as extensive as the Director General. The privileged position of the Director General can to some extent be rationalised on the basis that the collection of information relating to the contravention of competition law is particularly difficult and therefore an element of surprise is sometimes necessary to capture the necessary evidence. Nonetheless, it is clear from the extensive powers given to the Director General to investigate breaches of the 1998 Act that the operation of competitive markets has assumed a much greater significance not merely by comparison with the old framework of competition law but also in relation to other areas of business regulation.

NOTE: These powers are subject to limitations based on privileged communications (s. 30) and the right to self-incrimination. See Case 347/87 *Orkem* v *Commission* [1989] ECR 3283. See generally, DGFT's Guideline, Powers of Investigation, OFT 404. The DGFT has certainly utilised the new powers of investigation available under the Act. As at November 2001, over 40 cases had crossed the 'reasonable grounds for suspecting' threshold under s. 25 and were under active consideration. The OFT had conducted raids in 14 separate investigations, some at multiple locations, involving both s. 27 and s. 28 powers, obtained search warrants against 43 undertakings using s. 28, and carried out 27 site visits without notice under s. 27. An excellent example of an investigation leading to the discovery of a breach of the prohibition and the imposition of fines was in *Arriva/First Group*, DGFT Decision No CA98/9/2002, 30 January 2002.

Arriva/FirstGroup
DGFT Decision No CA98/9/2002, 30 January 2002. Decision, para. 7

7. Enquiries into the complaint began on 31 July 2000. They led to an investigation under the Competition Act 1998 Act ('the Act').[13] The Director General of Fair Trading ('the Director') applied to the High Court and the Court of Session for warrants to enter premises of the two undertakings in England and Scotland, and exercise powers under section 28 of the Act.[14] Warrants were issued on 4 and 6 October 2000. Unannounced visits to the premises[15] took place on 10 and 11 October 2000 and copies of documents were taken. On 16 March 2001, a Notice under section 26 of the Act[16] was issued to the TAS Partnership Limited ('TAS'), specialist consultants in public transport, and specified documents and information were received by the Director as required in the Notice. The Director also received documents from the Traffic Commissioner of the North Eastern Traffic Area in Leeds.[17]

NOTE: This was the first decision imposing a fine under the Chapter I prohibition and applying the leniency programme under the Act, see further below. Clause 198 of the Enterprise Bill amends the CA 1998 to allow people who are not employees of the OFT to accompany and assist OFT officers on raids conducted under warrant, and this will be helpful where they have, for instance, specialist IT expertise.

B: Enforcement

Breach of the prohibitions is to be enforced directly by the DGFT, utilising a range of effective sanctions. See DGFT's Guideline, Enforcement, OFT 407. The procedure for decision-making procedures following an investigation, are outlined in the Director General's Procedural Rules 2000 (SI 2000/93). The Director General issues a Rule 14 Notice, akin to the Commission's statement of objections, outlining the basis of any suspected infringement. The parties concerned are then given the opportunity to submit written and oral submissions in relation to the Notice. If the

---

13 Section 25 of the Act: 'The Director may conduct an Investigation if there are reasonable grounds for suspecting—(a) that the Chapter I prohibition has been infringed . . .'

14 Section 28 gives powers to enter and search premises and take copies of documents or remove originals.

15 For list of premises visited see Appendix, p. 21.

16 Section 26(1) of the Act: 'For the purposes of an investigation under section 25, the Director may require any person to produce to him a specified document, or to provide him with specified information, which he considers relates to any matter relevant to the investigation.'

17 Documents relating to the registration and de-registration of buses between March and July 2000.

DGFT proceeds to find a breach, there are a range of possible sanctions available. The first is to issue a direction relating to the agreement or conduct under ss. 32 and 33 respectively. The following is an excerpt from Directions issued in the *Napp* case:

Napp Pharmaceuticals Holdings Limited and Subsidiaries
4 May 2001, CA 98/2d/2001, pp. 1–2

Direction to bring the infringement to an end
1. Save as provided in paragraph 4 below, Napp shall bring the Infringement to an end and shall refrain from any conduct having the same or equivalent effect.

Pricing
2. Without prejudice to the generality of paragraph 1 above and save as provided in paragraph 4 below, Napp shall in respect of each strength of MST Tablet which it supplies or offers for supply in the United Kingdom:

(a) within fifteen Working Days from the date of these directions replace its Current NHS List Price with a revised NHS List Price which is equal to or lower than 85 per cent of the Current NHS List Price;

(b) not without the prior written consent of the Director increase its NHS List Price to a level which is higher than 85 per cent of the Current NHS List Price;

(c) where it offers supplies of MST Tablets in the United Kingdom, offer such supplies at a price which is equal to or lower than 87.5 per cent of the NHS List Price;

(d) not without the prior written consent of the Director supply or offer to supply MST Tablets to a Hospital at a price which is lower than 20 per cent of the NHS List Price; and

(e) where the effect of such supply would be to circumvent the object of paragraph (d) above, not without the prior written consent of the Director, either:

(i) supply or offer to supply MST Tablets to a Hospital on terms which make the supply or the terms of supply, including the price, conditional on the supply of any other product or service to the Hospital or to any other person; or

(ii) supply or offer to supply any other product or service to any person, including a Hospital, on terms which make the supply or the terms of supply, including the price, conditional on the supply of MST Tablets to a Hospital.

Existing contracts
3.(1) Napp shall within four months from the date of these directions cease to supply MST Tablets to Hospitals on the terms of its Existing Contracts.

(2) Napp shall in all good faith enter into negotiations with the other parties to its Existing Contracts with a view to agreeing revised terms for the supply of MST Tablets to the Hospitals covered by those contracts following the expiry of the period of four months from the date of these directions.

(3) Any agreements or arrangements made by Napp following the negotiations referred to in subparagraph (2) above shall be fully compliant with paragraphs 1 and 2 above.

NOTE: These directions, issued five weeks after the initial decision, required Napp to institute a revised list price and allowed it four months to renegotiate in good faith its existing contracts. A substantial fine was also imposed and both issues were considered by the CCAT, see further below, re the fines issue. Napp applied for the directions to be suspended, and ultimately a consent order was agreed as the CCAT was satisfied that the Act provided for directions to be varied by the tribunal and for these to be enforceable by the DGFT, paras 3(2), 3(3) and 10 of Sch. 8. The DGFT also has powers to impose interim measures under s. 35.

C: Penalties

The most important sanction in practice is the DGFT's power to impose penalties under s. 36. Section 36(8) merely provides that no penalty may be imposed which exceeds 10 per cent of the turnover of an undertaking. This is to be determined in accordance with the CA 1998 (Determination of Turnover for Penalties) Order 2000 (SI 2000/309) CA, reproduced in full in Middleton, K., *UK and EC Competition Documents*, 2nd edn, OUP, 2000.

Competition Act 1998 (Determination of Turnover for Penalties) Order 2000 (SI 2000/309)

3. The turnover of an undertaking for the purposes of section 36(8) is:

(1) the applicable turnover for the business year preceding the date when the infringement ended;

(2) where the length of the infringement is more than 12 months, in addition the amount of the applicable turnover for the business year preceding that identified under paragraph (1) which bears the same proportion to the applicable turnover for that business year as the period by which the length of infringement exceeds 12 months bears to 12 months; and

(3) where the length of the infringement is more than 24 months, in addition the amount of the applicable turnover for the business year preceding that identified under paragraph (2) which bears the same proportion to the applicable turnover for that business year as the period by which the length of infringement exceeds 24 months bears to 12 months;

save that the amount added under paragraph (2) or (3) shall not exceed the amount of the applicable turnover for the preceding business year in question.

NOTE: Although s. 36 is modelled on Article 15 of Regulation 17, it differs in three major respects. First, it is limited to UK turnover. Second, Article 3 of the Order makes clear that an undertaking can be fined effectively 30 per cent of its turnover, dependent upon the number of years during which the infringement has taken place. Finally, s. 38 requires the DGFT to publish guidelines on the application of the new fining powers and these are set out in the DGFT's Guidance as to the Appropriate Amount of a Penalty, OFT 423. The approach is distinct from that undertaken by the European Commission under Article 15 of Regulation 17, as discussed in Chapter 3.

DGFT's Guidance as to the Appropriate Amount of a Penalty
OFT 423

Policy objectives
1.8 The twin objectives of the Director's policy on financial penalties are to impose penalties on infringing undertakings which reflect the seriousness of the infringement and to ensure that the threat of penalties will deter undertakings from engaging in anti-competitive practices. The Director therefore intends, where appropriate, to impose financial penalties which are severe, in particular in respect of agreements[4] between undertakings which fix prices or share markets and other cartel activities,[5] as well as serious abuses of a dominant position, which the Director considers are among

---

4 The term 'agreement' includes a concerted practice and decision by an association of undertakings.

5 For the purposes of this guidance, cartel activities are agreements, decisions by associations of undertakings or concerted practices which infringe the Act and involve price fixing, bid rigging (collusive tendering), the establishment of output restrictions or quotas and/or market sharing or market dividing (based on the OECD definition of 'hard core cartels').

the most serious infringements caught under the Act. The deterrent is not aimed solely at the undertakings which are subject to the decision, but also at other undertakings which might be considering activities that are contrary to the Chapter I and Chapter II prohibitions.

1.9 The Director also wishes to encourage members of cartels to come forward with evidence on the existence and activities of any cartel in which they are involved and therefore the guidance sets out in Part 3 a clear policy on when lenient treatment will be given to such undertakings.

1.10 The guidance has been drafted to increase transparency by setting out the steps which the Director will follow when calculating the amount of a penalty.

2 Steps for determining the level of a penalty

Method of calculation

2.1 Any financial penalty imposed by the Director under section 36 of the Act will be calculated following a five step approach:

- calculation of the starting point by applying a percentage determined by the nature of the infringement to the 'relevant turnover' of the undertaking (see paragraph 2.3 below)
- adjustment for duration
- adjustment for other factors
- adjustment for further aggravating or mitigating factors
- adjustment if the maximum penalty of 10 per cent of the 'section 36(8) turnover' of the undertaking is exceeded and to avoid double jeopardy.

Details on each of these steps are set out in paragraphs 2.3 to 2.15 below.

2.2 A member of a cartel may benefit from total immunity from, or a significant reduction in the level of, a financial penalty, if the requirements set out in Part 3 of this guidance are satisfied.

Step 1—Starting point

2.3 The starting point for determining the level of financial penalty which will be imposed on an undertaking is calculated by applying a percentage rate to the 'relevant turnover' of the undertaking, up to a maximum of 10 per cent.[6] The 'relevant turnover' is the turnover of the undertaking in the relevant product market and relevant geographic market[7] affected by the infringement in the last financial year.[8] This may include turnover generated outside the United Kingdom if the relevant geographic market for the relevant product is wider than the United Kingdom.

2.4 The actual percentage rate which will be applied to the 'relevant turnover' will depend upon the nature of the infringement. The more serious the infringement, the higher the percentage rate is likely to be. Price-fixing or market-sharing agreements and other cartel activities are among the most serious infringements caught under the Chapter I prohibition. Conduct which infringes the Chapter II prohibition and which by virtue of the undertaking's dominant position and the nature of the conduct has, or is likely to have a particularly serious effect on competition, for example, predatory pricing, is also one of the most serious infringements under the Act. The starting point for such

---

6 In this Guidance, the expression 'turnover' is used in two separate contexts: 'relevant turnover' used to calculate the starting point and 'section 36(8) turnover' (calculated in accordance with The Competition Act 1998 (Determination of Turnover for Penalties) Order 2000 (SI 2000 No. 309)) which is used in Step 5 in the adjustment of the penalty figure to prevent the maximum amount for the penalty being exceeded The 'section 36(8) turnover' of the undertaking is not restricted to the turnover in the relevant product and relevant geographic market.

7 See the Competition Act guideline *Market Definition* for further information on the relevant product market and relevant geographic market. The relevant product market and relevant geographic market will be determined as part of the Director's decision that an infringement has taken place.

8 'Relevant turnover' will be calculated after the deduction of sales rebates and value added tax and other taxes directly related to turnover.

activities and conduct will be calculated by applying a percentage likely to be at or near 10 per cent of the 'relevant turnover' of the infringing undertakings.

2.5 It is the Director's assessment of the seriousness of the infringement which will determine the percentage of 'relevant turnover' which is chosen as the starting point for the financial penalty. When making his assessment, the Director will consider a number of factors, including the nature of the product, the structure of the market, the market share(s) of the undertaking(s) involved in the infringement, entry conditions and the effect on competitors and third parties. The damage caused to consumers whether directly or indirectly will also be an important consideration. The assessment will be made on a case by case basis for all types of infringement.

2.6 Where an infringement involves several undertakings, an assessment of the appropriate starting point will be carried out for each of the undertakings concerned, in order to take account of the real impact of the infringing activity of each undertaking on competition.

Step 2—Adjustment for duration

2.7 The starting point may be increased to take into account the duration of the infringement. Penalties for infringements which last for more than one year may be multiplied by not more than the number of years of the infringement. Part years may be treated as full years for the purpose of calculating the number of years of the infringement.

Step 3—Adjustment for other factors

2.8 The penalty figure reached after the calculations in steps 1 and 2 may be adjusted as appropriate to achieve the policy objectives, outlined in paragraph 1.8 above, in particular, of imposing penalties on infringing undertakings in order to deter undertakings from engaging in anti-competitive practices. The deterrent is not aimed solely at the undertakings which are subject to the decision, but also at other undertakings which might be considering activities which are contrary to the Chapter I and Chapter II prohibitions. Considerations at this stage may include, for example, the Director's estimate of the gain made or likely to be made by the infringing undertaking from the infringement. Where relevant, the Director's estimate would account for any gains which might accrue to the undertaking in other product or geographic markets as well as the 'relevant' market under consideration.[9] The assessment of the need to adjust the penalty will be made on a case by case basis for each individual infringing undertaking.

2.9 This step may result in a substantial adjustment of the financial penalty calculated at the earlier steps. The consequence may be that the penalty which is imposed is much larger than would otherwise have been imposed. The result of any one of steps 2 or 3 above or 4 below may well be to take the penalty over 10 per cent of the 'relevant turnover' identified at step 1, but the overall cap on penalties is 10 per cent of the 'section 36(8) turnover' referred to in step 5 below and must not be exceeded.

Step 4—Adjustment for further aggravating and mitigating factors

2.10 The basic amount of the financial penalty, adjusted as appropriate at steps 2 and 3, may be increased where there are other aggravating factors, or decreased where there are mitigating factors.

2.11 Aggravating factors include:

- role of the undertaking as a leader in, or an instigator of, the infringement;
- involvement of directors or senior management;
- retaliatory measures taken against other undertakings aimed at ensuring the continuation of the infringement;

---

9 For example, in a predation case the relevant market may be very small. However, the act of predation might provide an undertaking with a reputation for aggressive behaviour which it could use to its advantage in many other markets across the UK.

- continuing the infringement after the start of the investigation;
- repeated infringements by the same undertaking or other undertakings in the same group.

2.12 Mitigating factors include:

- role of the undertaking, for example, where the undertaking is acting under severe duress or pressure;
- genuine uncertainty as to whether the agreement or conduct constituted an infringement;
- adequate steps having been taken with a view to ensuring compliance with the Act;[10]
- infringements which are committed negligently rather than intentionally;
- cooperation which enables the enforcement process to be concluded more effectively and/or speedily than would otherwise be the case, over and above that expected of any undertaking.

NOTE: In cartel cases an undertaking which cooperates fully with the investigation may benefit from total immunity from, or a significant reduction in the level of, a financial penalty, if it meets the requirements set out in Part 3 of this guidance.

Step 5—Adjustment to prevent maximum penalty being exceeded and to avoid double jeopardy

2.13 The final amount of the penalty calculated according to the method set out above may not in any event exceed 10 per cent of the 'section 36(8) turnover' of the undertaking.[11]

2.14 The penalty will be adjusted if necessary to ensure that it does not exceed this maximum. This adjustment will be made *after* all the relevant adjustments have been made in steps 2 to 4 above and also, in cartel cases, *before* any adjustments are made under paragraph 3.8 of this guidance.

2.15 If a penalty or fine has been imposed by the European Commission, or by a court or other body in another Member State in respect of an agreement or conduct, the Director must take that penalty or fine into account when setting the amount of a penalty in relation to that agreement or conduct.

NOTE: Deterrence is a central plank of the fining policy and this was made clear in the *Aberdeen Journals* decision by the DGFT.

Decision of the DGFT in Aberdeen Journals Ltd
No CA98/5/2001, paras 130–132

Step 3: Adjustment for other factors

130. Aberdeen Journals, which had a turnover of £33.9 million is owned by Northcliffe, which publishes over 50 separate regional titles and achieved turnover of £59.3m (not including the turnovers of the subsidiaries it controls, including Aberdeen Journals), and is in turn owned by Daily Mail & General Trust plc, with a turnover of £1,620 million for the year ended 3 October 1999. The management of Northcliffe was intimately involved in Aberdeen Journals' conduct with regard to the *Herald & Post*, authorising, directing, and financing the losses the predatory conduct incurred. Further, the acquisition of a reputation for predation by Northcliffe could have far-reaching adverse effects on competition in several markets served by the newspaper publishing industry across the UK.[67]

---

10 See the Office of Fair Trading's booklet 'How your business can achieve compliance' which does not form part of this guidance, for more information on compliance issues.

11 See footnote 6 above regarding the terms 'relevant turnover' and 'section 36(8) turnover'.

67 See para. 2.4, footnote 9 of OFT423.

131. To ensure that the penalty acts as an adequate deterrent to predation to this undertaking, to the broader newspaper publishing industry, and more generally, the Director has increased the proposed penalty by a factor of four, i.e., to £1,897,200. While this increase is significant, the Director considers that any lesser increase would fail to act as a fully effective deterrent to predation.

Step 4: Adjustment for mitigating factors

132. The Director accepts first that Aberdeen Journals has cooperated fully throughout the investigation, and second, that it took rapid steps to cease its infringement (albeit in the face of an active investigation, and an explicit warning that it was at risk of infringing the Chapter II prohibition). He therefore has reduced the amount of the penalty by 10 per cent and 20 per cent respectively for each of these mitigating factors, and therefore imposes a penalty of £1,328,040.

NOTE: Fines can only be imposed if the infringement was intentional or negligent (s. 36(3)). The CCAT in *Napp* confirmed that these tests were alternatives. It should also be noted at this stage that the CCAT in *Napp* considered that it is not bound by the DGFT Guidelines when reviewing the amount of any penalty imposed by the DGFT. The limit imposed by Order (SI 2000/309) is binding and ss. 39 and 40 also provide for immunity from fines in relation to the Chapter I and II prohibitions in respect of small agreements and conduct of minor significance respectively. See the Competition Act (Small Agreements and Conduct of Minor Significance) Regulations 2000 (SI 2000/262).

In the US and the Community (see Chapter 3) there exists the possibility for members of a cartel to be granted partial or total immunity from competition law penalties in exchange for providing information about the cartel. The existence of a leniency programme can encourage members of cartels to 'whistleblow' and undermines the stability of the cartel. The OFT decided to adopt a leniency programme as part of its enforcement armoury under the CA 1998. The following passage contains the key elements of the programme, contained in the DGFT's Guidance as to the Appropriate Amount of a Penalty, OFT 423.

Guidance as to the Appropriate Amount of a Penalty
OFT 423

3 Lenient treatment for undertakings coming forward with information

Immunity from or reduction in financial penalty for undertakings coming forward with information in cartel cases

3.1 Undertakings participating in cartel activities[12] might wish to terminate their involvement and inform the Director of the existence of the cartel, but be deterred from doing so by the risk of incurring large financial penalties. To encourage such undertakings to come forward the Director will offer total immunity from financial penalties for an infringement of the Chapter I prohibition to a member of a cartel who is the first to come forward and who satisfies the requirements set out in paragraph 3.4. Alternatively, the Director may offer total immunity from financial penalties to a member of a cartel who is the first to come forward and who satisfies the requirements set out in paragraph 3.6. An undertaking which is not the first to come forward, or does not satisfy these requirements may benefit from a reduction in the amount of the penalty imposed if it satisfies the requirements set out in paragraph 3.8 below.

3.2 The Director considers that it is in the interest of the economy of the United Kingdom to grant favourable treatment to undertakings which inform him of cartels and which then cooperate with him in the circumstances set out below. It is the secret nature of cartels which justifies such a policy. The interests of customers and consumers in ensuring that such practices are detected and

12 See meaning of cartel activities as set out in footnote 5 above.

prohibited outweigh the policy objectives of imposing financial penalties on those undertakings which are members of the cartel and which cooperate with the Director.

Total immunity from financial penalties in cartel cases

3.3 Where an undertaking participating in a cartel is the *first to come forward* to provide evidence of the existence and activities of the cartel, and it fulfils all the requirements in paragraph 3.4, it will benefit from *total immunity* from financial penalties in respect of that infringement; if it is the first to come forward to provide such evidence and it fulfils all the requirements of paragraph 3.6 below, it may benefit from *total immunity* from financial penalties in respect of that infringement.

Total immunity for the first to come forward before an investigation has commenced

3.4 In order to benefit from total immunity under this paragraph, the undertaking must be the *first* to provide the Director with evidence of the existence and activities of a cartel *before* he has commenced an investigation[13] of the undertakings involved; provided that the Director does not already have sufficient information to establish the existence of the alleged cartel, and the following conditions are satisfied:

the undertaking must:

(a) provide the Director with all the information, documents and evidence available to it regarding the existence and activities of the cartel;
(b) maintain continuous and complete cooperation throughout the investigation;
(c) not have compelled another undertaking to take part in the cartel and not have acted as the instigator or played the leading role in the cartel; and
(d) refrain from further participation in the cartel from the time it discloses the cartel.

3.5 If an undertaking does not fulfil all the requirements in paragraph 3.4 above, it may still benefit from total immunity from financial penalties if it fulfils all the requirements in paragraph 3.6 below.

Total immunity for the first to come forward after an investigation[14] has commenced

3.6 In order to benefit from the possibility of total immunity under this paragraph:

- the undertaking seeking immunity under this paragraph must be the *first*[15] to provide the Director with evidence of the existence and activities of a cartel *before* the Director has given written notice of his proposal to make a decision that the Chapter I prohibition has been infringed[16]; and
- conditions (a) to (d) in paragraph 3.4 above must be satisfied.

3.7 The grant of immunity by the Director in these circumstances is, however, *discretionary*. In order for the Director to exercise his discretion to grant immunity to the undertaking he must be satisfied that the undertaking should benefit from immunity, taking into account the stage at which the undertaking comes forward and whether or not at that stage the Director has sufficient evidence to make a decision that the Chapter I prohibition has been infringed.

Reduction in the level of financial penalties in cartel cases

3.8 Undertakings which provide evidence of the existence and activities of a cartel *before written notice of a proposed infringement decision is given*, but are not the first to come forward, or do not meet all the requirements under paragraph 3.4 or 3.6 above, will be granted a *reduction* in the

---

13 By the exercise of powers under ss. 26–28 of the Act.
14 See footnote 13 above.
15 i.e. there must not be any undertaking which is benefiting from total immunity under paragraph 3.4 in relation to the same cartel
16 Under Rule 14 in the Competition Act 1998 (Director's rules) Order 2000 (SI 2000, 293).

amount of a financial penalty which would otherwise be imposed of up to 50 per cent, if the following conditions are met:

the undertakings must:

    (a) provide the Director with all the information, documents and evidence available to them regarding the existence and activities of the cartel;

    (b) maintain continuous and complete cooperation throughout the investigation; and

    (c) refrain from further participation in the cartel from the time they disclose the cartel.

NOTE: The scheme provides for partial or total immunity dependent on the fulfilment of the requisite conditions. Immunity can be granted even *after* an investigation has been started by the DGFT. The application of the leniency programme was first demonstrated in the *Arriva/ FirstGroup* decision.

DGFT Decision No CA98/9/2002, Market Sharing by Arriva plc and FirstGroup plc
30 January 2002

This was the first infringement decision by the DGFT under the Chapter I prohibition, and concerned a blatant market-sharing agreement involving bus routes in the Leeds area. The factual background demonstrates a flagrant disregard for the new Act, as the executives involved had each received training for the Act and were aware of their companies' compliance programmes. Dawn raids had taken place following the issue of warrants by the High Court yet the DGFT agreed to grant leniency as follows:

Leniency

70. Under the terms of the Director's leniency scheme, FirstGroup, as the first party to the cartel to approach the Director, after he had started his investigation, and provide evidence thereof, was granted 100 per cent immunity from any financial penalty.[73] The granting of leniency in a letter dated 2 November 2000, and signed on behalf of FirstGroup and the Director, was conditional on FirstGroup providing evidence of the cartel, co-operating with the Director throughout his investigation and complying with the other conditions set out in paragraph 3.4 of the Guidance on Penalties.[74] The Director is satisfied that FirstGroup complied with those conditions and accordingly, the penalty calculated for it is reduced to nil.

71. Arriva approached the Director with a request for leniency second and was granted leniency in a letter dated 8 December 2000, on the same conditions as FirstGroup but only to the extent that

---

73 Guidance on Penalties, paragraph 3.7. The grant of immunity by the Director after he has started an investigation is discretionary. 'In order for the Director to exercise his discretion to grant immunity to the undertaking he must be satisfied that the undertaking should benefit from immunity, taking into account the stage at which the undertaking comes forward and whether or not at that stage the Director has sufficient evidence to make a decision that the Chapter I prohibition has been infringed.'

74 Guidance on Penalties, paragraph 3.6, 'Total immunity for the first to come forward *after* an investigation has commenced. In order to benefit from the possibility of total immunity under this paragraph: the undertaking seeking immunity under this paragraph must be the first to provide the Director with evidence of the existence and activities of a cartel before the Director has given written notice of his proposal to make a decision that the Chapter I prohibition has been infringed; and conditions (a) to (d) in paragraph 3.4 must be satisfied' namely; 'the undertaking must: (a) provide the Director with all the information, documents and evidence available to it regarding the existence and activities of the cartel; (b) maintain continuous and complete cooperation throughout the investigation; (c) not have compelled another undertaking to take part in the cartel and not have acted as the instigator or played the leading role in the cartel; and (d) refrain from further participation in the cartel from the time it discloses the cartel.'

any penalty would be reduced by 36 per cent.[75] The Director is also satisfied that Arriva has complied with the conditions for its leniency and, as a result, the penalty for Arriva is reduced to £203,632.

NOTE: It is unclear why the DGFT selected the figure of 36 per cent in respect of Arriva in this case. The DGFT is hopeful that awareness of the leniency programme, and the creation of a 'race to the competition authority', will act as a deterrent to the formation of cartels and encourage members of existing cartels to come forward for leniency. Recent experience in the US has demonstrated the importance of an effective leniency, or 'corporate amnesty', policy to anti-trust enforcement. See Riley, A., 'Cartel Whistleblowing: Toward an American Model?' 9 MJ1 (2002).

QUESTION

On closer inspection of the background to the *Arriva/FirstGroup* decision, do you agree with the DGFT's decision to grant FirstGroup total immunity from penalty?

The DGFT's functions are to be assumed by the OFT under the Enterprise Bill. See below.

SECTION 3: **The Competition Commission Appeal Tribunal ('CCAT')/Competition Appeal Tribunal ('CAT')**

The CCAT is to be renamed the Competition Appeal Tribunal ('CAT') following the entry into force of Part 2 of the Enterprise Act, but in this section we refer to the practice to date of the CCAT.

The CCAT acts as an appeal tribunal under the CA 1998. Part 2 of the Enterprise Act (ss. 11–15 and Schs 2, 4, and 5) makes provision on the constitution of the CAT and for its rules. Appointments are to be made by the Lord Chancellor and the Tribunal will consist of a President, panel of chairmen and ordinary members. In fact, the President of the CCAT, Sir Christopher Bellamy, has acted as the Chairman in all appeals under the 1998 Act to date. Section 46(i) and (2) sets out what types of decision may be appealed to the CAT.

A: What can be appealed?

Section 46(3) details the type of decisions which can be appealed against:

---

75 Guidance on Penalties, paragraph 3.8. 'Undertakings which provide evidence of the existence and activities of a cartel before written notice of a proposed infringement decision is given, but are not the first to come forward, or do not meet all the requirements under paragraph 3.4 or 3.6 of the Guidance on Penalties will be granted a reduction in the amount of a financial penalty which would otherwise be imposed of up to 50 per cent, if the following conditions are met: the undertakings must: (a) provide the Director with all the information, documents and evidence available to them regarding the existence and activities of the cartel; (b) maintain continuous and complete co-operation throughout the investigation; and (c) refrain from further participation in the cartel from the time they disclose the cartel.'

Competition Act 1998

46. Appealable decisions

(1) Any party to an agreement in respect of which the Director has made a decision may appeal to the Competition Commission against, or with respect to, the decision.

(2) Any person in respect of whose conduct the Director has made a decision may appeal to the Competition Commission against, or with respect to, the decision.

(3) In this section 'decision' means a decision of the Director—

    (a) as to whether the Chapter I prohibition has been infringed,

    (b) as to whether the Chapter II prohibition has been infringed,

    (c) as to whether to grant an individual exemption,

    (d) in respect of an individual exemption—

        (i) as to whether to impose any condition or obligation under section 4(3)(a) or 5(1)(c),

        (ii) where such a condition or obligation has been imposed, as to the condition or obligation,

        (iii) as to the period fixed under section 4(3)(b), or

        (iv) as to the date fixed under section 4(5),

    (e) as to—

        (i) whether to extend the period for which an individual exemption has effect, or

        (ii) the period of any such extension,

    (f) cancelling an exemption,

    (g) as to the imposition of any penalty under section 36 or as to the amount of any such penalty,

    (h) withdrawing or varying any of the decisions in paragraphs (a) to (f) following an application under section 47(1), and includes a direction given under section 32, 33 or 35 and such other decision as may be prescribed.

NOTE: This gives the term 'decision' a fairly wide coverage. However, in one early case, the DGFT argued that no formal decision had been taken at all. Could an aggrieved complainant appeal on the basis of the rejection of a complaint?

Bettercare Group Ltd v *DGFT*
CCAT, Case No 1006/2/1/01, 26 March 2002

Bettercare is engaged in the provision of nursing homes and residential care services in Northern Ireland and complained to the DGFT that a local health and social services trust had abused its position as the sole purchaser of care services from Bettercare by offering unreasonably low contract prices and unfair terms. The complaint was 'rejected' on the basis of the view that the trust did not constitute an undertaking. Bettercare appealed under s. 46. The key issue was whether the communications between the DGFT and Bettercare, without the DGFT instituting the full administrative procedure, constituted a decision.

82. That takes us on to the main question, which is how the Director's decision to reject Bettercare's complaint in this case is to be analysed. Is it, as the Director submits, to be analysed merely as the exercise of the Director's discretion not to conduct an investigation under section 25 for lack of reasonable grounds to suspect an infringement? Or is it, as Bettercare submits, a decision that the Chapter II prohibition is not infringed because North & West is not acting as an undertaking when purchasing social care?

83. In addressing this central issue, it is not in our view helpful to use the concept of a 'decision to reject a complaint' because such a term is ambiguous. The Director may decide to 'reject a complaint' for many reasons. For example, he may have other cases that he wishes to pursue in priority (compare Case T-24 and 28/90 *Automec* v *Commission* [1992] ECR II-2223); he may have insufficient information to decide whether there is an infringement or not; he may suspect that there may be an infringement, but the case does not appear sufficiently promising, or the economic activity concerned sufficiently important, to warrant the commitment of further resources. None of these cases necessarily gives rise to a decision by the Director as to whether a relevant prohibition is infringed.

84. On the other hand, the Director may, in fact, decide to reject a complaint on the ground that there is no infringement. Nothing in the Act prevents the Director from taking a decision, following a complaint, that there has been no infringement. The Director has already done so in a number of decisions which seem to be plainly decisions, within the meaning of section 46(3)(a) or (b), to the effect that the Chapter I or Chapter II prohibitions has not been infringed, for example because there is no dominant position: (see e.g. *Dixon Stores Group Limited/Compaq Computer Limited/Packard Bell NEC Limited* UKCLR [2001] 670; *Consignia plc and Postal Preference Service Limited* UKCLR [2001] 846; *ICL/Synstar* UKCLR [2001] 902.

85. It is true that the decisions of this kind so far taken have a more formal appearance, have apparently been more fully investigated and are more fully reasoned than in the present case. However, we see nothing in the Act to exclude the possibility that the Director may legitimately decide that there is no infringement without conducting a formal investigation, and giving only brief reasons, because in his view the matter is sufficiently clear to enable him to reach a decision without further ado.

86. In our view that is the reality of the situation in this case. As already indicated, in our opinion the correspondence viewed objectively does disclose a decision by or on behalf of the Director to the effect that North & West is not an undertaking within the meaning of section 18 of the Act when acting as a purchaser of social care. As Bettercare submits, the question whether the conduct in question is that of 'an undertaking' within the meaning of section 18 is one of the essential ingredients in establishing an infringement of the Chapter II prohibition. We therefore accept Bettercare's submission that, in deciding that North & West is not acting as an undertaking in the relevant respect, the Director has necessarily decided that the Chapter II prohibition is not infringed as regards the subject matter of Bettercare's complaint. It follows that, in our respectful view, the Director, in this case, has taken a decision as to whether or not the Chapter II prohibition has been infringed, within the meaning of section 46(3)(b) of the Act.

87. It is true that, on the contested view of the facts and the law he takes, the Director's decision that North & West is not an undertaking also precludes him from launching an investigation under section 25 of the Act since, on the Director's view, it necessarily follows that he has 'no reasonable grounds for suspecting' an infringement. However, in our view, one cannot convert what is in substance an appealable decision into an unappealable decision by the simple device of describing it as the exercise of the Director's administrative discretion not to proceed further on the basis of lack of reasonable grounds for suspecting an infringement. It all depends on the substance. In our view, if, as a matter of substance, the Director's statement that he has no reasonable grounds for suspecting an infringement in fact masks a decision by the Director that the Chapter II prohibition is not infringed, there is still a 'relevant decision' for the purposes of section 47(1). In the present case, in our view, the Director has, in effect, decided that the conduct in question does not infringe the Chapter II prohibition, *with the consequence* that he cannot proceed under section 25. But that consequence, in our view, is merely the secondary result of the primary decision that there has been no infringement.

88. We thus reject the Director's submission that the decision in this case should be characterised

merely as an unappealable exercise of his discretion not to proceed further on the ground that the Director 'has no reasonable grounds for suspecting an infringement' under section 25. There may well be cases where the Director feels he has insufficient material in his possession to conduct an investigation under section 25, without being in a position to decide whether or not there is, in fact, an infringement. But in this case, it seems to us, the statements in the letters of 25 September and 2 November 2001, that the Director has 'no reasonable grounds for suspecting an infringement', while correct as far as they go, should not be allowed to conceal the fact that the Director has, in reality, decided that there is no infringement.

NOTE: Bettercare were using the provision in s. 47 to appeal as third parties, see further below. The CCAT stressed that whether the DGFT had taken a relevant decision was a question of fact. Appeal will not be available in all instances whereby the DGFT does not proceed to investigate a complaint fully, for instance on the basis of the prioritising of resources (*per Automec*). In that event, a third party has the alternative of seeking judicial review in the courts. In *Bettercare*, the next phase was the determination of the appeal on the substantive issue upon which the DGFT's decision was based.

B: Who can appeal?

Obviously a party to an agreement or a person in respect of whose conduct the Director has taken a decision can appeal, under s. 46(1) and 46(2) respectively. In addition, s. 47 makes provision for third-party appeals. The system at present is convoluted and first requires a request to the DGFT to withdraw or vary a decision. If the DGFT refuses the request because the applicant does not have a sufficient interest in the original decision or has not shown sufficient reason for it to be withdrawn or varied, the applicant can appeal to the CCAT.

In General Insurance Standards Council, the DGFT decided, on a notification from the GISC, that the rules in its constitution did not breach the Chapter I prohibition (*Notification by the GISC*, DGFT decision No CA98/1/2001). Two parties, the Institute of Independent Insurance Brokers (IIB) and the Association of British Travel Agents (ABTA) made s. 47 applications to the DGFT. It was accepted that both satisfied the sufficiently interested threshold but the DGFT maintained the position in its earlier decision. The third parties appealed, ultimately successfully, and the CCAT was critical of the s. 47 procedure:

Institute of Independent Insurance Brokers, The v **Director General of Fair Trading supported by the General Insurance Standards Council; Association of British Travel Agents Limited** v **The Director General of Fair Trading supported by the General Insurance Standards Council**
(Case Nos 1002/2/1/01 (Ir), 1003/2/1/01, 1004/2/1/01) [2002] CompAR 62

Procedure
270. Although not entirely relevant to the substance, this case has perhaps highlighted the somewhat cumbersome nature of the procedure under section 47 of the Act, which does not confer on an interested person, who is not a party to an agreement, the right to appeal directly to this Tribunal against an adverse decision of the Director, without going through the section 47 procedure. In this particular case, it is unfortunate that, for whatever reason, nearly six months passed before the IIB, in particular, was able to bring its complaint against the GISC Decision before this

Tribunal. That delay was detrimental to the IIB, who in the meantime had to close its regulatory division, and damaging to GISC because it has delayed for a substantial period the final resolution of its notification to the Director. We hope that this issue can be addressed in future, both from the administrative point of view and from the perspective of a possible modification to the Act. More generally, from the point of view of transparency in the procedure, we can see advantages in the Director adopting the administrative practice, in decisions such as the GISC Decision, of indicating briefly the substance of any adverse comments he has received and his response to them.

NOTE: In *Bettercare*, the CCAT rejected a formal approach to the s. 47 procedure by construing correspondence by Bettercare to the DGFT as an application to the DGFT to withdraw or vary the earlier decision. Section 16 of the Enterprise Act seeks to abolish the requirement for third parties to proceed via the DGFT in order to appeal. For fuller discussion of the CCAT judgment in relation to GISC, see Rodger, B.J., 'Early Steps to a Mature Competition Law System: Case Law Developments in the First 18 Months of the Competition Act 1998' [2002] ECLR 52.

QUESTION

Are individual end-product consumers 'interested' third parties for the purposes of an appeal under the Act in respect of, for example, a producers' cartel?

C: Determination of an appeal

The CCAT/CAT has a wide range of decision-making powers in respect of appeals, as set out, in particular in Sch. 8, para. 3(2) to the CA 1998.

Competition Act
Sch. 8, para. 3(2)

(2) The tribunal may confirm or set aside the decision which is the subject of the appeal, or any part of it, and may—
  (a) remit the matter to the Director,
  (b) impose or revoke, or vary the amount of, a penalty,
  (c) grant or cancel an individual exemption or vary any conditions or obligations imposed in relation to the exemption by the Director,
  (d) give such directions, or take such other steps, as the Director could himself have given or taken, or
  (e) make any other decision which the Director could himself have made.

NOTE: Following the Enterprise Act, reference to the 'Director' is replaced by the OFT. The CCAT has already utilised a number of these powers. In *GISC*, it withdrew the DGFT's GISC decision and set aside both s. 47 decisions. It also remitted various issues in connection with the notification and the market for further investigation. Similarly, in *Aberdeen Journals (Aberdeen Journals v DGFT*, 19 March 2002) the DGFT's decision on predatory pricing was set aside and the issue of market definition remitted to the DGFT for fuller consideration. In addition, to avoid undue delay, the DGFT was ordered to commence an administrative procedure within two months and to issue a decision within two months of its completion. Perhaps of greatest interest is the CCAT's power to review any fines imposed by the DGFT. This was a principal issue in the appeal by Napp and the CCAT discussed its role in this context at length. The following are key passages:

Napp Pharmaceutical Holdings Limited and Subsidiaries v *DGFT*
(Case 1000/1/1/01) (final judgment), 15 January 2002

Findings

General observations

497. We observe first, that the Tribunal is not bound by the *Director's Guidance*. The Act contains no provision which requires the Tribunal to even have regard to that *Guidance*.

498. Schedule 8, paragraph 3(2) of the Act, provides that 'the tribunal may confirm or set aside the decision which is the subject to the appeal, or any part of it, and may . . . (b) impose, or revoke, or vary the amount of, a penalty . . . or (e) make any other decision which the Director could have made'.

499. It follows, in our judgment, that the Tribunal has a full jurisdiction itself to assess the penalty to be imposed, if necessary regardless of the way the Director has approached the matter in application of the *Director's Guidance*. Indeed, it seems to us that, in view of Article 6(1) of the ECHR, an undertaking penalised by the Director is entitled to have that penalty reviewed *ab initio* by an impartial and independent tribunal able to take its own decision unconstrained by the *Guidance*. Moreover, it seems to us that, in fixing a penalty, this Tribunal is bound to base itself on its own assessment of the infringement in the light of the facts and matters before the Tribunal at the stage of its judgment.

500. That said, it does not seem to us appropriate to disregard the *Director's Guidance*, or the Director's own approach in the Decision under challenge, when reaching our own conclusion as to what the penalty should be. The *Director's Guidance* will no doubt over time take account of the various indications given by this Tribunal in appeals against penalties.

501. We emphasise, however, that the only constraint on the amount of the penalty binding on this Tribunal is that which flows from the Maximum Penalties Order. In the present case the maximum penalty under that Order is £5.56 million, for an infringement by Napp lasting from 1 March 2000 to 31 March 2001. It is clear from that Order that Parliament intended that it is the overall turnover of the undertaking concerned, rather than its turnover in the products affected by the infringement, which is the final determinant for the amount of the penalty. As the Director points out in the *Guidance*, any other approach would mean that abuses by powerful companies in small relevant markets might not be appropriately sanctioned.

502. We agree with the thrust of the *Director's Guidance* that while the turnover in the products affected by the infringement may be an indicative starting point for the assessment of the penalty, the sum imposed must be such as to constitute a serious and effective deterrent, both to the undertaking concerned and to other undertakings tempted to engage in similar conduct. The policy objectives of the Act will not be achieved unless this Tribunal is prepared to uphold severe penalties for serious infringements. As the *Guidance* makes clear, the achievement of the necessary deterrent may well involve penalties above, often well above, 10 per cent of turnover in the products directly concerned by the infringement, subject only to the overall 'cap' imposed by the Maximum Penalties Order. The position in this respect is no different in principle under Article 15(2) of Council Regulation No 17, albeit that the applicable maximum penalty under that provision is differently calculated.

503. We observe in parenthesis that since 1998 the European Commission has published *Guidelines on the Method of Setting Fines* OJ 1998 C9/3 ('the *Commission's Guidelines*') which have some similarities with, and some differences from, the *Director's Guidance*. The essential approach of the *Commission's Guidelines* is to indicate that the penalty will be made up of a fixed 'basic amount' depending on whether the infringement is categorised as 'minor', 'serious' or 'very serious'. The basic amount is then liable to be increased by reference to whether the infringement

has lasted more than a year, and then further adjusted, upwards or downwards, according to whether there are aggravating or mitigating circumstances. Where there are differences between the *Director's Guidance* and the *Commission's Guidelines*, it seems to us that the differences are probably 'relevant differences' for the purposes of section 60 of the Act, so that we are not required, at present, to take account of the *Commission's Guidelines*. Neither party has suggested that we should do so. However the principle of starting with a certain amount (either a percentage figure, as under the *Director's Guidance*, or a fixed sum, as under the *Commission's Guidelines*) and then adjusting that starting figure to meet the circumstances of the case, is common to both approaches.
. . .

The Tribunal's assessment of the penalty

535. This is the first occasion on which the Tribunal has considered the amount of a penalty under the Act. We propose to adopt a 'broad brush' approach. Each case will depend on its own circumstances.

536. In this case the Director considered an appropriate penalty to be some £3.2 million. Omitting the 'aggravating circumstance' that we are minded to exclude (paragraph 516 above) the Director's figure is £2.92 million.

537. We begin by taking the case as a whole. This is a serious case of predatory and selective pricing, lasting for thirteen months up to the date of the Decision, committed by a 'superdominant' undertaking in one segment of the market (the hospital segment) and tending to protect high prices and margins in another segment of the market where that undertaking is also a virtual monopolist (the community segment). In addition, Napp's prices in the community segment have been maintained well above the competitive level. If the objectives of the Act are to be achieved such conduct calls, in our judgment, for severe penalties. In those circumstances, absent any significant mitigating factors, we do not think that a penalty of £3 million, as a global figure, is outside the range of penalties that could reasonably be imposed, in a case such as the present, having regard to the permitted maximum of £5.56 million.

538. However, in view of the mitigating factors we have mentioned in paragraph 533 above, and to a slight extent those mentioned at paragraph 523 above, we have come to the conclusion that the overall penalty in this case should be fixed at the sum of £2.2 million.

539. If, as a 'cross-check', we were to apply the methodology of the *Director's Guidance*, the same result would be reached by taking the Director's starting percentage under Step 1, applying to that percentage a multiplier of slightly over three to reach £2.92 million under Step 3, and then reducing that figure by some 25 per cent for mitigating factors under Step 4. That in our view would equally have been a reasonable approach.

540. For the reasons already indicated, in paragraphs 507 *et seq.* above, we do not use the calculations of gain presented to us as the basis for our decision. However, we are satisfied that Napp's calculations of the gain do not adequately capture the full commercial advantage of the policy it has followed, for the reasons already given.

541. We consider that a penalty of £2.2 million is the lowest amount that can reasonably be arrived at to penalise Napp's conduct and to send an appropriate signal to the business community of the seriousness of infringements of the Competition Act 1998.

NOTE: Various points are of interest. The CCAT indicated that the Guidelines are not binding and that they would in time take account of CCAT pronouncements. This leaves the practice of determining the level of fines difficult to predict. In addition, the CCAT confirmed that it was not bound, under s. 60, to follow the European Commission approach to fines. The reasoning here is not convincing, as the CCAT relied on the existence of the DGFT Guidelines, which the

CCAT are not bound to adhere to, as a 'relevant difference' for the purposes of s. 60. In fact, ultimately, the CCAT approach is very similar to the Commission methodology, and could be criticised in a UK context for failing to provide any clear guidance for determining the appropriate level of fines at an early stage in the development of practice under the Act. The CCAT indicated the seriousness of the types of breach involved in *Napp*, and the importance of deterrence, but urged caution in relying on an assessment of any 'ill-gotten' gains as aggravating circumstances. This was the only appeal to date in which the CCAT has reviewed the imposition of penalties by the DGFT.

One key area which has been considered by the CCAT is the impact of human rights issues on enforcement under the CA 1998.

Napp Pharmaceutical Holdings Limited and Subsidiaries v *DGFT*
(Case 1000/1/1/01) (final judgment), 15 January 2002

98. As we have already stated in our interim judgment of 8 August 2001, we agree that the Director's concession that these proceedings are 'criminal', for the purposes of Article 6 of the ECHR, is properly made: see Case C-235/92P *Montecatini* v *Commission* [1999] ECR I-4575, paragraphs 175 and 176. That is particularly so since penalties under the Act are intended to be severe and to have a deterrent effect: see the Director's statutory *Guidance as to the appropriate amount of the Penalty*, (OFT 423, March 2000) issued under section 38(1) of the Act.

99. The fact that these proceedings may be classified as 'criminal' for the purposes of the ECHR gives Napp the protection of Article 6, and in particular the right to 'a fair and public hearing within a reasonable time by an independent and impartial tribunal established by law' (Article 6(1)), to the presumption of innocence (Article 6(2)), and to the minimum rights envisaged by Article 6(3) including the right 'to examine or have examined witnesses against him and to obtain the attendance and examination of witnesses on his behalf under the same conditions as witnesses against him' (Article 6(3)(d)).

100. In our view it follows from Article 6(2) that the burden of proof rests throughout on the Director to prove the infringements alleged.

101. However, as the Court of Appeal held in *Han*, cited above, to which we referred in our judgment of 8 August 2001, the fact that Article 6 applies does not of itself lead to the conclusion that these proceedings must be subject to the procedures and rules that apply to the investigation and trial of offences classified as criminal offences for the purposes of domestic law: see Potter LJ at paragraph 84, and Mance LJ at paragraph 88 of that judgment.

102. Neither the ECHR itself nor the European Court of Human Rights has laid down a particular standard of proof that must be applied in proceedings to which Article 6(2) or (3) apply, and still less that the standard should be that of 'proof beyond reasonable doubt', which is not a concept to be found in the domestic systems of many of the signatory States (see Sir Richard Buxton, cited above, at pp. 338 and 339).

103. In our view it follows that neither Article 6, nor the Human Rights Act 1998, in themselves oblige us to apply the criminal standard of proof as established in domestic law in cases where the Director seeks to impose a financial penalty in respect of alleged infringements of the Chapter I or Chapter II prohibitions under the Act.

104. In our view the standard of proof to be applied under the Act is to be decided in accordance with the normal rules of the United Kingdom domestic legal systems. Neither party has cited to us any decided domestic cases which suggest that, in circumstances such as these, the criminal standard should be applied, nor invited us to apply by analogy certain civil situations where traditionally the criminal standard of proof is required (e.g. committal proceedings).

105. Infringements of the Chapter I and Chapter II prohibitions imposed by sections 2 and 18 of the Act are not classified as criminal offences in domestic law, in contrast, for example, to the

criminal offences created under sections 42 to 44. Under section 38(8), penalties are recoverable by the Director as a civil debt. Directions are enforceable by civil proceedings under section 34. In our view the structure of the Act points to the conclusion that under domestic law the standard of proof we must apply in deciding whether infringements of the Chapter I or Chapter II prohibitions are proved is the civil standard, commonly known as the preponderance or balance of probabilities, notwithstanding that the civil penalties imposed may be intended by the Director to have a deterrent effect.

106. We add that in many cases under the Act the factual issues before this Tribunal will often relate to such matters as determining the relevant market, whether dominance exists, and assessing whether conduct characterised as an 'abuse' is economically justified. Issues of that kind involve a more or less complex assessment of mainly economic data and perhaps conflicting expert evidence. It seems to us more likely that Parliament would have intended us to apply the civil standard of proof to issues of this kind, rather than the time-honoured criminal standard of 'proof beyond reasonable doubt'.

107. In our view it follows from the speech of Lord Nicholls (with whom Lord Goff and Lord Mustill agreed) in Re H, cited above, at pp. 586 to 587, that under the law of England and Wales there are only two standards of proof, the criminal standard and the civil standard; there is no 'intermediate' standard. The position is the same in the law of Scotland and Northern Ireland. Within the civil standard, however, the more serious the allegation, the more cogent should be the evidence before the court concludes that the allegation is established on the preponderance of probability: see Lord Nicholls' speech in Re H, citing notably In re Dellow's Will Trusts [1964] 1 WLR 451, 455 and Hornal v Neuberger Products Ltd [1957] 1 QB 247, 266.

108. Since cases under the Act involving penalties are serious matters, it follows from Re H that strong and convincing evidence will be required before infringements of the Chapter I and Chapter II prohibitions can be found to be proved, even to the civil standard. Indeed, whether we are, in technical terms, applying a civil standard on the basis of strong and convincing evidence, or a criminal standard of beyond reasonable doubt, we think in practice the result is likely to be the same. We find it difficult to imagine, for example, this Tribunal upholding a penalty if there were a reasonable doubt in our minds, or if we were anything less than sure that the Decision was soundly based.

109. In those circumstances the conclusion we reach is that, formally speaking, the standard of proof in proceedings under the Act involving penalties is the civil standard of proof, but that standard is to be applied bearing in mind that infringements of the Act are serious matters attracting severe financial penalties. It is for the Director to satisfy us in each case, on the basis of strong and compelling evidence, taking account of the seriousness of what is alleged, that the infringement is duly proved, the undertaking being entitled to the presumption of innocence, and to any reasonable doubt there may be.

NOTE: The impact of human rights legislation is likely to have a wider impact and challenges are also to be anticipated in relation to the investigatory powers afforded the DGFT. The CCAT was also clearly aware of the human rights implications in the Aberdeen Journals appeal, where the CCAT did not allow reliance by the DGFT on material at the appeal stage as this would materially weaken the statutory right to be heard during the administrative phase.

QUESTION

If the sanctions under the CA 1998 are penal in nature, should it not follow that the authorities should adhere fully to the protections afforded to the defence under criminal proceedings?

NOTE: Under s. 49 of the Act a further appeal lies from decisions of an appeal tribunal either on a point of law or as to the amount of any penalty, or as to an award under s. 47A or 47B of the CA 1998. Any such appeal is to: the Court of Appeal in England and Wales in relation to proceedings before a tribunal in England and Wales; to the Court of Session in Scotland for proceedings before a tribunal in Scotland; and to the Court of Appeal in Northern Ireland for proceedings before a tribunal in Northern Ireland. Accordingly, any appeal in the *Aberdeen Journals* case would be to the Court of Session and in relation to *Bettercare*, to the Court of Appeal in Northern Ireland as the CCAT sat as a Scottish and Northern Irish tribunal respectively in those cases. Following the *Napp* judgment, Napp sought leave to appeal to the Court of Appeal and the CCAT adopted a very restricted definition of what constitutes a 'point of law'.

Napp Pharmaceutical Holdings Limited and Subsidiaries v *DGFT*

(Case 1000/1/1/01) (re reasons for refusing permission to appeal), 26 March 2002

Appeal on a point of law

25. In determining this request for permission to appeal, we have addressed, at least provisionally, what is meant by 'a point of law arising from a decision of an appeal tribunal' under section 49(1)(a) of the Act. This point is not addressed in Napp's application or skeleton argument, albeit it is briefly mentioned in Napp's further observations.

26. It is trite to say that a point of law is to be distinguished from a point of fact. As is well known, it may be difficult to say, in any given case, where the border lies between the two. In the present case, the issue is whether Napp has committed an 'abuse' within the meaning of the Chapter II prohibition. At one end of the spectrum, the Court of Justice and the Court of First Instance have laid down certain legal principles which apply when determining whether the Chapter II prohibition has been infringed. Whether we had, for example, ignored a relevant decision of the Court of Justice, would, we would have thought, be a point of law. At the other end of the spectrum, there will plainly be points of primary fact. For example, whether in this case Napp's prices to hospitals were or were not below the cost of raw materials is a point of fact. However, between these opposite ends of the spectrum there will, so it seems to us, often be questions arising under the Act which are essentially questions of appreciation or economic assessment of a more or less complex kind, depending on the circumstances, in which the Tribunal will be called upon to assess a range of factors, bringing to bear such expertise as it has, in order to determine such matters as the boundaries of the 'relevant market', the existence of 'barriers to entry', whether 'dominance' is established, whether a response by the dominant undertaking is 'proportionate' and so on.

27. In the present application, for example, a substantial part of Napp's argument on the hospital pricing abuse is that its pricing policy constituted 'normal competition' (grounds 1 (i), (ii), (iii) and (vi) of the request), this being, apparently, a reference to a dictum by the Court of Justice in Case 85/76 *Hoffman-La Roche* v *Commission* [1979] ECR 461, paragraph 91, which refers to a dominant undertaking committing an abuse 'through recourse to methods different from those which condition normal competition' (see paragraph 207 of the Tribunal's judgment). The issues surrounding this argument, from the many different angles it has been presented, are dealt with at paragraphs 231 to 352 of the Tribunal's judgment, Napp's contentions being rejected on every point. Whether, on the facts of this case what Napp did can be defended on the ground that it constituted 'normal competition' does not seem to us to be a 'point of law' as such, but rather a question of appreciation of the various interrelated facts and considerations discussed in paragraphs 231 to 352 of the judgment.

. . .

35. These cases, notably *Bairstow* v *Edwards* read with *South Yorkshire Transport*, cited above, seem to point to the conclusion that there is a 'point of law' under section 49(1)(a) where the issue is whether (i) there is a misdirection on a point of law; (ii) there is no evidence to support a relevant

finding of fact; or (iii) the tribunal's appreciation of the facts and issues before it is one that no reasonable tribunal could reach, that is to say the appreciation in question is outside 'the permissible field of judgment'. In the light of *Nipa Begum*, it may well be that the principles to be applied are not signficantly different from those applicable in judicial review proceedings. We bear these cases in mind in deciding whether Napp's arguments do involve 'a point of law' under section 49(1)(a), and if so whether any such point of law has a real prospect of success.

NOTE: This is a rather restrictive interpretation of what constitutes a 'point of law', limited to 'judicial review' type issues. The CCAT concluded that there were no real points of law raised in the appeal and no compelling reason to allow an appeal to proceed merely because this case involved the first infringement and penalty imposed under the Act. The Court of Appeal subsequently supported the refusal to allow permission to appeal as the appeal did not involve points of law (*Napp Pharmaceutical Holdings Ltd* v *DGFT* [2002] EWCA Civ 796, 8 May 2002). Interestingly, Buxton LJ, at para. 34, stated that even if the court had authority to review the CCAT's findings, it would be very reluctant to interfere with the conclusions of an expert and specialist tribunal.

For further reading, see Rayment, B., 'Practice and Procedure in the Competition Commission Appeal Tribunals' [2002] Comp Law, Issue 1.

SECTION 4:   **Private enforcement under the CA 1998**

One of the weaknesses identified in the proposals to reform UK competition law during the late 1980s and early 1990s was the absence of private rights of redress, notably under the FTA 1973. In the US, antitrust damages actions by claimants has played a significant role in the enforcement regime. See Jones, C., *Private Enforcement of Antitrust Law in the EU, UK, and USA*, Oxford: OUP, 1999. It is recognised that private enforcement of the competition rules, in tandem with administrative enforcement, can enhance their deterrent impact. As MacCulloch explains, the CA 1998 was introduced with the intention, albeit implied, of instituting a hybrid system of enforcement of the new prohibitions:

MacCulloch, A., Chapter 5 'Private Enforcement of the Competition Act Prohibitions', in Rodger, B.J., and MacCulloch, A. (eds), *The UK Competition Act: A New Era for UK Competition Law*
Oxford, Hart Publishing, 2000

The possibility of compensation actions following the breach of one of the prohibitions was heralded by the, then, President of the Board of Trade, Margaret Beckett, in the Draft Bill and explanatory document published in August 1997.[8] The change was undoubtedly to be welcomed, as it will give those who are directly affected by infringements an important new weapon. However, the exact manner in which such an action stems from the Act is uncertain. The main difficulty flows from the absence of a specific provision in the Act that states that private parties can bring an action based on an infringement of the Act's prohibitions. The lack of a specific provision leaves many important questions unanswered.

---

8 *A Prohibition Approach to Anti-Competitive Agreements and Abuse of a Dominant Position: Draft Bill* (London, DTI, 1997) ch 7.23.

The failure to provide directly for private actions received scant attention during debate in the Lords.[9] The only relevant provisions in the Act appear to be sections 55 and 58. Section 55(3)(b) provides that the Director General may disclose information to third parties if the disclosure is made for the purposes of civil proceedings. Section 58(1) provides that a finding of fact by the Director General in Part I proceedings is binding on the parties if the time for bringing an appeal has expired or an appeal tribunal has confirmed the decision. The reference to 'Part I proceedings' is defined in section 58(2) to include actions brought under Chapter I or II prohibitions by parties other than the Director General. The proceedings referred to in sections 55 and 58 must be actions brought by private individuals under the prohibitions, presumably for compensation, after administrative enforcement procedures have been completed.[10] This would be of obvious assistance to private claimants, as they would no longer need to prove the existence of an infringement to succeed in such an action, but could simply rely on any findings in the administrative action. This would enact a rule similar to that developed by the courts in *Iberian UK Ltd* v *BPB Industries*[11] for findings made by the European Commission during Community competition procedures or the rules developed in the USA under section 5(a) of the Clayton Act 1914.

It is submitted that the 1998 Act provides for a right of private action, but on what basis should a claimant proceed? The most obvious cause of action where a person seeks a remedy based on a statutory prohibition is that of breach of statutory duty. The common law rules surrounding the availability of such an action in the competition field were discussed recently in relation to sections 93 and 93A of the Fair Trading Act 1973 in *Mid Kent Holdings plc* v *General Utilities plc*.[12] The court came to the conclusion that there was no private right of action, even though section 93(2) and section 93A(2) appear, on their face, to give a right of action to a third party who apprehends the breach of an order, under section 93(2), or an undertaking, under section 93A(2). Without delving too deeply into the logic that led to that particular outcome, the reasons given by Knox J were based on the application of the general law governing the availability of civil remedies for the breach of a statutory provision.[13] The same principles will be used to establish if the prohibitions in the 1998 Act are enforceable by private parties. The fact that an ostensibly enabling provision was interpreted in that case in such a restrictive manner gives cause for concern.

The first general principle is that stated by Lord Simmons in *Cutler* v *Wandsworth Stadium Ltd*:[14]

> The only rule which in all the circumstances is valid is that the answer must depend on a consideration of the whole Act and the circumstances, including the pre-existing law, in which it was enacted.

As far as this principle is concerned, it appears that the Chapter I and II prohibitions of the 1998 Act may be amenable to a civil remedy. The arguments for the availability of civil remedies come from two main sources. The first potential argument rests upon the interpretation of the prohibitions themselves. Under the terms of section 60, the 1998 Act is designed to ensure that questions arising in the Act are 'dealt with in a manner which is consistent with the treatment of corresponding questions arising in Community law'. Concerns have been raised about the potential scope of this provision with regard to the particular needs of Community law, on one hand, and UK law, on the other.[15] Here we have an example of a potential difficulty. How far can the jurisprudence of

---

9 Hansard, HL, 17 November 1997, col 956.

10 A private action could seek injunctive relief, but as administrative action would have been completed it can be assumed that the infringing practices would have been discontinued.

11 [1996] 2 CMLR 601.

12 [1997] 1 WLR 14, [1996] 3 All ER 132.

13 The court's reasoning is explained fully in Rodger, B.J., 'Mid Kent Holdings plc v General Utilities plc: Remedies under the Fair Trading Act 1973' [1997] ECLR 273.

14 [1949] 1 All ER 544 at 548.

15 See J. Scholes and others, 'The UK Draft Competition Bill: Based on the Observations of the Competition Law Association' [1998] ECLR 32.

the European Court go in assisting a national court to discover Parliament's intention? The argument could run as follows.

- Parliament had the intention of making the UK provisions as consistent as possible with the corresponding Community provisions. Accordingly it copied the wording of Articles 81 and 82 of the EC Treaty, as far as possible in the UK context, in the Chapter I and II provisions; and added the interpretation provisions in section 60.
- The European Court in *BRT* v *SABAM*[16] held that, 'as the prohibitions in Articles 85(1) and 86 tend by their very nature to produce direct effects in relations between individuals, these Articles create direct rights in respect of the individuals concerned which the national courts must safeguard'.
- Therefore, Parliament must have intended that the Chapter I and II prohibitions in the 1998 Act create rights directly enforceable by individuals.

The Director General, in its Guideline on enforcement, is of the view that third party rights exist by implication in the Act.[17] In paragraph 5.1 the Guidance refers to section 60(6)(b) and states:

Section 60, which sets out certain principles to provide for the UK authorities to handle cases in such a way as to ensure consistency with EC law, expressly refers to decisions of the European Court and the European Commission as to the civil liability of an undertaking for harm caused by its infringement of Community law.

The express reference in the Act to expansive Community jurisprudence in the area of civil liability would be missed on all but the closest reading of the legislation. Section 60 appears to be a very general provision. The OFT's desire to give section 60 a broad inclusive interpretation does it credit but raises questions as to the scope of the wholesale adoption of Community competition law and policy. It also remains to be seen whether the UK courts will be as receptive to such an expansive interpretation. It is possible to view the interpretation provision as referring only to the application of the prohibitions themselves.[18]

While that argument is interesting, a second, more 'traditional', way of discovering Parliament's intention is also available to the courts. Since the decision of the House of Lords in *Pepper* v *Hart*[19] the courts may look back at parliamentary debates to assist them in their interpretation of statutes. There is sufficient evidence in the debates to come to the conclusion that private actions were envisaged. In response to a question on private remedies tabled by Lord Lucas in the Lords the government spokesman stated that there was 'no need to make explicit provision in the bill'.[20] While this may be evidence of their intention it certainly shows limited understanding of the canons of statutory interpretation.

It may therefore be possible to show that the general principle has been satisfied but there are also several more specific rules, one of which may cause problems with regard to the 1998 Act. Lord Simmons was of the opinion, in *Cutler* v *Wandsworth Stadium*,[21] that a court was not bound by the general principle. He went on to approve the statement by Lord Tenterden CJ in *Doe d. Rochester* v *Bridges*[22] that 'where an Act creates an obligation, and enforces the performance in a specified manner, we take it to be a general rule that performance cannot be enforced in any other manner'.

16 [1974] ECR 51, para 16.
17 *Enforcement* (OFT 407), para 5.1.
18 In other parts of the guidance the OFT stress that textual differences between the UK and EC provisions result in different interpretations. See *The Major Provisions* (OFT 400), para 6.3.
19 [1993] AC 593, [1992] 3 WLR 1032, [1993] All ER 42.
20 Hansard, HL, 17 November 1997, col 956. The Government's reasoning behind the lack of provision will be discussed in more detail *infra*.
21 [1949] AC 398.
22 (1831) 1 B & Ad 847 at 859, [1824–34] All ER Rep 167 at 170.

Obviously the 1998 Act gives the Director General broad powers to enforce the prohibitions; including the power to levy fines of up to 10 per cent of the UK turnover of the undertakings concerned. If one follows the 'general rule' in *Rochester* it would appear to be the case that private remedies would not be available in addition to the sweeping enforcement powers set out in the Act.

There is, of course, an exception to this rule. It is found in *Butler v Fife Coal Co Ltd*,[23] where it was held that 'when a duty of this kind is imposed for the benefit of particular persons, there arises at common law a correlative right in those persons who may be injured by its contravention'. Again, in this situation it could be valuable to return to the jurisprudence of the European Court. In *BRT v SABAM* it set out that Articles 81(1) and 82 EC, upon which the Chapter I and II prohibitions are based, 'produce direct effects in relations between individuals' and 'create direct rights in respect of the individuals concerned which the national courts must safeguard'. It may therefore be possible that the 1998 Act, with assistance from section 60, is to be interpreted as creating the same rights for individuals as a protected class, and therefore the general rule is to be displaced.

NOTE: It remains unclear why the government did not insert an express provision in the Act although the purported rationale was to retain harmony with the Community system. Neither of the facilitative provisions has, as yet, been utilised, although there have been a number of private actions raised in relation to the prohibitions. See, for discussion of some of the earlier cases, Rodger, B.J., 'Early Steps to a Mature Competition Law System: Case Law Developments in the First 18 Months of the Competition Act 1998' [2002] ECLR 52 at pp. 65–67. To a great extent, the earlier debate on the availability of private actions (see, for instance, Turner, J., 'The UK Competition Act 1998 and Private Rights' [1999] ECLR 62), has now been superseded as the issue has not been disputed in any of the judgments to date, for instance see *Getmapping plc v Ordnance Survey* (Laddie J, 31 May 2002, [2002] EWHC 1089 (Ch)).

Private enforcement does not solely consist of damages actions. Deterrence and effective protection of damaged parties can also be achieved by the availability of other forms of effective relief, such as an injunction or interdict, and a number of cases to date have involved this issue. The claimant in *Getmapping* was unsuccessful, see Chapter 2, but the claimant in *Network Multimedia Television Ltd (T/A Silicon.Com) v Jobserve Ltd* was granted an injunction, High Court, Chancery, Whightman QC, 5 April 2001, CA [2001] EWCA Civ 2018, 21 December 2001.

There are a number of hurdles facing any complaint in pursuing a successful damages claim, including the rules of domestic civil procedure. See Kon, S., and Maxwell, A.J., 'Enforcement in National Courts of the EC and New UK Competition Rules: Obstacles to Effective Enforcement' [1998] ECLR 443. In particular, there has been no final award of damages by a UK court under the Act and questions relating to the range of potential claimants, remoteness of damages and the quantification of damages remain unanswered.

Van Dijk, R., and Niels, G., 'The Economics of Quantifying Damages'
[2002] Comp Law, Issue 1

Who should be allowed to claim damages?
Arguably, only a party that suffers an injury that competition law was designed to prevent should be allowed to claim damages. This principle might mean that not only the direct purchasers of the cartel's products should be able to claim damages, but also the indirect purchasers—ie the customers of the customers of the cartel—if the direct purchasers' increased costs have been passed on to them.

However, in the US, a Supreme Court decision of 1977 generally denied indirect buyers such rights. Thus, in a cartel case involving an input into a final consumer good, only the immediate downstream producers of that final good are entitled to damages. End consumers are not allowed

23 [1912] AC 149 at 165.

standing, even if the downstream producers fully pass on the cartel price increase to consumer prices.

The main economic rationale behind this decision is that direct buyers have greater incentives to sue.

. . .

End consumers might be able to sue as a class, but this has the potential disadvantage that, in the end, the damages awarded must be divided among a large number of parties. This reduces the incentives for individuals to take active part in the class action, and may induce free riding. Direct buyers are normally fewer in numbers, so there is less of a free-rider problem.

The above may reflect a difference in the design of the legal framework for damages in the USA and the EU. Private competition law enforcement has two main objectives: first, to compensate the victims of anti-competitive behaviour; and, secondly, to deter companies from behaving anti-competitively in the first place. It may be that in the EU damages are mainly intended to compensate victims, while the US Supreme Court's decision referred to above attached relatively more weight to the deterrence effect.

. . .

Conclusion

The number of private competition law litigation cases in the national courts in Europe is still small, especially when contrasted with the situation in the USA. However, awareness and understanding of competition law are growing among European businesses and consumers, and policy initiatives are being taken to further facilitate private actions.

Quantifying damages is therefore becoming increasingly important. Courts are required to scrutinise damages claims. They have to judge whether claims are based on sound counterfactual analysis—and no doubt a few affected parties will tend to exaggerate the profits they would have made absent the anti-competitive behaviour. In US antitrust law, the principles and methodologies behind damages claims are now reasonably established. The challenge is to further develop such expertise and case-law in the national courts of Europe.

NOTE: US experience in quantifying damages will be instructive although it will be of less assistance in determining the types of remedies and range of potential claimants. In addition, developments in the private enforcement of Community law (discussed in Chapter 3 above), most notably in *Crehan* v *Courage*, are likely to provide little direct assistance, as it is left to national law to provide appropriate remedies. See Jones, A., and Beard, D., 'Co-Contractors, Damages and Article 81: The ECJ Finally Speaks' [2002] ECLR 246 at 252; and Rodger, B.J., 'The Interface Between Competition Law and Private Law: Article 81, Illegality and Unjustified Enrichment' (2002) 6/2 Edin LR 217–243. It has recently been suggested that the courts should consider the award of exemplary damages for breach of the CA 1998 prohibitions.

SECTION 5: **Enterprise Act provisions on private enforcement**

A principal aim of the Enterprise Act competition reforms is to enhance the rights of redress available to parties allegedly harmed by competition law infringements and thereby to enhance the deterrent effect of the competition rules. There are three provisions in Part 2 of the Act which merit brief consideration.

A: 'Damage' awards

Section 18 inserts a new s. 47A into the CA 1998 and allows claims for damages or any other sum of money to be brought before the Tribunal:

Enterprise Act

47A Monetary claims before Tribunal

(1) This section applies to—

(a) any claim for damages, or

(b) any other claim for a sum of money,

which a person who has suffered loss or damage as a result of the infringement of a relevant prohibition may make in civil proceedings brought in any part of the United Kingdom.

(2) In this section 'relevant prohibition' means any of the following—

(a) the Chapter I prohibition;

(b) the Chapter II prohibition;

(c) the prohibition in Article 81(1) of the Treaty;

(d) the prohibition in Article 82 of the Treaty;

(e) the prohibition in Article 65(1) of the Treaty establishing the European Coal and Steel Community;

(f) the prohibition in Article 66(7) of that Treaty.

(3) For the purpose of identifying claims which may be made in civil proceedings, any limitation rules that would apply in such proceedings are to be disregarded.

(4) A claim to which this section applies may (subject to the provisions of this Act and Tribunal rules) be made in proceedings brought before the Tribunal.

(5) But no claim may be made in such proceedings—

(a) until a decision mentioned in subsection (6) has established that the relevant prohibition in question has been infringed; and

(b) otherwise than with the permission of the Tribunal, during any period specified in subsection (7) or (8) which relates to that decision.

(6) The decisions which may be relied on for the purposes of proceedings under this section are—

(a) a decision of the OFT that the Chapter I prohibition or the Chapter II prohibition has been infringed

(b) a decision of the OFT that the prohibition in Article 81(1) or Article 82 of the Treaty has been infringed;

(c) a decision of the Tribunal on an appeal from a decision of the OFT that the Chapter I prohibition, the Chapter II prohibition or the prohibition in Article 81(1) or Article 82 of the Treaty has been infringed;

(d) a decision of the European Commission that the prohibition in Article 81(1) or Article 82 of the Treaty has been infringed; or

(e) a decision of the European Commission that the prohibition in Article 65(1) of the Treaty establishing the European Coal and Steel Community has been infringed, or a finding made by the European Commission under Article 66(7) of that Treaty.

(7) The periods during which proceedings in respect of a claim made in reliance on a decision mentioned in subsection (6) (a), (b) or (c) may not be brought without permission are—

(a) in the case of a decision of the OFT, the period during which an appeal may be made to the Tribunal under section 46, section 47 or the EC Competition Law (Articles 84 and 85) Enforcement Regulations 2001 (SI 2001/2916);

(b) in the case of a decision of the OFT which is the subject of an appeal mentioned in paragraph (a), the period following the decision of the Tribunal on the appeal during which a further appeal may be made under section 49 or under those Regulations;

(c) in the case of a decision of the Tribunal mentioned in subsection (5)(c), the period during which a further appeal may be made under section 49 or under those Regulations;

(d) in the case of any decision which is the subject of a further appeal, the period during which an appeal may be made to the House of Lords from a decision on the further appeal;

and, where any appeal mentioned in paragraph (a), (b), (c) or (d) is made, the period specified in that paragraph includes the period before the appeal is determined.

(8) The periods during which proceedings in respect of a claim made in reliance on a decision or finding of the European Commission may not be brought without permission are—

(a) the period during which proceedings against the decision or finding may be instituted in the European Court; and

(b) if any such proceedings are instituted, the period before those proceedings are determined.

(9) In determining a claim to which this section applies the Tribunal is bound by any decision mentioned in subsection (6) which establishes that the prohibition in question has been infringed.

(10) The right to make a claim to which this section applies in proceedings before the Tribunal does not affect the right to bring any other proceedings in respect of the claim.

NOTE: The tribunal can make monetary awards for breaches of both UK and EC competition law, but only if the relevant UK or EC authorities have made infringement decisions. The ability to raise 'follow-on' actions of this kind has been a particular success in the US. See Jones, and MacCulloch above. It is questionable at this stage whether the Tribunal, a body entrusted to deal with competition law issues, is suited to the task of awarding damages under s. 47A. In any event, aggrieved parties retain the option of commencing civil court proceedings under s. 47A. For alternative proposals, see Lever, J., 'Restructuring Courts and Tribunals Hearing UK and EC Competition Law Cases' [2002] Comp Law, Issue 1.

B: Claims on behalf of consumers

Section 19 inserts a new s. 47(B) which allows representative actions on behalf of consumers under s. 47(A) to be brought before the Tribunal:

Enterprise Act

47B Claims brought on behalf of consumers

(1) A specified body may (subject to the provisions of this Act and Tribunal rules) bring proceedings before the Tribunal which comprise consumer claims made or continued on behalf of at least two individuals.

(2) In this section 'consumer claim' means a claim to which section 47A applies which an individual has in respect of an infringement affecting (directly or indirectly) goods or services to which subsection (7) applies.

(3) A consumer claim may be included in proceedings under this section if it is—

(a) a claim made in the proceedings on behalf of the individual concerned by the specified body; or

(b) a claim made by the individual concerned under section 47A which is continued in the proceedings on his behalf by the specified body;

and such a claim may only be made or continued in the proceedings with the consent of the individual concerned.

(4) The consumer claims included in proceedings under this section must all relate to the same infringement.

(5) The provisions of section 47A(5) to (10) apply to a consumer claim included in proceedings under this section as they apply to a claim made in proceedings under that section.

(6) Any damages or other sum (not being costs or expenses) awarded in respect of a consumer claim included in proceedings under this section must be awarded to the individual concerned; but the Tribunal may, with the consent of the specified body and the individual, order that the sum awarded must be paid to the specified body (acting on behalf of the individual).

(7) This subsection applies to goods or services which—
   (a) the individual received, or sought to receive, otherwise than in the course of a business carried on by him (notwithstanding that he received or sought to receive them with a view to carrying on a business); and
   (b) were, or would have been, supplied to the individual (in the case of goods whether by way of sale or otherwise) in the course of a business carried on by the person who supplied or would have supplied them.

(8) A business includes—
   (a) a professional practice;
   (b) any other undertaking carried on for gain or reward;
   (c) any undertaking in the course of which goods or services are supplied otherwise than free of charge.

(9) 'Specified' means specified in an order made by the Secretary of State, in accordance with criteria to be published by the Secretary of State for the purposes of this section.

(10) An application by a body to be specified in an order under this section is to be made in a form approved by the Secretary of State for the purpose.

NOTE: There is provision in s. 47B for specifying appropriate consumer representative bodies for this purpose. This section contains a fairly wide definition of consumer for these purposes and reading subsections (2) and (7) together indicates that this procedure may be utilised in respect of indirect purchasers, in contrast with the current position in the US set out in *Illinois Brick* v *State of Illinois* 431 US 720 (1977). See Van Dijk and Niels, above.

C: Support for private enforcement

Section 20 inserts a new s. 58A which provides that in any action for damages for an infringement of the 1998 Act prohibitions or Article 81(1) or 82, a court will be bound by a decision of the OFT or Tribunal that any of the prohibitions have been infringed, provided that the requisite appeal process has taken place or the period for appeal lapsed.

Enterprise Act [s. 19 to end s. 58A(2)]

58A Findings of infringements
   (1) In any proceedings before the court for damages in respect of an infringement of—

(a) the Chapter I prohibition;
(b) the Chapter II prohibition;
(c) the prohibition in Article 81(1) of the Treaty;
(d) the prohibition in Article 82 of the Treaty;
the court is bound by a decision mentioned in subsection (2) in respect of the infringement.
(2) The decisions are—
    (a) a decision of the OFT that the Chapter I prohibition or the Chapter II prohibition has been infringed;
    (b) a decision of the OFT that the prohibition in Article 81(1) or Article 82 of the Treaty has been infringed;
    (c) a decision of the Tribunal that the Chapter I prohibition or the Chapter II prohibition has been infringed, or that the prohibition in Article 81(1) or Article 82 of the Treaty has been infringed.

NOTE: This provision widens the scope of the support in s. 58 and s. 55(3)(b) of the CA 1998 and is influenced by the system in the US whereby follow-on private actions are facilitated by the ability to rely on prior public law determinations. In addition, s. 16 of the Enterprise Act allows for the possibility of the transfer of proceedings between the CAT and the ordinary civil courts, with the long-term view of the development of the CAT as the specialist competition court in the UK.

The Enterprise Act reforms the enforcement of UK competition law in two major respects. The first is in relation to enforcement under the CA 1998, and the second concerns the replacement of the merger and monopoly control mechanisms under the FTA 1973 with the merger and market investigation control systems under Parts 3 and 4 of the Enterprise Act, see Chapter 9. In addition, there are new enforcement tasks under Part 6 of the Act in relation to the new cartel offence. In relation to the CA 1998, with the exception of private enforcement, discussed above, the changes are largely cosmetic, involving different bodies discharging essentially the same functions. The Competition Appeal Tribunal (CAT) is to replace the appeal tribunal of the Competition Commission (CCAT) (section 12 and Sch. 2), although it will also undertake certain new tasks such as awarding damages or other sums of money under s. 47A of the CA 1998 (above). A more significant change is the transfer of the DGFT's tasks and functions, not only for the purposes of the CA 1998 prohibitions but for all competition law functions to the newly constituted OFT.

SECTION 6: **The Enterprise Act: other main issues**

A: An independent competition authority

The Enterprise Act continues the trend towards the depoliticisation of UK competition law by reducing the role and influence of the Secretary of State and by the creation of the OFT as an independent authority.

DTI White Paper, World Class Competition Regime
July 2001

Strong, proactive and independent competition authorities
• The Government wishes to see truly independent competition authorities which work proactively to root out instances of anti-competitive behaviour.

- There will be clear legal duties for the OFT to promote competition.
- Government invites our competition authorities to advise on the impact of laws and regulations on competition. The Government is committed to responding publicly within 90 days.
- Government welcomes the OFT's move to introduce 'super-complaints' from consumer groups. This new power will be enshrined in legislation.
- Only those with expertise relevant to competition will be appointed to the Competition Commission. Only those with expertise relevant to competition or consumer affairs will be appointed to the Board of the OFT.
- Both the Competition Commission and the OFT will improve their staffing—with recruitment on the basis of expertise relevant to competition becoming the norm for those working in competition.
- The Government, the OFT and the Competition Commission, all share a common understanding of the aims of our competition regime—to increase the level of competition in the economy, to improve the UK's productivity performance and to make markets work well for consumers.
- The Government invites Parliament to actively scrutinise our competition regime. The mission statements of the Competition Commission, the OFT and Government will help it to do so.

4.1 While the Government can set a strong framework for competition, it is our competition authorities which carry responsibility for implementing it. For an effective competition regime, UK consumers and businesses rely on the OFT and the Competition Commission to detect instances where markets are not working well, and to take the necessary action to remedy the problems.

NOTE: Part I of the Enterprise Act establishes the Office of Fair Trading and sets out its general functions. At present, the OFT is an administrative support body to assist the DGFT in the exercise of his/her functions. Clause 1 establishes the OFT as a new corporate authority, a non-Ministerial Government Department, and all the DGFT's tasks and functions are transferred to it by s. 2. Schedule 1 makes detailed provision for the appointment of the Chairman, by the Chief Executive, and of the other members. The remainder of Part I of the Act sets out more detail on the OFT's functions, including the publication of an annual plan (clause 3), information gathering (s. 5) and the provision of information and advice to Ministers (s. 7).

QUESTION

To what extent will the creation of an independent authority weaken the accountability of the UK competition regime?

B: Super-complaints to the OFT

The Enterprise Act contains provisions on competition law, insolvency law and consumer law. The protection of the consumer is a cornerstone of the Act. The DTI White Paper, *World Class Competition Regime*, proposed the creation of a fast-track procedure for complaints by consumer bodies.

DTI, *Government Response to Consultation*
December 2001, Super-complaints

Super-complaints [paragraphs 4.25–4.27]
50. The White Paper proposed that the right for consumer groups to bring 'super-complaints' to the OFT where they suspect there are market structures or practices which are working against the interests of consumers should be enshrined in legislation. A majority of respondents either supported or had no strong objection to this proposal.

Government's response

The Government is aware that OFT may have a number of super-complaints per year, and will need to assess how it prioritises its investigative work. However, the Government and OFT are also keen to make use of the special skills that consumer bodies have in assessing which markets ought to be investigated. Thus they see this new approach as an enhancement to its trawling work.

The super-complaints procedure will be focused on cases where market structures or practices appear to be adversely affecting the interests of a significant number of consumers. The criteria for super-complainant status will be strict, to ensure a manageable list of designated bodies; and super-complainants will be expected to provide a reasoned case in support of their complaint.

The Government proposes that a similar procedure should apply to certain complaints by designated consumer bodies to the sector regulators who have concurrent powers under the Competition Act 1998. Super-complainants will be advised to discuss forthcoming super-complaints informally with the OFT (and any other relevant sector regulator if applicable) before submitting any complaint.

NOTE: The DGFT has already instituted an informal 'super-complaint' practice under the FTA 1973, but this system will be formalised under the statutory procedure set out in Clause 11 of the Enterprise Act:

Enterprise Act [s. 11(1)]

11 Super-complaints to OFT

(1) This section applies where a designated consumer body makes a complaint to the OFT that any feature, or combination of features, of a market in the United Kingdom for goods or services is or appears to be significantly harming the interests of consumers.

NOTE: This procedure is designed to encourage consumer representative groups to make collective complaints on their behalf. The benefit is that the OFT will be required to respond and make a considered response, in most cases, within 90 days (subsections (2) and (3)). Subsection (6) makes provision as to how consumer bodies can be designated as entitled to make super-complaints.

C: Mergers

One key difference is that the OFT refers mergers and is under a duty to refer a merger if it satisfies the requirements set out in Chapter I of Part III. Otherwise, the Enterprise Act retains the existing two-stage approach to merger control, with the Competition Commission carrying out the second-stage in-depth investigation if necessary, see Chapter 9. The Act introduces strict statutory timetables for the completion of each investigation stage (ss. 39 and 40). There is a new procedure for information to be obtained by the OFT in relation to mergers under s. 30. The CCAT's role, set out in ss. 35–41, is broadly similar as under the FTA 1973 but with the crucial change in status to that of being the determinative body in respect of all merger investigations, other than those involving public interest considerations. It has the investigative powers afforded to it under ss. 109–117, in order to complete its investigation and report. Section 109 gives the Competition Commission a power to serve notices requiring any person to attend to give evidence to the Competition Commission or to provide it with specified documents or information by specified dates. If it reports that there is a substantial lessening of competition, it is required to decide on appropriate remedial action to achieve as comprehensive a solution as is reasonable and practicable. Section 41 sets out the duty incumbent upon the Competition Commission:

Enterprise Act [s. 41]

41 Duty to remedy effects of completed or anticipated mergers

(1) Subsection (2) applies where a report of the Commission has been prepared and published under section 37 within the period permitted by section 38 and contains the decision that there is an anti-competitive outcome.

(2) The Commission shall take such action under section 79 or 81 as it considers to be reasonable and practicable—

  (a) to remedy, mitigate or prevent the substantial lessening of competition concerned; and

  (b) to remedy, mitigate or prevent any adverse effects which have resulted from, or may be expected to result from, the substantial lessening of competition.

(3) The decision of the Commission under subsection (2) shall be consistent with its decisions as included in its report by virtue of section 34(3) or (as the case may be) 35(2) unless there has been a material change of circumstances since the preparation of the report or the Commission otherwise has a special reason for deciding differently.

(4) In making a decision under subsection (2), the Commission shall, in particular, have regard to the need to achieve as comprehensive a solution as is reasonable and practicable to the substantial lessening of competition and any adverse effects resulting from it.

(5) In making a decision under subsection (2), the Commission may, in particular, have regard to the effect of any action on any relevant customer benefits in relation to the creation of the relevant merger situation concerned.

NOTE: There is a specialised regime in respect of mergers involving public interest considerations in relation to which the Secretary of State has retained an important role, and this is detailed in Chapter 2 of Part II of the Act. There are also provisions in Chapter 3 for other special cases including mergers involving Government defence contractors and the protection of legitimate interests in the mergers falling within the scope of the Community Merger Regulation.

Chapter 4 of Part III deals with enforcement (ss. 71–94 and Schs. 7 and 8). This is similar to the FTA 1973 scheme except that the Competition Commission can accept final undertakings (s. 82), and make an order (ss. 84 and Sch. 8) to remedy competition problems identified in its final report. The OFT has a duty to monitor undertakings and Orders (ss. 92–93).

Section 120 introduces a new level of review of the merger control process, whereby decisions taken in connection with a merger reference may be reviewed by the newly constituted CAT on the same grounds as a court on an application for judicial review.

D: Market investigations

Many of the changes, set out in Part 4 of the Enterprise Act, to the FTA 1973 system of investigation and enforcement are of a similar nature to those outlined above on mergers, and Part 4 should be consulted in detail. An initial difference is that OFT has a power and not a duty to make references in Part 4. However, the remainder is similar, including the separate public interest regime and the possibility of review of decisions under Part 4 by the CAT, see Chapter 7.

FURTHER READING

OFT, *Market Investigation references*, A Consultation Document, July 2002, OFT 501.

E: The new cartel offence

Part 6 of the Enterprise Act introduces a new cartel offence, discussed at greater length in Chapter 4. The OFT are to play a key role in the investigation and prosecution of the new offence.

Enterprise Act [s. 190]

190 Cartel offence: penalty and prosecution
(1) A person guilty of an offence under section 188 is liable—
    (a) on conviction on indictment, to imprisonment for a term not exceeding five years or to a fine, or to both;
    (b) on summary conviction, to imprisonment for a term not exceeding six months or to a fine not exceeding the statutory maximum, or to both.

(2) In England and Wales and Northern Ireland, proceedings for an offence under section 183 may be instituted only—
    (a) by the Director of the Serious Fraud Office, or
    (b) by or with the consent of the OFT.

(3) No proceedings may be brought for an offence under section 188 in respect of an agreement outside the United Kingdom, unless it has been implemented in whole or in part in the United Kingdom.

(4) Where, for the purpose of the investigation or prosecution of offences under section 188, the OFT gives a person written notice under this subsection, no proceedings for an offence under section 188 that falls within a description specified in the notice may be brought against that person in England and Wales or Northern Ireland except in circumstances specified in the notice.

NOTE: It is envisaged that the lead prosecutor in England and Wales will be the Serious Fraud Office and in Scotland, the Lord Advocate. There is provision for leniency in subsection (4) and the OFT have already issued a consultation document, 'The Cartel Offence: No-action Letters for Individuals', July 2002, OFT 503. ss. 192–202 make detailed provision on the investigatory powers, including surveillance powers (s. 199 and Sch. 26), afforded the OFT in relation to the criminal investigations. It remains to be seen how these investigations will interplay with civil investigations under the CA 1998, and in relation to potential breaches of Articles 81 and 82 EC.

Finally, the OFT also has a role in relation to the new provisions in Part 7 of the Act on directors' disqualification in relation to competition law breaches (s. 204). The OFT (or sectoral regulator) has investigatory powers for this purpose, can accept a disqualification undertaking or seek a court disqualification. See OFT Consultation Document, *Competition Disqualification Orders*, July 2002, OFT 500.

FURTHER READING

Rodger, B.J., and MacCulloch, A. (eds), *The UK Competition Act: A New Era for UK Competition Law*, Hart Publishing, Oxford, 2000.
DTI White Paper, 'World Class Competition Regime', July 2001, Cm 5233.

3

EC enforcement

Introduction

When examining the enforcement of the Community's competition rules, it is vital to start with the administrative structure which has developed EC competition law since the 1960s.

Regulation No 17 First Regulation Implementing Articles 81 and 82 of the Treaty
OJ, Sp Ed 1962, No 204/62, p. 87, as amended by Regulation 1216/1999/EC, OJ, 1999, L148/5

Article 1 Basic provision
Without prejudice to Articles 6, 7 and 23 of this Regulation, agreements, decisions and concerted practices of the kind described in Article 85(1) of the Treaty and the abuse of a dominant position in the market, within the meaning of Article 86 of the Treaty, shall be prohibited, no prior decision to that effect being required.

Article 2 Negative clearance
Upon application by the undertakings or associations of undertakings concerned, the Commission may certify that, on the basis of the facts in its possession, there are no grounds under Article 85(1) or Article 86 of the Treaty for action on its part in respect of an agreement, decision or practice.

Article 3 Termination of infringements
    1. Where the Commission, upon application or upon its own initiative, finds that there is infringement of Article 85 or Article 86 of the Treaty, it may by decision require the undertakings or associations of undertakings concerned to bring such infringement to an end.
    2. Those entitled to make application are:
      (a) Member States;
      (b) natural or legal persons who claim a legitimate interest.
    3. Without prejudice to the other provisions of this Regulation, the Commission may, before taking a decision under paragraph 1, address to the undertakings or associations of undertakings concerned recommendations for termination of the infringement.

Article 4 Notification of new agreements, decisions and practices
    1. Agreements, decisions and concerted practices of the kind described in Article 85(1) of the Treaty which come into existence after the entry into force of this Regulation and in respect of which the parties seek application of Article 85(3) must be notified to the Commission. Until they have been notified, no decision in application of Article 85(3) may be taken.

2. Paragraph 1 shall not apply to agreements, decisions or concerted practices where:

(1) the only parties thereto are undertakings from one Member State and the agreements, decisions or practices do not relate either to imports or to exports between Member States;

[2.(a) the agreements or concerted practices are entered into by two or more undertakings, each operating, for the purposes of the agreement, at a different level of the production or distribution chain, and relate to the conditions under which the parties may purchase, sell or resell certain goods or services;

(b) not more than two undertakings are party thereto, and the agreements only impose restrictions on the exercise of the rights of the assignee or user of industrial property rights, in particular patents, utility models, designs or trade marks, or of the person entitled under a contract to the assignment, or grant, of the right to use a method of manufacture or knowledge relating to the use and to the application of industrial processes.]

(3) they have as their sole object:

(a) the development or uniform application of standards or types; or

[(b) joint research and development;

(c) specialisation in the manufacture of products, including agreements necessary for the achievement thereof;

— where the products which are the subject of specialisation do not, in a substantial part of the common market, represent more than 15 per cent of the volume of business done in identical products or those considered by consumers to be similar by reason of their characteristics, price and use, and

— where the total annual turnover of the participating undertakings does not exceed 200 million units of account.

These agreements, decisions and concerted practices may be notified to the Commission.]

Article 5 Notification of existing agreements, decisions and practices

1. Agreements, decisions and concerted practices of the kind described in Article 85(1) of the Treaty which are in existence at the date of entry into force of this Regulation and in respect of which the parties seek application of Article 85(3) shall be notified to the Commission before 1 [November] 1962. [However, notwithstanding the foregoing provisions, any agreements, decisions and concerted practices to which not more than two undertakings are party shall be notified before 1 February 1963.]

2. Paragraph 1 shall not apply to agreements, decisions or concerted practices falling within Article 4(2); these may be notified to the Commission.

Article 6 Decisions pursuant to Article 85(3)

1. Whenever the Commission takes a decision pursuant to Article 85(3) of the Treaty, it shall specify therein the date from which the decision shall take effect. Such date shall not be earlier than the date of notification.

2. The second sentence of paragraph 1 shall not apply to agreements, decisions or concerted practices falling within Article 4(2) and Article 5(2), nor to those falling within Article 5(1) which have been notified within the time limit specified in Article 5(1).

Article 7 Special provisions for existing agreements, decisions and practices

1. Where agreements, decisions and concerted practices in existence at the date of entry into force of this Regulation and notified [within the limits specified in Article 5(1)] do not satisfy the requirements of Article 85(3) of the Treaty and the undertakings or associations of undertakings concerned cease to give effect to them or modify them in such manner that they no longer fall within the prohibition contained in Article 85(1) or that they satisfy the

requirements of Article 85(3), the prohibition contained in Article 85(1) shall apply only for a period fixed by the Commission. A decision by the Commission pursuant to the foregoing sentence shall not apply as against undertakings and associations of undertakings which did not expressly consent to the notification.

2. Paragraph 1 shall apply to agreements, decisions and concerted practices falling within Article 4(2) which are in existence at the date of entry into force of this Regulation if they are notified before 1 January [1967].

Article 8 Duration and revocation of decisions under Article 85(3)

1. A decision in application of Article 85(3) of the Treaty shall be issued for a specified period and conditions and obligations may be attached thereto.

2. A decision may on application be renewed if the requirements of Article 85(3) of the Treaty continue to be satisfied.

3. The Commission may revoke or amend its decision or prohibit specified acts by the parties:
>   (a) where there has been a change in any of the facts which were basic to the making of the decision;
>   (b) where the parties commit a breach of any obligation attached to the decision;
>   (c) where the decision is based on incorrect information or was induced by deceit;
>   (d) where the parties abuse the exemption from the provisions of Article 85(1) of the Treaty granted to them by the decision.

In cases to which subparagraphs (b), (c) or (d) apply, the decision may be revoked with retroactive effect.

Article 9 Powers

1. Subject to review of its decision by the Court of Justice, the Commission shall have sole power to declare Article 85(1) inapplicable pursuant to Article 85(3) of the Treaty.

2. The Commission shall have power to apply Article 85(1) and Article 86 of the Treaty; this power may be exercised notwithstanding that the time limits specified in Article 5(1) and in Article 7(2) relating to notification have not expired.

3. As long as the Commission has not initiated any procedure under Article 2, 3 or 6, the authorities of the Member States shall remain competent to apply Article 85(1) and Article 86 in accordance with Article 88 of the Treaty; they shall remain competent in this respect notwithstanding that the time limits specified in Article 5(1) and in Article 7(2) relating to notification have not expired.

Article 10 Liaison with the authorities of the Member States

1. The Commission shall forthwith transmit to the competent authorities of the Member States a copy of the applications and notifications together with copies of the most important documents lodged with the Commission for the purpose of establishing the existence of infringements of Article 85 or 86 of the Treaty or of obtaining negative clearance or a decision in application of Article 85(3).

2. The Commission shall carry out the procedure set out in paragraph 1 in close and constant liaison with the competent authorities of the Member States; such authorities shall have the right to express their views upon that procedure.

3. An Advisory Committee on Restrictive Practices and Monopolies shall be consulted prior to the taking of any decision following upon a procedure under paragraph 1, and of any decision concerning the renewal, amendment or revocation of a decision pursuant to Article 85(3) of the Treaty.

4. The Advisory Committee shall be composed of officials competent in the matter of restrictive practices and monopolies. Each Member State shall appoint an official to represent it who, if prevented from attending, may be replaced by another official.

5. The consultation shall take place at a joint meeting convened by the Commission; such meeting shall be held not earlier than fourteen days after dispatch of the notice convening it. The notice shall, in respect of each case to be examined, be accompanied by a summary of the case together with an indication of the most important documents, and a preliminary draft decision.

6. The Advisory Committee may deliver an opinion notwithstanding that some of its members or their alternates are not present. A report of the outcome of the consultative proceedings shall be annexed to the draft decision. It shall not be made public.

Article 11 Requests for information

1. In carrying out the duties assigned to it by Article 89 and by provisions adopted under Article 87 of the Treaty, the Commission may obtain all necessary information from the Governments and competent authorities of the Member States and from undertakings and associations of undertakings.

2. When sending a request for information to an undertaking or association of undertakings, the Commission shall at the same time forward a copy of the request to the competent authority of the Member State in whose territory the seat of the undertaking or association of undertakings is situated.

3. In its request the Commission shall state the legal basis and the purpose of the request and also the penalties provided for in Article 15(1)(b) for supplying incorrect information.

4. The owners of the undertakings or their representatives and, in the case of legal persons, companies or firms, or of associations having no legal personality, the persons authorised to represent them by law or by their constitution shall supply the information requested.

5. Where an undertaking or association of undertakings does not supply the information requested within the time limit fixed by the Commission, or supplies incomplete information, the Commission shall by decision require the information to be supplied. The decision shall specify what information is required, fix an appropriate time limit within which it is to be supplied and indicate the penalties provided for in Article 15(1)(b) and Article 16(1)(c) and the right to have the decision reviewed by the Court of Justice.

6. The Commission shall at the same time forward a copy of its decision to the competent authority of the Member State in whose territory the seat of the undertaking or association of undertakings is situated.

Article 12 Inquiry into sectors of the economy

1. If in any sector of the economy the trend of trade between Member States, price movements, inflexibility of prices or other circumstances suggest that in the economic sector concerned competition is being restricted or distorted within the common market, the Commission may decide to conduct a general inquiry into that economic sector and in the course thereof may request undertakings in the sector concerned to supply the information necessary for giving effect to the principles formulated in Articles 85 and 86 of the Treaty and for carrying out the duties entrusted to the Commission.

2. The Commission may in particular request every undertaking or association of undertakings in the economic sector concerned to communicate to it all agreements, decisions and concerted practices which are exempt from notification by virtue of Article 4(2) and Article 5(2).

3. When making inquiries pursuant to paragraph 2, the Commission shall also request undertakings or groups of undertakings whose size suggests that they occupy a dominant position within the common market or a substantial part thereof to supply to the Commission

such particulars of the structure of the undertakings and of their behaviour as are requisite to an appraisal of their position in the light of Article 86 of the Treaty.

4. Article 10(3) to (6) and Articles 11, 13 and 14 shall apply correspondingly.

Article 13 Investigations by the authorities of the Member States

1. At the request of the Commission, the competent authorities of the Member States shall undertake the investigations which the Commission considers to be necessary under Article 14(1), or which it has ordered by decision pursuant to Article 14(3). The officials of the competent authorities of the Member States responsible for conducting these investigations shall exercise their powers upon production of an authorisation in writing issued by the competent authority of the Member State in whose territory the investigation is to be made. Such authorisation shall specify the subject matter and purpose of the investigation.

2. If so requested by the Commission or by the competent authority of the Member State in whose territory the investigation is to be made, the officials of the Commission may assist the officials of such authorities in carrying out their duties.

Article 14 Investigating powers of the Commission

1. In carrying out the duties assigned to it by Article 89 and by provisions adopted under Article 87 of the Treaty, the Commission may undertake all necessary investigations into undertakings and associations of undertakings. To this end the officials authorised by the Commission are empowered:

(a) to examine the books and other business records;
(b) to take copies of or extracts from the books and business records;
(c) to ask for oral explanations on the spot;
(d) to enter any premises; land and means of transport of undertakings.

2. The officials of the Commission authorised for the purpose of these investigations shall exercise their powers upon production of an authorisation in writing specifying the subject matter and purpose of the investigation and the penalties provided for in Article 15(1)(c) in cases where production of the required books or other business records is incomplete. In good time before the investigation, the Commission shall inform the competent authority of the Member State in whose territory the same is to be made of the investigation and of the identity of the authorised officials.

3. Undertakings and associations of undertakings shall submit to investigations ordered by decision of the Commission. The decision shall specify the subject matter and purpose of the investigation, appoint the date on which it is to begin and indicate the penalties provided for in Article 15(1)(c) and Article 16(1)(d) and the right to have the decision reviewed by the Court of Justice.

4. The Commission shall take decisions referred to in paragraph 3 after consultation with the competent authority of the Member State in whose territory the investigation is to be made.

5. Officials of the competent authority of the Member State in whose territory the investigation is to be made may, at the request of such authority or of the Commission, assist the officials of the Commission in carrying out their duties.

6. Where an undertaking opposes an investigation ordered pursuant to this Article, the Member State concerned shall afford the necessary assistance to the officials authorised by the Commission to enable them to make their investigation. Member States shall, after consultation with the Commission, take the necessary measures to this end before 1 October 1962.

Article 15 Fines

1. The Commission may by decision impose on undertakings or associations of undertakings fines of from 100 to 5,000 units of account where, intentionally or negligently:

(a) they supply incorrect or misleading information in an application pursuant to Article 2 or in a notification pursuant to Articles 4 or 5; or

(b) they supply incorrect information in response to a request made pursuant to Article 11(3) or (5) or to Article 12, or do not supply information within the time limit fixed by a decision taken under Article 11(5); or

(c) they produce the required books or other business records in incomplete form during investigations under Article 13 or 14, or refuse to submit to an investigation ordered by decision issued in implementation of Article 14(3).

2. The Commission may by decision impose on undertakings or associations of undertakings fines of from 1,000 to 1,000,000 units of account, or a sum in excess thereof but not exceeding 10 per cent of the turnover in the preceding business year of each of the undertakings participating in the infringement where, either intentionally or negligently:

(a) they infringe Article 85(1) or Article 86 of the Treaty; or

(b) they commit a breach of any obligation imposed pursuant to Article 8(1).

In fixing the amount of the fine, regard shall be had both to the gravity and to the duration of the infringement.

3. Article 10(3) to (6) shall apply.

4. Decisions taken pursuant to paragraphs 1 and 2 shall not be of a criminal law nature.

5. The fines provided for in paragraph 2(a) shall not be imposed in respect of acts taking place:

(a) after notification to the Commission and before its decision in application of Article 85(3) of the Treaty, provided they fall within the limits of the activity described in the notification;

(b) before notification and in the course of agreements, decisions or concerted practices in existence at the date of entry into force of this Regulation, provided that notification was effected within the time limits specified in Article 5(1) and Article 7(2).

6. Paragraph 5 shall not have effect where the Commission has informed the undertakings concerned that after preliminary examination it is of opinion that Article 85(1) of the Treaty applies and that application of Article 85(3) is not justified.

Article 16 Periodic penalty payments

1. The Commission may by decision impose on undertakings or associations of undertakings periodic penalty payments of from 50 to 1,000 units of account per day, calculated from the date appointed by the decision, in order to compel them:

(a) to put an end to an infringement of Article 85 or 86 of the Treaty, in accordance with a decision taken pursuant to Article 3 of this Regulation;

(b) to refrain from any act prohibited under Article 8(3);

(c) to supply complete and correct information which it has requested by decision taken pursuant to Article 11(5);

(d) to submit to an investigation which it has ordered by decision taken pursuant to Article 14(3).

2. Where the undertakings or associations of undertakings have satisfied the obligation which it was the purpose of the periodic penalty payment to enforce, the Commission may fix the total amount of the periodic penalty payment at a lower figure than that which would arise under the original decision.

3. Article 10(3) to (6) shall apply.

Article 17 Review by the Court of Justice

The Court of Justice shall have unlimited jurisdiction within the meaning of Article 172 of the Treaty to review decisions whereby the Commission has fixed a fine or periodic penalty payment; it may cancel, reduce or increase the fine or periodic penalty payment imposed.

Article 18 Unit of account

For the purposes of applying Articles 15 to 17 the unit of account shall be that adopted in drawing up the budget of the Community in accordance with Articles 207 and 209 of the Treaty.

Article 19 Hearing of the parties and of third persons

1. Before taking decisions as provided for in Articles 2, 3, 6, 7, 8, 15 and 16, the Commission shall give the undertakings or associations of undertakings concerned the opportunity of being heard on the matters to which the Commission has taken objection.

2. If the Commission or the competent authorities of the Member States consider it necessary, they may also hear other natural or legal persons. Applications to be heard on the part of such persons shall, where they show a sufficient interest, be granted.

3. Where the Commission intends to give negative clearance pursuant to Article 2 or take a decision in application of Article 85(3) of the Treaty, it shall publish a summary of the relevant application or notification and invite all interested third parties to submit their observations within a time limit which it shall fix being not less than one month. Publication shall have regard to the legitimate interest of undertakings in the protection of their business secrets.

Article 20 Professional secrecy

1. Information acquired as a result of the application of Articles 11, 12, 13 and 14 shall be used only for the purpose of the relevant request or investigation.

2. Without prejudice to the provisions of Articles 19 and 21, the Commission and the competent authorities of the Member States, their officials and other servants shall not disclose information acquired by them as a result of the application of this Regulation and of the kind covered by the obligation of professional secrecy.

3. The provisions of paragraphs 1 and 2 shall not prevent publication of general information or surveys which do not contain information relating to particular undertakings or associations of undertakings.

Article 21 Publication of decisions

1. The Commission shall publish the decisions which it takes pursuant to Articles 2, 3, 6, 7 and 8.

2. The publication shall state the names of the parties and the main content of the decision; it shall have regard to the legitimate interest of undertakings in the protection of their business secrets.

Article 22 Special provisions

1. The Commission shall submit to the Council proposals for making certain categories of agreement, decision and concerted practice falling within Article 4(2) or Article 5(2) compulsorily notifiable under Article 4 or 5.

2. Within one year from the date of entry into force of this Regulation, the Council shall examine, on a proposal from the Commission, what special provisions might be made for exempting from the provisions of this Regulation agreements, decisions and concerted practices falling within Article 4(2) or Article 5(2).

Article 23 Transitional provisions applicable to decisions of authorities of the Member States

1. Agreements, decisions and concerted practices of the kind described in Article 85(1) of the Treaty to which, before the entry into force of this Regulation, the competent authority of a Member State has declared Article 85(1) to be inapplicable pursuant to Article 85(3) shall not be subject to compulsory notification under Article 5. The decision of the competent authority of

the Member State shall be deemed to be a decision within the meaning of Article 6; it shall cease to be valid upon expiration of the period fixed by such authority but in any event not more than three years after the entry into force of this Regulation. Article 8(3) shall apply.

2. Applications for renewal of decisions of the kind described in paragraph 1 shall be decided upon by the Commission in accordance with Article 8(2).

Article 24 Implementing provisions

The Commission shall have power to adopt implementing provisions concerning the form, content and other details of applications pursuant to Articles 2 and 3 and of notifications pursuant to Articles 4 and 5, and concerning hearings pursuant to Article 19(1) and (2).

[Article 25

1. As regards agreements, decisions and concerted practices to which Article 85 of the Treaty applies by virtue of accession, the date of accession shall be substituted for the date of entry into force of this regulation in every place where reference is made in this Regulation to this latter date.

2. Agreements, decisions and concerted practices existing at the date of accession to which Article 85 of the Treaty applies by virtue of accession shall be notified pursuant to Article 5(1) or Article 7(1) and (2) within six months from the date of accession.

3. Fines under Article 15(2)(a) shall not be imposed in respect of any act prior to notification of the agreements, decisions and practices to which paragraph 2 applies and which have been notified within the period therein specified.

4. New Member States shall take the measures referred to in Article 14(6) within six months from the date of accession after consulting the Commission.

5. The provisions of paragraphs (1) to (4) above shall apply in the same way in the case of accession of the Hellenic Republic, the Kingdom of Spain and of the Portuguese Republic.

6. The provisions of paragraphs 1 to 4 still apply in the same way in the case of the accession of Austria, Finland and Sweden. However, they do not apply to agreements, decisions and concerted practices which at the date of the accession already fall under Article 53 of the EEA Agreement.]

This Regulation shall be binding in its entirety and directly applicable in all Member States.

Done at Brussels, 6 February 1962.

NOTE: The adoption of Regulation 17 set the tone for the early development of the EC Competition rules, by securing the vital importance of the Commission within the enforcement system. The powers of the Commission under competition law are administered by the Directorate General for Competition (DG Comp), which is headed by the Director General. Political responsibility for competition policy is held by the Commissioner for Competition who has overall responsibility for all enforcement activity. Commission decisions within the competition sphere are not taken by the Competition Commissioner alone, but by the whole College of Commissioners. This ensures that all Community policies have an impact on Competition decisions.

Regulation 17 secures the Commission's position in two ways. First, it gives the Commission the authority and investigatory powers to enforce Articles 81 EC and 82 EC. Second, it secures the Commission's central role within Article 81 EC by reserving it the sole power to grant exemptions under Article 81(3) EC. The investigatory powers of the Commission under Articles 11 and 14 of Regulation 17 are broad, allowing it to seek wide categories of information from undertakings. Most of the Commission's investigations are carried out using the Article 11 powers but it does use Article 14 where it is concerned that a suspect undertaking may takes steps to dispose of evidence if the Article 11 procedure was used. Where the Commission wishes to undertake an investigation it should do so with the cooperation of the relevant Member State. Where, during an investigation, the Commission is concerned that it is necessary, it can adopt interim measures under Article 3 (see *Camera Care* v *Commission* (Case 792/79R) [1980] ECR 119, [1980] 1 CMLR 334). During an investigation two types of information are protected and need not be disclosed.

AM & S Europe Ltd v *Commission*
(Case 155/79) [1982] ECR 1575, [1982] 2 CMLR 264

The Commission sought to gather certain documents from AM & S relating to an alleged zinc cartel through an Article 14 procedure. AM & S refused to disclose certain documents, claiming that correspondence between an undertaking and its lawyers were subject to legal professional privilege.

[18] However, the above rules do not exclude the possibility of recognising, subject to certain conditions, that certain business records are of a confidential nature. Community law, which derives from not only the economic but also the legal interpenetration of the Member States, must take into account the principles and concepts common to the laws of those States concerning the observance of confidentiality, in particular, as regards certain communications between lawyer and client. That confidentiality serves the requirement, the importance of which is recognised in all of the Member States, that any person must be able, without constraint, to consult a lawyer whose profession entails the giving of independent legal advice to all those in need of it.

[19] As far as the protection of written communications between lawyer and client is concerned, it is apparent from the legal systems of the Member States that, although the principle of such protection is generally recognised, its scope and the criteria for applying it vary, as has, indeed, been conceded both by the applicant and by the parties who have intervened in support of its conclusions.

[20] Whilst in some of the Member States the protection against disclosure afforded to written communications between lawyer and client is based principally on a recognition of the very nature of the legal profession, inasmuch as it contributes towards the maintenance of the rule of law, in other Member States the same protection is justified by the more specific requirement (which, moreover, is also recognised in the first-mentioned States) that the rights of the defence must be respected.

[21] Apart from these differences, however, there are to be found in the national laws of the Member States common criteria inasmuch as those laws protect, in similar circumstances, the confidentiality of written communications between lawyer and client provided that, on the one hand, such communications are made for the purposes and in the interests of the client's rights of defence and, on the other hand, they emanate from independent lawyers, that is to say, lawyers who are not bound to the client by a relationship of employment.

[22] Viewed in that context Regulation 17 must be interpreted as protecting, in its turn, the confidentiality of written communications between lawyer and client subject to those two conditions, and thus incorporating such elements of that protection as are common to the laws of the Member States.

[23] As far as the first of those two conditions is concerned, in Regulation 17 itself, in particular in the eleventh recital in its preamble and in the provisions contained in Article 19, care is taken to ensure that the rights of the defence may be exercised to the full, and the protection of the confidentiality of written communications between lawyer and client is an essential corollary to those rights. In those circumstances, such protection must, if it is to be effective, be recognised as covering all written communications exchanged after the initiation of the administrative procedure under Regulation 17 which may lead to a decision on the application of Articles 85 and 86 of the

Treaty or to a decision imposing a pecuniary sanction on the undertaking. It must also be possible to extend it to earlier written communications which have a relationship to the subject-matter of that procedure.

[24] As regards the second condition, it should be stated that the requirement as to the position and status as an independent lawyer, which must be fulfilled by the legal adviser from whom the written communications which may be protected emanate, is based on a conception of the lawyer's rôle as collaborating in the administration of justice by the courts and as being required to provide, in full independence, and in the overriding interests of that cause, such legal assistance as the client needs. The counterpart of that protection lies in the rules of professional ethics and discipline which are laid down and enforced in the general interest by institutions endowed with the requisite powers for that purpose. Such a concept reflects the legal traditions common to the Member States and is also to be found in the legal order of the Community, as is demonstrated by Article 17 of the Protocols on the Statutes of the Court of Justice of the EEC and the EAEC, and also by Article 20 of the Protocol on the Statute of the Court of Justice of the ECSC.

NOTE: The privilege extends only to lawyers that are independent of the undertaking. Communications between an undertaking and its in-house lawyers are therefore not protected. This is somewhat unusual as, in many Member States, employed lawyers have the same rights as those who operate independently.

Mannesmannröhren-Werke AG v *Commission*
(Case T-112/98) [2001] ECR II-729, [2001] 5 CMLR 1

> The Commission undertook an investigation into producers of steel tubes in which it made various requests for information. The applicant refused to answer a number of questions as they were self-incriminatory. They claimed the Commission could not require them to answer such questions as it would be contrary to Article 6 of the ECHR.

[61] Next, it must be borne in mind that the purpose of the powers conferred on the Commission by Regulation 17 is to enable that institution to fulfil its duty under the Treaty to ensure that the rules on competition within the Common Market are observed.

[62] During the preliminary investigation procedure, Regulation 17 does not give an undertaking that is subjected to an investigative measure any right to avoid the application of that measure on the ground that the results thereof might provide evidence of an infringement by it of the competition rules. On the contrary, it places the undertaking under a duty of active co-operation, which means that it must be prepared to make available to the Commission any information relating to the subject-matter of the investigation (*Orkem*, para. [27] and *Societe Generale*, para. [72]).

[63] In the absence of any right to silence expressly provided for in Regulation 17, it is necessary to consider whether certain limitations on the Commission's powers of investigation during a preliminary investigation are, however, implied by the need to safeguard the rights of defence (*Orkem*, para. [32]).

[64] In this respect, it is necessary to prevent the rights of defence from being irremediably impaired during preliminary investigation procedures which may be decisive in providing evidence of the unlawful nature of conduct engaged in by undertakings (*Orkem*, para. [33] and *Societe Generale*, para. [73]).

[65] However, it is settled case law that, in order to ensure the effectiveness of Article 11(2) and (5) of Regulation 17, the Commission is entitled to compel an undertaking to provide all necessary

information concerning such facts as may be known to it and to disclose to the Commission, if necessary, such documents relating thereto as are in its possession, even if the latter may be used to establish, against it or another undertaking, the existence of anti-competitive conduct (*Orkem*, para. [34] and Case 27/88, *Solvay* v *EC Commission*, [[1989] ECR 3355; [1991] 4 CMLR 502] and *Societe Generale*, para. [74]).

[66] To acknowledge the existence of an absolute right to silence, as claimed by the applicant, would go beyond what is necessary in order to preserve the rights of defence of undertakings, and would constitute an unjustified hindrance to the Commission's performance of its duty under Article 89 of the EC Treaty (now, after amendment, Article 85 EC) to ensure that the rules on competiton within the Common Market are observed.

[67] It follows that an undertaking in receipt of a request for information pursuant to Article 11(5) of Regulation 17 can be recognised as having a right to silence only to the extent that it would be compelled to provide answers which might involve an admission on its part of the existence of an infringement which it is incumbent upon the Commission to prove (*Orkem*, para. [35]).

NOTE: The Court of First Instance approved the judgment of the Court in cases such as *Orkem* (Case 374/87, [1989] ECR 3283) and *Solvay* (Case 27/88, [1989] ECR 3355), which gives an undertaking under investigation relatively limited protection from self-incrimination. They can be required to produce all documentation demanded by the Commission, even if it may be considered incriminating, and the privilege as recognised in relation to competition cases only extends to material which would in effect constitute an admission of some sort. Several commentators have questioned the compatibility of this decision with judgments of the European Court of Human Rights, particularly *Funke* v *France* [1993] 1 CMLR 897, (1993) 16 EHRR 297. See Willis, P.R., ' "You Have The Right To Remain Silent . . .", Or Do You? The Privilege Against Self-Incrimination Following *Mannesmannröhren-Werke* and other Recent Decisions' [2001] ECLR 313.

Commission Regulation 2842/98/EC on the Hearing of Parties
OJ, 1998, L354/18

THE COMMISSION OF THE EUROPEAN COMMUNITIES,

Having regard to the Treaty establishing the European Community,
  Having regard to the Agreement on the European Economic Area,
  Having regard to Council Regulation No 17 of 6 February 1962, First Regulation implementing Articles 85 and 86 of the Treaty[1], as last amended by the Act of Accession of Austria, Finland and Sweden, and in particular Article 24 thereof,
  Having regard to Council Regulation (EEC) No 1017/68 of 19 July 1968 applying rules of competition to transport by rail, road and inland waterway[2], as last amended by the Act of Accession of Austria, Finland and Sweden, and in particular Article 29 thereof,
  Having regard to Council Regulation (EEC) No 4056/86 of 22 December 1986 laying down detailed rules for the application of Articles 85 and 86 of the Treaty to maritime transport[3], as last amended by the Act of Accession of Austria, Finland and Sweden, and in particular Article 26 thereof,
  Having regard to Council Regulation (EEC) No 3975/87 of 14 December 1987 laying down the procedure for the application of the rules on competition to undertakings in the air transport

1 OJ 13, 21. 2. 1962, p. 204/62.
2 OJ L 175, 23. 7. 1968, p. 1.
3 OJ L 378, 31. 12. 1986, p. 4.

sector[4], as last amended by Regulation (EEC) No 2410/92[5], and in particular Article 19 thereof,

Having consulted the appropriate Advisory Committees on Restrictive Practices and Dominant Positions,

(1) Whereas a great deal of experience has been acquired in the application of Commission Regulation No 99/63/EEC of 25 July 1963 on the hearings provided for in Article 19(1) and (2) of Regulation No 17[6], Commission Regulation (EEC) No 1630/69 of 8 August 1969 on the hearings provided for in Article 26(1) and (2) of Council Regulation (EEC) No 1017/68 of 19 July 1968[7], Section II of Commission Regulation (EEC) No 4260/88 of 16 December 1988 on the communications, complaints and applications and the hearings provided for in Council Regulation (EEC) No 4056/86 laying down detailed rules for the application of Articles 85 and 86 of the Treaty to maritime transport[8], as last amended by the Act of Accession of Austria, Finland and Sweden, and Section II of Commission Regulation (EEC) No 4261/88 of 16 December 1988 on the complaints, applications and hearings provided for in Council Regulation (EEC) No 3975/87 laying down the procedure for the application of the rules on competition to undertakings in the air transport sector[9];

(2) Whereas that experience has revealed the need to improve certain procedural aspects of those Regulations; whereas it is appropriate for the sake of clarity to adopt a single Regulation on the various hearing procedures laid down by Regulation No 17, Regulation (EEC) No 1017/68, Regulation (EEC) No 4056/86 and Regulation (EEC) No 3975/87; whereas, accordingly, Regulations No 99/63/EEC and (EEC) No 1630/69 should be replaced, and Sections II of Regulations (EEC) No 4260/88 and (EEC) No 4261/88 should be deleted and replaced;

(3) Whereas the provisions relating to the Commission's procedure under Decision 94/810/ECSC, EC of 12 December 1994 on the terms of reference of hearing officers in competition procedures before the Commission[10] should be framed in such a way as to safeguard fully the right to be heard and the rights of defence; whereas for these purposes, the Commission should distinguish between the respective rights to be heard of the parties to which the Commission has addressed objections, of the applicants and complainants, and of other third parties;

(4) Whereas in accordance with the principle of the rights of defence, the parties to which the Commission has addressed objections should be given the opportunity to submit their comments on all the objections which the Commission proposes to take into account in its decisions;

(5) Whereas the applicants and complainants should be granted the opportunity of expressing their views, if the Commission considers that there are insufficient grounds for granting the application or acting on the complaint; whereas the applicant or complainant should be provided with a copy of the non-confidential version of the objections and should be permitted to make known its views in writing where the Commission raises objections;

(6) Whereas other third parties having sufficient interest should also be given the opportunity of expressing their views in writing where they make a written application to do so;

(7) Whereas the various parties entitled to submit comments should do so in writing, both in their own interest and in the interests of sound administration, without prejudice to the possibility of an oral hearing where appropriate to supplement the written procedure;

(8) Whereas it is necessary to define the rights of persons who are to be heard and on what conditions they may be represented or assisted;

4 OJ L 374, 31. 12. 1987, p. 1.
5 OJ L 240, 24. 8. 1992, p. 18.
6 OJ 127, 20. 8. 1963, p. 2268/63.
7 OJ L 209, 21. 8. 1969, p. 11.
8 OJ L 376, 31. 12. 1988, p. 1.
9 OJ L 376, 31. 12. 1988, p. 10.
10 OJ L 330, 21. 12. 1994, p. 67.

(9) Whereas the Commission should continue to respect the legitimate interest of undertakings in the protection of their business secrets and other confidential information;

(10) Whereas compatibility should be ensured between the Commission's current administrative practices and the case-law of the Court of Justice and the Court of First Instance of the European Communities in accordance with the Commission notice on the internal rules of procedure for processing requests for access to the file in cases pursuant to Articles 85 and 86 of the Treaty, Articles 65 and 66 of the ECSC Treaty and Council Regulation (EEC) No 4064/89[1];

(11) Whereas to facilitate the proper conduct of the hearing it is appropriate to allow statements made by each person at a hearing to be recorded;

(12) Whereas in the interest of legal certainty, it is appropriate to set the time limit for the submissions by the various persons pursuant to this Regulation by defining the date by which the submission must reach the Commission;

(13) Whereas the appropriate Advisory Committee under Article 10(3) of Regulation No 17, Article 16(3) of Regulation (EEC) No 1017/68, Article 15(3) of Regulation (EEC) No 4056/86 or Article 8(3) of Regulation (EEC) No 3975/87 must deliver its opinion on the basis of a preliminary draft decision; whereas it should therefore be consulted on a case after the inquiry in that case has been completed; whereas such consultation should not prevent the Commission from reopening an inquiry if need be,

HAS ADOPTED THIS REGULATION:

CHAPTER 1
Scope

Article 1

This Regulation shall apply to the hearing of parties under Article 19(1) and (2) of Regulation No 17, Article 26(1) and (2) of Regulation (EEC) No 1017/68, Article 23(1) and (2) of Regulation (EEC) No 4056/86 and Article 16(1) and (2) of Regulation (EEC) No 3975/87.

CHAPTER II
Hearing of parties to which the Commission has addressed objections

Article 2

1. The Commission shall hear the parties to which it has addressed objections before consulting the appropriate Advisory Committee under Article 10(3) of Regulation No 17, Article 16(3) of Regulation (EEC) No 1017/68, Article 15(3) of Regulation (EEC) No 4056/86 or Article 8(3) of Regulation (EEC) No 3975/87.

2. The Commission shall in its decisions deal only with objections in respect of which the parties have been afforded the opportunity of making their views known.

Article 3

1. The Commission shall inform the parties in writing of the objections raised against them. The objections shall be notified to each of them or to a duly appointed agent.

2. The Commission may inform the parties by giving notice in the *Official Journal of the European Communities*, if from the circumstances of the case this appears appropriate, in particular where notice is to be given to a number of undertakings but no joint agent has been appointed. The notice shall have regard to the legitimate interests of the undertakings in the protection of their business secrets and other confidential information.

3. A fine or a periodic penalty payment may be imposed on a party only if the objections have been notified in the manner provided for in paragraph 1.

---

1 OJ C 23, 23. 1. 1997, p. 3.

4. The Commission shall, when giving notice of objections, set a date by which the parties may inform it in writing of their views.

5. The Commission shall set a date by which the parties may indicate any parts of the objections which in their view contain business secrets or other confidential material. If they do not do so by that date, the Commission may assume that the objections do not contain such information.

Article 4

1. Parties which wish to make known their views on the objections raised against them shall do so in writing and by the date referred to in Article 3(4). The Commission shall not be obliged to take into account written comments received after that date.

2. The parties may in their written comments set out all matters relevant to their defence. They may attach any relevant documents as proof of the facts set out and may also propose that the Commission hear persons who may corroborate those facts.

Article 5

The Commission shall afford to parties against which objections have been raised the opportunity to develop their arguments at an oral hearing, if they so request in their written comments.

CHAPTER III
Hearing of applicants and complainants

Article 6

Where the Commission, having received an application made under Article 3(2) of Regulation No 17 or a complaint made under Article 10 of Regulation (EEC) No 1017/68, Article 10 of Regulation (EEC) No 4056/86 or Article 3(1) of Regulation (EEC) No 3975/87, considers that on the basis of the information in its possession there are insufficient grounds for granting the application or acting on the complaint, it shall inform the applicant or complainant of its reasons and set a date by which the applicant or complainant may make known its views in writing.

Article 7

Where the Commission raises objections relating to an issue in respect of which it has received an application on a complaint as referred to in Article 6, it shall provide an applicant or complainant with a copy of the non-confidential version of the objections and set a date by which the applicant or complainant may make known its views in writing.

Article 8

The Commission may, where appropriate, afford to applicants and complainants the opportunity of orally expressing their views, if they so request in their written comments.

CHAPTER IV
Hearing of other third parties

Article 9

1. If parties other than those referred to in Chapters II and III apply to be heard and show a sufficient interest, the Commission shall inform them in writing of the nature and subject matter of the procedure and shall set a date by which they may make known their views in writing.

2. The Commission may, where appropriate, invite parties referred to in paragraph 1 to

develop their arguments at the oral hearing of the parties against which objections have been raised, if they so request in their written comments.

3. The Commission may afford to any other third parties the opportunity of orally expressing their views.

CHAPTER V

General provisions

Article 10

Hearings shall be conducted by the Hearing Officer.

Article 11

1. The Commission shall invite the persons to be heard to attend the oral hearing on such date as it shall appoint.

2. The Commission shall invite the competent authorities of the Member States to take part in the oral hearing.

Article 12

1. Persons invited to attend shall either appear in person or be represented by legal representatives or by representatives authorised by their constitution as appropriate. Undertakings and associations of undertakings may be represented by a duly authorised agent appointed from among their permanent staff.

2. Persons heard by the Commission may be assisted by their legal advisers or other qualified persons admitted by the Hearing Officer.

3. Oral hearings shall not be public. Each person shall be heard separately or in the presence of other persons invited to attend. In the latter case, regard shall be had to the legitimate interest of the undertakings in the protection of their business secrets and other confidential information.

4. The statements made by each person heard shall be recorded on tape. The recording shall be made available to such persons on request, by means of a copy from which business secrets and other confidential information shall be deleted.

Article 13

1. Information, including documents, shall not be communicated or made accessible in so far as it contains business secrets of any party, including the parties to which the Commission has addressed objections, applicants and complainants and other third parties, or other confidential information or where internal documents of the authorities are concerned. The Commission shall make appropriate arrangements for allowing access to the file, taking due account of the need to protect business secrets, internal Commission documents and other confidential information.

2. Any party which makes known its views under the provisions of this Regulation shall clearly identify any material which it considers to be confidential, giving reasons, and provide a separate non-confidential version by the date set by the Commission. If it does not do so by the set date, the Commission may assume that the submission does not contain such material.

Article 14

In setting the dates provided for in Articles 3(4), 6, 7 and 9(1), the Commission shall have regard both to the time required for preparation of the submission and to the urgency of the case. The time allowed in each case shall be at least two weeks; it may be extended.

CHAPTER VI
Final provisions

Article 15
1. Regulations No 99/63/EEC and (EEC) No 1630/69 are repealed.
2. Sections II of Regulations (EEC) No 4260/88 and (EEC) No 4261/88 are deleted.

Article 16
This Regulation shall enter into force on 1 February 1999.

NOTE: The role of the Hearing Officer was introduced to the administrative procedure to ensure the rights of the defence in competition proceedings. Before the introduction of this procedure, the Commission was in effect acting as investigator, prosecutor and judge. The Hearing Officer is an independent Officer, who ensures that the accused undertaking can properly defend themselves before an impartial body.

SECTION 2: **Power to fine**

For the procedure in Regulation 17 to be effective, an adverse finding must be supported by a proper deterrent. The Regulation sets out the importance of the Commission through its impressive power to fine undertakings that breach the competition rules. With a maximum fine of up to 10 per cent of global turnover, the Commission has the opportunity to impose major fines with real deterrent power. In 1998, the Commission produced Guidelines which indicate the manner in which the Commission will determine a fine appropriate to the circumstances of the case. The main determining factors are the seriousness of the breach (its *gravity*) and the length of the breach (its *duration*). Once the basic fine has been determined, other aggravating or attenuating circumstances will be taken into account.

Commission Guidelines on the Method of Setting Fines
OJ, 1998, C9/3

(Text with EEA relevance)
The principles outlined here should ensure the transparency and impartiality of the Commission's decisions, in the eyes of the undertakings and of the Court of Justice alike, while upholding the discretion which the Commission is granted under the relevant legislation to set fines within the limit of 10 per cent of overall turnover. This discretion must, however, follow a coherent and non-discriminatory policy which is consistent with the objectives pursued in penalizing infringements of the competition rules.

The new method of determining the amount of a fine will adhere to the following rules, which start from a basic amount that will be increased to take account of aggravating circumstances or reduced to take account of attenuating circumstances.

1. Basic amount
The basic amount will be determined according to the gravity and duration of the infringement, which are the only criteria referred to in Article 15(2) of Regulation No 17.

A. Gravity
In assessing the gravity of the infringement, account must be taken of its nature, its actual impact on the market, where this can be measured, and the size of the relevant geographic market.

Infringements will thus be put into one of three categories: minor infringements, serious infringements and very serious infringements.

— minor infringements:
These might be trade restrictions, usually of a vertical nature, but with a limited market impact and affecting only a substantial but relatively limited part of the Community market.
Likely fines: ECU 1,000 to ECU 1 million.

— serious infringements:
These will more often than not be horizontal or vertical restrictions of the same type as above, but more rigorously applied, with a wider market impact, and with effects in extensive areas of the common market. There might also be abuse of a dominant position (refusals to supply, discrimination, exclusion, loyalty discounts made by dominant firms in order to shut competitors out of the market, etc.).
Likely fines: ECU 1 million to ECU 20 million.

— very serious infringements:
These will generally be horizontal restrictions such as price cartels and market-sharing quotas, or other practices which jeopardize the proper functioning of the single market, such as the partitioning of national markets and clear-cut abuse of a dominant position by undertakings holding a virtual monopoly (see Decisions 91/297/EEC, 91/298/EEC, 91/299/EEC, 91/300/EEC and 91/301/EEC[1]—Soda Ash, 94/815/EC[2]—Cement, 94/601/EC[3]—Cartonboard, 92/163/EC[4]—Tetra Pak, and 94/215/ECSC[5]—Steel beams).
Likely fines: above ECU 20 million

Within each of these categories, and in particular as far as serious and very serious infringements are concerned, the proposed scale of fines will make it possible to apply differential treatment to undertakings according to the nature of the infringement committed.

It will also be necessary to take account of the effective economic capacity of offenders to cause significant damage to other operators, in particular consumers, and to set the fine at a level which ensures that it has a sufficiently deterrent effect.

Generally speaking, account may also be taken of the fact that large undertakings usually have legal and economic knowledge and infrastructures which enable them more easily to recognize that their conduct constitutes an infringement and be aware of the consequences stemming from it under competition law.

Where an infringement involves several undertakings (e.g. cartels), it might be necessary in some cases to apply weightings to the amounts determined within each of the three categories in order to take account of the specific weight and, therefore, the real impact of the offending conduct of each undertaking on competition, particularly where there is considerable disparity between the sizes of the undertakings committing infringements of the same type.

Thus, the principle of equal punishment for the same conduct may, if the circumstances so warrant, lead to different fines being imposed on the undertakings concerned without this differentiation being governed by arithmetic calculation.

B. Duration
A distinction should be made between the following:

— infringements of short duration (in general, less than one year): no increase in amount,

1 OJ L 152, 15.6.1991, p. 54.
2 OJ L 343, 30.12.1994, p. 1.
3 OJ L 243, 19.9.1994, p. 1.
4 OJ L 72, 18.3.1992, p. 1.
5 OJ L 116, 6.5.1994, p. 1.

— infringements of medium duration (in general, one to five years): increase of up to 50 per cent in the amount determined for gravity,

— infringements of long duration (in general, more than five years): increase of up to 10 per cent per year in the amount determined for gravity.

This approach will therefore point to a possible increase in the amount of the fine.

Generally speaking, the increase in the fine for long-term infringements represents a considerable strengthening of the previous practice with a view to imposing effective sanctions on restrictions which have had a harmful impact on consumers over a long period. Moreover, this new approach is consistent with the expected effect of the notice of 18 July 1996 on the non-imposition or reduction of fines in cartel cases[6]. The risk of having to pay a much larger fine, proportionate to the duration of the infringement, will necessarily increase the incentive to denounce it or to cooperate with the Commission.

The basic amount will result from the addition of the two amounts established in accordance with the above:

$$x \text{ gravity} + y \text{ duration} = \text{basic amount}$$

2. Aggravating circumstances

The basic amount will be increased where there are aggravating circumstances such as:

— repeated infringement of the same type by the same undertaking(s),

— refusal to cooperate with or attempts to obstruct the Commission in carrying out its investigations,

— role of leader in, or instigator of the infringement,

— retaliatory measures against other undertakings with a view to enforcing practices which constitute an infringement,

— need to increase the penalty in order to exceed the amount of gains improperly made as a result of the infringement when it is objectively possible to estimate that amount,

— other.

3. Attenuating circumstances

The basic amount will be reduced where there are attenuating circumstances such as:

— an exclusively passive or 'follow-my-leader' role in the infringement,

— non-implementation in practice of the offending agreements or practices,

— termination of the infringement as soon as the Commission intervenes (in particular when it carries out checks),

— existence of reasonable doubt on the part of the undertaking as to whether the restrictive conduct does indeed constitute an infringement,

— infringements committed as a result of negligence or unintentionally,

— effective cooperation by the undertaking in the proceedings, outside the scope of the Notice of 18 July 1996 on the non-imposition or reduction of fines in cartel cases,

— other.

4. Application of the notice of 18 July 1996 on the non-imposition or reduction of fines[7]

5. General comments

(a) It goes without saying that the final amount calculated according to this method (basic amount increased or reduced on a percentage basis) may not in any case exceed 10 per cent of the worldwide turnover of the undertakings, as laid down by Article 15(2) of Regulation No 17. In

---

6 OJ C 207, 18.7.1996, p. 4.

7 See footnote 6.

the case of agreements which are illegal under the ECSC Treaty, the limit laid down by Article 65(5) is twice the turnover on the products in question, increased in certain cases to a maximum of 10 per cent of the undertaking's turnover on ECSC products.

The accounting year on the basis of which the worldwide turnover is determined must, as far as possible, be the one preceding the year in which the decision is taken or, if figures are not available for that accounting year, the one immediately preceding it.

(b) Depending on the circumstances, account should be taken, once the above calculations have been made, of certain objective factors such as a specific economic context, any economic or financial benefit derived by the offenders (see Twenty-first report on competition policy, point 139), the specific characteristics of the undertakings in question and their real ability to pay in a specific social context, and the fines should be adjusted accordingly.

(c) In cases involving associations of undertakings, decisions should as far as possible be addressed to and fines imposed on the individual undertakings belonging to the association. If this is not possible (e.g. where there are several thousands of affiliated undertakings), and except for cases falling within the ECSC Treaty, an overall fine should be imposed on the association, calculated according to the principles outlined above but equivalent to the total of individual fines which might have been imposed on each of the members of the association.

(d) The Commission will also reserve the right, in certain cases, to impose a 'symbolic' fine of ECU 1,000, which would not involve any calculation based on the duration of the infringement or any aggravating or attenuating circumstances. The justification for imposing such a fine should be given in the text of the decision.

NOTE: The Commission has also published a Notice which introduces a 'leniency' or 'whistle-blowing' programme for cartel cases. Although large fines are an important deterrent within competition cases, there is a need to balance the importance of the deterrent with the administrative problems in detecting the existence of secret cartels. The leniency programme encourages those involved in cartels to come forward and inform the Commission of their involvement. If they do so, they will benefit from a reduction in the fine which would be imposed. The first undertaking to come forward will benefit from a 100 per cent reduction in the fine, with lesser benefits for subsequent whistle-blowers. The existence of the programme should greatly assist the Commission in detecting secret cartels and then once discovered, gathering evidence from those involved. Large fines may still be imposed upon those who do not cooperate with the Commission.

Commission Notice on immunity from fines and reduction of fines in cartel cases
OJ, 2002/C45/03

Introduction

1. This notice concerns secret cartels between two or more competitors aimed at fixing prices, production or sales quotas, sharing markets including bid-rigging or restricting imports or exports. Such practices are among the most serious restrictions of competition encountered by the Commission and ultimately result in increased prices and reduced choice for the consumer. They also harm European industry.

2. By artificially limiting the competition that would normally prevail between them, undertakings avoid exactly those pressures that lead them to innovate, both in terms of product development and the introduction of more efficient production methods. Such practices also lead to more expensive raw materials and components for the Community companies that purchase from such producers. In the long term, they lead to a loss of competitiveness and reduced employment opportunities.

3. The Commission is aware that certain undertakings involved in this type of illegal agreements

are willing to put an end to their participation and inform it of the existence of such agreements, but are dissuaded from doing so by the high fines to which they are potentially exposed. In order to clarify its position in this type of situation, the Commission adopted a notice on the non-imposition or reduction of fines in cartel cases[1], hereafter 'the 1996 notice'.

4. The Commission considered that it is in the Community interest to grant favourable treatment to undertakings which cooperate with it. The interests of consumers and citizens in ensuring that secret cartels are detected and punished outweigh the interest in fining those undertakings that enable the Commission to detect and prohibit such practices.

5. In the 1996 notice, the Commission announced that it would examine whether it was neces-sary to modify the notice once it had acquired sufficient experience in applying it. After five years of implementation, the Commission has the experience necessary to modify its policy in this matter. Whilst the validity of the principles governing the notice has been confirmed, experience has shown that its effectiveness would be improved by an increase in the transparency and certainty of the conditions on which any reduction of fines will be granted. A closer alignment between the level of reduction of fines and the value of a company's contribution to establishing the infringement could also increase this effectiveness. This notice addresses these issues.

6. The Commission considers that the collaboration of an undertaking in the detection of the existence of a cartel has an intrinsic value. A decisive contribution to the opening of an investigation or to the finding of an infringement may justify the granting of immunity from any fine to the undertaking in question, on condition that certain additional requirements are fulfilled.

7. Moreover, cooperation by one or more undertakings may justify a reduction of a fine by the Commission. Any reduction of a fine must reflect an undertaking's actual contribution, in terms of quality and timing, to the Commission's establishment of the infringement. Reductions are to be limited to those undertakings that provide the Commission with evidence that adds significant value to that already in the Commission's possession.

A. Immunity from fines

8. The Commission will grant an undertaking immunity from any fine which would otherwise have been imposed if:

(a) the undertaking is the first to submit evidence which in the Commission's view may enable it to adopt a decision to carry out an investigation in the sense of Article 14(3) of Regulation No 17[2] in connection with an alleged cartel affecting the Community; or

(b) the undertaking is the first to submit evidence which in the Commission's view may enable it to find an infringement of Article 81 EC[3] in connection with an alleged cartel affecting the Community.

9. Immunity pursuant to point 8(a) will only be granted on the condition that the Commission did not have, at the time of the submission, sufficient evidence to adopt a decision to carry out an investigation in the sense of Article 14(3) of Regulation No 17 in connection with the alleged cartel.

10. Immunity pursuant to point 8(b) will only be granted on the cumulative conditions that the Commission did not have, at the time of the submission, sufficient evidence to find an infringement of Article 81 EC in connection with the alleged cartel and that no undertaking had been granted conditional immunity from fines under point 8(a) in connection with the alleged cartel.

1 OJ C 207, 18.7.1996, p. 4.

2 OJ 13, 21.2.1962, p. 204/62. (Or the equivalent procedural regulations: Article 21(3) of Regulation (EEC) No 1017/68 of the Council; Article 18(3) of Council Regulation (EEC) No 4056/86 and Article 11(3) of Council Regulation (EEC) No 3975/87.)

3 Reference in this text to Article 81 EC also covers Article 53 EEA when applied by the Commission according to the rules laid down in Article 56 of the EEA Agreement.

11. In addition to the conditions set out in points 8(a) and 9 or in points 8(b) and 10, as appropriate, the following cumulative conditions must be met in any case to qualify for any immunity from a fine:

(a) the undertaking cooperates fully, on a continuous basis and expeditiously throughout the Commission's administrative procedure and provides the Commission with all evidence that comes into its possession or is available to it relating to the suspected infringement. In particular, it remains at the Commission's disposal to answer swiftly any request that may contribute to the establishment of the facts concerned;

(b) the undertaking ends its involvement in the suspected infringement no later than the time at which it submits evidence under point 8(a) or 8(b), as appropriate;

(c) the undertaking did not take steps to coerce other undertakings to participate in the infringement.

Procedure

12. An undertaking wishing to apply for immunity from fines should contact the Commission's Directorate-General for Competition. Should it become apparent that the requirements set out in points 8 to 10, as appropriate, are not met, the undertaking will immediately be informed that immunity from fines is not available for the suspected infringement.

13. If immunity from fines is available for a suspected infringement, the undertaking may, in order to meet condition 8(a) or 8(b), as appropriate:

(a) immediately provide the Commission with all the evidence relating to the suspected infringement available to it at the time of the submission; or

(b) initially present this evidence in hypothetical terms, in which case the undertaking must present a descriptive list of the evidence it proposes to disclose at a later agreed date. This list should accurately reflect the nature and content of the evidence, whilst safeguarding the hypothetical nature of its disclosure. Expurgated copies of documents, from which sensitive parts have been removed, may be used to illustrate the nature and content of the evidence.

14. The Directorate-General for Competition will provide a written acknowledgement of the undertaking's application for immunity from fines, confirming the date on which the undertaking either submitted evidence under 13(a) or presented to the Commission the descriptive list referred to in 13(b).

15. Once the Commission has received the evidence submitted by the undertaking under point 13(a) and has verified that it meets the conditions set out in point 8(a) or 8(b), as appropriate, it will grant the undertaking conditional immunity from fines in writing.

16. Alternatively, the Commission will verify that the nature and content of the evidence described in the list referred to in point 13(b) will meet the conditions set out in point 8(a) or 8(b), as appropriate, and inform the undertaking accordingly. Following the disclosure of the evidence no later than on the date agreed and having verified that it corresponds to the description made in the list, the Commission will grant the undertaking conditional immunity from fines in writing.

17. An undertaking which fails to meet the conditions set out in point 8(a) or 8(b), as appropriate, may withdraw the evidence disclosed for the purposes of its immunity application or request the Commission to consider it under section B of this notice. This does not prevent the Commission from using its normal powers of investigation in order to obtain the information.

18. The Commission will not consider other applications for immunity from fines before it has taken a position on an existing application in relation to the same suspected infringement.

19. If at the end of the administrative procedure, the undertaking has met the conditions set out in point 11, the Commission will grant it immunity from fines in the relevant decision.

B. Reduction of a fine

20. Undertakings that do not meet the conditions under section A above may be eligible to benefit from a reduction of any fine that would otherwise have been imposed.

21. In order to qualify, an undertaking must provide the Commission with evidence of the suspected infringement which represents significant added value with respect to the evidence already in the Commission's possession and must terminate its involvement in the suspected infringement no later than the time at which it submits the evidence.

22. The concept of 'added value' refers to the extent to which the evidence provided strengthens, by its very nature and/or its level of detail, the Commission's ability to prove the facts in question. In this assessment, the Commission will generally consider written evidence originating from the period of time to which the facts pertain to have a greater value than evidence subsequently established. Similarly, evidence directly relevant to the facts in question will generally be considered to have a greater value than that with only indirect relevance.

23. The Commission will determine in any final decision adopted at the end of the administrative procedure:

(a) whether the evidence provided by an undertaking represented significant added value with respect to the evidence in the Commission's possession at that same time;

(b) the level of reduction an undertaking will benefit from, relative to the fine which would otherwise have been imposed, as follows. For the:
   — *first* undertaking to meet point 21: a reduction of 30–50 per cent,
   — *second* undertaking to meet point 21: a reduction of 20–30 per cent,
   — *subsequent* undertakings that meet point 21: a reduction of up to 20 per cent.

In order to determine the level of reduction within each of these bands, the Commission will take into account the time at which the evidence fulfilling the condition in point 21 was submitted and the extent to which it represents added value. It may also take into account the extent and continuity of any cooperation provided by the undertaking following the date of its submission.

In addition, if an undertaking provides evidence relating to facts previously unknown to the Commission which have a direct bearing on the gravity or duration of the suspected cartel, the Commission will not take these elements into account when setting any fine to be imposed on the undertaking which provided this evidence.

Procedure

24. An undertaking wishing to benefit from a reduction of a fine should provide the Commission with evidence of the cartel in question.

25. The undertaking will receive an acknowledgement of receipt from the Directorate-General for Competition recording the date on which the relevant evidence was submitted. The Commission will not consider any submissions of evidence by an applicant for a reduction of a fine before it has taken a position on any existing application for a conditional immunity from fines in relation to the same suspected infringement.

26. If the Commission comes to the preliminary conclusion that the evidence submitted by the undertaking constitutes added value within the meaning of point 22, it will inform the undertaking in writing, no later than the date on which a statement of objections is notified, of its intention to apply a reduction of a fine within a specified band as provided in point 23(b).

27. The Commission will evaluate the final position of each undertaking which filed an application for a reduction of a fine at the end of the administrative procedure in any decision adopted.

General considerations

28. From 14 February 2002, this notice replaces the 1996 notice for all cases in which no undertaking has contacted the Commission in order to take advantage of the favourable treatment set out

in that notice. The Commission will examine whether it is necessary to modify this notice once it has acquired sufficient experience in applying it.

29. The Commission is aware that this notice will create legitimate expectations on which under-takings may rely when disclosing the existence of a cartel to the Commission.

30. Failure to meet any of the requirements set out in section A or B, as the case may be, at any stage of the administrative procedure may result in the loss of any favourable treatment set out therein.

31. In line with the Commission's practice, the fact that an undertaking cooperated with the Commission during its administrative procedure will be indicated in any decision, so as to explain the reason for the immunity or reduction of the fine. The fact that immunity or reduction in respect of fines is granted cannot protect an undertaking from the civil law consequences of its participation in an infringement of Article 81 EC.

32. The Commission considers that normally disclosure, at any time, of documents received in the context of this notice would undermine the protection of the purpose of inspections and investigations within the meaning of Article 4(2) of Regulation (EC) No 1049/2001 of the European Parliament and of the Council.

33. Any written statement made vis-à-vis the Commission in relation to this notice, forms part of the Commission's file. It may not be disclosed or used for any other purpose than the enforcement of Article 81 EC.

SECTION 3: **Notification under Article 81(3) EC**

Parties wishing to seek an individual exemption under Article 81(3) EC must notify the Commission of their agreement, pursuant to Article 4 of Regulation 17, on the appropriate Form, Form A/B. The Commission can issue an official exemption deci-sion according to Article 6 of Regulation 17, but in many instances they do not adopt the official procedure, preferring to close the procedure unofficially with an adminstrative letter stating that the agreement is one which the Commission believes would qualify for an exemption. This form of letter is known as a 'comfort letter' but is of limited legal status.

SA Lancôme and Cosparfrance Nederland BV v *Etos BV and Albert Heijn Supermart BV*
(Case 99/79) [1980] ECR 2511, [1981] 2 CMLR 164

Lancôme marketed perfumery, beauty products and toiletries through a selective distribution agreement. Following complaints and a Commission investigation, Lancôme amended its distribution agreements to the satisfaction of the Commis-sion. The procedure was closed by the Commission through a letter which stated, 'there is no longer any need, on the basis of the facts known to it, for it [the Commission] to take action in respect of the above-mentioned agreements under the provisions of Article [85(1)] of the Treaty of Rome. The file on this case may therefore be closed'. The status of that letter was questioned.

[11] Such a letter, which is based only upon the facts in the Commission's assessment and brings to an end the procedure of examination by the department of the Commission responsible for this, does not have the effect of preventing national courts before which the agreements in question are alleged to be incompatible with Article [85] from reaching a different finding as regards the agreements concerned on the basis of the information available to them. Whilst it does not bind the national courts, the opinion transmitted in such letters nevertheless constitutes a factor which the national courts may take into account in examining whether the agreements or conduct in question are in accordance with the provisions of Article [85].

NOTE: Negative comfort letters, such as this instance, are useful to the recipient. They are not binding on a national court, but may form an important part of their consideration of the individual case. However, a positive comfort letter, sometimes known as a 'discomfort letter', is not as helpful. The letter effectively says that the agreement is in breach of Article 81 EC but the Commission feels that it is the sort of agreement which might be granted an exemption, but no such exemption will be granted and the case is closed. In those circumstances, the national court is likely to find the agreement to be in breach of Article 81 EC, but has no power to grant an exemption, that power being reserved to the Commission. The following passage demonstrates the limitations of comfort letters.

Stevens, D., 'The "Comfort Letter": Old Problems, New Developments'
[1994] 15(2) ECLR 81, p. 86

The national court is required to respect the exemption decisions taken by the Commission . . . In this respect mention should be made of comfort letters in which the Commission services state that the conditions for applying Article 85(3) have been met. The Commission considers that national courts may take account of these letters as factual elements (emphasis added).

Thus, the national court could still, in theory, prohibit an agreement under Community law. Of course, the Notice does not affect the potential to apply conflicting domestic law. Nor does it dispense with the possibility that different national courts may adopt different approaches as to how to deal with the comfort letter dilemma, giving rise to lack of uniformity and possible forum shopping.

An example of the potential for confusion to arise in the national court is pointedly provided by the recent English case: *Inntrepreneur Estates Ltd* v *Mason*. The Deputy Judge, Mr Barnes QC, was clearly uneasy with the concept of a comfort letter. Attempting to apply the guidelines set out in the Notice, he drew attention to paragraph 25(a) of the Notice, which calls on the national court to take account of a comfort letter. The problem faced by Mr Barnes was that apparently he had no familiarity with the comfort letter:

> It is not, as I understand it, stated anywhere in the community legislation what precisely is a comfort letter nor does the guidance state in explicit terms what a comfort letter amounts to. [And further:] It is not entirely easy to know what comfort letters are or what letters amount to comfort letters.

Indeed, the two letters under consideration had none of the characteristics or language of the normal Commission comfort letter. Rather, they were notification by the Commission that the relevant agreement appeared to fulfil the requirements for an individual exemption and that the Commission would proceed with publication in accordance with Article 19(3) of Regulation 17. Mr Barnes, however, did not appear to recognise the difference. Having concluded that the letters in question were not comfort letters, he continued:

> On the one side there is the consideration that comfort letters are not a formal decision. . . . On the other hand it is clear that comfort letters are intended in many ways to be equivalent to a decision. . . . It may be that what is intended by [the] guidance [of

paragraph 25(a)] is that national courts are without further ado to treat comfort letters as being in their legal effect equivalent to a formal decision.

The Deputy Judge then proceeded to argue that, even if the letters were comfort letters, it would make no difference to his judgment. Having turned for guidance to Bellamy & Child's Common Market Law of Competition, he was advised that in circumstances where a comfort letter had been issued in preference to an Article 85(3) exemption, 'the national court would strive to find a means of upholding the validity of the agreement'. He was, however, unclear as to how, in such circumstances, this validity might be upheld, since it was not within his power to grant an exemption. He also noted that, in any case, there was disagreement under Community law as to the effect of comfort letters. Finally, and justifiably exasperated, the Deputy Judge closed the discussion by arguing that the defendants had a real prospect of succeeding in their contention that part of the agreement was void under Article 85(1): this was the case whether or not the letters were comfort letters. In other words, the Deputy Judge was prepared to ignore the suggestion in the letters that an individual exemption was imminent. It is quite clear from *Inntrepreneur* that the Notice has done little to ease the difficulties for the national courts created by the comfort letter and that it may, in fact, have added its own problems of interpretation.

NOTE: While comfort letters may be a highly advantageous mechanism for the Commission, to reduce its workload and allow it to dispose of a large number of cases swiftly, they create a great many problems for the national authorities, who must deal with cases closed by the Commission in this fashion. Problems are also faced by the parties to agreements themselves as they will also suffer from the uncertainty which is inherent within a comfort letter. The view of the Commission expressed in the letter is either unenforceable, in a 'negative clearance' letter, or unhelpful, in a 'discomfort' letter. For those reasons, there have been many calls for reform to give greater legal certainty for the parties and the national courts, See, Wodz, B., 'Comfort Letters and Other Informal Letters in EC Competition Proceedings: Why Is The Story Not Over?' [2000] ECLR 159.

SECTION 4: **Decentralisation**

The highly centralised system created by Regulation 17 was very successful for the Commission in the early years of competition law's development, but as the system became more mature a number of problems became more prevalent, the issues which surround the use of comfort letters being a pertinent example. In the early 1990s, the Commission began a process of decentralisation and modernisation which attempts to change its role. The Commission wants the National Competition Authorities and the undertaking themselves to take a larger role in the enforcement process, leaving the Commission to maintain an overarching policy role and deal with major pan-European cases.

Commission Notice on Cooperation between National Courts and the Commission
OJ, 1993, C39/6

I. Introduction

1. The abolition of internal frontiers enables firms in the Community to embark on new activities and Community consumers to benefit from increased competition. The Commission considers that

these advantages must not be jeopardized by restrictive or abusive practices of undertakings and that the completion of the internal market thus reaffirms the importance of the Community's competition policy and competition law.

2. A number of national and Community institutions have contributed to the formulation of Community competition law and are responsible for its day-to-day application. For this purpose, the national competition authorities, national and Community courts and the Commission each assume their own tasks and responsibilities, in line with the principles developed by the case-law of the Court of Justice of the European Communities.

3. If the competition process is to work well in the internal market, effective cooperation between these institutions must be ensured. The purpose of this Notice is to achieve this in relations between national courts and the Commission. It spells out how the Commission intends to assist national courts by closer cooperation in the application of Articles 85 and 86 of the EEC Treaty in individual cases.

II. Powers

4. The Commission is the administrative authority responsible for the implementation and for the thrust of competition policy in the Community and for this purpose has to act in the public interest. National courts, on the other hand, have the task of safeguarding the subjective rights of private individuals in their relations with one another[1].

5. In performing these different tasks, national courts and the Commission possess concurrent powers for the application of Article 85(1) and Article 86 of the Treaty. In the case of the Commission, the power is conferred by Article 89 and by the provisions adopted pursuant to Article 87. In the case of the national courts, the power derives from the direct effect of the relevant Community rules. In *BRT v Sabam*, the Court of Justice considered that 'as the prohibitions of Articles 85(1) and 86 tend by their very nature to produce direct effects in relations between individuals, these Articles create direct rights in respect of the individuals concerned which the national courts must safeguard'[2].

6. In this way, national courts are able to ensure, at the request of the litigants or on their own initiative, that the competition rules will be respected for the benefit of private individuals. In addition, Article 85(2) enables them to determine, in accordance with the national procedural law applicable, the civil law effects of the prohibition set out in Article 85[3].

7. However, the Commission, pursuant to Article 9 of Regulation No 17[4], has sole power to exempt certain types of agreements, decisions and concerted practices from this prohibition. The Commission may exercise this power in two ways. It may take a decision exempting a specific agreement in an individual case. It may also adopt regulations granting block exemptions for certain categories of agreements, decisions or concerted practices, where it is authorized to do so by the Council, in accordance with Article 87.

8. Although national courts are not competent to apply Article 85(3), they may nevertheless apply the decisions and regulations adopted by the Commission pursuant to that provision. The Court has on several occasions confirmed that the provisions of a regulation are directly applicable[5]. The

---

1 Case C-234/89, *Delimitis v Henninger Bräu*, [1991] ECR I-935, paragraph 44; Case T-24/90, *Automec v Commission*, judgment of 17 September 1992, paragraphs 73 and 85 (not yet reported).

2 Case 127/73, *BRT v Sabam*, [1974] ECR 51, paragraph 16.

3 Case 56/65, *LTM v MBU*, [1966] ECR 337; Case 48/72, *Brasserie de Haecht v Wilkin-Janssen*, [1973] ECR 77; Case 319/82, *Ciments et Bétons v Kerpen & Kerpen*, [1983] ECR 4173.

4 Council Regulation No 17 of 6 February 1962: First Regulation implementing Articles 85 and 86 of the Treaty (OJ No 13, 21.2.1962, p. 204/62; Special Edition 1959–62, p. 87).

5 Case 63/75, *Fonderies Roubaix v Fonderies Roux*, [1976] ECR 111; Case C-234/89, *Delimitis v Henninger Bräu*, [1991] ECR I-935.

Commission considers that the same is true for the substantive provisions of an individual exemption decision.

9. The powers of the Commission and those of national courts differ not only in their objective and content, but also in the ways in which they are exercised. The Commission exercises its powers according to the procedural rules laid down by Regulation No 17, whereas national courts exercise theirs in the context of national procedural law.

10. In this connection, the Court of Justice has laid down the principles which govern procedures and remedies for invoking directly applicable Community law.

Although the Treaty has made it possible in a number of instances for private persons to bring a direct action, where appropriate, before the Court of Justice, it was not intended to create new remedies in the national courts to ensure the observance of Community law other than those already laid down by national law. On the other hand . . . it must be possible for every type of action provided for by national law to be available for the purpose of ensuring observance of Community provisions having direct effect, on the same conditions concerning the admissibility and procedure as would apply were it a question of ensuring observance of national law[1].

11. The Commission considers that these principles apply in the event of breach of the Community competition rules; individuals and companies have access to all procedural remedies provided for by national law on the same conditions as would apply if a comparable breach of national law were involved. This equality of treatment concerns not only the definitive finding of a breach of competition rules, but embraces all the legal means capable of contributing to effective legal protection. Consequently, it is the right of parties subject to Community law that national courts should take provisional measures, that an effective end should be brought, by injunction, to the infringement of Community competition rules of which they are victims, and that compensation should be awarded for the damage suffered as a result of infringements, where such remedies are available in proceedings relating to similar national law.

12. Here the Commission would like to make it clear that the simultaneous application of national competition law is compatible with the application of Community law, provided that it does not impair the effectiveness and uniformity of Community competition rules and the measures taken to enforce them. Any conflicts which may arise when national and Community competition law are applied simultaneously must be resolved in accordance with the principle of the precedence of Community law[2]. The purpose of this principle is to rule out any national measure which could jeopardize the full effectiveness of the provisions of Community law.

III. The exercise of powers by the Commission

13. As the administrative authority responsible for the Community's competition policy, the Commission must serve the Community's general interest. The administrative resources at the Commission's disposal to perform its task are necessarily limited and cannot be used to deal with all the cases brought to its attention. The Commission is therefore obliged, in general, to take all organizational measures necessary for the performance of its task and, in particular, to establish priorities[3].

14. The Commission intends, in implementing its decision-making powers, to concentrate on

1 Case 158/80, *Rewe v Hauptzollant Kiel*, [1981] ECR 1805, paragraph 44; see also Case 33/76, *Rewe v Landwirtschaftskammer Saarland*, [1976] ECR 1989; Case 79/83, *Harz v Deutsche Tradax*, [1984] ECR 1921; Case 199/82, *Amministrazione delle Finanze dello Stato v San Giorgio*, [1983] ECR 3595.

2 Case 14/68, *Walt Wilhelm and Others v Bundeskartellamt*, [1969] ECR 1; Joined Cases 253/78 and 1 to 3/79, *Procureur de la République v Giry and Guerlain*, [1980] ECR 2327.

3 Case T-24/90, *Automec v Commission*, judgment of 17 September 1992, paragraph 77 (not yet reported).

notifications, complaints and own-initiative proceedings having particular political, economic or legal significance for the Community. Where these features are absent in a particular case, notifications will normally be dealt with by means of a comfort letter and complaints should, as a rule, be handled by national courts or authorities.

15. The Commission considers that there is not normally a sufficient Community interest in examining a case when the plaintiff is able to secure adequate protection of his rights before the national courts[4]. In these circumstances the complaint will normally be filed.

16. In this respect the Commission would like to make it clear that the application of Community competition law by the national courts has considerable advantages for individuals and companies:

— the Commission cannot award compensation for loss suffered as a result of an infringement of Article 85 or Article 86. Such claims may be brought only before the national courts. Companies are more likely to avoid infringements of the Community competition rules if they risk having to pay damages or interest in such an event,

— national courts can usually adopt interim measures and order the ending of infringements more quickly than the Commission is able to do,

— before national courts, it is possible to combine a claim under Community law with a claim under national law. This is not possible in a procedure before the Commission,

— in some Member States, the courts have the power to award legal costs to the successful applicant. This is never possible in the administrative procedure before the Commission.

IV. Application of Articles 85 and 86 by national courts

17. The national court may have to reach a decision on the application of Articles 85 and 86 in several procedural situations. In the case of civil law proceedings, two types of action are particularly frequent: actions relating to contracts and actions for damages. Under the former, the defendant usually relies on Article 85(2) to dispute the contractual obligations invoked by the plaintiff. Under the latter, the prohibitions contained in Articles 85 and 86 are generally relevant in determining whether the conduct which has given rise to the alleged injury is illegal.

18. In such situations, the direct effect of Article 85(1) and Article 86 gives national courts sufficient powers to comply with their obligation to hand down judgment. Nevertheless, when exercising these powers, they must take account of the Commission's powers in order to avoid decisions which could conflict with those taken or envisaged by the Commission in applying Article 85(1) and Article 86, and also Article 85(3)[1].

19. In its case-law the Court of Justice has developed a number of principles which make it possible for such contradictory decisions to be avoided[2]. The Commission feels that national courts could take account of these principles in the following manner.

1. Application of Article 85(1) and (2) and Article 86

20. The first question which national courts have to answer is whether the agreement, decision or concerted practice at issue infringes the prohibitions laid down in Article 85(1) or Article 86. Before answering this question, national courts should ascertain whether the agreement, decision or concerted practice has already been the subject of a decision, opinion or other official statement issued by an administrative authority and in particular by the Commission. Such statements provide national courts with significant, information for reaching a judgment, even if they are not formally bound by them. It should be noted in this respect that not all procedures before the Commission lead to an official decision, but that cases can also be closed by comfort letters. Whilst it is true that

---

4 Case T-24/90, cited above, paragraphs 91 to 94.

1 Case C-234/89, *Delimitis* v *Henninger Bräu*, [1991] ECR I-935, paragraph 47.

2 Case 48/72, *Brasserie de Haecht* v *Wilkin-Janssen*, [1973] ECR 77; Case 127/73, *BRT* v *Sabam*, [1974] ECR 51; Case C-234/89, *Delimitis* v *Henninger Bräu*, [1991] ECR I-935.

the Court of Justice has ruled that this type of letter does not bind national courts, it has nevertheless stated that the opinion expressed by the Commission constitutes a factor which the national courts may take into account in examining whether the agreements or conduct in question are in accordance with the provisions of Article 85[3].

21. If the Commission has not ruled on the same agreement, decision or concerted practice, the national courts can always be guided, in interpreting the Community law in question, by the case-law of the Court of Justice and the existing decisions of the Commission. It is with this in view that the Commission has, in a number of general notices[4], specified categories of agreements that are not caught by the ban laid down in Article 85(1).

22. On these bases, national courts should generally be able to decide whether the conduct at issue is compatible with Article 85(1) and Article 86. Nevertheless, if the Commission has initiated a procedure in a case relating to the same conduct, they may, if they consider it necessary for reasons of legal certainty, stay the proceedings while awaiting the outcome of the Commission's action[5]. A stay of proceedings may also be envisaged where national courts wish to seek the Commission's views in accordance with the arrangements referred to in this Notice[6]. Finally, where national courts have persistent doubts on questions of compatibility, they may stay proceedings in order to bring the matter before the Court of Justice, in accordance with Article 177 of the Treaty.

23. However, where national courts decide to give judgment and find that the conditions for applying Article 85(1) or Article 86 are not met, they should pursue their proceedings on the basis of such a finding, even if the agreement, decision or concerted practice at issue has been notified to the Commission. Where the assessment of the facts shows that the conditions for applying the said Articles are met, national courts must rule that the conduct at issue infringes Community competition law and take the appropriate measures, including those relating to the consequences that attach to infringement of a statutory prohibition under the civil law applicable.

2. Application of Article 85(3)

24. If the national court concludes that an agreement, decision or concerted practice is prohibited by Article 85(1), it must check whether it is or will be the subject of an exemption by the Commission under Article 85(3). Here several situations may arise.

25.(a) The national court is required to respect the exemption decisions taken by the Commission. Consequently, it must treat the agreement, decision or concerted practice at issue as compatible with Community law and fully recognize its civil law effects. In this respect mention should be made of comfort letters in which the Commission services state that the conditions for applying Article 85(3) have been met. The Commission considers that national courts may take account of these letters as factual elements.

26.(b) Agreements, decisions and concerted practices which fall within the scope of application of

---

3 Case 99/79, *Lancôme* v *Etos*, (1980) ECR 2511, paragraph 11.
4 See the notices on:
    — exclusive dealing contracts with commercial agents (OJ No 139, 24.12.1962, p. 2921/62),
    — agreements, decisions and concerted practices in the field of cooperation between enterprises (OJ No C 75, 29.7.1968, p. 3, as corrected in OJ No C 84, 28.8.1968, p. 14),
    — assessment of certain subcontracting agreements (OJ No C 1, 3.1.1979, p. 2),
    — agreements of minor importance (OJ No C 231, 12.9.1986, p. 2).
5 Case 127/73, *BRT* v *Sabam*, [1974] ECR 51, paragraph 21. The procedure before the Commission is initiated by an authoritative act. A simple acknowledgement of receipt cannot be considered an authoritative act as such; Case 48/72, *Brasserie de Haecht* v *Wilkin-Janssen*, [1973] ECR 77, paragraphs 16 and 17.
6 Case C-234/89, *Delimitis* v *Henninger Bräu*, [1991] ECR I-935, paragraph 53, Part V of this Notice.

a block exemption regulation are automatically exempted from the prohibition laid down in Article 85(1) without the need for a Commission decision or comfort letter[1].

27.(c) Agreements, decisions and concerted practices which are not covered by a block exemption regulation and which have not been the subject of an individual exemption decision or a comfort letter must, in the Commission's view, be examined in the following manner.

28. The national court must first examine whether the procedural conditions necessary for securing exemption are fulfilled, notably whether the agreement, decision or concerted practice has been duly notified in accordance with Article 4(1) of Regulation No 17. Where no such notification has been made, and subject to Article 4(2) of Regulation No 17, exemption under Article 85(3) is ruled out, so that the national court may decide, pursuant to Article 85(2), that the agreement, decision or concerted practice is void.

29. Where the agreement, decision or concerted practice has been duly notified to the Commission, the national court will assess the likelihood of an exemption being granted in the case in question in the light of the relevant criteria developed by the case law of the Court of Justice and the Court of First Instance and by previous regulations and decisions of the Commission.

30. Where the national court has in this way ascertained that the agreement, decision or concerted practice at issue cannot be the subject of an individual exemption, it will take the measures necessary to comply with the requirements of Article 85(1) and (2). On the other hand, if it takes the view that individual exemption is possible, the national court should suspend the proceedings while awaiting the Commission's decision. If the national court does suspend the proceedings, it nevertheless remains free, according to the rules of the applicable national law, to adopt any interim measures it deems necessary.

31. In this connection, it should be made clear that these principles do not apply to agreements, decisions and concerted practices which existed before Regulation No 17 entered into force or before that Regulation became applicable as a result of the accession of a new Member State and which were duly notified to the Commission. The national courts must consider such agreements, decisions and concerted practices to be valid so long as the Commission or the authorities of the Member States have not taken a prohibition decision or sent a comfort letter to the parties informing them that the file has been closed[2].

32. The Commission realizes that the principles set out above for the application of Articles 85 and 86 by national courts are complex and sometimes insufficient to enable those courts to perform their judicial function properly. This is particularly so where the practical application of Article 85(1) and Article 86 gives rise to legal or economic difficulties, where the Commission has initiated a procedure in the same case or where the agreement, decision or concerted practice concerned may become the subject of an individual exemption within the meaning of Article 85(3). National courts may bring such cases before the Court of Justice for a preliminary ruling, in accordance with Article 177. They may also avail themselves of the Commission's assistance according to the procedures set out below.

NOTE: This Notice sets out the difficulties that the Commission and the national courts face when trying to apply their concurrent jurisdiction under the competition rules. While it does suggest a number of procedural measures to help national courts (see, in particular, paras 33–44 of the Notice, not reproduced above), the Notice has not proved to be enormously useful in practice as the centralised structure of Regulation 17 continues to be an obstacle. See Waller, S.W.,

---

1 A list of the relevant regulations and of the official explanatory comments relating to them is given in the Annex to this Notice.
2 Case 48/72, *Brasserie de Haecht* v *Wilkin-Janssen*, [1973] ECR 77; Case 59/77, *De Bloss* v *Bouyer*, [1977] ECR 2359; Case 99/79, *Lancôme* v *Etos*, [1980] ECR 2511.

'Decentralization of the Enforcement Process of EC Competition Law—the Greater Role of National Courts' [1996] 2 LIEI 1, and MacCulloch, A., 'Inntrepreneur Estates: Co-operative application of the EC competition rules in the United Kingdom?' [1995] ECLR 380. The failure of this Notice to result in great practical change put further pressure on the Commission to take much more significant steps to allow the national authorities to play a greater role in the enforcement of EC competition law.

Masterfoods v *HB Ice Cream*
(Case C-344/98) [2000] ECR I-11369, [2001] 4 CMLR 14

HB, the leading manufacturer of ice-cream in Ireland supplied retail outlets with freezer cabinets free of charge, while retaining ownership of the cabinets, provided they were used exclusively for HB products. Masterfoods, a subsidiary of Mars Inc., entered the ice-cream market in 1989. A number of retailers subsequently began to stock Masterfoods products in cabinets supplied by HB, but HB demanded that the retailers comply with the 'exclusivity clause'. Masterfoods brought an action before the Irish courts seeking a declaration that the exclusivity clause was null and void under Articles 81 EC and 82 EC. HB brought a separate action seeking an injunction to restrain Masterfoods from inducing retailers to breach the exclusivity clause. Masterfoods' action was dismissed and HB were granted the injunction they sought. Masterfoods appealed to the Irish Supreme Court.

In parallel with those proceedings, Masterfoods lodged a complaint against HB with the European Commission. In 1998, by Decision 98/531/EC, the Commission ruled that the exclusivity clause constituted an infringement of Articles 81 EC and 82 EC. HB lodged an appeal against that decision under Article 230 EC and applied, under Article 242 EC, for the Decision to be suspended. In view of the proceedings in the European Courts, the Irish Supreme Court decided to stay proceedings and refer a number of questions to the Court of Justice for preliminary ruling under Article 234 EC.

[45] First of all, the principles governing the division of powers between the Commission and the national courts in the application of the Community competition rules should be borne in mind.

[46] The Commission, entrusted by Article 89(1) of the EC Treaty (now, after amendment, Article 85(1) EC) with the task of ensuring application of the principles laid down in Articles 85 and 86 of the Treaty, is responsible for defining and implementing the orientation of Community competition policy. It is for the Commission to adopt, subject to review by the Court of First Instance and the Court of Justice, individual decisions in accordance with the procedural rules in force and to adopt exemption regulations. In order effectively to perform that task, which necessarily entails complex economic assessments, it is entitled to give differing degrees of priority to the complaints brought before it (*Delimitis*, para. [44]; and Case C-119/97 P, *Ufex and Others* v *EC Commission* [[1999] ECR I-1341, [2000] 4 CMLR 266, para. [88]]).

[47] The Commission has exclusive competence to adopt decisions in implementation of Article 85(3) of the Treaty, pursuant to Article 9(1) of Regulation 17 [*Delimitis*, para. [44]]. However, it shares competence to apply Articles 85(1) and 86 of the Treaty with the national courts [*Delimitis*, para. [45]]. The latter provisions produce direct effects in relations between individuals and create direct rights in respect of the individuals concerned which national courts must safeguard [*BRT I*, cited at

fn. 114 above, para. [16]]. The national courts thus continue to have jurisdiction to apply the provisions of Articles 85(1) and 86 of the Treaty even after the Commission has initiated a procedure in application of Articles 2, 3 or 6 of Regulation 17 [*BRT I*, paras [17] to [20]].

[48] Despite that division of powers, and in order to fulfil the role assigned to it by the Treaty, the Commission cannot be bound by a decision given by a national court in application of Articles 85(1) and 86 of the Treaty. The Commission is therefore entitled to adopt at any time individual decisions under Articles 85 and 86 of the Treaty, even where an agreement or practice has already been the subject of a decision by a national court and the decision contemplated by the Commission conflicts with that national court's decision.

[49] It is also clear from the case law of the Court that the Member States' duty under Article 5 of the EC Treaty to take all appropriate measures, whether general or particular, to ensure fulfilment of the obligations arising from Community law and to abstain from any measure which could jeopardise the attainment of the objectives of the Treaty is binding on all the authorities of Member States including, for matters within their jurisdiction, the courts (see, to that effect, Case C-2/97, *IP v Borsana* [[1998] ECR I-8597, para. [26]]).

[50] Under the fourth paragraph of Article 189 of the Treaty, a decision adopted by the Commission implementing Article 85(1), 85(3) or 86 of the Treaty is to be binding in its entirety upon those to whom it is addressed.

[51] The Court has held, in paragraph [47] of *Delimitis*, that in order not to breach the general principle of legal certainty, national courts must, when ruling on agreements or practices which may subsequently be the subject of a decision by the Commission, avoid giving decisions which would conflict with a decision contemplated by the Commission in the implementation of Articles 85(1) and 86 and Article 85(3) of the Treaty.

[52] It is even more important that when national courts rule on agreements or practices which are already the subject of a Commission decision they cannot take decisions running counter to that of the Commission, even if the latter's decision conflicts with a decision given by a national court of first instance.

[53] In that connection, the fact that the President of the Court of First Instance suspended the application of Decision 98/531 until the Court of First Instance had given judgment terminating the proceedings before it is irrelevant. Acts of the Community institutions are in principle presumed to be lawful until such time as they are annulled or withdrawn (Case C-137/92 P, *EC Commission v BASF and Others* [[1994] ECR I-2555, para. [48]]). The decision of the judge hearing an application to order the suspension of the operation of the contested act, pursuant to Article 185 of the Treaty, has only provisional effect. It must not prejudge the points of law or fact in issue or neutralise in advance the effects of the decision subsequently to be given in the main action (order in Case C-149/95 P(R) *EC Commission v Atlantic Container Line and Others* [[1995] ECR I-2165; [1997] 5 CMLR 167, para. [22]]).

[54] Moreover, if a national court has doubts as to the validity or interpretation of an act of a Community institution it may, or must, in accordance with the second and third paragraphs of Article 177 of the Treaty, refer a question to the Court of Justice for a preliminary ruling.

[55] If, as here in the main proceedings, the addressee of a Commission decision has, within the period prescribed in the fifth paragraph of Article 173 of the Treaty, brought an action for annulment of that decision pursuant to that article, it is for the national court to decide whether to stay proceedings until a definitive decision has been given in the action for annulment or in order to refer a question to the Court for a preliminary ruling.

[56] It should be borne in mind in that connection that application of the Community competition rules is based on an obligation of sincere cooperation between the national courts, on the one hand, and the Commission and the Community Courts, on the other, in the context of which each acts on the basis of the role assigned to it by the Treaty.

[57] When the outcome of the dispute before the national court depends on the validity of the Commission decision, it follows from the obligation of sincere cooperation that the national court should, in order to avoid reaching a decision that runs counter to that of the Commission, stay its proceedings pending final judgment in the action for annulment by the Community Courts, unless it considers that, in the circumstances of the case, a reference to the Court of Justice for a preliminary ruling on the validity of the Commission decision is warranted.

[58] If a national court stays proceedings, it is incumbent on it to examine whether it is necessary to order interim measures in order to safeguard the interests of the parties pending final judgment.

NOTE: The *Masterfoods* judgment reaffirms the central importance of the Commission within the competition system and the subservient position of the national courts, which must wait for Community proceedings to be completed before they can deal effectively with a case. This decision is also stricter than the terms of the Commission Notice. It appears that a decision of the Commission is to be considered binding upon a national court and the national courts should not adopt a decision which runs counter to a Commission decision, even if it is subject to an appeal. The only option which appears to be open to a national court is to stay proceedings, and await the finalisation of the Community proceedings, or to make a reference to the Court of Justice under Article 234 EC. Both of these may be unsatisfactory in many cases because of their inherent delay. The position is less clear if the Commission has not yet adopted its initial decision. It seems that the national court is not required to stay proceedings or refer, but it may decide that it is the appropriate course of action.

Courage Ltd v *Crehan*
(Case C-453/99) [2001] ECR I-6297, [2001] 5 CMLR 28

Mr Crehan concluded two 20-year leases for public houses which imposed an obligation to purchase products from Courage. The tenant had to purchase a fixed minimum quantity of specified beers at the prices shown in the price list. Courage, the claimant in the main proceedings, brought an action for the recovery from Mr Crehan of the sums due for unpaid deliveries of beer. Mr Crehan contested the action on its merits, contending that the beer tie was contrary to Article 81 EC. He also counter-claimed for damages. Questions were raised before the Court of Justice under the Article 234 EC procedure concerning the compatibility of English law on damages with Community law.

[25.] As regards the possibility of seeking compensation for loss caused by a contract or by conduct liable to restrict or distort competition, it should be remembered from the outset that, in accordance with settled case-law, the national courts whose task it is to apply the provisions of Community law in areas within their jurisdiction must ensure that those rules take full effect and must protect the rights which they confer on individuals (see *inter alia* the judgments in Case 106/77 *Simmenthal* [1978] ECR 629, paragraph 16, and in Case C-213/89 *Factortame* [1990] ECR I-2433, paragraph 19).

[26.] The full effectiveness of Article 85 of the Treaty and, in particular, the practical effect of the prohibition laid down in Article 85(1) would be put at risk if it were not open to any individual to claim damages for loss caused to him by a contract or by conduct liable to restrict or distort competition.

[27.] Indeed, the existence of such a right strengthens the working of the Community competition rules and discourages agreements or practices, which are frequently covert, which are liable to restrict or distort competition. From that point of view, actions for damages before the national courts can make a significant contribution to the maintenance of effective competition in the Community.

[28.] There should not therefore be any absolute bar to such an action being brought by a party to a contract which would be held to violate the competition rules.

[29.] However, in the absence of Community rules governing the matter, it is for the domestic legal system of each Member State to designate the courts and tribunals having jurisdiction and to lay down the detailed procedural rules governing actions for safeguarding rights which individuals derive directly from Community law, provided that such rules are not less favourable than those governing similar domestic actions (principle of equivalence) and that they do not render practically impossible or excessively difficult the exercise of rights conferred by Community law (principle of effectiveness) (see Case C-261/95 *Palmisani* [1997] ECR I-4025, paragraph 27).

[30.] In that regard, the Court has held that Community law does not prevent national courts from taking steps to ensure that the protection of the rights guaranteed by Community law does not entail the unjust enrichment of those who enjoy them (see, in particular, Case 238/78 *Ireks-Arkady* v *Council and Commission* [1979] ECR 2955, paragraph 14, Case 68/79 *Just* [1980] ECR 501, paragraph 26, and Joined Cases C-441/98 and C-442/98 *Michaïlidis* [2000] ECR I-7145, paragraph 31).

[31.] Similarly, provided that the principles of equivalence and effectiveness are respected (see *Palmisani*, cited above, paragraph 27), Community law does not preclude national law from denying a party who is found to bear significant responsibility for the distortion of competition the right to obtain damages from the other contracting party. Under a principle which is recognised in most of the legal systems of the Member States and which the Court has applied in the past (see Case 39/72 *Commission* v *Italy* [1973] ECR 101, paragraph 10), a litigant should not profit from his own unlawful conduct, where this is proven.

[32.] In that regard, the matters to be taken into account by the competent national court include the economic and legal context in which the parties find themselves and, as the United Kingdom Government rightly points out, the respective bargaining power and conduct of the two parties to the contract.

[33.] In particular, it is for the national court to ascertain whether the party who claims to have suffered loss through concluding a contract that is liable to restrict or distort competition found himself in a markedly weaker position than the other party, such as seriously to compromise or even eliminate his freedom to negotiate the terms of the contract and his capacity to avoid the loss or reduce its extent, in particular by availing himself in good time of all the legal remedies available to him.

[34.] Referring to the judgments in Case 23/67 *Brasserie de Haecht* [1967] ECR 127 and Case C-234/89 *Delimitis* [1991] ECR I-935, paragraphs 14 to 26, the Commission and the United Kingdom Government also rightly point out that a contract might prove to be contrary to Article 85(1) of the Treaty for the sole reason that it is part of a network of similar contracts which have a cumulative effect on competition. In such a case, the party contracting with the person controlling the network cannot bear significant responsibility for the breach of Article 85, particularly where in practice the terms of the contract were imposed on him by the party controlling the network.

[35.] Contrary to the submission of Courage, making a distinction as to the extent of the parties' liability does not conflict with the case-law of the Court to the effect that it does not matter, for the purposes of the application of Article 85 of the Treaty, whether the parties to an agreement are on an equal footing as regards their economic position and function (see *inter alia* Joined Cases 56/64 and 58/64 *Consten and Grundig* v *Commission* [1966] ECR 382). That case-law concerns the conditions for application of Article 85 of the Treaty while the questions put before the Court in the present case concern certain consequences in civil law of a breach of that provision.

NOTE: The Court's ruling in *Crehan* is very important for the future of the enforcement in the UK courts as it clarifies the availability of damages in Article 81 EC cases. The Court clearly indicates that the English common law rules which prevented recovery were contrary to EC law as they severely reduced the effectiveness of Article 81 EC. The Court did make it clear that such a rule would be compatible with EC law in situations where one party would be unjustly enriched, or where that party bore responsibility for the creation of the agreement. That would not be applicable in Mr Crehan's situation where the brewery effectively dictated the terms of the contract though the use of their standard lease. Mr Crehan had no real responsibility for the anti-competitive restriction. This should encourage undertakings to seek damages for breaches of Article 81 EC as damages are available in a much wider range of situations.

Commission Notice on Cooperation between National Competition Authorities and the Commission
OJ, 1997, C313/3

I. Role of the Member States and of the Community
1. In competition policy the Community and the Member States perform different functions. Whereas the Community is responsible only for implementing the Community rules, Member States not only apply their domestic law but also have a hand in implementing Articles 85 and 86 of the EC Treaty.

2. This involvement of the Member States in Community competition policy means that decisions can be taken as closely as possible to the citizen (Article A of the Treaty on European Union). The decentralized application of Community competition rules also leads to a better allocation of tasks. If, by reason of its scale or effects, the proposed action can best be taken at Community level, it is for the Commission to act. Otherwise, it is for the competition authority of the Member State concerned to act.

3. Community law is implemented by the Commission and national competition authorities, on the one hand, and national courts, on the other, in accordance with the principles developed by the Community legislature and by the Court of Justice and the Court of First Instance of the European Communities.
It is the task of national courts to safeguard the rights of private persons in their relations with one another[1]. Those rights derive from the fact that the prohibitions in Articles 85(1) and 86[2] and the exemptions granted by regulation[3] have been recognized by the Court of Justice as being directly applicable. Relations between national courts and the Commission in applying Articles 85 and 86 were spelt out in a Notice published by the Commission in 1993[4]. This Notice is the counterpart, for relations with national authorities, to that of 1993 on relations with national courts.

4. As administrative authorities, both the Commission and national competition authorities act in the public interest in performing their general task of monitoring and enforcing the competition rules[5]. Relations between them are determined primarily by this common role of protecting the general interest. Although similar to the Notice on cooperation with national courts, this Notice accordingly reflects this special feature.

5. The specific nature of the role of the Commission and of national competition authorities is characterized by the powers conferred on those bodies by the Council regulations adopted under

---

1 Case T-24/90 *Automec v Commission ('Automec II')* [1992] ECR II-2223, paragraph 85.
2 Case 127/73 *BRT v SABAM* [1974] ECR 51, paragraph 16.
3 Case 63/75 *Fonderies Roubaix-Wattrelos v Fonderies A. Roux* [1976] ECR 111.
4 Notice on cooperation between national courts and the Commission in applying Articles 85 and 86 of the EEC Treaty (OJ C 39, 13.2.1993, p. 6).
5 *Automec II*, see footnote 1; paragraph 85.

Article 87 of the Treaty. Article 9(1) of Regulation No 17[6] thus provides: 'Subject to review of its decision by the Court of Justice[7], the Commission shall have sole power to declare Article 85(1) inapplicable pursuant to Article 85(3) of the Treaty'. And Article 9(3) of the same. Regulation provides: 'As long as the Commission has not initiated any procedure under Article 2[8], 3[9] or 6[10], the authorities of the Member States shall remain competent to apply Article 85(1) and Article 86 in accordance with Article 88 of the Treaty'.

It follows that, provided their national law has conferred the necessary powers on them, national competition authorities are empowered to apply the prohibitions in Articles 85(1) and 86. On the other hand, for the purposes of applying Article 85(3), they do not have any powers to grant exemptions in individual cases; they must abide by the decisions and regulations adopted by the Commission under that provision. They may also take account of other measures adopted by the Commission in such cases, in particular comfort letters, treating them as factual evidence.

6. The Commission is convinced that enhancing the role of national competition authorities will boost the effectiveness of Articles 85 and 86 of the Treaty and, generally speaking, will bolster the application of Community competition rules throughout the Community. In the interests of safeguarding and developing the single market, the Commission considers that those provisions should be used as widely as possible. Being closer to the activities and businesses that require monitoring, national authorities are often in a better position than the Commission to protect competition.

7. Cooperation must therefore be organized between national authorities and the Commission. If this cooperation is to be fruitful, they will have to keep in close and constant touch.

8. The Commission proposes to set out in this Notice the principles it will apply in future when dealing with the cases described herein. The Notice also seeks to induce firms to approach national competition authorities more often.

9. This Notice describes the practical cooperation which is desirable between the Commission and national authorities. It does not affect the extent of the powers conferred by Community law on either the Commission or national authorities for the purpose of dealing with individual cases.

10. For cases falling within the scope of Community law, to avoid duplication of checks on compliance with the competition rules which are applicable to them, which is costly for the firms concerned, checks should wherever possible be carried out by a single authority (either a Member State's competition authority or the Commission). Control by a single authority offers advantages for businesses.

Parallel proceedings before the Commission, on the one hand, and a national competition authority, on the other, are costly for businesses whose activities fall within the scope both of Community law and of Member States' competition laws. They can lead to the repetition of checks on the same activity, by the Commission, on the one hand, and by the competition authorities of the Member States concerned, on the other.

Businesses in the Community may therefore in certain circumstances find it to their advantage if some cases falling within the scope of Community competition law were dealt with solely by national authorities. In order that this advantage may be enjoyed to the full, the Commission thinks it is desirable that national authorities should themselves apply Community law directly or, failing that,

6 Council Regulation No 17 of 6 February 1962: First Regulation implementing Articles 85 and 86 of the Treaty; OJ 13, 21.2.1962, p. 204/62 (English Special Edition 1959–62, p. 87).

7 Now by the Court of First Instance and, on appeal, by the Court of Justice.

8 Negative clearance.

9 Termination of infringements—prohibition decisions.

10 Decisions pursuant to Article 85(3).

obtain, by applying their domestic law, a result similar to that which would have been obtained had Community law been applied.

11. What is more, in addition to the resulting benefits accruing to competition authorities in terms of mobilization of their resources, cooperation between authorities reduces the risk of divergent decisions and hence the opportunities for those who might be tempted to do so to seek out whichever authority seemed to them to be the most favourable to their interests.

12. Member States' competition authorities often have a more detailed and precise knowledge than the Commission of the relevant markets (particularly those with highly specific national features) and the businesses concerned. Above all, they may be in a better position than the Commission to detect restrictive practices that have not been notified or abuses of a dominant position whose effects are essentially confined to their territory.

13. Many cases handled by national authorities involve arguments based on national law and arguments drawn from Community competition law. In the interests of keeping proceedings as short as possible, the Commission considers it preferable that national authorities should directly apply Community law themselves, instead of making firms refer to the Community-law aspects of their cases to the Commission.

14. An increasing number of major issues in the field of Community competition law have been clarified over the last thirty years through the case-law of the Court of Justice and the Court of First Instance and through decisions taken on questions of principle and the exemption regulations adopted by the Commission. The application of that law by national authorities is thereby simplified.

15. The Commission intends to encourage the competition authorities of all Member States to engage in this cooperation. However, the national legislation of several Member States does not currently provide competition authorities with the procedural means of applying Articles 85(1) and 86. In such Member States conduct caught by the Community provisions can be effectively dealt with by national authorities only under national law.

In the Commission's view, it is desirable that national authorities should apply Article 85 or 86 of the Treaty, if appropriate in conjunction with their domestic competition rules, when handling cases that fall within the scope of those provisions.

16. Where authorities are not in a position to do this and hence can apply only their national law to such cases, the application of that law should 'not prejudice the uniform application throughout the common market of the Community rules on cartels and of the full effect of the measures adopted in implementation of those rules'[11]. At the very least, the solution they find to a case falling within the scope of Community law must be compatible with that law, Member States being forbidden, given the primacy of Community law over national competition law[12] and the obligation to cooperate in good faith laid down in Article 5 of the Treaty[13], to take measures capable of defeating the practical effectiveness of Articles 85 and 86.

17. Divergent decisions are more likely to be reached where a national authority applies its national law rather than Community law. Where a Member State's competition authority applies Community law, it is required to comply with any decisions taken previously by the Commission in the same proceedings. Where the case has merely been the subject of a comfort letter, then, according to the Court of Justice, although this type of letter does not bind national courts, the opinion expressed by the Commission constitutes a factor which the national courts may take into

---

11 Case 14/68 *Walt Wilhelm and Others* v *Bundeskartellamt* [1969] ECR 1, paragraph 4.

12 *Walt Wilhelm*, see footnote 11; paragraph 6; Case 66/86 *Ahmed Saeed Flugreisen and Others* v *Zentrale Zur Bekämpfung Unlauteren Wettbewerbs* [1989] ECR 803, paragraph 48.

13 Case C-165/91 *Van Munster* v *Rijksdienst voor Pensioenen* [1994] ECR I-4661, paragraph 32.

account in examining whether the agreements on conduct in question are in accordance with the provisions of Article 85[14]. In the Commission's view, the same holds true for national authorities.

18. Where an infringement of Article 85 or 86 is established by Commission decision, that decision precludes the application of a domestic legal provision authorizing what the Commission has prohibited. The objective of the prohibitions in Articles 85(1) and 86 is to guarantee the unity of the common market and the preservation of undistorted competition in that market. They must be strictly complied with if the functioning of the Community regime is not to be endangered[15].

19. The legal position is less clear as to whether national authorities are allowed to apply their more stringent national competition law where the situation they are assessing has previously been the subject of an individual exemption decision of the Commission or is covered by a block exemption Regulation. In *Walt Wilhelm*, the Court stated that the Treaty 'permits the Community authorities to carry out certain positive, though indirect, actions with a view to promoting a harmonious development of economic activities within the whole Community' (paragraph 5 of the judgment). In *Bundeskartellamt* v *Volkswagen and VAG Leasing*[16], the Commission contended that national authorities may not prohibit exempted agreements. The uniform application of Community law would be frustrated every time an exemption granted under Community law was made to depend on the relevant national rules. Otherwise, not only would a given agreement be treated differently depending on the law of each Member State, thus detracting from the uniform application of Community law, but the full effectiveness of an act giving effect to the Treaty—which an exemption under Article 85(3) undoubtedly is—would also be disregarded. In the case in point, however, the Court did not have to settle the question.

20. If the Commission's Directorate-General for Competition sends a comfort letter in which it expresses the opinion that an agreement or a practice is incompatible with Article 85 of the Treaty but states that, for reasons to do with its internal priorities, it will not propose to the Commission that it take a decision thereon in accordance with the formal procedures laid down in Regulation No 17, it goes without saying that the national authorities in whose territory the effects of the agreement or practice are felt may take action in respect of that agreement or practice.

21. In the case of a comfort letter in which the Directorate-General for Competition expresses the opinion that an agreement does restrict competition within the meaning of Article 85(1) but qualifies for exemption under Article 85(3), the Commission will call upon national authorities to consult it before they decide whether to adopt a different decision under Community or national law.

22. As regards comfort letters in which the Commission expresses the opinion that, on the basis of the information in its possession, there is no need for it to take any action under Article 85(1) or Article 86 of the Treaty, 'that fact cannot by itself have the result of preventing the national authorities from applying to those agreements' or practices 'provisions of national competition law which may be more rigorous than Community law in this respect. The fact that a practice has been held by the Commission not to fall within the ambit of the prohibition contained in Article 85(1) and (2) or Article 86, 'the scope of which is limited to agreements, or dominant positions capable of affecting trade between Member States, in no way prevents that practice from being considered by the national authorities from the point of view of the restrictive effects which it may produce nationally'. (Judgment of the Court of Justice in *Procureur de la République* v *Giry and Guerlain*[17].)

---

14 Case 99/79 *Lancôme* v *Etos* [1980] ECR 2511, paragraph 11, cited in the above mentioned notice on cooperation between national courts and the Commission in applying Articles 85 and 86.

15 Fourth Report on Competition Policy 1974, point 45.

16 Case C-266/93 [1995] ECR I-3477; see also the Opinion of Advocate-General Tesauro in the same case, paragraph 51.

17 Joined Cases 253/78 and 1 to 3/79 *Procureur de la République* v *Giry and Guerlain* [1980] ECR 2327, paragraph 18.

II. Guidelines on case allocation

23. Cooperation between the Commission and national competition authorities has to comply with the current legal framework. First, if it is to be caught by Community law and not merely by national competition law, the conduct in question must be liable to have an appreciable effect on trade between Member States. Secondly, the Commission has sole power to declare Article 85(1) of the Treaty inapplicable under Article 85(3).

24. In practice, decisions taken by a national authority can apply effectively only to restrictions of competition whose impact is felt essentially within its territory. This is the case in particular with the restrictions referred to in Article 4(2)(1) of Regulation No 17, namely agreements, decisions or concerted practices the only parties to which are undertakings from one Member State and which, though they do not relate either to imports or to exports between Member States, may affect intra-Community trade[18]. It is extremely difficult from a legal standpoint for such an authority to conduct investigations outside its home country, such as when on-the-spot inspections need to be carried out on businesses, and to ensure that its decisions are enforced beyond its national borders. The upshot is that the Commission usually has to handle cases involving businesses whose relevant activities are carried on in more than one Member State.

25. A national authority having sufficient resources in terms of manpower and equipment and having had the requisite powers conferred on it, also needs to be able to deal effectively with any cases covered by the Community rules which it proposes to take on. The effectiveness of a national authority's action is dependent on its powers of investigation, the legal means it has at its disposal for settling a case—including the power to order interim measures in an emergency—and the penalties it is empowered to impose on businesses found guilty of infringing the competition rules. Differences between the rules of procedure applicable in the various Member States should not, in the Commission's view, lead to outcomes which differ in their effectiveness when similar cases are being dealt with.

26. In deciding which cases to handle itself, the Commission will take into account the effects of the restrictive practice or abuse of a dominant position and the nature of the infringement.

In principle, national authorities will handle cases the effects of which are felt mainly in their territory and which appear upon preliminary examination unlikely to qualify for exemption under Article 85(3). However, the Commission reserves the right to take on certain cases displaying a particular Community interest.

Mainly national effects

27. First of all, it should be pointed out that the only cases at issue here are those which fall within the scope of Articles 85 and 86.

That being so, the existing and foreseeable effects of a restrictive practice or abuse of a dominant position may be deemed to be closely linked to the territory in which the agreement or practice is applied and to the geographic market for the goods or services in question.

28. Where the relevant geographic market is limited to the territory of a single Member State and the agreement or practice is applied only in that State, the effects of the agreement or practice must be deemed to occur mainly within that State even if, theoretically, the agreement or practice is capable of affecting trade between Member States.

Nature of the infringement: cases that cannot be exempted

29. The following considerations apply to cases brought before the Commission, to cases brought before a national competition authority and to cases which both may have to deal with.

18 It is possible that an agreement, 'although it does not relate either to imports or to exports between Member States' within the meaning of Article 4 of Regulation No 17, 'may affect trade between Member States' within the meaning of Article 85(1) of the Treaty (judgment of the Court of Justice in Case 43/69 *Bilger* v *Jehle* [1970] ECR 127, paragraph 5).

A distinction should be drawn between infringements of Article 85 of the Treaty and infringements of Article 86.

30. The Commission has exclusive powers under Article 85(3) of the Treaty to declare the provisions of Article 85(1) inapplicable. Any notified restrictive practice that *prima facie* qualifies for exemption must therefore be examined by the Commission, which will take account of the criteria developed in this area by the Court of Justice and the Court of First Instance and also by the relevant regulations and its own previous decisions.

31. The Commission also has exclusive responsibility for investigation complaints against decisions it has taken under its exclusive powers, such as a decision to withdraw an exemption previously granted by it under Article 85(3)[19].

32. No such limitation exists, however, on implementation of Article 86 of the Treaty. The Commission and the Member States have concurrent competence to investigate complaints and to prohibit abuses of dominant positions.

Cases of particular significance to the Community

33. Some cases considered by the Commission to be of particular Community interest will more often be dealt with by the Commission even if, inasmuch as they satisfy the requirements set out above (points 27–28 and 29–32), they can be dealt with by a national authority.

34. This category includes cases which raise a new point of law, that is to say, those which have not yet been the subject of a Commission decision or a judgment of the Court of Justice or Court of First Instance.

35. The economic magnitude of a case is not in itself sufficient reason for its being dealt with by the Commission. The position might be different where access to the relevant market by firms from other Member States is significantly impeded.

36. Cases involving alleged anti-competitive behaviour by a public undertaking, an undertaking to which a Member State has granted special or exclusive rights with the meaning of Article 90(1) of the Treaty, or an undertaking entrusted with the operation of services of general economic interest or having the character of a revenue-producing monopoly within the meaning of Article 90(2) of the Treaty may also be of particular Community interest.

III. Cooperation in cases which the Commission deals with first

37. Cases dealt with by the Commission have three possible origins: own-initiative proceedings, notifications and complaints. By their very nature, own-initiative proceedings do not lend themselves to decentralized processing by national competition authorities.

38. The exclusivity of the Commission's powers to apply Article 85(3) of the Treaty in individual cases means that cases notified to the Commission under Article 4(1) of Regulation No 17 by parties seeking exemption under Article 85(3) cannot be dealt with by a national competition authority on the Commission's initiative. According to the case-law of the Court of First Instance, these exclusive powers confer on the applicant the right to obtain from the Commission a decision on the substance of his request for exemption[20].

39. National competition authorities may deal, at the Commission's request, with complaints that do not involve the application of Article 85(3), namely those relating to restrictive practices which must be notified under Articles 4(1), 5(1) and 25 of Regulation No 17 but have not been notified to the Commission and those based on alleged infringement of Article 86 of the Treaty. On the other hand, complaints concerning matters falling within the scope of the Commission's exclusive powers, such as withdrawal of exemption, cannot be usefully handled by a national competition authority[21].

---

19 *Automec II*, see footnote 1; paragraph 75.
20 Case T-23/90 *Peugeot* v *Commission* [1991] ECR II-653, paragraph 47.
21 *Automec II*, see footnote 1; paragraph 75.

40. The criteria set out at points 23 to 36 above in relation to the handling of a case by the Commission or a national authority, in particular as regards the territorial extent of the effects of a restrictive practice or dominant position (points 27–28), should be taken into account.

Commission's right to reject a complaint

41. It follows from the case-law of the Court of First Instance that the Commission is entitled under certain conditions to reject a complaint which does not display sufficient Community interest to justify further investigation[22].

42. The Commission's resultant right to reject a complaint stems from the concurrent competence of the Commission, national courts and—where they have the power—national competition authorities to apply Articles 85(1) and 86 and from the consequent protection available to complainants before the courts and administrative authorities. With regard to that concurrent competence, it has been consistently held by the Court of Justice and the Court of First Instance that Article 3 of Regulation No 17 (the legal basis for the right to lodge a complaint with the Commission for alleged infringement of Article 85 or Article 86) does not entitle an applicant under that Article to obtain from the Commission a decision within the meaning of Article 189 of the Treaty as to whether or not the alleged infringement has occurred[23].

Conditions for rejecting a complaint

43. The investigation of a complaint by a national authority presupposes that the following specific conditions, derived from the case-law of the Court of First Instance, are met.

44. The first of these conditions is that, in order to assess whether or not there is a Community interest in having a case investigated further, the Commission must first undertake a careful examination of the questions of fact and law set out in the complaint[24]. In accordance with the obligation imposed on it by Article 190 of the Treaty to state the reasons for its decisions, the Commission has to inform the complainant of the legal and factual considerations which have induced it to conclude that the complaint does not display a sufficient Community interest to justify further investigation. The Commission cannot therefore confine itself to an abstract reference to the Community interest[25].

45. In assessing whether it is entitled to reject a complaint for lack of any Community interest, the Commission must balance the significance of the alleged infringement as regards the functioning of the common market, the probability of its being able to establish the existence of the infringement, and the extent of the investigative measures required for it to perform, under the best possible conditions, its task of making sure that Articles 85 and 86 are complied with[26]. In particular, as the Court of First Instance held in *BEMIM*[27], where the effects of the infringements alleged in a complaint are essentially confined to the territory of one Member State and where proceedings have been brought before the courts and competent administrative authorities of that Member State by the complainant against the body against which the complaint was made, the Commission is entitled to reject the complaint for lack of any sufficient Community interest in further investigation of the case, provided however that the rights of the complainant can be adequately safeguarded. As to whether the effects of the restrictive practice are localized, such is the case in particular with practices to

---

22 *Automec II*, see footnote 1; paragraph 85; cited in Case T-114/92 *BEMIM* v *Commission* [1995] ECR II-147, paragraph 80, and in Case T-77/95 *SFEI and Others* v *Commission* [1997] ECR II-1, paragraphs 29 and 55.

23 See in particular Case 125/78 *GEMA* v *Commission* [1979] ECR 3173, paragraph 17, and Case T-16/91 *Rendo and Others* v *Commission* [1992] ECR II-2417, paragraph 98.

24 *Automec II*, see footnote 1; paragraph 82.

25 *Automec II*, see footnote 1; paragraph 85.

26 *Automec II*, see footnote 1; paragraph 86, cited in *BEMIM*, paragraph 80.

27 See footnote 22; paragraph 86.

which the only parties are undertakings from one Member State and which, although they do not relate either to imports or to exports between Member States, within the meaning of point 1 of Article 4(2) of Regulation No 17[28], are capable of affecting intra-Community trade. As regards the safeguarding of the complainant's rights, the Commission considers that the referral of the matter to the national authority concerned needs must protect them quite adequately. On this latter point, the Commission takes the view that the effectiveness of the national authority's action depends notably on whether that authority is able to take interim measures if it deems it necessary, without prejudice to the possibility, found in the law of certain Member States, that such measures may be taken with the requisite degree of effectiveness by a court.

Procedure

46. Where the Commission considers these conditions to have been met, it will ask the competition authority of the Member State in which most of the effects of the contested agreement or practice are felt if it would agree to investigate and decide on the complaint. Where the competition authority agrees to do so, the Commission will reject the complaint pending before it on the ground that it does not display sufficient Community interest and will refer the matter to the national competition authority, either automatically or at the complainant's request. The Commission will place the relevant documents in its possession at the national authority's disposal[29].

47. With regard to investigation of the complaint, it should be stressed that, in accordance with the ruling given by the Court of Justice in Case C-67/91[30] (the 'Spanish banks' case), national competition authorities are not entitled to use as evidence, for the purposes of applying either national rules or the Community competition rules, unpublished information contained in replies to requests for information sent to firms under Article 11 of Regulation No 17 or information obtained as a result of any inspections carried out under Article 14 of that Regulation. This information can nevertheless be taken into account, where appropriate, to justify instituting national proceedings[31].

IV. Cooperation in cases which a national authority deals with first introduction

48. At issue here are cases falling within the scope of Community competition law which a national competition authority handles on its own initiative, applying Article 85(1) or 86, either alone or in conjunction with its national competition rules, or, where it cannot do so, its national rules alone. This covers all cases within this field which a national authority investigates before the Commission—where appropriate—does so, irrespective of their procedural origin (own-initiative proceedings, notification, complaint, etc.). These cases are therefore those which fulfil the conditions set out in Part II (Guidelines on case allocation) of this Notice.

49. As regards cases which they deal with under Community law, it is desirable that national authorities should systematically inform the Commission of any proceedings they initiate. The Commission will pass on this information to the authorities in the other Member States.

50. This cooperation is especially necessary in regard to cases of particular significance to the Community within the meaning of points 33–36. This category includes (a) all cases raising a new point of law, the aim being to avoid decisions, whether based on national law or on Community law,

---

28 See footnote 18.

29 However, in the case of information accompanied by a request for confidentiality with a view to protecting the informant's anonymity, an institution which accepts such information is bound, under Article 214 of the Treaty, to comply with such a condition (Case 145/83 *Adams v Commission* [1985] ECR 3539). The Commission will thus not divulge to national authorities the name of an informant who wishes to remain anonymous unless the person concerned withdraws, at the Commission's request, his request for anonymity *vis-à-vis* the national authority which may be dealing with his complaint.

30 Case C-67/91 *Dirección General de Defensa de la Competencia v Asociación Española de Banca Privada (AEB) and Others* [1992] ECR I-4785, operative part.

31 See footnote 30; paragraphs 39 and 43.

which are incompatible with the latter; (b) among cases of the utmost importance from an economic point of view, only those in which access by firms from other Member States to the relevant national market is significantly impeded; and (c) certain cases in which a public undertaking or an undertaking treated as equivalent to a public undertaking (within the meaning of Article 90(1) and (2) of the Treaty) is suspected of having engaged in an anti-competitive practice. Each national authority must determine, if necessary after consulting the Commission, whether a given case fits into one of these sub-categories.

51. Such cases will be investigated by national competition authorities in accordance with the procedures laid down by their national law, whether they are acting with a view to applying the Community competition rules or applying their national competition rules[32].

52. The Commission also takes the view that, like national courts to which competition cases involving Article 85 or 86 have been referred, national competition authorities applying those provisions are always at liberty, within the limits of their national procedural rules and subject to Article 214 of the Treaty, to seek information from the Commission on the state of any proceedings which the Commission may have set in motion and as to the likelihood of its giving an official ruling, pursuant to Regulation No 17, on cases which they are investigating on their own initiative. Under the same circumstances, national competition authorities may contact the Commission where the concrete application of Article 85(1) or of Article 86 raises particular difficulties, in order to obtain the economic and legal information which the Commission is in a position to supply to them[33].

53. The Commission is convinced that close cooperation with national authorities will forestall any contradictory decisions. But if, 'during national proceedings, it appears possible that the decision to be taken by the Commission at the culmination of a procedure still in progress concerning the same agreement may conflict with the effects of the decision of the national authorities, it is for the latter to take the appropriate measures' (*Walt Wilhelm*) to ensure that measures implementing Community competition law are fully effective. The Commission takes the view that these measures should generally consist in national authorities staying their proceedings pending the outcome of the proceedings being conducted by the Commission. Where a national authority applies its national law, such a stay of proceedings would be based on the principles of the primacy of Community law (*Walt Wilhelm*)[34] and legal certainty, and where it applies Community law, on the principle of legal certainty alone. For its part, the Commission will endeavour to deal as a matter of priority with cases subject to national proceedings thus stayed. A second possibility may, however, be envisaged, whereby the Commission is consulted before adopting the national decision. The consultations would consist, due regard being had to the judgment in the Spanish banks case, in exchanging any documents preparatory to the decisions envisaged, so that Member States' authorities might be able to take account of the Commission's position in their own decision without the latter having to be deferred until such time as the Commission's decision has been taken.

Procedure

In respect of complaints

54. Since complainants cannot force the Commission to take a decision as to whether the infringement they allege has actually occurred, and since the Commission is entitled to reject a complaint which lacks a sufficient Community interest, national competition authorities should not have any special difficulty in handling complaints submitted initially to them involving matters that fall within the scope of the Community competition rules.

---

32 See footnote 30; paragraph 32.
33 Case C-234/89 *Delimitis* v *Henninger Bräu* [1991] ECR I-935, paragraph 53.
34 See footnote 11; paragraphs 8, 9 and 5 respectively.

In respect of notifications

55. Although they form a very small percentage of all notifications to the Commission, special consideration needs to be given to notifications to the Commission of restrictive practices undergoing investigation by a national authority made for dilatory purposes. A dilatory notification is one where a firm, threatened with a decision banning a restrictive practice which a national authority is poised to take following an investigation under Article 85(1) or under national law, notifies the disputed agreement to the Commission and asks for it to be exempted under Article 85(3) of the Treaty. Such a notification is made in order to induce the Commission to initiate a proceeding under Article 2, 3 or 6 of Regulation No 17 and hence, by virtue of Article 9(3) of that Regulation, to remove from Member States' authorities the power to apply the provisions of Article 85(1). The Commission will not consider a notification to be dilatory until after it has contacted the national authority concerned and checked that the latter agrees with its assessment. The Commission calls upon national authorities, moreover, to inform it of their own accord of any notifications they receive which, in their view, are dilatory in nature.

56. A similar situation arises where an agreement is notified to the Commission with a view to preventing the imminent initiation of national proceedings which might result in the prohibition of that agreement[35].

57. The Commission recognizes, of course, that a firm requesting exemption is entitled to obtain from it a decision on the substance of its request (see point 38). However, if the Commission takes the view that such notification is chiefly aimed at suspending the national proceedings, given its exclusive powers to grant exemptions it considers itself justified in not examining it as a matter of priority.

58. The national authority which is investigating the matter and has therefore initiated proceedings should normally ask the Commission for its provisional opinion on the likelihood of its exempting the agreement now notified to it. Such a request will be superfluous where, 'in the light of the relevant criteria developed by the case-law of the Court of Justice and the Court of First Instance and by previous regulations and decisions of the Commission, the national authority has ascertained that the agreement, decision or concerted practice at issue cannot be the subject of an individual exemption'[36].

59. The Commission will deliver its provisional opinion on the likelihood of an exemption being granted, in the light of a preliminary examination of the questions of fact and law involved, as quickly as possible once the complete notification is received. Examination of the notification having revealed that the agreement in question is unlikely to qualify for exemption under Article 85(3) and that its effects are mainly confined to one Member State, the opinion will state that further investigation of the matter is not a Commission priority.

60. The Commission will transmit this opinion in writing to the national authority investigating the case and to the notifying parties. It will state in its letter that it will be highly unlikely to take a decision on the matter before the national authority to which it was referred has taken its final decision and that the notifying parties retain their immunity from any fines the Commission might impose.

61. In its reply, the national authority, after taking note of the Commission's opinion, should undertake to contact the Commission forthwith if its investigation leads it to a conclusion which differs from that opinion. This will be the case if, following its investigation, the national authority concludes that the agreement in question should not be banned under Article 85(1) of the Treaty or, if that provisions cannot be applied, under the relevant national law. The national authority should

---

35 With respect to agreements not subject to notification pursuant to point 1 of Article 4(2) of Regulation No 17, points 56 and 57 of this Notice also apply *mutatis mutandis* to express requests for exemption.
36 Points 29 and 30 of the Notice on cooperation between national courts and the Commission.

also undertake to forward a copy of its final decision on the matter to the Commission. Copies of the correspondence will be sent to the competition authorities of the other Member States for information.

62. The Commission will not itself initiate proceedings in the same case before the proceedings pending before the national authority have been completed; in accordance with Article 9(3) of Regulation No 17, such action would have the effect of taking the matter out of the hands of the national authority. The Commission will do this only in quite exceptional circumstances—in a situation where, against all expectations, the national authority is liable to find that there has been no infringement of Article 85 or 86 or of its national competition law, or where the national proceedings are unduly long drawn-out.

63. Before initiating proceedings the Commission will consult the national authority to discover the factual or legal grounds for that authority's proposed favourable decision or the reasons for the delay in the proceedings.

V. Concluding remarks

64. This Notice is without prejudice to any interpretation by the Court of First Instance and the Court of Justice.

65. In the interests of effective, consistent application of Community law throughout the Union, and legal simplicity and certainty for the benefit of undertakings, the Commission calls upon those Member States which have not already done so to adopt legislation enabling their competition authority to implement Articles 85(1) and 86 of the Treaty effectively.

66. In applying this Notice, the Commission and the competent authorities of the Member States and their officials and other staff will observe the principle of professional secrecy in accordance with Article 20 of Regulation No 17.

67. This Notice does not apply to competition rules in the transport sector, owing to the highly specific way in which cases arising in that sector are handled from a procedural point of view[37].

68. The actual application of this Notice, especially in terms of the measures considered desirable to facilitate its implementation, will be the subject of an annual review carried out jointly by the authorities of the Member States and the Commission.

69. This Notice will be reviewed no later than at the end of the fourth year after its adoption.

NOTE: This Commission Notice again tries to clarify what it sees as being its responsibility in the enforcement of the competition rules, and what it sees as being the responsibility of the National Competition Authorities. The benefits of a clear division of responsibility are largely practical in that undertakings with competition concerns can quickly identify the most appropriate authority for them to approach. The main problem with the notice is that it expressed the Commission's view, which was not necessarily shared by the Member States. The UK is a good example,

---

37 Council Regulation No 141/62 of 26 November 1962 exempting transport from the application of Council Regulation No 17 (OJ 124, 28.11.1962, p. 2753; English Special Edition 1959–62, p. 291), as amended by Regulations Nos 165/65/EEC (OJ 210, 11.12.1965, p. 314) and 1002/67/EEC (OJ 306, 16.12.1967, p. 1); Council Regulation (EEC) No 1017/68 of 19 July 1968 applying rules of competition to transport by rail, road and inland waterway (OJ L 175, 23.7.1968, p. 1; English Special Edition 1968 1, p. 302); Council Regulation (EEC) No 4056/86 of 22 December 1986 laying down detailed rules for the application of Articles 85 and 86 of the Treaty to maritime transport (OJ L 378, 31.12.1986, p. 4); Council Regulation (EEC) No 3975/87 of 14 December 1987 laying down the procedure for the application of the rules on competition to undertakings in the air transport sector (OJ L 374, 31.12.1987, p. 1); and Commission Regulation (EC) No 870/95 of 20 April 1995 on the application of Article 85(3) of the Treaty to certain categories of agreements, decisions and concerted practices between liner shipping companies (consortia) pursuant to Council Regulation (EEC) No 479/92 (OJ L 89, 21.4.1995, p. 7).

the Office of Fair Trading, the UK's NCA, is not empowered to enforce the EC competition rules and therefore the Notice is otiose in many UK situations. The DGFT's Guideline suggests that when a matter falls within EC law, undertakings should always go to the Commission, see, OFT Guideline, Enforcement, OFT 407. This indicates the limited impact of the Notice, and the need for more action if the Commission wishes to further its aim of true decentralisation.

SECTION 5: Modernisation

Because of the problems set out above within the current centralised system of enforcement, the Commission has brought forward proposals for dramatic reform of the enforcement system following consultation on the White Paper on Modernisation (Comm Prog 99/027, OJ, 1999, C132/1) and the Proposal for a Council Regulation (COM (2000) 582 final, OJ, 2000, C365E/284). The Regulation which was adopted by the Council on 16 December 2002 (Regulation 1/2003/EC, OJ, 2003, L1/1) is arguably the most important change to the EC enforcement regime since the introduction of Regulation 17. The Regulation comes into force on 1 May 2004 and effectively replaces Regulation 17/62. The lengthy lead-time is required to allow the various actors at both Community and national level to prepare for the new system.

Council Regulation 1/2003/EC on the implementation of the rules on competition laid down in Articles 81 and 82 of the Treaty, OJ, 2003, L1/1.
*** Articles 1—22, excluding recitals ***

CHAPTER I

PRINCIPLES

Article 1
Application of Articles 81 and 82 of the Treaty
    1. Agreements, decisions and concerted practices caught by Article 81(1) of the Treaty which do not satisfy the conditions of Article 81(3) of the Treaty shall be prohibited, no prior decision to that effect being required.
    2. Agreements, decisions and concerted practices caught by Article 81(1) of the Treaty which satisfy the conditions of Article 81(3) of the Treaty shall not be prohibited, no prior decision to that effect being required.
    3. The abuse of a dominant position referred to in Article 82 of the Treaty shall be prohibited, no prior decision to that effect being required.

Article 2
Burden of proof
In any national or Community proceedings for the application of Articles 81 and 82 of the Treaty, the burden of proving an infringement of Article 81(1) or of Article 82 of the Treaty shall rest on the party or the authority alleging the infringement.

The undertaking or association of undertakings claiming the benefit of Article 81(3) of the Treaty shall bear the burden of proving that the conditions of that paragraph are fulfilled.

Article 3
Relationship between Articles 81 and 82 of the Treaty and national competition laws
   1. Where the competition authorities of the Member States or national courts apply national competition law to agreements, decisions by associations of undertakings or concerted practices within the meaning of Article 81(1) of the Treaty which may affect trade between Member States within the meaning of that provision, they shall also apply Article 81 of the Treaty to such agreements, decisions or concerted practices. Where the competition authorities of the Member States or national courts apply national competition law to any abuse prohibited by Article 82 of the Treaty, they shall also apply Article 82 of the Treaty.
   2. The application of national competition law may not lead to the prohibition of agreements, decisions by associations of undertakings or concerted practices which may affect trade between Member States but which do not restrict competition within the meaning of Article 81(1) of the Treaty, or which fulfil the conditions of Article 81(3) of the Treaty or which are covered by a Regulation for the application of Article 81(3) of the Treaty. Member States shall not under this Regulation be precluded from adopting and applying on their territory stricter national laws which prohibit or sanction unilateral conduct engaged in by undertakings.
   3. Without prejudice to general principles and other provisions of Community law, paragraphs 1 and 2 do not apply when the competition authorities and the courts of the Member States apply national merger control laws nor do they preclude the application of provisions of national law that predominantly pursue an objective different from that pursued by Articles 81 and 82 of the Treaty.

CHAPTER II

POWERS

Article 4
Powers of the Commission
For the purpose of applying Articles 81 and 82 of the Treaty, the Commission shall have the powers provided for by this Regulation.

Article 5
Powers of the competition authorities of the Member States
The competition authorities of the Member States shall have the power to apply Articles 81 and 82 of the Treaty in individual cases. For this purpose, acting on their own initiative or on a complaint, they may take the following decisions:

   — requiring that an infringement be brought to an end,
   — ordering interim measures,

— accepting commitments,

— imposing fines, periodic penalty payments or any other penalty provided for in their national law.

Where on the basis of the information in their possession the conditions for prohibition are not met they may likewise decide that there are no grounds for action on their part.

Article 6
Powers of the national courts
National courts shall have the power to apply Articles 81 and 82 of the Treaty.

CHAPTER III

COMMISSION DECISIONS

Article 7
Finding and termination of infringement
1. Where the Commission, acting on a complaint or on its own initiative, finds that there is an infringement of Article 81 or of Article 82 of the Treaty, it may by decision require the undertakings and associations of undertakings concerned to bring such infringement to an end. For this purpose, it may impose on them any behavioural or structural remedies which are proportionate to the infringement committed and necessary to bring the infringement effectively to an end. Structural remedies can only be imposed either where there is no equally effective behavioural remedy or where any equally effective behavioural remedy would be more burdensome for the undertaking concerned than the structural remedy. If the Commission has a legitimate interest in doing so, it may also find that an infringement has been committed in the past.

2. Those entitled to lodge a complaint for the purposes of paragraph 1 are natural or legal persons who can show a legitimate interest and Member States.

Article 8
Interim measures
1. In cases of urgency due to the risk of serious and irreparable damage to competition, the Commission, acting on its own initiative may by decision, on the basis of a *prima facie* finding of infringement, order interim measures.

2. A decision under paragraph 1 shall apply for a specified period of time and may be renewed in so far this is necessary and appropriate.

Article 9
Commitments
1. Where the Commission intends to adopt a decision requiring that an infringement be brought to an end and the undertakings concerned offer commitments to meet the concerns expressed to them by the Commission in its preliminary assessment, the Commission may by decision make those commitments bind-

ing on the undertakings. Such a decision may be adopted for a specified period and shall conclude that there are no longer grounds for action by the Commission.

2. The Commission may, upon request or on its own initiative, reopen the proceedings:

(a) where there has been a material change in any of the facts on which the decision was based;

(b) where the undertakings concerned act contrary to their commitments; or

(c) where the decision was based on incomplete, incorrect or misleading information provided by the parties.

Article 10
Finding of inapplicability
Where the Community public interest relating to the application of Articles 81 and 82 of the Treaty so requires, the Commission, acting on its own initiative, may by decision find that Article 81 of the Treaty is not applicable to an agreement, a decision by an association of undertakings or a concerted practice, either because the conditions of Article 81(1) of the Treaty are not fulfilled, or because the conditions of Article 81(3) of the Treaty are satisfied.

The Commission may likewise make such a finding with reference to Article 82 of the Treaty.

CHAPTER IV

COOPERATION

Article 11
Cooperation between the Commission and the competition authorities of the Member States
1. The Commission and the competition authorities of the Member States shall apply the Community competition rules in close cooperation.

2. The Commission shall transmit to the competition authorities of the Member States copies of the most important documents it has collected with a view to applying Articles 7, 8, 9, 10 and Article 29(1). At the request of the competition authority of a Member State, the Commission shall provide it with a copy of other existing documents necessary for the assessment of the case.

3. The competition authorities of the Member States shall, when acting under Article 81 or Article 82 of the Treaty, inform the Commission in writing before or without delay after commencing the first formal investigative measure. This information may also be made available to the competition authorities of the other Member States.

4. No later than 30 days before the adoption of a decision requiring that an infringement be brought to an end, accepting commitments or withdrawing the benefit of a block exemption Regulation, the competition authorities of the Member States shall inform the Commission. To that effect, they shall provide the Commission with a summary of the case, the envisaged decision or, in the absence

thereof, any other document indicating the proposed course of action. This information may also be made available to the competition authorities of the other Member States. At the request of the Commission, the acting competition authority shall make available to the Commission other documents it holds which are necessary for the assessment of the case. The information supplied to the Commission may be made available to the competition authorities of the other Member States. National competition authorities may also exchange between themselves information necessary for the assessment of a case that they are dealing with under Article 81 or Article 82 of the Treaty.

5. The competition authorities of the Member States may consult the Commission on any case involving the application of Community law.

6. The initiation by the Commission of proceedings for the adoption of a decision under Chapter III shall relieve the competition authorities of the Member States of their competence to apply Articles 81 and 82 of the Treaty. If a competition authority of a Member State is already acting on a case, the Commission shall only initiate proceedings after consulting with that national competition authority.

Article 12
Exchange of information

1. For the purpose of applying Articles 81 and 82 of the Treaty the Commission and the competition authorities of the Member States shall have the power to provide one another with and use in evidence any matter of fact or of law, including confidential information.

2. Information exchanged shall only be used in evidence for the purpose of applying Article 81 or Article 82 of the Treaty and in respect of the subject-matter for which it was collected by the transmitting authority. However, where national competition law is applied in the same case and in parallel to Community competition law and does not lead to a different outcome, information exchanged under this Article may also be used for the application of national competition law.

3. Information exchanged pursuant to paragraph 1 can only be used in evidence to impose sanctions on natural persons where:

— the law of the transmitting authority foresees sanctions of a similar kind in relation to an infringement of Article 81 or Article 82 of the Treaty or, in the absence thereof,
— the information has been collected in a way which respects the same level of protection of the rights of defence of natural persons as provided for under the national rules of the receiving authority. However, in this case, the information exchanged cannot be used by the receiving authority to impose custodial sanctions.

Article 13
Suspension or termination of proceedings

1. Where competition authorities of two or more Member States have received a

complaint or are acting on their own initiative under Article 81 or Article 82 of the Treaty against the same agreement, decision of an association or practice, the fact that one authority is dealing with the case shall be sufficient grounds for the others to suspend the proceedings before them or to reject the complaint. The Commission may likewise reject a complaint on the ground that a competition authority of a Member State is dealing with the case.

2. Where a competition authority of a Member State or the Commission has received a complaint against an agreement, decision of an association or practice which has already been dealt with by another competition authority, it may reject it.

Article 14
Advisory Committee

1. The Commission shall consult an Advisory Committee on Restrictive Practices and Dominant Positions prior to the taking of any decision under Articles 7, 8, 9, 10, 23, Article 24(2) and Article 29(1).

2. For the discussion of individual cases, the Advisory Committee shall be composed of representatives of the competition authorities of the Member States. For meetings in which issues other than individual cases are being discussed, an additional Member State representative competent in competition matters may be appointed. Representatives may, if unable to attend, be replaced by other representatives.

3. The consultation may take place at a meeting convened and chaired by the Commission, held not earlier than 14 days after dispatch of the notice convening it, together with a summary of the case, an indication of the most important documents and a preliminary draft decision. In respect of decisions pursuant to Article 8, the meeting may be held seven days after the dispatch of the operative part of a draft decision. Where the Commission dispatches a notice convening the meeting which gives a shorter period of notice than those specified above, the meeting may take place on the proposed date in the absence of an objection by any Member State. The Advisory Committee shall deliver a written opinion on the Commission's preliminary draft decision. It may deliver an opinion even if some members are absent and are not represented. At the request of one or several members, the positions stated in the opinion shall be reasoned.

4. Consultation may also take place by written procedure. However, if any Member State so requests, the Commission shall convene a meeting. In case of written procedure, the Commission shall determine a time-limit of not less than 14 days within which the Member States are to put forward their observations for circulation to all other Member States. In case of decisions to be taken pursuant to Article 8, the time-limit of 14 days is replaced by seven days. Where the Commission determines a time-limit for the written procedure which is shorter than those specified above, the proposed time-limit shall be applicable in the absence of an objection by any Member State.

5. The Commission shall take the utmost account of the opinion delivered by

the Advisory Committee. It shall inform the Committee of the manner in which its opinion has been taken into account.

6. Where the Advisory Committee delivers a written opinion, this opinion shall be appended to the draft decision. If the Advisory Committee recommends publication of the opinion, the Commission shall carry out such publication taking into account the legitimate interest of undertakings in the protection of their business secrets.

7. At the request of a competition authority of a Member State, the Commission shall include on the agenda of the Advisory Committee cases that are being dealt with by a competition authority of a Member State under Article 81 or Article 82 of the Treaty. The Commission may also do so on its own initiative. In either case, the Commission shall inform the competition authority concerned.

A request may in particular be made by a competition authority of a Member State in respect of a case where the Commission intends to initiate proceedings with the effect of Article 11(6).

The Advisory Committee shall not issue opinions on cases dealt with by competition authorities of the Member States. The Advisory Committee may also discuss general issues of Community competition law.

Article 15
Cooperation with national courts

1. In proceedings for the application of Article 81 or Article 82 of the Treaty, courts of the Member States may ask the Commission to transmit to them information in its possession or its opinion on questions concerning the application of the Community competition rules.

2. Member States shall forward to the Commission a copy of any written judgment of national courts deciding on the application of Article 81 or Article 82 of the Treaty. Such copy shall be forwarded without delay after the full written judgment is notified to the parties.

3. Competition authorities of the Member States, acting on their own initiative, may submit written observations to the national courts of their Member State on issues relating to the application of Article 81 or Article 82 of the Treaty. With the permission of the court in question, they may also submit oral observations to the national courts of their Member State. Where the coherent application of Article 81 or Article 82 of the Treaty so requires, the Commission, acting on its own initiative, may submit written observations to courts of the Member States. With the permission of the court in question, it may also make oral observations.

For the purpose of the preparation of their observations only, the competition authorities of the Member States and the Commission may request the relevant court of the Member State to transmit or ensure the transmission to them of any documents necessary for the assessment of the case.

4. This Article is without prejudice to wider powers to make observations before

courts conferred on competition authorities of the Member States under the law of their Member State.

Article 16
Uniform application of Community competition law

1. When national courts rule on agreements, decisions or practices under Article 81 or Article 82 of the Treaty which are already the subject of a Commission decision, they cannot take decisions running counter to the decision adopted by the Commission. They must also avoid giving decisions which would conflict with a decision contemplated by the Commission in proceedings it has initiated. To that effect, the national court may assess whether it is necessary to stay its proceedings. This obligation is without prejudice to the rights and obligations under Article 234 of the Treaty.

2. When competition authorities of the Member States rule on agreements, decisions or practices under Article 81 or Article 82 of the Treaty which are already the subject of a Commission decision, they cannot take decisions which would run counter to the decision adopted by the Commission.

CHAPTER V

POWERS OF INVESTIGATION

Article 17
Investigations into sectors of the economy and into types of agreements

1. Where the trend of trade between Member States, the rigidity of prices or other circumstances suggest that competition may be restricted or distorted within the common market, the Commission may conduct its inquiry into a particular sector of the economy or into a particular type of agreements across various sectors. In the course of that inquiry, the Commission may request the undertakings or associations of undertakings concerned to supply the information necessary for giving effect to Articles 81 and 82 of the Treaty and may carry out any inspections necessary for that purpose.

The Commission may in particular request the undertakings or associations of undertakings concerned to communicate to it all agreements, decisions and concerted practices.

The Commission may publish a report on the results of its inquiry into particular sectors of the economy or particular types of agreements across various sectors and invite comments from interested parties.

2. Articles 14, 18, 19, 20, 22, 23 and 24 shall apply *mutatis mutandis*.

Article 18
Requests for information

1. In order to carry out the duties assigned to it by this Regulation, the Commis-

sion may, by simple request or by decision, require undertakings and associations of undertakings to provide all necessary information.

2. When sending a simple request for information to an undertaking or association of undertakings, the Commission shall state the legal basis and the purpose of the request, specify what information is required and fix the time-limit within which the information is to be provided, and the penalties provided for in Article 23 for supplying incorrect or misleading information.

3. Where the Commission requires undertakings and associations of undertakings to supply information by decision, it shall state the legal basis and the purpose of the request, specify what information is required and fix the time-limit within which it is to be provided. It shall also indicate the penalties provided for in Article 23 and indicate or impose the penalties provided for in Article 24. It shall further indicate the right to have the decision reviewed by the Court of Justice.

4. The owners of the undertakings or their representatives and, in the case of legal persons, companies or firms, or associations having no legal personality, the persons authorised to represent them by law or by their constitution shall supply the information requested on behalf of the undertaking or the association of undertakings concerned. Lawyers duly authorised to act may supply the information on behalf of their clients. The latter shall remain fully responsible if the information supplied is incomplete, incorrect or misleading.

5. The Commission shall without delay forward a copy of the simple request or of the decision to the competition authority of the Member State in whose territory the seat of the undertaking or association of undertakings is situated and the competition authority of the Member State whose territory is affected.

6. At the request of the Commission the governments and competition authorities of the Member States shall provide the Commission with all necessary information to carry out the duties assigned to it by this Regulation.

Article 19
Power to take statements

1. In order to carry out the duties assigned to it by this Regulation, the Commission may interview any natural or legal person who consents to be interviewed for the purpose of collecting information relating to the subject-matter of an investigation.

2. Where an interview pursuant to paragraph 1 is conducted in the premises of an undertaking, the Commission shall inform the competition authority of the Member State in whose territory the interview takes place. If so requested by the competition authority of that Member State, its officials may assist the officials and other accompanying persons authorised by the Commission to conduct the interview.

Article 20
The Commission's powers of inspection

1. In order to carry out the duties assigned to it by this Regulation, the Commis-

sion may conduct all necessary inspections of undertakings and associations of undertakings.

2. The officials and other accompanying persons authorised by the Commission to conduct an inspection are empowered:

(a) to enter any premises, land and means of transport of undertakings and associations of undertakings;

(b) to examine the books and other records related to the business, irrespective of the medium on which they are stored;

(c) to take or obtain in any form copies of or extracts from such books or records;

(d) to seal any business premises and books or records for the period and to the extent necessary for the inspection;

(e) to ask any representative or member of staff of the undertaking or association of undertakings for explanations on facts or documents relating to the subject-matter and purpose of the inspection and to record the answers.

3. The officials and other accompanying persons authorised by the Commission to conduct an inspection shall exercise their powers upon production of a written authorisation specifying the subject matter and purpose of the inspection and the penalties provided for in Article 23 in case the production of the required books or other records related to the business is incomplete or where the answers to questions asked under paragraph 2 of the present Article are incorrect or misleading. In good time before the inspection, the Commission shall give notice of the inspection to the competition authority of the Member State in whose territory it is to be conducted.

4. Undertakings and associations of undertakings are required to submit to inspections ordered by decision of the Commission. The decision shall specify the subject matter and purpose of the inspection, appoint the date on which it is to begin and indicate the penalties provided for in Articles 23 and 24 and the right to have the decision reviewed by the Court of Justice. The Commission shall take such decisions after consulting the competition authority of the Member State in whose territory the inspection is to be conducted.

5. Officials of as well as those authorised or appointed by the competition authority of the Member State in whose territory the inspection is to be conducted shall, at the request of that authority or of the Commission, actively assist the officials and other accompanying persons authorised by the Commission. To this end, they shall enjoy the powers specified in paragraph 2.

6. Where the officials and other accompanying persons authorised by the Commission find that an undertaking opposes an inspection ordered pursuant to this Article, the Member State concerned shall afford them the necessary assistance, requesting where appropriate the assistance of the police or of an equivalent enforcement authority, so as to enable them to conduct their inspection.

7. If the assistance provided for in paragraph 6 requires authorisation from a

judicial authority according to national rules, such authorisation shall be applied for. Such authorisation may also be applied for as a precautionary measure.

8. Where authorisation as referred to in paragraph 7 is applied for, the national judicial authority shall control that the Commission decision is authentic and that the coercive measures envisaged are neither arbitrary nor excessive having regard to the subject matter of the inspection. In its control of the proportionality of the coercive measures, the national judicial authority may ask the Commission, directly or through the Member State competition authority, for detailed explanations in particular on the grounds the Commission has for suspecting infringement of Articles 81 and 82 of the Treaty, as well as on the seriousness of the suspected infringement and on the nature of the involvement of the undertaking concerned. However, the national judicial authority may not call into question the necessity for the inspection nor demand that it be provided with the information in the Commission's file. The lawfulness of the Commission decision shall be subject to review only by the Court of Justice.

Article 21
Inspection of other premises
1. If a reasonable suspicion exists that books or other records related to the business and to the subject-matter of the inspection, which may be relevant to prove a serious violation of Article 81 or Article 82 of the Treaty, are being kept in any other premises, land and means of transport, including the homes of directors, managers and other members of staff of the undertakings and associations of undertakings concerned, the Commission can by decision order an inspection to be conducted in such other premises, land and means of transport.

2. The decision shall specify the subject matter and purpose of the inspection, appoint the date on which it is to begin and indicate the right to have the decision reviewed by the Court of Justice. It shall in particular state the reasons that have led the Commission to conclude that a suspicion in the sense of paragraph 1 exists. The Commission shall take such decisions after consulting the competition authority of the Member State in whose territory the inspection is to be conducted.

3. A decision adopted pursuant to paragraph 1 cannot be executed without prior authorisation from the national judicial authority of the Member State concerned. The national judicial authority shall control that the Commission decision is authentic and that the coercive measures envisaged are neither arbitrary nor excessive having regard in particular to the seriousness of the suspected infringement, to the importance of the evidence sought, to the involvement of the undertaking concerned and to the reasonable likelihood that business books and records relating to the subject matter of the inspection are kept in the premises for which the authorisation is requested. The national judicial authority may ask the Commission, directly or through the Member State competition authority, for detailed explanations on those elements which are necessary to allow its control of the proportionality of the coercive measures envisaged.

However, the national judicial authority may not call into question the necessity for the inspection nor demand that it be provided with information in the Commission's file. The lawfulness of the Commission decision shall be subject to review only by the Court of Justice.

4. The officials and other accompanying persons authorised by the Commission to conduct an inspection ordered in accordance with paragraph 1 of this Article shall have the powers set out in Article 20(2)(a), (b) and (c). Article 20(5) and (6) shall apply *mutatis mutandis*.

Article 22
Investigations by competition authorities of Member States

1. The competition authority of a Member State may in its own territory carry out any inspection or other fact-finding measure under its national law on behalf and for the account of the competition authority of another Member State in order to establish whether there has been an infringement of Article 81 or Article 82 of the Treaty. Any exchange and use of the information collected shall be carried out in accordance with Article 12.

2. At the request of the Commission, the competition authorities of the Member States shall undertake the inspections which the Commission considers to be necessary under Article 20(1) or which it has ordered by decision pursuant to Article 20(4). The officials of the competition authorities of the Member States who are responsible for conducting these inspections as well as those authorised or appointed by themshall exercise their powers in accordance with their national law.

If so requested by the Commission or by the competition authority of the Member State in whose territory the inspection is to be conducted, officials and other accompanying persons authorised by the Commission may assist the officials of the authority concerned.

NOTE: The Modernisation proposals aim to refocus the enforcement of EC competition law and rebalance the roles of the various national and EC authorities to create a more comprehensive overlapping structure (for a discussion of the White Paper see, Middleton, 'Modernisation of the Rules Implementing EC Competition Law' 1999 SLT 217, and Rodger, 'The Commission White Paper on Modernisation of the Rules Implementing Articles 81 and 82 of the EC Treaty' (1999) 24(6) ELRev 653). One of the main changes is to remove the Commission's monopoly over the power of exemption under Article 81(3) EC (Article 1). Following the modernisation it should be possible for both the NCAs and the national courts to utilise the exemption provisions in Article 81(3) EC (Articles 5 and 6). It will no longer be necessary to notify an agreement for an exemption. Undertakings will simply have to ensure that their agreement falls within the terms of Article 81(3) EC and the agreement will be enforceable. This has the effect of shifting all the EC enforcement of its antitrust rules to an *ex post* model—all enforcement will take place once conduct has been put in place on the market (mergers will retain their separate *ex ante* system). By releasing the Commission from its role in scrutinising notifications the proposals would also allow the Commission to re-focus its activities and concentrate on investigating serious pan-European competition breaches. In the majority of cases the front line enforcement role will fall to the NCAs who, in many instances, are closer to the national markets and may be in a better position to undertake first line investigations. To ensure consistency between the NCAs and allow for easier cross border investigations, the proposals would also set up mechanisms for exchange of information and support between the NCAs and between the NCAs and the Commission. If the Commission is to be allowed to refocus its activities it is vital that this network of competition authorities works effectively (see, Jones, 'Regulation 17: The Impact of the Current Application of Article 81 and 82 by the National Competition Authorities on the European Commission's Proposals for Reform' [2001] ECLR 405). The Commission also gains increased powers of investigation to assist where they take the lead in investigations, for example, to undertake sectoral investigations which do not necessarily lead to infringement actions (Article 17), to take statements from individuals (Article 19), or to carry out inspections on non-business premises such as the homes of company directors (Article 21).

Todino, M., 'Modernisation from the Perspective of National Competition Authorities: Impact of the Reform on Decentralised Application of EC Competition Law'
[2000] ECLR 348, pp. 351 & 352

On National Courts:
To sum up, it is submitted that the possibility for national courts to enforce Article 81.3 as a directly applicable provision would not dramatically increase the application of competition law by the judiciary, since the major impediments are to be found elsewhere: lack of familiarity in the national courts with subjects whereby economics and law are strictly interlinked; the difficulty of collecting evidence using the typical powers of a judge in the context of a civil dispute; the unlikelihood of getting damages; as well as the absence of procedural devices which act as incentives to private antitrust actions. Moreover, the different procedures in each Member State create an uneven system which at the moment cannot be harmonised, since in these matters Member States retain their sovereignty with the exception of the cooperation contemplated by the third pillar of the EU Treaty. In fact the Commission itself seems well aware of these problems.

Accordingly, while it is hoped that the proposed reform will enhance the role of national courts in the enforcement of EC rules, it would be surprising if the proposed shift to a directly applicable exemption system suddenly led to impressive developments in the judicial enforcement of competition rules.

On National Authorities:
With respect to the question of how to 'educate' national competition authorities to apply EC rules when dealing with national cases, a possible approach may be to further improve the relations between the Commission and national competition authorities so to develop a common culture and a mutual trust. The solution envisaged by the Commission to strengthen cooperation mechanisms with national competition authorities so as to set up an effective 'network' goes precisely in this direction. Indeed, flexible, rapid and efficient mechanisms for exchange of information and co-operation would foster a better understanding between authorities. To this end, as proposed by the Commission in the White Paper, it is important to reinforce the role of the Advisory Committee, which should become a full-scale forum in which important cases would be discussed irrespective of the national competition authorities dealing with them. Incidentally, the reinforcement of the network would also ensure that the consistency of competition policy would be preserved without resorting to more complicated solutions to conflicts in the application of Community law.

FURTHER READING

Ehlermann, C.D., 'The Modernisation of EC Antitrust Policy: A Legal and Cultural Revolution' (2000) CMLRev 537.

See generally Wessling, R., *The Modernisation of EC Antitrust*, Oxford, Hart Publishing, 2000.

Wessling, R., 'Unspoken Consequences and Incomplete Treatment of Alternative Options' [1999] ECLR 420.

Wessling, R., 'The draft-regulations modernising the competition rules: the Commission is married to one idea' (2001) 26 ELRev 357.

4

Control of anti-competitive agreements in the UK

Introduction

Prior to the UK Competition Act 1998 (CA 1998) the domestic competition law applicable to anti-competitive agreements could be found in the Restrictive Trade Practices Act 1976 (RTPA) which consolidated earlier restrictive trade practices legislation. By the late 1980s it became clear that reform of the legislative framework was necessary. Once an integral part of the commercial landscape in the UK, the RTPA lacked adequate investigative powers and effective sanctions and failed to catch certain significant agreements, particularly vertical agreements. The domestic regime was also out of step with Community competition law. The CA 1998, s. 1 repeals RTPA 1976 and 1977, the Resale Prices Act 1976 and much of the Competition Act 1980. The overriding objective of the CA 1998 is to align domestic competition law with the Community rules for the sake of consistency and to reduce the burden on business. The Enterprise Bill proposes to strengthen this regime even further with the introduction of US-style criminal sanctions for individuals involved in cartels, and disqualification of company directors.

A: Prior reform

Reform of domestic competition law has been a laborious process. The decade prior to enactment of the Competition Bill saw the publication of Green and White Papers, which both suggested that reform of the law on restrictive trade practices was necessary. See Department of Trade and Industry Consultation Document: *Review of Restrictive Trade Practices Policy* Cm 331 (March 1988); and *Opening Markets: New Policy on Restrictive Trade Practices* Cm 727, (July 1989). In 1992, a Green Paper on Monopoly Control proposed the introduction of an Article 82 prohibition, *Abuse of Market Power* Cm 2100 (November 1992). However, instead of the sweeping reforms desired, the government made minor amendments to the Fair Trading Act 1973 and the Competition Act 1980. In 1996, the government took heed of mounting criticism following a Select Committee investigation and published a further consultation document, *Tackling Cartels and the Abuse of Market Power* (March 1996) London: DTI, URN 96/905, this time accompanied by a draft Bill. The explanatory document observed that 'our present system is inflexible and slow, too often concerned with cases which are obviously harmless and not directed sufficiently at anti-competitive agreements'. (Cm 727 at para. 2.8.)

Despite widespread recognition that systematic reform was overdue, legislation was not enacted. Lack of Parliamentary time and the Conservative Party's stance on Europe were regarded as the primary obstacles to the introduction of 'pro-European' legislation. For an excellent exposition of the prior debate and reasons for the delay see Wilks, S., 'The Prolonged Reform of UK Competition Policy', in Doern B., and Wilks S. (eds), *Comparative Competition Policy: National Institutions in a Global Market* (Oxford, Clarendon Press, 1996).

As Wilks explains at p. 174:

The 'San Andreas' fault line within the Conservative Party was over attitudes to Europe. The proposed RTP reforms could have been presented as 'pro-European', adapting UK law to the Brussels model. This might in itself have been enough to make Ministers shy away from it.

Shortly after the general election in May 1997, the new Labour government made clear its intention to fulfil a manifesto commitment to reform domestic competition law and a second draft Bill was laid before Parliament in October 1997. Margaret Beckett, the former President of the Board of the Trade, stated in her foreword to the 1997 draft Bill that 'Present competition law is not working well . . . Consumers need a better deal. We need to prevent and remedy anti-competitive behaviour more effectively. We also need to do so efficiently, avoiding placing any unnecessary burden on business'.

FURTHER READING

See generally Whish, R., Chapter I, 'The Competition Act 1998 and the Prior Debate on Reform', in Rodger, B.J., and McCulloch, A. (eds), *The UK Competition Act: A New Era for UK Competition Law*, Oxford, Hart Publishing, 2000.

SECTION 2: **Competition Act 1998**

The (CA 1998) heralded a new era in domestic competition law. The Act, which entered into force on 1 March 2000, repealed the RTPA legislation and replaced it with a radically different prohibition system, modelled closely on the competition provisions of the EC Treaty. The primary objective was harmonisation of domestic law with the Community model, namely Articles 81 and 82 EC.

Middleton comments on the factors that have prompted harmonisation.

Middleton, K., Chapter 2, 'Harmonisation with Community Law—The Euro-clause', in Rodger, B. J., and MacCulloch, A. (eds), *The UK Competition Act: A New Era for UK Competition Law*
Oxford, Hart Publishing, 2000, pp. 22–24 [footnotes omitted]

One of the driving forces behind harmonisation is a recognition that commerce is no longer contained on a purely national or even European level, but one which is increasingly global. As companies expand their commercial activities, geographic and political boundaries become increasingly blurred. It is therefore appropriate that businesses operating in the single market should be subject to a uniform set of rules and principles. The primary objective behind reform of UK competition law is a desire to 'level the playing field' and make it easier for British business to compete effectively in global markets. Since the majority of the larger companies in the United Kingdom already have some exposure to the Community competition rules, it made sense to align domestic competition law with an established benchmark, namely Articles 81 and 82 EC.

The Minister responsible for the passage of the Competition Bill through the House of Lords, Lord Simon of Highbury, outlined the practical benefits of convergence:

> Such consistency would be of great benefit to so many of our businesses that currently have to worry about two different approaches to competition policy. It delivers a level playing field for our business community in the UK as firms become more and more engaged in European home markets.

Further, national competition authorities are able to cooperate more efficiently in cases with cross-border implications if the laws and procedures of the countries concerned are broadly similar. This is of particular importance in an enlarged Community where transactions with a cross-border aspect are likely to increase. Certainly, in recent years, there has been a discernible trend amongst the Member States to harmonise domestic competition law with Articles 81 and 82, despite the absence of any legal compulsion to do so. In the past few years, Member States such as Sweden, Denmark, Ireland, and The Netherlands, have introduced national competition legislation based on the Community rules, thereby reducing the risk of conflict between Community law and domestic law and encouraging competitiveness in international markets. A number of Central and Eastern European countries such as Romania and Hungary have done likewise. This trend towards harmonisation undoubtedly influenced the decision of the new Labour Government to choose Articles 81 and 82 EC as the appropriate model for new domestic laws.

NOTE: Maher also suggests that the 'current debates about international harmonisation of competition law and policy [make] it almost inevitable that the EC model be considered in the context of competition law reform'. Moreover, 'the considerable experience of the OFT of the EC rules also operates in favour of that model and on a more practical level, by harmonising the domestic and EC rules, reduces the regulatory demands on the OFT'. See Maher, I., 'Juridification, Codification and Sanction in UK Competition Law', MLR 63:4, July 2000, pp. 544–569 and an earlier article by the same author, 'Alignment of Competition Laws in the EC' (1996) YBEL 223. Cf. Rodger, B.J., and MacCulloch, A., who have suggested that 'the big debate on Euro-law harmonisation has little relevance except in relation to administration and enforcement powers. This is not to argue that these issues are not significant, merely that the debate on harmonisation has been misleading.' 'The Chapter I Prohibition: Prohibiting Cartels, or Permitting Verticals? Or Both?' Chapter 8 in *The UK Competition Act: A New Era for UK Competition Law*, Oxford, Hart Publishing. Which view do you share?

SECTION 3: **The Chapter I prohibition**

The 'Chapter I prohibition' is modelled closely on Article 81 EC. Section 2 contains the general prohibition and operates subject to s. 3 which provides for excluded agreements and ss. 4–11 which deal with exemptions. Section 60, the so-called 'Euro-clause', requires the UK courts and competition authorities to follow Community case-law for consistency, discussed at p. 143 below.

2. **Agreements etc. preventing, restricting or distorting competition**
    (1) Subject to section 3, agreements between undertakings, decisions by associations of undertakings or concerted practices which—
        (a) may affect trade within the United Kingdom, and
        (b) have as their object or effect the prevention, restriction or distortion of competition within the United Kingdom, are prohibited unless they are exempt in accordance with the provisions of this Part.
    (2) Subsection (1) applies, in particular, to agreements, decisions or practices which—
        (a) directly or indirectly fix purchase or selling prices or any other trading conditions;
        (b) limit or control production, markets, technical development or investment;
        (c) share markets or sources of supply;
        (d) apply dissimilar conditions to equivalent transactions with other trading parties, thereby placing them at a competitive disadvantage;
        (e) make the conclusion of contracts subject to acceptance by the other parties of supplementary obligations which, by their nature or according to commercial usage, have no connection with the subject of such contracts.
    (3) Subsection (1) applies only if the agreement, decision or practice is, or is intended to be, implemented in the United Kingdom.
    (4) Any agreement or decision which is prohibited by subsection (1) is void.
    (5) A provision of this Part which is expressed to apply to, or in relation to, an agreement is to be read as applying equally to, or in relation to, a decision by an association of undertakings or a concerted practice (but with any necessary modifications).
    (6) Subsection (5) does not apply where the context otherwise requires.
    (7) In this section 'the United Kingdom' means, in relation to an agreement which operates or is intended to operate only in a part of the United Kingdom, that part.
    (8) The prohibition imposed by subsection (1) is referred to in this Act as 'the Chapter I prohibition'.

QUESTIONS

1. Compare the wording of s. 2 with Article 81(1) EC. What differences, if any, do you notice?

2. Compare the Chapter I and II prohibitions with the previous regime. What are the advantages?

The CA 1998 enables the DGFT to publish Guidelines and Rules to assist those subject to it to adapt to the new regime. There are presently 20 published Guidelines and 2 in draft form and they are available from the OFT's website— *www.oft.gov.uk*. Although the Guidelines do not enjoy the status of legally binding rules they are equivalent to Commission Notices and may have some persuasive authority.

The following extract from OFT 'Chapter I Prohibition', OFT Guideline 401 demonstrates the similarities between the domestic prohibition and Article 81 EC.

OFT Guideline 401, The Chapter I prohibition

Terms used in the Chapter I prohibition

Undertakings

2.5 Undertaking includes any natural or legal person capable of carrying on commercial or economic activities relating to goods or services, whatever its legal status. It includes companies, firms, businesses, partnerships, individuals operating as sole traders, agricultural co-operatives, trade associations and non profit-making organisations.

2.6 The Chapter I prohibition does not apply to agreements where there is only one undertaking: that is, between undertakings which form a single economic unit. In particular, an agreement between a parent and its subsidiary company or between two companies which are under the control of a third will not be agreements between undertakings if the subsidiary has no real freedom to determine its course of action on the market and, although having a separate legal personality, enjoys no economic independence. Whether or not the undertakings form a single economic unit will depend on the facts of each case.

NOTE: The definition of the term 'undertaking' arose in the the the first 'substantive' judgment handed down by the Competition Commission Appeal Tribunal which set aside key aspects of the DGFT's earlier decision of 24 January 2001. The case concerned the application of the Chapter I prohibition to self-regulation in the insurance industry.

The CCAT distinguished statutory bodies exercising public and official powers from private contractual companies. Following the s. 60 requirement, the CCAT ruled that a regulator like the General Insurance Standards Council (GISC) pursued an economic activity in accordance with the definition of undertaking in Community law.

Institute of Independent Insurance Brokers, The v Director General of Fair Trading supported by the General Insurance Standards Council; Association of British Travel Agents Limited v The Director General of Fair Trading supported by the General Insurance Standards Council

(Case Nos 1002/2/1/01 (Ir), 1003/2/1/01, 1004/2/1/01) [2002] CompAR 62

252. It is common ground that Article 81 of the Treaty applies to the carrying on of 'economic activities' by 'undertakings'. As appears from the opinion of Advocate General Jacobs of 17 May 2001 in Case C-475/99 *Ambulanz Glöckner*, the concept of undertaking encompasses every entity engaged in an economic activity regardless of the legal status of the entity and the way it is financed. The basic test is whether the entity in question is engaged in an activity which consists in offering goods and services on a given market and which could, at least in principle, be carried out by a private actor in order to make a profit (paragraph 67). By contrast, while public bodies carrying on economic activities may be regarded as undertakings, 'activities in the exercise of official authority' are sheltered from the application of the competition rules (paragraph 72 of that opinion). The test is whether the activity in question is to be analysed as 'the exercise of public powers' or as 'economic activities': Case 118/85 *Commission* v *Italy* [1987] ECR 2599, paragraph 7. One test for whether the activity in question constitutes the exercise of public powers, or of official authority, is whether the activity in question 'is connected by its nature, its aim and the rules to which it is subject with the exercise of powers which are typically those of a public authority' (see paragraph 76 of the opinion of Advocate General Jacobs in *Ambulanz Glöckner*, citing Case 364/92 *Eurocontrol* [1994] ECR 1-43, paragraph 30).

253. To illustrate the difference between the exercise of 'public powers' or 'official authority' on the one hand and 'economic activity' on the other hand, in *Ambulanz Glöckner* itself Advocate General Jacobs concluded that the provision of ambulance services, including emergency services, was an 'economic activity' and thus within the rules on competition, since those were not services that must *necessarily* be carried out by public entities (paragraph 68 of his opinion). On the other hand, the grant or refusal by a public authority under statute of an authorisation to provide ambulance services fell outside the rules on competition, since it was 'a typical administrative decision taken in the exercise of prerogatives conferred by law which are usually reserved for public authorities' (paragraph 76). Other illustrative examples of the exercise of public authority falling outside Articles 81 and 82 of the Treaty include the arrangements for international air traffic control made by the European Organisation for the Safety of Air Navigation, an international organisation set up and run by 14 Contracting States in pursuance of an international Convention (see *Eurocontrol*, cited above); the fixing by public authorities under statute of tariffs for the use of German waterways (Case C-153/93 *Germany* v *Delta Schiffahrts* [1994] ECR I-2517); and anti-pollution surveillance carried out by virtue of a public authorisation which was held to be 'a task in the public interest which forms part of the essential functions of the State as regards protection of the environment in sensitive areas' and thus 'connected by its nature, its aim and the rules to which it is subject with the exercise of powers . . . which are typically those of a public authority . . .' (Case 343/95 *Cali & Figli* v *SEPG* [1997] ECR I-1547, at paragraphs 22 to 23).

254. Applying those principles to the present case, we note first that GISC is a private company that has been set up by the industry itself without any statutory basis. It exists solely by contract. GISC is not accountable to Parliament, nor to Ministers, nor indeed to anyone other than those in the industry who belong to GISC. As far as the constitution of GISC is concerned, GISC is run by a Board of Directors most of whom are, or have been, active in the industry. At present only two out of the Board of some 16 members are 'public interest' directors recruited, so we are told, through head-hunters and not appointed by a public authority. It is true that it is currently proposed that there should be five 'public interest directors', but that still leaves the 'outside' directors in a substantial minority vis-à-vis the ten 'industry' directors (see paragraphs 53 to 55 above). There is no independent chairman (without industry connections). It is also proposed that in future the directors will be elected by the Members of GISC, who will become shareholders in the company, six directors being elected by intermediaries and four directors elected by insurers. This change is proposed, notably, in order that 'the Board would be directly accountable to regulated businesses' and in order to give 'the regulated businesses a greater say in the running of the company'. There is to be weighted voting, on the basis that 'a large business in the industry should, in principle, have a greater number of votes than a small business'. A number of these changes are proposed on the basis of the principles of the Combined Code, which is a publicly available document dealing with the principles of corporate governance relevant to listed public companies in the United Kingdom (see paragraphs 55 to 58 above).

255. On this basis GISC appears to us to have the features normally to be found in a private sector organisation or company accountable to its members, rather than a publicly constituted body exercising 'public powers'. We note also that, in the cases cited to us where the exercise of official or public authority was held to fall outside the competition rules, the activity in question had been exercised on some statutory basis of one kind or another. In the present case, GISC lacks any such statutory foundation.

256. We doubt whether, as a matter of Community law, the notion of the exercise of 'official authority' or 'public powers' can extend to cases where the legal basis of the activity in question is not to be found in the public law of the Member State but relies entirely on contract between private parties. Even if the Government is supportive of the principle of self regulation in the general insurance sector—which may not be quite the same thing as supporting a monopoly regulator for

the whole sector, as shown by the Treasury paper of April 1998 cited at paragraph 38 above—the Government is not, constitutionally speaking, the legislature. Statements by Government ministers are not the same thing as a legal basis founded in public law. Again, as a matter of statutory interpretation, we would not expect to find that an activity could be taken outside section 2 of the Act on the basis of ministerial statements made in Parliament rather than on the basis of the various exclusions and order making powers to be found in section 3 and schedules 1 to 4 of the Act.

257. Lastly, while it is true that the assumption of regulatory powers in respect of general insurance could properly be an activity of the State, for example under the FSMA, the setting up of a framework for promoting professional standards and consumer protection in general insurance is not an activity which, by reason of its intrinsic nature, can *necessarily* only be carried out by public authorities, as the case law appears to require. Self evidently GISC, the IIB and ABTA are all private sector bodies who have sought to establish self-regulatory or quality assurance schemes of one kind or another in the industries in which they operate. While we do not doubt the good intentions of those concerned, it seems to us clear that each of those bodies is acting not solely in the public interest but also in the commercial interests of their members in promoting the various schemes in question. In the case of GISC, emphasis has been placed on developing the GISC brand, creating what GISC sees as a 'level playing field', and avoiding the threat of statutory intervention. Although GISC itself is not run for profit, the particular structure set up under the GISC Rules would hardly have been adopted if the industry did not see real commercial advantages in proceeding in the way it has. It seems to us that Advocate General Léger, at paragraphs 144 to 154 of his opinion in *Wouters*, was considering a different factual situation, namely regulatory powers conferred by statute (see paragraphs 154 and 258(3) of that opinion). Similarly, the two domestic cases cited to us, *Institute of Chartered Accountants* v *Customs & Excise* [1999] 1 WLR 701 and *R* v *Panel on Takeovers and Mergers ex p Datafin* [1987] 1 QB 815, were each decided in a different factual and legal context.

258. In all those circumstances we can see no compelling reason why GISC should not be regarded as itself an undertaking although, as we have said, we do not need to decide that point for the purposes of this judgment, nor make any reference to the Court of Justice under Article 234 of the Treaty.

The next extracts from OFT Guideline 401 illustrate the extent to which the domestic competition regime is aligned with the Community rules. Note the Guidelines refer to the Treaty numbering pre-Amsterdam.

OFT Guideline 401, The Chapter I prohibition

Agreement

2.7 Agreement has a wide meaning and covers agreements whether legally enforceable or not, written or oral; it includes so-called *gentlemen's agreements*. There does not have to be a physical meeting of the parties for an agreement to be reached: an exchange of letters or telephone calls may suffice if a consensus is arrived at as to the action each party will, or will not, take.

2.8 The fact that a party may have played only a limited part in the setting up of the agreement, or may not be fully committed to its implementation, or participated only under pressure from other parties does not mean that it is not party to the agreement (although the fact may be taken into account in deciding the level of any financial penalty).

Decisions by associations of undertakings

2.9 The Chapter I prohibition also covers decisions by associations of undertakings. Trade associations are the most common form of associations of undertakings but the provisions are not limited to any particular type of association. A decision may cover the constitution or rules of an association, decisions which are binding on its members and recommendations. A decision may be a resolution of the management committee of an association or of the full membership in general meeting, the effect of which is to limit the commercial freedom of action of the members in some respect. It will also cover any coordination of the members' conduct in accordance with its constitution even if that recommendation is not binding on the members, and may not have been fully complied with. It will be a question of fact in each case whether an association of undertakings is itself a party to an agreement.

2.10 The Competition Act guideline Trade Associations, Professions and Self-Regulating Bodies elaborates on the application and enforcement of the Act in respect of both trade associations and the rules of self-regulating bodies. Agreements constituting the rules regulating certain specified professional services are excluded from the prohibition; details are included in the same guideline.

Concerted practices

2.11 The Chapter I prohibition applies to concerted practices as well as to agreements. The boundary between the two concepts is imprecise. The key difference is that a concerted practice may exist where there is informal cooperation without any formal agreement or decision.

2.12 In considering if a concerted practice exists, the Director General will follow relevant Community precedents established under Article 85. An economic assessment of the relevant market will need to be made in each case and two main elements will need to be established:

- the existence of positive contacts between the parties; and
- the contact has the object or effect of changing the market behaviour of the undertakings in a way which may not be dictated by market forces.

2.13 The following are examples of factors which the Director General may consider in establishing if a concerted practice exists:

- whether the parties knowingly enter into practical cooperation;
- whether behaviour in the market is influenced as a result of direct or indirect contact between undertakings;
- whether parallel behaviour is a result of contact between undertakings which leads to conditions of competition which do not correspond to normal conditions of the market;
- the structure of the relevant market and the nature of the product involved;
- the number of undertakings in the market, and where there are only a few undertakings whether they have similar cost structures and outputs.

NOTE: Clearly the definition of agreement is wider than under the RTPA where 'the term interconnected bodies corporate' (s. 43) was restrictively interpreted. See *RE Austin Motor Car Ltd's Agreements* [1958] Ch 61; *British Basic Slag Ltd's Agreement* [1962] 3 All ER 247. Cf. with the comments of Lord Marnoch in *Aberdeen Solicitors Property Centre* v *Director General of Fair Trading* 1996 SLT 523. This suggests a departure from the general principle in common law that a subsidiary company possesses separate legal personality from the parent. See, e.g., the decision in *Schweppes Ltd* v *Registrar of Restrictive Trading Agreements* [1965] 1 All ER 195, LR 5 RP 103 in which Stamp J firmly rejected the so-called 'economic entity' doctrine on the grounds that the companies, parent and subsidiary, had separate legal personalities which could not be fused.

OFT Guideline 401, The Chapter I prohibition

The United Kingdom

2.14 The Chapter I prohibition applies only if the agreement is, or is intended to be, implemented in the United Kingdom.

2.15 The United Kingdom means Great Britain (England, Wales and Scotland and the subsidiary islands, excluding the Isle of Man and the Channel Islands) and Northern Ireland. For the purposes of the Chapter I prohibition, the United Kingdom includes any part of the United Kingdom where an agreement operates or is intended to operate.

2.16 Although the prohibition refers to a dual test, *'affect trade'* and *'restrict competition'*, in practice it is very unlikely that an agreement which restricts competition in the United Kingdom does not also affect trade in the United Kingdom. In applying the Chapter 1 prohibition the focus will be on the effect on competition.

NOTE: Section 2 (1)(a) CA 1998 provides that the Chapter I prohibition will only apply where 'trade is affected *within* the United Kingdom' and this is confirmed in OFT Guideline 401, para. 2.14 (above). Given the Community focus on the single market paradigm what purpose, if any, does this requirement serve in a domestic context? If an agreement affects both trade between Member States and trade within the UK, it will be subject to UK and EC competition rules. (Note however, Article 3 of the Commission's draft regulation which provides that 'if the agreement, practice or decision has an actual or potential effect on trade between Member States Article 81 EC shall apply to the exclusion of Chapter I of the CA 1998'. Accordingly, there will be no prospect of conflict between UK law and the Community rules since all transactions with a cross-border effect will be subject to the one set of rules. See generally Chapter 3 on Enforcement.)

The CA 1998 catches agreements that are *implemented* within the UK or any part of the UK. Does this mean the Chapter I prohibition has extraterritorial application? The validity of this practice remains controversial in both UK and Community law; the UK government preferring a more traditional view of jurisdiction based on the territorial and nationality principles of public international law. As Lord Simon explained during debate,

> by copying out the test in *Wood Pulp* on the fact of the Bill, we are also ensuring that in the event that EC jurisprudence develops and creates a pure effects-doctrine, the application of the UK prohibitions will not follow suit. Hansard (HL) 13 November 261.

Note however the distinction between implementation and effects remains unclear although the Court of First Instance's approach in Case T-102/96 *Gencor Ltd* v *Commission* [1999] 4 CMLR 971 tends to support a wide intepretation of the concept of implementation. Will it be necessary that undertakings have a subsidiary branch or other assets within the United Kingdom in order to exercise jurisdiction? If so, this would appear to be a wider view of jurisdiction than UK practice currently follows. See *Schweppes Ltd* v *Registrar of Restrictive Trading Agreements* [1965] 1 All ER 195, LR 5 RP 103 in which the Court firmly rejected the so-called 'economic entity' doctrine whereby a parent and subsidiary company are treated as a single entity in order to establish jurisdiction over one of the parties situated overseas. See also the position on extra-territoriality under the Enterprise Bill 2002 discussed at p. 151, and Chapter 12 generally.

A: Appreciability

The concept of appreciability has an important part to play in terms of delineating the scope of the Chapter I prohibition. Note the term 'appreciable' does not actually appear in the text of the Act. This is because an appreciability test increases uncertainty and is unnecessary since the Court's jurisprudence on appreciability applies through s. 60. This view is consistent with statements made in the House of Lords. Lord Simon noted that:

> an explicit appreciability test does not fit well with our approach of reliance on European

case law except in areas where it is clear a different approach is required. Worse, there is a risk that in apparently departing from established European principles, we might inadvertently create so high a threshold for action that we could impede the effective tackling of anti-competitive agreements. [Hansard HL 13 November 1997, col. 259.]

OFT Guideline 401, The Chapter 1 prohibition

The appreciable effect test

2.18 An agreement will infringe the Chapter I prohibition only if it has as its object or effect an appreciable prevention, restriction or distortion of competition in the United Kingdom. This follows from established case law of the European Court which the Director General and the United Kingdom courts will be bound to follow under Section 60 of the Act. *Any agreement which does not have an appreciable effect on competition in the United Kingdom should not be notified to the Director General.*

2.19 The Director General takes the view that an agreement will generally have no appreciable effect on competition if the parties' combined share of the relevant market does not exceed 25 per cent, although there will be circumstances in which this is not the case.

2.20 The Director General will, in addition, generally regard any agreement between undertakings which:

- directly or indirectly fixes prices or shares markets (referred to further in paragraphs 3.5–3.8 and 3.10–3.11 below); or
- imposes minimum resale prices; or
- is one of a network of similar agreements which have a cumulative effect on the market in question

as being capable of having an appreciable effect even where the combined market share falls below the 25 per cent threshold. Further details on networks of agreements are given in the Competition Act guideline *Vertical Agreements and Restraints*.

Other factors

2.21 Even where the parties' combined market share is higher than 25 per cent, the Director General may find that the effect on competition is not appreciable. Other factors, for example, the content of the agreement and the structure of the market or markets affected by the agreement, such as entry conditions or the characteristics of buyers and the structure of the buyers' side of the market, will be considered in determining whether the agreement has an appreciable effect (see the Competition Act guideline *Assessment of Market Power*).

Calculating market share

2.22 When applying the market share thresholds discussed in paragraphs 2.19–2.21 above, the relevant market share will be the combined market share not only of the parties to the agreement but also of other undertakings belonging to the same group of undertakings as the parties to the agreement. These will include, in the case of each party to the agreement, (i) undertakings over which it exercises control, and (ii) both undertakings which exercise control over it and any other undertakings which are controlled by those undertakings. Further details on defining the relevant market are given in the Competition Act guideline *Market Definition*.

Nonetheless, the OFT's Guideline lays down a higher appreciablity threshold of 25 per cent than is the case under Community law. Guideline 401 must be read in conjunction with the OFT's Enforcement Guideline OFT 407 which provides limited immunity for 'small agreements' and 'conduct of minor significance'.

OFT Guideline 407, Enforcement

Limited immunity for 'small agreements' and 'conduct of minor significance'

4.14 To ensure that smaller enterprises are not unduly burdened with the operation of the prohibitions the Act provides limited immunity from financial penalties for 'small agreements' in relation to infringements of the Chapter I prohibition and 'conduct of minor significance' in relation to infringements of the Chapter II prohibition. This immunity does not apply to price fixing agreements. 'Small agreements' and 'conduct of minor significance' can be defined (among other ways) by the turnover and/or the market share of the undertaking(s). The criteria to be used will be defined by the Secretary of State by order, and are expected to be based on the turnover of the undertaking(s) in the United Kingdom.

4.15 Undertakings will benefit from immunity if the Director General is satisfied that they acted on the reasonable assumption that they qualified for the limited immunity for 'small agreements' or 'conduct of minor significance'.

4.16 This concession confers provisional immunity from penalties only. The other possible sanctions (voidness of agreements or third party actions for breach of statutory duty) are still applicable.

SECTION 4: Examples of anti-competitive agreements

Section 2 of the CA 1998 mirrors Article 81(1) EC by prohibiting agreements etc., which 'have as their object or effect the prevention, restriction or distortion of competition'. This seemingly simple phrase has caused the Commission and the European Court great difficulties, as discussed in Chapter 5. A distinction has been made by the Court between agreements which have the object of restricting competition and those which have the effect of doing so, see e.g. Case 56/65 *STM* v *Maschinenbau Ulm*, discussed at p. 191.

Section 2(2) of the CA 1998 provides a list of agreements to which, in particular, the prohibition is to apply, namely those which:

(a) directly or indirectly fix purchase or selling prices or any other trading conditions;

(b) limit or control production, markets, technical development or investment;

(c) share markets or sources of supply;

(d) apply dissimilar conditions to equivalent transactions with other trading parties, thereby placing them at a competitive disadvantage;

(e) make the conclusion of contracts subject to acceptance by the other parties of supplementary obligations which, by their nature or according to commercial usage, have no connection with the subject of such contracts.

The list mirrors Article 81 EC; it is non-exhaustive and illustrates the types of behaviour that will infringe Chapter I. Further guidance may be sought from the OFT's Guideline OFT 401 at paras 3.5–3.28. The parallels with Community law on the requirement of object or effect are also clear in the judgment of the CCAT in the GISC.

Institute of Independent Insurance Brokers, The v *Director General of Fair Trading supported by the General Insurance Standards Council; Association of British Travel Agents Limited* v *The Director General of Fair Trading supported by the General Insurance Standards Council*

(Case Nos 1002/2/1/01 (Ir), 1003/2/1/01, 1004/2/1/01) [2002] CompAR 62

The General Insurance Standards Council (GISC) notified its Rules, which established a system of self-regulation for insurance sellers and brokers, to the DGFT in June 2000. Rule F42 prevented members of the GISC from dealing with intermediaries engaged in selling and broking insurance, unless the intermediaries were members of the GISC or their agents.

The main issue in the appeal was whether the GISC rules, and in particular Rule F42 had 'as their object or effect the prevention, restriction or distortion of competition within the United Kingdom' within the meaning of s. 2(1)(b) of the Act.

229. We next address the question whether the de facto exclusion, by GISC, of an alternative scheme of regulation for the independent broking sector gives rise, at first sight, to restrictions or distortions of competition which merited investigation by the Director.

230. In their article Kay & Vickers express the view that self regulatory organisations tend to act in the interests of their members, and may be inefficient in enforcing or promoting higher standards if they are under no competitive pressure to do so. For these reasons, Kay & Vickers suggest that competition between self regulatory organisations may be desirable (see pp. 239 to 241). In particular, situations in which persons cannot trade unless they are members of a particular self regulatory body 'should normally be resisted except where the service provided is a public rather than a private one' (see p. 238).

231. The GISC Rules give rise to a situation very close to that which Kay & Vickers suggest, at p. 238 of their article, 'should normally be resisted', in that intermediaries in the general insurance sector cannot in practice trade unless they are members of GISC. However, it is unnecessary for us in this case to enter into a theoretical debate. We are confronted by a specific factual situation, which is that the setting up of GISC has caused the collapse of a proposed alternative regulatory or certification scheme, namely IBRC Mk II, which was supported by some 1,000 broker firms, representing, we are told, half the independent broking sector, who did not wish to be regulated or certified by GISC. It seems to us, at first sight, that that situation in itself gives rise to a restriction or distortion of competition within the meaning of section 2(1)(b) of the Act.

232. In effect the evidence before us suggests that one way in which independent brokers are able to compete with insurers' direct selling operations and other intermediaries is by promoting themselves as offering higher 'quality' standards of professional competence and consumer protection. One potentially important means of competing in this way is for independent brokers to establish their own regulatory or 'quality assurance' scheme (such as IBRC Mk II) by means of which they may collectively promote themselves as meeting the quality standards of their own scheme. The evidence of the IIB with regards to its attempts to launch IBRC Mk II indicates the importance which a substantial part of the independent broking sector attaches to the establishment of its own regulatory or certification scheme as a means of competing with insurers and other intermediaries. We conclude that there is plainly a market for the provision of regulatory or certification services to independent brokers as an alternative to, and in competition with, GISC. To the extent that the Director found to the contrary at paragraph 18 of the IIB Decision, we reject that finding on the basis of the evidence before us.

233. It seems to us, therefore, at first sight, that the position of GISC as 'sole regulator' restricts or distorts competition in the provision of competing regulatory or certification services for which there is a demand from independent brokers in the general insurance sector. That, on the evidence before us, is potentially a restriction or distortion of competition in the market for regulatory or certification services in the general insurance sector which merited investigation by the Director.

234. We are reinforced in that view by the fact, already mentioned, that once compelled to join, an intermediary faces practical difficulties in leaving GISC, except by discontinuing its business altogether or ceding its business to another member (Rule F34). It follows that, however high the GISC fees were to become, however inappropriate were to be the standards it develops, or however inefficiently it were to conduct its business, the option of leaving to join an alternative regulatory scheme is not in practice open. Even if GISC does not misconduct itself, the option of belonging to an alternative regulatory scheme, for example one that does not exclude its own liability, as GISC does, or which promotes higher standards or, for example, offers a compensation fund, is not in practical terms an option for any intermediary in the general insurance industry. In preventing, apparently in perpetuity, the emergence of an alternative to GISC, it does seem to us that competition from alternative regulatory schemes is potentially eliminated altogether.

235. Moreover, in our view, at first sight, the elimination of an alternative regulatory or quality assurance scheme for the independent broking sector also tends to restrict or distort competition in the separate market in which independent brokers are competing against the direct sales organisations of insurance companies, and other intermediaries, in selling or advising on general insurance products.

236. As we have already indicated, a potentially important element of competition in this, as in most other markets, is the ability to differentiate the product offered, notably by establishing a particular brand or image. GISC itself places considerable emphasis on establishing the GISC logo as a brand (paragraphs 68 and 165 above). The evidence before us is, however, that the inability to launch schemes such as IBRC Mk II is likely to make it more difficult for the independent broking sector to differentiate itself from the generality of suppliers of insurance by promoting its own distinctive image, based (as the IIB sees it) on higher regulatory standards, through the medium of an alternative regulatory scheme. In the absence of GISC, the members of the IIB would have the competitive freedom to promote themselves distinctively on the basis of their membership of such an independent scheme. The effective exclusion of that possibility, by the establishment of GISC seems to us, at first sight, to be a potential restriction or distortion of competition in the market for the selling, advising or broking of general insurance services.

237. It seems to us that that potential restriction or distortion of competition is reinforced in the present case by the fact that GISC itself comprises of a number of constituencies with different and opposing interests. It is a particular (and unusual) feature of this case that GISC, a body partly composed of suppliers (the insurers), seeks to exercise regulatory and disciplinary powers over the customers of those suppliers (the intermediaries). In addition, the insurer members of GISC sell insurance direct, in competition with intermediaries. In some sectors, particularly the consumer sector, insurers may have a substantial interest at gaining market share at the expense of independent intermediaries, or in promoting sales through tied outlets through agency agreements. Independent brokers, for their part, have an overriding interest in preserving their independence from insurers, since the essence of the service they provide is that of offering impartial advice in the best interests of the client.

238. In such circumstances it seems to us, at first sight, that the independent broking sector has a particular competitive need to differentiate, even to distance, itself from other Members of GISC. That sector depends very largely on the public perception that there are advantages in seeking impartial advice from a broker, whose duty it is to act in the client's best interest independently of the insurers, whether it is in placing the business or in handling any subsequent claims. It seems to

us possible that that perception could be weakened if independent intermediaries are forced to belong to, and be disciplined by, a body in which insurers' interests are very strong.

239. The IIB also submits that GISC will have the effect of preventing higher standards emerging in the general insurance sector and has already had the effect of lowering standards. In this regard, there is some evidence before us that the GISC regime contemplates lower standards as compared with those of the previous IBRC regime or IBRC Mk II. For example, under the GISC Rules the liability of GISC is excluded, only firms rather than individuals are regulated, audit requirements may be waived by a procedure of 'self-certification', breach of the Commercial Code does not appear in itself to be a disciplinary matter and no compensation fund is provided. Since GISC seeks to bring within its net all kinds of intermediaries, it seems to us not implausible that the general standard of regulation may settle at a lower level than that desirable for certain specific sectors such as independent brokers. Again, without expressing any view on the relative advantages and disadvantages of the GISC Rules and IBRC Mk II, it seems to us that the question whether the establishment of GISC would tend to militate against the independent broking sector maintaining higher standards, and thus restrict or distort competition, was a question meriting investigation by the Director.

240. In the IIB Decision, the Director takes the view that it was unnecessary for him to take into account the possibility of the lowering of regulatory standards, and in particular, that 'it was not necessary and would not have been appropriate for the Director to carry out a comparative analysis of the different types of regulation that may currently or in the future exist in the industry' (paragraph 23).

241. We find ourselves unable to agree with that approach. It seems to us that, once it was appreciated that the GISC Rules created a monopoly, in this instance a monopoly in the regulation of the general insurance industry, it was incumbent on the Director to examine potential effects on competition of the creation of that regulatory monopoly. It having been submitted to him on credible evidence that one of the effects of that monopoly was to make more difficult the maintenance of higher regulatory standards, and thus to diminish competition on product quality, which is one of the essential aspects of competition, the Director should, in our view, have investigated whether that evidence did in fact support the conclusion that GISC's regulatory monopoly did tend to restrict or distort competition in the respect alleged.

242. We are unpersuaded that the restrictions of competition identified above are materially affected by GISC's submission that the threat of statutory regulation under the FSMA will suffice to ensure that GISC acts solely in the public interest. That is a quite different issue. In any event, the possibility that the present or any future Government might, at some unknown future date, wish to replace GISC with statutory regulation under the FSMA, and if so in what circumstances, is far too uncertain a consideration for us to take into account when analysing restrictions or distortions of competition under section 2(1)(b) of the Act.

243. We also observe that a number of the possible consequences of the exclusion of alternative regulatory or certification regimes would be avoided if there were a realistic possibility for a waiver of the GISC Rules where such an alternative scheme was in place. Any such waivers would have to be granted on the basis of objective and transparent criteria, and any refusals of waiver would have to be open to challenge by some appropriate and independent procedure. Since, however, that is not the case at present, it does not seem to us that the waiver provisions of the GISC Rules, as presently applied, affect the analysis set out above.

Rodger notes, 'Although some professional rules may encourage competition and fall outside the prohibition due to the rule of reason, this robust judgment by the tribunal will have implications in many areas of self-regulation in the economy.' (Rodger, B.J., 'Early Steps to a Mature Competition Law System' [2002] ECLR 61–67, at p. 64.) Certainly the case is likely to have implications for the professions. See generally the report conducted by the OFT on 'Competition in Professions', OFT 328, March 2001.

SECTION 5: **Exemptions**

A key feature of the CA 1998 is the possibility of obtaining an exemption from the Chapter I prohibition as is the case in Article 81(3) EC. Sections 4–11 contain the relevant provisions.

Exemptions

4. **Individual exemptions**

(1) The Director may grant an exemption from the Chapter I prohibition with respect to a particular agreement if—

   (a) a request for an exemption has been made to him under section 14 by a party to the agreement; and

   (b) the agreement is one to which section 9 applies.

(2) An exemption granted under this section is referred to in this Part as an individual exemption.

(3) The exemption—

   (a) may be granted subject to such conditions or obligations as the Director considers it appropriate to impose; and

   (b) has effect for such period as the Director considers appropriate.

(4) That period must be specified in the grant of the exemption.

(5) An individual exemption may be granted so as to have effect from a date earlier than that on which it is granted.

(6) On an application made in such way as may be specified by rules under section 51, the Director may extend the period for which an exemption has effect; but, if the rules so provide, he may do so only in specified circumstances.

5. **Cancellation etc. of individual exemptions**

(1) If the Director has reasonable grounds for believing that there has been a material change of circumstance since he granted an individual exemption, he may by notice in writing—

   (a) cancel the exemption;

   (b) vary or remove any condition or obligation; or

   (c) impose one or more additional conditions or obligations.

(2) If the Director has a reasonable suspicion that the information on which he based his decision to grant an individual exemption was incomplete, false or misleading in a material particular, he may by notice in writing take any of the steps mentioned in subsection (1).

(3) Breach of a condition has the effect of cancelling the exemption.

(4) Failure to comply with an obligation allows the Director, by notice in writing, to take any of the steps mentioned in subsection (1).

(5) Any step taken by the Director under subsection (1), (2) or (4) has effect from such time as may be specified in the notice.

(6) If an exemption is cancelled under subsection (2) or (4), the date specified in the notice cancelling it may be earlier than the date on which the notice is given.

(7) The Director may act under subsection (1), (2) or (4) on his own initiative or on a complaint made by any person.

6. Block exemptions

(1) If agreements which fall within a particular category of agreement are, in the opinion of the Director, likely to be agreements to which section 9 applies, the Director may recommend that the Secretary of State make an order specifying that category for the purposes of this section.

(2) The Secretary of State may make an order ('a block exemption order') giving effect to such a recommendation—

    (a) in the form in which the recommendation is made; or

    (b) subject to such modifications as he considers appropriate.

(3) An agreement which falls within a category specified in a block exemption order is exempt from the Chapter I prohibition.

(4) An exemption under this section is referred to in this Part as a block exemption.

(5) A block exemption order may impose conditions or obligations subject to which a block exemption is to have effect.

(6) A block exemption order may provide—

    (a) that breach of a condition imposed by the order has the effect of cancelling the block exemption in respect of an agreement;

    (b) that if there is a failure to comply with an obligation imposed by the order, the Director may, by notice in writing, cancel the block exemption in respect of the agreement;

    (c) that if the Director considers that a particular agreement is not one to which section 9 applies, he may cancel the block exemption in respect of that agreement.

(7) A block exemption order may provide that the order is to cease to have effect at the end of a specified period.

(8) In this section and section 7 'specified' means specified in a block exemption order.

7. Block exemptions: opposition

(1) A block exemption order may provide that a party to an agreement which—

    (a) does not qualify for the block exemption created by the order, but

    (b) satisfies specified criteria, may notify the Director of the agreement for the purposes of subsection (2).

(2) An agreement which is notified under any provision included in a block exemption order by virtue of subsection (1) is to be treated, as from the end of the notice period, as falling within a category specified in a block exemption order unless the Director—

    (a) is opposed to its being so treated; and

    (b) gives notice in writing to the party concerned of his opposition before the end of that period.

(3) If the Director gives notice of his opposition under subsection (2), the notification under subsection (1) is to be treated as both notification under section 14 and as a request for an individual exemption made under subsection (3) of that section.

(4) In this section 'notice period' means such period as may be specified with a view to giving the Director sufficient time to consider whether to oppose under subsection (2).

8. Block exemptions: procedure

(1) Before making a recommendation under section 6(1), the Director must—

    (a) publish details of his proposed recommendation in such a way as he thinks most suitable for bringing it to the attention of those likely to be affected; and

    (b) consider any representations about it which are made to him.

(2) If the Secretary of State proposes to give effect to such a recommendation subject to modifications, he must inform the Director of the proposed modifications and take into account any comments made by the Director.

(3) If, in the opinion of the Director, it is appropriate to vary or revoke a block exemption order he may make a recommendation to that effect to the Secretary of State.

(4) Subsection (1) also applies to any proposed recommendation under subsection (3).

(5) Before exercising his power to vary or revoke a block exemption order (in a case where there has been no recommendation under subsection (3)), the Secretary of State must—

    (a) inform the Director of the proposed variation or revocation; and

    (b) take into account any comments made by the Director.

(6) A block exemption order may provide for a block exemption to have effect from a date earlier than that on which the order is made.

9. The criteria for individual and block exemptions

This section applies to any agreement which—

    (a) contributes to—

        (i) improving production or distribution, or

        (ii) promoting technical or economic progress, while allowing consumers a fair share of the resulting benefit; but

    (b) does not—

        (i) impose on the undertakings concerned restrictions which are not indispensable to the attainment of those objectives; or

        (ii) afford the undertakings concerned the possibility of eliminating competition in respect of a substantial part of the products in question.

10. Parallel exemptions

(1) An agreement is exempt from the Chapter I prohibition if it is exempt from the Community prohibition—

    (a) by virtue of a Regulation,

    (b) because it has been given exemption by the Commission, or

    (c) because it has been notified to the Commission under the appropriate opposition or objection procedure and—

        (i) the time for opposing, or objecting to, the agreement has expired and the Commission has not opposed it; or

        (ii) the Commission has opposed, or objected to, the agreement but has withdrawn its opposition or objection.

(2) An agreement is exempt from the Chapter I prohibition if it does not affect trade between Member States but otherwise falls within a category of agreement which is exempt from the Community prohibition by virtue of a Regulation.

(3) An exemption from the Chapter I prohibition under this section is referred to in this Part as a parallel exemption.

(4) A parallel exemption—

    (a) takes effect on the date on which the relevant exemption from the Community prohibition takes effect or, in the case of a parallel exemption under subsection (2), would take effect if the agreement in question affected trade between Member States; and

    (b) ceases to have effect—

        (i) if the relevant exemption from the Community prohibition ceases to have effect; or

        (ii) on being cancelled by virtue of subsection (5) or (7).

(5) In such circumstances and manner as may be specified in rules made under section 51, the Director may—

(a) impose conditions or obligations subject to which a parallel exemption is to have effect;

(b) vary or remove any such condition or obligation;

(c) impose one or more additional conditions or obligations;

(d) cancel the exemption.

(6) In such circumstances as may be specified in rules made under section 51, the date from which cancellation of an exemption is to take effect may be earlier than the date on which notice of cancellation is given.

(7) Breach of a condition imposed by the Director has the effect of cancelling the exemption.

(8) In exercising his powers under this section, the Director may require any person who is a party to the agreement in question to give him such information as he may require.

(9) For the purpose of this section references to an agreement being exempt from the Community prohibition are to be read as including references to the prohibition being inapplicable to the agreement by virtue of a Regulation or a decision by the Commission.

(10) In this section— 'the Community prohibition' means the prohibition contained in—

(a) paragraph 1 of Article 85;

(b) any corresponding provision replacing, or otherwise derived from, that provision;

(c) such other Regulation as the Secretary of State may by order specify; and 'Regulation' means a Regulation adopted by the Commission or by the Council.

(11) This section has effect in relation to the prohibition contained in paragraph 1 of Article 53 of the EEA Agreement (and the EFTA Surveillance Authority) as it has effect in relation to the Community prohibition (and the Commission) subject to any modifications which the Secretary of State may by order prescribe.

11. Exemption for certain other agreements

(1) The fact that a ruling may be given by virtue of Article 88 of the Treaty on the question whether or not agreements of a particular kind are prohibited by Article 85 does not prevent such agreements from being subject to the Chapter I prohibition.

(2) But the Secretary of State may by regulations make such provision as he considers appropriate for the purpose of granting an exemption from the Chapter I prohibition, in prescribed circumstances, in respect of such agreements.

(3) An exemption from the Chapter I prohibition by virtue of regulations under this section is referred to in this Part as a section 11 exemption.

OFT Guideline 401, 'The Chapter I prohibition' explains the three types of exemption in more detail.

OFT Guideline 401, The Chapter I prohibition

Individual exemption

4.2 An individual exemption must be applied for by way of a notification on Form N and may be granted for individual agreements which satisfy the statutory exemption criteria. An individual exemption may be granted subject to conditions or obligations and/or for a specified period. The exemption can have effect from a date which is earlier than that on which it is granted.

Block exemption

4.3 Under the Act the Director General may, by order, make domestic block exemptions which exempt particular categories of agreement which he considers are likely to satisfy the statutory exemption criteria. An agreement which falls within a category specified in the block exemption will be automatically exempt from the Chapter I prohibition, and there is no need to notify such an agreement to the Director General. Any such block exemption may impose conditions or obligations subject to which the block exemption will have effect.

4.4 The breach of a *condition* imposed by the block exemption cancels the block exemption in respect of an agreement. The failure to comply with an *obligation* imposed by the block exemption enables the Director General to cancel the block exemption in respect of an agreement. Furthermore if the Director General thinks that an agreement does not satisfy the statutory exemption criteria he may cancel the block exemption in respect of an agreement.

4.5 The Act provides that a block exemption order may include an opposition procedure. This will enable an agreement which falls outside the scope of the block exemption to be treated as falling within it where:

- the agreement satisfies the specified criteria;
- the agreement has been notified to the Director General; and
- the Director General does not oppose it being so treated before the end of a specified period by giving notice in writing to the parties. If he does exercise that right, the notification made is automatically treated as a notification for decision in the normal way, and as a request for individual exemption (see paragraph 4.2 above).

Parallel exemption

4.6 A parallel exemption applies to an agreement which is covered by a European Commission individual or block exemption under Article 85(3), or would be covered by a European Commission block exemption if the agreement had an effect on trade between EC Member States. These types of agreement are automatically exempted under the Act without the need for individual exemption.

4.7 Where an agreement which benefits from a parallel exemption has produced, or may produce, significantly adverse effects on a market in the United Kingdom or part of it, the Director General may impose conditions on a parallel exemption or vary or cancel the exemption following procedures specified in rule 21 of the *Director General of Fair Trading's Procedural Rules*.

NOTE: A parallel exemption is not available for an agreement that has the benefit of an EC comfort letter.

OFT Guideline 401, The Chapter I prohibition

EC comfort letters

7.11 Many agreements notified to the European Commission receive an informal indication of the European Commission's likely assessment by means of a *comfort letter* rather than a formal decision. EC comfort letters are not legally binding but it is clear that the European Commission will re-open the file only in certain limited circumstances. The Act does not make provision for the informal procedures of the European Commission.

7.12 As a general policy, the Director General will not depart from the European Commission's assessment of an agreement as set out in an EC comfort letter, but the following exceptions to this policy should be noted:

- an agreement may raise particular concerns in relation to competition in the United Kingdom;
- the European Commission may indicate that there is an infringement of Article 85 which would not qualify for exemption, but that as a matter of its internal priorities it will not consider the matter further (a *discomfort letter*);

- the European Commission may indicate that the agreement does not have an *appreciable effect* on inter-state trade for the purposes of the application of Article 85(1).

In these circumstances, the parties will need to consider the application of the Chapter 1 prohibition and, if the agreement is subject to the prohibition, whether notification to the Director General is appropriate.

NOTE: The criteria for obtaining an individual exemption from the Chapter I prohibition set out in s. 9 mirror those articulated in Article 81(3) EC. The basic test for determining whether an agreement merits an exemption, is therefore, the effect, actual or potential, on competition. The Competition Authorities will have limited discretion to take any other factors into consideration as is the case in Community law, although see decisions of the European Court in Case 26/76 *Metro-SB-Grossmärkte GmbH* v *Commission (No 1)* and Case 1-17/93 *Matra Hachette* discussed at pp. 203–208, below.

OFT Guideline 401, The Chapter I prohibition

Exemption criteria

4.8 Section 9 of the Act sets out the criteria which must be met if an exemption is to be granted. That is any agreement which:

(a) contributes to
   (i)   improving production or distribution, or
   (ii) promoting technical or economic progress, while allowing consumers a fair share of the resulting benefit; but
(b) does not
   (i)   impose on the undertakings concerned restrictions which are not indispensable to the attainment of those objectives; or
   (ii) afford the undertakings concerned the possibility of eliminating competition in respect of a substantial part of the products in question.

4.9 The wording of the section is identical to that of Article 85(3) except that the latter refers to *'improving production or distribution of goods'*. The intention of the section is to make clear that (consistently with European Commission practice in relation to Article 85(3)) the domestic exemption provisions apply also to agreements which contribute to improvements in the provision of services.

4.10 The exemption criteria require that four conditions, two positive, two negative, are satisfied (see paragraphs 4.11–4.16 below). All of the conditions must be met. The objective and appreciable advantages must be sufficient to outweigh any disadvantages to competition. This must be judged objectively. The onus of demonstrating that the conditions are met falls upon the parties to an agreement.

The agreement contributes to improving production or distribution or promoting technical or economic progress . . .

4.11 Examples of improvements in production or distribution include lower costs from longer production or delivery runs, or from changes in the methods of production or distribution; improvements in product quality; increases in the range of products produced or services provided. In each case the nature of the improvement claimed must be clearly identified and justified.

4.12 Examples of the promotion of technical or economic progress include efficiency gains from economies of scale and specialisation in research and development with the prospect of an enhanced flow or speed of innovation, and technical progress.

. . . while allowing consumers a fair share of the resulting benefits

4.13 The second positive condition is not limited to final consumers. It can include the customers of the parties to the agreement. If an improvement, for example, a cost reduction, is seen as benefiting only the shareholders of the parties to the agreement, the condition would not be satisfied. The views of customers and consumers are likely to be important in the consideration of the case for exemption, and, in appropriate cases, they will be sought.

4.14 The resulting benefits are likely to be those which flow from improvements in production or distribution. An agreement may lead, for example, to the faster development of new products or of new markets or better distribution systems, so that the benefits to consumers also lie in the future. The Director General takes account of the dynamics of market conduct and competition in assessing whether or not this condition for exemption is satisfied.

Restrictions which are not indispensable to the attainment of the objectives set out in the two positive criteria

4.15 To qualify for exemption, agreements may not include restrictions beyond those necessary for the attainment of the benefits which the parties demonstrate are likely to flow from the agreement. The agreement should contain the least restrictive means of achieving its aims. The Director General will look carefully for any restrictions beyond those necessary to securing those benefits.

The possibility of eliminating competition in respect of a substantial part of the products in question

4.16 The Director General's assessment will consider this second negative condition in the overall context of the effect of the agreement on competition. If, after an appropriate market analysis, he concludes that it is not satisfied, there can be no possibility of an exemption. An application for an individual exemption is unlikely to succeed if the parties are unable to show that there will continue to be effective competition in the market(s) for the goods or services with which the agreement is concerned.

QUESTION

Do you notice any differences between s. 9 and Article 81(3) EC?

NOTE: There have been a number of notifications for individual exemption since CA 1998 came into force. One of the first notifications concerned the Memorandum of Understanding on the supply of fuels in an emergency, concluded in the aftermath of the fuel crisis in September 2000 by the government, major oil companies, road hauliers, police and trade unions. The purpose of the Memorandum was to preserve the supply of oil fuels and to protect supplies to essential users. Was an individual exemption likely? Rodger explains the circumstances surrounding the DGFT's decision.

Rodger, B.J., *Early Steps to a Mature Competition Law System*
[2002] ECLR, pp. 64–65

In its notice of consultation,[76] the DGFT was of the view that, subject to certain conditions and obligations, it merited an individual exemption. The Chapter I prohibition covered the Memorandum as this was an appreciable restriction on the basis that the applicants had a combined 82 per cent market share in the supply of all fuels at all levels of supply. The exemption criteria in section 9 were found to be satisfied, where restricted to the period surrounding a fuel crisis, in that the Memorandum improves distribution of oil in a crisis and consumers would benefit at least indirectly

---

76 Notice of consultation issued pursuant to r. 12 of the Competition Act 1998 (Director's Rules) Order 2000 (SI 2000 293) *Relating to a Notification of a Memorandum of Understanding on the supply of fuels in an emergency,* 12 July 2001 (Case CP/1730–00/S).

from the maintenance of essential supplies. The restrictions were deemed to be no more than necessary, and even information exchanges were indispensable to the efficient distribution of fuel in a crisis. The DGFT has intimated as a condition for the grant of the exemption that he would require to be informed as to any material change to the Memorandum and its activation. Almost inevitably, the least convincing aspect was the view that it would not eliminate competition in respect of a substantial part of the products, as 'a substantial amount of oil fuel will remain which could possibly be delivered to consumers' (paragraph 68). Following the consultation period, the DGFT has now decided to grant an exemption in respect of the Memorandum.[77]

The procedure for notifying agreements to the DGFT is discussed in Chapter 2. The next extract to be taken from the OFT Guideline however considers the issues in deciding which is the appropriate authority to notify in instances where there is overlap between Article 81 EC and Chapter I. The starting point in determining which is the more appropriate authority is to assess whether or not the agreement may affect trade between Member States.

OFT Guideline 401, The Chapter I prohibition

The appropriate authority to notify

7.4 In considering the appropriate authority to notify, there are several advantages in notifying agreements to the European Commission under Article 85 rather than to the Director General under the Chapter I prohibition:

- only the European Commission can give an exemption from Article 85(1). This exemption automatically exempts the agreement from the Chapter I prohibition (a *'parallel exemption,'* referred to in paragraphs 4.6 and 4.7 above). By contrast, however, exemption from the Chapter I prohibition does not preclude the application of Article 85(1);
- European Commission Article 85(3) exemption has effect in all the EC Member States, but exemption by the Director General has effect only in the United Kingdom;
- provisional immunity from financial penalties under the Chapter I prohibition is available without notification to the Director General; he may not impose a penalty under the Chapter I prohibition if an agreement has been notified to the European Commission and the European Commission has not yet determined the matter. It should be noted, however, that if the European Commission withdraws the benefit of provisional immunity from penalties with respect to the agreement before determining the matter, the immunity from penalty under the Chapter I prohibition will automatically cease on the same date.

7.5 The European Commission does not have the power to grant retroactive exemptions in all cases. The parties to an agreement may, therefore, consider it commercially beneficial to notify the European Commission at the earliest possible date. The Director General, however, does have the power to grant retroactive exemptions in all cases.

7.6 If the inter-state trade criterion is not met but the agreement does have an appreciable effect on competition in the United Kingdom, the Director General is the appropriate authority for notification. Where it is unclear whether the inter-state trade criterion is satisfied, the parties to an agreement may wish to consult with the Director General's officials as to the more appropriate authority to notify.

7.7 Where the parties to an agreement notify the European Commission and the European Commission takes the view that the agreement does not affect trade between Member States, the

77 PN 43a/01, 26 October 2001.

parties may choose to notify the Director General if the agreement has an appreciable effect on competition. The Director General will endeavour to give priority to such cases, and may grant individual exemptions where the agreements satisfy the section 9 exemption criteria.

Treatment of dual notifications

7.8 There are clear advantages in notifying to only one competition authority. However in the event of dual notifications the following points should be noted.

7.9 The Director General's officials will liaise closely with those of the European Commission in determining the more appropriate authority to assess the agreement. Where it is clear that the European Commission will deal with the agreement either by formal decision or by informal means, the Director General will generally take no action until the European Commission has completed its assessment and informed the parties. Where the European Commission formally exempts the agreement from Article 85 by a decision under Article 85(3), the agreement is automatically exempt from the Chapter I prohibition. If the case is closed by informal means, as a general policy the Director General will follow the European Commission's assessment of the agreement (see paragraphs 7.11 and 7.12 below). If the Director General does intend to depart from the European Commission's assessment of an agreement he will consult the European Commission before doing so.

7.10 The Director General may, however, proceed to consider a notification that has been made to both authorities and is already being considered by the European Commission, in particular where:

- the agreement raises particular concerns in relation to competition in the United Kingdom;
- he considers the agreement involves important legal, economic or policy developments.

NOTE: To date the OFT has published one block exemption order, backdated to 1 March 2000 in relation to travel cards, following a recommendation by the DGFT that public transport ticketing schemes should be exempted.

The Competition Act 1998 (Public Transport Ticketing Schemes Block Exemption) Order 2001
(SI 2001/319)

Citation, commencement, duration and interpretation

1. This Order may be cited as the Competition Act 1998 (Public Transport Ticketing Schemes Block Exemption) Order 2001 and shall come into force on 1st March 2001.

2. This Order shall have effect from the beginning of 1st March 2000 and shall cease to have effect at the end of the period of five years commencing on 1st March 2001.

3. In this Order—

'the Act' means the Competition Act 1998;

'block exemption' means the exemption from the Chapter I prohibition arising by virtue of this Order for the category of agreements specified in this Order;

'bus service' has the meaning given in section 159(1) of the Transport Act 1968 but excludes a bus service which is a tourist service;

'chartered service' means a public transport service:

    (a) for which the whole capacity of the vehicle, vessel or craft supplying that service has been purchased by one or more charterers for his or their own use or for resale;

    (b) which is a journey or trip organised privately by any person acting independently of the person operating the vehicle, vessel or craft supplying that service; or

    (c) on which the passengers travel together on a journey, with or without breaks, from one or more places to one or more places and back;

'complementary services' means local public transport services which are not in competition with each other over a substantial part of the route covered by the ticket in question;

'connecting service' means a service (other than a bus service, a chartered service or a tourist service) for the carriage of passengers by road, tramway, railway, inland waterway or air which is a long distance service and which runs between—

(a) a station or stopping place at or in the vicinity of which the relevant local public transport service stops; and

(b) any other place;

'Inland waterway' includes both natural and artificial waterways, and waterways within parts of the sea that are in the United Kingdom;

'journey' means any journey made by an individual passenger and includes a return journey;

'local public transport service' means:

(a) a bus service; or

(b) a scheduled public transport service (other than a bus service) using one or more vehicles or vessels for the carriage of passengers by road, railway, tramway or inland waterway at separate fares other than a long distance service, a chartered service or a tourist service;

'long distance add-on' means:

(a) a ticket (or tickets) entitling the holder to make a journey solely on the local public transport services of any one operator;

(b) a multi-operator travelcard; or

(c) a through ticket,

each being purchased as an add-on to a ticket (or tickets) entitling the holder to make a particular journey on one or more connecting services;

'long distance operator' means an undertaking (other than an operator) supplying a scheduled long distance service using one or more vehicles, vessels or craft for the carriage of passengers by road, railway, tramway, inland waterway or air at separate fares other than a chartered service or a tourist service;

'long distance service' means a public transport service in relation to which (except in an emergency) one or both of the following conditions are met with respect to every passenger using the service:

(a) the place where he is set down is fifteen miles or more, measured in a straight line, from the place where he was taken up;

(b) some point on the route between those places is fifteen miles or more, measured in a straight line, from either of those places,

and where a public transport service consists of one or more parts with respect to which one or both of these conditions are met, and one or more parts with respect to which neither of them is met, each of those parts shall be treated as a separate public transport service;

'members of the public' means any person other than an operator, potential operator, long distance operator or potential long distance operator;

'multi-operator individual ticket' means a ticket (or tickets) entitling the holder, where a particular journey could be made on local public transport services provided by any of two or more operators, to make that journey or any part of it on whichever service the holder chooses;

'multi-operator travel card' means a ticket (or tickets) entitling the holder to make three or more journeys on three or more specified local public transport services operating on three or more routes provided that:

(a) these routes are not substantially the same;

(b) these local public transport services are not substantially the same; and

(c) for each of these routes and local public transport services, the passenger usage and revenue received from the ticket and other such tickets purchased as a result of the relevant agreement, demonstrate that the ticket is not, in practice, a multi-operator individual ticket or a through ticket;

'operator' means an undertaking supplying local public transport services;

'posted price' means, where a ticket is purchased from one undertaking (the seller), a wholesale price set independently by another undertaking ('the creditor') for the carriage of passengers bearing that ticket on the public transport services of the creditor;

'public transport ticketing scheme' has the meaning given in Article 4(2);

'the register' means the register maintained by the Director under rule 8 of the Director's rules set out in the Schedule to the Competition Act 1998 (Director's rules) Order 2000;

'short distance add-on' means a multi-operator travelcard purchased as an add-on to a ticket (or tickets) entitling the holder to make a particular journey on a local public transport service pursuant to an agreement which provides for onward travel connections for passengers on complementary services;

'stopping place' means a point at which passengers are taken up or set down in the course of a public transport service;

'through ticket' means a ticket (or tickets) entitling the holder to make a particular journey on two or more local public transport services provided that such a journey is made on complementary services;

'ticket' means evidence of a contractual right to travel;

'tourist service' means a public transport service where the price charged for that service includes payment for a live or recorded commentary about the locality being a service primarily for the benefit of tourists;

'vehicle' includes vehicles constructed or adapted to run on flanged wheels but excludes hackney carriages, taxis, cabs, hire cars and any vehicle propelled by an animal; and

'working day' means a day which is not a Saturday, Sunday or any other day on which the Office of Fair Trading is closed for business.

Block exemption

4.(1) The category of agreements identified in paragraph (2) as public transport ticketing schemes is hereby specified for the purposes of section 6 of the Act.

(2) For the purpose of this Order a public transport ticketing scheme is one or more of the following:

(a) a written agreement between operators to the extent that it provides for members of the public to purchase, in a single transaction, a multi-operator travelcard;

(b) a written agreement between operators to the extent that it provides for members of the public to purchase, in a single transaction, a through ticket;

(c) a written agreement between operators to the extent that it provides for members of the public to purchase, in a single transaction, a multi-operator individual ticket;

(d) a written agreement between operators to the extent that it provides for members of the public to purchase, in a single transaction, a short distance add-on;

(e) a written agreement between one or more operators and one or more long distance operators to the extent that it provides for members of the public to purchase, in a single transaction, a long distance add-on;

5. This block exemption has effect subject to the conditions and the obligation specified in Articles 6 to 17.

Conditions and consequences of breach of conditions

6. Unless there is an objective, transparent and non-discriminatory reason, a public

transport ticketing scheme shall not, directly or indirectly, in isolation or in combination with other factors under the control of the parties:

(a) have the object or effect of preventing any operator or potential operator from participating in that public transport ticketing scheme; or

(b) to the extent that the scheme provides for members of the public to purchase a long distance add-on, have the object or effect of preventing any operator, potential operator, long distance operator or potential long distance operator from participating in that public transport ticketing scheme.

7. A public transport ticketing scheme shall not, directly or indirectly, in isolation or in combination with other factors under the control of the parties, have the object or effect of limiting:

(a) the variety or number of routes on which any operator or long distance operator provides or may provide public transport services; or

(b) the freedom of operators or long distance operators to set the price or availability of, the fare structure relating to, or the zones or geographical validity applicable for, any ticket entitling the holder to make a journey solely on the public transport services of any one operator or any one long distance operator.

8. A public transport ticketing scheme shall not, directly or indirectly, in isolation or in combination with other factors under the control of the parties, have the object or effect or limiting the frequency or timing of any public transport services operated by any operator or long distance operator, unless such restriction is indispensable to the effective operation of that scheme, pursuant to an agreement which provides for onward travel connections for passengers.

9.(1) Subject to paragraph (2), a public transport ticketing scheme shall not, directly or indirectly, in isolation or in combination with other factors under the control of the parties, have the object or effect of facilitating an exchange of information between the parties to that public transport ticketing scheme.

(2) Paragraph (1) shall not prevent an exchange of information between the parties to a public transport ticketing scheme which is directly related and indispensable to the effective operation of that scheme, provided that the relevant provision under which the information is exchanged is objective, transparent and non-discriminatory and that it does not breach any of the other conditions imposed by this Order.

10. Breach of any of the conditions imposed by any of Articles 6, 7, 8 or 9 shall have the effect of cancelling the block exemption in respect of that public transport ticketing scheme.

11. The parties to a public transport ticketing scheme which provides for members of the public to purchase a multi-operator travelcard shall not distribute between themselves the revenue received by virtue of the operation of that scheme other than pursuant to terms contained in that scheme which reflect, as far as is reasonably practicable, the actual passenger miles travelled on the vehicles or vessels of each party by passengers using tickets issued under that scheme during the accounting period in which such revenue was received.

12. Breach of the condition imposed by Article 11 shall have the effect of cancelling the block exemption in respect of the relevant public transport ticketing scheme to the extent that such scheme provides for members of the public to purchase a multi-operator travelcard.

13.(1) Subject to paragraph (2), a public transport ticketing scheme which provides for members of the public to purchase a through ticket, multi-operator individual ticket, short distance add-on or long distance add-on, shall not directly or indirectly, in isolation or in combination with other factors under the control of the parties have the object or effect of fixing a price at which the respective through ticket, multi-operator individual ticket, short distance add-on or long distance add-on is offered for sale.

(2) Paragraph (1) shall not prevent:

(a) the parties to a public transport ticketing scheme from agreeing to charge each other non-discriminatory posted prices for sales of the respective through ticket, short distance add-on or long distance add-on; or

(b) operators from fixing the price of a multi-operator travelcard which may be purchased as a short distance add-on or long distance add-on provided that such action does not breach any of the other conditions imposed by this Order.

14. Breach of the condition imposed by Article 13 shall have the effect of cancelling the block exemption in respect of the relevant public transport ticketing scheme to the extent that such scheme provides for members of the public to purchase the relevant through ticket, multi-operator individual ticket, short distance add-on or long distance add-on.

15. The parties to a public transport ticketing scheme which provides for members of the public to purchase a multi-operator individual ticket, shall not:

(a) include an operator as a party to that scheme unless that operator also makes available, concurrently with making available that multi-operator individual ticket, single and return tickets entitling the holder to make the particular journey covered by that multi-operator individual ticket solely on the local public transport services of that operator; or

(b) distribute between themselves the revenue received by virtue of the operation of that scheme other than pursuant to terms contained in that scheme whereby the operator which sells any particular multi-operator individual ticket retains exclusively all the revenue received from that sale.

16. Breach of the condition imposed by Article 15 shall have the effect of cancelling the block exemption in respect of the relevant public transport ticketing scheme to the extent that such scheme provides for members of the public to purchase a multi-operator individual ticket.

Obligation

17. A person shall, within ten working days from the date on which it receives notice in writing under this Article, supply to the Director such information in connection with those public transport ticketing schemes to which it is a party as the Director may require.

Cancellation by notice

18. If there is a failure to comply with the obligation imposed by Article 17 without reasonable excuse, the Director may, subject to Article 20, by notice in writing cancel this block exemption in respect of any public transport ticketing scheme to which the relevant request for information under Article 17 relates.

19. If the Director considers that a particular public transport ticketing scheme is not one to which section 9 of the Act applies, he may, subject to Article 20, by notice in writing cancel this block exemption in respect of that scheme.

20. If the Director proposes to cancel the block exemption in accordance with Article 18 or Article 19, he shall first give notice in writing of his proposal and shall consider any representations made to him.

21. For the purpose of Articles 18, 19 and 20, notice in writing is given by:

(a) the Director giving notice in writing of his decision or proposal to those persons whom he can reasonably identify as being parties to the relevant public transport ticketing scheme; or

(b) where it is not reasonably practicable for the Director to comply with paragraph (a), the Director publishing his decision or proposal in the register and:

(i) the London, Edinburgh and Belfast Gazettes;

(ii) at least one national daily newspaper; and

(iii) if there is in circulation an appropriate trade journal which is published at intervals not exceeding one month, in such trade journal,

stating the facts on which he bases it and his reasons for making it.

EXPLANATORY NOTE

(This note is not part of the Order)

This Order is a block exemption Order under section 6 of the Competition Act 1998 ('the Act'). It gives effect to the Director General of Fair Trading's recommendation that public transport ticketing schemes (as defined in the Order) for local public transport services constitute a category of agreements which are likely to be agreements to which section 9 of the Act applies. Agreements which fall within the category specified in the block exemption Order are exempt from the prohibition in Chapter I of the Act.

The recommendation was made by the Director following consultation in accordance with section 8(1) of the Act.

The block exemption has effect subject to certain conditions and obligations and concerns particularly agreements between local public transport operators (and in one case, together with long distance public transport operators) which provide for the purchase, in a single transaction, of:

(a) multi-operator travelcards (MTCs)

(b) through tickets (TTs)

(c) multi-operator individual tickets (MITs)

(d) short distance add-ons

(e) long distance add-ons

as defined in the Order.

The block exemption applies to such agreements to the extent that they fall within the scope of section 2 of the Act (agreements etc. preventing, restricting or distorting competition (the Chapter I prohibition)).

The Order includes provisions concerning the cancellation of the block exemption.

The block exemption is retrospective and has effect from 1st March 2000 and will cease to have effect at the end of the period of five years from the date of coming into force of the Order.

Guidance on the block exemption is available from the Director General of Fair Trading at www.oft.gov.uk

QUESTION

Will the UK competition authorities be able to apply stricter controls to an agreement which is the subject of a Community block or individual exemption? Community jurisprudence suggests that national competition authorities may *not* impose stricter controls on agreements exempted under block exemptions although the issue is far from clear. See Advocate General Tesauro's Opinion in Case C-266/93 *Bundeskartellamt* v *Volkswagen* [1995] ECR I-3477 at pp. 3500–3506 and Case C-70/93 *BMW* v *Ald* [1995] ECR I-3439 at pp. 3454–3458. The relationship between the Chapter I prohibition and Community law is a matter of some complexity and will become even more so once the draft regulation is implemented. On this issue, see Whish, R., *Competition Law*, 4th edn, Butterworths, Chapter 9, pp. 322–329.

SECTION 6:   **Exclusions**

One aspect of the new regime, which has no counterpart in Community competition law, is excluded agreements. Schedules 1–4 to the CA 1998 lists certain types of agreements to which the Chapter I prohibition does not apply; the details are expanded in the OFT Guideline:

OFT Guideline 401, The Chapter I prohibition

5.1 Schedules 1–4 of the Act specifically exclude from the Chapter I prohibition certain categories of agreement:

- to the extent to which an agreement would result in a merger or joint venture within the merger provisions of the Fair Trading Act 1973 (see the Competition Act guideline *Mergers and Ancillary Restrictions* for further detail);
- an agreement which would result in a concentration with a Community dimension and thereby be subject to the EC Merger Regulation;
- an agreement which is subject to competition scrutiny under the Financial Services Act 1986, the Companies Act 1989, the Broadcasting Act 1990, or the Environment Act 1995;
- an agreement which is required in order to comply with, and to the extent that it is, a planning obligation;
- an agreement which is the subject of a direction under section 21(2) of the Restrictive Trade Practices Act 1976;
- an agreement for the constitution of a European Economic Area regulated market, to the extent that it relates to the rules made or guidance issued by that market;
- an agreement made by an undertaking entrusted with the operation of services of general economic interest or of a revenue producing monopoly, insofar as the prohibition would obstruct the performance of those tasks (see the Competition Act guideline *General Economic Interest*);
- an agreement to the extent to which it is made to comply with a specified legal requirement;
- an agreement which is necessary to avoid conflict with international obligations and which is also the subject of an order by the Secretary of State;
- an agreement which is necessary for compelling reasons of public policy and which is also the subject of an order by the Secretary of State;
- an agreement which relates to a coal or steel product within the ECSC Treaty;
- an agreement where it relates to production of or trade in *'agricultural products'* as defined in the EC Treaty and in Council Regulation (EEC) No. 26/62, or to farmers' cooperatives;
- an agreement which constitutes a designated professional rule, imposes obligations arising from such a rule or constitutes an agreement to act in accordance with such rules.

5.2 The Secretary of State has the power to add, amend or remove exclusions in certain circumstances.

NOTES:
1. Where a merger falls within the ambit of the FTA 1973 it will not usually be subject to dual control under the CA 1998. Concerns were expressed during debate in the House of Lords that a wide exclusion of mergers would entail the risk of creating a loophole for anti-competitive agreements which might masquerade as mergers. Thus, the DGFT has power to claw back the benefit of the exclusion in para. 4 of Sch. 1 to the CA 1998.
2. A recent OFT report 'Competition in Professions' March 2001 OFT 328 proposes to revoke the Sch. 4 exclusion in respect of agreements constituting a designated professional rule from Chapter I; at para. 44.
3. The exclusion of vertical restraints from Chapter I of the CA 1998 was a key area of discussion during Parliamentary debate and a matter of some complexity for the government as it waited for the Community policy to be finalised. Ultimately, the government opted to exclude vertical agreements from the scope of the CA 1998 although a definition of a vertical agreement proved elusive. Thus, s. 50(1) states that the Secretary of State may by order provide for any provisions of Part 1 of the Act to apply to vertical agreements with such modifications as may be prescribed. The Competition Act 1998 (Land and Vertical Agreements) Exclusion Order 2000 SI 2000/310 (reproduced in full in Middleton, K., *UK and EC Competition Documents*, 2nd edn, Oxford, OUP at p. 219), which came into force the same day as the CA 1998, excludes all vertical agreements from the scope of the prohibition, although subject to a clawback provision. The treatment of vertical agreements under the Chapter I prohibition is discussed more fully in Chapter 5, and in OFT Guideline 419, Vertical agreements and restraints. The government discussed revoking the exclusion in its White Paper 'Productivity and Enterprise—A World Class Competition Regime', Cm 5233 (HMSO, July 2001), but the Enterprise Bill did not make any such provision.

NOTE: Land agreements do not generally give rise to competition concerns and the DGFT's Guideline on Land Agreements OFT 420 explains that the purpose of the Exclusion Order is to provide certainty for business concerning the scope of the Chapter I prohibition. There is no exclusion from the Chapter II prohibition for land agreements. What is meant by a land agreement?

OFT Guideline 420, Land Agreements

2.2 The Exclusion Order defines a *'land agreement'* in terms of:

- the creation, alteration, transfer or termination of an interest in land; and
- certain obligations and restrictions.

These elements are considered below.

Interest in land

2.3 A land agreement is defined in the Exclusion Order as an agreement which creates, alters, transfers or terminates an interest in land. Only agreements which have such results benefit from the exclusion. This includes, for example, transfers of freeholds, leases or assignments of leasehold interests and easements. The term *'interest in land'* is defined in the Exclusion Order. This covers what is usually understood to be an interest in land and includes licences, and, in Scotland, interests under a lease and other heritable rights in or over land including heritable securities. The exclusion also covers agreements to enter into land agreements.

2.4 The exclusion does not cover agreements which relate to land but which do not create, alter, transfer or terminate an interest in land. An agreement, for example, between landowners in a particular area to fix levels of rent to be charged to tenants or an agreement between tenants as to the nature of goods they will each sell in a particular area are not land agreements as defined in the

Exclusion Order because they do not create, alter, transfer or terminate an interest in land and therefore do not benefit from the exclusion.

FURTHER READING

Rodger, B.J., and MacCulloch, A., 'The Chapter I prohibition: Prohibiting Cartels, or Permitting Verticals? Or Both?', in *The UK Competition Act: A New Era for UK Competition Law*, Oxford, Hart Publishing, 2000.

SECTION 7: Consequences of infringement

A: Voidness

Section 2(4) CA 1998 provides, 'Any agreement or decision which is prohibited by subsection (1) is void'.

As is the case in Community law, only those elements of an agreement which are prohibited under s. 2 will be void, provided of course it is possible, as a matter of the general law of contract, to sever the offending clauses from the main body of the agreement. See the discussion of *Courage Ltd* v *Crehan* in Chapter 3, which decided that an agreement that infringes Article 81(1) EC is not only void and unenforceable, but is also illegal.

B: Sanctions

Financial penalties may be imposed for an infringement of Chapter I and these may be up to 10 per cent of annual turnover. The OFT Guideline 'Director General of Fair Trading's Guidance as to the Appropriate Amount of a Penalty' OFT 423 sets out how the amount is calculated and any mitigating circumstances to be considered. Penalties for infringement of either the Chapter I or Chapter II prohibition are discussed in Chapter 2.

The first cartel fine was handed out on 30 January 2002. The OFT imposed fines on FirstGroup plc and Arriva plc, two bus companies, for infringing the Chapter I prohibition by participating in a market-sharing cartel on certain routes. This was the first infringement decision made by the OFT under Chapter I. It was also the first occasion that the OFT had recourse to its Cartel Leniency Programme, under which companies participating in a cartel may benefit from immunity from fines in proportion to their cooperation before or during the OFT's investigation. The OFT decided that FirstGroup would benefit from a 100 per cent immunity from its fine for cooperating fully at an early stage. See OFT Press Release PN 6/02.

SECTION 8: **Requirement of consistency with Community law**

The overriding purpose of the CA 1998 is to harmonise domestic competition law with the Community model. This objective is articulated in s. 60(1) of the Act, the so-called 'Euro-clause', which seeks to:

> ensure that so far as is possible (having regard to any relevant differences between the provisions concerned), questions arising under this Part in relation to competition within the United Kingdom are dealt with in a manner which is consistent with the treatment of corresponding questions arising in Community law in relation to competition within the Community.

Where a question arises under Part I of the CA 1998, the competition authorities and the courts will be obliged to consider the Community position on the matter to ensure consistency; hence, the Act is deliberately silent on key terms and reference is to be made to the jurisprudence of the European Court and decisional practice of the Commission. OFT Guideline, The Chapter I prohibition explains how s. 60 will operate in practice.

OFT Guideline 401, The Chapter I prohibition

2.1 The Chapter I prohibition is modelled on Article 85. Section 60 of the Act sets out certain principles with a view to ensuring that the United Kingdom authorities handle cases in such a way as to ensure consistency with Community law. The Act therefore places a dual obligation on the United Kingdom authorities in considering and dealing with the application of the Chapter I prohibition. First, they must ensure that there is no inconsistency with either the principles laid down by the EC Treaty and the European Court or any relevant decision of the European Court. Secondly, the United Kingdom authorities must have regard to any relevant decision or statement of the European Commission. In the Director General's view this is limited to decisions or statements which have the authority of the European Commission as a whole, such as for example, decisions on individual cases under Article 85 and Article 86 of the EC Treaty. It would also include any clear statements which the European Commission has published about its policy approach in the Annual Report on Competition Policy.

2.2 The obligation to ensure consistency applies only to the extent that this is possible, having regard to any relevant differences between the provisions concerned. This means that there will be certain areas where the Community principles will not be relevant. For example the community single market objectives designed to establish a European common market would not be relevant to the domestic prohibition system.

2.3 The provisions of section 60 apply to all United Kingdom authorities which are involved with the administration and enforcement of the Act: the Director General, the Competition Commission and the domestic courts.

NOTE: A number of points merit consideration. Firstly, the enactment of the CA 1998 redefines the relationship between domestic law and Community law in competition matters and marks a significant shift in approach to statutory interpretation. The doctrine of supremacy is, of course, enshrined in Article 10 of the EC Treaty and is binding on the Member States; the enactment of the CA 1998 is, however, the first occasion in the United Kingdom in which the doctrine of supremacy has taken statutory form.

Secondly, the phrase 'in so far as is possible (having regard to any relevant differences between the relevant provisions concerned)' is clearly intended to permit departures from Community law. Lord Borrie explained the purpose of this phrase in Parliamentary debate: 'We have a structure, system and procedures which are not precisely the same as in the EU. Therefore, it is inevitable that one has to use words like "as far as possible" and others of that kind'. (Hansard, HL, 23 February 1998, col 515.) There are clear instances in which the Act intentionally departs from the Community model as Middleton explains:

Middleton, K., 'Harmonisation with Community Law—The Euro-clause', in Rodger, B.J., and MacCulloch, A. (eds), *The UK Competition Act: A New Era for UK Competition Law*

Oxford, Hart Publishing, 2000, pp. 26–29 [footnotes omitted]

. . . in a procedural context, the domestic appeal system is different from the Community system since appeals are not limited to the narrow judicial review-type grounds applicable to European Commission decisions. The Act is also silent regarding the availability of third party rights. Once again, the operation of the consistency principle will import the same right to sue that is available to parties under Articles 81 and 82 EC. Lord Haskel confirmed the Government's:

> clear intention in framing this [Bill] is that third parties may seek injunctions or damages in the courts if they have been adversely affected by the action of undertakings in breach of the prohibitions.

He went on to say: 'There is no need to make explicit provision in the Bill to achieve that result. Third party rights of action are to be the same as those under Articles 85 and 86'.

Section 60(6)(b) of the Act is also relevant in this context as it provides that decisions of the European Court and Commission on the question of the remedies available under Articles 81 and 82 EC will guide the UK courts in making a similar decision.

Further, section 30 of the Act confers a greater degree of legal professional privilege against production of documentation than exists under Community law. In contrast to the anomalous position in Community law, the Government has made it clear that legal privilege will extend to privileged communications between an in-house lawyer and the company. Privileged communications is defined in section 30 as being a communication 'between a professional legal adviser and his client' or 'made in connection with, or in contemplation of legal proceedings'. Any material that falls within this definition will not require to be produced to officials authorised by the Director General during an investigation.

An example of a 'relevant difference' that is intended to depart from Community law, is to be found in section 2(3), which provides that the prohibition set out in subsection (1) shall only apply 'if the agreement, decision or practice is, or intended to be, *implemented* in the United Kingdom'. The italicised phrase is an explicit reference to the European Court's decision in *Woodpulp*. Following the reasoning of the European Court in that case, it is possible that the Chapter I prohibition could be applied extra-territorially, where the agreement, having its origins outside the United Kingdom, is implemented within it. Although this is a much wider view of jurisdiction than UK practice currently follows the Government has made it clear that it does not wish to follow the Community position on the 'effects' doctrine. Lord Simon explained:

> by copying out the test in *Wood Pulp* on the face of the Bill, we are also ensuring that in the event that EC jurisprudence develops and creates a pure effects-doctrine, the application of the UK prohibitions will not follow suit.

It follows that where a domestic provision does not exactly mirror a Community definition the courts will have discretion to depart from established Community law. An analogy may be drawn from the experience of the Irish courts. The Irish Competition Act, which was introduced in 1991, is based closely on the Community model of competition legislation, although there are a number of explicit departures. For example, section 3(1) of the Act provides that:

> 'Undertaking' means a person being an individual, a body corporate or an unincorporated body of persons *engaged for gain* in the production, supply or distribution of goods or the provision of a service.

In *Deane* v *VHI*, the Supreme Court was asked to overturn the decision of the High Court which held that the defendant was not an undertaking within the meaning of section 3 of the Act. The issue was whether the defendant was a body corporate 'engaged for gain' in the supply of a service. The Court noted:

> the legislature in not adopting the general phrase 'undertaking', or any definition of it equivalent to that which has evolved in European Community law, but inserting into it the words 'engaged for gain', must be taken to have had a special purpose.

However, the court concluded that, whatever the intention of Parliament was in inserting the words 'engaged for gain' it could not have intended to exclude authorities or undertakings providing a public or national service whether or not the intention was to make profit. To exclude public authorities from the ambit of the Act, the court said, would mean that:

> the Act of 1991, so far from being a prohibition of distortion and abuse of dominant position by way of analogy to Articles 85 and 86, would be very extensively limited indeed, in its application of the provisions of those articles.

An analogous situation exists under section 2(1)(a) of the 1998 Act which provides that the Chapter I prohibition will only apply where 'trade is affected within the United Kingdom'. Since this test obviously departs from the Community test, which is linked to the goal of market integration, Community case law will not be determinative.

In addition to any 'relevant differences', which will be covered by section 60, there are several areas of the Act where divergence is intended. For example, the area of excluded agreements has no counterpart in Community law. Schedule 1 to the 1998 Act excludes agreements entered into as part of a merger; these will continue to be considered under the provisions of the Fair Trading Act 1973 or under the Merger Regulation (4064/89) where appropriate. Schedule 2 excludes certain agreements which are already subject to competition provisions in other domestic legislation, principally the Financial Services Act 1986, the Companies Act 1989, the Broadcasting Act 1990 and the Environment Act 1995. Other areas that are excluded include agreements concerning land, public undertakings, planning requirements or other legal requirements. The Secretary of State may also disapply the prohibitions to avoid conflict with international obligations or for exceptional or compelling reasons of public policy. Existing section 21(2) agreements under the Restrictive Trade Practices Act 1976 will also be excluded.

Section 60(2) and (3) provides that:

(2) At any time when the court determines a question arising under this Part, it must act (so far as is compatible with the provisions of this Part and whether or not it would otherwise be required to do so with a view to securing that there is no inconsistency between—
>> (a) the principles applied, and decision reached, by the court in determining that question; and
>> (b) the principles laid down by the Treaty and the European Court, and any relevant decision of that Court, as applicable at that time in determining any corresponding question arising in Community law.'

(3) The court must, in addition, have regard to any relevant decision or statement of the Commission.

NOTE: It is not obvious from s. 60(2) whether the obligation to ensure consistency with Community jurisprudence applies to general principles of Community law such as objectivity and proportionality. Reference to Hansard debates however confirms that the government's intention to import fundamental principles of Community law into the domestic regime extends beyond the substantive law, to include general procedural safeguards developed under Community law; for example, the rights against self-incrimination, the right to be heard and access to the file. Consider also the guarantees provided by the Human Rights Act 1998. Section 60(2) would not, however, appear to require consistency with the procedural practices of the Commission.

Section 60(3) does not impose a binding obligation on national courts to follow Commission decisions. Instead, the UK courts are merely to 'have regard' to statements, such as press releases, Policy Reports, Notices, and decisions. Comfort letters however, are regarded as sufficiently authoritative to constitute a statement of the Commission to which the Director General and courts are obliged to have regard.

Finally, there are risks in importing concepts from a supra-national system without proper consideration of the domestic context. Will Community case-law, which raises single market concerns, be regarded as 'corresponding', to any issues likely to arise under the domestic prohibitions? How will judges differentiate cases which are motivated by single market or other European policy considerations and hence not 'relevant' within the context of a national market? The next extract from Middleton notes the importance of the preliminary ruling procedure for national courts in discharging their obligation under s. 60(2).

Middleton, K., 'Harmonisation with Community Law—The Euro-clause', in *The UK Competition Act: A New Era for UK Competition Law*
pp. 33–37 [footnotes omitted]

Since the 1998 Act is a domestic statute, which does not fall within the European Court's jurisdiction, the competency of an Article 234 reference is, however, uncertain and merits detailed consideration.

First, it is clear from the text of Article 234 that the national courts may refer to the European Court any question of Community law, if clarification of that matter is essential to the determination of the case. Thus, in cases involving the application of Articles 81 and 82 EC before the national courts a request for a preliminary ruling would be competent. As a general rule, the European Court has no competence to interpret a provision of domestic law, or decide on the compatibility of domestic law with Community law. However, recent Community jurisprudence casts doubt on this position; particularly where a provision of national law is based on, or makes reference to, Community law.

The European Court, for instance, has recently held that it does have jurisdiction in appropriate circumstances to rule on the interpretation of provisions of national law. In *Bernd Giloy* v *Hauptzollamt Frankfurt am Main-Ost* the European Court stated:

> neither the wording of Article 177 nor the aim of the procedure established by that article indicates that the Treaty makers intended to exclude from the jurisdiction of the Court requests for a preliminary ruling on a Community provision where the domestic law of the Member State refers to [a] Community provision in order to determine the rules applicable to a situation which is purely internal to that State.

The Court went on to state:

> [it] has repeatedly held that it has jurisdiction to give preliminary rulings on questions concerning Community provisions in situations where the facts of the cases being considered by the national courts were outside the scope of Community law but where *those provisions had been rendered applicable either by domestic law* or merely by virtue of terms in a contract.

The European Court distinguished *Bernd Giloy* from its earlier judgment in *Kleinwort Benson Ltd* v *Glasgow City Council*. In that case the European Court declined a request from the English Court of Appeal for a preliminary ruling regarding the interpretation of Article 5(1) and (3) in Schedule 4 to the Civil Jurisdiction and Judgments Act 1982, which implemented the Brussels Convention on Jurisdiction and Judgments 1968. The Court noted:

> [while] certain provisions of the 1982 Act are taken almost word for word from the Convention, others depart from the wording of the corresponding Convention provision. That is true in particular of Article 5(3).

Thus, unlike the position in *Giloy*, and the *Dzodzi* cases, the provision of the Convention which the Court was asked to interpret in *Kleinwort Benson* had not been incorporated into domestic law. In addition, the Court noted:

> express provision was made in the Act for the authorities of the contracting State concerned to adopt modifications 'designed to produce divergence' between provisions of the Act and the corresponding provisions of the Convention.

Finally, the European Court observed that although the Civil Jurisdiction and Judgments Act 1982 provided in section 3(1) for questions of interpretation arising under the Brussels Convention to be decided consistently with Community case law, it was not a binding obligation and UK courts were merely to 'have regard' to Community principles when interpreting Schedule 4 provisions. Thus, the Court held that it could not give a preliminary ruling in *Kleinwort Benson* as its ruling would be advisory and not mandatory for UK courts.

Although the European Court has indicated that an *absolute* transposition of the relevant Community provision is necessary to ensure the competence of an Article 234 reference on matters wholly internal, the Court recently confirmed in *Oscar Bronner* v *Mediaprint* that:

> it is for the national courts alone which are seised of the case and are responsible for the judgment to be delivered to determine, in view of the special features of each case, both the need for a preliminary ruling in order to enable them to give their judgment and the relevance of the questions which they put to the Court. Consequently where the questions put by national courts concern the interpretation of a provision of Community law, the Court is, in principle, bound to give a ruling.

The Court then added that:

> Article 177 [234] of the Treaty, which is based on a clear separation of functions between a national court and this Court, does not allow this Court to review the reasons for which a reference is made.

In the key paragraph of its judgment the European Court states:

> the fact that a national court is dealing with a restrictive practices dispute by applying national competition law should not prevent it from making reference to the Court on the interpretation of Community law on the matter, and in particular on the interpretation of Article 86 of the Treaty in relation to that same situation, when it considers that a conflict between Community law and national law is capable of arising.

It is clear from its decisions in *Giloy* and *Oscar Bronner* that the European Court considers it is in the Community interest to ensure that Community provisions or concepts which have been transposed into domestic law are interpreted uniformly. Accordingly, the European Court seems favourably disposed to giving preliminary rulings on matters perceived to be wholly internal to a Member State. Further, unlike the case of *Kleinwort Benson* where the courts were merely to 'have regard' to Community jurisprudence under section 16(3) of the Civil Jurisdiction and Judgments Act 1982, section 60(2) of the 1998 Act obliges national courts to ensure consistency with Community law. On this basis, it is likely that the European Court will allow a request for a preliminary ruling where the national court requires clarification of a term directly transposed from Community law, for example, 'undertaking' or 'concerted practice'. Indeed, since the primary objective of section 60 is to ensure consistency with Community law, a preliminary ruling on 'corresponding' issues would be vital 'to ensure compliance with the rule of primacy of Community law and consequently, not to tolerate a situation in national law contrary to Community law'. Thus section 60 and Article 234 EC are complementary and will ensure Community law and UK law develop in parallel. It is only where the 1998 Act departs from Community law, for example, the requirement that trade is affected within the United Kingdom, and the matter would not be 'corresponding', that a preliminary ruling would not be competent.

None the less, the recent trend among Member States towards harmonisation with the Community rules may require the European Court to restrict the numbers of Article 234 references on grounds of expediency. The implications for the European Court's workload, should it be required to give preliminary rulings on provisions of national law in an enlarged Community, are obvious. Despite a dramatic upturn in its workload in recent years, the European Court has infrequently declined to exercise jurisdiction under Article 234. However, the UK courts have demonstrated a reluctance in the past to refer cases to Luxembourg and there is no indication that this will necessarily change when the 1998 Act comes into force. There is a concern that a reference merely results in unnecessary delay. Moreover, as judges gain expertise in competition matters, and confidence in their ability within the new regime, there may be a reduced need for national courts to refer questions to the European Court. It is doubtful in any case whether the potential overburdening of the European Court is a legitimate concern of the national courts.

NOTE: Section 60 acts as the cornerstone of the CA 1998 and marks the beginning of a new process of judicial interpretation in domestic law. Note however the remark made by the CCAT in GISC on the role of s. 60 at para. 215. 'In reaching that conclusion we bear in mind that, although s. 60 of the Act enjoins us to construe s. 2 consistently with Community law, our primary task, as a United Kingdom tribunal, is to construe the statute with which we are concerned.'

FURTHER READING

Willis, P.R., 'Procedural Nuggets from "The Klondike Clause": The Application of s. 60 of the Competition Act 1998 to the Procedures of the OFT' [1999] ECLR 314.

Nazerali, J., and Cowan, D., 'Importing the EU Model into the UK Competition Law: A Blueprint for Reform or a Step into "Euroblivion"?' [1999] ECLR 55.

Lord Borrie, 'Lawyers, Legislators and Lobbyists—the Making of the Competition Act 1998' [1999] JBL 205.

Rodger, B.J., 'Early Steps to a Mature Competition Law System: Case Law Developments in the First 18 Months of the Competition Act 1998' [2002] ECLR 52.

Barr, F., 'Has the UK gone European: is the European approach of the Competition Bill more than an illusion?' [1998] 3 ECLR 139.

SECTION 9: **The Enterprise Act**

In July 2001 the government published a White Paper (Cm 5233) 'A World Class Competition Regime', following an independent report by Sir Anthony Hammond QC and Roy Penrose OBE which recommended the adoption of US-style criminal sanctions for cartel perpetrators 'Proposed criminalisation of cartels in the UK', OFT 365 (HMSO, November 2001). The White Paper noted that the CA 1998 provides a sound basis for deterrence against inviduals and companies engaging in anti-competitive behaviour but that it fails to deter the most damaging form of anti-competitive behaviour—hard-core cartels. In March 2002, the government introduced the Enterprise Bill to Parliament which proposed the introduction of a new criminal offence for individuals involved in hard-core cartel activity. The Bill received Royal Assent on 6 November 2002 and the Competition Provisions will enter into force in May 2003. The criminal regime will coexist with the civil regime set out in s. 2 of the CA 1998. The government intends to provide a proper deterrent against cartels by allowing individuals to be prosecuted by the OFT. Imprisonment for up to five years of individuals will be possible, in addition to proceedings against companies and disqualification of company directors. The new criminal offence will be based on 'dishonesty' and the hard-core cartel activity will include price-fixing, bid-rigging, limitation of production and market sharing. Once in force, the UK will have one of the toughest competition regimes in the world; the transition from the pre-1997 regime, outlined at the beginning of this chapter, is remarkable.

The Enterprise Act 2002

Cartel offence

188 Cartel offence

(1) An individual is guilty of an offence if he dishonestly agrees with one or more other persons to make or implement, or to cause to be made or implemented, arrangements of the following kind relating to at least two undertakings (A and B).

(2) The arrangements must be ones which, if operating as the parties to the agreement intend, would—

(a) directly or indirectly fix a price for the supply by A in the United Kingdom (otherwise than to B) of a product or service,

(b) limit or prevent supply by A in the United Kingdom of a product or service,

(c) limit or prevent production by A in the United Kingdom of a product,

(d) divide between A and B the supply in the United Kingdom of a product or service to a customer or customers,

(e) divide between A and B customers for the supply in the United Kingdom of a product or service, or

(f) be bid-rigging arrangements.

(3) Unless subsection (2)(d), (e) or (f) applies, the arrangements must also be ones which, if operating as the parties to the agreement intend, would—

(a) directly or indirectly fix a price for the supply by B in the United Kingdom (otherwise than to A) of a product or service,

(b) limit or prevent supply by B in the United Kingdom of a product or service, or

(c) limit or prevent production by B in the United Kingdom of a product.

(4) In subsections (2)(a) to (d) and (3), references to supply or production are to supply or production in the appropriate circumstances (for which see section 189).

(5) 'Bid-rigging arrangements' are arrangements under which, in response to a request for

bids for the supply of a product or service in the United Kingdom, or for the production of a product in the United Kingdom—

(a) A but not B may make a bid, or

(b) A and B may each make a bid but, in one case or both, only a bid arrived at in accordance with the arrangements.

(6) But arrangements are not bid-rigging arrangements if, under them, the person requesting bids would be informed of them at or before the time when a bid is made.

(7) 'Undertaking' has the same meaning as in Part 1 of the 1998 Act.

189 Cartel offence: supplementary

(1) For section 188(2)(a), the appropriate circumstances are that A's supply of the product or service would be at a level in the supply chain at which the product or service would at the same time be supplied by B in the United Kingdom.

(2) For section 188(2)(b), the appropriate circumstances are that A's supply of the product or service would be at a level in the supply chain—

(a) at which the product or service would at the same time be supplied by B in the United Kingdom, or

(b) at which supply by B in the United Kingdom of the product or service would be limited or prevented by the arrangements.

(3) For section 188(2)(c), the appropriate circumstances are that A's production of the product would be at a level in the production chain—

(a) at which the product would at the same time be produced by B in the United Kingdom, or

(b) at which production by B in the United Kingdom of the product would be limited or prevented by the arrangements.

(4) For section 188(2)(d), the appropriate circumstances are that A's supply of the product or service would be at the same level in the supply chain as B's.

(5) For section 188(3)(a), the appropriate circumstances are that B's supply of the product or service would be at a level in the supply chain at which the product or service would at the same time be supplied by A in the United Kingdom.

(6) For section 188(3)(b), the appropriate circumstances are that B's supply of the product or service would be at a level in the supply chain—

(a) at which the product or service would at the same time be supplied by A in the United Kingdom, or

(b) at which supply by A in the United Kingdom of the product or service would be limited or prevented by the arrangements.

(7) For section 188(3)(c), the appropriate circumstances are that B's production of the product would be at a level in the production chain—

(a) at which the product would at the same time be produced by A in the United Kingdom, or

(b) at which production by A in the United Kingdom of the product would be limited or prevented by the arrangements.

190 Cartel offence: penalty and prosecution

(1) A person guilty of an offence under section 188 is liable—

(a) on conviction on indictment, to imprisonment for a term not exceeding five years or to a fine, or to both;

(b) on summary conviction, to imprisonment for a term not exceeding six months or to a fine not exceeding the statutory maximum, or to both.

(2) In England and Wales and Northern Ireland, proceedings for an offence under section 188 may be instituted only—

(a) by the Director of the Serious Fraud Office, or

(b) by or with the consent of the OFT.

(3) No proceedings may be brought for an offence under section 188 in respect of an agreement outside the United Kingdom, unless it has been implemented in whole or in part in the United Kingdom.

(4) Where, for the purpose of the investigation or prosecution of offences under section 188, the OFT gives a person written notice under this subsection, no proceedings for an offence under section 188 that falls within a description specified in the notice may be brought against that person in England and Wales or Northern Ireland except in circumstances specified in the notice.

191 Extradition

The offences to which an Order in Council under section 2 of the Extradition Act 1870 (c. 52) (arrangements with foreign states) can apply include—

(a) an offence under section 188,

(b) conspiracy to commit such an offence, and

(c) an attempt to commit such an offence.

Criminal investigations by OFT

192 Investigation of offences under section 188

(1) The OFT may conduct an investigation if there are reasonable grounds for suspecting that an offence under section 188 has been committed.

(2) The powers of the OFT under sections 193 and 194 are exercisable, but only for the purposes of an investigation under subsection (1), in any case where it appears to the OFT that there is good reason to exercise them for the purpose of investigating the affairs, or any aspect of the affairs, of any person ('the person under investigation').

193 Powers when conducting an investigation

(1) The OFT may by notice in writing require the person under investigation, or any other person who it has reason to believe has relevant information, to answer questions, or otherwise provide information, with respect to any matter relevant to the investigation at a specified place and either at a specified time or forthwith.

(2) The OFT may by notice in writing require the person under investigation, or any other person, to produce, at a specified place and either at a specified time or forthwith, specified documents, or documents of a specified description, which appear to the OFT to relate to any matter relevant to the investigation.

(3) If any such documents are produced, the OFT may—

(a) take copies or extracts from them;

(b) require the person producing them to provide an explanation of any of them.

NOTE: Not surprisingly, the cartel offence is controversial and a number of issues are unclear, not least the compatibility of the new criminal offence with the civil prohibition set out in Chapter I of the CA 1998. How will juries determine 'dishonesty'? Some of these issues are considered by Pickford, M., 'Introduction of a New Economic Crime', Competition Law Journal 1st edn, 2002 p. 35. There are also concerns arising from the interaction with substantive Community law. For example, is the proposal compatible with the Commission's Modernisation programme? Moreover, from a philosophical perspective, the introduction of US-style criminal sanctions does not sit comfortably alongside the alignment of UK competition law with the Community model. Finally, the phrase 'implement, or cause to be made or implemented' . . . in the UK suggests that the new offence will have extraterritorial effect, in contrast to the position under s. 2, CA 1998. See generally Joshua, J., 'A Sherman Act Bridgehead in Europe, or a Ghost Ship in Mid-Atlantic? A Close Look at the United Kingdom Proposals to Criminalise Hardcore Cartel Conduct' [2002] ECLR 231. On extraterritoriality generally, see Chapter 12.

The introduction of US-style sanctions is part of a growing trend in the Community and represents a commitment by the government to participate in the eradication of hard-core cartels at an international level. For example, the Irish Competition Amendement Act 1996 makes it a criminal offence under Irish competition law to enter into anti-competitive agreements (s. 2(2)) and to abuse a dominant position (s. 2(7)). France and Germany have similar criminal-type offences as do countries outside the Community, for example, Norway, Canada and Japan.

5

Article 81 EC

Introduction, Article 81 EC

Article 81 EC is concerned with collaborative behaviour between independent undertakings, the aim of which is to prevent, distort or restrict competition within the common market. An agreement which is caught by the prohibition in Article 81(1) EC is automatically null and void under Article 81(2) EC unless it merits an individual or block exemption in terms of the criteria set out in Article 81(3) EC. The Commission and the Court have applied Article 81 EC broadly in order to catch as much anti-competitive behaviour as possible. Article 81 EC is directly effective.

Article 81, EC

1. The following shall be prohibited as incompatible with the common market: all agreements between undertakings, decisions by associations of undertakings and concerted practices which may affect trade between Member States and which have as their object or effect the prevention, restriction or distortion of competition within the common market, and in particular those which:

   (a) directly or indirectly fix purchase or selling prices or any other trading conditions;
   (b) limit or control production, markets, technical development, or investment;
   (c) share markets or sources of supply;
   (d) apply dissimilar conditions to equivalent transactions with other trading parties, thereby placing them at a competitive disadvantage;
   (e) make the conclusion of contracts subject to acceptance by the other parties of supplementary obligations which, by their nature or according to commercial usage, have no connection with the subject of such contracts.

2. Any agreements or decisions prohibited pursuant to this Article shall be automatically void.

3. The provisions of paragraph 1 may, however, be declared inapplicable in the case of:
   — any agreement or category of agreements between undertakings;
   — any decision or category of decisions by associations of undertakings;
   — any concerted practice or category of concerted practices;

which contributes to improving the production or distribution of goods or to promoting technical or economic progress, while allowing consumers a fair share of the resulting benefit, and which does not:

   (a) impose on the undertakings concerned restrictions which are not indispensable to the attainment of these objectives;

(b) afford such undertakings the possibility of eliminating competition in respect of a substantial part of the products in question.

NOTE: The Community rules concerning the control of anti-competitive agreements have been inimical to the achievement of market integration. The drafters of the EC Treaty recognised that undertakings might erect their own barriers to trade and seek to maintain their position in a market by concluding agreements with actual or potential competitors situated in other Member States. According to the Court, Article 81 EC is 'a fundamental provision which is essential for the accomplishment of the tasks entrusted to the Community and, in particular, the functioning of the internal market'. See Case C-126/97 *Eco Swiss China Time* v *Benetton International* [1999] ECR I-3055 at 3092. Single market concerns have played a crucial part in the development of the Court's jurisprudence and sometimes this formalistic approach has been to the detriment of economic efficiency considerations. An appreciation of the tension between market integration and economic efficiency, and the close relationship between the Community competition rules and the free movement of goods, begins with the Court's seminal judgment in the following case:

Etablissements Consten SA and Grundig GmbH v Commission
(Cases 56 & 58/64) [1966] ECR 299, [1966] CMLR 418

Consten, a French distributor entered into an agreement with Grundig, a major manufacturer in West Germany of electrical and electronic products. Grundig agreed to supply only Consten in France and to ensure that its customers outside France were restrained from delivering the contract goods into France. Grundig granted exclusive rights to Grundig's trade mark GINT in France. In return, Consten agreed not to re-export Grundig products into any of the other Member States. This was an exclusive dealing agreement which conferred absolute territorial protection in France on Consten. Later, Consten discovered that UNEF, another French firm, had obtained Grundig's products from sources in another Member State and was selling them in France at a lower price than Consten. Consten sought to stop the resale of these goods and brought an action in the French courts against UNEF, the parallel importer, for unfair competition and infringement of its trade mark. UNEF complained to the Commission that the exclusive dealing agreement between Consten and Grundig breached Article 81(1) EC. The Commission decided that the agreement was unlawful under Article 81(1) EC because it segregated national markets, and refused to grant an exemption as the absolute territorial protection granted was not indispensable. Both parties appealed to the Court for an annulment of the Commission's decision under Article 230(4) (ex 173(2) EEC). Note that the case refers to Article 85 EC, now Article 81.

The Court ruled, in part, as follows:

The complaints concerning the applicability of Article 85(1) to sole distributorship contracts
The applicants submit that the prohibition in Article 85(1) applies only to so-called horizontal agreements. The Italian Government submits furthermore that sole distributorship contracts do not constitute 'agreements between undertakings' within the meaning of that provision, since the parties are not on a footing of equality. With regard to these contracts, freedom of competition may only be protected by virtue of Article 86 of the Treaty.

Neither the wording of Article 85 nor that of Article 86 gives any ground for holding that distinct areas of application are to be assigned to each of the two Articles according to the level in the economy at which the contracting parties operate. Article 85 refers in a general way to all agreements which distort competition within the Common Market and does not lay down any distinction between those agreements based on whether they are made between competitors operating at the same level in the economic process or between non-competing persons operating at different levels. In principle, no distinction can be made where the Treaty does not make any distinction.

Furthermore, the possible application of Article 85 to a sole distributorship contract cannot be excluded merely because the grantor and the concessionnaire are not competitors *inter se* and not on a footing of equality. Competition may be distorted within the meaning of Article 85(1) not only by agreements which limit it as between the parties, but also by agreements which prevent or restrict the competition which might take place between one of them and third parties. For this purpose, it is irrelevant whether the parties to the agreement are or are not on a footing of equality as regards their position and function in the economy. This applies all the more, since, by such an agreement, the parties might seek, by preventing or limiting the competition of third parties in respect of the products, to create or guarantee for their benefit an unjustified advantage at the expense of the consumer or user, contrary to the general aims of Article 85.

It is thus possible that, without involving an abuse of a dominant position, an agreement between economic operators at different levels may affect trade between Member States and at the same time have as its object or effect the prevention, restriction or distortion of competition, thus falling under the prohibition of Article 85(1).

In addition, it is pointless to compare on the one hand the situation, to which Article 85 applies, of a producer bound by a sole distributorship agreement to the distributor of his products with on the other hand that of a producer who includes within his undertaking the distribution of his own products by some means, for example, by commercial representatives, to which Article 85 does not apply. These situations are distinct in law and, moreover, need to be assessed differently, since two marketing organizations, one of which is integrated into the manufacturer's undertaking whilst the other is not, may not necessarily have the same efficiency. The wording of Article 85 causes the prohibition to apply, provided that the other conditions are met, to an agreement between several undertakings. Thus it does not apply where a sole undertaking integrates its own distribution network into its business organization. It does not thereby follow, however, that the contractual situation based on an agreement between a manufacturing and a distributing undertaking is rendered legally acceptable by a simple process of economic analogy—which is in any case incomplete and in contradiction with the said Article. Furthermore, although in the first case the Treaty intended in Article 85 to leave untouched the internal organization of an undertaking and to render it liable to be called in question, by means of Article 86, only in cases where it reaches such a degree of seriousness as to amount to an abuse of a dominant position, the same reservation could not apply when the impediments to competition result from agreement between two different undertakings which then as a general rule simply require to be prohibited.

Finally, an agreement between producer and distributor which might tend to restore the national divisions in trade between Member States might be such as to frustrate the most fundamental objections of the Community. The Treaty, whose preamble and content aim at abolishing the barriers between States, and which in several provisions gives evidence of a stern attitude with regard to their reappearance, could not allow undertakings to reconstruct such barriers. Article 85(1) is designed to pursue this aim, even in the case of agreements between undertakings placed at different levels in the economic process.

The submissions set out above are consequently unfounded.

The complaints relating to the concept of 'agreements . . . which may affect trade between Member States'

The applicants and the German Government maintain that the Commission has relied on a mistaken interpretation of the concept of an agreement which may affect trade between Member States and has not shown that such trade would have been greater without the agreement in dispute.

The defendant replies that this requirement in Article 85(1) is fulfilled once trade between Member States develops, as a result of the agreement, differently from the way in which it would have done without the restriction resulting from the agreement, and once the influence of the agreement on market conditions reaches a certain degree. Such is the case here, according to the defendant, particularly in view of the impediments resulting within the Common Market from the disputed agreement as regards the exporting and importing of Grundig products to and from France.

The concept of an agreement 'which may affect trade between Member States' is intended to define, in the law governing cartels, the boundary between the areas respectively covered by Community law and national law. It is only to the extent to which the agreement may affect trade between Member States that the deterioration in competition caused by the agreement falls under the prohibition of Community law contained in Article 85; otherwise it escapes the prohibition.

In this connexion, what is particularly important is whether the agreement is capable of constituting a threat, either direct or indirect, actual or potential, to freedom of trade between Member States in a manner which might harm the attainment of the objectives of a single market between States. Thus the fact that an agreement encourages an increase, even a large one, in the volume of trade between States is not sufficient to exclude the possibility that the agreement may 'affect' such trade in the abovementioned manner. In the present case, the contract between Grundig and Consten, on the one hand by preventing undertakings other than Consten from importing Grundig products into France, and on the other hand by prohibiting Consten from re-exporting those products to other countries of the Common Market, indisputably affects trade between Member States. These limitations on the freedom of trade, as well as those which might ensue for third parties from the registration in France by Consten of the GINT trade mark, which Grundig places on all its products, are enough to satisfy the requirement in question.

Consequently, the complaints raised in this respect must be dismissed.

The complaints concerning the criterion of restriction on competition

The applicants and the German Government maintain that since the Commission restricted its examination solely to Grundig products the decision was based upon a false concept of competition and of the rules on prohibition contained in Article 85(1), since this concept applies particularly to competition between similar products of different makes; the Commission, before declaring Article 85(1) to be applicable, should, by basing itself upon the 'rule of reason', have considered the economic effects of the disputed contrast upon competition between the different makes. There is a presumption that vertical sole distributorship agreements are not harmful to competition and in the present case there is nothing to invalidate that presumption. On the contrary, the contract in question has increased the competition between similar products of different makes.

The principle of freedom of competition concerns the various stages and manifestations of competition. Although competition between producers is generally more noticeable than that between distributors of products of the same make, it does not thereby follow that an agreement tending to restrict the latter kind of competition should escape the prohibition of Article 85(1) merely because it might increase the former.

Besides, for the purpose of applying Article 85(1), there is no need to take account of the concrete effects of an agreement once it appears that it has as its object the prevention, restriction or distortion of competition.

Therefore the absence in the contested decision of any analysis of the effects of the agreement on competition between similar products of different makes does not, of itself, constitute a defect in the decision.

It thus remains to consider whether the contested decision was right in founding the prohibition of the disputed agreement under Article 85(1) on the restriction on competition created by the agreement in the sphere of the distribution of Grundig products alone. The infringement which was found to exist by the contested decision results from the absolute territorial protection created the said contract in favour of Consten on the basis of French law. The applicants thus wished to eliminate any possibility of competition at the wholesale level in Grundig products in the territory specified in the contrast essentially by two methods.

First, Grundig undertook not to deliver even indirectly to third parties products intended for the area covered by the contract. The restrictive nature of that undertaking is obvious if it is considered in the light of the prohibition on exporting which was imposed not only on Consten but also on all the other sole concessionnaires of Grundig, as well as the German wholesalers. Secondly, the registration in France by Consten of the GINT trade mark, which Grundig affixes to all its products, is intended to increase the protection inherent in the disputed agreement, against the risk of parallel imports into France of Grundig products, by adding the protection deriving from the law on industrial property rights. Thus no third party could import Grundig products from other Member States of the Community for resale in France without running serious risks.

The defendant properly took into account the whole distribution system thus set up by Grundig. In order to arrive at a true representation of the contractual position the contract must be placed in the economic and legal context in the light of which it was concluded by the parties. Such a procedure is not to be regarded as an unwarrantable interference in legal transactions or circumstances which were not the subject of the proceedings before the Commission.

The situation as ascertained above results in the isolation of the French market and makes it possible to charge for the products in question prices which are sheltered from all effective competition. In addition, the more producers succeed in their efforts to render their own makes of product individually distinct in the eyes of the consumer, the more the effectiveness of competition between producers tends to diminish. Because of the considerable impact of distribution costs on the aggregate cost price, it seems important that competition between dealers should also be stimulated. The efforts of the dealer are stimulated by competition between distributors of products of the same make. Since the agreement thus aims at isolating the French market for Grundig products and maintaining artificially, for products of a very well-known brand, separate national markets within the Community, it is therefore such as to distort competition in the Common Market.

It was therefore proper for the contested decision to hold that the agreement constitutes an infringement of Article 85(1). No further considerations, whether of economic data (price differences between France and Germany, representative character of the type of appliance considered, level of overheads borne by Consten) or of the corrections of the criteria upon which the Commission relied in its comparisons between the situations of the French and German markets, and no possible favourable effects of the agreement in other respects, can in any way lead, in the face of abovementioned restrictions, to a different solution under Article 85(1).

NOTES:
1. The Court's judgment confirms that market integration lies at the heart of Article 81 EC. According to the Court, the object and effect of the agreement was to compartmentalise the French market '[making] it possible to charge for the products in question prices which are sheltered from all effective competition'. (Paras 342–3.)

   The Court also emphatically rejected claims that Article 81(1) EC only applies to horizontal agreements between parties operating at the same level of the economy and confirmed that vertical agreements between parties operating at different levels and not in direct competition with each other constitute an 'agreement between undertakings'. This part of the judgment attracted particular criticism. Although the exclusivity restrictions had the effect of tying Consten to Grundig in an exclusive dealing agreement and in turn, isolating the French market for the contract goods, French consumers were previously unable to obtain Grundig products in France. The arrangement enabled penetration of a new market which had been previously closed to German products and therefore contrary to the Court's conclusions, it was arguable that the agreement in fact encouraged competition and market integration. Furthermore, critics of the Court's judgment consider that the existence of market power is the real issue in these circumstances and point to the fact that inter-brand competition would prevent Grundig's products from being sold at a high price. In a subsequent case, Case 56/65 *Société Technique Minière (STM)*, the Court confirmed that market analysis is not necessary where the object of the agreement is clearly to restrict competition. It seems the Court will not countenance *absolute* territorial protection but may accept partial exclusivity where this is necessary to penetrate a new market. The issues raised in these cases, and subsequent developments are considered more generally in Chapter 5.

2. Three years later in Case 5/69 *Völk* v *Vervaecke* [1969] CMLR 273, the Court decided that an exclusive distribution agreement conferring absolute territorial protection fell outside the prohibition in Article 81(1) because of the small market share held by both parties. See p. 186, below.

SECTION 2: The elements of Article 81 EC

The simplest way to understand how Article 81 EC operates is to consider each element in turn.

A: Undertakings

The term used in Community competition law to describe commercial enterprises is 'undertakings'. The same term is also used in Article 82 EC and the Court has consistently held that the term has the same meaning in both contexts. The Court has, as in many other areas, given the term a broad meaning to maximise the scope of competition law. It will include any natural or legal person carrying on a commercial activity in the goods and services sector.

Polypropylene
[1986] OJ L 230/1, [1998] 4 CMLR 347, Commission decision

The subjects of [EC] competition rules are undertakings, a concept which is not identical with the question of legal personality for the purposes of company law or fiscal law. The term 'undertaking' is not defined in the Treaty. It may however refer to any entity engaged in commercial activities . . .

NOTE: Clearly this is a broad interpretation and has been confirmed by the Court in C-41/90 *Höfner and Elser* v *Macroton* [1991] ECR I-1979 to include 'every entity engaged in an economic activity regardless of the legal status of the entity and the way in which it is financed' (para. 21). The absence of a profit motive is irrelevant provided there is evidence of a commercial or economic activity being pursued. Does the definition extend to public authorities? The case-law has focused on whether the entity concerned carries out functions of an economic nature or performs an essential function of the state. In *Höfner*, the Court classified the German federal public employment agency, as an undertaking because it deemed employment procurement to be an economic activity. See also C-364/92 *SAT Fluggesellschaft* v *Eurocontrol* [1994] ECR I-43, [1994] 5 CMLR 208, paras 19–32 and Case-C343/95 *Diego Cali* v *SEPG* [1997] ECR I-1547, [1997]

5 CMLR 484, paras 22–23 in which the Court considered whether a private limited company entrusted with anti-pollution surveillance by the Genoese national port authority could constitute an undertaking for the purposes of Article 81 EC. The term undertaking also embraces entities concerned with the supply of goods or the provision of services for example, individuals (opera singers *RAI* v *UNITEL* [1978] OJ L157/39), professional bodies (Case C-221/99 *Conte* v *Rossi* 2001 I-9359) and even football associations e.g. *FIFA* (distribution of package tours during the 1990 World Cup) OJ 1992 L326/31. Can employees be regarded as undertakings? It appears from the Court's jurisprudence that the term undertaking does not include employees acting in their capacity as employees. However, trade unions and employees carrying on a business independently of their employer but in connection with that business have been held to be undertakings—see e.g. Case C-22/98 *Jean Claude Becu* [1999] ECR I-5665, paras 26 and 27.

B: Economic entity principle

Generally, Article 81(1) EC will only apply to the activities of two or more independent undertakings. The question of independence becomes an issue when companies belonging to the same group and having the status of parent and subsidiary are involved. In these circumstances the traditional definition of legal personality is irrelevant.

Béguelin Import v *GL Import-Export*
(Case 22/71) [1971] ECR 949, [1972] CMLR 81

Béguelin was the exclusive importer for WIN pocket lighters in Belgium and France. In 1967 a French subsidiary of Béguelin took over the concession for France. GL Import-Export imported a quantity of WIN lighters into France and were challenged by Béguelin. In defence, GL Import-Export claimed that the agreement between Béguelin and its French subsidiary was void under Article 81 EC. That argument was dependent upon whether Béguelin and its subsidiary were separate undertakings.

[5] A—The first question first seeks to establish whether, when a parent company established in a Member State and holder of an exclusive concession granted to it in respect of two Member States, grants to its subsidiary or allows it to acquire the exclusive concession in the second Member State, the prohibition in Article 85(1) applies in so far as the exclusive concession covers the territory of the said State.

[6] If the answer is in the affirmative, the question then seeks to establish what would be the consequences of infringement of the Treaty on the validity of the concession granted to the said subsidiary.

[7] Article 85(1) prohibits agreements which have as their object or effect an impediment to competition.

[8] This is not the position in the case of an exclusive sales agreement when in fact the concession granted under that agreement is in part transferred from the parent company to a subsidiary which, although having separate legal personality, enjoys no economic independence.

[9] Accordingly the relationship between the companies cannot be taken into account in determining the validity of an exclusive dealing agreement entered into between the subsidiary and a third party.

NOTE: This doctrine has become known as the 'economic entity' doctrine and makes clear that legally separate entities can be considered to be the same undertaking if they operate as a single entity on a market.

Viho Europe BV v *Commission*
(Case T-102/92) [1995] ECR II-17, [1997] 4 CMLR 469

Viho lodged complaints with the Commission about Parker Pen's distribution system which heavily utilised its subsidiary companies. Again the independence of the subsidiary companies was the key to Viho's complaint.

[47] As regards the appraisal under Article 85(1) of the Treaty of agreements concluded within a group of companies, the Court of Justice has held that 'where a subsidiary does not enjoy real autonomy in determining its course of action in the market, the prohibitions set out in Article 85(1) may be considered inapplicable in the relationship between it and the parent company with which it forms one economic unit' (judgment in Case 48/69 *ICI* v *Commission* [1972] ECR 619, paragraph 134). Similarly, in its judgment in *Ahmed Saeed Flugreisen and Others*, cited above, paragraph 35, the Court of Justice held that 'Article 85 does not apply where the concerted practice in question is between undertakings belonging to a single group as parent company and subsidiary if those undertakings form an economic unit within which the subsidiary has no real freedom to determine its course of action on the market' and added that '[h]owever, the conduct of such a unit on the market is liable to come within the ambit of Article 86'. It also follows from the case-law of the Court of First Instance that Article 85(1) of the Treaty refers only to relations between economic entities which are capable of competing with one another and does not cover agreements or concerted practices between undertakings belonging to the same group if the undertakings form an economic unit (judgment in Joined Cases T-68/89, T-77/89 and T-78/89 *SIV and Others* v *Commission* [1992] ECR II-1403, paragraph 357).

[48] It is not disputed in this case that Parker owns 100 per cent of the capital of its subsidiaries established in Germany, France, Belgium and the Netherlands. It is also apparent from the description given by Parker of the operation of its subsidiary companies, which the applicant has not disputed, that the sales and marketing activities of the subsidiaries are directed by an area team which is appointed by the parent company and which controls, in particular, sales targets, gross margins, sales costs, cash flow and stocks. That area team also lays down the range of products to be sold, monitors advertising and issues directives concerning prices and discounts.

[49] Consequently, the Court concludes that, in point 2 of its decision, the Commission correctly classifies the Parker group as 'one economic unit within which the subsidiaries do not enjoy real autonomy in determining their course of action in the market'.

[50] The Court of Justice has also held that 'in competition law, the term "undertaking" must be understood as designating an economic unit for the purpose of the subject-matter of the agreement in question even if in law that economic unit consists of several persons, natural or legal' (judgment in Case 170/83 *Hydrotherm* v *Compact* [1984] ECR 2999, paragraph 11). Similarly, the Court of First Instance has held that 'Article 85(1) of the EEC Treaty is aimed at economic units which consist of a unitary organization of personal, tangible and intangible elements which pursues a specific economic aim on a long-term basis and can contribute to the commission of an infringement of the kind referred to in that provision' (judgment in Case T-11/89 *Shell* v *Commission* [1992] ECR II-757, paragraph 311). Therefore, for the purposes of the application of the competition rules, the unified conduct on the market of the parent company and its subsidiaries takes precedence over the formal separation between those companies as a result of their separate legal personalities.

[51] It follows that, where there is no agreement between economically independent entities, relations within an economic unit cannot amount to an agreement or concerted practice between

undertakings which restricts competition within the meaning of Article 85(1) of the Treaty. Where, as in this case, the subsidiary, although having a separate legal personality, does not freely determine its conduct on the market but carries out the instructions given to it directly or indirectly by the parent company by which it is wholly controlled, Article 85(1) does not apply to the relationship between the subsidiary and the parent company with which it forms an economic unit.

NOTE: In deciding whether one undertaking is truly autonomous from another, it is necessary to examine its different aspects of independence including its financial and managerial independence. Wils suggests that the determinative factor is the degree of control.

Wils, W.P.J., 'The Undertaking as a Subject of EC Competition Law and the Imputation of Infringements to Natural or Legal Persons'
(2000) 25 ELRev 99, p 103

The distinctive characteristic of the firm is thus the existence of authority or the power to exercise control over people and physical assets. Employment relationships and ownership of physical assets usually provide the legal basis for such power, as they allow the employer-owner to direct human and physical assets. To some extent direction of inputs also takes place in the marketplace. An agreement for the provision of services by one firm to another may give the latter some specific control rights over some of the former's assets. A firm, however, is character-ised by the more general, residual control over physical assets and over the actions of employees.

Given that the use of authority and the price system are alternative coordination mechanisms, firms have a choice as to how much they rely on the one or the other. The choice is in fact a double one. First, firms can choose whether to produce certain goods or services in-house or rather to purchase them from other firms across a market. This choice will be made on the basis of a comparison of the respective costs of both options. Secondly, firms may decide to make some use of the market mechanism in their internal organization. Separate departments or divisions may supply one another as a result either of instructions from a higher authority or of what resemble market transactions between them. Some kinds of market may thus exist within firms, in that some transac-tions within the firm are coordinated by the price mechanism. However, as long as there is a higher authority which has the power to direct the departments' or divisions' operations, such markets within the firm can only exist by the grace of that higher authority, which wants this form of internal organization to exist and which could always interfere with it. The situation is thus quite different from market transactions between independent firms.

QUESTION

Wils concludes that 'for the purposes of competition law undertakings are to be identified with "economic units" rather than legal units'. Do you agree?

C: Agreements, decisions of associations and concerted practices

These terms essentially overlap with each other. Provided some form of collusion is identifiable, the Commission has not expressed any concern with categorising the 'arrangement' as an agreement, decision or concerted practice; the Court tends to agree. For example, the term 'agreement' encapsulates a broad range of behaviour and is not restricted to legally binding and enforceable agreements, as this would make it straightforward for undertakings to evade the prohibition. In the following case the Court held that so-called gentlemen's agreements fell within Article 81(1) EC. The case is commonly known as *Quinine*.

ACF Chemiefarma NV v *Commission*
(Case 41/69) [1970] ECR 661

I—The status and duration of the gentlemen's agreement
[106] The applicant complains that the Commission considered that the export agreement relating to trade with third countries and the gentlemen's agreement governing the conduct of its members in the Common Market constituted an indivisible entity as far as Article 85 was concerned.

[107] The applicant states that the gentlemen's agreement, unlike the export agreement, did not constitute an agreement within the meaning of Article 85(1) and in any event it definitively ceased to exist from the end of October 1962.

[108] The conduct of the parties to the export agreement does not in the applicant's view indicate that they continued the restrictions on competition which were originally provided for in the gentlemen's agreement.

[109] The opposite conclusions reached by the contested decision are therefore alleged to be vitiated because they are based on incorrect findings.

[110] The gentlemen's agreement, which the applicant admits existed until the end of October 1962, had as its object the restriction of competition within the Common Market.

[111] The parties to the export agreement mutually declared themselves willing to abide by the gentlemen's agreement and concede that they did so until the end of October 1962.

[112] This document thus amounted to the faithful expression of the joint intention of the parties to the agreement with regard to their conduct in the Common Market.

[113] Furthermore it contained a provision to the effect that infringement of the gentlemen's agreement would *ipso facto* constitute an infringement of the export agreement.

[114] In those circumstances account must be taken of this connexion in assessing the effects of the gentlemen's agreement with regard to the categories of acts prohibited by Article 85(1).

[115] The defendant bases its view that the gentlemen's agreement was continued until February 1965 on documents and declarations emanating from the parties to the agreement the tenor of which is indistinct and indeed contradictory so that it is impossible to conclude whether those undertakings intended to terminate the gentlemen's agreement at their meeting on 29 October 1962.

[116] The conduct of the undertakings in the Common Market after 29 October 1962 must therefore be considered in relation to the following four points: sharing out of domestic markets, fixing of common prices, determination of sales quotas and prohibition against manufacturing synthetic quinidine.

II—Protection of the producers' domestic markets
[117] The gentlemen's agreement guaranteed protection of each domestic market for the producers in the various Member States.

[118] After October 1962 when significant supplies were delivered on one of those markets by producers who were not nationals, as for example in the case of sales of quinine and quinidine in France, there was a substantial alignment of prices conforming to French domestic prices which were higher than the export prices to third countries.

[119] It does not appear that there were alterations in the insignificant volume of trade between the other Member States referred to by the clause relating to domestic protection in spite of considerable differences in the prices prevailing in each of those States.

[120] The divergences between the domestic legislation of those States cannot by itself explain those differences in price or the substantial absence of trade.

[121] Obstacles which might arise in the trade in quinine and quinidine from differences between national legislation governing pharmaceutical products under trademark cannot relevantly be invoked to explain those facts.

[122] The correspondence exchanged in October and November 1963 between the parties to the export agreement with regard to the protection of domestic markets merely confirmed the intention of those undertakings to allow this state of affairs to remain unchanged.

[123] This intention was subsequently confirmed by Nedchem during the meeting of the undertakings concerned in Brussels on 14 March 1964.

[124] From those circumstances it is clear that with regard to the restriction on competition arising from the protection of the producers' domestic markets the producers continued after the meeting on 29 October 1962 to abide by the gentlemen's agreement of 1960 and confirmed their common intention to do so.

[125] The applicant maintains that owing in particular to the shortage of raw materials the sharing out of domestic markets, as emerges from the exchange of letters of October and November 1963, had no effect on competition in the Common Market.

[126] Despite the scarcity of raw materials and an increase in the demand for the products in question, as the contested decision finds, a serious threat of shortage nevertheless emerged only in 1964 as a result of the interruption of Nedchem's supplies from the American General Service Administration.

[127] On the other hand such a situation cannot render lawful an agreement the object of which is to restrict competition in the Common Market and which affects trade between the Member States.

[128] The sharing out of domestic markets has as its object the restriction of competition and trade within the Common Market.

[129] The fact that, if there were a threatened shortage of raw materials, such an agreement might in practice have had less influence on competition and on international trade than in a normal period in no way alters the fact that the parties did not terminate their activities.

[130] Furthermore the applicant has furnished no conclusive evidence capable of proving that it had ceased to act in accordance with the agreement before the date of expiry of the export agreement.

[131] Consequently, the submissions concerning that part of the decision relating to the continuation of the agreement on the protection of the producers' domestic markets until the beginning of February 1965 are unfounded.

NOTE: Whish suggests that 'in a particular case, linguistically it is more natural to use one term than the other, but legally nothing turns on the distinction: the important distinction is between collusive and non-collusive behaviour', *Competition Law*, 4th edn, p. 78. See also Case 209/78 etc. *Van Landewyck* v *Commission* [1980] ECR 3125, [1981] 3 CMLR 134 *per* Advocate General Reischl at pp. 3310 and 185 respectively. This assertion seems to be supported firstly, by the Commission in *Cartonboard* 94/601 (1994) OJ L74/21 at para. 128, where the Commission states that '. . . it may not even be feasible or realistic to make any such distinction' and secondly, by the Court of First Instance in the following case:

Rhone-Poulenc SA v Commission (Polypropylene)
(Case T-1/89) [1991] ECR II-867

The Commission had carried out an investigation of a complex cartel in the petrochemicals sector involving 15 undertakings. The agreement was not in writing and instead comprised a series of oral, non-binding arrangements with no enforceable sanctions. Not all of the undertakings attended each meeting and those that did, did not always fully participate in discussions.

(c) Assessment by the Court

[118] It must be stated first of all that the question whether the Commission was obliged to characterize each factual element found against the applicant either as an agreement or a concerted practice within the meaning of Article 85(1) of the EEC Treaty is irrelevant. It is apparent from the second paragraph of point 80, the third paragraph of point 81 and the first paragraph of point 82 of the Decision, read together, that the Commission characterized each of those different elements primarily as an 'agreement'.

[119] It is likewise apparent from the second and third paragraphs of point 86, the third paragraph of point 87 and point 88 of the Decision, read together, that the Commission in the alternative characterized the elements of the infringement as 'concerted practices' where those elements either did not enable the conclusion to be drawn that the parties had reached agreement in advance on a common plan defining their action on the market but had adopted or adhered to collusive devices which facilitated the coordination of their commercial behaviour, or did not, owing to the complexity of the cartel, make it possible to establish that some producers had expressed their definite assent to a particular course of action agreed by the others, although they had indicated their general support for the scheme in question and conducted themselves accordingly. The Decision thus concludes that in certain respects the continuing cooperation and collusion of the producers in the implementation of an overall agreement may display the characteristics of a concerted practice.

[120] Since it is clear from the case-law of the Court of Justice that in order for there to be an agreement within the meaning of Article 85(1) of the EEC Treaty it is sufficient that the undertakings in question should have expressed their joint intention to conduct themselves on the market in a specific way (see the judgment in Case 41/69 *ACF Chemiefarma NV* v *Commission* [1970] ECR 661, paragraph 112, and the judgment in Joined Cases 209 to 215 and 218/78 *Heintz van Landewyck Sàrl* v *Commission* [1980] ECR 3125, paragraph 86), this Court holds that the Commission was entitled to treat the common intentions existing between the applicant and other polypropylene producers, which the Commission has proved to the requisite legal standard and which related to target prices for the period from July to December 1979 and sales volume targets for 1979 and 1980, as agreements within the meaning of Article 85(1) of the EEC Treaty.

[121] For a definition of the concept of concerted practice, reference must be made to the case-law of the Court of Justice, which shows that the criteria of coordination and cooperation previously laid down by that Court must be understood in the light of the concept inherent in the competition provisions of the EEC Treaty according to which each economic operator must determine independently the policy which he intends to adopt on the common market. Although this requirement of independence does not deprive economic operators of the right to adapt themselves intelligently to the existing and anticipated conduct of their competitors, it does, however, strictly preclude any direct or indirect contact between such operators the object or effect whereof is either to influence the conduct on the market of an actual or potential competitor or to disclose to such a competitor the course of conduct which they themselves have decided to adopt or contemplate adopting on the market (judgment in Joined Cases 40 to 48, 50, 54 to 56, 111, 113 and 114/73 *Suiker Unie and Others* v *Commission*, cited above, paragraphs 173 and 174).

[122] In the present case, the applicant participated in meetings concerning the fixing of price and sales volume targets during which information was exchanged between competitors about the prices they wished to see charged on the market, the prices they intended to charge, their profitability thresholds, the sales volume restrictions they judged to be necessary, their sales figures or the identity of their customers. Through its participation in those meetings, it took part, together with its

competitors, in concerted action the purpose of which was to influence their conduct on the market and to disclose to each other the course of conduct which each of the producers itself contemplated adopting on the market.

[123] Accordingly, not only did the applicant pursue the aim of eliminating in advance uncertainty about the future conduct of its competitors but also, in determining the policy which it intended to follow on the market, it could not fail to take account, directly or indirectly, of the information obtained during the course of those meetings. Similarly, in determining the policy which they intended to follow, its competitors were bound to take into account, directly or indirectly, the information disclosed to them by the applicant about the course of conduct which the applicant itself had decided upon or which it contemplated adopting on the market.

[124] The Commission was therefore justified, in the alternative, having regard to their purpose, in categorizing the EATP meeting of 22 November 1977 in which the applicant participated and the regular meetings of polypropylene producers in which the applicant participated between the end of 1978 or the beginning of 1979 and the end of 1980 as concerted practices within the meaning of Article 85(1) of the EEC Treaty.

NOTE: Moreover, it seems that the Commission and the Court are not prepared to absolve certain members of a cartel who express reservations about whether or not to participate in the agreed course of action. The Court of First Instance recently confirmed that an undertaking may be held responsible for a cartel even though it only participated in one of some of its constituent parts if it can be shown that it was aware of an overall plan to distort competition. See the CFI's judgment in Cases T-305/94 etc. *Limburgse Vinyl Maatschappij NV v Commission* [1999] ECR II-931, [1999] 5 CMLR 303, para. 773 (appeal pending). Expressions of reservation may, however, go some way towards mitigating any fine. See e.g. *Amino Acids*, Commission decision, paras 363–365. See also the Commission's Whistleblowing Guidelines. The existence of structural crisis cartels will not absolve guilt, but may substantially reduce any fine. See e.g. *Trefileurope Sales v Commission* [1995] ECR II-791 at para. 177.

D: Decisions by associations of undertakings

At first glance, it is difficult to appreciate why decisions by associations of undertakings where they restrict competition are prohibited given the wide interpretation of concerted practice. However, the difficulties faced by the Commission in proving a concerted practice, as we shall discover below, makes it easier to establish the existence of a decision by an association of undertakings. Undertakings often participate through the auspices of either a trade or professional association set up to represent their interests. The actual form of the decision is not important; what is crucial is the potential limits placed on the freedom of action of an association's members. A good example of how the decision of a trade association might affect competition in a market is COAPI.

Commission Decision 95/188
OJ L122/37, 1995 5 CMLR 468

[33] The Coapi, which incorporates all industrial property agents in Spain, therefore constitutes an association of undertakings within the meaning of Article 85(1) of the EC Treaty. The fact that it forms a professional association to which the public authorities have entrusted certain functions for the regulation of the profession and that in Spanish law it forms a legal person governed by public law, does not prevent Coapi from being regarded as an association of undertakings.

[34] The Coapi Regulations (which are concerned with both the establishment of the Coapi and its rules of procedure) form in their origins an agreement between undertakings. They were adopted by a meeting of industrial property agents. Subsequently, the general meeting of the Coapi has modified these regulations several times. Therefore, it follows from this that the Coapi Regulations also constitute a decision by an association of undertakings within the meaning of Article 85(1) of the EC Treaty.

[35] Likewise, the acts of the Coapi's general meeting and of its administrative board in fixing prices, which were adopted under the Coapi Regulations, constitute decisions by associations of undertakings within the meaning of Article 85(1). These acts are binding on all members and the Coapi ensures that they are applied, employing its power to impose penalties (fines and other sanctions extending to expulsion from the Coapi).

NOTE: Often, the trade association itself can act as a cloak, shielding the anti-competitive practices of its members. Thus, the Court has held that the constitution of a trade association in itself can amount to a decision for the purposes of Article 81 EC, see e.g. *National Sulphuric Acid Association* OJ [1980] L 260/24.

E: Concerted practices

The inclusion in Article 81 EC (1) of the term 'concerted practice' was designed to catch more informal means of cooperation. Although the Court infrequently differentiates an agreement from a concerted practice since both are caught by Article 81(1) EC, it is nevertheless crucial to distinguish collusion from genuine (and legitimate) parallel behaviour, particularly in an oligopolistic market. However, as we shall see, distinguishing parallel behaviour which is genuine from that which is not, is not always an easy task, the essential difficulty being one of proof. The Court expounded its famous definition of a concerted practice in the following case. The case is better known as the *Dyestuffs* case.

ICI v *Commission*
(Case 48/69) [1972] ECR 619, [1972] CMLR 557

On a number of occasions between 1964 and 1967, ten major producers of dyestuffs who held 80 per cent of the market for dyes sold in the Community, announced price rises of about 10 per cent. Telexed messages were sent from parent companies to their subsidiaries all within the space of an hour, and all containing similar wording. The Commission held that there was a concerted practice which contravened Article 81(1) EC and imposed heavy fines.

The concept of a concerted practice
[64] Article 85 draws a distinction between the concept of 'concerted practices' and that of 'agreements between undertakings' or of 'decisions by associations of undertakings'; the object is to bring within the prohibition of that article a form of coordination between undertakings which, without having reached the stage where an agreement properly so-called has been concluded, knowingly substitutes practical cooperation between them for the risks of competition.

[65] By its very nature, then, a concerted practice does not have all the elements of a contract but may *inter alia* arise out of coordination which becomes apparent from the behaviour of the participants.

[66] Although parallel behaviour may not by itself be identified with a concerted practice, it may however amount to strong evidence of such a practice if it leads to conditions of competition which do not correspond to the normal conditions of the market, having regard to the nature of the products, the size and number of the undertakings, and the volume of the said market.

[67] This is especially the case if the parallel conduct is such as to enable those concerned to attempt to stabilize prices at a level different from that to which competition would have led, and to consolidate established positions to the detriment of effective freedom of movement of the products in the Common Market and of the freedom of consumers to choose their suppliers.

[68] Therefore the question whether there was a concerted action in this case can only be correctly determined if the evidence upon which the contested decision is based is considered, not in isolation, but as a whole, account being taken of the specific features of the market in the products in question.

The characteristic features of the market in dyestuffs

[69] The market in dyestuffs is characterized by the fact that 80 per cent of the market is supplied by about ten producers, very large ones in the main, which often manufacture these products together with other chemical products or pharmaceutical specialities.

[70] The production patterns and therefore the cost structures of these manufacturers are very different, and this makes it difficult to ascertain competing manufacturers' costs.

[71] The total number of dyestuffs is very high, each undertaking producing more than a thousand.

[72] The average extent to which these products can be replaced by others is considered relatively good for standard dyes, but it can be very low or even non-existent for speciality dyes.

[73] As regards speciality products, the market tends in certain cases towards an oligopolistic situation.

[74] Since the price of dyestuffs forms a relatively small part of the price of the final product of the user undertaking, there is little elasticity of demand for dyestuffs on the market as a whole and this encourages price increases in the short term.

[75] Another factor is that the total demand for dyestuffs is constantly increasing, and this tends to induce producers to adopt a policy enabling them to take advantage of this increase.

[76] In the territory of the Community, the market in dyestuffs in fact consists of five separate national markets with different price levels which cannot be explained by differences in costs and charges affecting producers in those countries.

[77] Thus the establishment of the Common Market would not appear to have had any effect on this situation, since the differences between national price levels have scarcely decreased.

[78] On the contrary, it is clear that each of the national markets has the characteristics of an oligopoly and that in most of them price levels are established under the influence of a 'priceleader', who in some cases is the largest producer in the country concerned, and in other cases is a producer in another Member State or a third State, acting through a subsidiary.

[79] According to the experts this dividing-up of the market is due to the need to supply local technical assistance to users and to ensure immediate delivery, generally in small quantities, since, apart from exceptional cases, producers supply their subsidiaries established in the different Member States and maintain a network of agents and depots to ensure that user undertakings receive specific assistance and supplies.

[80] It appears from the data produced during the course of the proceedings that even in cases where a producer establishes direct contact with an important user in another Member State, prices are usually fixed in relation to the place where the user is established and tend to follow the level of prices on the national market.

[81] Although the foremost reason why producers have acted in this way is in order to adapt themselves to the special features of the market in dyestuffs and to the needs of their customers, the fact remains that the dividing-up of the market which results tends, by fragmenting the effects of competition, to isolate users in their national market, and to prevent a general confrontation between producers throughout the Common Market.

[82] It is in this context, which is peculiar to the way in which the dyestuffs market works, that the facts of the case should be considered.

[83] The increases of 1964, 1965 and 1967 covered by the contested decision are interconnected.

[84] The increase of 15 per cent in the prices of most aniline dyes in Germany on 1 January 1965 was in reality nothing more than the extension to another national market of the increase applied in January 1964 in Italy, the Netherlands, Belgium and Luxembourg.

[85] The increase in the prices of certain dyes and pigments introduced on 1 January 1965 in all the Member States, except France, applied to all the products which had been excluded from the first increase.

[86] The reason why the price increase of 8 per cent introduced in the autumn of 1967 was raised to 12 per cent for France was that there was a wish to make up for the increases of 1964 and 1965 in which that market had not taken part because of the price control system.

[87] Therefore the three increases cannot be isolated one from another, even though they did not take place under identical conditions.

[88] In 1964 all the undertakings in question announced their increases and immediately put them into effect, the initiative coming from Ciba-Italy which, on 7 January 1964, following instructions from Ciba-Switzerland, announced and immediately introduced an increase of 15 per cent. This initiative was followed by the other producers on the Italian market within two or three days.

[89] On 9 January ICI Holland took the initiative in introducing the same increase in the Netherlands, whilst on the same day Bayer took the same initiative on the Belgo-Luxembourg market.

[90] With minor differences, particularly between the price increases by the German undertakings on the one hand and the Swiss and United Kingdom undertakings on the other, these increases concerned the same range of products for the various producers and markets, namely, most aniline dyes other than pigments, food colourings and cosmetics.

[91] As regards the increase of 1965 certain undertakings announced in advance price increases amounting, for the German market, to an increase of 15 per cent for products whose prices had already been similarly increased on the other markets, and to 10 per cent for products whose prices had not yet been increased. These announcements were spread over the period between 14 October and 28 December 1964.

[92] The first announcement was made by BASF, on 14 October 1964, followed by an announcement by Bayer on 30 October and by Casella on 5 November.

[93] These increases were simultaneously applied on 1 January 1965 on all the markets except for the French market because of the price freeze in that State, and the Italian market where, as a result of the refusal by the principal Italian producer, ACNA, to increase its prices on the said market, the other producers also decided not to increase theirs.

[94] ACNA also refrained from putting its prices up by 10 per cent on the German market.

[95] Otherwise the increase was general, was simultaneously introduced by all the producers mentioned in the contested decision, and was applied without any differences concerning the range of products.

[96] As regards the increase of 1967, during a meeting held at Basel on 19 August 1967, which was attended by all the producers mentioned in the contested decision except ACNA, the Geigy under-

taking announced its intention to increase its selling prices by 8 per cent with effect from 16 October 1967.

[97] On that same occasion the representatives of Bayer and Francolor stated that their undertakings were also considering an increase.

[98] From mid-September all the undertakings mentioned in the contested decision announced a price increase of 8 per cent raised to 12 per cent for France, to take effect on 16 October in all the countries except Italy, where ACNA again refused to increase its prices, although it was willing to follow the movement in prices on two other markets, albeit on dates other than 16 October.

[99] Viewed as a whole, the three consecutive increases reveal progressive cooperation between the undertakings concerned.

[100] In fact, after the experience of 1964, when the announcement of the increases and their application coincided, although with minor differences as regards the range of products affected, the increases of 1965 and 1967 indicate a different mode of operation. Here, the undertakings taking the initiative, BASF and Geigy respectively, announced their intentions of making an increase some time in advance, which allowed the undertakings to observe each other's reactions on the different markets, and to adapt themselves accordingly.

[101] By means of these advance announcements the various undertakings eliminated all uncertainty between them as to their future conduct and, in doing so, also eliminated a large part of the risk usually inherent in any independent change of conduct on one or several markets.

[102] This was all the more the case since these announcements, which led to the fixing of general and equal increases in prices for the markets in dyestuffs, rendered the market transparent as regard the precentage rates of increase.

[103] Therefore, by the way in which they acted, the undertakings in question temporarily eliminated with respect to prices some of the preconditions for competition on the market which stood in the way of the achievement of parallel uniformity of conduct.

[104] The fact that this conduct was not spontaneous is corroborated by an examination of other aspects of the market.

[105] In fact, from the number of producers concerned it is not possible to say that the European market in dyestuffs is, in the strict sense, an oligopoly in which price competition could no longer play a substantial role.

[106] These producers are sufficiently powerful and numerous to create a considerable risk that in times of rising prices some of them might not follow the general movement but might instead try to increase their share of the market by behaving in an individual way.

[107] Furthermore, the dividing-up of the Common Market into five national markets with different price levels and structures makes it improbable that a spontaneous and equal price increase would occur on all the national markets.

[108] Although a general, spontaneous increase on each of the national markets is just conceivable, these increases might be expected to differ according to the particular characteristics of the different national markets.

[109] Therefore, although parallel conduct in respect of prices may well have been an attractive and risk-free objective for the undertakings concerned, it is hardly conceivable that the same action could be taken spontaneously at the same time, on the same national markets and for the same range of products.

[110] Nor is it any more plausible that the increases of January 1964, introduced on the Italian market and copied on the Netherlands and Belgo-Luxembourg markets, which have little in common

with each other either as regards the level of prices or the pattern of competition, could have been brought into effect within a period of two to three days without prior concertation.

[111] As regards the increases of 1965 and 1967 concertation took place openly, since all the announcements of the intention to increase prices with effect from a certain date and for a certain range of products made it possible for producers to decide on their conduct regarding the special cases of France and Italy.

[112] In proceeding in this way, the undertakings mutually eliminated in advance any uncertainties concerning their reciprocal behaviour on the different markets and thereby also eliminated a large part of the risk inherent in any independent change of conduct on those markets.

[113] The general and uniform increase on those different markets can only be explained by a common intention on the part of those undertakings, first, to adjust the level of prices and the situation resulting from competition in the form of discounts, and secondly, to avoid the risk, which is inherent in any price increase, of changing the conditions of competition.

NOTE: The coverage of Article 81 EC to the forms of practical cooperation discussed in *Dyestuffs* was expanded in the *'Sugar Cartel'* case. Various sugar producers argued that they had not participated in a concerted practice, contrary to Article 81 EC, as there was no plan to do so. The Court concluded that the absence of a plan was not detrimental to a finding of concertation, provided there was some form of mental consensus betweeen the parties.

Cooperative Vereniging 'Suiker Unie' v Commission
(Cases 40–48, 50, 54–56, 111 and 113–14/73) [1975] ECR 663, [1976] 1 CMLR 295

[173] The criteria of coordination and cooperation laid down by the case-law of the Court, which in no way require the working out of an actual plan, must be understood in the light of the concept inherent in the provisions of the Treaty relating to competition that each economic operator must determine independently the policy which he intends to adopt on the common market including the choice of the persons and undertakings to which he makes offers or sells.

[174] Although it is correct to say that this requirement of independence does not deprive economic operators of the right to adapt themselves intelligently to the existing and anticipated conduct of their competitors, it does however strictly preclude any direct or indirect contact between such operators, the object or effect whereof is either to influence the conduct on the market of an actual or potential competitor or to disclose to such a competitor the course of conduct which they themselves have decided to adopt or contemplate adopting on the market.

NOTE: Two points arise from the Court's jurisprudence. First the question of proof. The Commission and the Court have been criticised for relying on seemingly circumstantial evidence, for example, contemporaneous price rises. In *Dyestuffs*, the Court was persuaded by the discovery of telexed instructions by different undertakings to subsidiary companies on the same evening. Is this circumstantial evidence? Was there any other evidence that the Commission relied upon? The extract from the following case illustrates how the Court considers faxes, internal memoranda and telephone calls to prove the existence of a concerted practice.

Van Megen Sports v Commission
(Case T-49/95) [1996] ECR II-1799

Findings of the Court
[34] The applicant does not deny that Tretorn operated a system of exclusive distribution coupled with a prohibition of exports and with mechanisms intended to ensure that that prohibition was applied as effectively as possible. It acknowledges that it has been Tretorn's exclusive distributor in the Netherlands since 1985. It denies, on the other hand, that Tretorn imposed an export ban on *it*

and that *it* participated in the reporting and investigating of parallel imports. Until the Commission initiated the infringement procedure, it had not even been aware of the ban on parallel exports.

[35] According to the case-law of the Court of Justice and the Court of First Instance, the provisions of Article 85(1) of the Treaty may not be declared inapplicable to an exclusive distribution contract which does not in itself include a prohibition of re-exports of the products which are the subject of the contract, where the contracting parties are engaged in a concerted practice aimed at restricting parallel imports intended for an unauthorized dealer (see Case 86/82 *Hasselblad* v *Commission* [1984] ECR 883 and Case T-43/92 *Dunlop Slazenger* v *Commission* [1994] ECR II-441, paragraph 88).

[36] In the present case, the Commission had relied on the following two documents, described in points 24 and 25 of the Decision, as proof that the applicant had taken part in the Netherlands in the reporting and investigating of parallel imports:

— a fax of 16 July 1987 from Mr M of Tretorn to Mr A of Tretorn AB:

I just had a phone call from Will Van Megen to advise that XL boxes of 4 again turning up in a major shoe chain in Holland.

I have asked Will to forward the Code No to [Mr O] so that he can advise which country has shipped.

While I of course suspect our friends, we must wait for the proof.

If it is the UK, then obviously the shipment has been made to Holland in the past few weeks.

— a Tretorn internal memorandum of 20 June 1988 from Mr M to Mr O:

Please ring Will Van Megen. He has parallel from two different sources.

1 Box of 4, made in Ireland, no date code yet.

2 Box of 4, USTA approved, no date code yet.

He hopes to have date codes in a few days.

[37] Those two documents from Tretorn have probative force. As the Commission rightly observed, they were written by a well-informed third party who had no reason to give false information. Moreover, they were written outside the context of any procedure for defence or justification before the Commission or this Court.

[38] Those two pieces of evidence clearly establish that the applicant participated in the reporting and investigating of parallel imports of tennis balls, for the purposes of applying Tretorn's policy. It is clear from the fax of 16 July 1987 that the applicant informed Tretorn of the existence of parallel imports of Tretorn tennis balls in the Netherlands, that it was not the first time that it gave Tretorn such information, and that it had been asked to provide the date codes which might enable Tretorn to determine the country from which the balls came. As to the internal memorandum of 20 June 1988, that document shows that the applicant again informed Tretorn of the existence of parallel imports of Tretorn tennis balls in the Netherlands, that it had identified two different sources of those imports, and that it was investigating to obtain the date codes.

[39] With respect to the Tretorn internal memorandum of 23 August 1988, mentioned at point 46 of the Decision, recommending the stopping of deliveries to the American market because tennis balls delivered there were reappearing in the Netherlands via parallel imports, it is sufficient to observe that the Commission did not rely on that document with regard to the applicant. Point 46 of the

Decision comes under the heading 'Suspension of supplies to prevent parallel imports', under which the Commission mentions the measures adopted by Tretorn to deal with those imports. That document is thus relied on as against Tretorn, and not the applicant, in whose case the Commission rightly considered that it had sufficient evidence.

[40] As to the date codes, the fax of 16 July 1987, the internal memorandum of 20 June 1988 and the other evidence relied on by the Commission in the Decision (see points 36 to 38 and 40) show beyond doubt that Tretorn could identify the origin of parallel imports from the date codes. That can be seen in particular from a fax of 17 April 1987 from Tretorn to Formula Sport International Ltd (see point 37), in which Mr M of Tretorn stated: 'The date codes are all from the shipment to Formula.' It can also be seen from a fax of 15 May 1987, also from Tretorn to Formula Sport International Ltd, in which Mr M states: 'We are sure of our facts/date codes and the balls shipped to Formula ended up in Switzerland. . . . Formula is guilty so let's not have any more discussion'.

[41] As for the letter from Scapino, that document does not in any way contradict the Commission's evidence. The applicant could not itself prevent the parallel imports by Scapino. Had it wished to prevent them, it would have had to contact Tretorn, so that that company might take the necessary measures for that purpose. Moreover, it was naturally in the applicant's interest to sell as many Tretorn tennis balls as possible, to Scapino amongst others. It should also be noted that Tretorn's policy was to prohibit exports. There is nothing before the Court to suggest that Scapino would have exported the Tretorn tennis balls supplied by the applicant. The applicant therefore did not infringe Tretorn's policy by selling the balls to Scapino, which, like the applicant, is a Netherlands undertaking. Tretorn thus had no interest either in asking the applicant to refuse to supply Scapino, even assuming that it had been informed of those sales.

[42] The reasons given by the applicant to explain why it made reports to Tretorn cannot be accepted. If the applicant had wished to make those reports solely in order to find out whether Tretorn was making direct supplies to customers in the Netherlands and to strengthen its position in negotiations with Tretorn and thereby obtain a better price, it would not have needed to try to obtain the date codes of the tennis balls imported in parallel. It is thus apparent that it was in fact aware of Tretorn's policy of prohibiting parallel imports. It follows that the Commission was correct in finding, in point 70 of the Decision, that even if the interpretation given by the applicant was correct, 'the fact remains that the information was given in the context of a ban on parallel exports of which Van Megen was well aware and it actively participated in identifying the source of the parallel imports'.

[43] The applicant cannot, finally, argue that its two telephone conversations with Tretorn cannot be described as active participation, since it was the applicant which took the initiative in contacting Tretorn, not vice versa. Moreover, it can be seen from paragraph 38 above that the applicant made inquiries to obtain the date codes of the parallel imports. It follows that the applicant actively participated in Tretorn's policy.

[44] It follows from the foregoing that the pleas in law alleging that the Commission did not adduce sufficient evidence and did not give an adequate statement of reasons for its decision must be rejected.

F: Oligopoly as a defence

The second issue to arise from the Court's jurisprudence concerns behaviour which may in fact be a normal consequence of an oligopolistic market. As Furse explains '[I]n such a situation it is not the fact that prices have risen at the same time, by possibly the same level, that will induce condemnation under Article 81(1). The task of the Commission is to show that this has been achieved by other than the operation of normal market forces—it is the method, and not the result, that is being condemned' (*Competition Law of the UK and EC*, 2nd edn, Blackstone Press, 2000, p. 115). There is clearly a very fine line between innocent parallel behaviour, which is acceptable and indeed commercially prudent, and the 'knowing substitution of practical cooperation for the risks of competition'. This was exactly the difficulty faced by the Commission in the next case, better known as *Wood Pulp*. This important case confirms the importance of using economic analysis, where other means of proof may be impracticable or impossible, and the merits of obtaining expert economic advice.

A Ahlström Oy v *Commission*
(Cases C-89, 104, 114, 116, 117 and 125–29/85) [1993] ECR I-1307, [1993] 4 CMLR 407

The Commission concluded that 43 undertakings producing bleached sulphate pulp, used in the manufacture of fine quality paper, had participated in a concerted practice. The Commission based its findings partly on evidence of direct and indirect exchanges of information amongst the producers which had led to a situation whereby prices were announced in advance and followed quickly by similar announcements from competitors. The Commission concluded that 'the parallel conduct . . . following a proper economic analysis, cannot be explained as independently chosen parallel conduct in a narrow oligopolistic situation . . .' On appeal, the Court emphatically rejected the main thrust of the Commission's argument. The importance of the Court's judgment necessitates a lengthy extract.

A. The system of quarterly price announcements constitutes in itself the infringement of Article 85 of the Treaty

[59] According to the Commission's first hypothesis, it is the system of quarterly price announcements in itself which constitutes the infringement of Article 85 of the Treaty.

[60] First, the Commission considers that that system was deliberately introduced by the pulp producers in order to enable them to ascertain the prices that would be charged by their competitors in the following quarters. The disclosure of prices to third parties, especially to the press and agents working for several producers, well before their application at the beginning of a new quarter gave the other producers sufficient time to announce their own, corresponding, new prices before that quarter and to apply them from the commencement of that quarter.

[61] Secondly, the Commission considers that the implementation of that mechanism had the effect of making the market artificially transparent by enabling producers to obtain a rapid and accurate picture of the prices quoted by their competitors.

[62] In deciding on that point, it must be borne in mind that Article 85(1) of the Treaty prohibits all agreements between undertakings, decisions by associations of undertakings and concerted practices which may affect trade between Member States and which have as their object or effect the prevention, restriction or distortion of competition within the Common Market.

[63] According to the Court's judgment in *Suiker Unie* (cited above, at paragraphs 26 and 173), a concerted practice refers to a form of coordination between undertakings which, without having been taken to the stage where an agreement properly so-called has been concluded, knowingly substitutes for the risks of competition practical cooperation between them. In the same judgment, the Court added that the criteria of coordination and cooperation must be understood in the light of the concept inherent in the provisions of the Treaty relating to competition that each economic

operator must determine independently the policy which he intends to adopt on the Common Market.

[64] In this case, the communications arise from the price announcements made to users. They constitute in themselves market behaviour which does not lessen each undertaking's uncertainty as to the future attitude of its competitors. At the time when each undertaking engages in such behaviour, it cannot be sure of the future conduct of the others.

[65] Accordingly, the system of quarterly price announcements on the pulp market is not to be regarded as constituting in itself an infringement of Article 85(1) of the Treaty.

B. The infringement arises from concertation on announced prices
[66] In the second hypothesis, the Commission considers that the system of price announcements constitutes evidence of concertation at an earlier stage. In paragraph 82 of its decision, the Commission states that, as proof of such concertation, it relied on the parallel conduct of the pulp producers in the period from 1975 to 1981 and on different kinds of direct or indirect exchange of information.

[67] It follows from paragraphs 82 and 107 to 110 of the decision that the parallel conduct consists essentially in the system of quarterly price announcements, in the simultaneity or near-simultaneity of the announcements and in the fact that announced prices were identical. It is also apparent from the various telexes and documents referred to in paragraph 61 *et seq.* of the decision that meetings and contacts took place between certain producers with a view to exchanging information on their respective prices.

1. The telexes referred to in paragraph 61 et seq. of the decision
[68] In its questions of 6 March and 2 May 1990, the Court requested the Commission to specify what precise conclusions it drew from the telexes and documents referred to in paragraph 61 *et seq.* of its decision, that is to say to state between which producers the concertation established by each telex or document took place and for what period. In reply to that question, the Commission stated that those documents merely substantiated the evidence based on parallel conduct and that, accordingly, they were relevant not only as regards the undertakings and the period specifically mentioned therein but also as regards all the undertakings and the entire duration of the parallel conduct.

[69] In the light of that reply, those documents must be excluded from consideration. Since the identity of the persons taking part in concertation is one of the constituents of the infringement, it is impossible to rely as evidence of that infringement on documents whose probative value in that respect the Commission has been unable to specify.

2. The other evidence adduced by the Commission
[70] Since the Commission has no documents which directly establish the existence of concertation between the producers concerned, it is necessary to ascertain whether the system of quarterly price announcements, the simultaneity or near-simultaneity of the price announcements and the parallelism of price announcements as found during the period from 1975 to 1981 constitute a firm, precise and consistent body of evidence of prior concertation.

[71] In determining the probative value of those different factors, it must be noted that parallel conduct cannot be regarded as furnishing proof of concertation unless concertation constitutes the only plausible explanation for such conduct. It is necessary to bear in mind that, although Article 85 of the Treaty prohibits any form of collusion which distorts competition, it does not deprive economic operators of the right to adapt themselves intelligently to the existing and anticipated conduct of their competitors (see the judgment in *Suiker Unie*, cited above, paragraph 174).

[72] Accordingly, it is necessary in this case to ascertain whether the parallel conduct alleged by the Commission cannot, taking account of the nature of the products, the size and the number of the

undertakings and the volume of the market in question, be explained otherwise than by concertation.

(a) The system of price announcements

[73] As stated above, the Commission regards the system of quarterly price announcements as evidence of concertation at an earlier stage.

[74] In their pleadings, on the other hand, the applicants maintain that the system is ascribable to the particular commercial requirements of the pulp market.

[75] By orders of 25 October 1990 and 14 March 1991, the Court requested two experts to examine the characteristics of the market for bleached sulphate pulp during the period covered by the contested decision. Their report sets out the following considerations.

[76] The experts observe first that the system of announcements at issue must be viewed in the context of the long-term relationships which existed between producers and their customers and which were a result both of the method of manufacturing the pulp and of the cyclical nature of the market. In view of the fact that each type of paper was the result of a particular mixture of pulps having their own characteristics and that the mixture was difficult to change, a relationship based on close cooperation was established between the pulp producers and the paper manufacturers. Such relations were all the closer since they also had the advantage of protecting both sides against the uncertainties inherent in the cyclical nature of the market: they guaranteed security of supply to buyers and at the same time security of demand to producers.

[77] The experts point out that it is in the context of those long-term relationships that, after the Second World War, purchasers demanded the introduction of that system of announcements. Since pulp accounts for between 50 per cent and 75 per cent of the cost of paper, those purchasers wished to ascertain as soon as possible the prices which they might be charged in order to estimate their costs and to fix the prices of their own products. However, as those purchasers did not wish to be bound by a high fixed price in the event of the market weakening, the announced price was regarded as a ceiling price below which the transaction price could always be renegotiated.

[78] The explanation given for the use of a quarterly cycle is that it is the result of a compromise between the paper manufacturers' desire for a degree of foreseeability as regards the price of pulp and the producers' desire not to miss any opportunities to make a profit in the event of a strengthening of the market.

[79] The US dollar was, according to the experts, introduced on the market by the North American producers during the 1960s. That development was generally welcomed by purchasers who regarded it as a means of ensuring that they did not pay a higher price than their competitors.

(b) The simultaneity or near-simultaneity of announcements

[80] In paragraph 107 of its decision, the Commission claims that the close succession or even simultaneity of price announcements would not have been possible without a constant flow of information between the undertakings concerned.

[81] According to the applicants, the simultaneity or near-simultaneity of the announcements—even if it were established—must instead be regarded as a direct result of the very high degree of transparency of the market. Such transparency, far from being artificial, can be explained by the extremely well-developed network of relations which, in view of the nature and the structure of the market, have been established between the various traders.

[82] The experts have confirmed that analysis in their report and at the hearing which followed.

[83] First, they pointed out, a buyer was always in contact with several pulp producers. One reason for that was connected with the paper-making process, but another was that, in order to avoid becoming overdependent on one producer, pulp buyers took the precaution of diversifying their

sources of supply. With a view to obtaining the lowest possible prices, they were in the habit, especially in times of falling prices, of disclosing to their suppliers the prices announced by their competitors.

[84] Secondly, it should be noted that most of the pulp was sold to a relatively small number of large paper manufacturers. Those few buyers maintained very close links with each other and exchanged information on changes in prices of which they were aware.

[85] Thirdly, several producers who made paper themselves purchased pulp from other producers and were thus informed, in times of both rising prices and falling prices, of the prices charged by their competitors. That information was also accessible to producers who did not themselves manufacture paper but were linked to groups that did.

[86] Fourthly, that high degree of transparency in the pulp market resulting from the links between traders or groups of traders was further reinforced by the existence of agents established in the Community who worked for several producers and by the existence of a very dynamic trade press.

[87] In connection with the latter point, it should be noted that most of the applicants deny having communicated to the trade press any information on their prices and that the few producers who acknowledged having done so point out that such communications were sporadic and were made at the request of the press itself.

[88] Finally, it is necessary to add that the use of rapid means of communication, such as the telephone and telex, and the very frequent recourse by the paper manufacturers to very well-informed trade buyers meant that, notwithstanding the number of stages involved—producer, agent, buyer, agent, producer—information on the level of the announced prices spreads within a matter of days, if not within a matter of hours on the pulp market.

(c) Parallelism of announced prices

[89] The parallelism of announced prices on which the Commission relies as evidence of concertation is described in paragraph 22 of its decision. In that paragraph, the Commission, relying on Table 6 annexed to the decision, finds that the prices announced by the Canadian and United States producers were the same from the first quarter of 1975 to the third quarter of 1977 and from the first quarter of 1978 to the third quarter of 1981, that the prices announced by the Swedish and Finnish producers were the same from the first quarter of 1975 to the second quarter of 1977 and from the third quarter of 1978 to the third quarter of 1981 and, finally, that the prices of all the producers were the same from the first quarter of 1976 to the second quarter of 1977 and from the third quarter of 1979 to the third quarter of 1981.

[90] According to the Commission, the only explanation for such parallelism of prices is concertation between the producers. That contention is essentially based on the considerations that follow.

[91] In the first place, the single price charged by the producers during the period at issue cannot be regarded as an equilibrium price, that is to say a price resulting from the natural operation of the law of supply and demand. The Commission emphasizes that there was no testing of the market 'by trial and error', as evidenced by the stability of prices established between the first quarter of 1975 and the fourth quarter of 1976, and the fact that, generally in the case of softwood from the third quarter of 1979 to the second quarter of 1980, the first higher price demanded was always followed by the other producers.

[92] Nor can the argument concerning 'price leadership' be accepted: the similarity of announced prices, and that of transaction prices moreover, cannot be explained by the existence of a market leader whose prices were adopted by its competitors. The order in which the announcements were made continued to change from quarter to quarter and no one producer held a strong enough position to act as leader.

[93] Secondly, the Commission considers that, since economic conditions varied from one producer

to another or from one group of producers to another, they should have charged different prices. Pulp manufacturers with low costs should have lowered their prices in order to increase their market shares to the detriment of their least efficient competitors. According to the Commission, the divergences in question related to production and transport costs, the relationship between those costs (determined in the national currencies: Canadian dollar, Swedish krona or Finnish mark) and selling prices (fixed in US dollars), size of orders, variations in demand for pulp in the various importing countries, the relative importance of the European market, which was greater for Scandinavian producers than for United States and Canadian producers, and the production capacity utilization ratios which, generally speaking, were higher in the United States and Canada than in Sweden and Finland.

[94] So far as the size of orders is concerned, the Commission considers that since the sale of large quantities enabled producers to cut their costs substantially, the price records should have shown significant price differences between purchasers of large quantities and purchasers of small quantities. In practice, those differences rarely amounted to more than 3 per cent.

[95] Thirdly, the Commission claims that, at any rate for a time in 1976, 1977 and 1981, announced prices for pulp stood at an artificially high level which differed widely from that which might have been expected under normal competitive conditions. For example, it is inconceivable, without con-certation, for a single unchanged price of US$ 415 to have been announced for northern softwood from the first quarter of 1975 to the third quarter of 1977 and, especially during the second and third quarters of 1977, for the announced price to have stood at US$ 100 above the selling price actually obtainable on the market. The contention that prices stood at an abnormally high level is borne out by the fact that in 1977 and 1982 the fall in prices was particularly abrupt.

[96] Finally, the Commission relies on the grant of secret rebates and on changes in market shares.

[97] So far as concerns the grant of secret rebates, it should be noted that there is a contradiction between the decision and what has been said subsequently. In paragraph 112 of its decision, the Commission refers to the exclusion of secret competition but then states in its pleadings that, if the rebates were secret, it was because they undermined concertation and therefore had to remain concealed from the other producers.

[98] So far as concerns the shifts in market shares established between 1975 and 1981, the Commission considers that they do not justify the finding that there was no concertation. Those shifts were much less marked between 1975 and 1976 and between 1980 and 1981 than the shifts between 1978 and 1979 and between 1979 and 1980.

[99] The applicants disputed the view that parallelism of prices was attributable to concertation.

[100] In commissioning the second expert's report, the Court requested the experts to specify whether, in their opinion, the natural operation of the wood pulp market should lead to a differential price structure or to a uniform price structure.

[101] It is apparent from the expert's report, together with the ensuing discussion, that the experts regard the normal operation of the market as a more plausible explanation for the uniformity of prices than concertation. The main thrust of their analysis may be summarized as follows:

(i) Description of the market
[102] The experts describe the market as a group of oligopolies-oligopsonies consisting of certain producers and of certain buyers and each corresponding to a given kind of pulp. That market structure results largely from the method of manufacturing paper pulp: since paper is the result of a characteristic mixture of pulps, each paper manufacturer can deal only with a limited number of pulp producers and, conversely, each pulp producer can supply only a limited number of customers. Within the groupings so constituted, cooperation was further consolidated by the finding that it offered both buyers and sellers of pulp security against the uncertainties of the market.

[103] That organization of the market, in conjunction with its very high degree of transparency, leads in the short-term to a situation where prices are slow to react. The producers know that, if they were to increase their prices, their competitors would no doubt refrain from following suit and thus lure their customers away. Similarly, they would be reluctant to reduce their prices in the knowledge that, if they did so, the other producers would follow suit, assuming that they had spare production capacity. Such a fall in prices would be all the less desirable in that it would be detrimental to the sector as a whole: since overall demand for pulp is inelastic, the loss of revenue resulting from the reduction in prices could not be offset by the profits made as a result of the increased sales and there would be a decline in the producers' overall profits.

[104] In the long-term, the possibility for buyers to turn, at the price of some investment, to other types of pulp and the existence of substitute products, such as Brazilian pulp or pulp from recycled paper, have the effect of mitigating oligopolistic trends on the market. That explains why, over a period of several years, fluctuations in prices have been relatively contained.

[105] Finally, the transparency of the market could be responsible for certain overall price increases recorded in the short-term: when demand exceeds supply, producers who are aware—as was the case on the pulp market—that the level of their competitors' stocks is low and that their production capacity utilization rate is high would not be afraid to increase their prices. There would then be a serious likelihood of their being followed by their competitors.

(ii) Market trends from 1975 to 1981
[106] The various mechanisms described above offer explanations for some of the stages in the sequence of price changes regarded by the Commission as 'abnormal', particularly the stability of prices observed during the period from 1975 to 1976, the collapse of the market in 1977 and the fresh fall in prices at the end of 1981.

The period from 1975 to 1976
[107] In 1974 demand for pulp was very strong. Since production capacity utilization rates were very high and inventory levels were extremely low, excess demand led to an increase in prices.

[108] In 1975 and 1976, circumstances changed: there was an increase in inventory levels and a general decline in the production capacity utilization rate. Notwithstanding those changes, no producer took the initiative of reducing its prices, in the knowledge that, had it done so, its competitors would have followed suit. Conversely, had it decided to increase its prices, it would have remained isolated on the market and would have lost some, if not all, its customers.

[109] According to the experts, the oligopolistic characteristics of the market and its very high degree of transparency are not the only factors responsible for the price stability observed during the period from 1975 to 1977. A further explanation lies in the particular circumstances prevailing at the time.

[110] First, at the general level, it should be noted that in 1976 world demand for paper had recovered, which gave rise to optimistic forecasts. In addition, the rate of inflation was high, the real value of prices had fallen and interest rates were low. Furthermore, the Swedish producers qualified for a tax rebate on stock-building which was related to the value of inventories. Finally, the North American producers had an outlet on the United States market, which at the time was very buoyant, and for their part were operating close to capacity.

1977
[111] The price collapse in 1977 was the result of the massive increase in supply and the stagnant demand which characterized that period. The Swedish Government had ended the storage subsidy scheme, thereby generating a massive increase in supply at a time when inventory levels in the other producer countries were relatively high. The producers then found that the expected growth in demand had not materialized and that, consequently, an increase in prices was less likely. In those

circumstances, if an undertaking decided to lower its prices, it could be sure that its competitors would follow suit provided, however, that they had spare production capacity.

The period from 1978 to 1981

[112] As from the fourth quarter of 1978, demand recovered and came to exceed supply. The transparency of the market accordingly led to a rapid upward adjustment in prices. Undertakings which were aware that their competitors did not have any spare production capacity were then able to increase their prices without fear of remaining isolated and thus losing their share of the market.

[113] That period of rising prices was followed by a period of stability from mid-1980 to the end of 1981. That stability was attributable to the fact that inventory levels were low, production capacity utilization rates were high and demand, influenced by the appearance of new types of pulp on the market, was static.

[114] In the fourth quarter of 1981, the market again went into recession as a result of swollen inventories, the fall in production capacity utilization rates and the fall in world demand for paper. The absence of the special factors prevailing in 1975–1977, namely the higher rate of inflation and the existence in Sweden of a storage subsidy scheme, accounts for the more rapid fall in prices.

(iii) Several factors established on the market are incompatible with the explanation that there was concertation

[115] The experts analyse the structures of the market and price trends over the period at issue and maintain that several factors or mechanisms specific to that market are incompatible with an explanation based on concertation. Those factors are the existence of actual and potential outsiders not belonging to the group of undertakings alleged to have colluded, changing market shares and the absence of production quotas and the finding that producers did not take advantage of the differences between the various importing countries as regards elasticity of demand.

[116] So far as concerns the first point, it should be noted that in paragraph 137 of its decision, the Commission assesses production by outsiders at 40 per cent of total consumption of pulp in the Community. In view of the size of that market share, it would have been difficult for a cartel to operate only as between the undertakings found to have committed an infringement by engaging in concertation.

[117] The Commission's counterargument is that it refrained from initiating a proceeding against those other producers because, in its view, they had acted as followers during the period at issue.

[118] That argument cannot be accepted. It is wholly inconsistent with the reasoning adopted by the Commission as regards Table 6 in identifying the producers taking part in the concertation. If, in that regard, as already pointed out in paragraph 58 above, the mere fact of announcing the same price as another producer for the same period does indeed constitute sufficient evidence of concertation, the infringement procedure under Article 85 should clearly have been extended to those outsiders which, as the Commission acknowledges by its use of the term 'follower', announced the same price as the producers penalized in the context of Article 1(1) of the operative part of the decision.

[119] With regard to the second factor, the experts find that, having regard to Table 2 annexed to the decision, there were shifts in market shares between 1975 and 1981. Such changes reveal the existence of competition between the producers and the absence of quotas.

[120] Finally, so far as concerns the absence of differences in price between the various Member States, the experts consider that it is wrong to contend, as the Commission does in paragraphs 136 to 140 of the decision, that the pulp producers should have exploited the differences in price-elasticity in the different Member States. According to the experts, in order to do so, the undertakings would have had to be in a position to divide up the market, which would have been possible only if there had been an effective cartel embracing all existing and potential suppliers and capable

of ensuring compliance with barriers to resale and to transfer between Member States. In those circumstances, price uniformity constitutes on the contrary an argument militating in favour of the explanation based on the normal operation of the market.

(iv) Specific criticisms of the Commission's explanation made by the experts

[121] A number of specific criticisms are directed by the experts against the Commission's explanation. Those criticisms concern the impact on prices of transport costs, the size of orders and, in general, differences in costs and the grant of secret rebates.

[122] In the first place, in response to the Commission's contention that prices should have varied according to the destination, the experts state that the destination of the pulp—whether Atlantic ports or Baltic ports—had only a minor influence on transport costs. At most, it could have led to a difference in cost of US$ 10 a tonne. Contrary to what the Commission states, that difference is too small to affect prices within each of the two zones.

[123] Secondly, the experts explain why, in their view, very large orders for pulp did not lead to sharp price cuts. Such orders do not enable significant cost savings to be made for various reasons: first, wood pulp is normally a standard product delivered from anonymous stock; secondly, producers are in the habit of installing storage capacity at the great receiving ports; finally, because they use a wide range of pulps, the paper manufacturers prefer, when placing orders for large quantities, to have the pulp delivered in several consignments. Ultimately, the economies of scale associated with very large orders are confined to overheads and administrative costs.

[124] Thirdly, the experts consider that, even if there were real economies of scale, the differences in costs to which they led between the producers did not affect prices but the undertakings' profits.

[125] Finally, if the rebates granted were secret, that was for various reasons outside the pulp producers' control: to begin with, in some countries, such as France, rebates not justified by cost-savings are illegal; next, as rebates generally relate to annual tonnage, they cannot be calculated until the end of the financial year. Lastly, it is the buyers who ask for rebates to be kept confidential, partly in order to secure an advantage over their competitors by obtaining better prices, and partly in order to prevent paper buyers from seeking a reduction in price themselves.

3. Conclusions

[126] Following that analysis, it must be stated that, in this case, concertation is not the only plausible explanation for the parallel conduct. To begin with, the system of price announcements may be regarded as constituting a rational response to the fact that the pulp market constituted a long-term market and to the need felt by both buyers and sellers to limit commercial risks. Further, the similarity in the dates of price announcements may be regarded as a direct result of the high degree of market transparency, which does not have to be described as artificial. Finally, the parallelism of prices and the price trends may be satisfactorily explained by the oligopolistic tendencies of the market and by the specific circumstances prevailing in certain periods. Accordingly, the parallel conduct established by the Commission does not constitute evidence of concertation.

[127] In the absence of a firm, precise and consistent body of evidence, it must be held that concertation regarding announced prices has not been established by the Commission. Article 1(1) of the contested decision must therefore be annulled.

QUESTION

Following the Court's annulment of a substantial part of the Commission's decision in *Wood Pulp*, do you consider Article 81 EC to be an unsuitable tool for tackling collusion in an oligopolistic market?

NOTE: More recently the Commission has applied Article 82 EC to oligopolistic behaviour on the basis of collective dominance of the relevant market. See the landmark decision of the CFI in *Re Italian Flat Glass*: *Societa Italiano Vetio SpA* v *Commission* T-68, 77-78/89 [1992] ECR II-1403, [1992] 5 CMLR 302.

FURTHER READING

Joshua, J., 'Proof in Contested EEC Competition Cases' (1987) ELRev 315.

For an excellent exposition of the problem of oligopoly and conscious parallelism see Van Gerven, G., and Varona, E.N., 'The Wood Pulp Case and the Future of Concerted Practices' (1994) 31 CMLRev 575.

QUESTION

It is difficult to define in legal language the precise line between lawful and unlawful combinations. This must be left for the courts to determine in each particular case. All that we, as lawmakers, can do is to declare general principles, and we can be assured that the courts will apply them as to carry out the meaning of the law. . . . This bill is only an honest effort to declare a rule of action.

(Senator John Sherman on introducing the Bill to the US Senate, 1889)

Discuss.

G: Unilateral conduct

The general principle is that Article 81 EC applies to the activities of two or more undertakings and is thereby to be distinguished from Article 82 EC. However, the Commission has held that unilateral conduct can, in certain contexts, for example within a distribution system, amount to an agreement or concerted practice for the purposes of Article 81 EC. This is a view shared by the Court in a series of decisions.

AEG-Telefunken v *Commission*
(Case 107/82) [1983] ECR 3151, [1984] 3 CMLR 325

The Court accepted the Commission's findings that admission to a selective distribution system was based upon an acceptance, tacit or express, of the policies pursued by the manufacturer. It followed that a refusal to supply by AEG, to certain distributors which met the criteria set by the AEG, formed an integral part of the operation of the distribution network and thus constituted an agreement for the purposes of Article 81 EC.

[31] AEG contends that the acts complained of in the contested decision, namely the failure to admit certain traders and steps taken to exert an influence on prices, are unilateral acts and do not therefore, as such, fall within Article 85(1), which relates only to agreements between undertakings, decisions by associations of undertakings and concerted practices.

[32] In order properly to appreciate that argument it is appropriate to consider the legal significance of selective distribution systems.

[33] It is common ground that agreements constituting a selective system necessarily affect competition in the common market. However, it has always been recognized in the case-law of the Court that there are legitimate requirements, such as the maintenance of a specialist trade capable of providing specific services as regards high-quality and high-technology products, which may justify a reduction of price competition in favour of competition relating to factors other than price. Systems of selective distribution, in so far as they aim at the attainment of a legitimate goal capable of improving competition in relation to factors other than price, therefore constitute an element of competition which is in conformity with Article 85(1).

[34] The limitations inherent in a selective distribution system are however acceptable only on condition that their aim is in fact an improvement in competition in the sense above mentioned. Otherwise they would have no justification inasmuch as their sole effect would be to reduce price competition.

[35] So as to guarantee that selective distribution systems may be based on that aim alone and cannot be set up and used with a view to the attainment of objectives which are not in conformity with Community law, the Court specified in its judgment of 25 October 1977 (*Metro* v *Commission*, [1977] ECR 1875) that such systems are permissible, provided that resellers are chosen on the basis of objective criteria of a qualitative nature relating to the technical qualifications of the reseller and his staff and the suitability of his trading premises and that such conditions are laid down uniformly for all potential resellers and are not applied in a discriminatory fashion.

[36] It follows that the operation of a selective distribution system based on criteria other than those mentioned above constitutes an infringement of Article 85(1). The position is the same where a system which is in principle in conformity with Community law is applied in practice in a manner incompatible therewith.

[37] Such a practice must be considered unlawful where the manufacturer, with a view to maintaining a high level of prices or to excluding certain modern channels of distribution, refuses to approve distributors who satisfy the qualitative criteria of the system.

[38] Such an attitude on the part of the manufacturer does not constitute, on the part of the undertaking, unilateral conduct which, as AEG claims, would be exempt from the prohibition contained in Article 85(1) of the Treaty. On the contrary, it forms part of the contractual relations between the undertaking and resellers. Indeed, in the case of the admission of a distributor, approval is based on the acceptance, tacit or express, by the contracting parties of the policy pursued by AEG which requires inter alia the exclusion from the network of all distributors who are qualified for admission but are not prepared to adhere to that policy.

[39] The view must therefore be taken that even refusals of approval are acts performed in the context of the contractual relations with authorized distributors inasmuch as their purpose is to guarantee observance of the agreements in restraint of competition which form the basis of contracts between manufacturers and approved distributors. Refusals to approve distributors who satisfy the qualitative criteria mentioned above therefore supply proof of an unlawful application of the system if their number is sufficient to preclude the possibility that they are isolated cases not forming part of systematic conduct.

NOTE: In Cases 25 & 26/84 *Ford Werke AG* v *Commission* [1985] ECR 2725 the Court accepted the Commission's reasoning that a circular sent by a car manufacturer to its German dealers in which it suggested that it would not meet orders from them for right-hand-drive motor cars, thus isolating markets in the UK and Ireland, formed part of the contractual relations between manufacturer and dealer as an implied term. Similarly, in Case C-277/87 *Sandoz* [1990] ECR I-45 the Court concluded that:

> the Commission was justified in considering that the set of continuous commercial relations, of which the 'export prohibited' clause formed an integral part, established between Sandoz PF and

its customers was governed by a pre-established general agreement applicable to innumerable individual orders for Sandoz products. Such an agreement is covered by the provisions of Article 85(1) of the EEC Treaty.

However, the Commission and Court adopted different approaches in the following recent case, commonly known as the *Adalat* case.

Bayer v *Commission*
(Case T-41/96) [2000] ECR II-3383, [2001] 4 CMLR 4

Bayer, a large German pharmaceutical manufacturer, through its wholly owned subsidiaries in France and Spain, enjoyed long standing sales to wholesalers in those markets. The Commission concluded that, through these subsidiaries, Bayer had withheld from the wholesalers supplies of a broad range of medicinal products used in the treatment of cardiovascular diseases. Furthermore, the Commission held that the wholesalers 'complied' with this ban, despite evidence that they actually resisted attempts to limit supplies. The Commission formed the view that the export ban became an integral part of their commercial relations and that this amounted to an agreement for the purposes of Article 81(1) EC. However, the Commission's decision was overturned by the Court of First Instance.

[65.] In this case, it is found in the Decision that there is an agreement between undertakings within the meaning of that article. The applicant maintains, however, that the Decision penalises unilateral conduct on its part that falls outside the scope of the article. It claims that the Commission has given the concept of an agreement within the meaning of Article 85(1) of the Treaty an interpretation which goes beyond the precedents in the case-law and that its application to the present case infringes that provision of the Treaty. The Commission contends that it has fully followed the case-law in its evaluation of that concept and has applied it in a wholly appropriate manner to the facts of this case. It therefore needs to be determined whether, having regard to the definition of that concept in the case-law, the Commission was entitled to perceive in the conduct established in the Decision the factors constituting an agreement between undertakings within the meaning of Article 85(1) of the Treaty.

B. The concept of an agreement within the meaning of Article 85(1) of the Treaty
[66.] The case-law shows that, where a decision on the part of a manufacturer constitutes unilateral conduct of the undertaking, that decision escapes the prohibition in Article 85(1) of the Treaty (Case 107/82 *AEG* v *Commission* [1983] ECR 3151, paragraph 38; Joined Cases 25/84 and 26/84 *Ford and Ford Europe* v *Commission* [1985] ECR 2725, paragraph 21; Case T-43/92 *Dunlop Slazenger* v *Commission* [1994] ECR II-441, paragraph 56).

[67.] It is also clear from the case-law in that in order for there to be an agreement within the meaning of Article 85(1) of the Treaty it is sufficient that the undertakings in question should have expressed their joint intention to conduct themselves on the market in a specific way (Case 41/69 *ACF Chemiefarma* v *Commission* [1970] ECR 661, paragraph 112; Joined Cases 209/78 to 215/78 and 218/78 *Van Landewyck and Others* v *Commission* [1980] ECR 3125, paragraph 86; Case T-7/89 *Hercules Chemicals* v *Commission* [1991] ECR II-1711, paragraph 256).

[68.] As regards the form in which that common intention is expressed, it is sufficient for a stipulation to be the expression of the parties' intention to behave on the market in accordance with its terms (see, in particular, *ACF Chemiefarma*, paragraph 112, and *Van Landewyck*, paragraph

86), without its having to constitute a valid and binding contract under national law (*Sandoz*, paragraph 13).

[69.] It follows that the concept of an agreement within the meaning of Article 85(1) of the Treaty, as interpreted by the case-law, centres around the existence of a concurrence of wills between at least two parties, the form in which it is manifested being unimportant so long as it constitutes the faithful expression of the parties' intention.

[70.] In certain circumstances, measures adopted or imposed in an apparently unilateral manner by a manufacturer in the context of his continuing relations with his distributors have been regarded as constituting an agreement within the meaning of Article 85(1) of the Treaty (Joined Cases 32/78, 36/78 to 82/78 *BMW Belgium and Others* v *Commission* [1979] ECR 2435, paragraphs 28 to 30; *AEG*, paragraph 38; *Ford and Ford Europe*, paragraph 21; Case 75/84 *Metro* v *Commission* (*'Metro II'* [1986] ECR 3021, paragraphs 72 and 73; *Sandoz*, paragraphs 7 to 12; Case C-70/93 *BMW* v *ALD* [1995] ECR I-3439, paragraphs 16 and 17).

[71.] That case-law shows that a distinction should be drawn between cases in which an undertaking has adopted a genuinely unilateral measure, and thus without the express or implied participation of another undertaking, and those in which the unilateral character of the measure is merely apparent. Whilst the former do not fall within Article 85(1) of the Treaty, the latter must be regarded as revealing an agreement between undertakings and may therefore fall within the scope of that article. That is the case, in particular, with practices and measures in restraint of competition which, though apparently adopted unilaterally by the manufacturer in the context of its contractual relations with its dealers, nevertheless receive at least the tacit acquiescence of those dealers.

NOTE: The Commission's reasoning had serious implications for the principle of freedom of contract which underpins Article 81 EC and the Court's insistence at para. 69 on the existence of a 'concurrence of wills' is welcome. Lidgard suggests that:

> where a non-dominant company is unilaterally carrying out a strategy without seeking the assistance of others, there is simply no legal base for condemning the activity. From a general industry perspective it appears important to allow non-dominant companies to design their strategy to take products to the European market. Refusals to supply do not endanger the competitive climate. If Bayer is operating through wholesalers rather than integrating forwards, it should be entitled to require that these wholesalers perform their task, which is to provide Adalat on optimal terms to the French/Spanish market. If the wholesaler is more interested in performing a parallel trade function—in conflict with Bayer's interests—it should purchase freely available Adalat and sell it to the United Kingdom. Bayer is under this theory not only fully entitled to reduce requested quantities, but also to refuse supplies entirely.
>
> See Lidgard, H.H., 'Unilateral Refusal to Supply: An agreement in disguise?' [1997] ECLR 354 at 360.

Do you support this assertion?

FURTHER READING

Jakobsen, P.S., and Broberg, M., 'The Concept of Agreement in Article 81 EC: In the Manufacturers' Right to Prevent Parallel Trade Within the European Community' [2002] ECLR 127.

H: Effect on trade between Member States

This part of the prohibition sets out the jurisdictional line between Community law and domestic competition law. If behaviour has an 'effect on trade between

Member States' then Community law will apply to that behaviour. That does not mean that domestic law cannot apply, but the Member States, including the national courts, should not, through the operation of Article 10 EC, act in a manner which is inconsistent with Community law. The requirement of an 'effect on trade' has enjoyed a broad construction under Article 81 EC and the case-law demonstrates a firm focus on the promotion of the market integration paradigm. The classic definition is enunciated in *STM*, which sets out the extent of behaviour that is required to trigger Community competition law.

Société Technique Minière v *Maschinenbau Ulm GmbH*
(Case 56/65) [1966] ECR 337, [1966] CMLR 357

On the relations with trade between Member-States
The agreement should further be 'capable of affecting trade between Member-States'. This provision, clarified by the introductory clause of Article 85 which applies to agreements in so far as they are 'incompatible with the Common Market,' aims to fix the field of application of the prohibition by the requirement of a prior condition consisting in the possibility of hindering the realisation of a sole market among the Member-States. It is in fact to the extent that the agreement may effect trade between Member-States that the distortion of competition, induced by the agreement, involves the prohibitions of Community law in Article 85, whereas in the contrary case it escapes. To fulfil this condition, the agreement in question should, on the basis of a collection of objective legal or factual elements, allow one to expect, with a sufficient degree of probability, that it would exercise a direct or indirect, actual or potential, effect on the eddies of trade between Member-States.

NOTE: The Court decided in Cases 56 and 58/64 *Consten* and *Grundig* that 'the fact that an agreement encourages an increase, even a large one, in the volume of trade between states is not sufficient to exclude the possibility that the agreement may affect such trade' (p. 341). There is much greater focus on the structure of markets within the Article 82 EC jurisprudence whereas Article 81 EC is more concerned with attempts to partition markets on national lines. For example, an agreement between undertakings based in the same Member State may still have an effect on interstate trade. See e.g. Case C-193/83 *Windsurfing International Inc.* v *European Commission* [1986] ECR 611, [1986] 3 CMLR 489. In these circumstances the Court will consider the agreement in its proper economic context and in particular the so-called bundling effect of complex trade distribution systems. For instance, a particular market may become compartmentalised from the rest of the common market. This issue arose in *Almelo*.

Municipality of Almelo v *IJM*
(Case C-393/92) [1994] ECR I-1477

The Court decided '*inter alia*':

[34] Article 85 of the Treaty applies, in its own terms, to agreements between undertakings which restrict competition and affect trade between Member States.

[35] As regards the existence of an agreement between undertakings, it is to be observed, as the Commission found in the 1991 Decision, that the electricity distribution system in the Netherlands is based on a network of contractual legal relationships between generators, between generators and regional distributors, between regional distributors and local distributors and, finally, between local distributors and end-users. The exclusive purchasing clause in issue before the national court is contained in the general conditions for the supply of electric power by a regional distributor to local distributors and therefore constitutes a clause contained in an agreement as referred to in Article 85 of the Treaty.

[36] An agreement containing such a clause has a restrictive effect on competition, inasmuch as the clause prohibits the local distributors from obtaining electricity supplies from other suppliers.

[37] In order to determine whether such an agreement has an appreciable effect on trade between Member States, it is necessary, as the Court observed in its judgments in Case 23/67 *Brasserie de Haecht* [1967] ECR 525 and Case C-234/89 *Delimitis* [1991] ECR I-935, to assess it in its economic and legal context and to take account of any cumulative effect resulting from the existence of other exclusivity agreements.

[38] In that regard, it appears from the documents before the Court that the general conditions governing the relations between the parties to the main proceedings, which contain the exclusivity clause, follow the model General Terms and Conditions for the supply of electricity drawn up by the Association of Operators of Electricity Undertakings in the Netherlands.

[39] Those contractual relationships have the cumulative effect of compartmentalizing the national market, inasmuch as they have the effect of prohibiting local distributors established in the Netherlands from obtaining supplies of electricity from distributors or producers in other Member States.

NOTE: The importance of 'affect on interstate trade' has assumed even greater importance in the context of the Commission's Modernisation regulation. Article 3 of the Commission's regulation states that:

1.   Where the competition authorities of the Member States or national courts apply national competition law to agreements, decisions of associations of undertakings or concerted practices within the meaning of Article 81(1) of the Treaty which may affect trade between Member States within the meaning of that provision, they shall also apply Article 81 of the Treaty to such agreements, decisions or concerted practices

The original plan was that community law would apply to the exclusion of national law. This 'one for all, all for one', approach had considerable significance. J.M. Joshua suggested that 'it may well be that—disarmed by the siren call of "decentralisation"—the Member States have not fully appreciated how far the proposal involves a shift in the balance between national and EC law'. See Joshua, J.M., 'A Sherman Act Bridgehead in Europe, or a Ghost Ship in Mid-Atlantic? A Close Look at the United Kingdom Proposals to Criminalise Hardcore Cartel Conduct' [2002] ECLR 231 at 233. For a fuller discussion of this important development, see Chapter 3.

FURTHER READING

Burnley, R., 'Interstate Trade Revisited—The Jurisdictional Criterion for Articles 81 and 82 EC' [2002] ECLR 217.

I: *De minimis*

Article 81 EC requires any effect on competition or trade must be to an 'appreciable extent'; hence the *de minimis* doctrine can operate to limit the application of Article 81 EC. Where an agreement does not have an appreciable effect it will escape the prohibition in Article 81(1) EC and there is no need to notify. This principle emerged from the Court's judgment in an early case, Case 5/69 *Völk* v *Ets Vervaecke Sprl* [1969] ECR 295, [1969] CMLR 273. Here a German producer of washing machines, Völk, and a Belgian-based distributor, Vervaecke, entered into an exclusive distribution agreement which guaranteed absolute territorial protection for the distributor. The Court held that 'an agreement escapes the prohibition of Article [85(1)] where it has only an insignificant effect on the market, taking into account the weak position which the persons concerned have on the market of the product in question'. Völk's share of the market represented 0.6 per cent. The *de minimis* doctrine has since found expression in a Commission Notice, most recently revised in 2002 to ensure coherence with the Commission's revised rules for vertical and horizontal agreements. The Notice attempts to give undertakings important practical guidance as to whether an agreement falls within the scope of the *de minimis* doctrine. The 2002 Notice replaces the 1997 Notice (1997) OJ 1997, No C372/13, which introduced market-share thresholds. The 2002 Notice confirms this economic approach and the emphasis on a quantitative assessment. Note that the new Notice is not concerned with the effect on trade between Member States.

*Commission Notice on agreements of minor importance which do not appreciably restrict competition under Article 81(1) (*de minimis*)*[1]

I

1. Article 81(1) prohibits agreements between undertakings which may affect trade between Member States and which have as their object or effect the prevention, restriction or distortion of competition within the common market. The Court of Justice of the European Communities has clarified that this provision is not applicable where the impact of the agreement on intra-Community trade or on competition is not appreciable.

2. In this notice the Commission quantifies, with the help of market share thresholds, what is not an appreciable restriction of competition under Article 81 of the EC Treaty. This negative definition of appreciability does not imply that agreements between undertakings which exceed the thresholds set out in this notice appreciably restrict competition. Such agreements may still have only a negligible effect on competition and may therefore not be prohibited by Article 81(1)[2].

3. Agreements may in addition not fall under Article 81(1) because they are not capable of appreciably affecting trade between Member States. This notice does not deal with this issue. It does not quantify what does not constitute an appreciable effect on trade. It is however acknowledged that agreements between small and medium-sized undertakings, as defined in the Annex to Commission Recommendation 96/280/EC ([3]), are rarely capable of appreciably affecting trade between Member States. Small and medium-sized undertakings are currently defined in that recommendation as undertakings which have fewer than 250 employees and have either an annual turnover not exceeding EUR 40 million or an annual balance-sheet total not exceeding EUR 27 million.

---

1 This notice replaces the notice on agreements of minor importance published in OJ C 372, 9.12.1997.

2 See, for instance, the judgment of the Court of Justice in Joined Cases C-215/96 and C-216/96 *Bagnasco (Carlos)* v *Banca Popolare di Novara and Casa di Risparmio di Genova e Imperia* (1999) ECR 1-135, points 34–35. This notice is also without prejudice to the principles for assessment under Article 81(1) as expressed in the Commission notice 'Guidelines on the applicability of Article 81 of the EC Treaty to horizontal cooperation agreements', OJ C 3, 6.1.2001, in particular points 17–31 inclusive, and in the Commission notice 'Guidelines on vertical restraints', OJ C 291, 13.10.2000, in particular points 5–20 inclusive.

3 OJ L 107, 30.4.1996, p. 4. This recommendation will be revised. It is envisaged to increase the annual turnover threshold from EUR 40 million to EUR 50 million and the annual balance-sheet total threshold from EUR 27 million to EUR 43 million.

4. In cases covered by this notice the Commission will not institute proceedings either upon application or on its own initiative. Where undertakings assume in good faith that an agreement is covered by this notice, the Commission will not impose fines. Although not binding on them, this notice also intends to give guidance to the courts and authorities of the Member States in their application of Article 81.

5. This notice also applies to decisions by associations of undertakings and to concerted practices.

6. This notice is without prejudice to any interpretation of Article 81 which may be given by the Court of Justice or the Court of First Instance of the European Communities.

II

7. The Commission holds the view that agreements between undertakings which affect trade between Member States do not appreciably restrict competition within the meaning of Article 81(1):

(a) if the aggregate market share held by the parties to the agreement does not exceed 10 per cent on any of the relevant markets affected by the agreement, where the agreement is made between undertakings which are actual or potential competitors on any of these markets (agreements between competitors)[4]; or

(b) if the market share held by each of the parties to the agreement does not exceed 15 per cent on any of the relevant markets affected by the agreement, where the agreement is made between undertakings which are not actual or potential competitors on any of these markets (agreements between non-competitors).

In cases where it is difficult to classify the agreement as either an agreement between competitors or an agreement between non-competitors the 10 per cent threshold is applicable.

8. Where in a relevant market competition is restricted by the cumulative effect of agreements for the sale of goods or services entered into by different suppliers or distributors (cumulative fore-closure effect of parallel networks of agreements having similar effects on the market), the market share thresholds under point 7 are reduced to 5 per cent, both for agreements between competitors and for agreements between non-competitors. Individual suppliers or distributors with a market share not exceeding 5 per cent are in general not considered to contribute significantly to a cumulative foreclosure effect[1]. A cumulative foreclosure effect is unlikely to exist if less than 30 per cent of the relevant market is covered by parallel (networks of) agreements having similar effects.

9. The Commission also holds the view that agreements are not restrictive of competition if the market shares do not exceed the thresholds of respectively 10 per cent, 15 per cent and 5 per cent set out in points 7 and 8 during two successive calendar years by more than 2 percentage points.

10. In order to calculate the market share, it is necessary to determine the relevant market. This consists of the relevant product market and the relevant geographic market. When defining the

4 On what are actual or potential competitors, see the Commission notice 'Guidelines on the applicability of Article 81 of the EC Treaty to horizontal cooperation agreements', OJ C 3, 6.1.2001, paragraph 9. A firm is treated as an actual competitor if it is either active on the same relevant market or if, in the absence of the agreement, it is able to switch production to the relevant products and market them in the short term without incurring significant additional costs or risks in response to a small and permanent increase in relative prices (immediate supply-side substitutability). A firm is treated as a potential competitor if there is evidence that, absent the agreement, this firm could and would be likely to undertake the necessary additional investments or other necessary switching costs so that it could enter the relevant market in response to a small and permanent increase in relative prices.

1 See also the Commission notice 'Guidelines on vertical restraints', OJ C 291, 13.10.2000, in particular paragraphs 73, 142, 143 and 189. While in the guidelines on vertical restraints in relation to certain restrictions reference is made not only to the total but also to the tied market share of a particular supplier or buyer, in this notice all market share thresholds refer to total market shares.

relevant market, reference should be had to the notice on the definition of the relevant market for the purposes of Community competition law[2]. The market shares are to be calculated on the basis of sales value data or, where appropriate, purchase value data. If value data are not available, estimates based on other reliable market information, including volume data, may be used.

11. Points 7, 8 and 9 do not apply to agreements containing any of the following hardcore restrictions:

(1) as regards agreements between competitors as defined in point 7, restrictions which, directly or indirectly, in isolation or in combination with other factors under the control of the parties, have as their object[3]:

   (a) the fixing of prices when selling the products to third parties;

   (b) the limitation of output or sales;

   (c) the allocation of markets or customers;

(2) as regards agreements between non-competitors as defined in point 7, restrictions which, directly or indirectly, in isolation or in combination with other factors under the control of the parties, have as their object:

   (a) the restriction of the buyer's ability to determine its sale price, without prejudice to the possibility of the supplier imposing a maximum sale price or recommending a sale price, provided that they do not amount to a fixed or minimum sale price as a result of pressure from, or incentives offered by, any of the parties;

   (b) the restriction of the territory into which, or of the customers to whom, the buyer may sell the contract goods or services, except the following restrictions which are not hardcore:

   — the restriction of active sales into the exclusive territory or to an exclusive customer group reserved to the supplier or allocated by the supplier to another buyer, where such a restriction does not limit sales by the customers of the buyer,

   — the restriction of sales to end users by a buyer operating at the wholesale level of trade,

   — the restriction of sales to unauthorised distributors by the members of a selective distribution system, and

   — the restriction of the buyer's ability to sell components, supplied for the purposes of incorporation, to customers who would use them to manufacture the same type of goods as those produced by the supplier;

   (c) the restriction of active or passive sales to end users by members of a selective distribution system operating at the retail level of trade, without prejudice to the possibility of prohibiting a member of the system from operating out of an unauthorised place of establishment;

   (d) the restriction of cross-supplies between distributors within a selective distribution system, including between distributors operating at different levels of trade;

   (e) the restriction agreed between a supplier of components and a buyer who incorporates those components, which limits the supplier's ability to sell the components as spare parts to end users or to repairers or other service providers not entrusted by the buyer with the repair or servicing of its goods;

2 OJ C 372, 9.12.1997, p. 5.

3 Without prejudice to situations of joint production with or without joint distribution as defined in Article 5, paragraph 2, of Commission Regulation (EC) No 2658/2000 and Article 5, paragraph 2, of Commission Regulation (EC) No 2659/2000, OJ L 304, 5.12.2000, pp. 3 and 7 respectively.

(3) as regards agreements between competitors as defined in point 7, where the competitors operate, for the purposes of the agreement, at a different level of the production or distribution chain, any of the hardcore restrictions listed in paragraphs (1) and (2) above.

12.(1) For the purposes of this notice, the terms 'undertaking', 'party to the agreement', 'distributor', 'supplier' and 'buyer' shall include their respective connected undertakings.

(2) 'Connected undertakings' are:

(a) undertakings in which a party to the agreement, directly or indirectly:

— has the power to exercise more than half the voting rights, or

— has the power to appoint more than half the members of the supervisory board, board of management or bodies legally representing the undertaking, or

— has the right to manage the undertaking's affairs;

(b) undertakings which directly or indirectly have, over a party to the agreement, the rights or powers listed in (a);

(c) undertakings in which an undertaking referred to in (b) has, directly or indirectly, the rights or powers listed in (a);

(d) undertakings in which a party to the agreement together with one or more of the undertakings referred to in (a), (b) or (c), or in which two or more of the latter undertakings, jointly have the rights or powers listed in (a);

(e) undertakings in which the rights or the powers listed in (a) are jointly held by:

— parties to the agreement or their respective connected undertakings referred to in (a) to (d), or

— one or more of the parties to the agreement or one or more of their connected undertakings referred to in (a) to (d) and one or more third parties.

(3) For the purposes of paragraph 2(e), the market share held by these jointly held undertakings shall be apportioned equally to each undertaking having the rights or the powers listed in paragraph 2(a).

NOTE: The *'de minimis'* thresholds have been increased for agreements between competitors from 5 per cent under the previous Notice to 10 per cent and for agreements between non-competitiors from 10 per cent to 15 per cent. Furthermore, the Notice introduces, for the first time, a market share threshold for networks of agreements producing a cumulative anti-competitive effect. It contains the same list of hard-core restrictions, which cannot benefit from the *de minimis* Notice, as the vertical and horizontal block exemption regulations, see Chapter 6. The new Notice also confirms that agreements between small and medium-sized enterprises are in general *'de minimis'*.

A Commission Notice is not binding although it is unusual for the Commission to depart from its terms later. However, in several cases, the Court has departed from a quantitative *de minimis* approach and instead adopted a qualitative assessment. See, e.g. Case 30/78 *Distillers Co. Ltd* v *Commission* [1980] ECR 2229 in which the Court held at paras 27 and 28 that 'although an agreement may escape the prohibition in Article 85(1) when it affects the market only to an insignificant extent, having regard to the weak position which those concerned have in the market in the products in question, the same considerations do not apply in the case of a product of a large undertakings responsible for the entire production'.

J: Within the Common Market

This element concerns the territorial extent of Article 81 EC and suggests that only agreements which restrict competition within the Community are caught by the Community competition rules. Notwithstanding this territorial requirement, Article 81 EC may be applied to agreements concluded *outside* the territory of the Community which produce *effects within* the Community (the Commission's approach) or are *implemented* through a subsidiary situated within it (the Court's preferred approach). The extent to which Articles 81 and 82 EC can be applied to agreements between undertakings established outside the Community, known as extraterritoriality, is considered in Chapter 12.

K: Object or effect the prevention, restriction or distortion of competition

An agreement will not infringe Article 81 EC unless it has as its 'object or effect, the prevention, restriction or distortion of competition'. Although Article 81 EC provides some indication of the types of agreement prohibited, the list is not exhaustive, and, as we shall see, the Commission and Court have given the term, 'object or effect' an expansive interpretation. The 'object or effect' requirement has caused the Commission and the Court significant interpretative difficulties. The key problem concerns the drafting of the provision—is the phrase to be read disjunctively, or are the conditions cumulative? In *STM* the Court held that 'object or effect' was to be read disjunctively.

Société Technique Minière v *Maschinenbau Ulm GmbH*
Case 56/65 [1966] ECR 235, [1966] CMLR 357

On the relations of the agreement with competition
Finally, to be hit by the prohibition of Article 85(1), the agreement in the proceedings should 'be designed to prevent, restrict or distort competition within the Common Market or have that effect'. The fact that these are not cumulative but alternative conditions, indicated by the conjunction 'or', suggests first the need to consider the very object of the agreement, in the light of the economic context in which it is to be applied. The alterations in the play of competition envisaged by Article 85(1) should result from all or part of the clauses of the agreement itself. Where, however, an analysis of the said clauses does not reveal a sufficient degree of harmfulness with regard to competition, examination should then be made of the effects of the agreement and, if it is to be subjected to the prohibition, the presence of those elements which establish that competition has in fact been prevented, restricted or distorted to a noticeable extent should be required. The competition in question should be understood within the actual context in which it would occur in the absence of the agreement in question. In particular, the alteration of the conditions of competition may be thrown in doubt if the said agreement appears precisely necessary for the penetration of an undertaking into an area in which it was not operating. Therefore, to judge whether a contract containing a clause 'granting an exclusive right of sale' should be regarded as prohibited by reason of its object or its effect, it is necessary to take into account, in particular, the nature and the quantity, whether limited or not, of the products which are the object of the agreement, the position and size of the grantor and concessionaire on the market for the products concerned, the isolated nature of the

agreement in question or, on the contrary, its position in a series of agreements, the severity of the clauses aiming at protecting the exclusive right or, on the contrary, the possibilities left for other commercial currents upon the same products by means of re-exports and parallel imports.

NOTE: Article 81 EC includes a non-exhaustive list of the types of agreement that will 'prevent, restrict or distort' competition. The Court has confirmed, in a number of cases, that price-fixing agreements (*Dyestuffs*), agreements to share markets (*Quinine*), information exchanges (*Italian Flat Glass*) and export restrictions (*Consten* and *Grundig*) have the object of restricting competition. In these circumstances there is no need to assess the effect of the agreement on competition. Such restrictions may be weighed against any pro-competitive effects only in the context of Article 81(3) EC with a view to obtaining an exemption.

Anti-competitive behaviour does not exist in the abstract and, where the 'object' element is not satisfied, the Court has emphasised the importance of conducting a full market analysis to ascertain whether the agreement has prevented, restricted or distorted competition within the meaning of Article 81(1) EC.

Brasserie de Haecht SA v Wilkin
(Case 23/67) [1967] ECR 407, [1968] CMLR 26

A brewer and a café owner, both situated in Belgium, had entered into an exclusive purchasing agreement. The Court held that it was necessary to consider the whole economic context in which the agreement operated, in particular the existence of a network of such agreements which could have the effect of foreclosing competition.

. . . Article 85(1) mentions agreements, decisions and practices. By referring in the same sentence to agreements between undertakings, decisions by associations of undertakings and concerted practices, which may involve many parties, Article [85(1)] implies that the constituent elements of those agreements, decisions and practices may be considered together as a whole.

Furthermore, by basing its application to agreements, decisions or practices, not only their subject-matter but also on their effects in relation to competition, Article [85(1)] implies that regard must be had to such effects in the context in which they occur, that is to say, in the economic and legal context of such agreements, decisions or practices and where they might combine with others to have a cumulative effect on competition. In fact, it would be pointless to consider an agreement, decision or concerted practice by reason of its effects if those effects were to be taken distinct from the body of effects, whether convergent or not, surrounding their implementation. Thus in order to examine whether it is caught by Article [85(1)] an agreement cannot be examined in isolation from the above context, that is from the factual or legal circumstances causing it to prevent, restrict or distort competition. The existence of similar contracts may be taken into consideration for this objective to the extent to which the general body of contracts of this type is capable of restricting the freedom of trade.

Lastly, it is only to the extent to which agreements, decisions or practices are capable of affecting trade between Member States that the alteration of competition comes under Community prohibitions. In order to satisfy this condition, it must be possible for the agreement, decision or practice, when viewed in the light of a combination of the objective, factual or legal circumstances, to appear to be capable of having some influence, direct or indirect, on trade between Member States, of being conducive to a partitioning of the market and of hampering the economic interpenetration sought by the Treaty. When this point is considered the agreement, decision or practice cannot therefore be isolated from all the others of which it is one.

The existence of similar contracts is a circumstance which, together with others, is capable of being a factor in the economic and legal context within which the contract must be judged. Accordingly, whilst such a situation must be taken into account it should not be considered as decisive by itself, but merely as one among others in judging whether trade between Member States is capable of being affected through any alteration in competition.

In a further case involving beer supply agreements, the Court confirmed that where the object of an agreement is not to restrict competition, the agreement will only be caught by Article 81(1) EC if it produces anti-competitive effects.

Delimitis v *Henninger Bräu*
(Case C-234/89) [1991] ECR 1–935, [1992] 5 CMLR 210

The compatibility of beer supply agreements with Article 85(1) of the Treaty

[10] Under the terms of beer supply agreements, the supplier generally affords the reseller certain economic and financial benefits, such as the grant of loans on favourable terms, the letting of premises for the operation of a public house and the provision of technical installations, furniture and other equipment necessary for its operation. In consideration for those benefits, the reseller normally undertakes, for a predetermined period, to obtain supplies of the products covered by the contract only from the supplier. That exclusive purchasing obligation is generally backed by a prohibition on selling competing products in the public house let by the supplier.

[11] Such contracts entail for the supplier the advantage of guaranteed outlets, since, as a result of his exclusive purchasing obligation and the prohibition on competition, the reseller concentrates his sales efforts on the distribution of the contract goods. The supply agreements, moreover, lead to cooperation with the reseller, allowing the supplier to plan his sales over the duration of the agreement and to organize production and distribution effectively.

[12] Beer supply agreements also have advantages for the reseller, inasmuch as they enable him to gain access under favourable conditions and with the guarantee of supplies to the beer distribution market. The reseller's and supplier's shared interest in promoting sales of the contract goods likewise secures for the reseller the benefit of the supplier's assistance in guaranteeing product quality and customer service.

[13] If such agreements do not have the object of restricting competition within the meaning of Article 85(1), it is nevertheless necessary to ascertain whether they have the effect of preventing, restricting or distorting competition.

[14] In its judgment in Case 23/67 *Brassèrie De Haecht* v *Wilkin* [1967] ECR 407, the Court held that the effects of such an agreement had to be assessed in the context in which they occur and where they might combine with others to have a cumulative effect on competition. It also follows from that judgment that the cumulative effect of several similar agreements constitutes one factor amongst others in ascertaining whether, by way of a possible alteration of competition, trade between Member States is capable of being affected.

[15] Consequently, in the present case it is necessary to analyse the effects of a beer supply agreement, taken together with other contracts of the same type, on the opportunities of national competitors or those from other Member States, to gain access to the market for beer consumption or to increase their market share and, accordingly, the effects on the range of products offered to consumers.

[16] In making that analysis, the relevant market must first be determined. The relevant market is primarily defined on the basis of the nature of the economic activity in question, in this case the sale of beer. Beer is sold through both retail channels and premises for the sale and consumption of drinks. From the consumer's point of view, the latter sector, comprising in particular public houses

and restaurants, may be distinguished from the retail sector on the grounds that the sale of beer in public houses does not solely consist of the purchase of a product but is also linked with the provision of services, and that beer consumption in public houses is not essentially dependent on economic considerations. The specific nature of the public house trade is borne out by the fact that the breweries organize specific distribution systems for this sector which require special installations, and that the prices charged in that sector are generally higher than retail prices.

[17] It follows that in the present case the reference market is that for the distribution of beer in premises for the sale and consumption of drinks. That finding is not affected by the fact that there is a certain overlap between the two distribution networks, namely inasmuch as retail sales allow new competitors to make their brands known and to use their reputation in order to gain access to the market constituted by premises for the sale and consumption of drinks.

[18] Secondly, the relevant market is delimited from a geographical point of view. It should be noted that most beer supply agreements are still entered into at a national level. It follows that, in applying the Community competition rules, account is to be taken of the national market for beer distribution in premises for the sale and consumption of drinks.

[19] In order to assess whether the existence of several beer supply agreements impedes access to the market as so defined, it is further necessary to examine the nature and extent of those agreements in their totality, comprising all similar contracts tying a large number of points of sale to several national producers (judgment in Case 43/69 *Bilger* v *Jehle* [1970] ECR 127). The effect of those networks of contracts on access to the market depends specifically on the number of outlets thus tied to national producers in relation to the number of public houses which are not so tied, the duration of the commitments entered into, the quantities of beer to which those commitments relate, and on the proportion between those quantities and the quantities sold by free distributors.

[20] The existence of a bundle of similar contracts, even if it has a considerable effect on the opportunities for gaining access to the market, is not, however, sufficient in itself to support a finding that the relevant market is inaccessible, inasmuch as it is only one factor, amongst others, pertaining to the economic and legal context in which an agreement must be appraised (Case 23/67 *Brasserie De Haecht*, cited above). The other factors to be taken into account are, in the first instance, those also relating to opportunities for access.

[21] In that connection it is necessary to examine whether there are real concrete possibilities for a new competitor to penetrate the bundle of contracts by acquiring a brewery already established on the market together with its network of sales outlets, or to circumvent the bundle of contracts by opening new public houses. For that purpose it is necessary to have regard to the legal rules and agreements on the acquisition of companies and the establishment of outlets, and to the minimum number of outlets necessary for the economic operation of a distribution system. The presence of beer wholesalers not tied to producers who are active on the market is also a factor capable of facilitating a new producer's access to that market since he can make use of those wholesalers' sales networks to distribute his own beer.

[22] Secondly, account must be taken of the conditions under which competitive forces operate on the relevant market. In that connection it is necessary to know not only the number and the size of producers present on the market, but also the degree of saturation of that market and customer fidelity to existing brands, for it is generally more difficult to penetrate a saturated market in which customers are loyal to a small number of large producers than a market in full expansion in which a large number of small producers are operating without any strong brand names. The trend in beer sales in the retail trade provides useful information on the development of demand and thus an indication of the degree of saturation of the beer market as a whole. The analysis of that trend is, moreover, of interest in evaluating brand loyalty. A steady increase in sales of beer under new brand names may confer on the owners of those brand names a reputation which they may turn to account in gaining access to the public-house market.

[23] If an examination of all similar contracts entered into on the relevant market and the other factors relevant to the economic and legal context in which the contract must be examined shows that those agreements do not have the cumulative effect of denying access to that market to new national and foreign competitors, the individual agreements comprising the bundle of agreements cannot be held to restrict competition within the meaning of Article 85(1) of the Treaty. They do not, therefore, fall under the prohibition laid down in that provision.

[24] If, on the other hand, such examination reveals that it is difficult to gain access to the relevant market, it is necessary to assess the extent to which the agreements entered into by the brewery in question contribute to the cumulative effect produced in that respect by the totality of the similar contracts found on that market. Under the Community rules on competition, responsibility for such an effect of closing off the market must be attributed to the breweries which make an appreciable contribution thereto. Beer supply agreements entered into by breweries whose contribution to the cumulative effect is insignificant do not therefore fall under the prohibition under Article 85(1).

[25] In order to assess the extent of the contribution of the beer supply agreements entered into by a brewery to the cumulative sealing-off effect mentioned above, the market position of the contracting parties must be taken into consideration. That position is not determined solely by the market share held by the brewery and any group to which it may belong, but also by the number of outlets tied to it or to its group, in relation to the total number of premises for the sale and consumption of drinks found in the relevant market.

[26] The contribution of the individual contracts entered into by a brewery to the sealing-off of that market also depends on their duration. If the duration is manifestly excessive in relation to the average duration of beer supply agreements generally entered into on the relevant market, the individual contract falls under the prohibition under Article 85(1). A brewery with a relatively small market share which ties its sales outlets for many years may make as significant a contribution to a sealing-off of the market as a brewery in a relatively strong market position which regularly releases sales outlets at shorter intervals.

[27] The reply to be given to the first three questions is therefore that a beer supply agreement is prohibited by Article 85(1) of the EEC Treaty, if two cumulative conditions are met. The first is that, having regard to the economic and legal context of the agreement at issue, it is difficult for competitors who could enter the market or increase their market share to gain access to the national market for the distribution of beer in premises for the sale and consumption of drinks. The fact that, in that market, the agreement in issue is one of a number of similar agreements having a cumulative effect on competition constitutes only one factor amongst others in assessing whether access to that market is indeed difficult. The second condition is that the agreement in question must make a significant contribution to the sealing-off effect brought about by the totality of those agreements in their economic and legal context. The extent of the contribution made by the individual agreement depends on the position of the contracting parties in the relevant market and on the duration of the agreement.

NOTE: In the context of horizontal agreements, see the decision of the CFI in Cases T-374, 375, 384 & 388/94 *European Night Services* v *Commission* [1998] ECR II-3141 [1998] 5 CMLR 718 in which the CFI stressed at para. 137 'that the examination of conditions of competition is based not only on existing competition between undertakings already present on the relevant market but also on potential competition, in order to ascertain whether, in the light of the structure of the market and the economic and legal context within which it functions, there are either concrete possibilities both for the undertakings concerned to compete among themselves, or for a new competitor to penetrate the relevant market and compete with the undertakings already established'.

Over the years the Court has developed a rule of reason approach, partially borrowed from US antitrust law in an attempt to deal with the 'object or effect' issue. The Court tends to view many agreements containing restraints on the parties' conduct, with the exception of significant territorial or price restraints, as falling outside the scope of Article 81(1) altogether. For example, it has held that restraints in an agreement do not restrict competition within the meaning of Article 81(1) if they are necessary or ancillary to a pro-competitive agreement (*Remia*); are essential to induce a distributor to make a substantial investment necessary to ensure the commercial viability of the venture (*STM, Nungesser*); or are generally essential to the proper working of a selective distribution system (*Metro*).

Advocate General Leger's recent opinion in Case C-309/99 *Wouters* provides an excellent appraisal of 'object or effect' in the context of competition and the professions. Note in particular the discussion of the rule of reason at para. 99 where AG Leger explains the difficulty in drawing a dividing line between purely ethical rules which lie outside the scope of the competition provisions and rules or practices whose object or effect is contrary to Article 81 EC.

Wouters v *Netherlands Bar Council*
(Case C-309/99)

C—Restriction of competition
[88.] The second question seeks to ascertain whether, in forbidding lawyers to enter into multi-disciplinary partnership with accountants, the Regulation has as its 'object or effect the prevention, restriction or distortion of competition'.

[89.] In general, the Court passes through two successive stages in determining whether or not an agreement is compatible with Article 85(1) of the Treaty.

[90.] First, the Court ascertains whether the agreement has as its object the restriction of competition. To that end, it undertakes an objective examination of the aims pursued by the agreement in the light of the economic context in which it is to be applied. If an agreement has an anti-competitive object it is prohibited under Article 85(1) and there is no need to take account of its concrete effects. The same considerations apply to decisions of associations of undertakings.

The Court thus declares agreements or decisions of associations of undertakings the sole purpose of which is to restrict or distort competition between the parties or between the parties and third persons to be contrary to Article 85(1) of the Treaty. Such is the case as regards horizontal agreements for fixing the sale price of goods or services, horizontal agreements intended to partition national markets, vertical agreements including a clause prohibiting export and, in general, any agreement the object of which is to bring about an artificial partitioning of the market.

[91.] Where it is not the specific object of an agreement to restrict competition, the Court establishes whether its effect is the prevention, restriction or distortion of competition. In that respect, Article 85(1) of the Treaty prohibits both actual anti-competitive effects and purely potential effects, provided that those are sufficiently appreciable.

[92.] In either case, the criterion used to determine whether an agreement is liable to restrict competition consists of considering competition within the actual context in which it would occur in the absence of the agreement.

[93.] Furthermore, whether conduct is compatible with Article 85(1) must be assessed in the economic and legal context of the case, taking into account the nature of the product or service and the structure and actual conditions in which the market functions.

(a) The object of the Regulation

[94.] In the present case, the appellants in the main proceedings submit that the object of the Regulation is to restrict competition on the market for legal services in the Netherlands. They have put forward many facts, seeking to demonstrate that the Association adopted the contested Regulation for the sole purpose of thwarting the endeavours of firms of accountants to penetrate the relevant market.

[95.] On that point, I would note that proceedings under Article 234 EC are based on a clear separation of functions between the national courts and the Court of Justice, and that any assessment of the facts in the case is a matter for the national court. The Court of Justice is empowered only to give rulings on the interpretation or validity of a Community provision on the basis of the facts which the national court puts before it.

In its order for reference the Raad van State found that: 'the aim of the Regulation is to safeguard the independence and duty of loyalty of lawyers providing legal assistance'. In those circumstances, it is not open to the Court to examine the facts submitted by the appellants. The argument that the Regulation has an anti-competitive object must therefore be rejected.

(b) The effects of the Regulation

[96.] On the other hand, the Raad van State asks the Court to consider whether the effects produced by the Regulation are restrictive of competition on the Netherlands market for legal services.

[97.] The Association, the CCBE and some of the Governments which have intervened consider that this question calls for a negative answer. In support of their position, they in essence rely on Decision 1999/267 adopted by the Commission in the IPR case.

In that case, the Commission was called upon to decide on the legality of the rules in the code of conduct of the Institute of Professional Representatives before the European Patent Office (the IPR). The Commission took the view that most of the rules considered fell outside the prohibition laid down by Article 85(1) of the Treaty on the ground that:

> They are necessary, in view of the specific context of this profession, in order to ensure impartiality, competence, integrity and responsibility on the part of representatives, to prevent conflicts of interest and misleading advertising, to protect professional secrecy or to guarantee the proper functioning of the [Office].

According to the Commission, the provisions of the code of conduct laying down such rules are not liable to restrict competition if they are applied objectively and without discrimination.

[98.] The interveners submit that the Commission's reasoning, although it related to patent agents, applies to all professions. Inasmuch as the purpose of the contested prohibition on partnership is to guarantee the independence and loyalty to clients of lawyers, it will therefore fall outside the scope *ratione materiœ* of Article 85(1) of the Treaty.

In its written observations, the Commission did not take up a position on that matter. In answer to a question raised by the Court, it replied briefly that the contested regulation was not liable appreciably to restrict competition in that it seeks to guarantee the independence of lawyers and to avoid conflicts of interests.

[99.] In essence, the arguments put forward by the parties invite the Court to adopt a form of 'rule of reason'. That 'rule of reason' would enable all professional rules which are intended to ensure observance of the ethical rules particular to the legal profession to evade the prohibition laid down by Article 85(1) of the Treaty.

[100.] Before I examine that idea, it should be observed that the Treaty provisions on competition are set out according to a precise structure. Article 85(1) lays down the principle that agreements restrictive of competition are prohibited. In their respective spheres of application, Articles 85(3) and 90(2) provide opportunities for derogating from that principle.

[101.] The rule of reason theory was developed in the American law on agreements. In the United States, section 1 of the Sherman Act prohibits all obstacles to competition without distinction as to degree or motive. Unlike Article 85 of the Treaty, that legislation does not provide for any possibility that the authorities might exempt an agreement.

Faced with the rigidity of that provision, the United States courts swiftly found it necessary to interpret the Sherman Act in a more 'reasonable way'. In the first place, they developed the theory called 'ancillary restrictions': they held that restrictions of competition necessary to the performance of an agreement lawful in itself fell outside the prohibition laid down in section 1 of the Sherman Act. Then, the Supreme Court of the United States of America changed its point of view and adopted what might be called the 'competition balance-sheet method'. That method is defined as being:

> An analytical method intended to draw up, for every agreement in its own context, the balance-sheet of its anti- and pro-competitive effects. If it shows a positive balance, because the agreement stimulates competition more than it restricts it, section I of the Sherman Act will not apply.

[102.] In Community competition law, the 'rule of reason may carry several meanings'. However, it is not in the circumstances of this case necessary to recall the learned disputes concerning the definition of that concept or the advisability of its introduction into Community law.

[103.] For the needs of this case I shall simply say that the Court has made limited application of the 'rule of reason' in some judgments. Confronted with certain classes of agreement, decision or concerted practice, it has drawn up a competition balance-sheet and, where the balance is positive, has held that the clauses necessary to perform the agreement fell outside the prohibition laid down by Article 85(1) of the Treaty. The Court has thus held that:

— selective distribution systems constitute an aspect of competition which accords with Article 85(1) of the Treaty, provided that resellers are chosen on the basis of objective criteria of a qualitative nature and that such conditions are laid down uniformly for all potential resellers and are not applied in a discriminatory fashion;

— the dissemination of a new agricultural product encourages competition and the grant of an open exclusive licence for its cultivation and marketing in the territory of a Member State may be necessary if that competition-encouraging objective is to be achieved;

— a contract for the transfer of an undertaking contributes to competition and clauses requiring non-competition between the parties to the agreement escape the prohibition laid down in Article 85(1) provided that they are necessary to the transfer of the undertaking and that their duration and scope are strictly limited to that purpose;

— clauses essential to the performance of a franchise agreement do not constitute restrictions of competition within the meaning of Article 85(1) of the Treaty;

— a provision in the statutes of a cooperative purchasing association, forbidding its members to participate in other forms of organised cooperation which are in direct competition with it, is not caught by the prohibition in Article 85(1), so long as that provision is restricted to what is necessary to ensure that the cooperative functions properly and maintains its contractual power in relation to producers.

[104.] It follows from those judgments that, irrespective of any terminological dispute, the 'rule of reason' in Community competition law is strictly confined to a purely competitive balance-sheet of the effects of the agreement. Where, taken as a whole, the agreement is capable of encouraging competition on the market, the clauses essential to its performance may escape the prohibition laid down in Article 85(1) of the Treaty. The only 'legitimate goal which may be pursued in accordance with that provision is therefore exclusively competitive in nature'.

[105.] In this case, the argument put forward by the interveners and the Commission goes far beyond the scope of the competition balance-sheet allowed by the Court's case-law.

The parties do not maintain that the effect of the Regulation is to encourage competition on the market in legal services. As the observations made in response to the first question indicate, the parties believe that the prohibition of multi-disciplinary partnerships between lawyers and accountants is necessary in order to protect aspects of the profession—independence and loyalty to the client—which are essential in a State governed by the rule of law. Their reasoning therefore amounts to introducing into the provisions of Article 85(1) considerations which are linked to the pursuit of a public-interest objective.

[106.] In that regard, I regret the fact that the Commission has not set out the legal reasoning supporting its position. As academic legal writing has shown, it is possible that Decision 1999/267 in the IPR case is explained more by the concern to avoid notifying the professional rules adopted by the association authorities in the various Member States. We know that as Community law now stands the Commission alone has power to adopt decisions providing for exemption pursuant to Article 85(3) of the Treaty.

However, if we attempt to analyse the Commission's reasoning, it would appear to fall into several successive stages. The point is to establish whether:

(1) the professional rule in question involves a restriction of competition on the relevant market;

(2) the professional rule pursues a legitimate objective, having regard to the characteristics of the profession (the preservation of the independence, loyalty to clients, powers, integrity or responsibility of lawyers, the protection of professional secrecy or the need to avoid conflicts of interest);

(3) the professional rule is necessary if the objective it pursues is to be attained; and

(4) the professional rule is applied objectively and without discrimination.

[107.] Having regard to those various components, I think that the interveners' argument misconstrues the *ratio legis* and the structure of the Treaty provisions.

In the first place, it amounts to introducing into the wording of Article 85(1) of the Treaty considerations which are linked to the pursuit of a public-interest objective. In the second, it sets all the questions of fact and of law in the context of that provision. It implies that the Court should consider, in the light of Article 85(1) of the Treaty exclusively, not only the question of determining whether a restriction of competition exists but also whether or not it might be justified. Such an interpretation is liable to negate a great part of the effectiveness of Articles 85(3) and 90(2) of the Treaty.

My evaluation of this point is confirmed by the judgment of the Court of First Instance in *Institute of Professional Representatives* v *Commission*. The Court held that: 'it cannot be accepted that rules which organise the exercise of a profession fall as a matter of principle outside the scope of Article 81(1) EC merely because they are classified as rules of professional conduct by the competent bodies'.

[108.] In consequence, I propose that the Court should dismiss the argument put forward by the interveners.

[109.] Before I explain my position, it is important to point out that we cannot rely simply on reading the provisions of the Treaty in order to examine the rules adopted by professional associations.

[110.] In his Opinion in *Pavlov*, Mr Jacobs stated that: 'Owing to the heterogeneity of the professions and the specificities of the markets on which they operate, no general formula can be applied'. I fully concur with that analysis.

It seems to me to be impossible to identify a single formula which might cover all the professional rules relating to all the professions in the various Member States. Each professional rule must be examined on a case-by-case basis, depending on its subject-matter, context and purpose.

[111.] One of the challenges raised by the issue of the application of Community competition law to the professions is how to identify solutions which will reflect the structure and broad logic of the Treaty provisions. In this connection, I think it necessary to make a distributive application of the Community competition rules. From that viewpoint, it may be helpful to refer to a reading plan including the following three guidelines.

[112.] First, it is not inconceivable that, having regard to the characteristics of the market for legal services, certain professional rules may be likely to encourage competition within the meaning of the Court's case-law as it now stands.

As Mr Jacobs has observed, the markets for professional services are notable for asymmetric information. In so far as the consumer is rarely in a position to assess the quality of the services provided, certain rules might prove necessary in order to ensure that the market operates in normal competitive conditions. Thus, there are those who claim that rules restricting advertising make it possible to avoid introducing systematic enticement into the market and, in the long term, a falling-off in the general quality of the services.

Following that line of thought, academic writers have put forward the idea that the rules forbidding lawyers to fix their fees on the basis of the result obtained could have pro-competitive effects. However that may be, professional rules which are in fact capable of encouraging or guaranteeing normal competition on the market for legal services might fall outside the prohibition laid down in Article 85(1) by virtue of the 'rule of reason'.

[113.] Second, I would point out that in Community competition law there are no infringements which are inherently incapable of qualifying for an exemption under Article 85(3) of the Treaty.

According to the case-law, the wording of Article 85(3) makes it possible to take account of the particular nature of different branches of the economy, social concerns and, to a certain extent, considerations connected with the pursuit of the public interest. Professional rules which, in the light of those criteria, produce economic effects which are positive, taken as a whole, should therefore be eligible for exemption under Article 85(3) of the Treaty.

[114.] Finally, Article 90(2) of the Treaty applies specifically to undertakings entrusted with the operation of services of general economic interest. It is therefore possible that professional rules aimed at the preservation, in the public interest, of certain essential features of the profession of lawyer may fall within the ambit of that provision. That is, in addition, the subject of the fifth question.

[115.] Inasmuch as I propose that the interveners' argument be rejected, it remains to be considered whether the Regulation produces effects restricting competition on the Netherlands market for legal services.

[116.] In that regard, the arguments put forward by the appellants in the main proceedings are persuasive. In the absence of the contested prohibition on partnership, competition would be likely to develop in various ways.

[117.] First, by entering into multi-disciplinary partnerships with lawyers, accountants would be in a position to improve their services qualitatively and quantitatively.

In general, lawyers have a monopoly of pre-trial work and representation. In most cases, they alone are able to represent natural and legal persons before the judicial authorities of a State. As a result of their activity, lawyers therefore have solid experience in the field of litigation. In addition, they enjoy prestige which frequently prompts them to uphold their clients' interests before extra-judicial authorities (administrative bodies, supranational bodies, the press, etc.).

By being associated with members of the legal profession, accountants could benefit from their experience. Their opinions, consultations and the documents they draw up in various areas of the law could be more reliable, better informed and, as a result, offer significant gains. Furthermore, accountants would be able to extend the range of services they offer to their clients. As a result of their partnership with lawyers, the common structure could undertake the representation of their clients' interests before the judicial authorities in the event of litigation.

[118.] Conversely, lawyers in association with accountants could also improve the quality and diversity of their services.

Taking account of their activities, accountants have gained real experience in some legal spheres, such as tax law, the law of accountancy, financial law, legislation on aid to undertakings and the rules relating to the (re)structuring of undertakings. Lawyers could benefit from the experience acquired by accountants in those various fields and, thus, improve the quality of the legal services offered.

Furthermore, accountants operate on markets other than that of the provision of legal services. They also offer services in such areas as the certification of accounts, auditing, book-keeping and management consultancy. Creating an associative structure with accountants would enable lawyers to offer a distinctly more varied range of services to their clients.

[119.] Second, integrating those various services into a single structure would bring additional advantages both for the professionals concerned and for consumers.

In the first place, lawyers and accountants should be able to achieve economies of scale since the common structure would comprise a greater number of service providers. Those economies of scale ought to be reflected in the cost of providing the services and, eventually, have positive effects for consumers in terms of price.

Next, clients would be able to turn to a single structure for a large part of the services required for the organisation, management and operation of their businesses. They would, as a result, obtain services which were better adapted to their needs since the structure would possess overall and in-depth knowledge of their policies (commercial policy, sales strategy, personnel management, etc.) and the difficulties they encounter. In addition, clients ought to be able to save both time and money. They would not themselves need to coordinate the services offered by the two professional categories (lawyers and accountants), and could simply communicate to just one person all the information necessary for handling their business.

[120.] In this connection, a study carried out at national level indicates that undertakings are not unanimous in demanding the establishment of such multi-disciplinary structures. In those States in which they are authorised, it seems that each undertaking individually chooses the type of organisation which it finds most suited to its needs (single structure or multiple providers). None the less, the conclusion to be drawn from that study is that there is a genuine demand for that kind of structure, including lawyers and members of the professional category of accountants.

[121.] In those circumstances, I consider that the effect of the contested regulation is to restrict competition within the common market. It hinders the appearance on the market of associative structures capable of offering 'integrated services' for which there exists potential demand on the part of consumers. The effect of the contested Regulation is therefore to 'limit or control production, markets, technical development or investment within the meaning of Article 85(1)(b) of the Treaty'.

(c) Whether the restriction of competition is appreciable

[122.] It is clear from established case-law that Article 85(1) of the Treaty prohibits only those restrictions of competition that are appreciable.

[123.] In this case, several factors make it possible to state that the Regulation appreciably restricts competition on the Netherlands market for legal services.

[124.] First, the contested Regulation applies to all lawyers registered in the Netherlands. In accordance with Article 29 of the Advocatenwet, the Regulation also applies to visiting lawyers, that is to say, to persons authorised to practise their professional activity in another Member State under the title of lawyer or an equivalent title. Plainly, competition is less affected where the Association's bodies adopt an individual decision concerning just one member of the profession.

[125.] Second, the parties concerned by the contested Regulation occupy a major position on the Netherlands market for legal services.

According to information supplied by the parties to the main proceedings, the market share held by the legal profession on the market for legal services in the Netherlands amounts to between 35 and 50 per cent. The market shares held by firms of accountants have not been communicated to the Court.

Nevertheless, certain official documents indicate that Arthur Andersen Worldwide and Price Waterhouse achieve 17 to 20 per cent of turnover from the one area of tax advisory services. The turnover of each firm worldwide is between 8,000,000,000 and 10,000,000,000 euros.

[126.] Lastly, the restriction imposed by the Regulation affects an essential element of competition, since it has a direct effect on the services which operators are authorised to offer on the market. According to the Court's case-law, the competition on services between operators constitutes an important factor in the context of Article 85(1) of the Treaty.

[127.] It follows from the above that the Regulation has the effect of restricting competition to an appreciable degree.

NOTE: The rule of reason has particular resonance in the context of distribution agreements and is discussed alongside the Commission's Green Paper on *Vertical Restraints in EC Competition Policy* (COM C96) 721 (final) and subsequent developments in Chapter 6, e.g. the Commission's revised policy as set out in the Guidelines accompanying Regulation 2790/99.

FURTHER READING

Odudu, O., 'Interpreting Article 81(1): object as subjective intention', ELRev 2001, 26(1) pp. 60–75.

SECTION 3: Consequences of infringement: Article 81(2) EC

Parties face severe consequences for infringement of Article 81(1) EC. First, there are important civil consequences. Article 81(2) EC provides that 'any agreements or decisions prohibited pursuant to this Article shall be automatically void' unless the provisions which infringe Article 81(1) EC are severable and are not sufficiently serious to render the whole agreement void. The prohibited clauses are unenforceable although the parties may be required to implement the remainder of the agreement, subject to the possiblity of severance. Reference however must be made to the important judgment of the English Court of Appeal in *Passmore* v *Morland* in which the Court of Appeal determined that the automatic nullity of Article 81(2) is of a 'temporaneous or transient character' (*Passmore* v *Morland* [1999] EuLR [1999] 1 CMLR 1129 (*per* Chadwick L). Accordingly, the agreement may move 'in and out' of the prohibition in paragraph 1.

The landmark decision of the Court in Case C-453/99 *Courage* v *Crehan* [2001] ECR I-6297 [2001] 5 CMLR 28 (see the Opinion of Advocate General Mischo in particular, 22 March 2001) highlights the tension between the application of

Community law in the national courts and national procedural autonomy. See *The Times*, 4 October, 2001. The Court confirmed that Community law precludes a rule of national law which prevents the recovery of damages merely by reason of being a party to an illegal contract. This decision is of great potential significance and is discussed more fully in Chapter 3.

A: Fines

Parties to a prohibited agreement face substantial fines by the Commission of up to 10 per cent of annual turnover based on worldwide turnover. The largest fine to date, imposed on 21 November 2001, totalled 855.22 million euros in respect of eight companies (e.g. Hoffman-La Roche) involved in various market-sharing and price-fixing cartels in the vitamins market between 1989 and 1999. The sums included a 50 per cent reduction granted under the Leniency Notice of 1996 in view of the undertaking's cooperation in the investigation.

SECTION 4: Exemptions: Article 81(3) EC

Article 81(3) EC has had an important role given the large number of agreements which are potentially caught by Article 81(1) EC. To recap: an agreement caught by the prohibition contained in Article 81(1) EC is null and void under Article 81(2) EC unless it merits an individual or block exemption in terms of the criteria set out in Article 81(3) EC. There are two types of exemption—an individual exemption decision by the Commission, or exemption for a 'category of agreement', under a Commission Block Exemption Regulation. At present, Regulation 17/62 gives the Commission exclusive power to grant an exemption under Article 81(3) EC although the Commission proposes further radical changes to the exemption system, discussed below, p. 209 and Chapter 3. We shall begin our discussion with individual exemptions.

A: Individual exemptions

At present, the Commission is the sole determinant of the Article 81(3) EC criteria and deals with notifications for an exemption on a case-by-case approach. All four criteria, set out above, two positive and two negative must be met. The following case demonstrates the operation of Article 81(3) EC.

Matra Hachette SA v *Commission*
(Case T-17/93) [1994] ECR II-595

> The Commission had determined that the agreement between two competing motor-vehicle undertakings to combine manufacturing activities in the relevant market fell within Article 81(1). The question for the Court was whether the agreement fulfilled the criteria set out in Article 81(3) EC.

[104] It must first be borne in mind that the Commission may only grant an individual exemption decision if, in particular, the four conditions laid down by Article 85(3) of the Treaty are all met by the agreement, with the result that an exemption must be refused if any of the four conditions is not met (judgment of the Court of Justice in Joined Cases 43/82 and 63/82 *VBVB* and *VBBB* v *Commission* [1984] ECR 19; judgment of the Court of First Instance in Case T-66/89 *Publishers Association* v *Commission* [1992] ECR II-1995); secondly, it is incumbent upon notifying undertakings to provide the Commission with evidence that the conditions laid down by Article 85(3) are met (judgment in *VBVB* and *VBBB* v *Commission*, cited above), an obligation which, in the proceedings before the Court, must be assessed in the light of the onus which falls on the applicant to provide information to challenge the Commission's appraisal; thirdly, where complex economic facts are involved, judicial review of the legal characterization of the facts is limited to the possibility of the Commission having committed a manifest error of assessment (judgment of the Court of Justice in Case 42/84 *Remia and Others* v *Commission* [1985] ECR 2545).

[105] With regard more particularly to the first of the four conditions laid down by Article 85(3), it should be borne in mind that, by virtue of that provision, the agreements which may qualify for an exemption are those which contribute 'to improving the production or distribution of goods or to promoting technical or economic progress'.

. . .

[108] The Court therefore considers that, having regard to paragraph 24 of the Decision, as analysed above, the discussion of the appraisal in this case of the first of the four conditions is limited to the question whether, as maintained by the Commission and contrary to the arguments put forward by the applicant, the manufacturing process for the 'VX62' vehicle, as described in paragraph 25 of the Decision, together with the improvements to the product referred to in paragraph 26, are such as to justify the application of the provisions in question to the present case.

[109] As regards, first, the manufacturing process, it is clear from the unambiguous statements from the intervener, Ford, which have not been seriously challenged by the applicant, that the manufacturing process to be used at Setúbal constitutes the first application by a European car manufacturer of the enhanced form of the manufacturing process recommended in 1990 by the most authoritative researchers in the field of technological development, such as the Massachusetts Institute of Technology (MIT). The Court considers, despite the applicant's assertions to the contrary, that an optimization of the manufacturing process of that kind is in conformity with the meaning and purpose of the first of the four conditions laid down by Article 85(3) of the Treaty.

[110] As regards, secondly, the technical improvements made to the product, described as 'cosmetic' by the applicant, they must be assessed in relation to the state of development of car construction techniques in Europe when the Decision was adopted. Adopting that approach, the Court considers that, as maintained by the Commission, the technical improvements made to the vehicle fall within the scope of Article 85(3), since they bring together in a single product techniques which, where they exist, are at present used in isolation, on different models.

[111] It follows that the Commission's assessment, according to which the manufacturing process for the vehicle and the technical improvements made to the product are conducive to improvement of the production or distribution of products or to the promotion of technical or economic progress, does not contain any manifest error.

. . .

[120] The Court would point out in the first place that, according to the second of the four conditions laid down by Article 85(3) of the Treaty, agreements qualifying for exemption are those which allow consumers 'a fair share of the resulting benefit'. The question whether the project in

question satisfies that condition is examined in paragraph 27 of the Decision, according to which the exempted project will enable economies of scale to be achieved and promote intensified competition in the market, to the benefit of the European consumer.

[121] Examination of the applicant's criticisms on this point shows that they raise two main questions.

[122] The first question is whether, as contended, the advantage given to the consumer must be assessed by reference to the present state of the market or by reference to the advantage that might have been afforded to the consumer in the event of the founders having chosen to penetrate the market individually. The Court considers that, as rightly maintained by the Commission, the applicant's reasoning is based on false premises. At that stage of the examination of the application for exemption, it is incumbent upon the Commission to appraise the project submitted to it as objectively as possible, without in any way considering the appropriateness of the project by reference to other technically possible or economically viable choices, since it is common ground that it is when considering the third of the four conditions laid down by Article 85(3) of the Treaty that the Commission may, in order to appraise the indispensability of the restrictions on competition resulting from the project in question, take account of other possible choices. The applicant's view that the advantage made available to the consumer by the project in question should be assessed by reference to the advantage accruing to the consumer from other technologically possible or economically viable choices is therefore, to that extent, unfounded.

[123] The applicant's argument then raises the question whether the project at issue is capable of affording the founders a collective dominant position. In that regard, the applicant's reasoning is based on the idea that the existence of considerable excess production capacity, linked with substantial State aid, enables the founders to engage in unfair practices, ousting the competition and, in the longer term, giving the founders a collective dominant position, which they will abuse to the detriment of the consumer (see below, paragraph 153).

[124] The Court considers that the applicant's reasoning takes for granted, successively, the acquisition by the founders of a collective dominant position, then the abuse by those undertakings of that position. Such reasoning is purely hypothetical and can only be rejected, without its being necessary for the Court to say whether, in the presence of an adequately substantiated infringement of Article 86 of the Treaty, the Commission is required to reject a request for an exemption (see below, paragraph 154).

. . .

[135] According to the terms of the third and fourth conditions laid down by Article 85(3) of the Treaty, exemption is available for agreements which do not 'impose on the undertakings concerned restrictions (of competition) which are not indispensable to the attainment of (the) objectives' of improving the production or distribution of products and promoting technical or economic progress, while allowing consumers a fair share of the resulting benefit. It follows that the Decision must establish that any adverse effects on competition resulting from the project are proportionate to the contribution made by it to economic or technical progress. As stated in the judgment of the Court of Justice in Joined Cases 56/64 and 58/64 *Consten and Grundig* v *Commission* [1966] ECR 299, 'this improvement must in particular show appreciable objective advantages of such a character as to compensate for the disadvantages which they cause in the field of competition'. It is therefore for the Court to verify whether, as contended by the founders, any adverse affects on competition deriving from the project in question are indispensable in order to attain the objectives of achieving economic and technical progress.

. . .

[138] The Court considers that, as the Commission maintains, the central question to be answered, in assessing the legality of the Decision in relation to the third of the four conditions laid down in Article 85(3) of the Treaty, is whether the joint venture is strictly indispensable to enable the founders to penetrate the market in question. If that question is answered in the affirmative, it will *ipso facto* be established that the restrictions of competition deriving from the agreement are indispensable in order to attain the objectives pursued by the two conditions examined above, in particular the first one. The answer is indeed affirmative, since the Commission maintains, without being contradicted in any serious way by the applicant, whose reasoning is based on non-comparable situations, that, if each of the founders actually was technically and financially capable of penetrating the market individually, such penetration could be achieved only at a loss, in view of the particularly high level of the joint venture's 'break-even point' and of the information available concerning forecasts of sales and market shares.

. . .

[150] The Court would point out, first, that, by virtue of the last of the four conditions imposed by Article 85(3) of the Treaty, an individual exemption decision may be available for agreements which do not 'afford . . . undertakings the possibility of eliminating competition in respect of a substantial part of the products in question'.

[151] In the present case, that point is covered by paragraphs 37 and 38 of the Decision. According to paragraph 37, cooperation between Ford and VW, far from eliminating competition in the multi-purpose vehicle segment, will on the contrary stimulate it, in view of the important position occupied by the 'Espace'. In paragraph 38, the Decision states that the differentiation of the products offered by each of the two founders will have a positive effect on competition between car manufacturers in Europe at the distribution stage.

[152] In challenging those two paragraphs of the Decision, the applicant argues, first, that the Setúbal plant will give rise to excess production capacity in the market concerned. However, the Court notes that the applicant has not established that the Decision is incorrect in that respect, in particular paragraphs 6 and 14 thereof, which are confirmed by Ford's statements. Moreover, in its judgment in *Matra* v *Commission*, cited above, the Court of Justice held that 'as regards the evaluation of the risk of excess production capacity, . . . the Commission carried out a comprehensive and detailed examination of this question before concluding that no such risk exists. . . . In those circumstances, the arguments put forward by Matra . . . are not such as to establish that the Commission based its decision on a manifestly incorrect assessment of the economic data' (paragraphs 26 and 28). The applicant's argument must therefore be rejected, without its being necessary for the Court to consider whether, as contended by the applicant, which relies in particular on an expert's report from Professor Encaoua, the existence of excess production capacity will necessarily have the effect of ousting competitors.

[153] The applicant claims, secondly, that the existence of excess production capacity will, in time, enable the founders to achieve a collective dominant position. However, the Court considers that, as stated by the Commission, the achievement or strengthening of a dominant position, whether individual or collective, is not as such prohibited by Articles 85 and 86 of the Treaty. Article 86 merely prohibits the abuse of a dominant position by one or more undertakings. Accordingly, an alleged risk that the founders might in time collectively achieve a dominant position cannot in any event constitute legal justification for withholding an exemption, the likelihood of that risk materializing during the period of validity of the Decision not having been established by the applicant.

[154] Accordingly, the Court considers that, as already stated in paragraph 124 above, the argument based on the risk of the achievement and abuse of a collective dominant position must be rejected in any event, without its being necessary for the Court to decide whether—as the applicant

necessarily implies—the Commission should, in the presence of a sufficiently clear infringement of Article 86 of the Treaty, reject an application for an individual exemption.

NOTE: Amato observes that 'the decision eloquently symbolises the infiltrations of industrial policy that have long marked European antitrust law', *Antitrust and the Bounds of Power: The Dilemma of Liberal Democracy in the History of the Market* (see below) at p. 59. In the following extract, he criticises the weight the Court gives to non-competition criteria:

Amato, G., *Antitrust and the Bounds of Power: The Dilemma of Liberal Democracy in the History of the Market*
Oxford, Hart Publishing, 1997, pp. 61–62

In the first place, there is the ambiguous relevance/irrelevance allowed to the social profile of the affair: the expected jobs in a depressed area. It is an aspect that certainly interests the European Community, is in fact protected by specific instruments (from the Community regional policies to the review of State aids directed at similar ends), but does not fall within the antitrust purview, given that Article 85(3), analytical as it is, does not mention it among the grounds for exemption. In this case, however, it ended up having some weight; otherwise it would not have been mentioned, and certainly not to say it led to 'exceptional circumstances', however additional.

Secondly, there are the very broad concepts both of productive improvement, and of technical progress, both detached from the proven presence of innovations that are the outcome of research and development and made instead to include in principle any organizational pattern capable of promising higher productivity. In these circumstances it amounts to an almost unbounded concept, applicable accordingly to the bulk of new manufacturing plants that replace previous installations. Thirdly, there is the basing of the benefit to consumers on the relationship with the existing position, and not instead with the one resulting from continuing competition between the two parties to the agreement. Under the apparent good sense of the arguments used . . . there is, for a competition authority assessing the practices of firms in relation to their restrictive potential, a real error in law, explicable only by the specific features of the case: the complainant is the firm that (almost) dominates the market and will see a stronger competitor emerge from the agreement. If that is so, however, the argument ought to have been different, with the comparison involving on the one hand the competitive efficiency—against Matra-Renault—of the joint product, and on the other what separate products by VW and Ford might instead have led to.

. . . [T]he principles of argument that result show surprising permeability of the antitrust principles, which are hybridized and weakened by the joint presence of industrial policy and social cohesion objectives. The original subsidiarity of the competition principle in relation to other principles laid down by the Treaty thus displays continuing vitality that goes well beyond the capacity for these principles to act as a merely external limit, going instead as far as corroding the sense and logic of the antitrust machinery from within.

NOTE: There has been considerable debate since the inception of the Community concerning the purpose of the Article 81(3) EC criteria. What are the criteria designed to achieve? Should Article 81(3) EC permit a discussion of non-competition considerations? In the next case, the Court certainly seemed prepared to countenance non-competition factors as a basis for exemption.

Metro-SB-Grossmärkte GmbH v *Commission (No 1)*
Case 26/76 [1977] ECR 1875, [1978] 2 CMLR 1

[43] With regard to the first condition set out above, the conclusion of supply contracts for six months taking account of the probable growth of the market should make it possible to ensure both a certain stability in the supply of the relevant products, which should allow the requirements of persons obtaining supplies from the wholesaler to be more fully satisfied, and, since such supply

contracts are of relatively short duration, a certain flexibility, enabling production to be adapted to the changing requirements of the market. Thus a more regular distribution is ensured, to the benefit both of the producer, who takes his share of the planned expansion of the market in the relevant product, of the wholesaler, whose supplies are secured, and, finally, of the undertakings which obtain supplies from the wholesaler, in that the variety of available products is increased. Another improvement in distribution is provided under the clause in the cooperation agreement obliging SABA to compensate wholesalers for service performed under guarantee and to supply spare parts necessary for repairs under guarantee. Furthermore, the establishment of supply forecasts for a reasonable period constitutes a stabilising factor with regard to the provision of employment which, since it improves the general conditions of production, especially when the market conditions are unfavourable, comes within the framework of the objectives to which reference may be had pursuant to Article 85 (3).

NOTE: The 'search for the soul of Article 81(3) EC' has assumed greater relevance in the context of the Community's Modernisation regulation which will give national courts and the NCA's power to apply the exemption criteria. The Commission's White Paper on Modernisation rejected the consideration of non-economic concerns as part of the balancing test to be carried out under Article 81(3) EC. The Commission stated at para. 56 that Article 81(3) EC is intended 'to provide a legal framework for the economic assessment of restrictive practices and not to allow the application of the competition rules to be set aside because of political considerations'. This statement is puzzling given the Court's insistence that the EC competition rules must be interpreted in light of the Treaty objectives, and it is also difficult to reconcile with some of the Commission's previous decisions, which confirm the relevance of a broad range of factors under Article 81(3) EC not only economic factors but also social, cultural, industrial and environmental issues. The Commission appears to be concerned that the criteria would be open to subjective interpretation by the national courts. Some commentators have suggested that national courts are not appropriate fora for making determinations under Article 81(3) EC, a view the authors of the following extract emphatically reject.

Whish, R., and Sufrin, B., 'Community Competition Law: Notification and Exemption-Goodbye to All That', in Hayton, D., *Law's Future(s): British Legal Developments in the 21st Century*
Oxford, Hart Publishing, 2000, p. 150

In considering whether national courts are appropriate fora for making determinations under Article 81(3), the authors of this chapter stress that in their view the problem is emphatically *not* that economics is too difficult for judges. The issue of whether there is a restriction of competition, which is already within the ambit of national judges given that Article 81(1) is directly applicable, in itself demands economic analysis, which may be more complex than the application of Article 81(3) in its narrow 'competition' sense. The point is rather that, if the question asked by Article 81(3) does require the consideration of *non-competition matters*, it is arguable that this needs a public body to do it because the nature of the decision, which involves a balancing of public and private interests and of the requirements of different Community policies, is unsuited to judicial determination. Other Member States, in adopting Community style competition provisions in their domestic laws, have not taken on board the broad sweep of Article 81(3), and exemptions under the Competition Act 1998 in the United Kingdom will be given by the Director General of Fair Trading, not the courts. There seems little judicial enthusiasm in the United Kingdom for applying Article 81(3).

To sum up: whether or not non-competition policies *should* be taken into account under Article 81(3), the conclusion must be that it is inconvenient in terms of the White Paper if they *are*, because interpreted broadly the Article 81(3) criteria are inimical to direct applicability. If the Commission says long and hard enough in the lead up to any implementation of the White Paper that the purpose of

Article 81(3) is only to provide for additional economic analysis, and follows a self-denying ordinance in any exemptions it issues, that interpretation may for practical purposes become the orthodoxy. The difficulty, of course, would be if the Court were to continue to interpret Article 81(3) to admit other policies, as it has been prepared to do in the past. It is, in any event, impossible to disguise the fact that the White Paper proposals do not merely concern matters of procedure, but go to the meaning of Article 81(3) itself. It may be that the Commission should go further than the White Paper proposal and advocate the abolition of Article 81(3) altogether, leaving the entire analysis of agreement to the test set out in Article 81(1): that, however, would require a Treaty amendment.

NOTE: Cf. Rein Wessling, 'The draft regulation modernising the competition rules: The Commission is married to one idea' (2001) 26 ELRev 357.

B: Block exemptions

Block exemptions offer practical benefits for undertakings since they exempt 'categories of agreements' without requiring prior approval by the Commission. The four criteria articulated in Article 81(3) EC equally apply in Block Exemption regulations. Block exemptions offer the business world greater certainty and, provided an agreement conforms with the terms of the Block Exemption, it will not require to be notified to the Commission and is deemed compatible with the Community competition rules. The Commission has adopted block exemptions for a number of different types of agreement: Research and development 2659/2000; motor-vehicle distribution 1400/2002; specialisation agreements 2658/2000; technology transfer 240/96 (under review); and the so-called single umbrella regulation for vertical agreements 2790/99.

C: Reform of the exemption procedure

Article 81(3) EC presented the Commission with a unique opportunity to develop the Community's competition policy in a way that it saw fit. Certainly, in the early days of the Community, the Commission seized the chance to promote market integration through the competition rules. However, the wide construction afforded to the notion of *'object or effect the prevention, restriction or distortion'* has meant that a vast number of essentially benign agreements have been caught within the general prohibition in Article 81(1) EC, only to be considered for exemption under the four criteria articulated in Article 81(3) EC. Although this policy proved successful in the early years, enabling the Commission to gather information about the ways in which undertakings conducted their business throughout the Community, it quickly became the victim of its own success, and the Commission has had difficulties in coping with a vast workload. The formalism of the block exemption system has also been heavily criticised over the years. Although block exemptions avoided the need for notification, companies faced problems in tailoring their agreements to fit the narrow terms of the Regulations, often at the expense of the most appropriate and efficient forms of business. A number of quick-fix measures were implemented, for example the introduction of an 'opposition procedure' in some block exemption regulations and the use of so-called 'comfort letters'. See generally Chapter 3. The Commission recently published a Regulation which introduces radical changes to the exemption procedure. The regulation will devolve power to the national competition authorities and courts. This is a bold initiative and given its significance for the competition law enforcement process, is discussed in detail in Chapter 3.

SECTION 5:   Horizontal agreements

Collusion in a market is generally prohibited under Article 81(1) (see p. 166 above). However, there may be occasions when cooperation between independent undertakings is desirable, for instance research and developments projects (R & D). The Commission has tended to adopt a strict approach to horizontal cooperation agreements; any efficiency gains are only considered under Article 81(3). This approach attracted criticism for much the same reasons as vertical agreements— undertakings were required to notify agreements to the Commission in order to be considered for an exemption, or tailor their agreement in order to meet the narrow and formalistic requirements of the block exemptions, see for instance in relation to specialisation agreements, Regulation 417/85, and for R & D agreements, Regulation 418/85. In keeping with its new economic-oriented approach to verticals implemented in 2000 (Regulation 2790/99), the Commission adopted two new block exemptions, Regulation 2658/2000 for specialisation agreements, ([2000] OJ L304/3) and Regulation 2659/2000 for R & D agreements, ([2000] OJ L304/7). They both introduce market share thresholds and are accompanied by detailed Guidelines on Horizontal Cooperation Agreements ([2001] OJ C3/2). The Guidelines articulate the Commission's new economic-oriented approach in relation to horizontal cooperation agreements and establish an analytical framework for the most common types of agreements.

Guidelines on the applicability of Article 81 of the EC Treaty to horizontal cooperation agreements
OJ 2001 C3/2

2. Horizontal cooperation may lead to competition problems. This is for example the case if the parties to a cooperation agree to fix prices or output, to share markets, or if the cooperation enables the parties to maintain, gain or increase market power and thereby causes negative market effects with respect to prices, output, innovation or the variety and quality of products.

3. On the other hand, horizontal cooperation can lead to substantial economic benefits. Companies need to respond to increasing competitive pressure and a changing market place driven by globalisation, the speed of technological progress and the generally more dynamic nature of markets. Cooperation can be a means to share risk, save costs, pool know-how and launch innovation faster. In particular for small and medium-sized enterprises cooperation is an important means to adapt to the changing market place.

. . .

6. Changing markets have generated an increasing variety and use of horizontal cooperation. More complete and updated guidance is needed to improve clarity and transparency regarding the applicability of Article 81 in this area. Within the assessment greater emphasis has to be put on

economic criteria to better reflect recent developments in enforcement practice and the case law of the Court of Justice and Court of First Instance of the European Communities.

7. The purpose of these guidelines is to provide an analytical framework for the most common types of horizontal cooperation. This framework is primarily based on criteria that help to analyse the economic context of a cooperation agreement. Economic criteria such as the market power of the parties and other factors relating to the market structure, form a key element of the assessment of the market impact likely to be caused by a cooperation and therefore for the assessment under Article 81. Given the enormous variety in types and combinations of horizontal cooperation and market circumstances in which they operate, it is impossible to provide specific answers for every possible scenario. The present analytical framework based on economic criteria will neverthe-less assist businesses in assessing the compatibility of an individual cooperation agreement with Article 81.

. . .

Market power and market structure
27. The starting point for the analysis is the position of the parties in the markets affected by the cooperation. This determines whether or not they are likely to maintain, gain or increase market power through the cooperation, i.e. have the ability to cause negative market effects as to prices, output, innovation or the variety or quality of goods and services. To carry out this analysis the relevant market(s) have to be defined by using the methodology of the Commission's market def-inition notice. Where specific types of markets are concerned such as purchasing or technology markets, these guidelines will provide additional guidance.

. . .

29. In addition to the market position of the parties and the addition of market shares, the market concentration, i.e. the position and number of competitors, may have to be taken into account as an additional factor to assess the impact of the cooperation on market competition. As an indicator the Herfindahl-Hirshman Index ('HHI'), which sums up the squares of the individual market shares of all competitors, can be used: With an HHI below 1,000 the market concentration can be characterised as low, between 1,000 and 1,800 as moderate and above 1,800 as high. Another possible indicator would be the leading firm concentration ratio, which sums up the individual market shares of the leading competitors.

30. Depending on the market position of the parties and the concentration in the market, other factors such as the stability of market shares over time, entry barriers and the likelihood of market entry, the countervailing power of buyers/suppliers or the nature of the products (e.g. homogeneity, maturity) have to be considered as well. Where an impact on competition in innovation is likely and cannot be assessed adequately on the basis of existing markets, specific factors to analyse these impacts may have to be taken into account.

NOTE: The full text of the Guidelines on Horizontal Cooperation is reproduced in Middleton, K., UK/EC Competition Documents, OUP, 2nd edn, p. 580.

FURTHER READING

Frazer, T., 'Competition Policy after 1992: The Next Step' [1990] 53 MLR 609.

Ehlermann, C.D., 'The Contribution of EC Competition Policy to the Single Market' (1992) 29 CML Rev 257.

6

Vertical restraints

SECTION 1: Introduction

What are vertical restraints? Vertical agreements are agreements concluded between undertakings operating at different levels of a market, for example between the producer of a product and a retailer. Vertical restraints are the contractual restrictions employed in such agreements. Why are they of special concern to Community competition policy?

The application of the Community competition rules to vertical restraints has been considerably stricter than, for instance, those in the US, with the exception of price-fixing, which is per se illegal in both the US and the EU. The Community's strict approach can be partly explained by the extreme hostility with which the Commission views any restriction that threatens market integration. The Commission believes that the appointment of exclusive distributors on a Member State basis contributes to the partitioning of the single market, as well as creating barriers to entry for a new producer to enter the market see e.g. Case 56 and 58/64 *Consten & Grundig*, [1966] ECR 299, [1966] CMLR 418. By contrast, the European Court has shown more of a readiness to consider economic justifications for vertical restriction see e.g. Case 258/78 *Nungesser (L.C) KG & Kurt Eisele* v *Commission* [1982] ECR 2015, [1983] 1 CMLR 278 and Case 42/84 *Remia BV* v *Commission* [1985] ECR 2545, [1987] 1 CMLR 1. The Commission's hostile attitude has been almost universally criticised by industry, economists and legal practitioners and in particular, its failure to analyse properly the impact of the vertical restriction on the market.

Our discussion begins with an analysis of the economic debate.

SECTION 2: The economic debate

Vertical restraints can produce either positive or negative effects. They can, for instance, restrict intra-brand competition (competition between market operators at the same level of market and in relation to the same brand). This is a particular concern in selective and exclusive distribution systems where such restraints can lead to a reduction in consumer choice and higher prices. For example, the nature of selective and exclusive distribution in the European car industry is widely believed to be the reason for the disparity in car prices across the EU and the lack of intra-brand competition in the market. (See Commission's Evaluation Report 2000. A New Block Exemption Regulation 1400/2002 came into force on 1 October 2002.) It is clear, however, that vertical agreements can also work to stimulate inter-brand competition (competition between different brands of competing products), encouraging the entry of new products on the market and enhancing consumer welfare. Note for example, the US Supreme Court's attitude towards inter-brand competition: 'Interbrand competition . . . is the primary concern of antitrust law. . . . When interbrand competition exists . . . it provides a significant check on the exploitation of intrabrand market power because of the ability of consumers to substitute a different brand of the same product', *Continental TV Inc.* v *GTE Sylvania Inc.* 433 US 36 (1977) p. 581.

Given the importance of vertical restraints in competition policy, it is not surprising that there has been considerable academic debate on this issue. There are essentially two schools of thought. Proponents of the powerful Chicago school, notably Bork and Posner, advocate a non-interventionist approach towards vertical restraints and have based their favourable approach on the free rider rationale as explained by Gyselen.

Gyselen, L., 'Vertical Restraints in the Distribution Process: Strength and Weakness of the Free Rider Rationale under EEC Competition Law'
21 CMLRev (1984) 647

The free rider argument is above all a dealer service argument and is most powerful with respect to luxury or technically complex products. Restraints upon intrabrand competition can be designed to prevent 'parasite' dealers from taking a free ride on the promotional or servicing efforts of other dealers offering the same brand. Insofar as the restraints prevent the former from reaping where they have not sown, they induce the latter to continue their presale promotion (advertising, display, demonstration) and post sale servce (maintenance, repair). They will therefore enhance the brand's competitive position in a market governed *arguendo* by substantial non-price competition. Hence, restraints upon intrabrand competition have the redeeming virtue of promoting interbrand competition.

Bork's contribution to the economic debate has been particularly important.

Bork, R.H., *The Antitrust Paradox: A Policy at War with Itself*
Oxford, Maxwell Macmillan, 1993, pp. 297–8

We have seen that vertical price fixing (resale price maintenance), vertical market division (closed dealer territories), and, indeed, all vertical restraints are beneficial to consumers and should for that reason be completely lawful. Basic economic theory tells us that the manufacturer who imposes such restraints cannot intend to restrict and must (except in the rare case of price discrimination, which the law should regard as neutral) intend to create efficiency. The most common efficiency is the inducement or purchase by the manufacturer of extra reseller sales, service or promotional effort.

The proposal to legalize all truly vertical restraints is so much at variance with conventional thought on the topic that it will doubtless strike many readers as troublesome, if not bizarre. But I have never seen any economic analysis that shows how manufacturer-imposed resale price maintenance, closed dealer territories, customer allocation clauses, or the like can have the net effect of restricting output. We have too quickly assumed something that appears untrue.

Perhaps the ambiguity of the word 'restraint' accounts for some of our confusion on this topic. When the Supreme Court speaks of a restraint it often, or even usually, refers to the manufacturer's control of certain activities of his resellers or to the elimination by the manufacturer of some forms of rivalry among his resellers. There is, of course, nothing sinister or unusual about using 'restraint' in that sense. It is merely a form of vertical integration by contract, a less complete integration than that which would obtain if the manufacturer owned his outlets and directed their activities. It is merely one instance of the coordination of economic activities which is ubiquitous in the economic world and upon which our wealth depends. The important point is that such vertical control never creates 'restraint' in that other common meaning, restriction of output. Perhaps, if we are more careful about the ambiguity of the word and make it clear in which sense we use it, our reasoning about antitrust problems, including the problem of vertical restraints, will improve.

NOTE: Bork's thesis that all vertical agreements should be lawful on the grounds of efficiency has been challenged by several US scholars, and more recently by researchers in a UK context. (See Dobson P., and Waterson, M., 'Vertical Restraints and Competition Policy', December 1996 OFT Research Paper 12.) See also Whish R., and Bishop, B., 'The treatment of vertical agreements under the Competition Bill: a report for the Competition Bill Team of the Department and Trade and Industry' (London, DTI, 1998). Comanor suggests that the key consideration is whether vertical restraints are in the consumer interest.

Comanor, W.S., 'Vertical Price-fixing, Vertical Market Restrictions and the New Antitrust Policy'
98 Harvard L. Review 983 (1984–1985) at pp. 1000–1002

When vertical restraints are used to promote the provision of distribution services, the critical issue for antitrust purposes remains whether consumers are better served by lower prices and fewer services or by higher prices and more services. In its *Spray-Rite* brief, the Department of Justice suggested that pure vertical restraints always lead to increased consumer welfare. This position is unfounded, and a more hostile treatment of vertical restraints is appropriate.

Because vertical restraints can either enhance or diminish consumer welfare, depending upon the situation; it is tempting to apply the rule of reason on a case-by-case basis. After all, restraints that augment consumer welfare should be deemed 'reasonable' under existing antitrust standards. Yet it is no easy task to determine whether particular restraints increase or decrease efficiency: the answer in each case depends largely on the relative preferences of different groups of consumers. In the interests of judicial economy, therefore, it may be more expeditious to set general policy standards, even though they will sometimes lead to improper results.

Vertical restraints that concern established products are more likely to reduce consumer welfare. Large numbers of consumers are already familiar with such products and are therefore unlikely to place much value on acquiring further information about them. In this context, stringent antitrust standards should be applied to vertical price and non-price restraints alike. This approach could take the form either of a direct per se prohibition, or of a modified rule of reason analysis under which the defendant would be required to demonstrate that the restraints have benefited consumers generally. By contrast, in the case of new products or products of new entrants into the market, vertical restraints are less likely to lessen consumer welfare, because their novelty should create greater demand for information. In these circumstances, the restraints should be permissible, or at least should be treated more leniently in any modified rule of reason analysis.

FURTHER READING

See Posner, R.A., *Antitrust Law: An Economic Perspective*, Chicago, University of Chicago Press, 1976 and more specifically in the context of vertical agreements Posner, R.A., 'The Next Step in the Antitrust Treatment of Restricted Distribution: *per se* legality', 48 U Chi L Rev 6 (1981).

NOTE: The 'battle for the soul of antitrust' continues. In the context of vertical agreements, however, a consensus has emerged among economists that vertical agreements do not generally give rise to competition concerns unless one of the parties to the agreement has significant market power, or there exists a large network of similar agreements with the possibility of foreclosure. See for example, Case 234/89 *Delimitis* v *Henninger Bräu* [1991] ECR I-935, [1992] 5 CMLR 210. This is a view now shared by the European Commission as reflected in its Green Paper on Vertical Restraints (COM (96) 721 final) and subsequent legislative reform discussed at p. 231 below.

SECTION 3: **Vertical restraints and Article 81(1) EC**

Article 81(1) EC provides the basic framework for the treatment of vertical restraints in Community law. Article 82 EC has a limited role in Community policy on vertical restraints.

The broad scope of Article 81(1) EC, catching all agreements which prevent, restrict or distort competition means that most vertical agreements fall within the general prohibition, but may benefit from an individual or block exemption under Article 81(3) EC. This regime is reinforced by Regulation 17/62, which established a centralised system of notification and authorisation. At present, only the Commission may grant an individual exemption following notification. However, the Commission's Modernisation will abolish notification and give national competition authorities a much wider role in the exemption procedure. See Chapter 3.

The application of Article 81(1) EC to vertical agreements has proved controversial. The Commission has tended to prohibit all distribution agreements under Article 81(1) EC, irrespective of any pro-competitive effects unless the agreement does not have an appreciable impact on competition or upon interstate trade. See e.g. the 2001 '*de minimis*' Notice discussed at p. 190. For instance, the Commission regards territorial restraints as restrictions of competition regardless of their market effects. This strict approach is largely attributable to the Commission's concern (some might say obsession) with achieving market integration.

The seminal decision of the Court in Cases 56 and 58/64 *Consten* and *Grundig* illustrates the Community's concern to preserve parallel trade at the expense of economic and pro-competitive considerations. The background to this case is discussed in Chapter 5. The Court accepted the Commission's findings that absolute territorial protection, which sought to prevent any parallel imports of the contract goods, is prohibited under Article 81(1) EC, but stressed that the Commission should not have prohibited the whole agreement. Thus, the provision of territorial exclusivity does not in itself infringe Article 81(1) EC.

Amato explains the Community's position.

Amato, G., *Antitrust and the Bounds of Power: The Dilemma of Liberal Democracy in the History of the Market*
Oxford, Hart Publishing, 1997, pp. 48–49

The parties maintained, first before the Commission itself and then before the Court of Justice, that Article 85 referred primarily to inter-brand competition, and that as far as intra-brand restrictions went, one had to presume efficiency in promoting inter-brand competition failing proof of the contrary. This argument copied word-for-word approaches of the Chicago School, which in fact at the time the American courts themselves had rejected, in the name of protection (dropped later in the *Sylvania* case) for the right of each distributor or retailer to exercise freedom of trade without restraint.

Our Court did not accept the arguments either, but for very different reasons. It accepted that inter-brand competition was the most relevant for the purposes of prohibition under Article 85, but added that this did not *a priori* exempt intra-brand restrictions, with the consequence— inconceivable today (and perhaps in earlier times too) for an American court—that the fact that the Commission was not concerned to ascertain the size of inter-brand competition was irrelevant. On this basis, the absolute territorial protection by which the exclusivity for France was guaranteed was illegitimate. It is indeed true, said the Court, that imports have an effect on the supply planning that Consten may engage in and on the organization of services it may offer customers. But a margin of risk is inherent in commercial activity, and in any case 'the more manufacturers isolate themselves from each other in consumers' eyes, the more competition among them is reduced. Moreover, competition among wholesale distributors of products of one and the same brand enlivens the downstream market of sales to final consumers'.

As we can see, these are very important assertions of principle that bring the decision close to the American ones of the 1960s. But there are two important differences, one explicit and the other implicit. The explicit one is that the need for intra-brand competition is based on protection not of an individual right (freedom of trade) but of a general and objective principle (competitiveness of the market in all its segments). The implicit one is that such a pervasive and rigorous principle is asserted to the extent that it serves to protect another principle, a higher one in 1966, that of market integration. For the territory protected by Consten's rigid exclusivity coincided with that of the French State, and both the Commission and the Court saw this protection as persistence of the segmentation of economic activities along national frontiers, violating the 'Grundnorm' of the whole Community system.

NOTE: Certainly the goal of full market integration must have seemed a distant dream in 1962 and the Court's strict approach is perhaps understandable. Hawk suggests that this approach in fact 'furthers the Commission's institutional interests; more specifically, it reinforces its monopoly to grant [85(3)] exemptions. If an economic analysis were made under Article [85(1)] far fewer vertical arrangements would be subject to the Commission's exclusive jurisdiction to grant individual exemptions under Article [85(3)]. Economic analysis also would be within the competence of national courts when applying Article 85(1)', Hawk, B.E., 'System Failure: Vertical Restraints and EC Competition Law' (1995) 32 CMLRev 973 at p. 982. Hawk's comments demonstrate the significance of the Commission's Modernisation regulation.

There was a notable relaxation of Community policy on vertical restraints following the Court's decision in Cases 56 and 58/64 *Consten* and *Grundig*. Although the Commission continued to outlaw any restriction conferring exclusivity or absolute territorial protection, it introduced a series of block exemption regulations, which enabled legal advisers to draft distribution agreements according to established Commission policy. Thus distribution agreements continued to be prohibited in terms of Article 81(1) EC, but benefited from a block exemption under Article 81(3) EC. The Commission finally issued a block exemption for exclusive distribution agreements in 1967, Regulation 67/67 which offered companies some legal certainty, avoiding the need for notification. Exclusive distribution agreements now fall under the umbrella of block exemption regulation 2790/99 (see p. 231 below).

In contrast to the Commission's approach, the Court indicated that it would countenance some restrictions based on an economic analysis of the effects of an agreement, provided the restrictions did not go beyond what was necessary to secure the commercial viability of the arrangement. This became known as the '*ancillary restraints*' doctrine. There have been a number of cases on this issue, mostly in the context of selective distribution. In Case 258/78 *Nungesser* v *Commission* the Court quashed the Commission's finding that an exclusive licence of plant breeders' rights infringed Article 81(1) as the Commission had failed to take into account that 'open exclusivity' might be reasonable in the circumstances to secure the considerable financial investment which was required to develop the product.

Nungesser v *Commission*
(Case 258/78) [1982] ECR 2015, [1983] 1 CMLR 278

The Court was asked to annul the Commission's decision relating to the lawfulness of an exclusive licence agreement.

B—The application of Article 85 of the EEC Treaty to exclusive licences

44 By this submission the applicants criticize the Commission for wrongly taking the view that an exclusive licence of breeders' rights must by its very nature be treated as an agreement prohibited by Article 85(1) of the Treaty. They submit that the Commission's opinion in that respect is unfounded in so far as the exclusive licence constitutes the sole means, as regards seeds which have been recently developed in a Member State and which have not yet penetrated the market of another Member State, of promoting competition between the new product and comparable products in that other Member State; indeed, no grower or trader would take the risk of launching the new product on a new market if he were not protected against direct competition from the holder of the breeders' rights and from his other licensees.

45 This contention is supported by the German and British Governments and by the *Caisse de Gestion des Licences Végétales*. In particular, the two governments claim that the general character of the reasons given for the contested decision is incompatible with the terms of Article 85 of the Treaty and conflicts with a sensible competition policy. The reasons given for the decision are said to be based on the ill-conceived premise that every exclusive licence of an industrial or commercial property right, whatever its nature, must be regarded as an agreement prohibited by Article 85(1) and that it is therefore for the Commission to judge whether, in a given case, the conditions for the grant of an exemption under Article 85 (3) are satisfied.

. . .

53 It should be observed that those two sets of considerations relate to two legal situations which are not necessarily identical. The first case concerns a so-called open exclusive licence or assignment and the exclusivity of the licence relates solely to the contractual relationship between the owner of the right and the licensee, whereby the owner merely undertakes not to grant other licences in respect of the same territory and not to compete himself with the licensee on that

territory. On the other hand, the second case involves an exclusive licence or assignment with absolute territorial protection, under which the parties to the contract propose, as regards the products and the territory in question, to eliminate all competition from third parties, such as parallel importers or licensees for other territories.

54 That point having been clarified, it is necessary to examine whether, in the present case, the exclusive nature of the licence, in so far as it is an open licence, has the effect of preventing or distorting competition within the meaning of Article 85(1) of the Treaty.

55 In that respect the Government of the Federal Republic of Germany emphasized that the protection of agricultural innovations by means of breeders' rights constitutes a means of encouraging such innovations and the grant of exclusive rights for a limited period, is capable of providing a further incentive to innovative efforts.

From that it infers that a total prohibition of every exclusive licence, even an open one, would cause the interest of undertakings in licences to fall away, which would be prejudicial to the dissemination of knowledge and techniques in the Community.

56 The exclusive licence which forms the subject-matter of the contested decision concerns the cultivation and marketing of hybrid maize seeds which were developed by INRA after years of research and experimentation and were unknown to German farmers at the time when the co-operation between INRA and the applicants was taking shape. For that reason the concern shown by the interveners as regards the protection of new technology is justified.

57 In fact, in the case of a licence of breeders' rights over hybrid maize seeds newly developed in one Member State, an undertaking established in another Member State which was not certain that it would not encounter competition from other licensees for the territory granted to it, or from the owner of the right himself, might be deterred from accepting the risk of cultivating and marketing that product; such a result would be damaging to the dissemination of a new technology and would prejudice competition in the Community between the new product and similar existing products.

58 Having regard to the specific nature of the products in question, the Court concludes that, in a case such as the present, the grant of an open exclusive licence, that is to say a licence which does not affect the position of third parties such as parallel importers and licensees for other territories, is not in itself incompatible with Article 85(1) of the Treaty.

59 Part B of the third submission is thus justified to the extent to which it concerns that aspect of the exclusive nature of the licence.

60 As regard to the position of third parties, the Commission in essence criticizes the parties to the contract for having extended the definition of exclusivity to importers who are not bound to the contract, in particular parallel importers. Parallel importers or exporters, such as Louis David KG in Germany and Robert Bomberault in France who offered INRA seed for sale to German buyers, had found themselves subjected to pressure and legal proceedings by INRA, Frasema and the applicants, the purpose of which was to maintain the exclusive position of the applicants on the German market.

61 The Court has consistently held (cf. Joined Cases 56 and 58/64 *Consten and Grundig* v *Commission* [1966] ECR 299) that absolute territorial protection granted to a licensee in order to enable parallel imports to be controlled and prevented results in the artificial maintenance of separate national markets, contrary to the Treaty.

NOTE: It should be clear by now that the Court will condone an open exclusive licence where the exclusivity can be justified on commercial grounds, but will not tolerate absolute territorial protection. For further discussion of absolute territorial restrictions in distribution contracts, see Lidgard, H.H., 'Territorial Restrictions in Vertical Relations' (1997) 21 World Competition 71. Compare the Community approach to territorial restrictions in vertical agreements with the lenient approach in the US. See 'US Antitrust Guidelines for the Licensing of Intellectual

Property, Antitrust Enforcement Guidelines for International Operations; Antitrust & Trade Regulation'; Report Vol. 68, No 1708.

Clearly the application of the ancillary restraints doctrine established in *Nungesser* depends on the circumstances in each case and in particular the nature of the product. In Case 42/84 *Remia* [1985] ECR 2545, [1987] 1 CMLR 1, the Court held that a restriction on a seller not to compete with a business sold with its goodwill does not infringe Article 81(1) provided it is reasonably limited in time and geographical extent. In Case 161/SA *Pronuptia* the Court adopted the '*Nungesser* principle' in respect of certain restrictions, this time in the context of a franchising agreement, and accepted that sometimes such restrictions are necessary to maintain the identity and reputation of a franchising network.

Pronuptia de Paris GmbH v *Pronuptia de Paris Irmgaard Schillgalis*
(Case 161/84) [1986] ECR 353, [1986] 1 CMLR 414

In an Article 234 EC (ex 177) reference the question put to the European Court by the German court was 'Is Article 85(1) of the Treaty applicable to franchise agreements such as the contracts between the parties, which have as their object the establishment of a special distribution system whereby the franchisor provides to the franchisee, in addition to goods, certain trade names, trademarks, merchandising material and services?'

27 In view of the foregoing, the answer to the first question must be that:

   (1) The compatibility of franchise agreements for the distribution of goods with Article 85 (1) depends on the provisions contained therein and on their economic context.

   (2) Provisions which are strictly necessary in order to ensure that the know-how and assistance provided by the franchisor do not benefit competitors do not constitute restrictions of competition for the purposes of Article 85(1).

   (3) Provisions which establish the control strictly necessary for maintaining the identity and reputation of the network identified by the common name or symbol do not constitute restrictions of competition for the purposes of Article 85(1).

   (4) Provisions which share markets between the franchisor and the franchisees or between franchisees constitute restrictions of competition for the purposes of Article 85(1).

   (5) The fact that the franchisor makes price recommendations to the franchisee does not constitute a restriction of competition, so long as there is no concerted practice between the franchisor and the franchisees or between the franchisees themselves for the actual application of such prices.

   (6) Franchise agreements for the distribution of goods which contain provisions sharing markets between the franchisor and the franchisees or between franchisees are capable of affecting trade between Member States.

NOTE: Shortly after this decision the Commission published a block exemption regulation on franchise agreements, Regulation 4087/88 (Commission regulation (EEC) No 4087/88 of 30 November 1988 on the application of Article 85(3) of the Treaty to Categories of Franchise Agreements [OJ 1988, No L359/46]). This has now been replaced by block exemption regulation 2790/99.

Another form of distribution commonly used throughout the Community is selective distribution whereby (a) a producer limits the sale of his products to appointed distributors chosen according to certain qualitative and quantitative criteria; and (b) appointed distributors are not permitted to resell to anyone other than the other appointed distributors, end users or consumers. Selective distribution tends to be limited to branded products which are either highly technical and require qualified staff to advise customers e.g. computers or are luxury goods, e.g. perfume or cosmetics, which demand protection. The legal framework applicable to selective distribution was established in *Metro (No 1)*.

Metro-SB-Grossmärkte GmbH v *Commission (No 1)*
(Case 26/76), [1977] ECR 1875, [1978] 2 CMLR 1

SABA manufacturered televisions, radios and tape-recorders, which it distributed through a selective distribution network. Only specialist dealers who could meet SABA's selection criteria could sell the products. Metro was refused admission to the network on the basis that it failed to meet SABA's criteria. The Commission held that Article 81(1) EC did not apply to certain aspects of the selective distribution network and granted an exemption in respect of the other provisions caught by Article 81(1) EC. Metro appealed to the Court against the Commission's decision to grant an exemption to SABA under Article 230 EC.

19 The applicant maintains that Article 2 of the contested Decision is vitiated by misuse of powers inasmuch as the Commission has failed to recognize 'what is protected under Article [85] (namely) freedom of competition for the benefit of the consumer, not the coincident interests of a manufacturer and a given group of traders who wish to secure selling prices which are considered to be satisfactory by the latter'.

Furthermore, if it were to be considered that an exemption from the prohibition might be granted in respect of the distribution system in dispute pursuant to Article [85](3), the applicant maintains that the Commission has misapplied that provision by granting an exemption in respect of restrictions on competition which are not indispensable to the attainment of the objectives of improving production or distribution or promoting technical or economic progress and which lead to the elimination of competition from self-service wholesale traders.

A—misuse of powers
20 The requirement contained in Articles 3 and [85] of the EEC Treaty that competition shall not be distorted implies the existence on the market of workable competition, that is to say the degree of competition necessary to ensure the observance of the basic requirements and the attainment of the objectives of the Treaty, in particular the creation of a single market achieving conditions similar to those of a domestic market.

In accordance with this requirement the nature and intensiveness of competition may vary to an extent dictated by the products or services in question and the economic structure of the relevant market sectors.

In the sector covering the production of high quality and technically advanced consumer durables, where a relatively small number of large- and medium-scale producers offer a varied range of items which, or so consumers may consider, are readily interchangéable, the structure of the market does not preclude the existence of a variety of channels of distribution adapted to the peculiar characteristics of the various producers and to the requirements of the various categories of consumers.

On this view the Commission was justified in recognizing that selective distribution systems constituted, together with others, an aspect of competition which accords with Article [85](1), provided that resellers are chosen on the basis of objective criteria of a qualitative nature relating to the technical qualifications of the reseller and his staff and the suitability of his trading premises and that such conditions are laid down uniformly for all potential resellers and are not applied in a discriminatory fashion.

21 It is true that in such systems of distribution price competition is not generally emphasized either as an exclusive or indeed as a principal factor.

This is particularly so when, as in the present case, access to the distribution network is subject to conditions exceeding the requirements of an appropriate distribution of the products.

However, although price competition is so important that it can never be eliminated it does not constitute the only effective form of competition or that to which absolute priority must in all circumstances be accorded.

The powers conferred upon the Commission under Article [85](3) show that the requirements for the maintenance of workable competition may be reconciled with the safeguarding of objectives of a different nature and that to this end certain restrictions on competition are permissible, provided that they are essential to the attainment of those objectives and that they do not result in the elimination of competition for a substantial part of the common market.

For specialist wholesalers and retailers the desire to maintain a certain price level, which corresponds to the desire to preserve, in the interests of consumers, the possibility of the continued existence of this channel of distribution in conjunction with new methods of distribution based on a different type of competition policy, forms one of the objectives which may be pursued without necessarily falling under the prohibition contained in Article [85](1), and, if it does fall thereunder, either wholly or in part, coming within the framework of Article [85](3).

This argument is strengthened if, in addition, such conditions promote improved competition inasmuch as it relates to factors other than prices.

NOTE: Selective distribution is now covered by Regulation 2790/99, although the Court's jurisprudence will continue to have relevance.

A: Rule of reason

The development of the *'Nungesser* principle' led some commentators to call for the formal adoption of a US-style rule of reason into Community competition law. Protagonists of the rule of reason argue that there are certain restrictions for example, in exclusive dealing, exclusive purchasing and franchise agreements that do not actually prevent or restrict competition within the meaning of Article 81(1) EC. They argue that the balancing of the pro- and anti-competitive effects of these agreements should take place under Article 81(1), rather than under the exemption criteria in Article 81(3) EC. There are difficulties however, in adopting a rule of reason approach into Community competition law and analogies with US antitrust are not always helpful. The rule of reason was developed by the US courts to resolve the intellectual burden created by the early legislation. Section 1 of the Sherman Act 1890 provides that '. . . Every contract, combination in the form of trust or otherwise, or conspiracy, in restraint of trade or commerce is declared illegal'. Clearly every contract is prima facie in restraint of trade and the US courts set about distinguishing between those restraints which were illegal per se, and those which required further analysis to determine their status under s. 1. Price-fixing restrictions for example, are usually always per se prohibited by the US judiciary as are horizontal market restrictions. See *White Motor Co* v *United States*, 372 US 253 (1963). All other restrictions are subject to the rule of reason test whereby the restraint is viewed in its market context to assess its pro- and anti-competitive effects. The following extract from the Supreme Court's decision in *Continental TV Inc.* v *GTE Sylvania* 433 US 36 (1977) demonstrates the Court's willingness to accept a rule of reason approach.

Continental TV Inc. v *GTE Sylvania Inc.*
433 US 36 (1977)

Vertical restrictions promote interbrand competition by allowing the manufacturer to achieve certain efficiencies in the distribution of his products. These 'redeeming virtues' are implicit in every decision sustaining vertical restrictions under the rule of reason. Economists have identified a number of ways in which manufacturers can use such restrictions to compete more effectively against other manufacturers. See, e.g., Preston, Restrictive Distribution Arrangements: Economic Analysis and Public Policy Standards, 30 Law & Contemp Prob 506, 511 (1965).[23] For example, new manufacturers and manufacturers entering new markets can use the restrictions in order to induce competent and aggressive retailers to make the kind of investment of capital and labor that is often required in the distribution of products unknown to the consumer. Established manufacturers can use them to induce retailers to engage in promotional activities or to provide service and repair facilities necessary to the efficient marketing of their products. Service and repair are vital for many products, such as automobiles and major household appliances. The availability and quality of such services affect a manufacturer's goodwill and the competitiveness of his product. Because of market imperfections such as the so-called 'free rider' effect, these services might not be provided by retailers in a purely competitive situation, despite the fact that each retailer's benefit would be greater if all provided the services than if none did. Posner, supra, n 13, at 285; cf. P. Samuelson, Economics 506–507 (10th ed 1976).

FURTHER READING

For a discussion of the rule of reason in US antitrust see the Symposium: The Future Course of the Rule of Reason in Antitrust 68/2 Antitrust L.J. (2000). The following article also provides a useful discussion of the US rule of reason and the Nungesser principle, concluding with a comparative analysis.

Peeters, J., 'The Rule of Reason revisited: Prohibition on Restraints of Competition in the Sherman Act and the EEC Treaty' (1989) 37 AJ of Comparative Law, p. 521.

NOTE: There are obvious differences in the competition law regimes of the US and the European Union, not least the fact that the dominant concern of Community competition law is market integration, which does not feature in US antitrust decisionmaking. Can you think of other differences that call into question analogies with US law? Whish and Sufrin for example, have resisted calls for transposition of a rule of reason into the Community competition law framework.

Whish, R., and Sufrin, B., 'Article 85 and the Rule of Reason'
(1987) 7 YEL 1, pp. 36–38

In the light of the foregoing considerations, the call for the adoption of a US-style rule of reason should be resisted and, indeed, there is much to be said for dropping this term (and the terms

---

23 Marketing efficiency is not the only legitimate reason for a manufacturer's desire to exert control over the manner in which his products are sold and serviced. As a result of statutory and common-law developments, society increasingly demands that manufacturers assume direct responsibility for the safety and quality of their products. For example, at the federal level, apart from more specialized requirements, manufacturers of consumer products have safety responsibilities under the Consumer Product Safety Act, 15 USC §§ 2051 et seq. (1970 ed Supp V) [15 USCS §§ 2051 et seq.], and obligations for warranties under the Consumer Product Warranties Act, 15 USC §§ 2301 et seq. (1970 ed Supp V) [15 USCS §§ 2301 et seq.]. Similar obligations are imposed by state law. See e.g., Cal Civ Code §§ 1790 et seq. (West 1973). The legitimacy of these concerns has been recognized in cases involving vertical restrictions. See, e.g., *Tripoli Co.* v *Wella Corp.* 425 F2d 932 (CA3 1970).

'ancillary restraint' and 'per se illegality') from EEC antitrust law altogether, on the basis that they do more to confuse than to clarify. EEC competition law requires its own vocabulary, carefully honed to express its own particular tensions.

Quite apart from the issue of terminology, the writers have other doubts about the wisdom of analysing Article 85(1) in a way that relies on an approach similar to that in the Sherman Act. It would not help the cause of certainty. As Joliet himself said:

> Generally business groups in Europe, just as in America, complain about the lack of certainty in Antitrust law. At the same time, they are inclined to demand more flexibility. Such demands are irreconcilable. *A rule of reason under Article 85(1) would bring about more uncertainty for business men*. [Emphasis added.]

The matter of certainty is, of course, important. It is in no one's interest to retard beneficial collaboration between firms striving to compete in a competitive international market. However, the best answer to this problem is for the Commission to continue to improve its procedures, to publish block exemptions where this is possible, and to develop such notions as objective necessity and potential competition. We also expect its sophistication in dealing with economics to continue to improve, but do not consider that this goes hand in hand with rule-of-reason analysis. This would stifle the proper application of Article 85 which, precisely because of its more ample wording, does not bear the same intellectual burden that the words 'restraint of trade' do in the Sherman Act. We doubt, too, that it would be helpful to draw the national courts further into the application of Article 85 by asking them to undertake extensive economic analysis under Article 85(1). We are happy for them to enforce the competition rules against blatant cartels and abuses of a dominant position. We do not consider them to be appropriate fora for deciding upon complex economic issues.

We are also of the opinion that protagonists of the rule of reason fail to give due consideration to the significance of single market integration. Even if this is not a goal approved by all observers, to call for the application of the competition rules in a way which ignores it is fundamentally to misconstrue the context in which EEC law is applied. Also, there is a certain disingenuousness in complaining about EEC competition law when it (with other provisions of the Treaty) has done so much to open up markets which until relatively recently were difficult to penetrate. Competition law in one sense benefits everyone on the market—even those who object to some of the particular ways in which it is applied.

Our conclusion, therefore, is that there are sound reasons for resisting the call for a rule of reason under Article 85(1).

FURTHER READING

See also Forrester, I., and Norall, C., 'The Laicisation of Community Law: Self-help and the Rule of Reason—How Competition Law is and Could be Applied' (1984) 21 CMLRev 11.

B: Block exemption debate

The block exemption regulations were introduced with the principal aim of increasing legal certainty and thereby reducing the Commission's workload. The difficulties with block exemptions quickly became clear. The absence of any market-share criteria meant companies without significant market power incurred unnecessary regulation, whereas companies with significant market power could escape regulation altogether. Criticism also centred on the so-called *straitjacket* effect, which obliged advisers to structure a commercial agreement to meet certain form-based requirements, in the process compromising the commercial benefits.

An agreement that did not meet these strict requirements did not qualify for exemption. Although the Commission argued that such formalism (as opposed to economic or commercial criteria) provided undertakings with legal certainty, it has been argued that 'these formalistic categories have nothing to do with competition policy'.

Professor Barry Hawk was particularly critical of the Commission's approach in his seminal article on vertical restraints in EC Competition Law.

Hawk, B.E., 'System Failure: Vertical Restraints and EC Competition Law'
(1995) 32 CMLRev, p. 973 [footnotes omitted]

It was evident as early as the 1960s that DG IV lacked the resources to deal with notifications seeking individual exemptions. This should not be surprising. No competition authority in the world has the resources to examine the vast number of vertical agreements (and licenses) whose enforceability has been called into question by the overbroad application of 85(1). The Emperor wears no clothes. The notification system set up in Regulation 17 has never worked and will never work. Like the 1976 Restrictive Practices Act in the UK, the notification system serves mostly to increase transaction costs and transfer income from firms to outside antitrust lawyers. It has no redeeming enforcement virtues and should be scrapped.

But rather than abandon an obviously deficient and inoperable notification system, the Commission has resorted to block exemptions. These vary considerably in their provision of legal certainty. One extreme is Regulation 83/83 covering exclusive distributorships, which does provide a fair degree of legal certainty for simple stand-alone exclusive distributor agreements. At the other extreme is probably the joint R & D block exemption that appears, on the basis of anecdotal evidence, rarely ever to cover a real-world arrangement.

2.4 Step D—Legal formalisms and 'analysis' by pigeonholing
The Commission largely applies Article 85(1) to distribution arrangements according to formal legal categories. One set of rules applies to exclusive distribution, another to selective distribution, another to franchising, and a chaotic array of considerations apply to distribution arrangements that are not neatly pigeonholed. Paradoxically, these rules have become enshrined by the very block exemptions that were issued to relieve the harsher aspects of the Commission's rigid application of Article 85(1).

The Commission's treatment of specific provisions in *selective distribution* and *franchises* illustrates the formalistic approach.

Commission decisions on *selective distribution* frequently are marked by conclusory reasoning and neglect of economic analysis. Some restraints are placed under 85(1) (e.g. minimum sales and stocking obligations) with no apparent economic analysis at all; the restriction on economic freedom notion apparently supports this result. However, other provisions that clearly 'restrain the economic freedom' of the dealer are placed outside 85(1) (e.g. a restriction on wholesalers not to supply end-users and restrictions on dealers supplying certain classes of customers). The result is intellectual incoherence and a substitution of formal categories for analysis.

Franchise agreements provide a second example. The Commission (and the Court) generally accord more favourable treatment to restrictive clauses in franchising agreements as compared to distribution agreements. For example, dealer location clauses, minimum purchasing obligations and stocking requirements in franchise agreements do not even fall within Article 85(1), while in selective distribution agreements the same clauses not only fall within Article 85(1) but might also be denied an exemption under Article 85(3). This is problematic: many distribution agreements have elements that are characteristic of franchises, i.e. the transfer of commercial knowhow to independent parties operating under the supplier's trademark and not dealing in certain competing goods.

2.5 Step E—Lack of substantive analysis

The legal formalisms described above ultimately eliminate what should be the heart of the matter: an antitrust (i.e. economics/law) substantive analysis of a particular agreement or practice, i.e. its competitive harms and benefits. Competition law is economic law, and economics must play a predominant (if not exclusive) role in the examination of particular agreements. That is why the Commission's frequent inattention to market power and effects on price and output is so sorely criticized.

The legal formalisms under Article 85 contrast starkly with US antitrust counselling practice. When dealing with non-territorial vertical restraints under EC law, lawyers spend the great majority of their time in pigeonholing exercises and in textual exegesis of block exemptions and interpretative guidelines. It is shocking how little time is devoted to assessing the competitive risks and benefits of the vertical restraints at issue. The practice under the Sherman Act is exactly the opposite. It is difficult to believe that EC competition policy is furthered where there is far more attention and intellectual resources devoted to doctrinal formalisms than to substantive analysis.

For further comment on the *straitjacket* effect and other difficulties, see the concluding chapter in Korah, V., *An Introductory Guide to EC Competition Law and Practice*, 7th edn, (Hart) 2000, Chapter 13, in particular, pp. 358–359.

SECTION 4: The Green Paper on vertical restraints

It is clear the Commission has applied Article 81(1) EC broadly to vertical agreements and restraints because of their threat to market integration and their anti-competitive effects. Criticism of the Community's strict approach and the expiry of three block exemption regulations at the end of 1999 covering exclusive buying, selling and franchising (later extended to 31 December 1999 and finally 31 May 2000) presented the Commission with an obvious opportunity to revise its treatment of vertical restraints. Consequently, the Commission published a Green Paper on Vertical Restraints in EC Competition Policy, in January 1997, (COM (96) 721 final, adopted by the Commission on 22.1.1997, available from the Competition Directorate General home page *http://europa.eu.int/en/comm/competition/antitrust/96721en-en.pdf*). By publishing the Green Paper the Commission sought a period of consultation with interested parties. The Green Paper represented a radical change in Community policy towards vertical restraints, not least the realisation of the importance of market structure rather than legal form in determining whether an agreement is anti-competitive or not.

The Commission invited comments on a number of issues and proposed a number of possible options for change, some more radical than others, and discussed in full in Chapter VIII, 'Options', pp. 75–79 of the Green Paper.

Green Paper on vertical restraints in competition policy, COM (96) 721

II. Economic analysis of vertical restraints and the single market

10. The heated debate among economists concerning vertical restraints has calmed somewhat and a consensus is emerging. Vertical restraints are no longer regarded as per se suspicious or per se pro-competitive. Economists are less willing to make sweeping statements. Rather, they rely more on the analysis of the facts of a case in question. However, one element stands out: the importance

of market structure in determining the impact of vertical restraints. The fiercer is interbrand competition, the more likely are the pro-competitive and efficiency effects to outweigh any anti-competitive effects of vertical restraints. Anti-competitive effects are only likely where interbrand competition is weak and there are barriers to entry at either producer or distributor level. In addition it is recognised that contracts in the distribution chain reduce transaction costs, and can allow the potential efficiencies in distribution to be realised. In contrast, there are cases where vertical restraints raise barriers to entry or further dampen horizontal competition in oligopolistic markets.

Option I—Maintain current system

281. Option I consists of maintaining the current system (including the special arrangements for beer and petrol).

NOTE: Given the extent of criticism of the Community's approach towards vertical restraints an option for 'no change' might seem strange. The Commission, however, believes that its policy which spanned 40 years was largely successful. (See section VII, paras 25, 26, 27, 28 of Exec. summary, Green Paper.)

Option II—Wider block exemptions

282. It is sometimes suggested that current block exemptions are too limited. Option II would maintain the current system, with some changes in the provisions of the block exemption Regulations. There would be no significant procedural changes. The block exemptions would apply more widely than hitherto by an extension of their coverage to different clauses set out below thus broadening legal certainty. Fewer individual cases would require notification. Some of these changes may be made by the Commission acting under the powers already granted to it under Council Regulation 19/65. Others would require amendment of that Council Regulation. Some suggested changes are listed below and comments on their appropriateness and on other possible changes are welcome.

283. Measures to increase flexibility in general could include one or more of the following:

— the block exemptions would cover not only the precise clauses listed, but also clauses which are similar or less restrictive;

— the inclusion of prohibited clauses might not deny the benefit of the exemption for the rest of the agreement;

— the block exemption could apply to agreements involving more than two parties;

— a block exemption or a Commission notice for selective distribution could be enacted.

284. Specific measures to increase flexibility could include one or more of the following:

— the block exemptions for exclusive distribution and exclusive purchasing could be extended to cover services or to permit the distributor to transform or process the contract goods. Distributors could be allowed to add significant value by changing the economic identity of the goods without losing the benefit of the block exemption;

— the block exemption for exclusive purchasing agreements could be extended to cover partial as well as exclusive supply;

— the block exemption for franchising agreements could be extended to cover maximum resale price maintenance as an exception to the general principle that resale price maintenance will not be exempted;

— associations of independent retailers could be permitted to benefit from block exemption regulations, provided that the independent retailers are small and medium-sized enterprises[77] and that the market share of the association remains below a certain threshold;

77 In the sense of the Commission recommendation of 3 April 1996 concerning the definition of small and medium-sized enterprises, O.J. no L107 of 30.4.1996.

— an arbitration procedure could be set up for distributors denied admission to a selective distribution network.

285. Under this option the special provisions in Regulation No 1984/83 for beer and petrol would remain in force with certain changes to increase the flexibility of the application of the Regulation. One possibility could be to limit the requirement to specify the 'tied' beers to the type of beer concerned, instead of identifying the individual brands as required under the current Regulation. This gives the brewer the possibility of adding or replacing brands of a type of beer for which the tenant is already tied, instead of requiring an additional agreement with the tenant for such changes, as required by the Regulation. As regards petrol one could consider how to deal with forms of distribution other than exclusive purchase in relation to goods sold in convenience stores that form part of the service station business. Additionally, one could consider whether it is justified to maintain the requirement that the supplier should make available or finance lubrication equipment in order to benefit from an exemption for exclusivity of supply of lubricants.

Option III—More focused block exemptions

286. This option stresses Community competition policy's market integration objectives. Territorial protection and vertical restraints are seen as a significant contributory factor to the maintenance of considerable price differentials between Member States. It is certainly the case that many markets are becoming more concentrated at the production and distribution level, while vertical restraints can foreclose markets and raise barriers to entry. The value added by distribution is an important element in its own right. Intrabrand competition can play an important role in promoting competition in markets where interbrand competition is not fierce.

287. The current block exemptions apply without any market share limits. They could be amended so as to apply only where each party has less than, for instance, 40 per cent market share of the relevant market in the contract territory. There would be no block exemption above that threshold, at least in respect of the following restrictions:

— protection against active sales from outside the territory

— protection for exclusive dealing (prohibition to sell competing products/services).

288. Within the framework of the present option, comments are also welcome about the appropriateness to adopt a block exemption regulation in respect of selective distribution agreements, to the extent that these agreements fall within Article 85(1). In case such a regulation would be adopted, it would apply only where the producer or distributor does not hold more than for instance, 40 per cent share of the relevant market or a lower figure in an oligopolistic market.

289. The suggestions made in Option II could be applied to agreements below the market share threshold.

290. Parties may have doubts about the correct definition of a market and calculation of their share thereof, which could lead them to notify agreements to the Commission in a search for legal certainty. There would also be notifications of agreements where the parties have market shares in excess of the threshold.

291. The Commission would appreciate estimates of the number and type of cases likely to be notified, and views on whether guidelines explaining the circumstances in which the Commission would grant exemptions under Article 85(3) could solve this problem. Possible grounds for exemption could include the condition that there be no significant price discrimination to the detriment of customers.

292. In line with the general rule above, no protection would be given to exclusive beer-supply agreements in favour of a brewer with a share above e.g. 40 per cent on a given national on-trade market. However, a sector specific alternative could be to limit the extent of the exclusivity either to a given percentage of the total beer throughput of a particular pub (e.g. 3/4 tied, 1/4 free) or to certain

containers (e.g. draught tied, bottles and cans free). A further alternative could be to limit the scope of the exclusivity to beer only. In the context of filling stations, it should be considered whether, in cases where the supplier has a market share in excess of a certain percentage, e.g. 40 per cent, the maximum contract term permitted by the exemption should be reduced.

Option IV—Block exemptions with measure to specify the economic circumstances in which Article 85(1) applies

293. The idea underlying this option is that economic analysis of vertical restraints should be implemented by legal instruments which give undertakings a considerable degree of legal certainty. The economic criteria designed to determine the market conditions in which Article 85(1) would apply could be developed, in the first place, within the framework of a new Commission notice and subsequently, in the light of the experience acquired, within the framework of a negative clearance regulation.

294. This option would provide for more flexible treatment of vertical arrangements for agreements between parties with no significant market power. The alleged limiting effect of block exemptions and emphasis on the legal classification of different forms of distribution would be reduced.

295. For parties with less than, for instance, 20 per cent market share in the contract territory, there would be a rebuttable presumption of compatibility with Article 85(1) (*'the negative clearance presumption'*). In other words, vertical restraints in such circumstances would not normally be caught by Article 85(1). This presumption would cover all vertical restraints except those relating to minimum resale prices, impediments to parallel trade or passive sales, or those contained in distribution agreements between competitors.

296. This negative clearance presumption could be rebutted by the Commission on the basis of a market analysis which would take account of factors such as:

— market structure (e.g. oligopoly)

— barriers to entry

— the degree of integration of the single market, evaluated on the basis of indicators such as the price differential existing between Member States and the level of market penetration in each Member State of products imported from other Member States, or

— the cumulative impact of parallel networks.

297. Agreements which, as a result of this market analysis, were shown to fall within Article 85(1) could benefit from a block exemption if they fulfilled the necessary conditions (see below variants I and II). The negative clearance presumption could be implemented by a Commission Notice and subsequently in the light of the experience acquired, within the framework of a negative clearance regulation which would require a new Council enabling Regulation under Article 87 of the Treaty.

298. For cases with market share above for instance 20 per cent and for those below 20 per cent which fall within Article 85(1), there could be two possibilities, as follows:

Variant I

299. All cases over 20 per cent could be covered by the block exemption described in Option II (wider block exemption).

Variant II

300. All cases over 20 per cent would be covered by the block exemption described in Option III (i.e. inapplicability of block exemption to certain restrictions above 40 per cent market share).

Beer and petrol

301. The presumption of non-applicability of Article 85(1) as described above would apply to the exclusive beer- and petrol-supply agreements only insofar as the cumulative impact of parallel networks has no significant foreclosure effect.

The Commission published a 'Follow up Communication to the Green Paper on Vertical Restraints' (COM (98) 544, [1999] 4 CMLR 281) in which it outlined in more detail its plans for reform. Despite marked opposition to the use of market share tests, the European Commission favoured Option 4, Variant 2—i.e. automatic exemption for agreements below a market share threshold and individual examination for agreements above that threshold. The Commission explained its reasoning as follows.

Follow-up Communication (COM (98))

2. Need for a more economics based approach

To remedy these three shortcomings and better protect competition, the primary objective of Community competition policy, a more economics based approach is required. Such an approach should be based on the effects on the market; vertical agreements should be analysed in their market context. It is only when inter-brand competition is weak and market power exists that it becomes important to control vertical agreements. This should facilitate a relaxation of the form-based requirements, ensure that fewer agreements are covered by Article 85(1) and afford a better scrutiny of agreements of companies having substantial market power.

The policy proposal set out in this Communication is based on a more economic approach. This is required, as was explained above, to remedy the shortcomings of current policy. For situations without significant market power a safe harbour needs to be created, thus providing a presumption of legality for those vertical restraints that are likely to have no net negative effects. Vertical restraints falling outside the safe harbour will not be presumed to be illegal but may need individual examination. In the context of individual examination, the Commission will have the burden of proof that the agreement in question infringes Article 85(1) and will have to examine whether the agreement does or does not fulfil the conditions of Article 85(3).

The proposed safe harbour consists of one broad umbrella Block-Exemption regulation covering all vertical restraints for the distribution of goods and services. This regulation uses market-share thresholds to distinguish between agreements that are or are not block-exempted. By being based primarily on a black-clause approach, i.e. defining what is not block-exempted instead of defining what is exempted, it avoids the strait-jacket effect and facilitates the simplification of the applicable rules. The policy will ensure that the vast majority of vertical agreements where no significant net negative effect can be expected no longer require individual scrutiny. It will thereby allow the Commission and national competition authorities to concentrate on the important cases. It treats different forms of vertical agreements having similar effects in a similar way, preventing unjustified differentiation in policy between forms or sectors and avoiding a policy bias in the choice companies make concerning their formats of distribution. In order to maintain a sufficient level of legal certainty the Block-Exemption regulation will be supplemented by guidelines detailing the Commission's policy concerning individual examination above the market-share thresholds and possible withdrawal of the Block-Exemption below the thresholds.

NOTE: Most commentators supported a shift towards a more economic approach, although not all were in support of the introduction of market shares. The level at which the market-share threshold was to be fixed and whether there would be any variation according to the seriousness of the restraint, was hotly debated following publication of the follow-up communication. See for example, Schroeder, D., 'The Green Paper on Vertical Restraints: Beware of Market Share Thresholds' [1997] ECLR 430 and Kellaway, R., 'Vertical Restraints: Which Option' [1997] ECLR 387.

FURTHER READING

For an economic perspective on the treatment of vertical restraints following the Green Paper proposals see Biro Z., and Fletcher, A., 'The EC Green Paper on Vertical Restraints: An Economic Comment', Editorial [1998] ECLR 129.

SECTION 5: **Legislative changes**

A: Enabling regulations

Two enabling regulations were passed to implement the Commission's new policy articulated in the Follow-up Communication.

1. The first of these is Regulation 1216/99 (Regulation 1216/99 of 10 June 1999 amending Regulation 17/62 OJ 1999, No L148/5). The original function of Article 4(2) of Regulation 17/62 was to filter out cases that on a preliminary assessment appeared to be less harmful to competition by exempting them from prior notification. This provision has been amended by Regulation 1216/99 to take into account a number of criticisms, principally the Commission's acceptance that as vertical agreements are less harmful to competition they should benefit from a more flexible procedure.

A new subparagraph in Regulation 17/62 provides that the obligation to notify shall not apply to vertical agreements. The purpose of retroactivity is to reduce the number of notifications. Parties will be less inclined to notify in advance of implementation of the agreement if exemption can be retrospective to the date the contract is made.

Article 4(2) now applies to vertical agreements where one or more parties has market power. This is an important legislative change and enables the Commission to grant individual exemption for specified kinds of agreements retrospectively to the time the agreement was entered into.

Retroactive application does not however protect undertakings from fines. Immunity from fines still requires an advance notification pursuant to Article 15, para. (5)(a) of Regulation 17/62. Note, however, there does not appear to be a major risk of fines as the Commission, in the case of vertical agreements, only imposes fines for hard-core restrictions, for instance, resale price maintenance. The Commission has already started to pre-empt this reform in the field of beer-supply agreements by retroactively exempting the agreements of distributors such as Whitbread [1999] OJ L88/26, and Scottish and Newcastle plc [1999] OJ L88/26.

2. The second legislative change is brought about by Regulation 1215/99 which amends Regulation 19/65. Council Regulation 19/65 was adopted to facilitate the handling of notifications and it empowers the Commission to adopt appropriate regulations for the application of Article 81(3) EC. Regulation 19/65 has been amended to extend the scope of the Commission's powers to cover *all* types of

vertical agreements concluded between two or more firms, each operating at a different stage of the economic process. These agreements are, according to the Commission, supply and/or purchase of goods for resale or processing or marketing of services including exclusive distribution, exclusive purchasing, franchising, selective distribution or indeed any combinations.

B: Regulation 2790/99

As explained in the Follow-up communication, the Commission proposed a new block exemption regulation to replace the existing system of sector-specific block exemptions with a single broad 'umbrella' exemption regulation. The principal aim was to move away from a form-based system to a system which allows for greater economic analysis. In order to remove the so-called *'straitjacket* effect', the regulation was to be based mainly on a black-clause approach. Thus, instead of defining what *is* exempted, by reference to a positive list of provisions, the new regulation represents a shift in emphasis towards a black-list. The purpose of this new approach is to reduce the regulatory burden on companies and make it easier for legal advisers to draft more flexible commercial agreements. The black-list approach abandons the differentiation in policy between types of sectors and agreements.

The new block exemption, Regulation 2790/99 (Commission Regulation No 2790/99 of 22 December 1999 on the application of Article 81(3) to categories of vertical agreements and concerted practices, OJ, 999, L336/21) came into force on 1 June 2000 (hereinafter referred to as 'BER').

Commission Regulation (EC) No 2790/1999 of 22 December 1999 on the application of Article 81(3) of the Treaty to categories of vertical agreements and concerted practices

(Text with EEA relevance)

THE COMMISSION OF THE EUROPEAN COMMUNITIES,

Having regard to the Treaty establishing the European Community,

Having regard to Council Regulation No 19/65/EEC of 2 March 1965 on the application of Article 85(3) of the Treaty to certain categories of agreements and concerted practices(1), as last amended by Regulation (EC) No 1215/1999(2), and in particular Article 1 thereof,

Having published a draft of this Regulation(3),

Having consulted the Advisory Committee on Restrictive Practices and Dominant Positions, Whereas:

(1) Regulation No 19/65/EEC empowers the Commission to apply Article 81(3) of the Treaty (formerly Article 85(3)) by regulation to certain categories of vertical agreements and corresponding concerted practices falling within Article 81(1).

(2) Experience acquired to date makes it possible to define a category of vertical agreements which can be regarded as normally satisfying the conditions laid down in Article 81(3).

(3) This category includes vertical agreements for the purchase or sale of goods or services where these agreements are concluded between non-competing undertakings, between certain

competitors or by certain associations of retailers of goods; it also includes vertical agreements containing ancillary provisions on the assignment or use of intellectual property rights; for the purposes of this Regulation, the term 'vertical agreements' includes the corresponding concerted practices.

(4) For the application of Article 81(3) by regulation, it is not necessary to define those vertical agreements which are capable of falling within Article 81(1); in the individual assessment of agreements under Article 81(1), account has to be taken of several factors, and in particular the market structure on the supply and purchase side.

(5) The benefit of the block exemption should be limited to vertical agreements for which it can be assumed with sufficient certainty that they satisfy the conditions of Article 81(3).

(6) Vertical agreements of the category defined in this Regulation can improve economic efficiency within a chain of production or distribution by facilitating better coordination between the participating undertakings; in particular, they can lead to a reduction in the transaction and distribution costs of the parties and to an optimisation of their sales and investment levels.

(7) The likelihood that such efficiency-enhancing effects will outweigh any anti-competitive effects due to restrictions contained in vertical agreements depends on the degree of market power of the undertakings concerned and, therefore, on the extent to which those undertakings face competition from other suppliers of goods or services regarded by the buyer as interchangeable or substitutable for one another, by reason of the products' characteristics, their prices and their intended use.

(8) It can be presumed that, where the share of the relevant market accounted for by the supplier does not exceed 30 per cent, vertical agreements which do not contain certain types of severely anti-competitive restraints generally lead to an improvement in production or distribution and allow consumers a fair share of the resulting benefits; in the case of vertical agreements containing exclusive supply obligations, it is the market share of the buyer which is relevant in determining the overall effects of such vertical agreements on the market.

(9) Above the market share threshold of 30 per cent, there can be no presumption that vertical agreements falling within the scope of Article 81(1) will usually give rise to objective advantages of such a character and size as to compensate for the disadvantages which they create for competition.

(10) This Regulation should not exempt vertical agreements containing restrictions which are not indispensable to the attainment of the positive effects mentioned above; in particular, vertical agreements containing certain types of severely anti-competitive restraints such as minimum and fixed resale-prices, as well as certain types of territorial protection, should be excluded from the benefit of the block exemption established by this Regulation irrespective of the market share of the undertakings concerned.

(11) In order to ensure access to or to prevent collusion on the relevant market, certain conditions are to be attached to the block exemption; to this end, the exemption of non-compete obligations should be limited to obligations which do not exceed a definite duration; for the same reasons, any direct or indirect obligation causing the members of a selective distribution system not to sell the brands of particular competing suppliers should be excluded from the benefit of this Regulation.

(12) The market-share limitation, the non-exemption of certain vertical agreements and the conditions provided for in this Regulation normally ensure that the agreements to which the block exemption applies do not enable the participating undertakings to eliminate competition in respect of a substantial part of the products in question.

(13) In particular cases in which the agreements falling under this Regulation nevertheless have effects incompatible with Article 81(3), the Commission may withdraw the benefit of the block exemption; this may occur in particular where the buyer has significant market power in

the relevant market in which it resells the goods or provides the services or where parallel networks of vertical agreements have similar effects which significantly restrict access to a relevant market or competition therein; such cumulative effects may for example arise in the case of selective distribution or non-compete obligations.

(14) Regulation No 19/65/EEC empowers the competent authorities of Member States to withdraw the benefit of the block exemption in respect of vertical agreements having effects incompatible with the conditions laid down in Article 81(3), where such effects are felt in their respective territory, or in a part thereof, and where such territory has the characteristics of a distinct geographic market; Member States should ensure that the exercise of this power of withdrawal does not prejudice the uniform application throughout the common market of the Community competition rules or the full effect of the measures adopted in implementation of those rules.

(15) In order to strengthen supervision of parallel networks of vertical agreements which have similar restrictive effects and which cover more than 50 per cent of a given market, the Commission may declare this Regulation inapplicable to vertical agreements containing specific restraints relating to the market concerned, thereby restoring the full application of Article 81 to such agreements.

(16) This Regulation is without prejudice to the application of Article 82.

(17) In accordance with the principle of the primacy of Community law, no measure taken pursuant to national laws on competition should prejudice the uniform application throughout the common market of the Community competition rules or the full effect of any measures adopted in implementation of those rules, including this Regulation,

HAS ADOPTED THIS REGULATION:

Article 1

For the purposes of this Regulation:
- (a) 'competing undertakings' means actual or potential suppliers in the same product market; the product market includes goods or services which are regarded by the buyer as interchangeable with or substitutable for the contract goods or services, by reason of the products' characteristics, their prices and their intended use;
- (b) 'non-compete obligation' means any direct or indirect obligation causing the buyer not to manufacture, purchase, sell or resell goods or services which compete with the contract goods or services, or any direct or indirect obligation on the buyer to purchase from the supplier or from another undertaking designated by the supplier more than 80 per cent of the buyer's total purchases of the contract goods or services and their substitutes on the relevant market, calculated on the basis of the value of its purchases in the preceding calendar year;
- (c) 'exclusive supply obligation' means any direct or indirect obligation causing the supplier to sell the goods or services specified in the agreement only to one buyer inside the Community for the purposes of a specific use or for resale;
- (d) 'selective distribution system' means a distribution system where the supplier undertakes to sell the contract goods or services, either directly or indirectly, only to distributors selected on the basis of specified criteria and where these distributors undertake not to sell such goods or services to unauthorised distributors;
- (e) 'intellectual property rights' includes industrial property rights, copyright and neighbouring rights;
- (f) 'know-how' means a package of non-patented practical information, resulting from experience and testing by the supplier, which is secret, substantial and identified: in this context, 'secret' means that the know-how, as a body or in the precise configuration and assembly of its components, is not generally known or easily accessible;

'substantial' means that the know-how includes information which is indispensable to the buyer for the use, sale or resale of the contract goods or services; 'identified' means that the know-how must be described in a sufficiently comprehensive manner so as to make it possible to verify that it fulfils the criteria of secrecy and substantiality;

(g) 'buyer' includes an undertaking which, under an agreement falling within Article 81(1) of the Treaty, sells goods or services on behalf of another undertaking.

Article 2

1. Pursuant to Article 81(3) of the Treaty and subject to the provisions of this Regulation, it is hereby declared that Article 81(1) shall not apply to agreements or concerted practices entered into between two or more undertakings each of which operates, for the purposes of the agreement, at a different level of the production or distribution chain, and relating to the conditions under which the parties may purchase, sell or resell certain goods or services ('vertical agreements').

This exemption shall apply to the extent that such agreements contain restrictions of competition falling within the scope of Article 81(1) ('vertical restraints').

2. The exemption provided for in paragraph 1 shall apply to vertical agreements entered into between an association of undertakings and its members, or between such an association and its suppliers, only if all its members are retailers of goods and if no individual member of the association, together with its connected undertakings, has a total annual turnover exceeding EUR 50 million; vertical agreements entered into by such associations shall be covered by this Regulation without prejudice to the application of Article 81 to horizontal agreements concluded between the members of the association or decisions adopted by the association.

3. The exemption provided for in paragraph 1 shall apply to vertical agreements containing provisions which relate to the assignment to the buyer or use by the buyer of intellectual property rights, provided that those provisions do not constitute the primary object of such agreements and are directly related to the use, sale or resale of goods or services by the buyer or its customers. The exemption applies on condition that, in relation to the contract goods or services, those provisions do not contain restrictions of competition having the same object or effect as vertical restraints which are not exempted under this Regulation.

4. The exemption provided for in paragraph 1 shall not apply to vertical agreements entered into between competing undertakings; however, it shall apply where competing undertakings enter into a non-reciprocal vertical agreement and:

(a) the buyer has a total annual turnover not exceeding EUR 100 million, or

(b) the supplier is a manufacturer and a distributor of goods, while the buyer is a distributor not manufacturing goods competing with the contract goods, or

(c) the supplier is a provider of services at several levels of trade, while the buyer does not provide competing services at the level of trade where it purchases the contract services.

5. This Regulation shall not apply to vertical agreements the subject matter of which falls within the scope of any other block exemption regulation.

Article 3

1. Subject to paragraph 2 of this Article, the exemption provided for in Article 2 shall apply on condition that the market share held by the supplier does not exceed 30 per cent of the relevant market on which it sells the contract goods or services.

2. In the case of vertical agreements containing exclusive supply obligations, the exemption provided for in Article 2 shall apply on condition that the market share held by the buyer does

not exceed 30 per cent of the relevant market on which it purchases the contract goods or services.

Article 4
The exemption provided for in Article 2 shall not apply to vertical agreements which, directly or indirectly, in isolation or in combination with other factors under the control of the parties, have as their object:

(a) the restriction of the buyer's ability to determine its sale price, without prejudice to the possibility of the supplier's imposing a maximum sale price or recommending a sale price, provided that they do not amount to a fixed or minimum sale price as a result of pressure from, or incentives offered by, any of the parties;

(b) the restriction of the territory into which, or of the customers to whom, the buyer may sell the contract goods or services, except:
   — the restriction of active sales into the exclusive territory or to an exclusive customer group reserved to the supplier or allocated by the supplier to another buyer, where such a restriction does not limit sales by the customers of the buyer,
   — the restriction of sales to end users by a buyer operating at the wholesale level of trade,
   — the restriction of sales to unauthorised distributors by the members of a selective distribution system, and
   — the restriction of the buyer's ability to sell components, supplied for the purposes of incorporation, to customers who would use them to manufacture the same type of goods as those produced by the supplier;

(c) the restriction of active or passive sales to end users by members of a selective distribution system operating at the retail level of trade, without prejudice to the possibility of prohibiting a member of the system from operating out of an unauthorised place of establishment;

(d) the restriction of cross-supplies between distributors within a selective distribution system, including between distributors operating at different levels of trade;

(e) the restriction agreed between a supplier of components and a buyer who incorporates those components, which limits the supplier to selling the components as spare parts to end-users or to repairers or other service providers not entrusted by the buyer with the repair or servicing of its goods.

Article 5
The exemption provided for in Article 2 shall not apply to any of the following obligations contained in vertical agreements:

(a) any direct or indirect non-compete obligation, the duration of which is indefinite or exceeds five years. A non-compete obligation which is tacitly renewable beyond a period of five years is to be deemed to have been concluded for an indefinite duration. However, the time limitation of five years shall not apply where the contract goods or services are sold by the buyer from premises and land owned by the supplier or leased by the supplier from third parties not connected with the buyer, provided that the duration of the non-compete obligation does not exceed the period of occupancy of the premises and land by the buyer;

(b) any direct or indirect obligation causing the buyer, after termination of the agreement, not to manufacture, purchase, sell or resell goods or services, unless such obligation:
   — relates to goods or services which compete with the contract goods or services, and

- is limited to the premises and land from which the buyer has operated during the contract period, and
- is indispensable to protect know-how transferred by the supplier to the buyer, and provided that the duration of such non-compete obligation is limited to a period of one year after termination of the agreement; this obligation is without prejudice to the possibility of imposing a restriction which is unlimited in time on the use and disclosure of know-how which has not entered the public domain;

(c) any direct or indirect obligation causing the members of a selective distribution system not to sell the brands of particular competing suppliers.

Article 6
The Commission may withdraw the benefit of this Regulation, pursuant to Article 7(1) of Regulation No 19/65/EEC, where it finds in any particular case that vertical agreements to which this Regulation applies nevertheless have effects which are incompatible with the conditions laid down in Article 81(3) of the Treaty, and in particular where access to the relevant market or competition therein is significantly restricted by the cumulative effect of parallel networks of similar vertical restraints implemented by competing suppliers or buyers.

Article 7
Where in any particular case vertical agreements to which the exemption provided for in Article 2 applies have effects incompatible with the conditions laid down in Article 81(3) of the Treaty in the territory of a Member State, or in a part thereof, which has all the characteristics of a distinct geographic market, the competent authority of that Member State may withdraw the benefit of application of this Regulation in respect of that territory, under the same conditions as provided in Article 6.

Article 8
1. Pursuant to Article 1 a of Regulation No 19/65/EEC, the Commission may by regulation declare that, where parallel networks of similar vertical restraints cover more than 50 per cent of a relevant market, this Regulation shall not apply to vertical agreements containing specific restraints relating to that market.

2. A regulation pursuant to paragraph 1 shall not become applicable earlier than six months following its adoption.

Article 9
1. The market share of 30 per cent provided for in Article 3(1) shall be calculated on the basis of the market sales value of the contract goods or services and other goods or services sold by the supplier, which are regarded as interchangeable or substitutable by the buyer, by reason of the products' characteristics, their prices and their intended use; if market sales value data are not available, estimates based on other reliable market information, including market sales volumes, may be used to establish the market share of the undertaking concerned. For the purposes of Article 3(2), it is either the market purchase value or estimates thereof which shall be used to calculate the market share.

2. For the purposes of applying the market share threshold provided for in Article 3 the following rules shall apply:
(a) the market share shall be calculated on the basis of data relating to the preceding calendar year;
(b) the market share shall include any goods or services supplied to integrated distributors for the purposes of sale;

(c) if the market share is initially not more than 30 per cent but subsequently rises above that level without exceeding 35 per cent the exemption provided for in Article 2 shall continue to apply for a period of two consecutive calendar years following the year in which the 30 per cent market share threshold was first exceeded;

(d) if the market share is initially not more than 30 per cent but subsequently rises above 35 per cent, the exemption provided for in Article 2 shall continue to apply for one calendar year following the year in which the level of 35 per cent was first exceeded;

(e) the benefit of points (c) and (d) may not be combined so as to exceed a period of two calendar years.

Article 10

1. For the purpose of calculating total annual turnover within the meaning of Article 2(2) and (4), the turnover achieved during the previous financial year by the relevant party to the vertical agreement and the turnover achieved by its connected undertakings in respect of all goods and services, excluding all taxes and other duties, shall be added together. For this purpose, no account shall be taken of dealings between the party to the vertical agreement and its connected undertakings or between its connected undertakings.

2. The exemption provided for in Article 2 shall remain applicable where, for any period of two consecutive financial years, the total annual turnover threshold is exceeded by no more than 10 per cent.

Article 11

1. For the purposes of this Regulation, the terms 'undertaking', 'supplier' and 'buyer' shall include their respective connected undertakings.

2. Connected undertakings are:

(a) undertakings in which a party to the agreement, directly or indirectly:
— has the power to exercise more than half the voting rights, or
— has the power to appoint more than half the members of the supervisory board, board of management or bodies legally representing the undertaking, or
— has the right to manage the undertaking's affairs;

(b) undertakings which directly or indirectly have, over a party to the agreement, the rights or powers listed in (a);

(c) undertakings in which an undertaking referred to in (b) has, directly or indirectly, the rights or powers listed in (a);

(d) undertakings in which a party to the agreement together with one or more of the undertakings referred to in (a), (b) or (c), or in which two or more of the latter undertakings, jointly have the rights or powers listed in (a);

(e) undertakings in which the rights or the powers listed in (a) are jointly held by:
— parties to the agreement or their respective connected undertakings referred to in (a) to (d), or
— one or more of the parties to the agreement or one or more of their connected undertakings referred to in (a) to (d) and one or more third parties.

3. For the purposes of Article 3, the market share held by the undertakings referred to in paragraph 2(e) of this Article shall be apportioned equally to each undertaking having the rights or the powers listed in paragraph 2(a).

Article 12

1. The exemptions provided for in Commission Regulations (EEC) No 1983/83(4), (EEC) No 1984/83(5) and (EEC) No 4087/88(6) shall continue to apply until 31 May 2000.

2. The prohibition laid down in Article 81(1) of the EC Treaty shall not apply during the

period from 1 June 2000 to 31 December 2001 in respect of agreements already in force on 31 May 2000 which do not satisfy the conditions for exemption provided for in this Regulation but which satisfy the conditions for exemption provided for in Regulations (EEC) No 1983/83, (EEC) No 1984/83 or (EEC) No 4087/88.

Article 13
This Regulation shall enter into force on 1 January 2000.

It shall apply from 1 June 2000, except for Article 12(1) which shall apply from 1 January 2000. This Regulation shall expire on 31 May 2010.

NOTE: The BER is accompanied by detailed Guidelines which set out the Commission's policy on agreements above the thresholds and the circumstances which would warrant the withdrawal of the block exemption. These Guidelines were published in draft form in December 1999 and were adopted by the Commission on 24 May 2000 OJ 2000, No C291/1. A key aspect of the new block exemption is the introduction of market-share thresholds. This is the first time a Community block exemption has contained market-share criteria and the Guidelines must be consulted regarding specific issues that arise in the context of vertical restraints. The Commission's Notice on the definition of the relevant market for the purposes of Community competition law should still be consulted when considering market definition issues (OJ 1997, No C372/5). Although the Guidelines are rather technical they set out in great detail how the 30 per cent market share threshold should be calculated. The full text of the Guidelines is reproduced in Middleton, K., *UK and EC Competition Documents*, 2nd edn, OUP 2002.

Guidelines on Vertical Restraints
OJ 2000, C291/1

2 The relevant market for calculating the 30 per cent market share threshold under the BER
89. Under Article 3 of the BER, it is in general the market share of the supplier that is decisive for the application of the BER. In the case of vertical agreements concluded between an association of retailers and individual members, the association is the supplier and needs to take into account its market share as a supplier. Only in the case of exclusive supply as defined in Article 1(c) of the BER is it the market share of the buyer, and only that market share, which is decisive for the application of the BER.

90. In order to calculate the market share, it is necessary to determine the relevant market. For this the relevant product market and the relevant geographic market must be defined. The relevant product market comprises any goods or services which are regarded by the buyer as interchangeable, by reason of their characteristics, prices and intended use. The relevant geographic market comprises the area in which the undertakings concerned are involved in the supply and demand of relevant goods or services, in which the conditions of competition are sufficiently homogeneous, and which can be distinguished from neighbouring geographic areas because, in particular, conditions of competition are appreciably different in those areas.

91. For the application of the BER, the market share of the supplier is its share on the relevant product and geographic market on which it sells to its buyers.[31] In the example below, this is market A. The product market depends in the first place on substitutability from the buyers' perspective. When the supplied product is used as an input to produce other products and is generally not recognisable in the final product, the product market is normally defined by the direct buyers'

---

31 For example, the Dutch market for new replacement truck and bus tyres in the *Michelin* case (Case 322/81, *Nederlandsche Banden-Industrie Michelin NV* v *Commission*, [1983] ECR 3461), the various meat markets in the Danish slaughter-house case: Commission Decision 2000/42/EC (*Danish Crown/Vestjyske Slagterier*, IV/M. 1313) OJ L20, 25.01.2000, p. 1.

preferences. The customers of the buyers will normally not have a strong preference concerning the inputs used by the buyers. Usually the vertical restraints agreed between the supplier and buyer of the input only relate to the sale and purchase of the intermediate product and not to the sale of the resulting product. In the case of distribution of final goods, what are substitutes for the direct buyers will normally be influenced or determined by the preferences of the final consumers. A distributor, as reseller, cannot ignore the preferences of final consumers when it purchases final goods. In addition, at the distribution level the vertical restraints more often do not only concern the sale of products between supplier and buyer, but also their resale. As different distribution formats usually compete, markets are in general not defined by the form of distribution that is applied. Where suppliers generally sell a portfolio of products, the entire portfolio may determine the product market when the portfolios and not the individual products are regarded as substitutes by the buyers. As the buyers on market A are professional buyers, the geographic market is usually wider than the market where the product is resold to final consumers. Often, this will lead to the definition of national markets or wider geographic markets.

92. In the case of exclusive supply, the buyer's market share is its share of all purchases on the relevant purchase market.[32] In the example below, this is also market A.

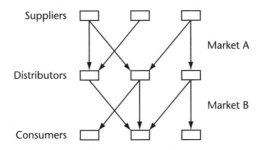

93. Where a vertical agreement involves three parties, each operating at a different level of trade, their market shares will have to be below the market share threshold of 30 per cent at both levels in order to benefit from the BER. If for instance, in an agreement between a manufacturer, a wholesaler (or association of retailers) and a retailer, a non-compete obligation is agreed, then the market share of both the manufacturer and the wholesaler (or association of retailers) must not exceed 30 per cent in order to benefit from the BER.

94. Where a supplier produces both original equipment and the repair or replacement parts for this equipment, the supplier will often be the only or the major supplier on the after-market for the repair and replacement parts. This may also arise where the supplier (OEM supplier) subcontracts the manufacturing of the repair or replacement parts. The relevant market for application of the BER may be the original equipment market including the spare parts or a separate original equipment market and after-market depending on the circumstances of the case, such as the effects of the restrictions involved, the lifetime of the equipment and importance of the repair or replacement costs.

NOTE: In addition to the introduction of market share criteria, the Guidelines make it clear that 'the Commission will adopt an economic approach which is based on the effects on the market; vertical agreements have to be analysed in their legal and economic context' (para. 7) (with the exception of hard-core restrictions).

32 For an example of purchase markets see Commission Decision 1999/674/EC (*Rewe/Meinl* case, IV/M.1221), OJ L274, 23.10.1999, p. 1.

QUESTIONS

Do you think the Commission is right to introduce market share criteria? Do market share criteria reflect market power? Explain how market share thresholds will increase legal uncertainty and security. Will they necessarily make it difficult for undertakings properly to assess whether an agreement is caught by Article 81(1) or benefits from a block exemption?

SECTION 6: *De minimis*

The relationship between the BER and the Commission's *'de minimis'* Notice is complex. The Commission revised its Notice on Agreements of Minor Importance in 1997 (OJ 1997 C29/3) to coincide with the Green Paper proposals. The Notice provided that vertical agreements between undertakings with a market share of less than 10 per cent fall outside the scope of Article 81(1) EC altogether. However, Article 81(1) EC may still apply below the 10 per cent threshold with respect of hard-core restrictions provided that there is an appreciable effect on trade between Member States and on competition. Where this is the case, the relevant case-law of the European Court will be applicable, see e.g. Case 5/69 *Völk* v *Vervaecke* [1969] ECR 295. The 1997 Notice was replaced in 2001 by a new Notice OJ 2001 C368/7. See Chapter 5.

SECTION 7: **Withdrawal of block exemption**

Article 7 of the BER provides for the benefit of the block exemption to be withdrawn if a vertical agreement, considered either in isolation or alongside similar agreements enforced by competing suppliers or buyers, falls within the scope of Article 81(1) EC. The Guidelines explain the circumstances in which this might happen.

Guidelines on Vertical Restraints
OJ 2000, C291/1

(71) This may occur when a supplier, or a buyer in the case of exclusive supply agreements, holding a market share not exceeding 30 per cent, enters into a vertical agreement which does not give rise to objective advantages such as to compensate for the damage which it causes to competition. This may particularly be the case with respect to the distribution of goods to final consumers, who are often in a much weaker position than professional buyers of intermediate goods. In the case of sales to final consumers, the disadvantages caused by a vertical agreement may have a stronger impact than in a case concerning the sale and purchase of intermediate goods. When the conditions of Article 81(3) are not fulfilled, the Commission may withdraw the benefit of the Block Exemption Regulation under Article 6 and establish an infringement of Article 81(1).

(72) Where the withdrawal procedure is applied, the Commission bears the burden of proof that the agreement falls within the scope of Article 81(1) and that the agreement does not fulfil all four conditions of Article 81(3).

(73) The conditions for an exemption under Article 81(3) may in particular not be fulfilled when access to the relevant market or competition therein is significantly restricted by the cumulative effect of parallel networks of similar vertical agreements practised by competing suppliers or buyers. Parallel networks of vertical agreements are to be regarded as similar if they contain restraints producing similar effects on the market. Similar effects will normally occur when vertical restraints practised by competing suppliers or buyers come within one of the four groups listed in paragraphs 104 to 114. Such a situation may arise for example when, on a given market, certain suppliers practise purely qualitative selective distribution while other suppliers practise quantitative selective distribution. In such circumstances, the assessment must take account of the anti-competitive effects attributable to each individual network of agreements. Where appropriate, withdrawal may concern only the quantitative limitations imposed on the number of authorised distributors. Other cases in which a withdrawal decision may be taken include situations where the buyer, for example in the context of exclusive supply or exclusive distribution, has significant market power in the relevant downstream market where he resells the goods or provides the services.

(74) Responsibility for an anti-competitive cumulative effect can only be attributed to those undertakings which make an appreciable contribution to it. Agreements entered into by undertakings whose contribution to the cumulative effect is insignificant do not fall under the prohibition provided for in Article 81(1)[1] and are therefore not subject to the withdrawal mechanism. The assessment of such a contribution will be made in accordance with the criteria set out in paragraphs 137 to 229.

(75) A withdrawal decision can only have ex nunc effect, which means that the exempted status of the agreements concerned will not be affected until the date at which the withdrawal becomes effective.

(76) Under Article 7 of the Block Exemption Regulation, the competent authority of a Member State may withdraw the benefit of the Block Exemption Regulation in respect of vertical agreements whose anti-competitive effects are felt in the territory of the Member State concerned or a part thereof, which has all the characteristics of a distinct geographic market. Where a Member State has not enacted legislation enabling the national competition authority to apply Community competition law or at least to withdraw the benefit of the Block Exemption Regulation, the Member State may ask the Commission to initiate proceedings to this effect.

(77) Often, such cases lend themselves to decentralised enforcement by national competition authorities. However, the Commission reserves the right to take on certain cases displaying a particular Community interest, such as cases raising a new point of law.

(78) National decisions of withdrawal must be taken in accordance with the procedures laid down under national law and will only have effect within the territory of the Member State concerned. Such national decisions must not prejudice the uniform application of the Community competition rules and the full effect of the measures adopted in implementation of those rules[1]. Compliance with this principle implies that national competition authorities must carry out their assessment under Article 81 in the light of the relevant criteria developed by the Court of Justice and the Court of First Instance and in the light of notices and previous decisions adopted by the Commission.

(79) The Commission considers that the consultation mechanisms provided for in the Notice on cooperation between national competition authorities and the Commission[2] should be used to avert the risk of conflicting decisions and duplication of procedures.

---

1 Judgment in the *Delimitis* Case.

1 Judgment of the Court of Justice in Case 14/68 *Walt Wilhelm and Others* v *Bundeskartellamt* [1969] ECR 1, paragraph 4, and judgment in *Delimitis*.

2 OJ C 313, 15.10.1997, p. 3, points 49 to 53.

NOTE: Moreover, Article 8 of the block exemption regulation enables the Commission to exclude, by regulation, from the block exemption parallel networks of similar vertical restraints where these cover more than 50 per cent of a relevant market.

(81) Whereas the withdrawal of the benefit of the Block Exemption Regulation under Article 6 implies the adoption of a decision establishing an infringement of Article 81 by an individual company, the effect of a regulation under Article 8 is merely to remove, in respect of the restraints and the markets concerned, the benefit of the application of the Block Exemption Regulation and to restore the full application of Article 81(1) and (3). Following the adoption of a regulation declaring the Block Exemption inapplicable in respect of certain vertical restraints on a particular market, the criteria developed by the relevant case-law of the Court of Justice and the Court of First Instance and by notices and previous decisions adopted by the Commission will guide the application of Article 81 to individual agreements. Where appropriate, the Commission will take a decision in an individual case, which can provide guidance to all the undertakings operating on the market concerned.

(82) For the purpose of calculating the 50 per cent market coverage ratio, account must be taken of each individual network of vertical agreements containing restraints, or combinations of restraints, producing similar effects on the market. Similar effects normally result when the restraints come within one of the four groups listed in paragraphs 104 to 114.

(83) Article 8 does not entail an obligation on the part of the Commission to act where the 50 per cent market-coverage ratio is exceeded. In general, disapplication is appropriate when it is likely that access to the relevant market or competition therein is appreciably restricted. This may occur in particular when parallel networks of selective distribution covering more than 50 per cent of a market make use of selection criteria which are not required by the nature of the relevant goods or discriminate against certain forms of distribution capable of selling such goods.

(84) In assessing the need to apply Article 8, the Commission will consider whether individual withdrawal would be a more appropriate remedy. This may depend, in particular, on the number of competing undertakings contributing to a cumulative effect on a market or the number of affected geographic markets within the Community.

(85) Any regulation adopted under Article 8 must clearly set out its scope. This means, first, that the Commission must define the relevant product and geographic market(s) and, secondly, that it must identify the type of vertical restraint in respect of which the Block Exemption Regulation will no longer apply. As regards the latter aspect, the Commission may modulate the scope of its regulation according to the competition concern which it intends to address. For instance, while all parallel networks of single-branding type arrangements shall be taken into account in view of establishing the 50 per cent market coverage ratio, the Commission may nevertheless restrict the scope of the disapplication regulation only to non-compete obligations exceeding a certain duration. Thus, agreements of a shorter duration or of a less restrictive nature might be left unaffected, in consideration of the lesser degree of foreclosure attributable to such restraints. Similarly, when on a particular market selective distribution is practised in combination with additional restraints such as non-compete or quantity-forcing on the buyer, the disapplication regulation may concern only such additional restraints. Where appropriate, the Commission may also provide guidance by specifying the market share level which, in the specific market context, may be regarded as insufficient to bring about a significant contribution by an individual undertaking to the cumulative effect.

(86) The transitional period of not less than six months that the Commission will have to set under Article 8(2) should allow the undertakings concerned to adapt their agreements to take account of the regulation disapplying the Block Exemption Regulation.

(87) A regulation disapplying the Block Exemption Regulation will not affect the exempted status of the agreements concerned for the period preceding its entry into force.

NOTE: Regulation 2790/99 only applies to exclusive dealing, purchasing and franchise agreements. Discussion has centred on whether it could be extended to other sectors which have previously benefited from their own block exemption, for example the motor industry. The block exemption applicable to the car industry, Regulation 1475/95, expired on 30 September 2002 and was replaced by a new block exemption regulation, 1400/2002 on 1 October 2002. Pressure to remove block exemption Regulation 1475/95 was intense and its demise seemed inevitable. It is hoped the new regulation will increase competition in the European car industry. For comment, see Middleton, K., *European Current Law*, May 2002, xi–xv.

BER 2790 is a significant development in the Community's treatment of vertical restraints and the Commission notes its success in its annual report.

Foreword to the Commission's 30th Report on Competition Policy, 2000

The full set of regulations and guidelines on vertical and horizontal agreements establishes a comprehensive framework for the application of competition rules to the great majority of agreements between undertakings. It also responds to the intention to bring the competition analysis more in line with economic reasoning, to give economic operators a clearer understanding of competition issues and concepts and to relieve enterprises from burdensome administrative obligations.

What is also important to underline, is that in the present year we were already able to harvest some of the benefits of the new approach. The number of notifications fell by nearly 40 per cent over the previous year, undoubtedly following the new rules on vertical and horizontal agreements. On the other hand, almost 30 per cent of the new cases were opened ex officio, compared to only 20 per cent in 1999. These developments are fully in line with the policy objective of dealing with standard agreements through legislative action, while using the available resources to pursue a more proactive policy and concentrate on the most dangerous anticompetitive practices.

NOTE: The significance of the vertical restraints reform will be greatly reduced when the Commission's Modernisation regulation (2000) is adopted. The regulation will abolish the notification and authorisation system and give NCAs a much greater role in Community competition law enforcement than is presently the case under BER 2790/99. Clearly further legislative reform in this area of Community competition law will be required. Implementation of the draft regulation will also impact on the treatment of vertical agreements in a domestic context.

FURTHER READING

For comment on the relationship between the new Community policy on vertical agreements and the White Paper on Modernisation, see Rodger, B.J., Chapter 3, in Rodger, B.J., and MacCulloch, A. (eds) *The UK Competition Act: A New Era for UK Competition Law*. Oxford, Hart Publishing, 2000, see pp. 67 and 73 in particular.

SECTION 8: **UK competition law and vertical restraints**

The CA 1998, whilst seeking to ensure symmetry between UK and Community competition law to simplify compliance for companies, disapplies the Chapter I prohibition of anti-competitive agreements from a broad range of vertical agreements. The question of how to treat vertical agreements in the Competition Act was a difficult issue for the UK Government, and the Competition Bill did not contain any specific arrangements for vertical agreements. The government appeared to be waiting for the new Community vertical restraints policy to be made clear. This attempt at harmonisation would have been highly unsatisfactory given the strict treatment of vertical agreements under Community law. In any case, it appears that the delay in formulating the UK position was partly to ensure technical consistency in terms of the definition of a vertical restraint as opposed to substantive harmonisation. The government was also keen to avoid being over-burdened with unnecessary notifications in respect of agreements where there was no restriction of competition. In the end, the government decided to exclude vertical agreements from the ambit of the 1998 Act by secondary legislation. Lord Simon confirmed that:

> There remains a case therefore for special treatment of vertical agreements under the [Act] to avoid the burden of unnecessary notification and to ease the so-called *'straitjacket'* which existing European block exemptions impose. (Hansard, HL Report Stage, 9 February 1998, col. 901.)

Departure from the Community position on vertical restraints has been welcomed given the Community's preoccupation with the goal of market integration. Thus, s. 50(1) of the CA 1998 provides the Secretary of State with power to make an Order modifying the application of the Chapter I prohibition to vertical agreements. The Competition Act 1998 (Land and Vertical Agreements Exclusion No 310) Order 2000 was published in draft form in February 2000 together with a consultation document and came into force on 1 March 2000.

The Competition Act 1998 (Land and Vertical Agreements Exclusion) Order 2000

Citation and commencement

1. This Order may be cited as the Competition Act 1998 (Land and Vertical Agreements Exclusion) Order 2000 and shall come into force on 1st March 2000.

Definitions

2. In this Order—

'the Act' means the Competition Act 1998;

'interest in land' includes any estate, interest, easement, servitude or right in or over land (including any interest or right created by a licence), and in Scotland also includes any interest under a lease and other heritable right in or over land including a heritable security;

'land' includes buildings and other structures and land covered with water;

'land agreement' means an agreement between undertakings which creates, alters, transfers or terminates an interest in land, or an agreement to enter into such an agreement, together with any obligation and restriction to which Article 6 applies; and to the extent that an agreement is a vertical agreement it is not a land agreement;

'party to an agreement' in respect of a land agreement includes a successor in title to a party to the agreement;

'relevant land' means the land in respect of which a land agreement creates, alters, transfers or terminates an interest, or in respect of which it constitutes an agreement to do so; and 'other relevant land' means other land in which a party to a land agreement has an interest; and 'vertical agreement' means an agreement between undertakings, each of which operates, for the purposes of the agreement, at a different level of the production or distribution chain, and relating to the conditions under which the parties may purchase, sell or resell certain goods or services and includes provisions contained in such agreements which relate to the assignment to the buyer or use by the buyer of intellectual property rights, provided that those provisions do not constitute the primary object of the agreement and are directly related to the use, sale or resale of goods or services by the buyer or its customers.

Exclusion of vertical agreements from the Chapter 1 prohibition

3. The Chapter 1 prohibition shall not apply to an agreement to the extent that it is a vertical agreement.

4. Article 3 shall not apply where the vertical agreement, directly or indirectly, in isolation or in combination with other factors under the control of the parties has the object or effect of restricting the buyer's ability to determine its sale price, without prejudice to the possibility of the supplier imposing a maximum sale price or recommending a sale price, provided that these do not amount to a fixed or minimum sale price as a result of pressure from, or incentives offered by, any of the parties.

Exclusion of land agreements from the Chapter 1 prohibition

5. The Chapter 1 prohibition shall not apply to an agreement to the extent that it is a land agreement.

Obligations and restrictions

6.—(1) This article applies to an obligation which is accepted by a party to a land agreement in his capacity as holder of an interest:

    (a) in the relevant land or other relevant land and is for the benefit of another party to the agreement in his capacity as holder of an interest in the relevant land; or

    (b) in other relevant land and relates to the imposition in respect of that land of:

        (i) restrictions of a kind described in paragraph (2)(a) which correspond to those accepted by a party to the agreement in his capacity as holder of an interest in the relevant land; or

        (ii) obligations which correspond to those accepted by a party to the agreement in his capacity as holder of an interest in the relevant land.

(2) This article applies to a restriction which:

    (a) restricts the activity that may be carried out on, from, or in connection with the relevant land or other relevant land and is accepted by a party to the agreement in his capacity as holder of an interest in the relevant land or other relevant land and is for the benefit of another party to the agreement in his capacity as holder of an interest in the relevant land;

    (b) is accepted by a party to the agreement in his capacity as holder of an interest in other relevant land and relates to the imposition of restrictions on the activity that may be carried out on, from, or in connection with the other relevant land which correspond to those accepted by a party to the agreement in his capacity as holder of an interest in the relevant land; or

    (c) restricts the freedom of a party to the agreement to create or transfer an interest in the relevant land to another person.

Withdrawal of exclusion etc.

7. The power in paragraph 4 of Schedule 1 to the Act to withdraw the benefit of the exclusion from the Chapter 1 prohibition applies (with the exception of sub-paragraph (5)(b)) to the

exclusion provided by Articles 3 and 5 as it applies to the exclusion provided by paragraph 1 of Schedule 1.

8. Articles 3 and 5 do not apply to an agreement to the extent that it takes effect between the same parties and is to the like object or effect as an agreement which has been the subject of a direction under Article 7.

NOTE: Note that the Order also excludes Land Agreements from the ambit of the Act. This contrasted with earlier drafts of the Order which did not include Land Agreements. Why do you think the government excluded agreements relating to land from the legislation?

Consider also the definition of 'vertical agreement' in s. 2. Can you identify any difficulties with this definition? How does this depart from the Community definition?

The OFT Guideline on Vertical Agreements and Restraints OFT 419, para. 2.1 provides that exclusion is automatic and no individual notification needs to be made to the Director General to benefit from its provisions. The Guidelines also make it clear that there are two elements to the definition of vertical agreement.

2.2 The Exclusion Order states that 'vertical agreement':

> means an agreement between undertakings, each of which operates, for the purposes of the agreement, at a different level of the production or distribution chain, and relating to the conditions under which the parties may purchase, sell or resell certain goods or services and includes provisions contained in such agreements which relate to the assignment to the buyer or use by the buyer of intellectual property rights, provided that those provisions do not constitute the primary object of the agreement and are directly related to the use, sale or resale of goods or services by the buyer or its customers.

The Director General considers that there are two elements to this definition:

- the economic relationship between the undertakings involved in the agreement; and
- the provisions of the agreement, which may include certain provisions relating to the assignment or use of intellectual property rights.

These two elements are considered below.

Economic relationship between the undertakings involved

2.3 For an agreement to fall within the definition of a 'vertical agreement' in the Exclusion Order and benefit from the exclusion, the economic relationship between the parties must be such that each of the undertakings involved in the agreement operates '*at a different level of the production or distribution chain*'. Examples of activities at different levels of the production or distribution chain include supplying raw materials, manufacturing, wholesaling and retailing. An agreement between a wood supplier and a paper manufacturer for the supply of wood to make paper would be an example of a vertical agreement between undertakings operating at different levels of the production or distribution chain.

2.4 Different levels of the production or distribution chain may be found within each of the broad categories mentioned above. Within manufacturing, for example, one undertaking may manufacture a component part of a final product (such as a light bulb) and make an agreement to sell that part to a second undertaking which uses that part in its manufacture of the final product (such as a car). Although each of these undertakings is a manufacturer (one of light bulbs and one of cars), they would be regarded as operating at different levels of the production or distribution chain when they entered into an agreement for the supply of light bulbs to be incorporated into a car. Such an agreement may, therefore, benefit from the exclusion.

2.5 'Each' undertaking must operate at a different level of the production or distribution chain for an agreement to benefit from the exclusion. Therefore, for example, an agreement between one manufacturer and a group of six competing wholesalers (where each of the six wholesalers operates at the same level of the production or distribution chain), while being an agreement between undertakings at different levels of the production or distribution chain (that is, manufacturing and wholesaling), would not benefit from the exclusion. The agreement would involve more than one undertaking at one particular level of the production or distribution chain (wholesaling). An agreement between a supplier of raw materials, a manufacturer, a distributor and a retailer could, however, benefit from the exclusion because each undertaking operates at a different level of the production or distribution chain.

2.6 Undertakings often operate at more than one level of the production or distribution chain. An agreement between undertakings that operate at one or more of the same levels of the production or distribution chain may benefit from the exclusion for vertical agreements. This will only be the case, however, where the agreement concerns only respective activities of those undertakings which are at different levels of the production or distribution chain. The agreement can benefit from the exclusion because the undertakings involved each operate at different levels of the production or distribution chain 'for the purposes of the agreement'.

2.7 If, for example, a manufacturer which also distributes its product enters into a supply agreement with a distributor, that supply agreement may benefit from the exclusion even though the manufacturer also has sales activities which operate at the same level of the production or distribution chain as the distributor's activities. The two undertakings are operating at different levels of the production or distribution chain for the purposes of the agreement: the first is acting as a manufacturer and the second as a distributor. A supply agreement between them in these respective capacities (that is, as a manufacturer and as a distributor) may fall within the definition of a vertical agreement in the Exclusion Order and may therefore benefit from the exclusion.

NOTE: The government has recognised that in some cases vertical restraints can have serious competition concerns, for example, where there is significant market power, although this has not been defined. Article 7 of the Order provides the Director General with a 'clawback' power to terminate the exclusion if there are individual cases where vertical agreements give rise to competition concerns. The power of clawback does not exist in relation to categories of agreements. This is an important safeguard to protect against agreements which although excluded might have serious competition concerns and the OFT Guideline explains how this will operate in practice.

OFT Guideline 419, Vertical Agreements and Restraints

5 Withdrawal of the exclusion for vertical agreements

5.1 The Exclusion Order excludes vertical agreements because they do not generally give rise to competition concerns unless one of the parties to the agreement has significant market power or a network of similar agreements exists which has a cumulative effect on the market. The Director General does, however, have the power to remove the benefit of the exclusion from individual vertical agreements which will enable them to be considered under the Chapter 1 prohibition. He can exercise this power only:

- if he is considering whether to withdraw the benefit of the exclusion, and, by written notice, requires any party to the agreement to provide him with information in connection with the agreement, and, without reasonable excuse, that party fails to comply with such requirement within 10 working days; or
- where he considers that a vertical agreement will, if not excluded, infringe the Chapter 1 prohibition, and he is not likely to grant it an unconditional individual exemption.[12]

12 An individual exemption is unconditional if no conditions or obligations are attached to it by the Director General—see the Competition Act guideline *The Chapter 1 Prohibition*.

5.2 In practice, it is likely that the Director General will exercise these powers only rarely. To infringe the Chapter 1 prohibition, the agreement must have an 'appreciable' effect on competition (see part 1 above and the Competition Act guidelines *The Chapter 1 Prohibition* and *Assessment of Market Power*). The Director General will consider carefully complaints in respect of agreements which have the benefit of the exclusion.

5.3 Where the Director General intends to give a direction withdrawing the benefit of the exclusion from an agreement he must consult the parties to that agreement. Such a direction must specify the date from which it is to take effect; it may not take effect from a date earlier than the date on which it was given. If the Director General gives such a direction he will publish it on the public register that he maintains.

Consequences of withdrawal

5.4 If the benefit of the exclusion is withdrawn from a particular agreement, the agreement does not automatically infringe the Chapter 1 prohibition. A withdrawal direction merely allows the Director General to consider the application of the Chapter 1 prohibition to the agreement. He may then be able to use the information-gathering powers in the Act to require the parties to the agreement (and any third parties) to provide information. He will be able to consider the effect of the whole of an agreement on competition and decide whether it infringes the Chapter 1 prohibition.

5.5 If the Director General withdraws the benefit of the exclusion from an agreement, and finds that it does infringe the Chapter 1 prohibition, such an infringement finding can have effect only from the date of the withdrawal. The agreement will be void only from the date of withdrawal and any financial penalties imposed in respect of that agreement can relate only to the period after the withdrawal of the exclusion.

5.6 The Exclusion Order prevents undertakings from avoiding the consequences of a withdrawal direction. If, following a direction withdrawing the benefit of the exclusion from an agreement, the undertakings enter into another agreement which is to the like object or effect as the agreement which was the subject of the withdrawal direction that subsequent agreement will not benefit from the exclusion.

NOTE: Price-fixing agreements, however, will always be prohibited.

OFT Guideline 419, Vertical Agreements and Restraints

Price-fixing

3.1 The benefit of the exclusion does not apply to vertical agreements that fix prices. The Exclusion Order provides that the exclusion for vertical agreements does not apply to any vertical agreement which directly or indirectly has the object or effect of restricting a buyer's ability to determine its sale price.

3.2 Agreements where the seller imposes a maximum or recommended sale price may benefit from the exclusion except where such a maximum or recommended sale price results, in practice, in a fixed or minimum sale price because of pressure from, or any incentives offered by, any of the undertakings involved. Where recommended or maximum prices have such an effect the agreements will not benefit from the exclusion for vertical agreements. Examples of types of practices that may result in fixed or minimum sale prices include:

- agreements fixing the maximum level of discount a distributor can grant;
- intimidation, delay or suspension of deliveries and contract terminations in relation to the observance of a certain price level; and
- measures aimed at identifying price-cutting distributors, such as the implementation of a price monitoring system.

3.3 Price-fixing agreements that do not benefit from the exclusion are subject to scrutiny under the Chapter 1 prohibition and are capable of having an appreciable effect on competition even if the parties' combined share of the relevant market is less than 25 per cent. Details of how agreements that fix prices will be treated by the Director General under the Act are given in the Competition Act guideline *The Chapter 1*.

SECTION 9: Relationship between the UK and EC treatment of vertical agreements

The exclusion of vertical agreements from the CA 1998 is clearly designed to reduce the regulatory burden on British business of having to notify agreements under two different systems. The definition of a vertical agreement in the Exclusion Order therefore closely mirrors that in the BER for technical consistency. OFT Guideline 419 explains the relationship between the UK and EC treatment of vertical agreements.

OFT Guideline 419, Vertical Agreements and Restraints

4.1 Article 81(1) of the EC Treaty prohibits anti-competitive agreements which 'may affect trade between Member States', whereas the Chapter 1 prohibition applies only to anti-competitive agreements which 'may affect trade within the United Kingdom'. The phrase 'may affect trade between Member States' has been broadly interpreted by the European Court which has found that even where the parties to an agreement are within the same Member State inter-state trade may still be affected.[9] Many agreements will therefore be caught by both Article 81(1) and the Chapter 1 prohibition.

4.2 Agreements that benefit from a European Commission individual or block exemption, or would do so if the agreement had an effect on trade between Member States, are automatically exempt from the Chapter 1 prohibition under the Act without the need for notification to the Director General. Such agreements benefit from a 'parallel exemption' (see the Competition Act guideline *The Chapter 1 Prohibition*).

4.3 An exclusion (or exemption) from the Chapter 1 prohibition does not, however, preclude the application of Article 81(1).

NOTE: Besides achieving technical consistency with Community law, the exclusion of vertical agreements from the CA will also enable the UK competition authorities to focus attention on serious restrictions of competition instead of being concerned with essentially benign agreements. In all other respects the UK position diverges from the Community approach.

OFT Guideline 419, Vertical Agreements and Restraints

4.5 The definition of a vertical agreement in the Exclusion Order reflects that in the EC Verticals Block Exemption. The most significant differences between the scope of the Exclusion Order and that of the EC Verticals Block Exemption are that:

- the EC Verticals Block Exemption applies only to agreements where the market share of the supplier (or buyer, in the case of an agreement with an exclusive supply obligation) does not exceed 30 per cent of the relevant market. There is no market share cap in order to benefit from the Exclusion Order; and

9 Case 56/65 *Société Technique Minière* v *Maschinenbau Ulm GmbH* [1966] ECR 235; and Case 8/72 *Vereniging van Cementhandelaren* v *Commission* [1972] ECR 977, [1973] CMLR 7.

• the EC Verticals Block Exemption contains a number of 'hardcore' restrictions which, if included in the vertical agreement, have the effect of taking the agreement outside its scope. The only equivalent restriction in the Exclusion Order relates to price-fixing vertical agreements.

NOTE: The Exclusion Order only excludes vertical agreements from the scope of the Chapter I prohibition and vertical agreements may be subject to scrutiny under the Chapter II prohibition (s. 8). This is consistent with the new economic consensus that vertical agreements do not pose a threat to competition unless there is market power. Thus, where an undertaking has abused a dominant position in the form of a vertical agreement of restraints it will be assessed the same way as any other type of conduct under the Chapter II prohibition (see OFT Guideline 419, Vertical Agreements and Restraints, para. 6.1).

Vertical agreements may also be subject to scrutiny under the FTA 1973. Thus, in certain circumstances the scale and complex monopoly provisions of the FTA 1973 may be appropriate for dealing with vertical relationships and the potential competition problems that might arise. For example, it is increasingly often the case that vertical agreements are prevalent in a market as a result of the *structure* of the market as opposed to there being an actual agreement or evidence of collusion between the undertakings concerned to cause such a situation. Can you think of a particular sector where the structure of the market might cause there to be concern over the use of certain vertical restraints?

In its White Paper 'A World Class Competition Regime' July 2001, the government suggested 'that there is a risk that the more permissive domestic exclusion may have the effect of discouraging some private actions. Now that a European-level block exemption is in place (with parallel effect in the UK), there is no strong case for retaining the domestic exclusion. Therefore, the Government intends to repeal the domestic exclusion of vertical agreements'. The Enterprise Act did not however, make any provision for repeal of the domestic exclusion of vertical agreements.

QUESTIONS

1. To what extent was harmonisation the driving force behind reform of UK policy on vertical restraints?

2. Discuss the key differences between UK and EC policy on vertical restraints.

3. To what extent does the treatment of vertical restraints under the CA 1998 offer companies legal certainty? Is this a better regime than the Community system?

4. What role do you believe market integration will play in the new Community policy on vertical restraints?

FURTHER READING

Rodger, B.J., and MacCulloch, A., Chapter 6, 'The Chapter I prohibition—prohibiting cartels or permitting verticals? Or both?', in *The UK Competition Act: A New Era for UK Competition Law*, Oxford, Hart Publishing, 2000.

Subiotto, R., and Amato, F., 'Preliminary Analysis of the Commission's Reform Concerning Vertical Restraints', Journal of World Competition 23(2): 5–26, 2000.

Whish, R., 'Regulation 2790/99: The Commission's "New Style" Block Exemption for Vertical Agreements' (2000) 37 CMLRev 887.

7

UK monopoly control

SECTION 1: **Introduction**

The control of monopoly in the UK has undergone an extensive transformation recently with the introduction of the Competition Act 1998 (CA 1998), particularly its Chapter II prohibition. The Fair Trading Act 1973 (FTA 1973), based on the public interest test for assessing market structure and conduct was retained, but is set to be replaced by the provisions for market investigations contained in Part IV of the Enterprise Act. Nonetheless, it is clear that the new prohibition under the CA 1998 is to be the key competition law tool in the UK for dealing with issues of market power.

**Whish, R., 'The Competition Act 1998 and the prior debate on reform',
Chapter 1 in Rodger, B.J., and MacCulloch, A. (eds),** *The UK Competition Act:
A New Era for UK Competition Law*
Oxford, Hart Publishing, 2000, at pp. 1–4

The Competition Act 1998, which entered into force on 1 March 2000, radically reforms the domestic law of the United Kingdom on restrictive agreements and anti-competitive practices. To understand just how radical the 1998 Act is, it is interesting to review briefly the pragmatic growth of legislation on this subject in the United Kingdom over the preceding fifty years: much of the complexity of the law arose from the fact that there was an accretion of several layers of competition control in a number of different Acts of Parliament. The years 1948, 1973 and 1998 can be seen to have been particularly important in the evolution of the law. This would suggest that the next major piece of legislation can be expected in 2023, the end of the next cycle of twenty-five years; however it may be that further change will come much sooner than this if reform follows the European Commission's White Paper on Modernisation,[1] and in particular its proposal that the system of notification of agreements should be abandoned, necessitating amendment of the Competition Act 1998. A central feature of the Act is the procedure of notification for guidance and/or a decision, which was itself modelled on the system in Regulation 17/62 which the Commission now proposes to abandon.

A review of the period from 1948 to 1998 shows that competition law in the United Kingdom has been in a continual process of formation, with the legislature having extended the law in a pragmatic, ad hoc, way. Competition law in the United Kingdom cannot be traced back to a 'Big Bang', as could be said of the Sherman Act of 1890 in the USA or Articles 81 and 82 in the EC Treaty. Instead there have been a series of explosions at intervals of, normally, about four or five years, some quite minor, with the more substantial ones tending to occur at twenty-five year intervals. The 1998 Act

---

1 On this issue, see further Barry Rodger, Chapter 3.

sweeps away much of the system that has formed over the preceding fifty years, while retaining the investigative system for mergers and monopolies that has its origins in the first modern statute, the Monopolies and Restrictive Practices (Inquiry and Control) Act 1948. The system of merger control is now itself the subject of a consultation procedure, pursuant to a Department of Trade and Industry document published in August 1999.[2]

The first twenty-five years

The Monopolies and Restrictive Practices (Inquiry and Control) Act 1948[3] established the Monopolies and Restrictive Practices Commission, a direct ancestor of the Competition Commission created by the 1998 Act. The 1948 Act can be traced back to the White Paper published during the Second World War on Employment Policy,[4] which considered that a policy of full employment was most likely to be successful in a competitive economy. The 1948 Act enabled monopolies and restrictive practices to be investigated. The President of the Board of Trade was given the power to instigate investigations and to determine the appropriate remedy in the event that the Commission found there to be a detriment to the public interest. The function of the Commission was simply to investigate and report: it did not have an original jurisdiction of its own and it did not make decisions or impose remedies itself. Although the Competition Commission's role is more complex under the legislation in force today, including regulatory Acts such as the Telecommunications Act 1984 and the Railways Act 1993, much of its current work conforms to the original model in 1948.

After the 1948 Act, there followed numerous additions to the domestic legislation: a review of the legislative history shows that it has taken a long time to 'form' a system of competition law in the United Kingdom. As we shall go on to see, it also took a long time to determine how best to 'reform' it. Certain dates stand out in the years after 1948. In 1955 the Monopolies and Restrictive Practices Commission published its *Report on Collective Discrimination*,[5] the minority opinion in which led to the adoption of the Restrictive Trade Practices Act 1956. It was at this point that the treatment of 'monopoly situations' and restrictive trade practices diverged, the latter being subject to a stricter regime, albeit not strict enough; much of the motivation behind the new legislation was the need for effective sanctions. A controversial issue as the recent Competition Bill passed through Parliament was whether the provisions for the investigation of monopoly situations should be retained after the introduction of the new prohibitions for restrictive agreements and abuse of dominance. This matter is discussed further below by Mark Furse, Chapter 7.

The next important date was 1964, when the Resale Prices Act was passed; that Act, prohibiting collective resale price maintenance and rendering individual resale price maintenance unlawful unless authorised by the Restrictive Practices Court according to specified criteria, was enormously controversial at the time. Some of this controversy resurfaced as the Competition Bill passed through Parliament, where considerable time was spent on the position of pharmacies, the authorisation granted by the court to price maintenance for medicaments and the position that would obtain under the new regime.[6]

In 1965 the Monopolies and Mergers Act introduced for the first time a system of merger control in the United Kingdom, as part of the new Labour Government's policy of encouraging rationalisation and consolidation of industry but not at the expense of creating firms with excessive market power. This Act used the model of 1948, including reference to the Monopolies and Mergers Commission

---

2 *Mergers: A Consultation Document on Proposals for Reform* (London, DTI, August 1999).

3 On the background to this Act, see R. Whish, *Competition Law* (3rd edn, London, Butterworths, 1993) pp. 60–2; S. Wilks, 'The Prolonged Reform of UK Competition Policy' in G.B. Doern and S. Wilks (eds), *Comparative Competition Policy: National Institutions in a Global Market* (Oxford, Clarendon Press, 1996) pp. 139–84 at 141–3; T. Freyer, *Regulating Big Business* (Cambridge, Cambridge University Press, 1992), ch 7.

4 Cm 6527 (1944).

5 Cmd 9504 (1955).

6 See discussion *infra*.

and action by the Secretary of State following the Commission's investigation and adverse report. This system for the control of mergers has remained in place ever since, but is currently under review by the Department of Trade and Industry.[7] Three years later the Restrictive Trade Practices Act 1968 made various changes to the 1956 Act, including the provision of powers to extend the legislation to catch 'information agreements'[8] and the introduction of the notion that unregistered, registrable agreements would be void in respect of any 'relevant restrictions' In the years that followed, obedience to the legislation was much more likely to be attributable to firms needing to ensure that their agreements were enforceable than to their fear of action being taken against them by the Registrar of Restrictive Trading Agreements or, after 1973, the Director General of Fair Trading. One of the most unsatisfactory features of the restrictive practices legislation was that serious cartels, which should be prohibited, continued because the legislation lacked the investigatory powers and the sanctions to make it bite, while innocuous agreements were often registrable as a result of the form-based and highly complex provisions on 'restrictions', in consequence of which it was necessary to 'furnish particulars' of them to the Office of Fair Trading in order to avoid the risk of unenforceability.

The second twenty-five years
The Fair Trading Act 1973 was of major importance. The significance of this Act lay not so much in the substantive law, although this was the legislation that gave the power to the Secretary of State to bring the services sector within the scope of the Restrictive Trade Practices Act[9] and also reduced the 'monopoly situation' threshold from 33 per cent to 25 per cent. What was more significant was that this Act created the role of the Director General of Fair Trading and radically revised the institutional structure of competition law in the United Kingdom. The creation of this role, and of the Office of Fair Trading, meant that there was now an institution which, among its other roles, had responsibility for competition policy. At last it was beginning to be possible to see that there was 'competition law' in the United Kingdom; the fact that this was also the year in which the United Kingdom joined the European Economic Community, as it then was, and therefore that Articles 85 and 86 of the EC Treaty, as they then were, became directly applicable, made this point even clearer. Competition law achieved early adulthood in the United Kingdom in 1973, a rare example in the modern world of minority being abandoned at the advanced age of twenty-five.

Following the Fair Trading Act, further competition legislation continued to come onto the statute book at fairly regular intervals. The Restrictive Trade Practices Act 1976 consolidated the legislation, and the Restrictive Trade Practices Act 1977 introduced complex new provisions on 'financing terms'. The legislation on resale price maintenance was consolidated in the Resale Prices Act 1976. The Competition Act 1980 arose out of two consultation documents known as the Liesner Reports, which began the long process of reform. These Reports, and many subsequent ones, are discussed *infra*. Numerous statutes in the 1980s and 1990s made additional changes to the system of competition law, for example the Financial Services Act 1986, the Channel Tunnel Act 1987, the Companies Act 1989, the Courts and Legal Services Act 1990, the Deregulation and Contracting Out Act 1994 and the Broadcasting Act 1996. However by the late 1980s it had become clear that a major reform of the law had become necessary, and the Conservative Government committed itself in a White Paper as early as July 1989 to radical reform of the legislation on restrictive trade practices. Its inability to find parliamentary time for a Bill in the eight subsequent years that it remained in office caused great frustration for many, not least the Director General of Fair Trading who lacked the powers to pursue cartels that should be prohibited, and yet whose office had to spend inordinate amounts of time registering innocuous agreements that were nevertheless caught by the complex restrictive practices legislation.

---

7 See *supra* n. 2.

8 The power was exercised in 1969 by the Restrictive Trade Practices Act (Information Agreements) Order (SI 1969/1842).

9 The power was exercised in 1976 by the Restrictive Trade Practices Act (Services) Order (SI 1976/98).

NOTE: The CA 199 certainly marked a 'radical' change from the traditional public interest test model which had been developed in the UK. (See further Wilks, below.) The influence of the European tradition of competition law over the past 40 years cannot be underestimated in the new legislation. Whish's prediction that further major reform was unlikely to await another 25 years was accurate and the Enterprise Bill makes further radical reform to UK competition law, based largely on the DTI White Paper, *A World Class Competition Regime*, CM 5233, July 2001.

This chapter will look at the monopoly provisions of the FTA 1973. Although these will be superseded by the provisions in the Enterprise Act for market investigations, which will also be outlined, the development of policy and practice under this key piece of legislation is crucial to understanding the development of competition law in the UK. The Enterprise Act provisions on market investigations, when in force, will replace and build on, to a great extent, the monopoly provisions of the Fair Trading Act 1973. The chapter will also look in detail at the CA 1998 Chapter II prohibition and practice thereunder.

SECTION 2: **Fair Trading Act 1973**

The Monopolies and Restrictive Trade Practices (Inquiry and Control) Act 1948, following upon the White Paper on Employment policy in 1944, introduced the UK system for dealing with monopoly which was adopted by the FTA 1973. The following passage by Wilks sets out the background to the FTA 1973:

Wilks, S., *In the Public Interest, Competition Policy and the Monopolies and Mergers Commission*
Manchester, MUP, 1999, pp. 172–173

The British vocabulary talked similarly of 'monopolies' and 'restrictive practices' but it did not regard them as unlawful and was not 'anti' anything. Indeed, although nowadays these terms have become pejorative, the normative coloration was more muted in the 1940s when both monopoly and restrictive practices had proved their worth in responding to depression and mobilising for war. The term 'monopoly' is an especially curious shorthand with which the MMC has had to live. Cases of true monopoly, where 100 per cent of production is concentrated in one undertaking, are extremely rare and in principle indefensible. The MMC has in practice dealt with oligopoly. The economic illiteracy of its title underlines the way in which the MMC has found 'monopoly' not to be harmful—in cases such as flat glass or soluble coffee, where a principled stress on competition would have indicated remedial action but where an efficiency defence has been accepted. Thus British policy came late to a wholehearted commitment to competition. The focus of competition policy on 'competition'; the high salience of competition policy within the mix of economic policies; and the insertion of principles of competition into a range of unrelated policies—all these are developments of the Thatcher years. It is therefore important to set aside the preconceptions of the 1990s in evaluating earlier and more agnostic views of competition, and to appreciate that the machinery of government was designed as much to restrict competition as to encourage it.

The complexity and ambiguity of British competition agencies and law, as they stood in 1997 ahead of the Labour reforms, therefore reflected peculiar policy dynamics. The policies did not grow from a clear design or a policy vision. They were not forged in a furnace of public outrage (as in the United States); they were not imposed as part of the fruits of victory (as in Japan and, partially, Germany); neither were they conceived as part of a vision of political and economic integration (as with the European Economic Community (EEC)). Instead British policy emerged incrementally and piecemeal as a product of consensus building by a powerful civil service, heavily influenced by business lobbying, increasingly responding to developments in economic thought, and operating under a benign and exceptional mantle of political bi-partisanship.

The creation of the Fair Trading Act

The 1973 Fair Trading Act is a deceptive piece of legislation. It dominated British competition policy for twenty-five years but it signified both more and less than at first appears. It was less significant in that its substantive contribution to the design of policy was minimal. Essentially it was a consolidating statute which re-enacted the principles, methods and powers of the main extant legislation. For the MMC its direct impact was slight. The MMC's functions and methods were unchanged. The Fair Trading Act gave it a new name, new partners and revised public interest guidance. On the other hand, it was more significant in creating a dedicated agency and a spokesman responsible for articulating competition concerns. The impact of the legislation should be assessed with regard to the way in which the DGFT and his Office exploited their position, rather than with regard to the stipulation of new principles or objectives of policy.

The Fair Trading Act could be portrayed as a gradual and almost inevitable policy development. Nothing could be further from the truth. It was the third of three radically different attempts at legislation and its genesis was marked by virtually every variety of political uncertainty, including elections, ministerial reshuffles, inter-departmental in-fighting, lobbying, expediency and accident. It constitutes a classic study in pragmatic policy making, of 'muddling through' in a process dominated and energised by officials in the DTI who responded, more or less ably, and more or less willingly, to the political pressures placed upon them.

NOTE: Wilks has provided an excellent account of the history of the Monopolies and Mergers Commission and the development of the institution of competition policy in the UK. This passage, which is set out in Chapter 6, focused on the 'unique and idiosyncratic model' of British competition policy. Of particular interest in the genesis of the 1973 Act is the bi-partisan character of policy development and his critique of the 'shotgun marriage' between consumerism and competition law embedded in the 1973 Act due to a lack of Parliamentary time.

Wilks also highlights the crucial role afforded the DGFT under the FTA 1973. (Following the Enterprise Act's entry into force, this task will be assumed by the OFT.) Chapter 2 discussed the institutional framework for the enforcement of UK competition law, with the DGFT playing a key role alongside the Secretary of State for Trade and Industry and the Competition Commission. The reporting panel of the Competition Commission has assumed the MMC's role under the FTA 1973 since 1 April 1999.

A: Monopoly references

The first formal stage in a monopoly inquiry under the 1973 Act is for a monopoly reference to be made to the Competition Commission by either the Secretary of State or the DGFT.

Most monopoly references have been made under s. 49 of the Act. These are references 'not limited to the facts' and require the Competition Commission to assess the public interest in addition to the factual situation. (Cf. s. 48 references limited to the facts.) The Secretary of State has certain exclusive powers, for instance to refer specified anti-competitive practices s. 50 (see *Parallel Pricing*, Cmnd 5330, 1973), but otherwise competence is shared with the DGFT.

The following is an example of a press release notifying the reference of a monopoly situation to the Commission:

OFT Press Release PN 11/99

8 April 1999, Bridgeman refers supermarkets

John Bridgeman, Director General of Fair Trading, today referred the, 60bn a year grocery retailing sector to the Competition Commission (formerly MMC) for investigation.

The Commission has 12 months to report to the Secretary of State for Trade and Industry on:

- whether a monopoly exists in the sector—which includes all companies in Great Britain with 10 or more stores where more than 600 square metres of retail sales space is devoted to grocery sales and more than 300 square metres is devoted to food and non alcoholic drinks—and, if so, in whose favour
- whether the situation is being exploited
- whether the monopoly operates, or may be expected to operate, against the public interest.

The reference follows an eight-month OFT competition inquiry. The OFT looked at the profit levels of the four largest supermarket chains—Tesco, Sainsbury, Safeway and Asda—over five years (1993–98) and competition issues such as barriers to entry and pricing policies. The study was based on data from 1630 stores in Great Britain and also included an independent assets evaluation of land and buildings.

John Bridgeman said:

> After analysing the profits of the four largest supermarket chains using a range of conventional and specialist economic measures I have to conclude that there is a level of profitability here which requires further investigation by the Competition Commission. The Commission will be able to carry out a wide-ranging and transparent study of this important industry.

The OFT inquiry had raised several competition issues, he said. The most important of which were:

- the nature, extent and existence of barriers to entering the market on a competitive scale
- the extent to which land is increasingly impacting on the cost structure of competing firms
- the intensity of price competition at local, regional and national levels
- the nature of the relationship between the multiples and their suppliers, including agricultural producers and the ways in which buyer power is exerted

Mr Bridgeman said:

> My interest has been in trying to find out whether excessive profits are being earned and I have considered the results in the context of wider concerns such as whether there are barriers to entering this industry or other factors affecting competition.
>
> I believe that there are now significant barriers to new competitors in high-volume grocery retailing in Britain. For example, sites for new stores are dwindling and this gives the existing stores an advantage. Planning delays, site development costs and the ability of the largest stores to outbid smaller rivals add to the problem. This should not be seen as criticism of planning policy—it is simply to state the fact that there are significant barriers to entry and they limit the impact new competitors could be expected to have on the behaviour of the current main players.
>
> In this situation it becomes imperative that the competition authorities are satisfied that competition between existing grocery retailers is effective. I am not. I am concerned, for instance, that grocery prices are often set to match competitors rather than to undercut them particularly in catchment areas where consumers have a limited choice of supermarkets.
>
> Supermarkets have become an important and vital part of the national economy and they have brought the benefits of greater convenience and choice to the consumer. Their size has brought them tremendous buyer power which can be used to deliver better

quality and lower prices to customers. I have had concerns for some time, though, that this power may become exploitative and the many responses from suppliers during our inquiry suggests that it is something which needs to be looked at by the Competition Commission.

The supermarkets have been co-operative and helpful at every stage of the OFT's inquiry and I have considered their representations carefully. I note, in particular, what has been said about the measures we have used to assess profitability. Considerable effort was made to explain our methods and assumptions to all the parties and I am satisfied that we have been as fair as possible in our analysis. It is not possible to determine whether excessive profits are being made by simply comparing profits and margins across different UK businesses. Sophisticated economic modelling is required to take into account the firms' levels of investment and risk. We have used a number of measures and have not exclusively relied upon any one indicator of profitability.

NOTE: As exemplified by the supermarkets reference, monopoly references normally concern a particular market, although in some cases the Commission are directed to look at the specific practices of a company. (See e.g. OFT Press release PN 7/00, 3 February 2000, Scottish Milk Inquiry, directed at the practices of Wiseman Dairies plc.) In the supermarkets inquiry the Commission did not consider that the profits of the major supermarket companies' operated against the public interest. (Cm 4842, 2000.)

SECTION 3: **Monopoly situations**

FTA 1973 provides for monopoly situations to be referred to the Commission. The Act makes separate, but similar, provision in relation to goods (s. 6), services (s. 7) and exports (s. 8), and there are two broad types of monopoly situation: scale/structural and complex/behavioural. The provisions in relation to goods alone shall be referred to for simplicity:

Fair Trading Act 1973 [s. 6(1)(a)]

Monopoly situation in relation to supply of goods

6.—(1) For the purposes of this Act a monopoly situation shall be taken to exist in relation to the supply of goods of any description in the following cases, that is to say, if—

    (a) at least one-quarter of all the goods of that description which are supplied in the United Kingdom are supplied by one and the same person, or are supplied to one and the same person, or . . .

NOTE: The 25 per cent criterion was introduced by the 1973 Act to replace the earlier 33 per cent threshold. This scale/structural monopoly provision can be met by an individual company or by 'interconnected bodies corporate' (s. 6(1)(b)). This type of monopoly situation is directed at a company with market power and has been largely rendered otiose by the introduction of the CA 1998 Chapter II prohibition.

On the other hand, the primary complex/behavioural monopoly situation under the Act (see also s. 6(1)(d)) is designed to cover more general market failure, not necessarily associated with the market power of an individual undertaking.

Fair Trading Act 1973 [s. 6(2)]

(2) The two or more persons referred to in subsection (1) (c) of this section, in relation to goods of any description, are any two or more persons (not being a group of interconnected bodies corporate) who whether voluntarily or not, and whether by agreement or not, so conduct their respective affairs as in any way to prevent, restrict or distort competition in connection with the production or supply of goods of that description, whether or not they themselves are affected by the competition and whether the competition is between persons interested as producers or suppliers or between persons interested as customers of producers or suppliers.

NOTE: This provision has been utilised widely as it allows markets to be investigated where there is market failure but not necessarily any anti-competitive activity confined to one undertaking. These provisions have been particularly useful in relation to oligopolistic markets, see Rodger, B.J., 'Oligopolistic Market Failure, Collective Dominance v Complex Monopoly' [1995] ECLR 21, and the appropriateness for dealing with such markets under the FTA 1973 where it is difficult to attach blame was one of the reasons noted for the retention of these provisions when the CA 1998 was introduced, see Furse, M., 'Monopolies, the Public Interest, the Fair Trading Act and the Chapter II Prohibition' Chapter 7 in Rodger, B.J., and MacCulloch, A. (eds), *The UK Competition Act: A New Era for UK Competition Law*. However, the requirement for a restriction of competition to be identified in advance has been criticised by Brent, R., 'The Certain Pursuit of Oligopoly: A Reply' [1996] ECLR 163. In the recent Banking report by the Competition Commission (The Supply of Banking Services by Clearing Banks to Small and Medium sized Enterprises, 2002 Cm 5319), the Commission found the existence of both a scale and complex monopoly:

> We found that RBSG, which includes National Westminster Bank and Ulster Bank as well as RBS Bank, itself has a scale monopoly situation in that it supplies over 25 per cent of the reference services. We also identified a number of practices, each carried out by some or all of the clearing banks (together accounting for over 25 per cent of supply of the reference services), which constitute a complex monopoly situation in that they restrict and/or distort price competition in the supply of the reference services. These include generally confining the provision of free banking services to startups and switchers; generally not paying interest on current accounts; giving discriminatory discounts through negotiations; and refraining from price competition in setting prices such that they more than adequately finance an efficient SME banking business. (Summary of Report)

NOTE: The existence of a complex monopoly does not automatically lead to a finding that it operates against the public interest. However, in the Bank's report, the monopoly position was found to be against the public interest and led to excessive prices.

QUESTION

Is it necessary to have specific competition law provisions for dealing with the problems in oligopopolistic markets?

FURTHER READING

See, for instance, Rodger, B.J., 'Oligopolistic Market Failure: Collective Dominance Versus Market Failure' [1995] 1 ECLR 1.

SECTION 4: **Competition Commission Report**

The Competition Commission is required to conduct its investigation and produce a report to the Secretary of State within the time limit specified (s. 55). In addition to considering the factual issues, such as whether a monopoly situation exists, in whose favour and what conduct is attributable to it, in references under s. 49, the Commission is also required to consider the public interest implications of the monopoly situation and make appropriate recommendations in order to remedy any adverse effects identified.

Fair Trading Act 1973 [s. 84]

Public interest

84—(1) In determining for any purposes to which this section applies whether any particular matter operates, or may be expected to operate, against the public interest, the Commission shall take into account all matters which appear to them in the particular circumstances to be relevant and, among other things, shall have regard to the desirability—

   (a) of maintaining and promoting effective competition between persons supplying goods and services in the United Kingdom;
   (b) of promoting the interests of consumers, purchasers and other users of goods and services in the United Kingdom in respect of the prices charged for them and in respect of their quality and the variety of goods and services supplied;
   (c) of promoting, through competition, the reduction of costs and the development and use of new techniques and new products, and of facilitating the entry of new competitors into existing markets;
   (d) of maintaining and promoting the balanced distribution of industry and employment in the United Kingdom; and
   (e) of maintaining and promoting competitive activity in markets outside the United Kingdom on the part of producers of goods, and of suppliers of goods and services, in the United Kingdom.

   (2) This section applies to the purposes of any functions of the Commission under this Act other than functions to which section 59(3) of this Act applies.

NOTE: The Commission is required to identify 'particular effects, adverse to the public interest' (s. 72(2)). The breadth of the public interest test is notable and it has been criticised in the past because it creates uncertainty and unpredictability (see Hutchings, M.B., 'The Need for Reform of UK Competition Policy' [1995] ECLR 211; cf. Rodger, B.J., 'Decentralisation, the Public Interest and the Pursuit of Certainty' [1995] ECLR 395. The impact on competition is only one factor to be considered, although it has clearly been the predominant issue in Commission reports under these provisions. The public interest test is to be replaced in the Enterprise Act with a competition-based test. (See further below and the DTI White Paper, 'A World Class Competition Regime' (Cm 5233, July 2001.)

   A notable feature of the public interest test and of the role of competition law in general under the FTA 1973 is the role of consumer protection. Competition law aims to ensure effective competition which will ultimately be in the interests of the consumer but it appears that the consumer interest has a more direct role under the FTA 1973. The following passage is set in the context of a discussion on the genesis of the FTA 1973.

Wilks, S., *In the Public Interest, Competition Policy and the Monopolies and Mergers Commission*

Manchester, MUP, 1999, pp. 183–184 and 187–188

Thus, although Howe was appointed as a consumer minister, and took enthusiastically to that role, the mission which put him into the DTI was price control. His appointment was 'in Ted Heath's eyes as the "Minister for Keeping Prices Down"'. The legislation on competition policy was thus over-shadowed by the re-launch of consumer protection policy, and by a preoccupation with anti-inflation measures.

As Howe jovially conceded, he was the midwife of the Fair Trading Act, not the parent. All the same, he did introduce some last minute changes and he also agreed to allow a film crew to follow through the legislation for a 'fly on the wall' TV documentary. The film makes interesting viewing and made minor celebrities of some of the officials. Howe greatly expanded section 2 of the Act which gives the Director General a duty 'to keep under review' commercial activities. This was much wider than officials had planned. In the very last meeting to approve the draft Bill he also inserted 'and Mergers' into the title of the Monopolies Commission. No one felt bold enough to stand out against this change, which discomposed the typists and caused some surprise for the Commission. The two pieces of draft legislation—on competition and on consumer protection—were hastily stapled together, there was no time for a White Paper, and the draft Bill was published at the beginning of December 1972. It was long and complex; in Cunningham's words, 'the Act itself is not a model of clarity, it is more an example of what legislation should not be'. The consumer protection sections came in Part II, which created the Consumer Protection Advisory Committee. The statutory con-sumer protection powers have barely been used but, as we see below, Directors General have given at least equal weight to that side of their responsibilities.

Successive DGFTs have repeated John Methven's initial assertion that the consumer/competition combination was a great advantage. Geoffrey Howe also made a great virtue of this necessity both during the debates on the Bill and in his retrospective assessments. In practice, however, the two activities have been administered in substantial separation from one another and it is not very clear that there are great benefits. Consumer protection policy is concerned with developing and applying quite detailed rules about commercial behaviour. There is no obvious or logical link with market structure or competitive conditions, and the clients tend to be the public, consumer groups and local authorities through their trading standards offices. In contrast, competition policy is about business structure and strategy, and the clients tend to be businesses, lawyers and economists. Clearly 'the consumer' should be the ultimate beneficiary but that statement verges on pious moralising. The downside of the marriage has been the diversion of energies, the consumer preoccupation of Directors General, and the diffusion of attention away from the competition brief.

NOTE: Geoffrey Howe was appointed as Minister for Trade and Consumer Affairs at the DTI with the role of guiding the legislation through Parliament. This passage demonstrates the political context in which competition law was linked to an anti-inflation strategy. This also highlights how the preoccupations of competition law can change in time. Nonetheless, successive DGFTs have stressed the important role the consumer interest plays under the FTA competition provisions in particular.

DGFT Annual Report, 1999

Introduction

'Rip-off Britain'

The issue of high prices has always been an important one, but has been an especially major theme in the media throughout 1999. Reckless talk of high prices can itself begin to erode consumer confidence. It may even reduce the attractiveness of the UK as a place to visit, or distort patterns of investment. The headlines and debate on 'rip-off Britain' are therefore something I have taken very seriously.

The UK has not operated a policy of general price control for many years. Nor have most other nations of the developed world. They, and increasingly also the former managed economies of Eastern Europe and the third world countries, have all concluded that a free market in which there is vigorous and genuine competition both rewards efficient businesses and gives the best deal to consumers. This is because entrepreneurs can enter new markets without encountering artificial barriers. They can study consumer needs and endeavour to increase their profits and market share by competing on price, quality, convenience or innovation. In an ideal market the consumer is in the driving seat and the supply of the right products at the right price matches the requirements of a discerning demand.

Unfortunately, we do not yet live in a perfect world and market failures occur. The task of making competition policy a success falls on enforcers such as the Competition Policy Division of my Office. My competition powers enable me to act on behalf of consumers in a direct way and many of the consumer issues which have featured so strongly in the headlines have, in fact, related to issues of competition policy. The view, sometimes expressed, that the consumer affairs and competition policy roles in regulation should be separated is, in my view, mistaken and would be a disservice to consumer welfare. Our system is mirrored by those of the United States, Canada, Australia and France.

Market failures occur because some businesses would prefer to make profits by preventing competition through abuse of dominant positions, or by adopting anti-competitive agreements which, under the new Competition Act, are now prohibited by law. High prices can sometimes be a symptom of such anti-competitive activity. My power to act under the Competition Act 1998 will depend on the ability to establish a breach of law. As with any other investigative process, it is dangerous to start with a presumption of guilt. Investigation must be fair and impartial. In such a case the Act provides the strong safeguard of a swift appeal system through the Competition Commission. In monopoly cases, which will continue to be investigated under the provisions of the Fair Trading Act, I must be satisfied that one or more companies may be involved in a monopoly situation. While there is no question of financial penalties, the disruption, expense and uncertainty of a monopoly reference to the Competition Commission should not be underestimated, nor should the threat of an imposed remedy by the Secretary of State. The stakes are high for all parties but the OFT will implement the law with vigour.

NOTE: The DGFT has traditionally combined two roles: supervising competition policy and championing the rights of the consumer. Pricing policies, where a monopoly situation exists, would appear to be a clear concern of the competition authorities. This has not always been the case but the cyclical nature of competition law and its concerns has been demonstrated by the recent 'rip-off Britain' strategy including in particular the Competition Commission report on new car pricing. (Cm 4660, 2000) The position of the consumer will be further facilitated by the Enterprise Act provision to allow consumer bodies to bring super-complaints to the OFT involving a fast-track procedure (DTI White Paper *op. cit.* at paras 4.25–4.27).

QUESTION

Is competition law merely consumer law in a different guise? Is consumer protection the sole, or main, purpose of competition law enforcement?

FURTHER READING

Ahdar, R., 'Consumers, Redistribution of Income and the Purpose of Competition Law' [2002] ECLR 314.

The following are merely selected examples of issues which the Commission has looked at under the monopoly provisions of the FTA 1973:

A: Monopoly situations per se

The Commission is required to assess whether the monopoly position itself operates against the public interest. This has been established in very few reports, partly because the obvious remedy of divestiture—breaking up the monopoly—is fairly radical, although it has become more frequent in recent years.

The Supply of Beer
Cm 651, 1989, paras 1.9–1.110, 1.18–1.20 and 1.25

1.9. One of the most prominent features of the United Kingdom beer industry is the extent of vertical integration. Brewing companies differ greatly in size, but the majority of them brew beer *and* wholesale it *and* retail it. In order to retail beer, brewing companies own a substantial proportion of the public houses. We estimate that brewers own about 75 per cent of the public houses in Great Britain. Brewer-owned houses fall into two categories—managed, in which the publican and, as a rule, the staff are employees of the brewing company; and tenanted, where the publican is not an employee of the brewer-landlord, but pays the brewer a rent for the premises and earns his living from the retail profit made by the outlet. In both categories, the brewer specifies what beers may be sold in the public house, and where they must be bought (usually from the brewer himself). In the case of managed public houses, the brewer sets retail prices as well.

1.10. The on-licensed trade available outside brewer-owned outlets is usually described as the 'free trade'. Here, too, brewer influence is strong through the mechanism of the loan tie. In order to secure either exclusivity for his own products in a 'free house', or a minimum throughput, a brewer will offer a loan to the owner(s) of the house at below market rates of interest. It is open to the owners of free houses to have one loan, more than one, or none at all, but loan-tying is a widespread practice throughout the United Kingdom. We estimate that half of the 25 per cent of public houses that are not owned by brewers are tied to them by loans. About half of members' clubs are loan-tied as well. About two-thirds of all the beer that brewers sell, including that supplied for consumption at home, is sold to premises that they either own or tie by a loan.

. . .

Our view
1.18. Eloquently though the industry's case has been put, we are not persuaded that all is well. We have confirmed our provisional finding that a complex monopoly situation exists in favour of the brewers with tied estates and loan ties.

1.19. This complex monopoly restricts competition at all levels. Brewers are protected from competition in supplying their managed and tenanted estates because other brewers do not have access to them. Even in the free trade many brewers prefer to compete by offering low-interest loans, which then tie the outlet to them, rather than by offering beer at lower prices. Wholesale prices are higher than they would be in the absence of the tie. This inevitably feeds through into high retail prices.

1.20. The ownership and loan ties also give little opportunity for an independent wholesaling sector to prosper and offer competition to the brewers' wholesaling activities, for example by offering a mix of products from different producers.

Our recommendations

The property tie

1.25. It has been put to us repeatedly that smaller brewers in particular need their tied estates to stay in business. In present circumstances, if the tie were to be abolished altogether we believe that many regional and local brewers would withdraw from brewing, concentrate on retailing, and leave the market to domination by national and international brand owners. This would substantially reduce consumer choice. We therefore recommend, not the complete abolition of the tie, but a ceiling of 2,000 on the number of on-licensed premises, whether public houses, hotels or any other type of on-licensed outlet, which any brewing company or group may own. This ceiling will require the divestment of some 22,000 premises by United Kingdom national brewers. (No regional or local brewer currently reaches the 2,000 ceiling we recommend.) We do not believe that United Kingdom property or capital markets will have any difficulty in absorbing the change; we are recommending a maximum of three years for the divestments to take place.

NOTE: The Secretary of State subsequently made significant Orders, of interest here including The Supply of Beer (Tied Estate) Order 1989, No 2390/1989. Following a recent review, the limitations on ownership are now to be removed due to changes in the beer market, DTI P/2000/805, 1 December 2000; DTI P/2002/107, 19 February 2002. Divestiture was also recommended in Gas and British Gas plc (Cm 2317, 1993) and more recently in the Supply of Raw Milk report (Cm 4286, 1999).

More commonly, the Commission proceeds to report upon aspects of the conduct of parties within a market under investigation:

B: Pricing policies

A concern with pricing policies reflects the close links in the FTA 1973 between competition and consumer policy. A number of Commission reports have investigated the issues of excessive and oligopolistic pricing. Excessive pricing has not been defined and the Commission calculates profitability and proceeds to make a qualitative judgment on its reasonableness as demonstrated in their classic report on drugs, valium and librium:

Chlordiazepoxide and Diazepam
(1972–73) HCP 197 at paras 229–235 and 237

Profits

229. Roche Products does not accept that profitability should be, or in any realistic terms can be, examined in terms of individual drugs . . . We accept that the profitability of the Roche Group's drug business as a whole would be a factor to take into account if we had been afforded any precise information on the subject. But in the present context we have to reach conclusions about the prices for particular drugs; and it is at least clear that the prices charged for these drugs, in the United Kingdom and elsewhere, must play a major part in determining the profitability of the Group's drug business as a whole.

230. It is arguable that the pharmaceutical industry could not be expected to invest in speculative research of the kind that leads to innovations unless it were offered the prospect of an above average level of reward when it successfully introduces a new drug. If it were our task to determine a fair price for a recently introduced drug we would regard this as an argument to take seriously into account. But, for reasons which we explain in paragraphs 231 and 232, the level of profit which

might have been allowed for in determining what should have been fair prices for the reference drugs up to the present is barely relevant to our present problem. For purposes of illustration only we have, as indicated in paragraphs 165 to 170, estimated the effect of adding a profit of 25 per cent on capital to the cost figures as set out in appendix 5, table 2 and arrived at notional prices of £421 and £964 per kilo of Librium and Valium respectively (as compared with the actual average prices in 1970 of £734 and £1,962 respectively). But we regard these figures only as providing a starting point for arriving at fair current and future prices.

Effects of past excessive prices

231. Successful patented drugs, whose sales as in the present case exceed the conservative estimates on which the innovator's pricing policy is likely to have been based, often give a high return (in terms of recovery of research costs and profit), particularly if there is no price reduction. The public interest issues involved have been considered in principle many times over the years, both in relation to the patent law generally and also with particular regard to the situation in the pharmaceutical industry. There is a continuing conflict between the needs on the one hand to provide pharmaceutical manufacturers with an incentive (in the form of attractive profit potential) to produce innovations, and on the other hand to set limits to the exploitation of successful innovations through excessively high prices under patent protection.

232. In considering what would be a reasonable limit to exploitation in a particular case, regard must be had to the profitability of the drug over its patent life as a whole. Thus after a few years, during which sales have increased and very high rates of profit indeed may have been achieved, exploitation could be kept within reasonable limits by adequate, regular price reductions. Where, as in the present case, no such reduction has been made over two-thirds or more of the patent life, a more drastic price cut may therefore be required thereafter. Accordingly, in determining what are the maximum prices that should be charged for the reference drugs in future, we need to take into account, so far as this is possible, the return the Roche Group has obtained from them over their patent lives up to the present. It is quite clear that since the introduction of the reference drugs the Group must have earned very high levels of profit indeed from the sale of these drugs in the United Kingdom, besides recovering increasingly large contributions to its current expenditure on research, the scale of which it was able, as one consequence of such profits in this country and elsewhere, to expand with a view to developing future product innovations. Because of the conflict of factors affecting the public interest to which we have referred, it can only be a matter of judgment at what stage undue exploitation of success can be said to begin. But we have no doubt that in the present exceptional case this stage has long been passed.

233. On the basis of cost figures which, as we have shown, we regard as higher than are acceptable for the purpose of arriving at fair prices, we have estimated the Group profit on the sale of Librium and Valium in the United Kingdom in 1970 at about £4m after allowing for a Group research contribution of about £1m from those two drugs. . . . More approximately but on the same conservative basis, we have estimated that the total Group profits for the sale of all reference drugs in the United Kingdom in the seven years from 1966 to the end of 1972 were in the region of £25m, out of which the Group repaid to DHSS, in response to pressure from the Department, about £1m in respect of reference goods trading up to the end of 1969. . . . These profits are calculated after allowing for recovery of research expenditure as a charge against sales of the reference goods amounting probably to some £6m to £7m over the seven years.

234. In the light of these facts, the question of what rate of profit should be allowed in determining a fair price becomes, as we have said in paragraph 230, barely relevant to our problem, since the Roche Group has already obtained from the sale of these drugs in this country profits far in excess of what is justifiable.

Recommendations

235. Among the points we bear in mind in reaching a conclusion on the appropriate level of prices in future are the following:

(a) Even if we could accept the cost figures in appendix 5, table 2, fair prices based upon these costs might have been lower than those actually charged in 1970 by at least 40 per cent for Librium and at least 50 per cent for Valium (paragraph 230).

(b) For reasons we have given in detail (paragraphs 219 to 227) we are satisfied that some of the cost figures referred to—in particular those for research and promotion costs—grossly exceed the levels that should be taken into account to arrive at fair prices. It follows that fair prices should in any case be substantially below the levels indicated in (a).

(c) There are no grounds for maintaining the particular price differential between Valium and Librium which existed in 1970 (paragraph 228).

(d) The excessive prices charged up to the present have already produced excessive profits on a very large scale (paragraph 234).

Although we have made a number of calculations in an attempt to quantify the effects of (b) and (c) above, none has proved entirely satisfactory having regard to our incomplete knowledge of the business of the Roche Group. But in the event this scarcely matters in the light of (d).

. . .

237. We recommend that Roche Products' selling prices for the reference drugs should be reduced (i) as regards Librium, to not more than 40 per cent of the selling prices in 1970, (ii) as regards Valium, to not more than 25 per cent of the selling prices in 1970, (iii) as regards other drugs covered by the reference, by corresponding proportions as may be determined by DHSS.

NOTE: During the 1970s a number of reports focused on excessive pricing and price monitoring was considered an appropriate remedy, for instance by undertakings not to increase prices without government approval (following Ready Cooked Breakfast Cereal foods (1972–73) HCP 2). During the 1980s and 1990s price regulation became less a feature of the monopoly controls as attitudes to the operation of the market changed. (See also the report, 'Supply of Recorded Music', Cm 2599, 1994 where the Commission did not find the pricing of CDs in the UK, higher in comparison with the US and EC, to be against the public interest.) The rip-off Britain campaign instituted in the late 1990s again placed pricing for consumers at the forefront of the FTA's concerns, although not all Commission reports have been critical of pricing strategies. (See 'Supply of New Cars', CM 4660, 2000 and cf. 'Supermarket pricing' Cm 4842, 2000.) Parallel pricing, a concern in oligopolistic industries, whereby pricing effectively increases without any formal collusion (see 'Parallel Pricing', Cmnd 5330, 1973), has been criticised as it can also lead to excessive prices for the consumer. (See 'White Salt', Cm 9778, 1986.)

C: Contractual controls over distributors

The Commission has often criticised the extent to which contractual restraints are imposed by undertakings with a degree of market power, as this may lead to market foreclosure. The Supply of Beer report provides an example of a particular type of restraint, exclusive purchasing requirements:

The Supply of Beer
Cm 651, 1999, paras 1.22 and 1.28

1.22. Chapters 11 and 12 set out in detail the detriments which we see as arising from this lack of competition. In summary, the main ones are:

— the price of a pint of beer in a public house has risen too fast in the last few years;
— the high price of lager is not justified by the cost of producing it;
— the variation in wholesale prices between regions of the country is excessive;
— consumer choice is restricted because one brewer does not usually allow another brewer's beer to be sold in the outlets which he owns: this restriction often happens in loan-tied outlets as well;
— consumer choice is further restricted because of brewers' efforts to ensure that their own brands of cider and soft drinks are sold in their outlets;
— tenants are unable to play a full part in meeting consumer preferences, both because of the tie and because the tenant's bargaining position is so much weaker than his landlord's; and
— independent manufacturers and wholesalers of beer and other drinks are allowed only limited access to the on-licensed market.
. . .

The product tie

1.28. In order to improve the market opportunity in the tenanted trade, we recommend that a tenant should be allowed to purchase a minimum of one brand of draught beer from a supplier other than his landlord. We also recommend that there should be no tie whatever for non-alcohol or low-alcohol beers, nor for wines, spirits, ciders, soft drinks or mineral waters.

NOTE: The subsequent Supply of Beer (Loan Ties, Licensed Premises and Wholesale Prices) Order 1989 (SI 1989/2258) required brewers *inter alia* to allow tied houses to supply a 'guest' beer and prohibited the compulsory tie of non-alcoholic drinks to the supply of beer (also to be revoked, see DTI P/2002/107, 19 February 2002). This report and subsequent action demonstrate the important social impact which monopoly reports can produce, in this case clearly enhancing consumer choice. On the other hand, the Commission recognised, in its general report on 'Tie-ins and Full Line Forcing' ((1980–81) HCP 232) that a case-by-case approach should be adopted as there may be countervailing economies of scale benefits in certain tying practices.

D: Price discrimination/predatory pricing

Price discrimination consists of charging different prices to different customers without objective cost justification, and predatory pricing is the classic monopolistic action of reducing prices, normally to below cost, for a sufficient period to drive out competitors or foreclose new competition. Price discrimination is often effected through discounts and selective pricing and it is increasingly recognised that the two forms of pricing—discriminatory and predatory—are intertwined (see Case T-228/97 *Irish Sugar plc* v *Commission* [1999] 5 CMLR 1300).

Bus Services in Mid and West Kent, Summary
Cm 2309, 1993

In a reference made on 15 December 1992 (see Appendix 1.1) the Director General of Fair Trading asked us to investigate and report on whether a monopoly situation existed in the supply of bus services in Mid and West Kent. This reference area stretches from the Medway towns in the north through the rural High Weald to the East Sussex border and includes the Maidstone, Sevenoaks, Tonbridge and Tunbridge Wells areas.

Within this area the dominant supplier of bus services is The Maidstone & District Motor Services Ltd (M&D). We established that it provides about two-thirds of the local bus services in the area and thus that a scale monopoly situation exists. There are about 20 other operators, some of these very small businesses, offering commercial and tendered local bus services within the reference area. Of these operators, three, Bygone Buses, Turners of Maidstone and Mercury Passenger Services, were operating commercial services during the course of our inquiry in direct competition with M&D.

We received a number of complaints about M&D's response to competition in the area. These included complaints about the frequency, timing and operation of M&D's services on routes where competition was occurring and about fares charged. M&D's main response to the entry of a competitor on its routes has been to introduce extra journeys, usually timed to run immediately before the competitor's, and sometimes combined with selective fare cuts confined to these journeys. M&D argued that its responses were appropriate to protect the profitability of its network and that the costs of providing the additional journeys were small and covered by the revenue generated.

We do not accept these arguments. We do not consider that the immediate costs of a response are an adequate basis for assessing its acceptability in competition terms. We consider that the costs and revenue of such responses must be measured over a longer term, with a realistic assessment of the costs incurred, and that M&D's operation of additional journeys not covering such costs operates or may be expected to operate against the public interest.

Furthermore, we consider that, even where a competitive response meets the cost criteria above, it is not necessarily in the public interest. We accept that adjusting the timing and frequency of services is one of the ways in which operators can justifiably compete for passengers. However, we consider that the introduction by the dominant operator of additional journeys, timed immediately before a competitor's, was designed to target competitors without the resources to retaliate in kind, and to encourage their withdrawal from the routes. We conclude that this behaviour by M&D operates or may be expected to operate against the public interest.

We also found that M&D's registration of commercial services against a competitor's tendered service, operation of unregistered buses and use of selective fare reductions on journeys immediately in front of a competitor's journeys operate or may be expected to operate against the public interest.

We considered action to remedy these effects. Our main recommendation is that, where another operator registers on a route in competition with M&D, M&D should not then register journeys before the competitor's journeys, on this or substantially similar competitive routes, within a shorter interval than the competitor has itself registered in front of the M&D service. In framing this recommendation we have noted M&D's arguments about the practical difficulties any remedy of this kind would cause for it. We recognize that some difficulties may arise in implementing such a remedy across a network but we have not attempted to deal with these by laying down detailed rules. We think the intention of our remedy is clear and, if complaints arose, it would be for the Office of Fair Trading (OFT) to determine, in the particular circumstances, whether the M&D registration was justified. While we cannot be sure that this untried remedy will fully meet the detriments we have identified, we think it will significantly constrain M&D's future behaviour.

We also recommend that:

(a) if a competitor withdraws from a route after M&D has registered additional journeys immediately before it, M&D should maintain its frequency of service and not increase fares on the route for at least one year;
(b) M&D should not register commercial services against competitors' tendered services; and
(c) it should not make selective fare reductions on services running immediately before a competitor's.

NOTE: This was one of a number of reports into the activities of Stagecoach under the monopoly and merger provisions of the FTA 1973 during what became known as the 'Bus Wars' following deregulation of the bus industry in the late 1980s. The charging of predatory prices to force out competitors was one of the key competitive strategies of Stagecoach plc. Bork suggests that predatory pricing should never be illegal, Bork, R.H., *The Antitrust Paradox: A Policy at War with Itself*, Oxford, Maxwell Macmillan, 1993, Chapter 14, and there has been criticism of the Community approach to the issue of what constitutes 'meeting but not beating' competition. See Andrews, P., 'Is Meeting Competition a Defence to Predatory Pricing?' [1998] ECLR 49. Nonetheless, the UK authorities have adopted a pragmatic approach to what constitutes predatory pricing. (See also 'Concrete Roofing Tiles' (1981–82) HCP; OFT Research paper 5, and Myers, G., 'Predatory Behaviour in UK Competition Policy', 1994.)

SECTION 5:   Action following a Commission Report

Where the Commission reports that there are specific public interest detriments, and provided that a majority of two-thirds of the group support the conclusions (see Supply of Scottish Milk, Cm 4286, 1999) there are two alternative methods of enforcement. Most commonly, the Secretary of State will request the DGFT to negotiate and obtain appropriate undertakings from parties in order to remedy the public interest effects specified by the Commission.

DTI Press Release
P2000/260 7 April 2000

Stephen Byers, Secretary of State for Trade and Industry, today announced that he had accepted further undertakings from Birds Eye Wall's and from Nestlé and Mars in connection with the Impulse Ice Cream Monopoly Report. Mr Byers said:

> This is the second stage of remedying the problems identified by the Competition Commission. Together with the undertakings I accepted from Birds Eye Wall's in February in connection with their supply to wholesale distributors, these undertakings will help to underpin stronger competition and more choice in the shops for the consumer this summer.

The outlet exclusivity undertakings given by Birds Eye Wall's, Mars and Nestlé apply with effect from 29 January 2000. As of that date these companies undertake not to enter into or renew outlet exclusivity agreements with shops. They may enter into exclusivity agreements with single mobile vans or seasonal kiosks until the end of 2002, provided these agreements do not apply to all outlets on a single site.

The undertakings from Birds Eye Wall's on freezer exclusivity and retrospective discounts for retailers come into effect on April 15. From that date Birds Eye Wall's will no longer be able to reserve more than 50 per cent of the freezer display space for its products, and none of the freezer storage space.

Notes for editors

1. The Competition Commission report 'The Supply of Impulse Ice Cream: a report on the supply in the UK of ice cream purchased for immediate consumption', Cm 4510 (#35.40), was published on 28 January 2000. Copies are available from the Stationery Office.

2. The Secretary of State announced on 14 February that he had accepted undertakings from Birds Eye Wall's on terms of supply to wholesalers. These are interim, and will apply until the Secretary of State decides on a final remedy on distribution by Birds Eye Wall's.

3. The Secretary of State is consulting on the distribution remedy. Comments should be sent to the Director General of Fair Trading by 15 April.

4. Media copies of the undertakings on outlet and freezer exclusivity and on Birds Eye's retrospective discounts to retailers, are available from the DTI Newsroom.

NOTE: These undertakings followed the most recent report into the supply of ice-cream under the FTA 1973. ('The Supply of Ice Cream', Cm 4510, 2000. See earlier report, 'Ice Cream', Cm 2524, 1994.) On this occasion the Commission was concerned that effectively, freezer/outlet exclusivity in any tobacconist's, confectioner's and newsagent's of ice-cream for 'immediate consumption' excluded competition and restricted consumer choice. Subsequently, undertakings were also given by Birds Eye Wall's ('BEW') regarding their distribution arrangements in order to further enhance competition. For further discussion of this issue see Robertson, A., and Williams, M., 'An Ice-Cream War: the Law and Economics of Freezer Exclusivity' [1995] ECLR 7.

If undertakings are considered to be inappropriate, are not given, or are breached, the Secretary of State may resort to his Order-making powers in Sch. 8. These powers include the power to control prices, order the publication of prices and prohibit discriminatory practices. Orders tend to be fairly technical, (for example see The Supply of New Cars Order 2000 (SI 2000/2088) following Commission Report, Cm 4660, 2000) and the explanatory note and accompanying DTI press release are instructive. The following are excerpts from an Order and a DTI press release respectively.

The Foreign Package Holidays (Tour Operators and Travel Agents) Order 2000 (SI 2000/2110), Articles 2–4

Market share test

2. This Order shall apply where—
    (a) the linked travel agent or the travel group of which it is part has a share of the market in travel agents' services exceeding 5 per cent;
    (b) the linked tour operator or the travel group of which it is part has a share of the market in tour operators' services exceeding 5 per cent; or
    (c) paragraphs (a) and (b) are both satisfied.

Transparency of ownership links

3. Subject to article 5, from the date this Order comes into force it shall be unlawful for a travel agent and a tour operator who are linked to make or carry out an agreement (whenever made) between—
    (a) such linked travel agent and tour operator; or
    (b) such linked travel agent and another person in its travel group;
for the supply or offer to supply by the linked travel agent to a consumer of a foreign package holiday organised by the linked tour operator ('the linked supply or offer to supply of foreign package holidays') unless article 4 is satisfied.

4.—(1) This article is satisfied where—
    (a) there is displayed on the front of the linked travel agent's retail premises in a prominent position so that it may be easily read, the name of the travel agent and the name of the travel group of which the travel agent is part together with an explanation of the link between the travel agent and that travel group;
    (b) there is displayed on the front of every foreign package holiday brochure of the linked tour operator, available to consumers in the linked travel agent's retail premises, in a prominent position so that it may easily be read, a notice stating the name of the travel agent together with an explanation of the link between the tour operator and the travel agent;
    (c) there is displayed in the linked travel agent's retail premises in a prominent position so that it may easily be read by consumers in those premises, a notice which states the

name under which the linked tour operator trades in foreign package holidays through linked travel agents, an explanation of the link between the tour operator and the travel agent and, where the condition specified in paragraph (b) is required to be satisfied, the fact that the brochures display the requisite notice;

(d) there is stated in legible characters on all business stationery of the linked travel agent used for the purposes of the linked supply or offer to supply of foreign package holidays the name of the travel group of which the travel agent is part together with an explanation of the link between the travel agent and that travel group; and

(e) all advertisements made on behalf of the linked travel agent or linked tour operator, which are connected with the linked supply or offer to supply of foreign package holidays and which refer to both the linked travel agent and tour operator, contain a statement explaining the link between them.

(2) The conditions specified in sub-paragraphs (a), (b), (d) and (e) of paragraph (1) above do not apply where the name of the travel agent and the tour operator are the same or are so similar to each other that members of the public might reasonably conclude from that fact that the travel agent and tour operator are linked.

(3) In this article 'business stationery' means business letters, invoices and receipts issued in the course of business and written demands for payment of debts arising in the course of business which are used in respect of the linked supply or offer of supply of foreign package holidays to consumers.

(4) In this article 'name' means the name under which, as the case may be, the tour operator, travel agent or travel group, trade in the United Kingdom with consumers of foreign package holidays.

DTI Press Release P/98/397

20 May 1998

Margaret Beckett takes action to cut prices of TVs, washing machines and other electrical goods

Margaret Beckett, President of the Board of Trade and Secretary of State for Trade and Industry, has made an Order under the Fair Trading Act 1973 to remedy the problems identified by the Monopolies and Mergers Commission (MMC) in their 1997 reports on the domestic electrical goods markets (televisions, video cassette recorders, hi-fi systems and camcorders, washing machines, tumble driers, dishwashers and cold food storage equipment).

Mrs Beckett said:

> The aim of the Order is to increase price competition in these markets. The MMC found that price competition in these markets is muted. I am determined that practices which restrict competition should be stopped. Retailers should be free to set their own prices and should not be refused supply because of their pricing. Consumers should not be denied the benefits of strong price competition. I agree with the MMC that a prohibition of the use of recommended retail prices is necessary to deal effectively with the adverse effects they found in these markets.
>
> The Order will make it illegal for suppliers to try to restrict the freedom of retailers to price products as they choose. It will be illegal for suppliers to recommend retail prices to retailers. It will also be illegal for suppliers to discriminate in their prices or terms and conditions of supply against retailers who sell at discounted prices.
>
> Suppliers will not be able to simply refuse to supply retailers whose prices they do not like. Suppliers must make their supply criteria available to requesting retailers and it will be illegal for suppliers to refuse to supply retailers wanting supplies and meeting those criteria. Retailers will be entitled to a written explanation if they are refused supplies. It will

also be illegal for a retailer to induce a supplier to refuse supplies to, or otherwise put pressure on, a rival retailer who sells at discounted prices.

These remedies should ensure that discount retailers can obtain supplies and all retailers have the freedom to sell goods at prices of their choosing. Consumers will have a wider choice of outlets, and benefit from more competitive pricing.

These are tough remedies, but tough action is needed to remedy the problems identified by the MMC and bring benefits to consumers. I announced my proposals for action on publication of the MMC reports in July 1997. Comments from consumers and all sectors of the industry have been given full and careful consideration. Suppliers have also had an opportunity to comment on a draft of the Order. I have borne in mind the concerns of business and taken these on board where appropriate to ensure that the burden of the Order is not disproportionate to the benefit. But I am not prepared to compromise the effectiveness of my remedies.

I am asking the Director General of Fair Trading to write to leading suppliers and dealers to ask what steps they are taking to comply with the Order. If the response is not satisfactory, I will make directions requiring action from those concerned. Smaller businesses will not be required to demonstrate compliance to the Office of Fair Trading unless there is cause for concern.

When the reports were published in July 1997, Mrs Beckett accepted the MMC's findings that a variety of widespread and entrenched practices by suppliers and retailers of domestic electrical goods operated against the public interest. She proposed a package of remedies to prohibit the use of recommended retail prices, and practices designed to enforce recommended retail prices, and to help retailers who want to compete on price but have difficulty getting supplies.

The Order will not come into force until 1 September 1998 to give those companies affected time to comply with its terms.

The Director General of Fair Trading was also asked to seek undertakings from certain companies or organisations to remedy several further findings made by the MMC. These undertakings have been provided.

General Domestic Appliances Holdings Ltd (GDA) has undertaken not to reintroduce into its terms and conditions of sale to any dealer a clause to the effect that if the dealer's margin needs on any goods change then the level of support provided by GDA might be subject to change. Empire Stores Group plc has undertaken to remove a clause from its contracts by which it seeks information about prices charged by competitors. Dixons Group plc has undertaken not to include in its terms and conditions of purchase a clause allowing them to renegotiate prices or delivery dates or to cancel a contract in the event that the supplier allows so called disorderly market forces to prevail.

Undertakings given by Combined Independent (Holdings) Limited (CIH) and its 21 local groups ensure that CIH will not make any recommendation restricting the resale of goods purchased from the company or the local groups. CIH has also undertaken not to refuse membership to any dealer who meets its membership criteria. It will no longer require prospective members to provide three years' audited accounts, although it will still be able to require an applicant to demonstrate the ability to pay for the goods ordered. CIH's role as a buying group serving the interests of small electrical retailers therefore remains unaffected.

Notes to editors

1. The eight references were made by the Director General of Fair Trading on 27 April 1995 under sections 10(3), 10(7), 47(1), 49(2) and 50(1) of the Fair Trading Act 1973 (the Act). The MMC were asked to investigate the existence or possible existence of a monopoly situation in relation to the supply in the UK, otherwise than by retail sale or hire, of televisions, video-cassette recorders, hi-fi systems, camcorders, washing machines, tumble driers, dishwashers and cold food storage equipment, in respect of:

(a) steps taken, by recommending or suggesting prices to be charged by dealers, or otherwise, to influence the prices at which dealers resell these goods; and

(b) withholding supplies of these goods from dealers;

and if so, whether any aspect of the situation might be expected to operate against the public interest.

2. The MMC reports 'Domestic Electrical Goods I: a report on the supply in the UK of televisions, video cassette recorders, hi-fi systems and camcorders' (Cm 3675) and 'Domestic Electrical Goods II: a report on the supply in the UK of washing machines, tumble driers, dishwashers and cold food storage equipment' (Cm 3676) were published on 30 July 1997. The MMC found that two complex monopoly situations existed for each of these goods. The first was in favour of all suppliers who quoted RRPs (the great majority) and of those dealers who had discussions with suppliers which influenced RRPs or who took account of RRPs when setting their own selling prices. The second complex monopoly situation existed in favour of suppliers who selected dealers to be supplied on the basis of certain criteria and of all those dealers supplied by them.

3. The MMC found that a variety of widespread and entrenched practices by suppliers and dealers of domestic electrical goods operate against the public interest. Retail prices are higher than they would otherwise be, price competition in these markets is muted, new retailers have difficulty getting supplies, and innovation in retailing is discouraged. As a result, consumers have to pay more than they should. The MMC made a number of recommendations to deal with the practices they found to be against the public interest. The MMC also made several further findings concerning additional features of the behaviour of certain companies or organisations.

4. Under section 56 of the Fair Trading Act 1973, the Secretary of State has the power to make an Order to remedy the adverse effects identified by the MMC in a monopoly report. Under section 88 of the Fair Trading Act 1973, the Secretary of State has the power to accept undertakings to remedy the adverse effects identified by the MMC in a monopoly report.

5. Copies of the Order SI 1998/1271 Monopolies and Mergers—The Restriction on Agreements and Conduct (Specified Electrical Goods) Order 1998 will be available from the Stationery Office.

6. Copies of the final draft of the Order and the undertakings can be obtained by telephoning [0171] 215 6125. Media copies are available from the DTI press office.

NOTE: The Order was introduced following the Commission's report on *Foreign Package Holidays* (Cm 3183, 1997) in order to enhance transparency and ensure consumer awareness of the ownership links between travel agents and tour operators. (See also the later related Order in relation to favoured customers, The Foreign Package Holidays (Tour Operators and Travel Agents) Order 2001 (SI 2001/2581).) The Restriction on Agreements and Conduct (Specified Domestic Electrical Goods) Order 1998 (SI 1998/1271) was introduced in response to the Commission reports, 'Domestic Electrical Goods I and II' (Cm 3676, 1997) in order to increase price competition in a range of electrical goods.

Part II of Sch. 8 provides the remedy of divestiture, resorted to following the Beer Report, as follows:

The Supply of Beer (Tied Estate) Order 1989 (SI 1989/2390), Art. 2(1)

2.—(1) Every brewer who before 1st November 1992 holds interests in more than two thousand licensed premises shall do all such things as may be necessary to secure that on that date either—

(a) he is no longer a brewer, or

(b) he no longer holds interests in more than two thousand licensed premises, or

(c) the provisions of the Schedule to this Order are satisfied with respect to him.

NOTE: As a result of changed market circumstances, the Beer orders were reviewed in 2000 and they are to be amended, including the abolition of this particular restriction (DTI Press Release P/2000/805, 1 December 2000; DTI P/2002/107, 19 February 2002).

The Secretary of State is not obliged to follow either the advice of the DGFT or the recommendations of the Competition Commission, and in one notable recent instance, the Commission's proposed structural remedy was rejected ('Supply of Raw Milk', Cm 4286, 1999).

QUESTION

Is divestiture too radical a competition law remedy?

SECTION 6:   **Reform—the Enterprise Act**

During the late 1980s and 1990s the existing UK provisions for the control of monopoly, including the provisions on anti-competitive practices contained in the Competition Act 1980, were the subject of numerous criticisms and proposals for reform. Notable in this regard was the DTI Green Paper, *Abuse of Market Power* (November 1992, Cm 2100 see particularly paras 4.3, 4.7, 4.12–13). Legislation was not introduced following these proposals although ultimately the CA 1998 adopted a version of model 3 in the Green Paper which stressed the versatility of the FTA provisions but recommended adoption of rules in harmony with the main Community competition rules, Article 82 EC in this context. We shall deal with the CA 1998 in the final section of this chapter, but it should be noted here that it retained the existing provisions of the FTA 1973. However, shortly after the entry into force of the CA 1998 prohibitions, the DTI produced proposals to reform dramatically the monopoly provisions of the FTA 1973 and replace them with a new scheme for investigating markets.

DTI, A World Class Competition Regime
Cm 5233, July 2001, paras 6.12–6.15 and 6.21–6.24

The new regime for investigating markets
6.12   The new regime for investigating markets will have a similar scope to the existing monopoly provisions, but will operate along the same lines as the new merger regime. It will be used for market wide inquiries. It is not Government's intention that it will be used to deal with scale monopoly problems except in exceptional circumstances (see paragraphs 6.58 to 6.59 below).

- The OFT will work pro-actively to keep markets under review—where it appears that markets may not be working well, it will be able to refer them to the Competition Commission for further investigation.
- The Competition Commission will carry out a full investigation—assessing the market against a new competition-based test.
- The Competition Commission will itself determine what remedies are necessary. If appropriate, it will ask the OFT to negotiate undertakings on its behalf.

- Occasionally, even though there are adverse competition effects, the way a market operates may bring countervailing benefits to consumers. If this is the case, then the Competition Commission may decide to take no action or modify its remedies.
- Ministers will retain the power to decide the very small minority of cases where clearly defined exceptional public interest issues arise.
- There may be a case for Ministers retaining a limited role in relation to divestment remedies recommended by the Competition Commission.

Making references

6.13 The Fair Trading Act enables a reference to the Competition Commission to address complex monopoly questions when:

- it can name or define companies in a market who collectively have a share of supply of 25 per cent more; and
- it appears that the companies, whether voluntarily or not, and whether by agreement or not, so conduct their affairs as in any way to prevent, restrict or distort competition.

6.14 The Government believes that this test should be changed. The first limb is of little value—as in almost every market, it is possible to name or define companies who collectively have a share of supply of 25 per cent or more. The second limb is also problematic, as it asks the OFT to make an assessment that is not directly related to the substantive test applied by the Competition Commission in its subsequent inquiry.

A new reference test

6.15 For the new regime for investigating markets, the Government will develop a more flexible reference test—which allows the OFT to refer markets when it believes that conduct, or circumstances surrounding the operation of a market, suggest a Competition Commission investigation would be merited. The Government invites views on the following replacement test:

> The OFT believes (or has a reasonable suspicion) that a market may operate in a manner which adversely affects competition.

Or, alternatively, and closer to the proposed merger test:

> The OFT believes (or has a reasonable suspicion) that the market may operate in a manner which substantially lessens competition.

. . .

A new competition-based test

6.21 When a market is referred for investigation, a key question that the Competition Commission needs to answer is whether any facts found by the Commission during their investigations operate, or may be expected to operate, against the public interest. The test is concerned with the public interest rather than competition issues.

6.22 With the advent of the Competition Act 1998, monopolies and restrictive agreements are considered against a competition test. The continued presence of the public interest test in the Fair Trading Act now looks anomalous and outdated.

6.23 The Government intends to replace the public interest test with a narrower, more focused competition test.

6.24 In a merger case, the Competition Commission will assess whether a merger will lead to a substantial lessening of competition. A similar analysis may be applicable in a market-wide investigation (ie whether the conduct or performance of any firm or any other aspect of the market has the effect of substantially lessening competition). Alternatively, the test may be based on adverse effects (ie whether the conduct or performance of any firm or any other aspect of the market means that the market operates in a manner which adversely affects competition). The Government invites views on these two approaches. One issue is whether the test should include some degree of appreciability such as 'substantial'.

NOTE: Part IV of the Enterprise Act contains a complicated set of provisions to implement these proposals and the new system will merely be outlined in the following section. There are three major issues: the removal (largely) of the Minister from the process to enhance independence and reduce potential political interference in the application of the system; the abandonment of the public interest test in favour of a new competition test; and a widening of the scheme from 'monopoly' investigations to 'market' investigations.

SECTION 7: **Referral**

The reference test is to be dramatically reformed.

DTI, *Government Response to Consultation*
October 2001, pp. 11–12

Reference test [paragraphs 6.13–6.15]

29. The White Paper offered two alternative reference tests:

- 'The OFT believes (or has a reasonable suspicion) that a market may operate in a manner which *adversely affects* competition'; or
- 'The OFT believes (or has a reasonable suspicion) that a market may operate in a manner which *substantially lessens competition*.'

30. Of those respondents who gave a view on the reference test, most favoured the substantial lessening of competition test. However, a significant minority supported the adverse effects test. A number of respondents also advocated different tests of their own devising. While a number of those who favoured the substantial lessening of competition test gave consistency with the new mergers regime as a reason for their view, all were clearly attracted to it principally because the word 'substantial' set a 'materiality threshold' for the launching of market investigations.

Government's response
The Government has concluded that the reference test should be based on the more flexible concept of 'adverse effects', rather than on a 'substantial lessening of competition'. Although the new merger regime proposes a 'substantial lessening of competition' test, a merger inquiry is linked to a definite event, unlike a market investigation. It is easier to say with certainty and precision that competition in a market will be substantially lessened if two companies operating in a market merge, than it is to say that competition in a market is substantially less than it would be if the market structure or the behaviour of players in the market was different in some hypothetical way.

The Government does not consider that such a test will lead to references being made where the economic impact of any adverse effects on competition are trivial. The OFT will be required to consider that a reference is an appropriate response to any competition concerns about a market.

The Government has also concluded that the OFT should only be required to have a reasonable suspicion that a market may be operating in a manner which adversely affects competition in order to refer it to the CC, rather than a belief that this is the case.

Enterprise Act [section 131(1) and (2)]

131 Power of OFT to make references

(1) The OFT may, subject to subsection (4), make a reference to the Commission if the OFT has reasonable grounds for suspecting that any feature, or combination of features, of a market in the United Kingdom for goods or services prevents, restricts or distorts competition in connection with the supply or acquisition of any goods or services in the United Kingdom or a part of the United Kingdom.

(2) For the purposes of this Part any reference to a feature of a market in the United Kingdom for goods or services shall be construed as a reference to—

(a) the structure of the market concerned or any aspect of that structure;

(b) any conduct (whether or not in the market concerned) of one or more than one person who supplies or acquires goods or services in the market concerned; or

(c) any conduct relating to the market concerned of customers of any person who supplies or acquires goods or services.

NOTE: The 25 per cent threshold under the FTA 1973 has disappeared. Note that the DTI's favoured approach has not been adopted in the Act and a more complicated test has been introduced. A feature of a market can include both conduct and structural issues. Note in particular that the Secretary of State, in addition to the role in relation to exceptional public interest issues, has a power, under section 132, to make a reference where not satisfied with the OFT decision not to refer a market.

SECTION 8: **The competition test**

The key feature of Part IV of the Enterprise Act is the new test to be applied by the Competition Commission in place of the public interest test.

DTI Government Response to Consultation
October 2001, pp. 13–14

Substantive Analysis of Markets by the CC

Competition-based test [paragraphs 6.21–6.24]

34. The White Paper proposed that the public interest test should be replaced with a narrower, more focused competition test. Specifically, it invited views on whether a test should be based on a 'substantial lessening of competition' or on 'adverse effects'.

35. The majority of respondents who commented on this issue favoured the 'substantial lessening of competition' test. These respondents were influenced by the element of appreciability implied by the word 'substantial'. As with the reference test, a small number of respondents proposed different competition-based tests of their own devising. A few respondents were opposed to the introduction of a competition test, preferring the retention of a public interest test.

Government response
As with the reference test, the Government has concluded that the competition-based test should be based on the more flexible concept of 'adverse effects on competition', rather than on 'a substantial lessening of competition'. The reasons for the choice of this formulation for the competition-based test are the same as the reasons for the choice of the reference test.

The Government has also concluded that the CC should reach a higher standard of proof when assessing markets (a 'belief') than the OFT should reach when referring markets, as the CC has the power to impose intrusive remedies if they make an adverse finding.

Consumer benefits [paragraphs 6.25–6.29]

36. The White Paper asked for views on two alternative models for consumer benefits. Under the 'merger model', benefits to consumers are more tightly defined, in terms of price, innovation, quality or choice. Under the alternative Article 81(3)/Competition Act model, a broader range of factors may be taken into account.

37. The majority of respondents who commented on this issue favoured following the Article 81(3)/Competition Act model. However, a number of respondents thought the more tightly defined merger model was preferable.

Government response

The Government has concluded that the merger model of assessing consumer benefits should be followed for market investigations. This model takes into account factors on which a competition authority's judgment can be readily considered authoritative and ensures consistency across both the markets and merger regimes.

The Government recognises that in certain regulated markets, firms must comply with statutory terms and conditions in order to operate in them. These terms and conditions are expressed in their licences, franchise agreements, or conditions of appointment. The Government has therefore concluded that—to the extent that the CC proposes to introduce remedies which would involve changes to the licence conditions under which firms operate in a regulated sector, conditions of appointment (in the water sector) or franchise agreements (in the rail sector)—the CC should, in reaching their final decision on remedies, take account of the statutory duties, aims or objectives of the regulator or Ministers responsible for the sector under investigation (including any statutory guidance on such duties given by Ministers).

Enterprise Act [s. 133]

129 Variation of market investigation references

(1) The OFT or (as the case may be) the appropriate Minister may at any time vary a market investigation reference made by it or (as the case may be) him.

(2) The OFT or (as the case may be) the appropriate Minister shall consult the Commission before varying any such reference.

(3) Subsection (2) shall not apply if the Commission has requested the variation concerned.

(4) No variation under this section shall be capable of altering the period permitted by section 135 within which the report of the Commission under section 134 is to be prepared and published or (as the case may be) the period permitted by section 142 within which the report of the Commission under section 140 is to be prepared and published or given.

NOTE: The term 'adverse effect' is used here as a shorthand for the test to be employed by the Commission. In line with the general pro-consumer ethos in the Act, subsection (4) allows the Commission to take action either to remedy the adverse effect on competition or any detrimental effect on customers arising from such adverse effect. In addition, the Commission can take into account any countervailing consumer benefits of the market features concerned.

SECTION 9: Exceptional public interest issues

Contrary to the general theme of reducing ministerial involvement in Part IV, the Secretary of State has retained an important role in relation to public interest considerations. The 'public interest' has not disappeared altogether although it has been retained in a very limited fashion:

DTI Government Response to Consultation
October 2001, p. 15

Exceptional public interest issues [paragraphs 6.41–6.45]
40. The White Paper proposed that the legislation will set out areas where exceptional public interest issues can arise. In the new merger regime this will be limited to national security with a reserve power for the Government to create new EPI issues by affirmative resolution. Views on whether to use the same approach for market investigations were invited.

41. The majority of respondents favoured the same approach to EPI issues as mergers, although it was commented that the White Paper proposal for Ministers to register their interest at any stage of the inquiry and for a short period after the report is published was unsatisfactory in terms of business certainty.

Government response
The Government has concluded that where EPI issues arise in a market investigation, Ministers will be able to intervene in a case. The CC will still investigate the market and make a finding against the competition-based test, but instead of implementing remedies they will make recommendations to Ministers who will take the final decisions on remedies. The market investigation regime, like the merger regime, will specify national security as an EPI issue. There will also be a reserve power for the Government to list further grounds by secondary legislation subject to affirmative resolution. In order to ensure certainty for those affected by an inquiry, the Government has concluded that the Secretary of State would have to claim a case on EPI grounds within the first four months of a CC investigation, and that it will not be possible to refer a case on EPI grounds.

NOTE: Chapter 2 of Part IV introduces a particularly complex set of provisions in relation to public interest intervention notices by the Secretary of State. (Section 139–40.) There was considerable debate in Parliament on the scope of these fall-back provisions, and Government Ministers stressed that they would be used rarely. Indeed, section 153 sets out the only public interest consideration at present as national security although new considerations can be specified by delegated legislation.

SECTION 10: **Remedies under Part IV**

The FTA 1973 contained a fairly convoluted system for enforcement involving each of the bodies in the tripartite enforcement process. Enforcement is given detailed treatment under Chapter 3 of Part IV of the Enterprise Act, where it has been streamlined and the role of the Competition Commission considerably enhanced.

DTI Government Consultation Document
October 2001, pp. 14–15

Remedy setting [paragraphs 6.30–6.36]
38. The White Paper said that the CC would be required to determine what remedies are necessary to address the competition problem that it has identified. Respondents' comments on the pro-

posal for the CC to devise and implement remedies were overwhelmingly favourable. Several respondents also welcomed the proposals to change the CC's procedures in relation to remedy setting, with discussion on remedies being properly informed by the CC's publication of provisional findings.

39. The White Paper invited views as to whether Ministers should retain a role where a major divestment remedy is proposed. The overwhelming majority of respondents commented that continuing Ministerial involvement in divestment remedies is anomalous in reforms which are guided by the principle of removing political influence from the enforcement of competition law.

Government response
The Government has concluded that the CC will determine what remedies are necessary to address the competition problems that they have identified. They will be able to impose a specified range of remedies, including divestment remedies, without reference to Ministers. The CC will have no power to vary or alter any laws or regulations that give rise or contribute to the competition problem. Instead, they will make recommendations to the public authority which has responsibility for this law or regulation.

NOTE: The provisions are inevitably more detailed than this simplistic outline. Undertakings may still be given in lieu of a reference. The key feature is the role of the Competition Commission to accept final undertakings (section 159) and make appropriate orders (section 160), although the Secretary of State has also retained an enforcement role under these provisions where there is a public interest consideration and an intervention notice has been given. The OFT is entrusted with monitoring undertakings and orders. Section 179 provides for judicial review by the CAT of decisions taken under Part IV of the Enterprise Act.

QUESTION

Are market investigations likely to be an unnecessary burden for business? Should the authorities focus solely on abusive conduct under the CA 1998?

SECTION 11: **The Competition Act 1998**

In 1998, the UK's 25-year competition law cycle was maintained with the introduction of the CA 1998. The aims of the legislation were to enhance the deterrent effect of UK competition law and to harmonise our system with the Community provisions, Articles 81 and 82 EC. The Act introduced two new prohibitions, the Chapter II prohibition being modelled very closely on the prohibition on the abuse of a dominant position in Article 82 EC. Chapter III of the Act introduced important powers of investigation and enforcement of the new prohibitions (see Chapter 2).

Wilks, S., *In the Public Interest, Competition Policy and the Monopolies and Mergers Commission*
Manchester, MUP, 1999, pp. 322–324

The Competition Act 1998
With an elegant accident of symmetry the Act comes exactly fifty years after the Monopolies and Restrictive Practices Act 1948. It is potentially a revolutionary piece of legislation which has

considerable implications for the institutions of British capitalism. As explored in the concluding chapter, the 1948 Act catered to the voluntarism, the self-regulation and the accommodative arm's-length relationship between government and industry which permeated the political economy of the 1940s. The 1998 Act creates a more formal and legally objective framework for industry. It provides didactic guidance rather than the co-operative exploration which underlay its 1948 predecessor. The formal provisions of the Act are briefly reviewed in chapter 10.

Despite its European provenance, the new Act is a piece of British legislation although it builds in novel provisions to employ European jurisprudence. It is designed to dovetail with the European regime and doubtless many hope that this new, more effective, Act will increase the element of real subsidiarity. It represents something of a compromise, as can be seen if it is considered in the context of the debates reviewed above. In respect of the first debate it almost certainly represents a more active British competition policy, and one that stresses 'competition' as a principle rather than 'the public interest'. In respect of the second debate it adopts the European stance of prohibition and an effects doctrine, and does so for monopolies as well as restrictive practices. But the monopolies element is enacted with due caution and the mergers regime remains unaltered. In respect of the third debate the institutions have changed in their relationships with one another and in the abolition of one court and the creation of a new tribunal. These changes have been the product of wide consultation. The Government has pursued a neo-pluralist path of involvement of the policy network through a proliferation of Green and White Papers and by giving every indication of listening to the responses. There is nothing impetuous or dogmatic about this legislation. Government has sought advice, built consensus and moved with judicious caution. This is indicative of a neo-pluralist policy stance which seeks to build consensus but which also requires technical support. The Government was genuinely uncertain about the potential effects of new legislation and in true civil service style (and very unlike the sweeping Thatcherite policy initiatives) it enrolled the views and the advice of business, lawyers and other specialists. It is indicative of this caution that the new model has perhaps embraced the European certainties too emphatically. After years of being reproached as not being European enough, some lawyers are now suggesting that the Government has become too European. The European blueprint does indeed involve some major shifts in the regime of monopoly control. In order to evaluate the extent of change consider the following:

- the shift from agnostic investigation to prohibition
- the replacement of the 'public interest' test by an 'effect on competition' test
- the exclusion of the Secretary of State from the administrative process as regards actions and remedies
- the incorporation of the principles of European competition law jurisprudence into British administration
- hence the likely growth of legal involvement through defence, appeal and third-party action
- the empowerment of third parties through rights of appeal and the potential to pursue damages in the courts
- the imposition of substantial penalties.

Change of this magnitude is potentially of extraordinary significance and it is curious that press coverage of the Act was relatively subdued. What really matters, however, is the fashion in which the new procedures will be administered and it is here that civil service caution has come into its own. There is a sense in which the UK Competition Act is an expression of 'beating them at their own game'. The European law is accepted but it is brought firmly under national control by British institutions.

NOTE: As Wilks notes, the CA 1998 is certainly more legalistic than its predecessors. Wilks discusses the main changes, the key issue being the 'Europeanisation' of domestic competition policy.

A: Harmonisation

The key to understanding the Chapter II prohibition and its impact is the basic rule that it should be interpreted consistently with Community law. This is provided through the operation of s. 60 of the CA 1998, otherwise known as the governing principles provision or 'Euro-clause'. The objective, set out in s. 60(1), is enshrined in s. 60(2) which seeks to ensure that the UK authorities and courts must interpret the prohibition in accordance with European Court jurisprudence. They are also required under s. 60(3) to have regard to relevant decisions or statements by the Commission. Section 60(1) permits departure from Community law where there are relevant differences. See generally Chapter 4 and specifically, Middleton, K., 'Harmonisation with Community Law; The Euro Clause' Chapter 3 in Rodger, B.J., and MacCulloch, A. (eds), *The UK Competition Act: A New Era for UK Competition Law*, Hart Publishing: Oxford, 2000 at pp. 21–23, pp. 26–29 and 33–39.

B: The prohibition

Section 18 provides:

Competition Act 1998 [s. 18]

Abuse of dominant position

   18.—(1) Subject to section 19, any conduct on the part of one or more undertakings which amounts to the abuse of a dominant position in a market is prohibited if it may affect trade within the United Kingdom.

   (2) Conduct may, in particular, constitute such an abuse if it consists in—

   (a) directly or indirectly imposing unfair purchase or selling prices or other unfair trading conditions;

   (b) limiting production, markets or technical development to the prejudice of consumers;

   (c) applying dissimilar conditions to equivalent transactions with other trading parties, thereby placing them at a competitive disadvantage;

   (d) making the conclusion of contracts subject to acceptance by the other parties of sup-plementary obligations which, by their nature or according to commercial usage, have no connection with the subject of the contracts.

   (3) In this section—

   'dominant position' means a dominant position within the United Kingdom; and

   'the United Kingdom' means the United Kingdom or any part of it.

   (4) The prohibition imposed by subsection (1) is referred to in this Act as 'the Chapter II prohibition'.

NOTE: This basically replicates Article 82 EC but places the provision in a UK context. As discussed more fully in Chapter 2 the DGFT has been afforded a similar role to that of the Commission under Community law with powers to investigate and fine companies for breaching the prohibition. This was a crucial change in the direction of UK competition policy and one would have anticipated extensive Parliamentary debates on the nature and likely impact of the prohibition.

Sufrin, B., 'The Chapter II prohibition' Chapter 6 in Rodger B.J., and MacCulloch, A. (eds), *The UK Competition Act: A New Era for UK Competition Law*
Oxford, Hart Publishing, 2000, at pp. 120–121 and pp. 146–147

The effect of the Competition Act 1998 and in particular section 60, however, is that the adoption of the Chapter II, and Chapter I, prohibition is unlike other radical innovations in UK law.[7] The Chapter II prohibition is born trailing clouds, if not of glory, then at least of three decades of case law, and comes with the stipulation that UK courts are to follow future developments in its interpretation fashioned in Luxembourg and, to a lesser extent, in Brussels. The fact that the Competition Act brings into domestic law not only an Article 82-type system but also the substantive content of Article 82 as developed by the European Court was deliberate and was presented by the Government as a positively beneficial feature of the new law in that UK companies will no longer be subject to 'differing approaches and potentially differing judgments on the same competition issues'.[8]

There was little debate during the progress of the Competition Bill about what makes undertakings 'dominant', and therefore subject to the Chapter II prohibition, or about what conduct it prohibits, partly because the discussion was repeatedly side-tracked on to the issue of predatory pricing in the newspaper industry. In the Second Reading in the Commons John Redwood, the Shadow Secretary of State, asked the President of the Board of Trade 'what current legal business practices she hopes and expects the Bill to make illegal?' but was told this was a 'vague and wandering question' and that 'no one can be expected to give case-by-case definitions, especially not a Minister', these things being matters for the Director General of Fair Trading.[9] Parliament was assured that two cases called *AKZO*[10] and *Tetra Pak*[11] would take care of predatory pricing in newspapers. Although, in that context, the Minister of State did describe what dominance meant in European jurisprudence,[12] the scope and philosophy of the Community rules which were being brought into domestic law were not subjected to any detailed examination. This was 'a Bill for consumers, for business and for jobs . . . another step in the creation of strong markets that will make Britain a more competitive economy'[13] but exactly *how* the Chapter II prohibition would do this in terms of substantive law was not described.

Conclusion
The Chapter II prohibition cannot be expected to solve all problems concerning the abuse of market power by firms in the United Kingdom. We have bought Article 82 with all its complexities and uncertainties 'off the peg' so to speak, aware of its shortcomings, but its attractions are that it provides for the deterrence, enforcement and penalties which UK law on monopolies lacked before, and it produces harmony with Community law.

The latter feature has been widely welcomed, in that undertakings have only to comply with one set of rules rather than two, but that argument is fallacious. If rules are unsatisfactory or imperfect, subjecting undertakings to them twice over is not necessarily an advantage, and subjecting undertakings which operate only domestically to those rules because it is supposedly easier for undertakings who must already comply with Article 82 in their inter-Member State dealings is

7 There is a tempting analogy with the Human Rights Act 1998, ss. 2 and 3, but the interpretation provisions there are significantly different from the Competition Act 1998, s. 60. See S. Marshall, 'Interpreting Interpretation in the Human Rights Bill' [1998] *PL* 197 and D. Feldman, 'The Human Rights Act 1998 and Constitutional Principles' (1999) 19 *Legal Studies* 165.

8 See Margaret Beckett, Second Reading, Hansard, HC, 11 May 1998, col 25.

9 Hansard, HC, 11 May 1998, cols 23 and 24.

10 See *infra*, n. 79.

11 See *infra*, n. 80.

12 Hansard, HC, 11 May 1998, col 118.

13 Ibid., col 23.

unacceptable. If Article 82 is to be applied as domestic law it should be because Parliament believes that its substantive content provides the rules which should govern the conduct of dominant undertakings in the United Kingdom in order to promote consumer welfare. The fact that many UK undertakings already have to take account of Article 82 itself should be no reason for failing to subject the law introduced by section 18 of the 1998 Act to proper scrutiny.

Article 82 EC, in the name of competition, subjects dominant undertakings to a high degree of regulation but, despite section 60 of the 1998 Act, the nature of the issues raised in the control of market power inevitably gives a considerable margin of appreciation to the UK competition authorities. It is the way in which the Director General exercises that discretion which will determine how far the Chapter II prohibition really promotes competition.

NOTE: Sufrin points out that in fact there was very little debate on the substance of the prohibition. Indeed, one of the principal criticisms of Article 82 EC is the lack of certainty it allows for parties to determine what constitutes legitimate competitive behaviour as opposed to illegal and abusive conduct which is prohibited. One of the key debates during the passage of the Bill was whether to include a specific rule on predatory pricing in the newspaper industry, but ultimately this was rejected. Sufrin's chapter discusses recent developments under Article 82 EC (see Chapter 8) and notes the potential difficulties for the UK authorities in applying the case-law, for instance in relation to refusal to supply, see Case C-7/97 *Oscar Bronner* v *Mediaprint* [1998] ECR I-7791 and predatory pricing, see Case T-228/97 *Irish Sugar plc* v *Commission* [1999] 5 CMLR 1300.

As Sufrin notes, ascertaining the impact of the new prohibition will be facilitated by the development of practice and case-law, noted below, and also by the production of guidelines by the DGFT under s. 52(1) of the Act. The following is an excerpt from the Chapter II prohibition Guideline (OFT 402).

OFT Guideline 402, The Chapter II prohibition

4.5 Abusive conduct generally falls into one of the following categories: conduct which *exploits* customers or suppliers through, for example:

- excessively high prices; or
- discriminatory prices, or other terms or conditions; or

conduct which is *anti-competitive* (sometimes called '*exclusionary behaviour*', because it removes or limits competition from existing competitors, or because it excludes new undertakings from entering the market by, for example:

- *predatory* behaviour;
- vertical restraints; or
- refusing to supply existing or potential competitors.

4.6 The following explanations do not constitute an exhaustive list of behaviour which the Director General might regard as an abuse. They are likely to cover many potential cases, but each case will be considered on its own merits.

Excessively high prices

4.7 Perhaps the most obvious form of abuse is where a dominant undertaking charges prices higher than it would do if it faced effective competition.[7] The European Court has held that:

---

7 Authority for the principle that charging unfairly high prices is an abuse is found in the *General Motors* case (Case 26/75, *General Motors Continental NV* v *Commission*, [1975] ECR 1367; [1976] 1 CMLR 95), in which the European Commission found the pricing strategy of the dominant undertaking to be excessive and imposed a fine. The Commission's decision was annulled by the European Court on the basis of the facts, but the principle was upheld.

charging a price which is excessive because it has no reasonable relation to the economic value of the product supplied is . . . an abuse.[8]

4.8 The essential issue is when a price becomes *excessively high*: in general to be excessively high the price must be higher than it would normally be in a competitive market. Clearly all companies must earn some level of profits in order to finance investments. The profits of a dominant undertaking in the relevant market consistently exceeding its relevant cost of capital (the return which could be earned from investing elsewhere having regard to the risks incurred by investing in the particular company) might, however, indicate that its prices were excessive.

4.9 There may, however, be many objective justifications for prices which are apparently 'excessively high'. First, in competitive markets, prices and costs vary over time and there are likely to be periods when high profits can be earned. This is an important part of the competitive process since it can encourage increased output or entry to a market. Secondly, undertakings in competitive markets may be able to sustain high profits for a period of time if they are more efficient than their competitors. This might occur if an undertaking has developed lower-cost techniques of production, supplies higher quality products or is more effective at identifying market opportunities. (Exclusive access to low-cost inputs, such as exclusive rights to certain raw materials, is not, however, the same thing as superior efficiency.) To be an abuse, prices would have to be *persistently* excessive without stimulating new entry or innovation.

4.10 Given the uncertainties in estimating what an undertaking's cost of capital should be, prices would have to allow profits which *significantly* and persistently exceeded its cost of capital before an abuse could be established. The assessment of this question is explained in more detail in the Competition Act guideline. Assessment of Individual Agreements and Conduct.

Individual agreements and conduct

4.11 In markets where there is a high rate of innovation it may be natural to see high prices for a period of time. Persistently high profits which result from successive innovations will provide both a return on previous innovations and incentives for further innovation. In these circumstances high profits will not indicate an abuse.

4.12 In applying the Chapter II prohibition the Director General will therefore be mindful of the need not to interfere in natural market mechanisms where high prices will encourage new entry or innovation and thereby serve to increase competition. Excessive prices are likely to be regarded as an abuse only in markets where an undertaking is so dominant, and new entry so unlikely, that it is clear that high profits will not stimulate successful new entry or innovation within a reasonable period.

4.13 Where joint dominance exists, undertakings might engage in some form of *tacit collusion*—failing to compete on price even though there is no agreement between them. In some cases this type of behaviour may be prohibited under Chapter I as a concerted practice, but if the level of collusion falls short of a concerted practice, it might in principle be considered under the Chapter II prohibition if the undertakings were jointly dominant. The fact that different undertakings charge the same price is not, of itself, however, an abuse: in competitive markets, undertakings which sell similar products and incur similar costs will tend to charge the same price. To show that tacit collusion was an abuse of joint dominance would usually require other evidence—that opportunities to cut prices following a significant fall in input costs were deliberately ignored, or that prices were excessive (as defined above), for example.

NOTE: Sufrin believes 'The Guidelines walk a delicate line between stating a Community position which might not always be thought ideal but which has to be recognised because of

---

8 Case 27/76 *United Brands* v *Commission* [1978] ECR 207, [1978] 1 CMLR 429.

s. 60, and explaining how the Director General might wish to approach the matter.' (above at p. 24.) However, as with other Guidelines, this excerpt is fairly anodyne and highlights that very little practical advice is actually gained from the text.

C: Practice to date

The DGFT and CCAT have already developed a body of case-law under the Chapter II prohibition. The following is an excerpt from the first decision by the DGFT finding a breach of the prohibition:

Napp Pharmaceutical Holdings Limited and Subsidiaries (Napp)
CA 98/2/2001 30 March 2001, paras 138 and 236–237

Napp sells sustained release morphine tablets and capsules in the UK. It was alleged that Napp had abused its dominant position by predatory discounting of drugs to hospitals and charged excessive prices to other customers.

(e) Conclusion on dominance

138. The presumption of dominance created by Napp's very high market share is reinforced by the existence of high barriers to entry: regulation, first mover advantage, high sunk promotional costs, and strategic barriers to entry arising from Napp's pricing strategy in the hospital segment. Neither limited buyer power in the hospital segment of the market nor the operation of the PPRS provide significant evidence to the contrary. Napp therefore holds a dominant position in the supply of sustained release morphine tablets and capsules in the UK.

. . .

E Conclusion

236. Napp has:

(a) while charging high prices to customers in the community segment of the market, supplied sustained release morphine tablets and capsules to hospitals at discounts which have the object and effect of hindering competition in the market for the supply of sustained release morphine tablets and capsules in the UK. The pricing behaviour of Napp has to be considered as a whole, but the particular aspects in which, in the circumstances of the present case, its discounting behaviour is abusive under section 18 of the Act are as follows:

    (i) selectively supplying sustained release morphine tablets and capsules to customers in the hospital segment at lower prices than to customers in the community segment;

    (ii) more particularly, targeting competitors, both by supplying at higher discounts to hospitals where it faced (or anticipated) competition and by supplying at higher discounts on those strengths of sustained release morphine tablets and capsules where it faced competition; and

    (iii) supplying sustained release morphine tablets and capsules to hospitals at excessively low prices.

Moreover, Napp has engaged in the above conduct with the intention of eliminating competition.

(b) charged excessive prices to customers in the community segment of the market for the supply of sustained release morphine tablets and capsules in the UK.

237. In doing so, Napp has abused its dominant position in the market for the supply of sustained release morphine tablets and capsules in the UK and thereby infringed the Chapter II prohibition imposed by section 18 of the Act.

NOTE: The DGFT relied heavily throughout on European Court jurisprudence and Commission practice. The DGFT used his powers to impose penalties under s. 36 of the Act of £3.21 million (calculated in accordance with the Guidance on Penalties, OFT 423, March 2000) and issued Directions (4 May 2001) under s. 33 in respect of their pricing. The CCAT supported the findings of abuse and the following excerpt focuses on the issue of predatory pricing:

Napp Pharmaceutical Holdings Limited and Subsidiaries v *DGFT*
(Case 1000/1/01, (final judgment) 15 January 2002, paras 228–230)

228. On the basis of *AKZO* and *Tetra Pak II*, and having regard to our duty under section 60(2) of the Act to secure, so far as compatible with Part I of the Act, that there is no inconsistency between the principles we apply and the principles laid down by the Court of Justice, in our judgment it follows, on the foregoing facts alone, that Napp has abused its dominant position in offering prices below average variable costs to hospitals contrary to the Chapter II prohibition, as the Director found in the Decision, without it being necessary to find that Napp had a specific intention to eliminate competition. In view of the fact that the *AKZO* approach was laid down in a case where the dominant undertaking had only 50 per cent of the market, it seems to us that it is only in the most exceptional of circumstances that a similar approach should not be applied in cases of 'superdominance' where the undertaking concerned has around 95 per cent of the market.

229. It is true, however, that in paragraph 127 of his opinion in *Compagnie Maritime Belge*, Advocate General Fennelly stated that while sales below average variable costs (for which in this case direct costs are considered to be a proxy) are 'in effect presumed to be abusive', he went on to say that 'a dominant firm, would be permitted to rebut this presumption by showing that such pricing was not part of a plan to eliminate its competitor'. In view of the remarks at paragraphs 132 and 137 of his opinion, we doubt whether Mr Fennelly would necessarily have taken the same approach on this point had he been considering a case, such as the present, of a virtual monopolist selling well below direct costs. Nonetheless, as a precaution we consider in this judgment whether it is shown that Napp had no plan or intention to eliminate competition, so as to bring itself within the exception to the *AKZO* test envisaged by Mr Fennelly.

230. In that connection we begin by considering Napp's fundamental argument that the *AKZO* and *Tetra Pak II* approach is not the right starting point in this case because, properly understood, Napp's hospital sales did not 'generate a loss' because of the 'follow-on effects'. That issue has to be considered also in the light of *Compagnie Maritime Belge* and *Irish Sugar*, cited above, which show that even if the prices of a dominant firm remain above costs, and simply match the price of a competitor, there may still be an abuse, at least where a superdominant firm is concerned, if the reduced prices in question are made on a selective basis and have no economic rationale other than the elimination of competition.

NOTE: The CCAT judgment is an excellent example of the application of Community law jurisprudence, following closely recent case-law such as *Maritime Belge* Case T-228/97, *Irish Sugar* v *Commission* [1999] ECR II-2969 and *Irish Sugar* Cases C-395/96P and 396/96P, *Compagnie Maritime Belge* v *Commission* [2000] ECR I-1442, and the novel Community concept of 'super-dominance'. The CCAT went on to reject the 'net revenue' defence to the predatory pricing abuse. However, the CCAT reduced the overall fine to be imposed on Napp (see further in Chapter 2).

A more straightforward example of predatory pricing was involved in a decision against Aberdeen Journals Ltd:

Summary, CA98/5/2001
Decision of the Director General of Fair Trading No CA98/5/2001

The *Aberdeen & District Independent* newspaper complained that Aberdeen Journals Limited was predating in the pricing of advertising space in its *Herald & Post*. Aberdeen Journals is owned by Northcliffe Newspapers Group Ltd, itself part of the Daily Mail & General Trust group.

Aberdeen Journals is dominant in the market for the supply of advertising space in local newspapers (paid-for and free) within the Aberdeen area.

Aberdeen Journals has deliberately incurred losses on the *Herald & Post* in an attempt to expel the *Aberdeen & District Independent*, its only rival in the relevant market. Aberdeen Journals has therefore infringed the Chapter II prohibition by predating. A penalty of £1,328,040 is imposed.

NOTE: Aberdeen Journals appealed to the CCAT. Further emphasising the importance of Community jurisprudence, the CCAT considered that the DGFT had not set out the assessment of the relevant product market in sufficient detail. The issue was remitted to the DGFT and the DGFT subsequently restated and confirmed the earlier decision on the basis of an expanded treatment of the issue of the relevant market (No CA98/14/2002, 16 September 2002). The DGFT has also made a number of Decisions in which there has been found to be no breach of the prohibition. For instance he issued a decision that by granting Postal Preference Service Limited (PPS) a licence to use Royal Mail trade marks on its consumer lifestyle surveys, Consignia plc has not infringed the Chapter II prohibition, CA98/4/2001, 15 June 2001. See other decisions in the OFT website *www.oft.gov.uk* and Rodger, B.J., 'Early Steps to a Mature Competition Law System: Case Law Developments in the First 18 Months of the Competition Act 1998' [2002] ECLR 52.

Decisions of the DGFT can be appealed to the CCAT (CAT, following the Enterprise Act 2002) and thereafter to the Court of Appeal in England and Wales and Court of Session in Scotland. The courts will also be involved in determining disputes based on the Chapter II prohibition. (For further discussion of the possibility of private enforcement, see Chapter 2 above, and MacCulloch, A., 'Private Enforcement of the Competition Act Prohibitions' Chapter Five, in Rodger B.J., and MacCulloch A. (eds), *The UK Competition Act: A New Era for UK Competitive Law*.) The first judgment on the substance of the Chapter II prohibition was delivered in *Claritas (UK) Limited* v *The Post Office and Postal Preference Service Limited* [2001] UKCLR 2. There have been a number of subsequent judgments in relation to the prohibition, the most notable recently being *Getmapping plc* v *Ordnance Survey*, Laddie J, 31 May 2002, [2002] EWHC 1089 (Ch).

Laddie J, High Court of Justice
Chancery Division, 31 May 2002, para. 49

Getmapping ('GM') sought interlocutory relief against Ordnance Survey ('OS'), in order to ensure that OS, in the light of the obligations imposed by s. 18 of the CA 1998, placed GM's digital photographs on its website or made them accessible from it.

49. In the absence of contrary authority, it seems to me that the provenance of the funds which enable a dominant trader to enter a new market is irrelevant to the issue of abuse. As long as those funds are not obtained by abusive behaviour in the market in which the trader is dominant and are not used in an abusive way in the new market, there is no breach of s. 18 of the Act. In relation to this I accept Mr Barnes' submission that using funds from the dominant market to allow predatory pricing in the new market would be an abuse, but merely entering the market and enjoying a commercial advantage over others is not. It follows that even if, as GM complains, OS is obtaining a competitive advantage in the imagery market, that does not indicate an abuse of a dominant position.

NOTE: The judgment relied heavily on the limitations imposed on the scope of the abuse prohibition as identified by the ECJ in *Oscar Bronner* v *Mediaprint* (Case C-7/97 [1998] ECR P7791) and the CFI in *Deutsche Post* (Case T-175/99 *UPS* v *Commission*).

QUESTION

Do you agree that the source of funds allowing a competitor to enter a new market should be irrelevant for abuse purposes?

D: The future operation of the prohibition

The DGFT and CCAT have already established a body of practice under the CA 1998 and it was clear at the outset, from the emphasis placed on education and compliance, that the Chapter II prohibition was likely to have a significant impact on business practice.

Rodger, B.J., 'Early Steps to a Mature Competition Law System: Case Law Developments in the First 18 Months of the Competition Act 1998'
[2002] ECLR p. 52

Introduction
The Competition Act 1998 has introduced a sea change in the way competition law is dealt with in the United Kingdom at a time when competition law has been developing a considerably higher profile. With the notable exceptions of the House of Lords debates regarding newspaper pricing and over-the-counter medicine pricing/community pharmacies, analysis of the likely impact of particular provisions during the passage of the Bill through Parliament, particularly in relation to section 18 and the Chapter II prohibition, was limited, and the Competition Act did not attract the attention of the broader public. However, the impact of the prohibitions on business practice, and the requirement for effective compliance strategies to be set up, is already becoming clearer.

In the space of a little over 18 months, there have been a considerable number of decisions taken under the Act by the Director General of Fair Trading (DGFT) and the Competition Commission has delivered one final judgment and a number of interim judgments. A wide range of issues have been dealt with in a short space of time, from excessive pricing to predatory pricing (*Napp, Aberdeen Journals*), the application of the Chapter I prohibition to self-regulation in the insurance industry (*GISC*), the grant of block exemptions (*travel cards*) and individual exemptions, and the acceptance of voluntary assurances in lieu of the imposition of interim measures, to the procedures and process of appeal against decision by the DGFT (as explored in *Napp*). The importance of section 60 of the Act and the role for Community jurisprudence in interpreting and applying the prohibitions has been clearly demonstrated (*Napp, Claritas*, etc.). The range of issues has varied from the small and localised, notably the warning about price-fixing to members of the Bury Private Hire Association, to the £27 billion insurance industry in the United Kingdom and the competitive strategy of BSkyB, demonstrating the importance of compliance with the Act across the whole spectrum of industry in the United Kingdom. Although there have been a number of fresh investigations under the Act, it is also notable that some investigations and decisions have followed from prior practice, under either the 1973 Act or 1980 Act (*Aberdeen Journals/Napp* below). Inevitably, and particularly since the Competition Commission Appeal Tribunal (CCAT) has become involved in appeals under the Act, we have witnessed a move towards a more formalistic and legalistic competition law system, at least in terms of process. This is partly inevitable, due to the punitive consequences of breach of the new rules, and the need for clarity, certainty and the rights of the defence to be respected. It perhaps also reflects the involvement of the courts, given that private enforcement is a central plank of enforcement under the Act.

NOTE: The Enterprise Act makes no substantive reform to the Chapter II prohibition, although it alters the institutional structure by replacing the DGFT with the newly constituted OFT, and it provides for parties damaged by an infringement of either prohibition to claim damages from the Competition Appeal Tribunal. These issues were discussed in Chapter 2 on UK Enforcement.

QUESTION

Do you think the CA 1998 has been given sufficient time to 'bed-down' prior to the introduction of the Enterprise Act?

FURTHER READING

Wilks, *In the Public Interest*, MUP, Manchester, 1999.

Rodger B.J., and MacCulloch, A. (eds), *The UK Competition Act: A New Era for UK Competition Law*, Hart Publishing, Oxford, 2000.

8

Article 82 EC

SECTION 1: **Introduction, Article 82 EC**

One of the primary purposes of Article 82 EC is to prevent businesses which possess power through their position on the market from distorting competition within the Single Market. The protection of competition can be see as supporting the four freedoms in the Single Market project from the damaging effects which may be caused by the use, and abuse, of the power wielded by businesses within the Community. The prohibition of the 'abuse' of this power is set out in Article 82 EC.

Article 82

Any abuse by one or more undertakings of a dominant position within the common market or in a substantial part of it shall be prohibited as incompatible with the common market insofar as it may affect trade between Member States.

Such abuse may, in particular, consist in:

> (a) directly or indirectly imposing unfair purchase or selling prices or other unfair trading conditions;
> (b) limiting production, markets or technical development to the prejudice of consumers;
> (c) applying dissimilar conditions to equivalent transactions with other trading parties, thereby placing them at a competitive disadvantage;
> (d) making the conclusion of contracts subject to acceptance by the other parties of supplementary obligations which, by their nature or according to commercial usage, have no connection with the subject of such contracts.

NOTE: The indicative list of abuses in paragraphs (a) to (d) is simply that, an indicative list. The prohibition contained in the first paragraph has been interpreted widely by the Commission and the Courts.

SECTION 2: **The elements of Article 82 EC**

A: Undertakings

The term used in Community competition law to describe commercial enterprises is 'undertakings'. The same term is also used in Article 81 EC and the Court has consistently held that the term has the same meaning in both contexts. See Chapter 5.

B: Effect on trade between Member States

Because of the particular features of Article 82 EC, there is much greater focus on the structure of markets within the Article 82 EC jurisprudence in this area.

Commercial Solvents v *Commission*
(Cases 6 & 7/73) [1974] ECR 223, [1974] 1 CMLR 309

> Istituto/Commercial Solvents were the dominant producers of a number of intermediate chemical products, including 'nitropropane' and 'aminobutanol'. Those chemicals were used for the manufacture of 'ethambutol', used as an anti-tuberculosis drug. A customer of Commercial Solvents, Zoja SpA, used the intermediary products to produce ethambutol. At the end of 1970, Zoja attempted to source further supplies of the intermediary but Commercial Solvents made it clear that none would be available. The refusal to supply Zoja would result in its removal from the market for anti-tuberculosis drugs.

[30] The applicants argue that in this case it is principally the world market which is affected, since Zoja sells 90 per cent of its production outside the Common Market and in particular in the developing countries, and that constitutes a much more important market for anti-tuberculosis drugs than the countries of the Community, where tuberculosis has largely disappeared. The sales outlets of Zoja in the Common Market are further reduced by the fact that in many member-States Zoja was blocked by the patents of other companies, in particular American Cyanamid, which prevented it from selling its specialities based on ethambutol. Therefore abuse of the dominant position, even if it were established, would not come within the ambit of Article 86, which prohibits such an abuse only 'in so far as it may effect trade between member-States'.

[31] This expression is intended to define the sphere of application of Community rules in relation to national laws. It cannot therefore be interpreted as limiting the field of application of the prohibition which it contains to industrial and commercial activities supplying the member-States.

[32] The prohibitions of Articles 85 and 86 must in fact be interpreted and applied in the light of Article 3(f) of the Treaty, which provides that the activities of the Community shall include the institution of a system ensuring that competition in the Common Market is not distorted, and Article 2 of the Treaty, which gives the Community the task of promoting 'throughout the Community harmonious development of economic activities'. By prohibiting the abuse of a dominant position within the market in so far as it may affect trade between member-States *Article 86* therefore covers abuse which may directly prejudice consumers as well as abuse which indirectly prejudices them by impairing the effective competitive structure as envisaged by Article 3(f) of the Treaty.

[33] The Community authorities must therefore consider all the consequences of the conduct complained of for the competitive structure in the Common Market without distinguishing between production intended for sale within the market and that intended for export. When an undertaking in a dominant position within the Common Market abusively exploits its position in such a way that a competitor in the Common Market is likely to be eliminated, it does not matter whether the conduct relates to the latter's exports or its trade within the Common Market, once it has been established that this elimination will have repercussions on the competitive structure within the Common Market.

[34] Moreover the contrary argument would in practice mean that the control of Zoja's production and outlets would be in the hands of Commercial Solvents Corp. and Istituto. Finally its cost prices

would have been so affected that the ethambutol produced by it would possibly become unmarketable.

[35] Moreover it emerged at the hearing that Zoja is at present able to export and does indeed export the products in question to at least two member-States. These exports are endangered by the difficulties caused to this company and, by reason of this, trade between member-States may be affected.

NOTE: The existence of a large market participant may, in itself, hamper the proper development of the Single Market.

Soda-ash—Solvay, Commission Decision
91/299/EEC, OJ, 1991, L152/21

> Soda-ash is a substance used in glass production and the chemical industry. Most glass producers needed a continuous and secure supply of soda-ash which they tended to secure from a supplier in their own Member State. The Commission took action as it was concerned that suppliers were not competing outside their traditional 'spheres of influence'.

4. Effect on trade between Member States
[65] Article 86 covers not only abuse which may directly prejudice consumers but also abuse which indirectly prejudices them by impairing the effective competitive structure in the common market as envisaged by Article 3(f) of the EEC Treaty.

The fidelity rebates and other inducements to exclusivity applied by Solvay affect trade between Member States by reinforcing the links between the customers and the dominant supplier. The opportunities for competing suppliers to enter new markets or obtain new customers are effectively removed since the customer's marginal tonnage requirements for which they would be competing are currently being supplied by Solvay at prices which they would be unable to meet. The various devices employed by Solvay to tie customers had the result of reinforcing the structural rigidity and the division of the soda-ash market on national lines, and thus harmed or threatened to harm the attainment of the objective of a single market between Member States.

[66] The fact that Solvay's measures were aimed principally at imports from the United States does not affect the application of Article 86. Imports of natural ash from the United States were seen as the main threat to Solvay's domination of the soda-ash market in continental western Europe. The arrival in substantial quantities of natural ash would also have had a considerable effect upon the agreed division of the market between ICI and Solvay. The activities therefore affected the basic competitive structure of the soda-ash industry within the Community.

It should also be noted that were the major glass producers to import soda-ash from the United States in substantial quantities, they would probably do so in order to supply their works in several Member States. Furthermore, Solvay's exclusionary measures were aimed not only at the United States producers but also at smaller producers of synthetic ash located inside the Community. All of these producers have since 1982 made deliveries from their own national market to other Community Member States although their opportunities were severely constrained by Solvay's pricing policies.

NOTE: The protection of the development of the Single Market means that Article 82 may apply to conduct that only occurs within one Member State, if that conduct has the potential effect of retarding the development of intra-Community trade by denying potential sales to producers in other Member States.

C: Dominant position

It is vital to ensure that the undertaking that is suspected of abusing its power does indeed have market power—a dominant position in EC terminology. Without that market power, the undertaking will be constrained by its competitors and competition law will not need to intervene. To establish whether an undertaking has such power it is necessary first to establish in which market they operate, and second, to establish if they are dominant in that market.

Relevant product market

The importance of the relevant market was explained by the Court in:

Continental Can v Commission
(Case 6/72) [1973] ECR 215

[14] The definition of the relevant market is of essential significance, for the possibilities of competition can only be judged in relation to those characteristics of the products in question by virtue of which those products are particularly apt to satisfy an inelastic need and are only to a limited extent interchangeable with other products. In order to be regarded as constituting a distinct market, the products in question must be individualized not only by the mere fact that they are used for packing certain products, but by particular characteristics of production which make them specifically suitable for this purpose.

NOTE: Deciding whether a product is interchangeable with another is not always an easy task. To assist in that task, the Commission has published detailed guidance explaining its view of the process. The Commission's practice is not legally binding—merely persuasive.

Commission Notice on Market Definition
OJ C372/5, 1997, paras 7–34

II. Definition of relevant market

Definition of relevant product market and relevant geographic market
[7] The Regulations based on Articles [85] and [86] of the Treaty, in particular in section 6 of Form A/B with respect to Regulation No 17, as well as in section 6 of Form CO with respect to Regulation (EEC) No 4064/89 on the control of concentrations having a Community dimension have laid down the following definitions, 'Relevant product markets' are defined as follows:

'A relevant product market comprises all those products and/or services which are regarded as interchangeable or substitutable by the consumer, by reason of the products' characteristics, their prices and their intended use'.

[8] 'Relevant geographic markets' are defined as follows:

'The relevant geographic market comprises the area in which the undertakings concerned are involved in the supply and demand of products or services, in which the conditions of competition are sufficiently homogeneous and which can be distinguished from neighbouring areas because the conditions of competition are appreciably different in those areas'.

[9] The relevant market within which to assess a given competition issue is therefore established by the combination of the product and geographic markets. The Commission interprets the definitions

in paragraphs 7 and 8 (which reflect the case-law of the Court of Justice and the Court of First Instance as well as its own decision-making practice) according to the orientations defined in this notice. Concept of relevant market and objectives of Community competition policy.

[10] The concept of relevant market is closely related to the objectives pursued under Community competition policy. For example, under the Community's merger control, the objective in controlling structural changes in the supply of a product/service is to prevent the creation or reinforcement of a dominant position as a result of which effective competition would be significantly impeded in a substantial part of the common market. Under the Community's competition rules, a dominant position is such that a firm or group of firms would be in a position to behave to an appreciable extent independently of its competitors, customers and ultimately of its consumers. Such a position would usually arise when a firm or group of firms accounted for a large share of the supply in any given market, provided that other factors analysed in the assessment (such as entry barriers, customers' capacity to react, etc.) point in the same direction.

[11] The same approach is followed by the Commission in its application of Article 86 of the Treaty to firms that enjoy a single or collective dominant position. Within the meaning of Regulation No 17, the Commission has the power to investigate and bring to an end abuses of such a dominant position, which must also be defined by reference to the relevant market. Markets may also need to be defined in the application of Article [85] of the Treaty, in particular, in determining whether an appreciable restriction of competition exists or in establishing if the condition pursuant to Article [85(3)(b)] for an exemption from the application of Article [85(1)] is met.

[12] The criteria for defining the relevant market are applied generally for the analysis of certain types of behaviour in the market and for the analysis of structural changes in the supply of products. This methodology, though, might lead to different results depending on the nature of the competition issue being examined. For instance, the scope of the geographic market might be different when analysing a concentration, where the analysis is essentially prospective, from an analysis of past behaviour. The different time horizon considered in each case might lead to the result that different geographic markets are defined for the same products depending on whether the Commission is examining a change in the structure of supply, such as a concentration or a cooperative joint venture, or examining issues relating to certain past behaviour.

Basic principles for market definition

Competitive constraints

[13] Firms are subject to three main sources or competitive constraints: demand substitutability, supply substitutability and potential competition. From an economic point of view, for the definition of the relevant market, demand substitution constitutes the most immediate and effective disciplinary force on the suppliers of a given product, in particular in relation to their pricing decisions. A firm or a group of firms cannot have a significant impact on the prevailing conditions of sale, such as prices, if its customers are in a position to switch easily to available substitute products or to suppliers located elsewhere. Basically, the exercise of market definition consists in identifying the effective alternative sources of supply for the customers of the undertakings involved, in terms both of products/services and of geographic location of suppliers.

[14] The competitive constraints arising from supply side substitutability other then those described in paragraphs 20 to 23 and from potential competition are in general less immediate and in any case require an analysis of additional factors. As a result such constraints are taken into account at the assessment stage of competition analysis.

Demand substitution

[15] The assessment of demand substitution entails a determination of the range of products which are viewed as substitutes by the consumer. One way of making this determination can be viewed as

a speculative experiment, postulating a hypothetical small, lasting change in relative prices and evaluating the likely reactions of customers to that increase. The exercise of market definition focuses on prices for operational and practical purposes, and more precisely on demand substitution arising from small, permanent changes in relative prices. This concept can provide clear indications as to the evidence that is relevant in defining markets.

[16] Conceptually, this approach means that, starting from the type of products that the undertakings involved sell and the area in which they sell them, additional products and areas will be included in, or excluded from, the market definition depending on whether competition from these other products and areas affect or restrain sufficiently the pricing of the parties' products in the short term.

[17] The question to be answered is whether the parties' customers would switch to readily available substitutes or to suppliers located elsewhere in response to a hypothetical small (in the range 5 per cent to 10 per cent) but permanent relative price increase in the products and areas being considered. If substitution were enough to make the price increase unprofitable because of the resulting loss of sales, additional substitutes and areas are included in the relevant market. This would be done until the set of products and geographical areas is such that small, permanent increases in relative prices would be profitable. The equivalent analysis is applicable in cases concerning the concentration of buying power, where the starting point would then be the supplier and the price test serves to identify the alternative distribution channels or outlets for the supplier's products. In the application of these principles, careful account should be taken of certain particular situations as described within paragraphs 56 and 58.

[18] A practical example of this test can be provided by its application to a merger of, for instance, soft-drink bottlers. An issue to examine in such a case would be to decide whether different flavours of soft drinks belong to the same market. In practice, the question to address would be whether consumers of flavour A would switch to other flavours when confronted with a permanent price increase of 5 per cent to 10 per cent for flavour A. If a sufficient number of consumers would switch to, say, flavour B, to such an extent that the price increase for flavour A would not be profitable owing to the resulting loss of sales, then the market would comprise at least flavours A and B. The process would have to be extended in addition to other available flavours until a set of products is identified for which a price rise would not induce a sufficient substitution in demand.

[19] Generally, and in particular for the analysis of merger cases, the price to take into account will be the prevailing market price. This may not be the case where the prevailing price has been determined in the absence of sufficient competition. In particular for the investigation of abuses of dominant positions, the fact that the prevailing price might already have been substantially increased will be taken into account.

Supply substitution

[20] Supply-side substitutability may also be taken into account when defining markets in those situatons in which its effects are equivalent to those of demand substitution in terms of effectiveness and immediacy. This means that suppliers are able to switch production to the relevant products and market them in the short term without incurring significant additional costs or risks in response to small and permanent changes in relative prices. When these conditions are met, the additional production that is put on the market will have a disciplinary effect on the competitive behaviour of the companies involved. Such an impact in terms of effectiveness and immediacy is equivalent to the demand substitution effect.

[21] These situations typically arise when companies market a wide range of qualities or grades of one product; even if, for a given final customer or group of consumers, the different qualities are not substitutable, the different qualities will be grouped into one product market, provided that most of the suppliers are able to offer and sell the various qualities immediately and without the significant increases in costs described above. In such cases, the relevant product market will encompass all

products that are substitutable in demand and supply, and the current sales of those products will be aggregated so as to give the total value or volume of the market. The same reasoning may lead to group different geographic areas.

[22] A practical example of the approach to supply-side substitutability when defining product markets is to be found in the case of paper. Paper is usually supplied in a range of different qualities, from standard writing paper to high quality papers to be used, for instance, to publish art books. From a demand point of view, different qualities of paper cannot be used for any given use, i.e. an art book or a high quality publication cannot be based on lower quality papers. However, paper plants are prepared to manufacture the different qualities, and production can be adjusted with negligible costs and in a short time-frame. In the absence of particular difficulties in distribution, paper manufacturers are able therefore, to compete for orders of the various qualities, in particular if orders are placed with sufficient lead time to allow for modification of production plans. Under such circumstances, the Commission would not define a separate market for each quality of paper and its respective use. The various qualities of paper are included in the relevant market, and their sales added up to estimate total market value and volume.

[23] When supply-side substitutability would entail the need to adjust significantly existing tangible and intangible assets, additional investments, strategic decisions or time delays, it will not be considered at the stage of market definition. Examples where supply-side substitution did not induce the Commission to enlarge the market are offered in the area of consumer products, in particular for branded beverages. Although bottling plants may in principle bottle different beverages, there are costs and lead times involved (in terms of advertising, product testing and distribution) before the products can actually be sold. In these cases, the effects of supply-side substitutability and other forms of potential competition would then be examined at a later stage.

Potential competition

[24] The third source of competitive constraint, potential competition, is not taken into account when defining markets, since the conditions under which potential competition will actually represent an effective competitive constraint depend on the analysis of specific factors and circumstances related to the conditions of entry. If required, this analysis is only carried out at a subsequent stage, in general once the position of the companies involved in the relevant market has already been ascertained, and when such position gives rise to concerns from a competition point of view.

III. Evidence relied on to define relevant markets

The process of defining the relevant market in practice

Product dimension

[25] There is a range of evidence permitting an assessment of the extent to which substitution would take place. In individual cases, certain types of evidence will be determinant, depending very much on the characteristics and specificity of the industry and products or services that are being examined. The same type of evidence may be of no importance in other cases. In most cases, a decision will have to be based on the consideration of a number of criteria and different items of evidence. The Commission follows an open approach to empirical evidence, aimed at making an effective use of all available information which may be relevant in individual cases. The Commission does not follow a rigid hierarchy of different sources of information or types of evidence.

[26] The process of defining relevant markets may be summarized as follows: on the basis of the preliminary information available or information submitted by the undertakings involved, the Commission will usually be in a position to broadly establish the possible relevant markets within which, for instance, a concentration or a restriction of competition has to be assessed. In general, and for all practical purposes when handling individual cases, the question will usually be to decide on a few alternative possible relevant markets. For instance, with respect to the product market, the issue will

often be to establish whether product A and product B belong or do not belong to the same product market, it is often the case that the inclusion of product B would be enough to remove any competition concerns.

[27] In such situations it is not necessary to consider whether the market includes additional products, or to reach a definitive conclusion on the precise product market. If under the conceivable alternative market definitions the operation in question does not raise competition concerns, the question of market definition will be left open, reducing thereby the burden on companies to supply information.

Geographic dimension

[28] The Commission's approach to geographic market definition might be summarized as follows: it will take a preliminary view of the scope of the geographic market on the basis of broad indications as to the distribution of market shares between the parties and their competitors, as well as a preliminary analysis of pricing and price differences at national and Community or EEA level. This initial view is used basically as a working hypothesis to focus the Commission's enquiries for the purposes of arriving at a precise geographic market definition.

[29] The reasons behind any particular configuration of prices and market shares need to be explored. Companies might enjoy high market shares in their domestic markets just because of the weight of the past, and conversely, a homogeneous presence of companies throughout the EEA might be consistent with national or regional geographic markets. The initial working hypothesis will therefore be checked against an analysis of demand characteristics (importance of national or local preferences, current patterns of purchases of customers, product differentiation/brands, other) in order to establish whether companies in different areas do indeed constitute a real alternative source of supply for consumers. The theoretical experiment is again based on substitution arising from changes in relative prices, and the question to answer is again whether the customers of the parties would switch their orders to companies located elsewhere in the short term and at a negligible cost.

[30] If necessary, a further check on supply factors will be carried out to ensure that those companies located in differing areas do not face impediments in developing their sales on competitive terms throughout the whole geographic market. This analysis will include an examination of requirements for a local presence in order to sell in that area the conditions of access to distribution channels, costs associated with setting up a distribution network, and the presence or absence of regulatory barriers arising from public procurement, price regulations, quotas and tariffs limiting trade or production, technical standards, monopolies, freedom of establishment, requirements for administrative authorizations, packaging regulations, etc. In short, the Commission will identify possible obstacles and barriers isolating companies located in a given area from the competitive pressure of companies located outside that area, so as to determine the precise degree of market interpenetration at national, European or global level.

[31] The actual pattern and evolution of trade flows offers useful supplementary indications as to the economic importance of each demand or supply factor mentioned above, and the extent to which they may or may not constitute actual barriers creating different geographic markets. The analysis of trade flows will generally address the question of transport costs and the extent to which these may hinder trade between different areas, having regard to plant location, costs of production and relative price levels.

Market integration in the Community

[32] Finally, the Commission also takes into account the continuing process of market integration, in particular in the Community, when defining geographic markets, especially in the area of concentrations and structural joint ventures. The measures adopted and implemented in the internal market programme to remove barriers to trade and further integrate the Community markets cannot be

ignored when assessing the effects on competition of a concentration or a structural joint venture. A situation where national markets have been artifically isolated from each other because of the existence of legislative barriers that have now been removed will generally lead to a cautious assessment of past evidence regarding prices, market shares or trade patterns. A process of market integration that would, in the short term, lead to wider geographic markets may therefore be taken into consideration when defining the geographic market for the purposes of assessing concentrations and joint ventures.

The process of gathering evidence

[33] When a precise market definition is deemed necessary, the Commission will often contact the main customers and the main companies in the industry to enquire into their views about the boundaries of product and geographic markets and to obtain the necessary factual evidence to reach a conclusion. The Commission might also contact the relevant professional associations, and companies active in upstream markets, so as to be able to define, in so far as necessary, separate product and geographic markets, for different levels of production or distribution of the products/ services in question. It might also request additional information to the undertakings involved.

[34] Where appropriate, the Commission will address written requests for information to the market players mentioned above. These requests will usually include questions relating to the perceptions of companies about reactions to hypothetical price increases and their views of the boundaries of the relevant market. They will also ask for provision of the factual information the Commission deems necessary to reach a conclusion on the extent of the relevant market. The Commission might also discuss with marketing directors or other officers of those companies to gain a better understanding on how negotiations between suppliers and customers take place and better understand issues relating to the definition of the relevant market. Where appropriate, they might also carry out visits or inspections to the premises of the parties, their customers and/or their competitors, in order to better understand how products are manufactured and sold.

NOTE: The Commission's practice has largely been welcomed, see e.g., Baker, S., and Wu, L., 'Applying the Market Definition Guidelines of the European Commission' [1998] ECLR 273. However, Arnull questions the merits of the Commission's Notice.

Arnull, 'Competition, the Commission and Some Constitutional Questions of More than Minor Importance'
[1998] 23 ELRev 1 [footnotes omitted]

On the vexed question of defining the relevant market, the Commission refers to a Notice devoted to that issue published in the same edition of the Official Journal. That Notice breaks new ground by adopting the so-called SSNIP test developed in the United States in the early 1980s and now applied around the world. SSNIP stands for 'small but significant non-transitory increase in prices' and the test is used to assess demand substitution. As the Commission explains: 'The question to be answered in whether the parties' customers would switch to readily available substitutes or to suppliers located elsewhere in response to a hypothetical small (in the range 5 per cent–10 per cent) but permanent relative price increase in the products and areas being considered'. The Notice goes on to explain the techniques used by the Commission in applying the SSNIP test. Importance is attached to a method known as 'shock analysis', which involves analysing recent events or shocks in the market that offer concrete examples of substitution between two products. The Commission states that this sort of information, when available, 'will normally be fundamental for market definition'. A striking aspect of the Notice is the apparent rejection by the Commission of factors which have traditionally been thought relevant to the definition of the relevant market. The Notice declares: '. . . product characteristics and intended use are insufficient to show whether two products are demand substitutes. Functional interchangeability or similarity in characteristics may not, in themselves, provide sufficient criteria, because the responsiveness of customers to relative price changes may be determined by other considerations as well'.

There are two constitutional difficulties with the burgeoning use by the Commission of instruments such as these. One is that, because such instruments do not in themselves produce any legal effects, their validity cannot be challenged before the Community Courts. Of course, decisions taken pursuant to the policies set out in them are susceptible to review, but by the time a challenge is brought, large numbers of cases may already have been resolved in accordance with the contested policy, even if it is ultimately found to be unlawful. The second difficulty is that the Commission is not required to comply with any external procedural requirements before issuing these instruments. Although it often invites comments before doing so, neither the other institutions nor the authorities of the Member States nor the Advisory Committee on Restrictive Practices and Monopolies have any formal right to be consulted. It seems undesirable for initiatives of such importance taken by a Community institution to lie beyond proper political and judicial scrutiny.

Even the objective of legal certainty may prove elusive. Whatever the theoretical merits of the Commission's new approach to defining the relevant product market, it is not easy to reconcile with the Court's case law on Article 86 EC. Until it is sanctioned by the Community Courts, national judges are likely to find decisions of those Courts more persuasive than a mere notice issued by the Commission. There even appear to be some in the Commission who have yet to be converted to the merits of the new approach. Although the 1997 version of the Notice on agreements of minor importance contains a reference to the Notice of defining the relevant market, it also states that '[t]he relevant product market comprises any products or services which are regarded as interchangeable or substitutable by the consumer, by reason of their characteristics, prices and intended use'. Old habits evidently die hard.

NOTE: While the Commission's views are expressed in the Notice, the jurisprudence of the Court is still invaluable in properly understanding this area.

United Brands v *Commission*
(Case 27/76) [1978] ECR 207, [1978] 1 CMLR 429

> United Brands was the world's largest producer on the world banana market. Its European subsidiary was responsible for coordinating banana sales across the EC, except in the UK and Italy. It was important to decide if the banana market was a market in its own right, or merely a part of the market for fresh fruit.

[12] As far as the product market is concerned it is first of all necessary to ascertain whether, as the applicant maintains, bananas are an integral part of the fresh fruit market, because they are reasonably interchangeable by consumers with other kinds of fresh fruit such as apples, oranges, grapes, peaches, strawberries, etc. Or whether the relevant market consists solely of the banana market which includes both branded bananas and unlabelled bananas and is a market sufficiently homogeneous and distinct from the market of other fresh fruit.

[13] The applicant submits in support of its argument that bananas compete with other fresh fruit in the same shops, on the same shelves, at prices which can be compared, satisfying the same needs: consumption as a dessert or between meals.

[14] The statistics produced show that consumer expenditure on the purchase of bananas is at its lowest between June and December when there is a plentiful supply of domestic fresh fruit on the market.

[15] Studies carried out by the food and agriculture organization (FAO) (especially in 1975) confirm that banana prices are relatively weak during the summer months and that the price of apples for

example has a statistically appreciable impact on the consumption of bananas in the Federal Republic of Germany.

[16] Again according to these studies some easing of prices is noticeable at the end of the year during the 'orange season'.

[17] The seasonal peak periods when there is a plentiful supply of other fresh fruit exert an influence not only on the prices but also on the volume of sales of bananas and consequently on the volume of imports thereof.

[18] The applicant concludes from these findings that bananas and other fresh fruit form only one market and that UBC's operations should have been examined in this context for the purpose of any application of Article 86 of the Treaty.

[19] The Commission maintains that there is a demand for bananas which is distinct from the demand for other fresh fruit especially as the banana is a very important part of the diet of certain sections of the Community.

[20] The specific qualities of the banana influence customer preference and induce him not to readily accept other fruits as a substitute.

[21] The Commission draws the conclusion from the studies quoted by the applicant that the influence of the prices and availabilities of other types of fruit on the prices and availabilities of bananas on the relevant market is very ineffective and that these effects are too brief and too spasmodic for such other fruit to be regarded as forming part of the same market as bananas or as a substitute therefor.

[22] For the banana to be regarded as forming a market which is sufficiently differentiated from other fruit markets it must be possible for it to be singled out by such special features distinguishing it from other fruits that it is only to a limited extent interchangeable with them and is only exposed to their competition in a way that is hardly perceptible.

[23] The ripening of bananas takes place the whole year round without any season having to be taken into account.

[24] Throughout the year production exceeds demand and can satisfy it at any time.

[25] Owing to this particular feature the banana is a privileged fruit and its production and marketing can be adapted to the seasonal fluctuations of other fresh fruit which are known and can be computed.

[26] There is no unavoidable seasonal substitution since the consumer can obtain this fruit all the year round.

[27] Since the banana is a fruit which is always available in sufficient quantities the question whether it can be replaced by other fruits must be determined over the whole of the year for the purpose of ascertaining the degree of competition between it and other fresh fruit.

[28] The studies of the banana market on the court's file show that on the latter market there is no significant long term cross-elasticity any more than—as has been mentioned—there is any seasonal substitutability in general between the banana and all the seasonal fruits, as this only exists between the banana and two fruits (peaches and table grapes) in one of the countries (West Germany) of the relevant geographic market.

[29] As far as concerns the two fruits available throughout the year (oranges and apples) the first are not interchangeable and in the case of the second there is only a relative degree of substitutability.

[30] This small degree of substitutability is accounted for by the specific features of the banana and all the factors which influence consumer choice.

[31] The banana has certain characteristics, appearance, taste, softness, seedlessness, easy handling, a constant level of production which enable it to satisfy the constant needs of an important section of the population consisting of the very young, the old and the sick.

[32] As far as prices are concerned two FAO studies show that the banana is only affected by the prices—falling prices—of other fruits (and only of peaches and table grapes) during the summer months and mainly in July and then by an amount not exceeding 20 per cent.

[33] Although it cannot be denied that during these months and some weeks at the end of the year this product is exposed to competition from other fruits, the flexible way in which the volume of imports and their marketing on the relevant geographic market is adjusted means that the conditions of competition are extremely limited and that its price adapts without any serious difficulties to this situation where supplies of fruit are plentiful.

[34] It follows from all these considerations that a very large number of consumers having a constant need for bananas are not noticeably or even appreciably enticed away from the consumption of this product by the arrival of other fresh fruit on the market and that even the personal peak periods only affect it for a limited period of time and to a very limited extent from the point of view of substitutability.

[35] Consequently the banana market is a market which is sufficiently distinct from the other fresh fruit markets.

NOTE: As can be seen from the discussion in *United Brands*, the key factor in deciding whether bananas were on the same market as other fruit was its interchangeability, sometimes also expressed as substitutability, with other fruit. To analyse that interchangeability, the Court examined the cross-elasticity of demand between fruits, a less technical version of the later SSNIP test, and other factors such as the particular characteristics of the banana to distinguish it from the rest of the fruit market.

Hilti AG v *Commission*
(Case T-30/89) [1991] ECR II-1439, [1992] 4 CMLR 16

Hilti was the largest European producer of PAF nail guns, nails and cartridge strips ('PAF' stands for 'powder-actuated fastening'). Following complaints from undertakings supplying Hilti compatible nails, that they were being excluded from the market by Hilti's behaviour, the Commission instigated an investigation. The Commission found Hilti to be dominant on the nail gun, cartridge strip, and nail markets. Hilti appealed to the Court of First Instance.

Legal appraisal
[64] It should be observed at the outset that in order to assess Hilti's market position it is first necessary to define the relevant market, since the possibilities of competition can only be judged in relation to those characteristics of the products in question by virtue of which those products are particularly apt to satisfy an inelastic need and are only to a limited extent interchangeable with other products (judgment of the Court of Justice of 21 February 1973 in Case 6/72 *Continental Can*, paragraph 32).

[65] In order to determine, therefore, whether Hilti, as a supplier of nail guns and of consumables designed for them, enjoys such power over the relevant product market as to give it a dominant position within the meaning of Article 86, the first question to be answered is whether the relevant market is the market for all construction fastening systems or whether the relevant markets are those for PAF tools and the consumables designed for them, namely cartridge strips and nails.

[66] The Court takes the view that nail guns, cartridge strips and nails constitute three specific markets. Since cartridge strips and nails are specifically manufactured, and purchased by users, for a single brand of gun, it must be concluded that there are separate markets for Hilti-compatible cartridge strips and nails, as the Commission found in its decision (paragraph 55).

[67] With particular regard to the nails whose use in Hilti tools is an essential element of the dispute, it is common ground that since the 1960s there have been independent producers, including the interveners, making nails intended for use in nail guns. Some of those producers are specialized and produce only nails, and indeed some make only nails specifically designed for Hilti tools. That fact in itself is sound evidence that there is a specific market for Hilti-compatible nails.

[68] Hilti's contention that guns, cartridge strips and nails should be regarded as forming an indivisible whole, 'a powder-actuated fastening system' is in practice tantamount to permitting producers of nail guns to exclude the use of consumables other than their own branded products in their tools. However, in the absence of general and binding standards or rules, any independent producer is quite free, as far as Community competition law is concerned, to manufacture consumables intended for use in equipment manufactured by others, unless in doing so it infringes a patent or some other industrial or intellectual property right. Even on the assumption that, as the applicant has argued, components of different makes cannot be interchanged without the system characteristics being influenced, the solution should lie in the adoption of appropriate laws and regulations, not in unilateral measures taken by nail gun producers which have the effect of preventing independent producers from pursuing the bulk of their business.

[69] Hilti's argument that PAF tools and consumables form part of the market in PAF systems for the construction industry generally cannot be accepted either. The Court finds that PAF systems differ from other fastening systems in several important respects. The specific features of PAF systems, set out in paragraph 62 of the Decision, are such as to make them the obvious choice in a number of cases. It is evident from the documents before the Court that in many cases there is no realistic alternative either for a qualified operator carrying out a job on site or for a technician instructed to select the fastening methods to be used in a given situation.

[70] The Court considers that the Commission's description of those features in its decision is sufficiently clear and convincing to provide sound legal justification for the conclusions drawn from it.

[71] Those findings leave no real doubt as to the existence, in practice, of a variety of situations, some of which inherently favour the use of a PAF system whilst others favour one or more other fastening systems. As the Commission notes, the fact that several different fastening methods have each continued for long periods to account for an important share of total demand for fastening systems shows that there is only a relatively low degree of substitutability between them.

[72] In such circumstances the Commission was entitled to base its conclusions on arguments which took account of the qualitative characteristics of the products at issue.

[73] Its conclusions are, moreover, corroborated by the opinion prepared by Mr Yarrow and the survey conducted by Rosslyn Research Ltd, mentioned above, inasmuch as they disclose the existence of a large number of nail gun users who could see no realistic alternative to the PAF system in circumstances corresponding to most of those in which nail guns have in fact been used.

[74] Moreover, the evidence produced by the applicant is not such as to weaken the findings made by the Commission.

[75] In the first place it must be observed that the opinion of Mr Yarrow and the survey by Rosslyn Research Ltd do not demonstrate—as their authors claim—a high degree of economic substitutability between the relevant products. The questions put to construction undertakings are not apt to provide an answer to the fundamental question in this case, namely whether slight but significant differences in the price of nails are likely to shift demand to a significant extent. In a market in which, as here, very large discounts on catalogue prices are common, the mere fact that a number of those questioned referred first to price as a decisive factor, without elaborating on the impact which a change in price would have on the choice of method to be used, cannot prove that there is a high degree of cross-price-elasticity.

[76] In the second place, it may be noted that Professor Albach's econometric analyses take account of only one factor—price—when it is clear from the documents before the Court, in particular the survey conducted by Rosslyn Research Ltd, that the choice of the consumer depends to a large extent on unquantifiable circumstances.

[77] The conclusion must be that the relevant product market in relation to which Hilti's market position must be appraised is the market for nails designed for Hilti nail guns.

[78] That finding is corroborated by the above mentioned letter of 23 March 1983 from Hilti to the Commission, in which the opinion was expressed that there were separate markets for guns, cartridge strips and nails. Although that did not, at the time, represent an interpretation of the term 'relevant market' for the purposes of Article 86 of the Treaty, the content of the letter is nevertheless quite revealing as to Hilti's own commercial view of the markets in which it operated at the time. Hilti has explained that the letter was prepared by an in-house lawyer, in conjunction with an outside legal adviser and the product manager concerned. The letter was therefore drafted by persons who may be assumed to have had a sound knowledge of the undertaking and its business.

NOTE: In *Hilti* the Court had to decide on two questions. First, whether PAFs, such as nail guns, were interchangeable with other fastening systems, such as drilling and screwing. And, second, whether there were separate markets for nail guns and its consumables, cartridge strips and nails, or if they were to be considered as a single product market for the whole PAF system. The Court decided there was no sufficient interchangeability with other fastening systems on the basis of the particular characteristics of the nail gun and its suitability for particular uses over other systems. The second argument was more controversial: the Court decided that there were three separate markets for nail guns, Hilti cartridge strips, and Hilti compatible nails. The evidence upon which they based their decision was largely that there were several competing producers of Hilti compatible nails, whose complaints brought about the Commission investigation. This finding has been challenged by a number of commentators. See e.g. Price, D.R., 'Abuse of a Dominant Position—The Tale of Nails, Milk Cartons and TV Guides' [1990] ECLR 80. Many would argue that any attempt to exploit Hilti customers by raising the price of Hilti consumables would quickly result in customers switching to use other brands of nail gun. This is particularly the case where the cost of consumables is relatively high compared to the cost of the original product. Similar arguments may also arise with other related products such as photocopiers and their related toner cartridges.

Nederlandsche Banden-Industrie Michelin NV v *Commission*
(Case 322/81) [1983] ECR 3461, [1985] 1 CMLR 282

Complaints were made regarding Michelin's policies towards tyre dealers, especially regarding the discounts and bonuses granted to them. As Michelin produced tyres for a wide range of vehicles and sold to manufacturers and retailers, it was important to define correctly the market in question.

[37] As the court has repeatedly emphasized, most recently in its judgment of 11 December 1980 in Case 31/80 *NV l'Oreal and SA l'Oreal* v *PVBA de Nieuwe Amck* (1980) ECR 3775, for the purposes of investigating the possibly dominant position of an undertaking on a given market, the possibilities of competition must be judged in the context of the market comprising the totality of the products which, with respect to their characteristics, are particularly suitable for satisfying constant needs and are only to a limited extent interchangeable with other products. However, it must be noted that the determination of the relevant market is useful in assessing whether the undertaking concerned is in a position to prevent effective competition from being maintained and behave to an appreciable extent independently of its competitors and customers and consumers. For this purpose, therefore,

an examination limited to the objective characteristics only of the relevant products cannot be sufficient: the competitive conditions and the structure of supply and demand on the market must also be taken into consideration.

[38] Moreover, it was for that reason that the Commission and Michelin NV agreed that new, original-equipment tyres should not be taken into consideration in the assessment of market shares. Owing to the particular structure of demand for such tyres characterized by direct orders from car manufacturers, competition in this sphere is in fact governed by completely different factors and rules.

[39] As far as replacement tyres are concerned, the first point which must be made is that at the user level there is no interchangeability between car and van tyres on the one hand and heavy-vehicle tyres on the other. Car and van tyres therefore have no influence at all on competition on the market in heavy-vehicle tyres.

[40] Furthermore, the structure of demand for each of those groups of products is different. Most buyers of heavy-vehicle tyres are trade users, particularly haulage undertakings, for whom, as the Commission explained, the purchase of replacement tyres represents an item of considerable expenditure and who constantly ask their tyre dealers for advice and long-term specialized services adapted to their specific needs. On the other hand, for the average buyer of car or van tyres the purchase of tyres is an occasional event and even if the buyer operates a business he does not expect such specialized advice and service adapted to specific needs. Hence the sale of heavy-vehicle tyres requires a particularly specialized distribution network which is not the case with the distribution of car and van tyres.

[41] The final point which must be made is that there is no elasticity of supply between tyres for heavy vehicles and car tyres owing to significant differences in production techniques and in the plant and tools needed for their manufacture. The fact that time and considerable investment are required in order to modify production plant for the manufacture of light-vehicle tyres instead of heavy-vehicle tyres or vice versa means that there is no discernible relationship between the two categories of tyre enabling production to be adapted to demand on the market. Moreover, that was why in 1977, when the supply of tyres for heavy vehicles was insufficient, Michelin NV decided to grant an extra bonus instead of using surplus production capacity for car tyres to meet demand.

[42] The Commission rightly examined the structure of the market and demand primarily at the level of dealers to whom Michelin NV applied the practice in question. Michelin NV has itself stated, although in another context, that it was compelled to change its discount system to take account of the tendency towards specialization amongst its dealers, some of whom, such as garage owners, no longer sold tyres for heavy vehicles and vans. This confirms the differences existing in the structure of demand between different groups of dealers. Nor has Michelin NV disputed that the distinction drawn between tyres for heavy vehicles, vans and cars is also applied by all its competitors, especially as regards discount terms, even if in the case of certain types of tyre the distinctions drawn by different manufacturers may vary in detail.

[43] Nevertheless, it cannot be deduced from the fact that the conduct to which exception is taken in this case affects dealers that Michelin NV's position ought to be assessed on the basis of the proportion of Michelin heavy-vehicle tyres in the dealers' total turnover. Since it is a question of investigating whether Michelin NV holds a dominant position in the case of certain products, it is unimportant that the dealers also deal in other products if there is no competition between those products and the products in question.

[44] On the other hand, in deciding whether a dominant position exists, neither the absence of elasticity of supply between different types and dimensions of tyres for heavy vehicles, which is due to differences in the conditions of production, nor the absence of interchangeability and elasticity of demand between those types and dimensions of tyre from the point of view of the specific needs

of the user allow a number of smaller markets, reflecting those types and dimensions, to be distinguished, as Michelin NV suggests. Those differences between different types and dimensions of tyre are not vitally important for dealers, who must meet demand from customers for the whole range of heavy-vehicle tyres. Furthermore, in the absence of any specialization on the part of the undertakings concerned, such differences in the type and dimensions of a product are not a crucial factor in the assessment of an undertaking's market position because in view of their similarity and the manner in which they complement one another at the technical level, the conditions of competition on the market are the same for all the types and dimensions of the product.

[45] In establishing that Michelin NV has a dominant position the Commission was therefore right to assess its market share with reference to replacement tyres for lorries, buses and similar vehicles and to exclude consideration of car and van tyres.

NOTE: In this decision the Court focused on the structure of supply and demand to assist it in the proper delineation of the market. Interchangeability of supply is also important to the market, as if other suppliers could easily enter the market, they must be considered as being potential competitors within the product market. In this case, suppliers of car and van tyres could not easily switch production to heavy-vehicle tyres and therefore they could be discounted from that market. The structure of demand was also important, as the Court was able to differentiate between original equipment tyres, which are fitted to cars as they are manufactured, and replacement cars, fitted by car owners once the original tyres are worn. Although the products are identical, the way in which demand operates, between individual purchases and manufacturer bulk purchases, is very different allowing the markets to be treated separately.

Continental Can v *Commission*
(Case 6/72) [1973] ECR 215, [1973] CMLR 199

> Continental Can acquired majority stakes in a German company and a Dutch company. The Commission challenged these acquisitions as the abuse of a dominant position.

[31] The applicant contests the exactitude of the data on which the Commission bases its Decision. It cannot be concluded from SLW's market share, amounting to 70 to 80 per cent in meat cans, 80 to 90 per cent in cans for fish and crustacea and 50 to 55 per cent in metal closures with the exception of crown corks—percentages which moreover are too high and could not be proved by the defendant—that this undertaking dominates the market for light metal containers. The Decision, moreover, excluded the possibility of competition arising from substitute products (glass and plastic containers) relying on reasons which do not stand up to examination. The statements about possibilities of real and potential competition as well as about the allegedly weak position of the consumers are therefore, in the applicants' view, irrelevant.

[32] For the appraisal of SLW's dominant position and the consequences of the disputed merger, the definition of the relevant market is of essential significance, for the possibilities of competition can only be judged in relation to those characteristics of the products in question by virtue of which those products are particularly apt to satisfy an inelastic need and are only to a limited extent interchangeable with other products.

[33] In this context recitals Nos 5 to 7 of the second part of the Decision deal in turn with a 'market for light containers for canned meat products', a 'market for light containers for canned seafood', and a 'market for metal closures for the food packing industry, other than crown corks', all allegedly dominated by SLW and in which the disputed merger threatens to eliminate competition. The Decision does not, however, give any details of how these three markets differ from each other, and

must therefore be considered separately. Similarly, nothing is said about how these three markets differ from the general market for light metal containers, namely the market for metal containers for fruit and vegetables, condensed milk, olive oil, fruit juices and chemico-technical products. In order to be regarded as constituting a distinct market, the products in question must be individualized, not only by the mere fact that they are used for packing certain products, but by particular character-istics of production which make them specificialy suitable for this purpose. Consequently, a domin-ant position on the market for light metal containers for meat and fish cannot be decisive, as long as it has not been proved that competitors from other sectors of the market for light metal containers are not in a position to enter this market, by a simple adaptation, with sufficient strength to create a serious counterweight.

NOTE: This judgment shows the vital importance of correctly defining the market in respect of both supply and demand sides. Because the Commission had failed satisfactorily to adduce evidence to support its findings the Court quashed its Decision.

D: Geographic market

Once the product market is correctly defined it is necessary to define the geo-graphical extent of the market. Some markets will be necessarily localised, while others may be global. Such a decision will have an obvious impact on the level of competition on a market.

United Brands v *Commission*
(Case 27/76) [1978] ECR 207, [1978] 1 CMLR 429

As United Brands were not active in certain EC markets the inclusion of those markets would have weakened the argument that they were in a dominant position.

[44] The conditions for the application of Article 86 to an undertaking in a dominant position presuppose the clear delimitation of the substantial part of the common market in which it may be able to engage in abuses which hinder effective competition and this is an area where the objective conditions of competition applying to the product in question must be the same for all traders.

[45] The Community has not established a common organization of the agricultural market in bananas.

[46] Consequently import arrangements vary considerably from one Member State to another and reflect a specific commercial policy peculiar to the states concerned.

[47] This explains why for example the French market owing to its national organization is re-stricted upstream by a particular import arrangement and obstructed downstream by a retail price monitored by the administration.

[48] This market, in addition to adopting certain measures relating to a 'target price' (*'prix objectif'*) fixed each year and to packaging and grading standards and the minimum qualities required, reserves about two thirds of the market for the production of the overseas departments and one third to that of certain countries enjoying preferential relations with France (Ivory Coast, Madagas-car, Cameroon) the bananas whereof are imported duty-free, and it includes a system the running of which is entrusted to the *'comite interprofessionnel bananier'* ('c.i.b.').

[49] The United Kingdom market enjoys 'commonwealth preferences', a system of which the main feature is the maintenance of a level of production favouring the developing countries of the

commonwealth and of a price paid to the associations of producers directly linked to the selling price of the green banana charged in the United Kingdom.

[50] On the Italian market, since the abolition in 1965 of the state monopoly responsible for marketing bananas, a national system of quota restrictions has been introduced, the ministry for shipping and the exchange control office supervising the imports and the charterparties relating to the foreign ships which carry the bananas.

[51] The effect of the national organization of these three markets is that the applicant's bananas do not compete on equal terms with the other bananas sold in these states which benefit from a preferential system and the Commission was right to exclude these three national markets from the geographic market under consideration.

[52] On the other hand the six other states are markets which are completely free, although the applicable tariff provisions and transport costs are of necessity different but not discriminatory, and in which the conditions of competition are the same for all.

[53] From the standpoint of being able to engage in free competition these six states form an area which is sufficiently homogeneous to be considered in its entirety.

[54] UBC has arranged for its subsidiary in Rotterdam—UBCBV—to market its products. UBCBV is for this purpose a single centre for the whole of this part of the Community.

[55] Transport costs do not in fact stand in the way of the distribution policy chosen by UBC which consists in selling f.o.r. Rotterdam and Bremerhaven, the two ports where the bananas are unloaded.

[56] These are factors which go to make relevant market a single market.

[57] It follows from all these considerations that the geographic market as determined by the Commission which constitutes a substantial part of the common market must be regarded as the relevant market for the purpose of determining whether the applicant may be in a dominant position.

NOTE: The Court confirmed that the special characteristics of the markets in France, Italy, and the UK meant that those markets operated in very different ways to the rest of the Community. As Community markets become increasingly integrated, it is likely that many markets will be Community wide, but in a number of cases, because of the particular nature of the some products, markets will still be locally defined, see e.g. *Sealink/B&I-Holyhead: Interim Measures* [1992] 5 CMLR 255.

E: Temporal market

Markets may also need to be defined in terms of time. It may be the case that the market conditions considered were limited in time or operate on a seasonal basis.

Commission Decision (77/327/EEC)
ABG, OJ L117/1, 1977, [1977] 2 CMLR D1

Firms hold a dominant position where they are able to act fully independently—in other words where they may conduct their business without regard for the reactions of competitors and customers. This can happen when general economic circumstances and particular market conditions combine so that firms with an established market position, access to raw materials and adequate industrial capacity and capital resources find themselves in a position to control production and distribution in a substantial proportion of the market.

The market under consideration is that of motor spirit.

The general economic scene was set towards 1 November 1973 with the outbreak of the oil crisis, which was caused by a simultaneous reduction in the supply of oil offered on the world market combined with a substantial increase in the price demanded for it.

In this situation, the only people who still had access to oil supplies at economically viable prices were the large international oil companies refining or having oil refined in the Netherlands. This was because of their special relationships with the oil-producing countries of the Middle East, their integrated structures and the multinational nature of their installations and organizations.

Such a sudden shortage, especially one that was not brought about by economic considerations, led to a restriction of both actual and potential competition among the small group of companies concerned, a restriction that was particularly marked at the level of distribution.

The general fear of shortage, the sudden reduction in supplies of oil offered and the fact that the maximum prices for motor spirit fixed by the Dutch government were below international prices meant that the independent firms in the Netherlands could only obtain supplies from the world market at prices giving rise to losses; hence they could no longer import petroleum products in large quantities without endangering their longer-term survival. Imports were no longer available on the Dutch market and the independent buyers could only obtain their supplies from companies with refineries in the Netherlands. Thus, the relevant market for this case is the Netherlands, which constitutes a substantial part of the common market.

Economic restrictions such as existed in the Netherlands during the oil crisis can substantially alter existing commercial relations between suppliers who have a substantial share of the market and quantities available and their customers. For reasons completely outside the control of the normal suppliers, their customers can become completely dependent on them for the supply of scarce products. Thus, while the situation continues, the suppliers are placed in a dominant position in respect of their normal customers.

With the general shortage of supplies, all the oil companies were faced with the same problem—that of maintaining supplies to their regular customers. Thus, they were not able to make up the deficiencies of the other companies with substantial market shares and they were in no way in competition with each other to supply each other's customers.

In the prevailing circumstances each of these companies found itself in a dominant position relative to its customers.

NOTE: The Commission made it clear that the Decision was limited to the time during the 1970s oil crisis when petrol supplies could only be acquired in the Netherlands from the limited number of refineries within that Member State. The dramatic change from the normal conditions of the market meant that it was only proper that the market be differentiated from 'normal market conditions' that existed before and after the crisis. Another discussion of a possible temporal limit to the market can be seen in *United Brands*, discussed above, where the Court eventually rejected a claim that the banana market was affected by the seasonal nature of competitor fruit such as oranges or apples.

F: Dominance

Once the correct market has been established it is then possible to examine that market to see if the undertaking under investigation is in a dominant position. The classic definition of dominance was expounded by the Court in:

United Brands v *Commission*
(Case 27/76) [1978] ECR 207, [1978] 1 CMLR 429

[63] Article 86 is an application of the general objective of the activities of the Commission laid down by Article 3(f) of the Treaty: the institution of a system ensuring that competition in the Common Market is not distorted.

[64] This Article prohibits any abuse by an undertaking of a dominant position in a substantial part of the Common Market in so far as it may affect trade between member-States.

[65] The dominant position referred to in this Article relates to a position of economic strength enjoyed by an undertaking which enables it to prevent effective competition being maintained on the relevant market by giving it the power to behave to an appreciable extent independently of its competitors, customers and ultimately of its consumers.

[66] In general a dominant position derives from a combination of several factors which, taken separately, are not necessarily determinative.

NOTE: This definition largely corresponds with the economic understanding of a 'price-maker', an undertaking which no longer takes its price from the market but can independently make its own price. But the definition itself gives little indication of the correct manner in which to establish the existence of dominance. The Court has developed a number of important factors which should be taken into account when examining the position of an undertaking, but as it notes in para. 66, none of those factors is necessarily determinative.

Hoffmann-La Roche v *Commission*
(Case 85/76) [1979] ECR 461, [1979] 3 CMLR 211

> La Roche were the largest producer of vitamins within the Community and were challenged by the Commission for a number of allegedly abusive discounting practices within a number of vitamin markets.

[38] Article 86 is an application of the general objective of the activities of the Community laid down by Article 3(f) of the Treaty, namely, the institution of a system ensuring that competition in the Common Market is not distorted. Article 86 prohibits any abuse by an undertaking of a dominant position in a substantial part of the Common Market in so far as it may affect trade between Member States. The dominant position thus referred to relates to a position of economic strength enjoyed by an undertaking which enables it to prevent effective competition being maintained on the relevant market by affording it the power to behave to an appreciable extent independently of its competitors, its customers and ultimately of the consumers.

[39] Such a position does not preclude some competition, which it does where there is a monopoly or a quasi-monopoly, but enables the undertaking which profits by it, if not to determine, at least to have an appreciable influence on the conditions under which that competition will develop, and in any case to act largely in disregard of it so long as such conduct does not operate to its detriment. A dominant position must also be distinguished from parallel courses of conduct which are peculiar to oligopolies in that in an oligopoly the courses of conduct interact, while in the case of an undertaking occupying a dominant position the conduct of the undertaking which derives profits from that position is to a great extent determined unilaterally. The existence of a dominant position may derive from several factors which, taken separately, are not necessarily determinative but among these factors a highly important one is the existence of very large market shares.

[40] A substantial market share as evidence of the existence of a dominant position is not a constant factor and its importance varies from market to market according to the structure of

those markets, especially as far as production, supply and demand are concerned. Even though each group of vitamins constitutes a separate market, these different markets, as has emerged from the examination of their structure, nevertheless have a sufficient number of features in common to make it possible for the same criteria to be applied to them as far as concerns the importance of the market shares for the purpose of determining whether there is a dominant position or not.

[41] Furthermore although the importance of the market shares may vary from one market to another the view may legitimately be taken that very large shares are in themselves, and save in exceptional circumstances, evidence of the existence of a dominant position. An undertaking which has a very large market share and holds it for some time, by means of the volume of production and the scale of the supply which it stands for—without those having much smaller market shares being able to meet rapidly the demand from those who would like to break away from the undertaking which has the largest market share—is by virtue of that share in a position of strength which makes it an unavoidable trading partner and which already because of this secures for it, at the very least during relatively long periods, that freedom of action which is the special feature of a dominant position.

NOTE: As can be seen from this judgment, the Court puts great store in market shares as an indication of market strength. The larger the market share, the stronger an undertaking must be in comparison to its competitors in that market. Market share is usually established by calculating the undertaking's share of total sales in the relevant market. See also Articles 9 and 10 of Commission Regulation 2790/1999/EC, OJ, L336/21, 1999.

AKZO Chemie BV v *Commission*
(Case C-62/86) [1991] ECR I-3359, [1993] 5 CMLR 215

AKZO was a large Dutch chemicals group who were active on the market for flour additives. It was accused of abusing its position on the market to exclude a competitor, ECS.

[59] It should be further observed that according to its own internal documents AKZO had a stable market share of about 50 per cent from 1979 to 1982 (Annexes 2 and 4 to the statement of objections and Table A annexed to that statement). Furthermore, AKZO has not adduced any evidence to show that its share decreased during subsequent years.

[60] With regard to market shares the Court has held that very large shares are in themselves, and save in exceptional circumstances, evidence of the existence of a dominant position: Case 85/76, *Hoffmann-La Roche* v *EC Commission* ([1979] ECR 461, [1979] 3 CMLR 211, at para. [41]). That is the situation where there is a market share of 50 per cent such as that found to exist in this case.

NOTE: The *AKZO* judgment sets out an important 'rule of thumb' which is still used in many instances. There is a presumption that a market share of 50 per cent gives rise to a presumption of dominance. Such a presumption could, of course, be rebutted if the undertaking could adduce evidence to indicate that its apparent strength shown by its market share does not in reality give rise to dominance and true independence. A number of the reasons why apparent market strength may not lead to dominance are discussed later in the chapter. See Barriers to Entry, below at p. 313.

United Brands v *Commission*

(Case 27/76) [1978] ECR 207, [1978] 1 CMLR 429

> During the Court's discussion of United Brands' dominance on the banana market it considered market shares to be important, but other factors were also considered.

[105] In the second place the Commission states that it estimates UBC's market share at 45 per cent.

[106] However UBC points out that this share dropped to 41 per cent in 1975.

[107] A trader can only be in a dominant position on the market for a product if he has succeeded in winning a large part of this market.

[108] Without going into a discussion about percentages, which when fixed are bound to be to some extent approximations, it can be considered to be an established fact that UBC's share of the relevant market is always more than 40 per cent and nearly 45 per cent.

[109] This percentage does not however permit the conclusion that UBC automatically controls the market.

[110] It must be determined having regard to the strength and number of the competitors.

[111] It is necessary first of all to establish that on the whole of the relevant market the said percentage represents *grosso modo* a share several times greater than that of its competitor Castle and Cooke which is the best placed of all the competitors, the others coming far behind.

[112] This fact together with the others to which attention has already been drawn may be regarded as a factor which affords evidence of UBC's preponderant strength.

[113] However an undertaking does not have to have eliminated all opportunity for competition in order to be in a dominant position.

[114] In this case there was in fact a very lively competitive struggle on several occasions in 1973 as Castle and Cooke had mounted a large-scale advertising and promotion campaign with price rebates on the Danish and German markets.

[115] At the same time Alba cut prices and offered promotional material.

[116] Recently the competition of the Villeman et Tas firm on the Netherlands market has been so lively that prices have dropped below those on the German market which are traditionally the lowest.

[117] It must however be recorded that in spite of their exertions these firms have not succeeded in increasing their market share on the national markets where they launched their attacks.

[118] It must be noted that these periods of competition limited in time and space did not cover the whole of the relevant market.

[119] Even if the local attacks of some competitors can be described as 'fierce' it can only be placed on record that UBC held out against them successfully either by adapting its prices for the time being (in the Netherlands in answer to the challenge from Villeman et Tas) or by bringing indirect pressure to bear on the intermediaries.

[120] Furthermore if UBC's position on each of the national markets concerned is considered it emerges that, except in Ireland, it sells direct and also, as far as concerns Germany, indirectly through Scipio, almost twice as many bananas as the best placed competitor and that there is no appreciable fall in its sales figures even when new competitors appear on these markets.

[121] UBC's economic strength has thus enabled it to adopt a flexible overall strategy directed against new competitors establishing themselves on the whole of the relevant market.

NOTE: Although United Brands' market share fell below the 50 per cent threshold discussed in

AKZO, the Court had no problem establishing that a market share between 40 and 45 per cent could indicate dominance. By examining the market shares of all operating on the banana market it became clear that United Brands had a significant advantage compared to its nearest rival, which had a market share of 16 per cent, and its other competitors were in a much weaker position. Even with a market share of only 40 per cent, that meant that United Brands could exert considerable strength over the market. The judgment in *United Brands* has led to the adoption of another rule of thumb, that undertakings with market shares over 40 per cent should be very careful as to their position as they may well be considered dominant. But such a finding could be easily challenged if another competitive undertaking had a market share approaching 30 per cent to counterbalance the strength of the suspect undertaking.

Several other rules of thumb appear to be developing. If an undertaking has a very low market share, below 20 per cent, it is highly likely that they will not be considered dominant, even if the nearerst competitor is considerably weaker. Another, very different, result may occur if an undertaking has a very strong position with a market share reaching very high levels, perhaps as high as 80 per cent. The Court has suggested that undertakings with very high market shares may be treated differently from those who are in a less strong position.

Irish Sugar plc v *Commission*
(Case T-228/97) [1999] ECR II-2969, [1999] 5 CMLR 1300

Irish Sugar was the sole producer of sugar beet in Ireland and Northern Ireland and was challenged by the Commission, *inter alia*, for abusing its position through the use of targeted rebates. During the period in question, the suspect undertaking held an 88 per cent share of the retail sugar market.

[188] In this case, the applicant has been unable to establish an objective economic justification for the rebates. They were given to certain customers in the retail sugar market by reference solely to their exposure to competition resulting from cheap imports from another Member State and, in this case, by reference to their being established along the border with Northern Ireland. It also appears, according to the applicant's own statements, that it was able to practise such price rebates owing to the particular position it held on the Irish market. Thus, it states that it was unable to practise such rebates over the whole of Irish territory owing to the financial losses it was making at the time. It follows that, by the applicant's own admission, its economic capacity to offer rebates in the region along the border with Northern Ireland depended on the stability of its prices in other regions, which amounts to recognition that it financed those rebates by means of its sales in the rest of Irish territory. By conducting itself in that way, the applicant abused its dominant position in the retail sugar market in Ireland, by preventing the development of free competition on that market and distorting its structures, in relation to both purchasers and consumers. The latter were not able to benefit, outside the region along the border with Northern Ireland, from the price reductions caused by the imports of sugar from Northern Ireland.

[189] Thus, even if the existence of a dominant position does not deprive an undertaking placed in that position of the right to protect its own commercial interests when they are threatened (see paragraph [112] above), the protection of the commercial position of an undertaking in a dominant position with the characteristics of that of the applicant at the time in question must, at the very least, in order to be lawful, be based on criteria of economic efficiency and consistent with the interests of consumers. In this case, the applicant has not shown that those conditions were fulfilled.

NOTE: It is not immediately apparent from para. 189 that the Court is potentially developing a new doctrine, but some commentators have suggested that the reference to undertakings in a dominant position 'with the characteristics of that of the applicant at the time in question', is a reference to undertakings with very high market shares and are therefore in, what is sometimes referred to as, a 'super-dominant' position, see Sufrin, B., 'The Chapter II Prohibition', in Rodger, B.J., and MacCulloch, A. (eds), *The UK Competition Act: A New Era for UK Competition Law*, Oxford, Hart Publishing, 2000. Although an undertaking's 'super dominance' usually results in a stricter definition of abuse, it appears clear that the stronger the market position of an undertaking, the more strictly they will be controlled by Community competition law.

G: Barriers to entry

Market strength, as usually denoted by market share, does not in itself establish dominance. For an undertaking to have true market power, it must be in a position to protect that strength over time. If an undertaking has a high market share, it merely gives a snapshot of its current position and does not indicate its ability to maintain that position. Even if an undertaking has retained a high market share for a lengthy period, it does not mean that it is effectively constrained by competition. One of the key aspects of establishing dominance is not the pressure from existing competitors, as that will be indicated by market share over time, but potential competition from undertakings which are not currently active on the market. If potential competitors could enter a market quickly, their potential competition would constrain the activities of the current market leader. Therefore, any barrier which makes entry to a market difficult is very important in establishing if an undertaking has true dominance.

The precise meaning of the term 'barriers to entry' has proved controversial. We will first examine the economic debate that began in the United States in the 1970s.

Bork, R.H., *The Antitrust Paradox*
New York, Free Press, 1993, pp. 310 and 328

We may begin by asking what a 'barrier to entry' is. There appears to be no precise definition, and in current usage a 'barrier' often seems to be anything that makes the entry of new firms into an industry more difficult. It is at once apparent that an ambiguity lurks in the concept, and it is this ambiguity that causes the trouble. When existing firms are efficient and possess valuable plants, equipment, knowledge, skill, and reputation, potential entrants will find it correspondingly more difficult to enter the industry, since they must acquire those things. It is harder to enter the steel industry than the business of retailing shoes or pizzas, and it is harder to enter either of these fields than to become a suburban handyman. But these difficulties are natural; they inhere in the nature of the tasks to be performed. There can be no objection to barriers of this sort. Their existence means only that when market power is achieved by means other than efficiency, entry will not dissipate the objectionable power instantaneously, and law may therefore have a role to play. If entry were instantaneous, market forces would break up cartels before a typist in the Antitrust Division could rap out a form complaint. Antitrust is valuable because in some cases it can achieve results more rapidly than can market forces. We need not suffer losses while waiting for the market to erode cartels and monopolistic mergers . . .

The concept of barriers to entry is badly misunderstood. We have seen that the confusion of natural barriers with artificial barriers has led to a number of mistaken decisions. It leads economists to suppose that ordinary market forces do not control the structure of industries, and hence to recommend governmental intervention or investigation. A final example—dozens could be chosen—is Mark Schupack's application of the ideas of Bain:

'Consider what a potential entrant to the automobile industry would have to face in order to successfully overcome the product differentiation barrier. It would have to undertake heavy advertising expenditures to woo consumers away from other firms where they have already established some brand loyalty. It would have to spend money to differentiate its product successfully from closely related automobiles. It would have to undertake annual model changes. And perhaps most important, it would have to build a large nationwide network of dealers who are pretty much committed to the new manufacturer's products.'

This catalogue is intended to suggest that competition would not necessarily shape the structure of the automobile industry, that something artificial, something other than the efficiency of existing firms, keeps potential entrants out. Schupack might just as well have said: the new entrant would have to make an automobile with appealing features, change models to keep up with competition, spend money to inform consumers of what it had to sell, and find people who thought the car would sell well enough to make it profitable to retail and service the product. He might, with equal pertinence, have added that the entrant would also have to build a plant, hire engineers, sales experts, designers, accountants, lawyers, and managers, buy steel and fabric and paint, and so on. He actually says nothing more than that a new entrant would have to do the things other companies have found essential to please consumers. In that respect, there is no difference whatever between advertising or finding dealers and building a plant.

This is true of any and all industries. Where the product and its service are complex and expensive, it is natural that the entrant will have to do many complex and expensive things, and do them well, in order to succeed. These are natural barriers or costs of entry. To identify them is merely to make a descriptive statement, one that does not imply the propriety of invoking law to alter the size or behavior of firms already in the market.

The argument of this chapter in no way suggests that there are no artificial barriers to entry. It does suggest that the only artificial barriers of interest to antitrust are those capable of creation by private parties, and that such barriers are always instances of deliberate predation. The next two chapters deal with types of predation that may be employed either to block entry or to injure existing rivals. Unlike the faulty theory of entry barriers now in vogue, however, the possibility of predation does not require or justify such steps as prohibiting mergers or outlawing the vertical division of dealer territories. Prophylactic rules for predation are not justified, as we have seen, and the law should concern itself with entry blocking only in those instances where a deliberate attempt to block entry by means other than efficiency is proved.

NOTE: As we can see from Bork's description of the difficulties facing entrants to markets he feels that these are natural requirements of efficiency that will have to be achieved if an undertaking wants to enter a market with any success. The school of thought to which Bork is linked would define barriers to entry very narrowly, and would only accept that a true barrier exists where a cost is borne by a new entrant which was not borne by the incumbent market players.

Posner, R., *Antitrust Law*
Chicago, CUP, 1976, p. 59

In discussing the relevance of new entry to the propensity to collude I have carefully avoided using that confusing term 'barrier to entry'. A barrier to entry is commonly used in a quite literal sense to mean anything which a new entrant must overcome in order to gain a foothold in the market, such as the capital costs of entering the market on an efficient scale. This is a meaningless usage, since it is obvious that a new entrant must incur costs to enter the market, just as his predecessors, the firms now occupying the market, did previously. A more precise definition has been offered by Stigler: a barrier to entry is a condition that imposes higher long-run costs of production on a new entrant than are borne by the firms already in the market. A barrier to entry in Stigler's sense has important policy implications: it implies the existence of a range within which the firms in the market can increase the market price above the competitive level without having to worry at all about losing sales to a new entrant. But, as we shall see in the next chapter, barriers to entry in this sense appear to be rare. Of greater practical importance are factors that do not create a barrier to entry but increase the length of time required for new entry to take place, by making the production process a complex one which requires substantial time to organize efficiently. Such factors include vertical integration and economies of scale, which increase the optimum size of the new entrant.

NOTE: Posner's view is similar to Bork's, but makes the distinction between a true barrier to entry, in his view, and other factors which make entry more difficult and lengthy. The views of both Bork and Posner can be described as being nearer the narrow definition of barriers to entry. By taking such a view they would favour a more limited role for the competition authorities. As entry is still possible any anti-competitive activity by a strong undertaking on a market would be constrained by the potential of entry, and therefore there would be no need for intervention by the competition authorities. Only where entry is restricted by a true barrier to entry should the authorities need to intervene. Given the different nature of US antitrust law, and the different political emphasis of these US scholars from that of the European Commission and the Court, it is not surprising that EC law has taken a very different approach.

Centre Belge d'Etudes de Marche-Tele-Marketing SA v *Compagnie Luxembourgeoise de Telediffusion SA*
(Case 311/84) [1985] ECR 3261, [1986] 2 CMLR 558

Centre Belge brought an action before the Luxembourg courts, seeking an injunction restraining CLT from refusing to sell it television time on its TV station for telephone marketing operations, using a telephone number other than that operated by CLT. Centre Belge advertised using a technique known as telemarketing whereby products were advertised with a telephone number where they could see further information. CLT had an effective statutory monopoly on the TV advertising for the market in question.

[11] In substance the first question asks whether Article 86 of the Treaty applies to an undertaking holding a dominant position on a particular market where that position is due not to the activities of the undertaking itself but to the fact that by reason of provisions laid down by law there can be no competition or only very limited competition on the market.

[12] The Centre Belge proposes that the Court should answer that question in the affirmative. It maintains that, according to the case law of the Court, an undertaking holding a monopoly in a particular service has a dominant position on the market in that service within the meaning of Article 86 and that that Article applies to the conduct of broadcasting organisations. Compagnie Luxembourgeoise cannot rely on the proviso in Article 90(2), since it is not an undertaking 'entrusted with the operation of services of general economic interest' for the purposes thereof.

[13] Compagnie Luxembourgeoise states that the Court held, in its judgment in Case 155/73 (*Sacchi*) ([1974] ECR 409, [1974] 2 CMLR 177) that a State may, for reasons of public interest of a non-economic nature, remove radio and television broadcasting from competition by conferring a monopoly on an undertaking. Extending the scope of the question put to the Court, Compagnie Luxembourgeoise proposes, therefore, that the Court should reply that it is not as such incompatible

with Article 86 of the Treaty for an undertaking to which a State has granted exclusive rights within the meaning of Article 90 to enjoy a monopoly.

[14] Information Publicite does not agree with the abstract definition of a dominant position which in its opinion is suggested by the question. It maintains that it is not possible to disregard the product or service at issue or the extent of the relevant market. Further, to fall within the provisions of Article 86 the dominant position must affect trade between Member States and exist within a substantial part of the Common Market. Information Publicite therefore proposes that the Court should reply that the existence of a statutory monopoly does not in itself entail a dominant position within the meaning of Article 86.

[15] In the Commission's view, the notion of a dominant position, as defined by the Court, refers to a factual situation independent of the reasons giving rise to that situation. The question must therefore be answered in the affirmative.

[16] With regard to the first question, it must first of all be remembered that, according to the established case law of the Court most recently confirmed by the judgment in Case 322/81 (*Michelin* v *EC Commission*) ([1983] ECR 3461, [1985] 1 CMLR 282), an undertaking occupies a dominant position for the purposes of Article 86 where it enjoys a position of economic strength which enables it to hinder the maintenance of effective competition on the relevant market by allowing it to behave to an appreciable extent independently of its competitors and customers and ultimately of consumers. The fact that the absence of competition or its restriction on the relevant market is brought about or encouraged by provisions laid down by law in no way precludes the application of Article 86, as the Court has held, *inter alia*, in Case 26/75 (*General Motors* v *EC Commission*) ([1975] ECR 1367, [1976] 1 CMLR 95), Case 13/77 (*INNO* v *ATAB*) ([1977] ECR 2115, [1978] 1 CMLR 283) and most recently in its judgment of 20 March 1985 in Case 41/83 (*Italy* v *EC Commission*) ([1985] 2 CMLR 368).

[17] Although it is true, as Compagnie Luxembourgeoise has pointed out, that it is not incompatible with Article 86 for an undertaking to which a Member State has granted exclusive rights within the meaning of Article 90 of the Treaty to enjoy a monopoly, it is none the less apparent from the same Article that such undertakings remain subject to the Treaty rules on competition and in particular those contained in Article 86. In *Sacchi*, the Court also stressed that, if certain Member States treat undertakings entrusted with the operation of television, even as regards their commercial activities and in particular advertising, as undertakings entrusted with the operation of services of general economic interest, the prohibitions of Article 86 apply, as regards their behaviour within the market, by reason of Article 90(2), so long as it is not shown that the said prohibitions are incompatible with the performance of their tasks.

[18] The reply to the first question must therefore be that Article 86 of the EEC Treaty must be interpreted as applying to an undertaking holding a dominant position on a particular market, even where that position is due not to the activities of the undertaking itself but to the fact that by reason of provisions laid down by law there can be no competition or only very limited competition on that market.

NOTE: In this instance it was clear that there was no effective competition for CLT and such competition was unlikely to develop while they retained a statutory monopoly. This would be considered as a barrier to entry by Bork, Posner and, obviously, by the Court. CLT's position was protected by law and therefore their activities were not constrained by potential competitors. This is one of the few areas where the US scholars and the European Court are of a similar view.

Hilti AG v *Commission*
(Case T-30/89) [1991] ECR II-1439, [1992] 4 CMLR 16

[89] The Commission has proved that Hilti holds a market share of around 70 per cent to 80 per cent in the relevant market for nails. That figure was supplied to the Commission by Hilti following a

request by the Commission for information pursuant to Article 11 of Regulation 17. As the Commission has rightly emphasised, Hilti was therefore obliged to supply information which, to the best of its knowledge, was as accurate as possible. Hilti's subsequent assertion that the figures were unsound is not corroborated by any evidence or by any examples showing them to be unreliable. Moreover, Hilti has supplied no other figures to substantiate its assertion. This argument of the applicant must therefore be rejected.

[90] The Court of Justice has held: Case 27/76 *United Brands* v *EC Commission* ([1978] ECR 207, [1978] 1 CMLR 429) and Case 85/76 *Hoffmann-La Roche* v *EC Commission* ([1979] ECR 461, [1979] 3 CMLR 211) that the dominant position referred to in Article 86 EEC relates to a position of economic strength enjoyed by an undertaking which enables it to prevent effective competition being maintained on the relevant market by giving it the power to behave to an appreciable extent independently of its competitors, customers and ultimately of its consumers; the existence of a dominant position may derive from a combination of several factors which, taken separately, are not necessarily determinative but among which a highly important one is the existence of very large market shares.

[91] With particular reference to market shares, the Court of Justice has held (*Hoffmann-La Roche*, cited above, paragraph [41]) that very large shares are in themselves, and save in exceptional circumstances, evidence of a dominant position.

[92] In this case it is established that Hilti holds a share of between 70 per cent and 80 per cent in the relevant market. Such a share is, in itself, a clear indication of the existence of a dominant position in the relevant market: Case 62/86 *AKZO Chemie BV* v *EC Commission*. (Not yet reported, para. [60].)

[93] Furthermore, as regards the other factors noted by the Commission as helping to maintain and reinforce Hilti's position in the market, it must be pointed out that the very fact that Hilti holds a patent and, in the United Kingdom, invokes copyright protection in relation to the cartridge strips designed for use in its own tools strengthens its position in the markets for Hilti-compatible consumables. Hilti's strong position in those markets was enhanced by the patents which it held at the time on certain elements of its DX 450 nail gun. It should be added that, as the Commission rightly contended, it is highly improbable in practice that a non-dominant supplier will act as Hilti did, since effective competition will normally ensure that the adverse consequences of such behaviour outweigh any benefits.

[94] On the basis of all those considerations, the Court holds that the Commission was entitled to take the view that Hilti held a dominant position in the market in nails for the nail guns which it manufactures.

NOTE: In this judgment, high market shares held by Hilti were clearly relevant, but the CFI also relied on other factors which helped 'maintain and reinforce' their position (para. 93). Those factors could also be described as barriers to entry. As they held patent rights over cartridge strips it made it very difficult for any other undertaking to produce such strips without breaching Hilti's patent. Their position in the market for nail guns was also protected to some extent by patent rights, but not as strongly as their position in the consumables market. The combination of the high market shares and the protective IP rights ensured Hilti's position.

Hoffmann-La Roche v *Commission*
(Case 85/76) [1979] ECR 461, [1979] 3 CMLR 211

Having defined the relevant vitamins markets and examined Hoffman's market shares, the Court went on to look at other factors which indicated their dominance.

[42] The contested decision has mentioned besides the market shares a number of other factors which together with Roche's market shares would secure for it in certain circumstances a dominant position. These factors which the decision classifies as additional criteria are as follows:

(a) Roche's market shares are not only large but there is also a big disparity between its shares and those of its next largest competitors (Recitals 5 and 21 to the decision);

(b) Roche produces a far wider range of vitamins than its competitors (Recital 21 to the decision);

(c) Roche is the world's largest vitamin manufacturer whose turnover exceeds that of all the other producers and is at the head of a multinational group which in terms of sales is the world's leading pharmaceuticals producer (Recitals 5, 6 and 21 to the decision);

(d) Although Roche's patents for the manufacture of vitamins have expired Roche, since it has played a leading role in this field, still enjoys technological advantages over its competitors of which the highly developed customer information and assistance service which it has is evidence (Recitals 7 and 8 to the decision);

(e) Roche has a very extensive and highly specialised sales network (Recital 21 to the decision);

(f) There is no potential competition (Recital 21 to the decision).

Furthermore during the proceedings before the Court the Commission adduced as a factor establishing Roche's dominant position the latter's ability, notwithstanding lively competition, to maintain its market shares substantially intact.

[43] Before considering whether the factors taken into account by the Commission can in fact be confirmed in Roche's case it is necessary to ascertain, since the applicant challenges their relevance, whether these factors, in the light of the special features of the relevant markets and of the market shares, are of such a kind as to disclose the existence of a dominant position.

[44] In this connexion it is necessary to reject the criterion based on retention of market shares, since this may just as well result from effective competitive behaviour as from a position which ensures that Roche can behave independently of competitors, and the Commission, while admitting that there is competition, has not mentioned the factors which may account for the stability of market shares where it has been found to exist. However, if there is a dominant position then retention of the market shares may be a factor disclosing that this position is being maintained, and, on the other hand, the methods adopted to maintain a dominant position may be an abuse within the meaning of Article 86 of the Treaty.

[45] The fact that Roche produces a far wider range of vitamins than its competitors must similarly be rejected as being immaterial. The Commission regards this as a factor establishing a dominant position and asserts that 'since the requirements of many users extend to several groups of vitamins, Roche is able to employ a sales and pricing strategy which is far less dependent than that of the other manufacturers on the conditions of competition in each market'.

[46] However, the Commission has itself found that each group of vitamins constitutes a specific market and is not, or at least not to any significant extent, interchangeable with any other group or with any other products (Recital 20 to the decision) so that the vitamins belonging to the various groups are as between themselves products just as different as the vitamins compared with other products of the pharmaceutical and food sector. Moreover, it is not disputed that Roche's competitors, in particular those in the chemical industry, market besides the vitamins which they manufacture themselves, other products which purchasers of vitamins also want, so that the fact that Roche is in a position to offer several groups of vitamins does not in itself give it any advantage over its competitors, who can offer, in addition to a less or much less wide range of vitamins, other products which are also required by the purchasers of these vitamins.

[47] Similar considerations lead also to the rejection as a relevant factor of the circumstance that Roche is the world's largest vitamin manufacturer, that its turnover exceeds that of all the other

manufacturers and that it is at the head of the largest pharmaceuticals group in the world. In the view of the Commission these three considerations together are a factor showing that there is a dominant position, because 'it follows that the applicant occupies a preponderant position not only within the Common Market but also on the world market; it therefore enjoys very considerable freedom of action, since its position enables it to adapt itself easily to the developments of the different regional markets. An undertaking operating throughout the markets of the world and having a market share which leaves all its competitors far behind it does not have to concern itself unduly about any competitors within the Common Market.' Such reasoning based on the benefits reaped from economies of scale and on the possibility of adopting a strategy which varies according to the different regional markets is not conclusive, seeing that it is accepted that each group of vitamins constitutes a group of separate products which require their own particular plant and form a separate market, in that the volume of the overall production of products which are different as between themselves does not give Roche a competitive advantage over its competitors, especially over those in the chemical industry, who manufacture on a world scale other products as well as vitamins and have in principle the same opportunities to set off one market against the other as are offered by a large overall production of products which differ from each other as much as the various groups of vitamins do.

[48] On the other hand the relationship between the market shares of the undertaking concerned and of its competitors, especially those of the next largest, the technological lead of an undertaking over its competitors, the existence of a highly developed sales network and the absence of potential competition are relevant factors, the first because it enables the competitive strength of the under-taking in question to be assessed, the second and third because they represent in themselves technical and commercial advantages and the fourth because it is the consequence of the existence of obstacles preventing new competitors from having access to the market. As far as the existence or non-existence of potential competition is concerned it must, however, be observed that, although it is true—and this applies to all the groups of vitamins in question—that because of the amount of capital investment required the capacity of the factories is determined according to the anticipated growth over a long period so that access to the market by new producers is not easy, account must also be taken of the fact that the existence of considerable unused manufacturing capacity creates potential competition between established manufacturers. Nevertheless Roche is in this respect in a privileged position because, as it admits itself, its own manufacturing capacity was, during the period covered by the contested decision, in itself sufficient to meet world demand without this surplus manufacturing capacity placing it in a difficult economic or financial situation.

[49] It is in the light of the preceding considerations that Roche's shares of each of the relevant markets, complemented by those factors which in conjunction with the market shares make it possible to show that there may be a dominant position, must be evaluated. Finally, it will also be necessary to consider whether Roche's submissions relating to the implication of its conduct on the market, mainly as far as concerns prices, are of such a kind as to alter the findings to which the examination of the market shares and the other factors taken into account might lead.

NOTE: A number of factors put forward by the Commission were rejected by the Court: reten-tion of market shares, the fact that La Roche produced a wide range of vitamins, and La Roche was the world's largest vitamin producer. These were largely discounted as their use would have been contrary to the reasoning used by the Commission to define the relevant markets. The Court did accept a number of factors as being important. First, the technical lead La Roche possessed over its rivals. Second, the existence of a developed sales network. And third, the absence of potential competition. The latter of these adds little to the previous two without the Court's further explanation that this is because of the capital investment required to enter the market and the market's existing overcapacity. In effect, the Court had utilised four separate barriers to entry to support its finding of dominance in *Hoffman-La Roche*. All of these barriers would fail to meet Bork and Posner's definition of a true barrier and fit into the category of factors which merely make it more difficult to enter a market. By adopting these barriers in their jurisprudence the Court clearly take a much wider stance than the US scholars. The Court takes the view that any factor which would discourage entry, no matter whether the incumbent faced the same problems, is a barrier which can be used to support a finding of dominance. Sometimes these barriers are known are 'strategic' or 'first-mover' advantages as they are related to advantages possessed by an undertaking which is first to develop experience in the industry. The fact that 'second movers' have to spend heavily to develop that experience to begin to compete with the incumbent is considered a barrier to their entry.

United Brands v *Commission*
(Case 27/76) [1978] ECR 207, [1978] 1 CMLR 429

> Having defined the relevant market and examined United Brands' market share, the Court moved on to consider if there were any other factors which might indicate or reinforce their dominance.

[69] It is advisable to examine in turn UBC's resources for and methods of producing, packaging, transporting, selling and displaying its product.

[70] UBC is an undertaking vertically integrated to a high degree.

[71] This integration is evident at each of the stages from the plantation to the loading on wagons or lorries in the ports of delivery after those stages, as far as ripening and sale prices are concerned, UBC even extends its control to ripener/distributors and wholesalers by setting up a complete network of agents.

[72] At the production stage UBC owns large plantations in Central and South America.

[73] In so far as UBC's own production does not meet its requirements it can obtain supplies without any difficulty from independent planters since it is an established fact that unless circumstances are exceptional there is a production surplus.

[74] Furthermore several independent producers have links with UBC through contracts for the growing of bananas which have caused them to grow the varieties of bananas which UBC advised them to adopt.

[75] The effects of natural disasters which could jeopardise supplies are greatly reduced by the fact that the plantations are spread over a wide geographic area and by the selection of varieties not very susceptible to diseases.

[76] This situation was born out by the way in which UBC was able to react to the consequences of hurricane 'Fifi' in 1974.

[77] At the production stage UBC therefore knows that it can comply with all the requests which it receives.

[78] At the stage of packaging and presentation on its premises UBC has at its disposal factories, manpower, plant and material which enable it to handle the goods independently.

[79] The bananas are carried from the place of production to the port of shipment by its own means of transport including railways.

[80] At the carriage by sea stage it has been acknowledged that UBC is the only undertaking of its kind which is capable of carrying two thirds of its exports by means of its own banana fleet.

[81] Thus UBC knows that it is able to transport regularly, without running the risk of its own ships not being used and whatever the market situation may be, two thirds of its average volume of sales

and is alone able to ensure that three regular consignments reach Europe each week, and all this guarantees it commercial stability and well being.

[82] In the field of technical knowledge and as a result of continual research UBC keeps on improving the productivity and yield of its plantations by improving the draining system, making good soil deficiencies and combating effectively plant disease.

[83] It has perfected new ripening methods in which its technicians instruct the distributor/ripeners of the 'Chiquita' banana.

[84] That is another factor to be borne in mind when considering UBC's position since competing firms cannot develop research at a comparable level and are in this respect at a disadvantage compared with the applicant.

[85] It is acknowledged that at the stage where the goods are given the final finish and undergo quality control UBC not only controls the distributor/ripeners which are direct customers but also those who work for the account of its important customers such as the Scipio group.

[86] Even if the object of the clause prohibiting the sale of green bananas was only strict quality control, it in fact gives UBC absolute control of all trade in its goods so long as they are marketable wholesale, that is to say before the ripening process begins which makes an immediate sale unavoidable.

. . .

[122] The particular barriers to competitors entering the market are the exceptionally large capital investments required for the creation and running of banana plantations, the need to increase sources of supply in order to avoid the effects of fruit diseases and bad weather (hurricanes, floods), the introduction of an essential system of logistics which the distribution of a very perishable product makes necessary, economies of scale from which newcomers to the market cannot derive any immediate benefit and the actual cost of entry made up *inter alia* of all the general expenses incurred in penetrating the market such as the setting up of an adequate commercial network, the mounting of very large-scale advertising campaigns, all those financial risks, the costs of which are irrecoverable if the attempt fails.

[123] Thus, although, as UBC has pointed out, it is true that competitors are able to use the same methods of production and distribution as the applicant, they come up against almost insuperable practical and financial obstacles.

[124] That is another factor peculiar to a dominant position.

NOTE: The Court sets out a number of barriers to entry that it considers important to United Brands' ability to retain its dominant position. The first of those was United Brands' vertical integration. It has control of every stage of production from research and development to final ripening and distribution to retailers. As the Court notes at para. 122, it would be very difficult and expensive for a market entrant to replicate all these facilities to enter the market with the same scope as United Brands. The second barrier entry discussed by the Court was United Brands' expertise developed through its research and development facilities (paras 82–84). Again it would be very difficult for a competitor to replicate the R & D facilities and know-how. The third barrier to entry invoked by the Court is that of 'product differentiation' through advertising (paras 87–96, not reproduced above). By investing heavily in advertising their 'Chiquita' brand, United Brands had created a demand for that product in particular which would make customers less likely to switch their preference to bananas from competing suppliers. Again, it would be very costly for a potential competition to invest heavily in brand promotion to compete with the established 'Chiquita' brand.

Some commentators would argue that such brand promotion is not a significant barrier to entry:

Paterson, L. 'The Power Of The Puppy—Does Advertising Deter Entry'
[1997] ECLR 337, pp. 341–342 [footnotes omitted]

Brand loyalty and entry [footnotes omitted]

Suppose that economic analysis does point to the existence of strong brand loyalty. Why does this matter? The Commission's response to date has been that brand loyalty makes entry harder, as entrants have to sink costs into advertising and promotion if they are to persuade brand loyal customers to try something new.

In some circumstances, however, brand loyalty may actually facilitate entry, albeit of a market-segmenting or 'niche' variety. On the other hand, if an entrant is to compete head-to-head with incumbents for brand loyal customers, then the Commission is probably right to assert that this will require some sinking of advertising and promotional costs. What is less clear is whether these costs will deter entry.

Brand loyalty and market segmentation

In some markets, brand loyalty can facilitate entry of the 'market segmenting' variety. This is probably best illustrated by way of a simple example.

Suppose that, in a given market, the incumbent's brand, Brand X, enjoys some brand loyalty. In particular, suppose that 70 per cent of Brand X's customers are brand loyal and would never consider switching to another brand. An entrant comes into the market, with Brand Y. Brand Y is priced below Brand X. Brand Y is effectively targeting the 30 per cent of Brand X's customers who are not brand loyal. In this case, Brand X's best response may not be to enter into direct competition with Brand Y. Instead, the incumbent could let Brand Y take the 30 per cent of its customers that are non-brand loyal, and charge a higher price to its brand loyal customers.

However, brand loyalty will only facilitate this 'market segmenting' type of entry in certain circumstances.

First, there need to be at least some people who are prepared to buy from an entrant (i.e. are not completely brand loyal to Brand X), otherwise market segmentation of this type can never occur.

Second, there needs to be a sufficient number of customers who will not switch away from the incumbent's brand in response to price changes. If many of Brand X's customers are not brand loyal, and switch to lower priced Brand Y, then Brand X may do better by entering into direct price competition with Brand Y for the non brand loyal customers.

Third, there needs to be no substantial cost advantage from being a large market player. Suppose that economies of scale are very important, implying that large companies have much lower unit costs than small companies. If Brand Y only targets a market segment, it may be unable to cover its average unit costs of supply. In this case, if Brand Y is to be successful, it may have to target Brand X's loyal customers, as discussed further below.

So, in certain circumstances, brand loyalty may facilitate entry as it can imply that post-entry price competition will be relatively soft. However, the type of entry that is facilitated tends to be of the 'market segmenting' variety. This type of entry may lead to an increase in sales and a reduction in the price paid by some customers, but does not constrain the incumbent's power over its brand loyal customers. From an antitrust perspective, this may be a matter of concern.

Brand loyalty and head-to-head competition

Now suppose that, perhaps because of a combination of customer preferences and economies of scale, potential entrants have to compete head-to-head with incumbents for their brand loyal customers. In this case, by the very definition of brand loyalty, an entrant will have to incur significant advertising and promotional costs if he is to persuade brand loyal customers to try a new product. So, in these circumstances, the Commission is right to assert that:

The establishment of a new brand would require heavy investment in advertising and promotion in order to persuade brand loyal consumers to switch away from their usual brand.

But even if entry necessitates the sinking of advertising and promotional costs to persuade brand loyal customers to try something new, it is not clear that entry is impossible, or even improbable. The probability of entry rests crucially upon whether these sunk costs are large or small in the context of the likely scale of entry, as well as the nature of post-entry price competition.

How would one begin to assess whether sunk entry costs were 'large' or 'small'? The first step is to estimate the absolute size of advertising and promotional sunk costs. In doing this it is imperative to distinguish between entry-related advertising and promotional costs (which obviously do not have to be incurred by incumbents) and day-to-day advertising and promotional costs which need to be incurred by incumbents and entrants alike. Only the former cost plays any role in entry decisions. In other words, a competition authority has to measure the additional costs that an entrant will have to incur over and above the normal costs of doing business incurred by the incumbent (including any ongoing expenditures incumbents need to incur to maintain brand loyalty). It is, for example, insufficient to estimate the costs that an entrant will have to incur in its first year of business (which was in fact the figure calculated by the Commission in the *KC/Scott* decision).

After having estimated the size of any sunk advertising and promotional costs an entrant may have to incur (and these are likely to be larger the stronger is the degree of incumbent brand loyalty), the next step is to put these costs into their market context. One way might be to ask, given the likely scale of entry, what would be the mark-up over the incumbent's unit cost that the entrant would need to earn to break even.

BPB Industries plc
(Commission Decision 89/22/EEC) OJ, 1989, L10/50

BPB Industries plc was the British holding company of a major group having worldwide interests notably in gypsum products, other building materials, paper and board. BPB was the largest producer of plasterboard in the world outside the US. The Commission defined the relevant market as being plasterboard, a material used to line ceilings and walls in the construction industry.

C. Dominant position

[115] The issue of dominance must be considered in relation to the period to which this decision relates, namely June 1985 to August 1986. In considering the issue of dominance or market power, it is necessary to consider not only the position of BPB in the market but also its technological and financial resources and the competitive position of its rivals.

[116] In 1985 and 1986, BPB's share of the plasterboard market in Great Britain was between 98 and 96 per cent and in the island of Ireland between about 100 and 92 per cent. As BG has pointed out, BPB enjoys substantial economies in producing on a large scale in integrated industrial complexes, extracting gypsum and producing plaster then plasterboard. BPB has very extensive technical and financial resources. As the sole producer in the relevant geographical markets it alone benefited from the economies which flow from the placing of plasterboard production close to its markets.

. . .

[120] The impact of potential competition on the market position of BPB has been limited in particular by the cost of establishing new plasterboard production and sales and technical support networks. In view of the strength of BPB's market position and its policy of maintaining capacity to meet the domestic demand for plasterboard at all times, it could expect to maintain a dominant position for a considerable period in the face of market entry by competitors on any realistic scale. The position of BPB is reinforced by the need for a new producer to incur the yet greater financial risk of developing gypsum mines in Britain or Ireland, or to accept the cost disadvantage of importing gypsum.

NOTE: Notwithstanding the very strong position of BPB on the market, a near monopoly with a market share above 95 per cent, the Commission still relied on the existence of a number of barriers to entry to bolster their finding of dominance. The economies of scale that BPB benefited from were signalled as a barrier to entry (para. 116). Because BPB produced plasterboard on such a large scale compared to any other produced they benefited from reduction in costs which could not be matched by existing producers, and if a new competitor were to enter the market they would find it very expensive to enter on the same scale as BPB. Another barrier to entry was the cost of developing gypsum mines, a raw material vital for the production of plaster, or undertake the risks of importing gypsum from distant mines outside the market (para. 120).

AKZO Chemie BV v *Commission*
(Case C–62/86) [1991] ECR I-3359, [1993] 5 CMLR 215

AKZO was a large Dutch chemicals group who were active on the market for flour additives. It was accused of abusing its position on the market to exclude a competitor, ECS. After defining the relevant market as the market for organic peroxides the Commission looked at various factors which might support a finding of dominance.

2. The dominant position
[55] The Commission considers that AKZO has a dominant position within the organic peroxides market. It bases its view on AKZO's market share and on the existence of a number of factors which, combined with that market share, is said to give it a marked predominance.

[56] The Commission describes these factors at paragraph 69 of the decision as follows:

(i)   AKZO's market share is not only large in itself but is equivalent to all the remaining producers put together;
(ii) apart from Interox and Luperox the remaining producers have a limited product range and/or are of local significance only;
(iii) AKZO's market share (as well as that of the second and third placed producers Interox and Luperox) has remained steady over the period under consideration and AKZO has always successfully repulsed any attacks on its position by smaller producers;
(iv) AKZO was able even during periods of economic downturn to maintain its overall margin by regular price increases and/or increases in sales volume;
(v)   AKZO offers a far broader range of products than any rival, has the most highly developed commercial and technical marketing organisation, and possesses the leading knowledge in safety and toxicology;
(vi) AKZO has on its own account been able effectively to eliminate 'troublesome' competitors (besides ECS) from the market or weaken them substantially: the example of SCADO for one shows that AKZO is in a position, if it so wishes, to exclude a less powerful producer;
(vii) once such small but potentially dangerous competitors are neutralised, AKZO has been able to raise the price for the particular product in respect of which their competition was felt.

[61] Moreover, the Commission rightly pointed out that other factors confirmed AKZO's predominance in the market. In addition to the fact that AKZO regards itself as the world leader in the peroxides market, it should be observed that, as AKZO itself admits, it has the most highly developed marketing organisation, both commercially and technically, and wider knowledge than that of its competitors with regard to safety and toxicology (Annexes 2 and 4 to the statement of objections).

[62] The pleas put forward by AKZO in order to deny that it had a dominant position within the organic peroxides market as a whole must therefore be rejected.

NOTE: The judgment in *AKZO* refers to a number of factors which the Commission used to support its decision but it is arguable that several of these were factors which properly should be considered as matters relating to market strength, for example, comparability of market shares and market share stability over time. Only two of the Commission's factors raised by the Court could be seen as being barriers to entry, even under the broad definition adopted by the Court. The first being that it has specialised know-how and experience which its competitors would find difficult to replicate (para. 59(v)). This is a well-established barrier which the Court has utilised on many occasions. The second barrier is far more controversial and is perhaps an example of the widest use of the concept within EC jurisprudence. The Commission suggests that AKZO's previous behaviour on the market may have, in itself, have acted as a barrier to entry (para. 56(vi)–(vii)). This is problematic as such behaviour was also alleged to be the abuse in the instant case. Normally, one considers the dominance and abuse as separate issues but here they become increasingly intertwined. The Court does not specifically address that assertion but its inclusion is indicative that it garners some support. There is an argument that this reasoning is circular in nature and should not be used, but it does give a real indication of the European view of barriers to entry being broadly drawn. Any factor in the market structure or because of the previous behaviour of an undertaking on the market which would discourage potential competitors from entering the market may be considered as a barrier to entry by the Community authorities.

H: Abuse

Once it has been established that an undertaking has a dominant position, it is necessary to investigate whether their behaviour could be categorised as being abusive. The Treaty itself sets out an indicative list of behaviour which was envisaged as being abusive by the drafters of the Treaty.

Such abuse may, in particular, consist in:

(a) directly or indirectly imposing unfair purchase or selling prices or other unfair trading conditions

(b) limiting production, markets or technical development to the prejudice of consumers

(c) applying dissimilar conditions to equivalent transactions with other trading parties, thereby placing them at a competitive disadvantage

(d) making the conclusion of contracts subject to acceptance by the other parties of supplementary obligations which, by their nature or according to commercial usage, have no connection with the subject of such contracts.

This list is only indicative and the Court has used its teleological style of reasoning to expand the categories of abuse to cover many differing types of behaviour, which harm the competitive process within the EC. For the purposes of categorisation it is useful to split the different abuses into two, somewhat overlapping, categories; namely exploitative and exclusionary abuses. Each of the categories has different characteristics and the reasons that competition law finds them damaging is different.

I: Exploitative abuses

Exploitative abuse would describe a situation in which a dominant undertaking uses its position of power to exploit the market and make a supra-competitive profit. This behaviour is suggested as being rational for a monopolist who wishes to maximise their profits and its avoidance is therefore considered to be one of the main aims of any competition law system. A dominant undertaking may be able to raise the prices on its goods by creating an artificial scarcity of its product and prices will increase above the level at which they would be priced on a 'competitive' market, thus the prices, and the profits, gained are described as being supra-competitive. There are several different ways a dominant undertaking may try to exploit its position on the market and its customers.

(a) *Excessive pricing*

The most obvious manner in which a dominant undertaking may attempt to exploit its customers is to charge an excessive price through creating an artificial scarcity of the dominant product. The major problem for competition lawyers is deciding what is an excessive price.

General Motors v *Commission*
(Case 26/75) [1975] ECR 1367, [1976] 1 CMLR 95

Vehicles to be used in Belgium have to satisfy certain technical standards set out in a Royal Decree. Each type of vehicle manufactured in or imported into Belgium must be approved. Once a type of vehicle has been approved the manufacturer should issue a certificate of conformity for all vehicles of that type. Vehicles registered abroad and reimported into Belgium had to gain a certificate of conformity from the manufacturer's agent. For all GM cars the manufacturer's agent was the appellant. They charged the same for approval checks on European imports as they did for the import of US models. This was challenged as being an excessive price.

The abuse

[11] It is possible that the holder of the exclusive position referred to above may abuse the market by fixing a price—for a service which it is alone in a position to provide—which is to the detriment of any person acquiring a motor vehicle imported from another Member State and subject to the approval procedure.

[12] Such an abuse might lie, *inter alia*, in the imposition of a price which is excessive in relation to the economic value of the service provided, and which has the effect of curbing parallel imports by neutralising the possibly more favourable level of prices applying in other sales areas in the Community, or by leading to unfair trade in the sense of Article 86(2)(a).

[13] However, the applicant maintains on this point that the conduct complained of did not constitute an 'abuse' within the meaning of Article 86.

[14] In order to demonstrate this point the applicant puts forward a number of arguments based on the actual circumstances in which the charge in question was imposed and, subsequently, largely refunded in the five cases referred to by the Commission.

The Court decided that the excessive price was not abusive as GM had quickly realised the price was too high and reduced the charge. It had then of its own volition refunded the excess charge to importers before the Commission investigation had started. The judgment clarified that excessive pricing could be abusive but that not all excessive pricing was abusive.

United Brands v Commission
(Case 27/76) [1978] ECR 207, [1978] 1 CMLR 429

In its decision the Commission argued that UBC had abused its dominant position by charging excessive prices to its customers in Germany, Denmark and the Netherlands when compared to the price it charged its customers in Ireland.

[248] The imposition by an undertaking in a dominant position directly or indirectly of unfair purchase or selling prices is an abuse to which exception can be taken under Article 86 of the Treaty.

[249] It is advisable therefore to ascertain whether the dominant undertaking has made use of the opportunities arising out of its dominant position in such a way as to reap trading benefits which it would not have reaped if there had been normal and sufficiently effective competition.

[250] In this case charging a price which is excessive because it has no reasonable relation to the economic value of the product supplied is such an abuse.

[251] This excess could, inter alia, be determined objectively if it were possible for it to be calculated by making a comparison between the selling price of the product in question and its cost of production, which would disclose the amount of the profit margin; however the Commission has not done this since it has not analysed UBC's costs structure.

[252] The question therefore to be determined is whether the difference between the costs actually incurred and the price actually charged is excessive and, if the answer to this question is in the affirmative, to consider whether a price has been imposed which is either unfair in itself or when compared to competing products.

[253] Other ways may be devised—and economic theorists have not failed to think up several—of selecting the rules for determining whether the price of a product is unfair.

[254] While appreciating the considerable and at times very great difficulties in working out production costs which may sometimes include a discretionary apportionment of indirect costs and general expenditure and which may vary significantly according to the size of the undertaking, its object, the complex nature of its set up, its territorial area of operations, whether it manufactures one or several products, the number of its subsidiaries and their relationship with each other, the production costs of the banana do not seem to present any insuperable problems.

NOTE: United Brands highlights the difficulties in proving the existence of excessive pricing. Ultimately, the Commission had not adduced enough evidence to show that the price charged by United Brands was indeed excessive. The method the Court suggests that the Commission should use to support a finding of excessive pricing is a complex 'cost-plus' approach, which will be difficult and complex to utilise in practice. It is for that reason, that the Commission has not brought many cases on the basis of excessive prices since the 1970s (cf. the approach of the OFT in the UK seen in Napp).

Merci Convenzionali Porto Genova SpA v Siderurgica Gabrielli
(Case C-179/90) [1991] ECR I-5889, [1994] 4 CMLR 422.

The port of Genova is administered by a public authority which regulates work within the port. All dock work, including the loading and unloading of ships, was reserved to certain groups of enrolled dockworkers. Siderurgica imported a consignment of steel in a vessel which was capable of direct unloading, but that was not allowed as the work would not be performed by the reserved workers. A dispute arose following the delay caused by the ship's inability directly to unload quickly and because of strikes by dockworkers.

[18] According to Article 86(2)(a), (b) and (c) EEC, such abuse may in particular consist in imposing on the persons requiring the services in question unfair purchase prices or other unfair trading conditions, in limiting technical development, to the prejudice of consumers, or in the application of dissimilar conditions to equivalent transactions with other trading parties.

[19] In that respect it appears from the circumstances described by the national court and discussed before the Court of Justice that the undertakings enjoying exclusive rights in accordance with the procedures laid down by the national rules in question are, as a result, induced either to demand payment for services which have not been requested, to charge disproportionate prices, to refuse to have recourse to modern technology, which involves an increase in the cost of the operations and a prolongation of the time required for their performance, or to grant price reductions to certain consumers and at the same time to offset such reductions by an increase in the charges to other consumers.

. . .

[22] In the main proceedings it may be seen from the national court's findings that the unloading of the goods could have been effected at a lesser cost by the ship's crew, so that compulsory recourse to the services of the two undertakings enjoying exclusive rights involved extra expense and was therefore capable, by reason of its effect on the prices of the goods, of affecting imports.

NOTE: This judgment focuses on another form of exploitative abuse by which a dominant undertaking could exploit its customers. This phenomenon is sometimes known as 'x-inefficiency' and occurs when the dominant undertaking uses its dominance to relax and no longer strives to produce their products or deliver their service in the most efficient and cost-effective manner possible. It is also sometimes said that the dominant undertaking is 'enjoying the quiet life'. If that is the case the consumers of the undertaking's product or service will not benefit from the cost savings that you would expect the undertaking to make and will in time have to pay more than would have occurred if there was a competitive market. Here the port authorities employed inefficient techniques which incurred higher costs on those who used the facility. If there was a competitive market they would have been forced to adopt more efficient practices, but without that competition they could afford not to change their ways.

J: Exclusionary abuses

Exclusionary abuses are problematic and can result in a dominant undertaking strengthening their position in the market. As they are already in a very strong position, this may be particularly damaging for competition. Many of the abuses which Community competition law focuses on can be described as being exclusionary in nature. This is because Community law takes a particular focus on protecting the competitive structure of the market rather than just protecting the consumer.

Nederlandsche Banden Industrie Michelin NV v *Commission*
(Case 322/81) [1983] ECR 3461, [1985] 1 CMLR 282

The appellant manufactured new tyres for vans and lorries. The Commission took action against Michelin for, *inter alia*, operating a system of selective and discriminatory discounts.

[70] As regards the application of Article 86 to a system of discounts conditional upon the attainment of sales targets, such as described above, it must be stated first of all that in prohibiting any abuse of a dominant position on the market in so far as it may affect trade between Member-States Article 86 covers practices which are likely to affect the structure of a market where, as a direct result of the presence of the undertaking in question, competition has already been weakened and which, through recourse to methods different from those governing normal competition in products or services based on traders' performance, have the effect of hindering the maintenance or development of the level of competition still existing on the market.

NOTE: This approach by the Court has raised a number of questions about the Commission's focus in Competition law terms. Is it Commission policy to protect consumers, the process of competition, or a dominant undertakings competitors? See, Springer, U., 'Meeting Competition: Justification of Price Discrimination under EC and US Antitrust Law' [1997] ECLR 251 and Andrews, P., 'Is Meeting Competition a Defence to Predatory Pricing? The Irish Sugar Decision Suggests a New Approach' [1998] ECLR 49.

(a) *Exclusionary pricing*

Complaints about the pricing practices of dominant undertakings are common in competition law. The main concern here is not that the dominant undertaking is charging high prices to its customers, but that it is pricing in a way which is designed to drive its competitors out of the market or make it difficult for them to compete with the dominant player.

(b) *Predatory pricing*

AKZO Chemie BV v *Commission*
(Case C-62/86) [1991] ECR I-3359, [1993] 5 CMLR 215

Following an investigation, the Commission had found that AKZO had adopted a course of conduct on the market designed to secure ECS's withdrawal from the organic peroxides market. One of the abuses concerned systematically providing products to customers of ECS at unreasonably low prices designed to damage ECS.

[69] It should be observed that, as the Court held in Case 85/76, *Hoffmann-La Roche* v *EC Commission*, the concept of abuse is an objective concept relating to the behaviour of an undertaking in a dominant position which is such as to influence the structure of a market where, as a result of the very presence of the undertaking in question, the degree of competition is weakened and through recourse to methods which, different from those which condition normal competition in products or services on the basis of the transactions of commercial operations, has the effect of hindering the maintenance of the degree of competition still existing in the market or the growth of that competition.

[70] It follows that Article 86 prohibits a dominant undertaking from eliminating a competitor and

thereby strengthening its position by using methods other than those which come within the scope of competition on the basis of quality. From that point of view, however, not all competition by means of price can be regarded as legitimate.

[71] Prices below average variable costs (that is to say, those which vary depending on the quantities produced) by means of which a dominant undertaking seeks to eliminate a competitor must be regarded as abusive. A dominant undertaking has no interest in applying such prices except that of eliminating competitors so as to enable it subsequently to raise its prices by taking advantage of its monopolistic position, since each sale generates a loss, namely the total amount of the fixed costs (that is to say, those which remain constant regardless of the quantities produced) and, at least, part of the variable costs relating to the unit produced.

[72] Moreover, prices below average total costs, that is to say, fixed costs plus variable costs, but above average variable costs, must be regarded as abusive if they are determined as part of a plan for eliminating a competitor. Such prices can drive from the market undertakings which are perhaps as efficient as the dominant undertaking but which, because of their smaller financial resources, are incapable of withstanding the competition waged against them.

[73] These are the criteria that must be applied to the situation in the present case.

[74] Since the criterion of legitimacy to be adopted is a criterion based on the costs and the strategy of the dominant undertaking itself, AKZO's allegation concerning the inadequacy of the Commission's investigation with regard to the cost structure and the pricing policy of its competitors must be rejected at the outset.

NOTE: The *AKZO* formula has been used on many subsequent occasions but has caused several problems, namely the difficulties in categorising costs as either fixed or variable costs. The test for predatory pricing was extended in *Tetra Pak II* (Case T-51/89) [1990] ECR II-309, [1991] 4 CMLR 334 to a situation whereby the dominant undertaking abused its strength on one market to undercut competition on another related market.

Another form of predatory price discrimination was discussed in:

Irish Sugar plc v *EC Commission*
(Case T-228/97) [1999] ECR II-2969, [1999] 5 CMLR 1300

Irish Sugar was the dominant supplier of white granulated sugar in the Republic of Ireland. One of the alleged abuses addressed by the Commission was Irish Sugar's policy of offering selective low prices to potential customers of rival sugar suppliers from the Northern Ireland. Irish Sugar granted so-called 'border rebates' to its customers who may have been tempted to source supplies outside the Republic. In its Decision (*Irish Sugar plc*, Commission Decision 97/624/EC, OJ, 1997, L258/1), the Commission specifically referred to the Court's judgment in *AKZO* on a number of occasions, particularly at para. 134:

[134] There is no doubt that a firm in a dominant position is entitled to defend that position by competing with other firms on its market. However, the dominant firm must not deliberately attempt to effectively shut out competitors. It has a special responsibility not to diminish further the degree of competition remaining on the market. Firms which may be strong or even dominant on one geographic market are in a different position with respect to other geographic markets where they are confronted with a local dominant undertaking. The maintenance of a system of effective competition does, however, require that competition from undertakings which are only small competitors on the geographic market where dominance prevails, regardless of their position on geographic markets which are separate for the purpose of assessing dominance, be protected against

behaviour by the dominant undertaking designed to exclude them from the market not by virtue of greater efficiency or superior performance but by an abuse of market power. In the Commission's final decision in *ECS/AKZO* it was held to be abusive for a company with a 50 per cent or more market share to offer selectively low prices to customers of a small competitor while maintaining substantially higher prices for its existing customers. This principle was upheld by the Court. In the period in which it sought to restrict imports, Irish Sugar had over 90 per cent of both the Irish industrial and retail sugar markets.

NOTE: This was important in that the prices charged by Irish Sugar were not below ATC and therefore they would not appear to fall within the traditional reading of the *AKZO* test. This was confirmed by the Court of First Instance.

[184] In the particular circumstances of the case, the applicant cannot rely, in order to show that the special rebates granted between 1986 and 1988 to certain retailers established in the border area with Northern Ireland were lawful, either on the pricing policy of operators on the British market, or on its financial situation, or on the defensive nature of its conduct, or on the alleged existence of an illegal trade.

[185] First of all, the influence of the pricing policy of operators active principally on a neighbouring market, in this case the British and Northern Ireland market, on that of operators active on another national market is of the very essence of a common market. Anything which restricts that influence must therefore be regarded as an obstacle to the achievement of that common market and prejudicial to the outcome of effective and undistorted competition, especially with regard to the interests of consumers. Therefore, where such obstacles are brought about by an undertaking holding a dominant position as extensive as that enjoyed by the applicant, that is an abuse incompatible with Article 86. The applicant has, moreover, nowhere argued that the prices charged by its competitors along the border with Northern Ireland were below the cost price of the product, or supplied any evidence to that effect.

[186] Secondly, the applicant cannot rely on the insufficiency of the financial resources at its disposal at the time to justify the selective and discriminatory granting of those border rebates and thereby escape the application of Article 86, without making a dead letter of the prohibition contained in that article. The circumstances in which an undertaking in a dominant position may be led to react to the limited competition which exists on the market, especially where that undertaking holds more than 88 per cent of the market as in this case, form part of the competitive process which Article 86 is precisely designed to protect. Moreover, the applicant has several times underlined the high level of retail sale prices in Ireland, explaining it by the influence of the high level of the guaranteed intervention price in the context of the common organisation of the market in sugar.

[187] Finally, the defensive nature of the practice complained of in this case cannot alter the fact that it constitutes an abuse for the purposes of Article 86(c).

[188] In this case, the applicant has been unable to establish an objective economic justification for the rebates. They were given to certain customers in the retail sugar market by reference solely to their exposure to competition resulting from cheap imports from another Member State and, in this case, by reference to their being established along the border with Northern Ireland. It also appears, according to the applicant's own statements, that it was able to practise such price rebates owing to the particular position it held on the Irish market. Thus it states that it was unable to practise such rebates over the whole of Irish territory owing to the financial losses it was making at the time. It follows that, by the applicant's own admission, its economic capacity to offer rebates in the region along the border with Northern Ireland depended on the stability of its prices in other regions, which amounts to recognition that it financed those rebates by means of its sales in the rest of Irish territory. By conducting itself in that way, the applicant abused its dominant position in the retail

sugar market in Ireland, by preventing the development of free competition on that market and distorting its structures, in relation to both purchasers and consumers. The latter were not able to benefit, outside the region along the border with Northern Ireland, from the price reductions caused by the imports of sugar from Northern Ireland.

[189] Thus, even if the existence of a dominant position does not deprive an undertaking placed in that position of the right to protect its own commercial interests when they are threatened (see paragraph [112] above), the protection of the commercial position of an undertaking in a dominant position with the characteristics of that of the applicant at the time in question must, at the very least, in order to be lawful, be based on criteria of economic efficiency and consistent with the interests of consumers. In this case, the applicant has not shown that those conditions were fulfilled.

NOTE: Although the Court was not clear that this was a case of predatory pricing, it appears certain that where a dominant undertaking adopts a course of conduct reducing pricing selectively and there is an intention to drive a competitor from the market, that behaviour will certainly be seen as abusive. The benefits of such an approach are discussed by Andrews.

Andrews, P., 'Is Meeting Competition A Defence To Predatory Pricing? The Irish Sugar Decision Suggests A New Approach'
[1998] ECLR 49–57, pp. 55–56 [footnotes omitted]

Justification for a non-discrimination rule for predatory pricing
The objective of any rule on predatory pricing must be to prohibit the dominant firm, replete with funds gathered by exploiting its dominant position, from reducing its price to an unreasonably low level to discipline or eliminate rivals, or to discourage new entrants. At the same time, the rule must be flexible enough so that a producer who faces new competition should not be expected to stand aside impotently and watch its market collapse. Indeed, it is the essence of competition that firms should compete for custom by reducing price.

A further complicating factor is that, in establishing the intention or otherwise of the dominant firm to remove its competitors from the market by unfair means, it is difficult to distinguish between, on the one hand, a deliberate attempt to exclude a rival from the market, and, on the other hand, an intention held by the dominant firm to act bona fide in its own interest, since the two apparently distinguishable intentions are in effect different ways of looking at the same thing. The Commission acknowledged as much when it said in *AKZO* that 'it does not consider an intention even by a dominant firm to prevail over its rival as unlawful'.

Clearly, any rule on predatory pricing that must juggle these competing concerns will necessarily require flexibility in its application. Below is an attempt to summarise some of the arguments likely to be raised for and against the use of a non-discrimination rule to identify predatory behaviour.

The effect of the rule on prices in the market generally
Most serious of the possible arguments against a prohibition on selective below-cost pricing is the allegation that such a rule, by restricting dominant firms from meeting competition, would have the effect of accepting a higher price in the market. This argument runs as follows. Smaller rivals of the dominant firm will naturally concentrate their competitive efforts on the most attractive customers ('cream-skimming'). If the dominant company is deprived of the right to single out those customers and offer prices aligned with those of the smaller rival, the competitor will be free to raise its price to just below the level of the dominant company's prices. In the meantime, cream-skimming will have caused the dominant company's prices to rise generally, so that eventually the customer's new price for service may be higher than the price it paid before the competitor won the contract in the first place. Those customers who originally switched to the lower-price rival are therefore deprived of lower prices for having the willingness to switch.

One possible counter-argument is that although the rule may lead to a possible price increase in relation to the individual company with whom the dominant firm is competing, by increasing competition in the market as a whole, the rule will have a downward effect on prices. To illustrate, where a dominant firm is allowed to meet competition below cost, the price will fall as between the dominant firm and the rival and the choice of the consumer will thus be increased. However, eventually the dominant firm will eliminate all competition by pursuing such a pricing policy which, in the long run, will lead to a fall-off of competition and an increase in price. Thus, it could be argued that a general non-discrimination rule would have a price-reducing effect on a much wider group of customers since it would allow competitors access to the market, whereafter price competition could develop.

The rule would be easier to apply than the current test in *AKZO*

The *AKZO* rule is notoriously difficult to apply. The very limited number of cases in which the Commission has successfully been able to establish and prosecute predatory behaviour testifies to this fact—other than *AKZO*, *Tetra Pak II* is the only case in which such an action has successfully been taken, and in that case most of the condemned pricing was below AVC.

One reason for this is that costs are often very difficult to assess, particularly where undertakings produce or supply a multiplicity of products. Also, there remains considerable controversy as to the classification of costs as variable or fixed. Indeed, in *AKZO*, there was much dispute over the classification of labour, with the court finally upholding AKZO's claim that on this occasion labour costs were fixed rather than variable.

The second reason is that in the 'grey' area between average variable and total cost, intention is crucial. Intention, however, may be difficult to ascertain, especially when harming competitors is of the essence of the competitive process and bringing an intention to inflict harm into the predatory pricing equation is economic nonsense.

Certainly, the non-discrimination rule would reduce the burden on the Commission of establishing the exclusionary intention of the dominant firm by having greater regard for the objective pricing strategy of the dominant firm, in line with the court's ruling in *AKZO*. But would it limit the necessity of assessing costs? To determine whether the dominant firm had selectively priced below ATC would, of course, require an analysis of its cost structure.

The rule would favour the new entrant and the smaller rival

The rule would favour new entrants and smaller competitors on the market of dominance by providing them with a lifeline on entrance into the market, since until sufficient competition is established to make it worthwhile for the dominant firm to reduce its prices to all equivalent customers, they will not face price competition with the dominant firm at below cost.

This is explained as follows: the rule as proposed allows a dominant firm the option to meet competition provided it does so on a non-selective basis and without predatory intent. Thus, faced with a smaller rival offering prices below its own, the dominant firm has a choice either (i) to compete with the lower prices of the smaller rival provided it is prepared to offer the same price to all its equivalent customers, or (ii) to allow the smaller rival to enter the market without reacting to the prices. In all likelihood, the dominant firm will not react to the lower prices until a sufficient amount of its clients are threatened to make it worthwhile to drop its prices. Thus, the new entrant is allowed to capture the first few accounts. At some point in the future, however, when a sufficient number of accounts are attacked, the dominant firm will meet competition for all its customers in order to protect its traditional customer base. In many ways, this is exactly the process the Commission wants to see happening—new entrants are allowed a foothold in the market place, and once competition is sufficiently established, price competition may begin in earnest, when the dominant firm chooses the point in time when it will change its policy to respond to competitors' prices.

Clearly, however, there is significant detriment to the dominant company in the restraint such a rule imposes on its ability to defend its traditional customer base from attack. The accusation again would fly that 'the competition rules are not being used to enable efficient firms to expand at the expense of the less efficient, but to protect smaller and medium-sized firms at the expense of efficient or larger firms'.

The rule would hit at cross-subsidisation by dominant firms

Dominant firms have a special responsibility to maintain undistorted competition and must not use the additional revenue generated as a result of their dominance to engage in wrongful behaviour. A dominant firm that prices selectively below cost to meet competition is not competing on efficiency but on the basis of its greater financial reserves enjoyed by reason of its dominance. As per the court in *AKZO*, such pricing permits the dominant firm to carry on its behaviour 'by setting off losses resulting from the sales to customers of the competitor against profits made on the sales to traditional customers'. The dominant company is cross-subsidising its losses on the targeted customers with its profits from traditional customers charged above total cost. This is the very act that the non-discrimination rule seeks to prohibit.

However, cross-subsidisation is not per se illegal. Moreover, in the case of a ban on selective below-cost pricing, is it fair that the new entrant or smaller rival on the market of dominance may be permitted to cross-subsidise its promotional campaign while the dominant firm is prohibited from responding in kind?

There is objective justification for below-cost pricing

The Commission has recognised that '[t]he pursuit of activities having inadequate profitability to cover all the costs involved may indeed be economically justified in the short term, provided income remains above variable costs and the said activities contribute in part to covering fixed costs'. The rationale behind this is that dominant companies, like other companies, often have good reasons for charging, or needing to charge, below ATC. While, over the long term, a company's revenues must exceed its costs, in the short and medium term, prices above AVC will contribute to defray variable and at least some of the firm's fixed costs.

Examples of cases where pricing below cost would be justified are (i) low or promotional pricing due to the market launch of a new product (any attempt by any firm, whatever its market strength, to introduce a new product is often characterised by heavy advertising and an initial period of loss-making), (ii) selling off technically obsolescent products, and (iii) for cashflow reasons during a down-turn of the business.

Nevertheless, the fact that there are cases where it may be justified for a dominant company to price below total cost, does not mean that a non-discrimination rule is unjustified. Rather it suggests that the rule must be carefully applied. Moreover, in the above examples, the below-cost pricing is likely to be carried out on a non-selective basis which would not fall within the scope of the prohibition.

(c) Discounts and rebates

While consumers may feel that they benefit from the savings made through discounts and rebates, they can be used by dominant undertakings to 'tie' customers to them and stifle the development of true competition on a market. For that reason some discounting practices have been challenged in the EC, while others are seen as justifiable.

Hoffmann-La Roche v Commission
(Case 85/76) [1979] ECR 461, [1979] 3 CMLR 211

Hoffmann-La Roche were held to have a dominant position in the market for a number of vitamins. The Commission had challenged a number of discounts offered by Hoffmann-La Roche in its contracts with customers on the basis that they were abusive.

[89] An undertaking which is in a dominant position on a market and ties purchasers—even if it does so at their request—by an obligation or promise on their part to obtain all or most of their requirements exclusively from the said undertaking abuses its dominant position within the meaning of Article 86 of the Treaty, whether the obligation in question is stipulated without further qualification or whether it is undertaken in consideration of the grant of a rebate. The same applies if the said undertaking, without tying the purchasers by a formal obligation, applies, either under the terms of agreements concluded with these purchasers or unilaterally, a system of fidelity rebates, that is to say discounts conditional on the customer's obtaining all or most of its requirements—whether the quantity of its purchases be large or small—from the undertaking in a dominant position.

[90] Obligations of this kind to obtain supplies exclusively from a particular undertaking, whether or not they are in consideration of rebates or of the granting of fidelity rebates intended to give the purchaser an incentive to obtain his supplies exclusively from the undertaking in a dominant position, are incompatible with the objective of undistorted competition within the Common Market, because—unless there are exceptional circumstances which may make an agreement between undertakings in the context of Article 85 and in particular of paragraph (3) of that Article, permissible—they are not based on an economic transaction which justifies this burden or benefit but are designed to deprive the purchaser of or restrict his possible choices of sources of supply and to deny other producers access to the market. The fidelity rebate, unlike quantity rebates exclusively linked with the volume of purchases from the producer concerned, is designed through the grant of a financial advantage to prevent customers from obtaining their supplies from competing producers. Furthermore, the effect of fidelity rebates is to apply dissimilar conditions to equivalent transactions with other trading parties in that two purchasers pay a different price for the same quantity of the same product depending on whether they obtain their supplies exclusively from the undertaking in a dominant position or have several sources of supply. Finally, these practices by an undertaking in a dominant position and especially on an expanding market tend to consolidate this position by means of a form of competition which is not based on the transactions effected and is therefore distorted.

[91] For the purpose of rejecting the finding that there has been an abuse of a dominant position the interpretation suggested by the applicant that an abuse implies that the use of the economic power bestowed by a dominant position is the means whereby the abuse has been brought about cannot be accepted. The concept of abuse is an objective concept relating to the behaviour of an undertaking in a dominant position which is such as to influence the structure of a market where, as a result of the very presence of the undertaking in question, the degree of competition is weakened and which, through recourse to methods different from those which condition normal competition in products or services on the basis of the transactions of commercial operators, has the effect of hindering the maintenance of the degree of competition still existing in the market or the growth of that competition.

Section 5: The English clause
[102] All the contracts in question except five (the Animedica International, Guyomarc'h, Merck B sub6, Protector and Upjohn contracts) contain a clause, called the English clause, under which the customer, if he obtains from competitors offers at prices which are more favourable than those under the contracts at issue may ask Roche to adjust its prices to the said offers; if Roche does not comply with this request, the customer, in derogation from his undertaking to obtain his requirements exclusively from Roche, is entitled to get his supplies from the said competitor without for that reason losing the benefit of the fidelity rebates provided for in the contracts in respect of the other purchases already effected or still to be effected by him from Roche.

[103] In the applicant's view this clause destroys the restrictive effect on competition both of the exclusivity agreements and of the fidelity rebates. In particular in the case of those contracts which do not contain an express undertaking by the purchaser to obtain his requirements exclusively from Roche the English clause eliminates 'the attractive effect' of the rebates at issue since the customer does not have to choose between acceptance of Roche's less attractive offers or losing the benefit of the fidelity rebates on all purchases which he has already effected from Roche.

[104] There is no doubt whatever that this clause makes it possible to remedy some of the unfair consequences which undertakings by purchasers to obtain their requirements exclusively from Roche or the provision for fidelity rebates on all purchases accepted for relatively long periods, might have in so far as those purchasers are concerned. Nevertheless it is necessary to point out that the purchaser's opportunities for exploiting competition for his own benefit are more restricted than appears at first sight.
. . .

[107] It is particularly necessary to stress that, even in the most favourable circumstances, the English clause does not in fact remedy to a great extent the distortion of competition caused by the clauses obliging purchasers to obtain their requirements exclusively from Roche and by the fidelity rebates on a market where an undertaking in a dominant position is operating and where for this reason the structure of competition has already been weakened. In fact the English clause under which Roche's customers are obliged to inform it of more favourable offers made by competitors together with the particulars above mentioned—so that it will be easy for Roche to identify the competitor—owing to its very nature, places at the disposal of the applicant information about market conditions and also about the alternatives open to, and the actions of, its competitors which is of great value for the carrying out of its market strategy. The fact that an undertaking in a dominant position requires its customers or obtains their agreement under contract to notify it of its competitors' offers, whilst the said customers may have an obvious commercial interest in not disclosing them, is of such a kind as to aggravate the exploitation of the dominant position in an abusive way. Finally by virtue of the machinery of the English clause it is for Roche itself to decide whether, by adjusting its prices or not, it will permit competition.

[108] It is able in this way, owing to the information which its own customers supply, to vary its market strategy in so far as it affects them and its competitors. It follows from all these factors that the Commission's view that the English clauses incorporated in the contracts at issue were not of such a kind as to take them out of the category of abuse of a dominant position has been arrived at by means of a proper construction and application of Article 86 of the Treaty.

Nederlandsche Banden-Industrie Michelin NV v *Commission*
(Case 322/81) [1983] ECR 3461, [1985] 1 CMLR 282

Michelin NV were found to have a dominant position on the market for replacement tyres for lorries and buses. They were accused of abusing that dominant position by operating a series of abusive discounting schemes.

(b) The application of Article 86 to a system of target discounts
[70] As regards the application of Article 86 to a system of discounts conditional upon the attainment of sales targets, such as described above, it must be stated first of all that in prohibiting any abuse of a dominant position on the market in so far as it may affect trade between Member States Article 86 covers practices which are likely to affect the structure of a market where, as a direct result of the presence of the undertaking in question, competition has already been weakened and which, through recourse to methods different from those governing normal competition in products or services based on traders' performance, have the effect of hindering the maintenance or development of the level of competition still existing on the market.

[71] In the case more particularly of the grant by an undertaking in a dominant position of discounts to its customers the Court has held in its judgments of 16 December 1975 in Joined Cases 40–48/73 etc. *Cooperatieve Vereniging 'Suiker Unie' ua* v *EC Commission* and of 13 February 1979 in Case 85/76 *Hoffmann-La Roche* v *EC Commission* that in contrast to a quantity discount, which is linked solely to the volume of purchases from the manufacturer concerned, a loyalty rebate, which by offering customers financial advantages tends to prevent them from obtaining their supplies from competing manufacturers, amounts to an abuse within the meaning of Article 86 of the Treaty.

[72] As regards the system at issue in this case, which is characterised by the use of sales targets, it must be observed that this system does not amount to a mere quantity discount linked solely to the volume of goods purchased since the progressive scale of the previous year's turnover indicates only the limits within which the system applies. Michelin NV has moreover itself pointed out that the majority of dealers who bought more than 3,000 tyres a year were in any case in the group receiving the highest rebates. On the other hand the system in question did not require dealers to enter into any exclusive dealing agreements or to obtain a specific proportion of their supplies from Michelin NV, and that this point distinguishes it from loyalty rebates of the type which the Court had to consider in its judgment of 13 February 1979 in *Hoffmann-La Roche*.

[73] In deciding whether Michelin NV abused its dominant position in applying its discount system it is therefore necessary to consider all the circumstances, particularly the criteria and rules for the grant of the discount, and to investigate whether, in providing an advantage not based on any economic service justifying it, the discount tends to remove or restrict the buyer's freedom to choose his sources of supply, to bar competitors from access to the market, to apply dissimilar conditions to equivalent transactions with other trading parties or to strengthen the dominant position by distorting competition.

NOTE: When comparing these cases, it is clear that although the discounting schemes were different in nature, the reason that they were considered as abusive was the tying effect that they had on a market already distorted by the presence of the dominant undertaking. In both cases, the undertakings operated discounting schemes which were not challenged as those schemes were linked to quantity of sales and therefore could be justified on the basis of saving made by the dominant undertaking.

(d) *Refusal to supply and essential facilities*

As a dominant undertaking is, by definition, in a powerful position with regard to a particular product it is of concern to those who desire such a product that they can gain supplies from the dominant undertaking. Thus, a refusal to supply a potential customer can be problematic in relation to dominant undertakings. A complication in this area stems from the basic legal tenet that an undertaking may choose to deal with any customers in the manner of their choosing. To compel an undertaking to trade with another is a breach of their basic freedom of contract. It has been vital for competition law to set out the limited circumstances in which the law will interfere with an undertaking's basic freedom.

Istituto Chemioterapico Italiano SpA & Commercial Solvents Corporation v *EC Commission*
(Cases 6–7/73) [1974] ECR 223, [1974] 1 CMLR 309

Istituto/Commercial Solvents were the dominant producers of a number of intermediate chemical products, including 'nitropropane' and 'aminobutanol'. Those chemicals were used for the manufacture of 'ethambutol', used as an anti-tuberculosis drug. A customer of Commercial Solvents, Zoja SpA, used the intermediary products to produce ethambutol. At the end of 1970 Zoja attempted to source further supplies of the intermediary but Commercial Solvents made it clear that none would be available.

[23] The applicants state that they ought not to be held responsible for ceasing to supply aminobutanol to Zoja for this was due to the fact that in the spring of 1970 Zoja itself informed Istituto that it was cancelling the purchase of large quantities of aminobutanol which had been provided for in a contract then in force between Istituto and Zoja. When at the end of 1970 Zoja again contacted Istituto to obtain this product, the latter was obliged to reply, after consulting Commercial Solvents Corp., that in the meantime Commercial Solvents Corp. had changed its commercial policy and that the product was no longer available. The change of policy by Commercial Solvents Corp. was, they claim, inspired by a legitimate consideration of the advantage that would accrue to it of expanding its production to include the manufacture of finished products and not limiting itself to that of raw material or intermediary products. In pursuance of this policy it decided to improve its product and no longer to supply aminobutanol save in respect of commitments already entered into by its distributors.

[24] It appears from the documents and from the hearing that the suppliers of raw material are limited, as regards the EEC, to Istituto, which, as stated in the claim by Commercial Solvents Corp., started in 1968 to develop its own specialities based on ethambutol, and in November 1969 obtained the approval of the Italian government necessary for the manufacture and in 1970 started manufacturing its own specialities. When Zoja sought to obtain further supplies of aminobutanol, it received a negative reply. Commercial Solvents Corp. had decided to limit, if not completely to cease, the supply of nitropropane and aminobutanol to certain parties in order to facilitate its own access to the market for the derivatives.

[25] However, an undertaking being in a dominant position as regards the production of raw material and therefore able to control the supply to manufacturers of derivatives cannot, just because it decides to start manufacturing these derivatives (in competition with its former customers), act in such a way as to eliminate their competition which, in the case in question, would have amounted to eliminating one of the principal manufacturers of ethambutol in the Common Market. Since such conduct is contrary to the objectives expressed in Article 3(f) of the Treaty and set out in greater detail in Articles 85 and 86, it follows that an undertaking which has a dominant position in the market in raw materials and which, with the object of reserving such raw material for manufacturing its own derivatives, refuses to supply a customer, which is itself a manufacturer of these derivatives, and therefore risks eliminating all competition on the part of this customer, is abusing its dominant position within the meaning of Article 86. In this context it does not matter that the undertaking ceased to supply in the spring of 1970 because of the cancellation of the purchases by Zoja, because it appears from the applicants' own statement that, when the supplies provided for in the contract had been completed, the sale of aminobutanol would have stopped in any case.

NOTE: While the judgment in *Commercial Solvents* made it clear that a refusal to supply a customer could be abusive, it was an extreme case whereby the refusal would result in the *de facto* elimination of a major competitor. One of the major questions raised by the judgment was the extent of this obligation to supply customers and competitors. Did it only cover existing customers, or could it be extended to supplying new customers to create a competitor?

Particular problems exist when a dominant undertaking can protect its position through the exclusivity granted to it via intellectual property rights. There is always an uneasy relationship between competition law and IP law. Competition law attempts to deal with the problems created by an undertaking's power over the market where there are no other providers of a product; IP law attempts to reward innovation by ensuring that an innovator can retain exclusivity for a period of time. If an innovator is forced to provide protected material to competitors surely that would remove the reward that their exclusivity was supposed to create.

Radio Telefis Eireann and Independent Television Publications Limited v EC Commission

(Joined Cases C 241-242/91P) [1995] ECR I-743, [1995] 4 CMLR 718

Most households in Ireland and a sizeable minority in Northern Ireland can receive television programmes broadcast by RTE, ITV and BBC. No comprehensive weekly television guide was available on the market in Ireland or in Northern Ireland. Each television station published a television guide covering its own programmes and claimed, under Irish and United Kingdom legislation, copyright protection for its own weekly programme listings in order to prevent their reproduction by third parties. The copyright holders provided their programme schedules free of charge, on request, to daily and periodical newspapers, accompanied by a licence for which no charge was made, setting out the conditions under which that information could be reproduced. Daily listings could thus be published in the press. Magill TV Guide Ltd attempted to publish a comprehensive weekly television guide but was prevented from doing so by RTE, ITP and the BBC, which obtained injunctions prohibiting publication of weekly television listings. Magill lodged a complaint with the Commission which adopted a decision against RTE, ITP and BBC. In that decision the Commission found that there had been a breach of Article 82 EC and ordered the three organisations to put an end to that breach.

[48] With regard to the issue of abuse, the arguments of the appellants and IPO wrongly presuppose that where the conduct of an undertaking in a dominant position consist of the exercise of a right classified by national law as 'copyright', such conduct can never be reviewed in relation to Article 86 of the Treaty.

[49] Admittedly, in the absence of Community standardisation or harmonisation of laws, determination of the conditions and procedures for granting protection of an intellectual property right is a matter for national rules. Further, the exclusive right of reproduction forms part of the author's rights, so that refusal to grant a licence, even if it is the act of an undertaking holding a dominant position, cannot in itself constitute abuse of a dominant position. (See *Volvo* v *Veng*, above, at paras [7] and [8].)

[50] However, it is also clear from that judgment (at para. 9) that the exercise of an exclusive right by the proprietor may, in exceptional circumstances, involve abusive conduct.

[51] In the present case, the conduct objected to is the appellants' reliance on copyright conferred by national legislation so as to prevent Magill—or any other undertaking having the same intention—from publishing on a weekly basis information (channel, day, time and title of programmes) together with commentaries and pictures obtained independently of the appellants.

[52] Among the circumstances taken into account by the Court of First Instance in concluding that such conduct was abusive was, first, the fact that there was, according to the findings of the Court of First Instance, no actual or potential substitute for a weekly television guide offering information on the programmes for the week ahead. On this point, the Court of First Instance confirmed the Commission's finding that the complete lists of programmes for a 24-hour period—and for a 48-hour period at weekends and before public holidays—published in certain daily and Sunday newspapers,

and the television sections of certain magazines covering, in addition, 'highlights' of the week's programmes, were only to a limited extent substitutable for advance information to viewers on all the week's programmes. Only weekly television guides containing comprehensive listings for the week ahead would enable users to decide in advance which programmes they wished to follow and arrange their leisure activities for the week accordingly. The Court of First Instance also established that there was a specific, constant and regular potential demand on the part of consumers (see the RTE judgment, paragraph [62], and the ITP judgment, paragraph [48]).

[53] Thus the appellants—who were, by force of circumstance, the only sources of the basic information on programme scheduling which is the indispensable raw material for compiling a weekly television guide—gave viewers wishing to obtain information on the choice of programmes for the week ahead no choice but to buy the weekly guides for each station and draw from each of them the information they needed to make comparisons.

[54] The appellants' refusal to provide basic information by relying on national copyright provisions thus prevented the appearance of a new product, a comprehensive weekly guide to television programmes, which the appellants did not offer and for which there was a potential consumer demand. Such refusal constitutes an abuse under heading (b) of the second paragraph of Article 86 of the Treaty.

[55] Second, there was no justification for such refusal either in the activity of television broadcasting or in that of publishing television magazines (RTE judgment, paragraph [73], and ITP judgment, paragraph [58]).

[56] Third, and finally, as the Court of First Instance also held, the appellants, by their conduct, reserved to themselves the secondary market of weekly television guides by excluding all competition on that market (see 6/73 and 7/73, *Commercial Solvents* v *EC Commission* [1974] ECR 223, [1974] 1 CMLR 309, at para. [25]) since they denied access to the basic information which is the raw material indispensable for the compilation of such a guide.

[57] In the light of all those circumstances, the Court of First Instance did not err in law in holding that the appellants' conduct was an abuse of a dominant position within the meaning of Article 86 of the Treaty.

[58] It follows that the plea in law alleging misapplication by the Court of First Instance of the concept of abuse of a dominant position must be dismissed as unfounded.

NOTE: The *'Magill'* judgment, as this series of litigation is sometimes known, made it clear that the Court may require an undertaking to supply a new customer with a product or service, especially when that refusal to supply would stop the creation of a new product for which there is a demand, or deserve a secondary market to the supplier. But the Court also made clear this was an exceptional circumstance, particularly because of the complications introduced because the material in question was copyright. Is the position the same where there are no IP rights in question?

Oscar Bronner GmbH & Co KG v *Mediaprint Zeitungs- und Zeitschriftenverlag GmbH & Co KG*
(Case C-7/97) [1998] ECR I-7791, [1999] 4 CMLR 112

Oscar Bronner published a daily newspaper in Austria. Its share of the market was 3.6 per cent of circulation. Mediaprint published two newspapers which had a combined market share of 46.8 per cent of circulation. In the domestic courts Bronner sought an order requiring Mediaprint to allow Bronner access to its nationwide home-delivery service for daily newspapers against payment of reasonable remuneration. Mediaprint refused such access to their network, which was the only nationwide network in Austria. The domestic court referred a number of questions to the Court of Justice under Article 234 EC.

[23] In its first question, the national court effectively asks whether the refusal by a press undertaking which holds a very large share of the daily newspaper market in a Member State and operates the only nationwide newspaper home-delivery scheme in that Member State to allow the publisher of a rival newspaper, which by reason of its small circulation is unable either alone or in co-operation with other publishers to set up and operate its own home-delivery scheme in economically reasonable conditions, to have access to that scheme for appropriate remuneration constitutes the abuse of a dominant position within the meaning of Article 86 of the Treaty.

[24] In that respect, Oscar Bronner argues that the supply of services consisting in the home delivery of daily newspapers constitutes a separate market, inasmuch as that service is normally offered and requested separately from other services. Oscar Bronner also argues that, under the doctrine of 'essential facilities' as established by the Court of Justice in Joined Cases, C 241 & 242/91 P, *RTE and Itp* v *EC Commission* ([1995] ECR I-743; [1995] 4 CMLR 418) (the '*Magill* judgment'), the service performed by placing a facility at the disposal of others and that supplied by using that facility in principle constitute separate markets. It therefore maintains that, as the owner of such an 'essential facility', in this case the only economically viable home-delivery scheme existing in Austria on a national scale, Mediaprint is obliged to allow access to the scheme by competing products on market conditions and at market prices.

[25] Oscar Bronner also refers in this context to Joined Cases 6 and 7/73, *Commercial Solvents* v *EC Commission*, ([1974] ECR 223; [1974] 1 CMLR 309, para. [25]) which, in its submission, demonstrates that the refusal by an undertaking in a dominant position to supply undertakings immediately downstream is lawful only if objectively justifed. Referring to the judgment of the Court of Justice in Case 311/84, *CBEM* v *CLT and IPB*, ([1985] ECR 3261; [1986] 2 CMLR 558) in which it held that an abuse within the meaning of Article 86 is committed where, without any objective necessity, an undertaking holding a dominant position on a particular market reserves to itself or to an undertaking belonging to the same group an ancillary activity which might be carried out by another undertaking as part of its activities on a neighbouring but separate market, with the possibility of eliminating all competition from such undertaking, Oscar Bronner maintains that that consideration applies equally to the case of an undertaking holding a dominant position in the market for a given supply of services, which is indispensable for the activity of another undertaking in a different market.

[26] Mediaprint objects that, in principle, undertakings in a dominant position are also entitled to the freedom to arrange their own affairs, in that they are normally entitled to decide freely to whom they wish to offer their services and, in particular, to whom they wish to allow access to their own facilities. Thus, as the Court expressly held in *Magill*, an obligation to contract, to which an undertaking holding a dominant position would be subject, can be based on Article 86 of the Treaty only in exceptional circumstances.

[27] In Mediaprint's submission, the judgments in *Commercial Solvents* v *EC Commission and CBEM*, (cited above) show that such exceptional circumstances exist only if the dominant undertaking's refusal to supply is likely to eliminate all competition in a downstream market, which is not the case in the main proceedings, where, in parallel with home delivery, other distribution systems enable Oscar Bronner to sell its daily newspapers in Austria.

[28] Mediaprint adds that, even if such exceptional circumstances did exist, a dominant undertaking's refusal to contract is not abusive if it is objectively justified. That would be the case in the main proceedings if the inclusion of Der Standard were likely to compromise the functioning of Mediaprint's home-delivery scheme or were to be shown to be impossible for reasons relating to the capacity of that scheme.

[29] The Commission points out that it is for the national court to assess whether the conditions for

applying Article 86 of the Treaty are met, and maintains that it is only if a separate market in home-delivery schemes exists and Mediaprint holds a dominant position in that market that it needs to be examined whether its refusal to include Oscar Bronner in that network constitutes an abuse.

. . .

[37] Finally it would need to be determined whether the refusal by the owner of the only nationwide home-delivery scheme in the territory of a Member State, which uses that scheme to distribute its own daily newspapers, to allow the publisher of a rival daily newspaper access to it constitutes an abuse of a dominant position within the meaning of Article 86 of the Treaty, on the ground that such refusal deprives that competitor of a means of distribution judged essential for the sale of its newspaper.

[38] Although in *Commercial Solvents* v *EC Commission and CBEM*, (cited above) the Court of Justice held the refusal by an undertaking holding a dominant position in a given market to supply an undertaking with which it was in competition in a neighbouring market with raw materials (*Commercial Solvents* v *EC Commission*, para. [25]) and services (*CBEM*, para. [26]) respectively, which were indispensable to carrying on the rival's business, to constitute an abuse, it should be noted, first, that the Court did so to the extent that the conduct in question was likely to eliminate all competition on the part of that undertaking.

[39] Secondly, in *Magill*, at paras [49] and [50], the Court held that refusal by the owner of an intellectual property right to grant a licence, even if it is the act of an undertaking holding a dominant position, cannot in itself constitute abuse of a dominant position, but that the exercise of an exclusive right by the proprietor may, in exceptional circumstances, involve an abuse.

[40] In *Magill*, the Court found such exceptional circumstances in the fact that the refusal in question concerned a product (information on the weekly schedules of certain television channels) the supply of which was indispensable for carrying on the business in question (the publishing of a general television guide), in that, without that information, the person wishing to produce such a guide would find it impossible to publish it and offer it for sale, (para. [53]) the fact that such refusal prevented the appearance of a new product for which there was a potential consumer demand, (para. [54]) the fact that it was not justified by objective considerations, (para. [55]) and that it was likely to exclude all competition in the secondary market of television guides. (para. [56])

[41] Therefore, even if that case law on the exercise of an intellectual property right were applicable to the exercise of any property right whatever, it would still be necessary, for the *Magill* judgment to be effectively relied upon in order to plead the existence of an abuse within the meaning of Article 86 of the Treaty in a situation such as that which forms the subject-matter of the first question, not only that the refusal of the service comprised in home delivery be likely to eliminate all competition in the daily newspaper market on the part of the person requesting the service and that such refusal be incapable of being objectively justified, but also that the service in itself be indispensable to carrying on that person's business, inasmuch as there is no actual or potential substitute in existence for that home-delivery scheme.

[42] That is certainly not the case even if, as in the case which is the subject of the main proceedings, there is only one nationwide home-delivery scheme in the territory of a Member State and, moreover, the owner of that scheme holds a dominant position in the market for services constituted by that scheme or of which it forms part.

[43] In the first place, it is undisputed that other methods of distributing daily newspapers, such as by post and through sale in shops and at kiosks, even though they may be less advantageous for the distribution of certain newspapers, exist and are used by the publishers of those daily newspapers.

[44] Moreover, it does not appear that there are any technical, legal or even economic obstacles capable of making it impossible, or even unreasonably difficult, for any other publishers of daily

newspapers to establish, alone or in cooperation with other publishers, its own nationwide home-delivery scheme and use it to distribute its own daily newspapers.

[45] It should be emphasised in that respect that, in order to demonstrate that the creation of such a system is not a realistic potential alternative and that access to the existing system is therefore indispensable, it is not enough to argue that it is not economically viable by reason of the small circulation of the daily newspaper or newspapers to be distributed.

[46] For such access to be capable of being regarded as indispensable, it would be necessary at the very least to establish, as the Advocate General has pointed out at paragraph 68 of his Opinion, that it is not economically viable to create a second home-delivery scheme for the distribution of daily newspapers with a circulation comparable to that of the daily newspapers distributed by the existing scheme.

[47] In the light of the foregoing considerations, the answer to the first question must be that the refusal by a press undertaking which holds a very large share of the daily newspaper market in a Member State and operates the only nationwide newspaper home-delivery scheme in that Member State to allow the publisher of a rival newspaper, which by reason of its small circulation is unable either alone or in cooperation with other publishers to set up and operate its own home-delivery scheme in economically reasonable conditions, to have access to that scheme for appropriate remuneration does not constitute abuse of a dominant position within the meaning of Article 86 of the Treaty.

NOTE: *Oscar Bronner* settled a number of questions regarding the extent of the 'essential facilities' doctrine whereby a competitor should be given access to a facility owned and operated by a dominant undertaking. It restricts the doctrine to a limited number of circumstances where it is not practicable to replicate the facility. This would tend to limit its application to situations where there is a 'natural' monopoly, in that the market will only bear one such facility and it does not make economic sense to require a competitor to invest in replicating that which is currently operated by the dominant undertaking.

The situation in which an 'essential facility' can become a problem is explained by Ridyard.

Ridyard, D., 'Essential Facilities and the Obligation to Supply Competitors Under the UK and EC Competition Law'
[1996] 17(8) ECLR 438, pp. 438–440, [footnotes omitted]

Introduction to the Essential Facilities Doctrine

In the *Sealink* decision, the Commission describes an essential facility as follows: 'a facility or infra-structure, without access to which competitors cannot provide services to their customers'. The decision goes on to assert that refusal to grant access to an essential facility without 'objective justification', or the granting of access to that facility on 'discriminatory terms' represents an infringement of Article 86. This suggests that there are two central issues to the evaluation of essential facilities problems:

— First, what are the circumstances in which an essential facility can be said to exist?
— Second, where an essential facility has been identified, what are the terms on which access to that facility by competitors should be granted?

Although there are many cases involving essential facility issues, it is remarkable how little light these cases shed on these two central questions. In a review of the US cases, Areeda sums up the problem with the essential facilities doctrine as follows:

You will not find any case that provides a consistent rationale for the doctrine that explores the social costs and benefits of the administration costs of requiring the creator of an asset to share it with a rival. It is less a doctrine than an epithet indicating some exceptions to the right to keep one's creations to oneself, but not telling us what those exceptions are.

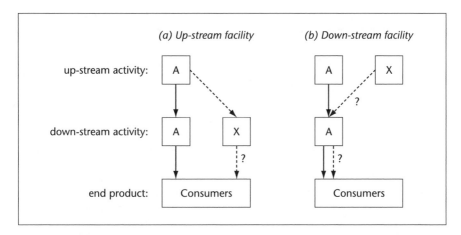

Figure 1 The Essential Facilities Problem

Areeda's conclusion is that there is a need for a 'limiting principle' to inject some discipline into the application of essential facilities arguments. A similar conclusion can readily be reached on the UK and EC cases. Before discussing some of these cases in more detail, it may first be helpful to describe the essential facilities dilemma in terms of a simplified model into which most cases can be made to fit.

The market situation underlying the essential facilities problem is one involving two related activities, both of which form components of the product that is purchased by the end consumer. For convenience, these two components can be characterised as 'up-stream' and 'down-stream' activities, such as manufacture and distribution. The essential facilities problem might arise at either the up-stream or down-stream levels, and can be depicted as shown in Figure 1.

In the scenario of the up-stream facility, Firm A supplies consumers with its product, which is a combination or 'bundle' of the up-stream and down-stream activities. The question is, should firm X, which has a capability to perform the down-stream activity only, have access to the up-stream facility of firm A in order to supply consumers as well? Conceptually similar considerations apply in the case of the down-stream facility.

Since most products purchased by consumers go through a number of separate processing stages, almost any product market could in principle become subject to this kind of dispute. This explains why the concept of essential facility obligations is so threatening to business, and underlines the need for some form of discipline (or Areeda's 'limiting principle') to control its application. To illustrate, the up-stream/down-stream dichotomy depicted in Figure 1 can apply in the following cases:

'Up-stream'	'Down-stream'
Transport infrastructure	Transport operator
(eg rail, port, airport)	(eg train, ferry, airline)
Pipeline/Wire	Supply of water, gas, electricity, telephone services through pipe/wire
Manufacture	Retail/distribution
R & D	Manufacture
Raw material	Processing
Manufacture	Marketing/branding
Spare parts	Maintenance service

Whatever the precise context of the case, the basic arguments of both sides in an essential facilities case (firm 'X' the complainant, firm 'A' the defendant as depicted in Figure 1) are along the following lines:

— The complainant (firm X) typically argues that A's refusal to deal prevents firm X from entering the market, and that this reduces consumer choice, protects firm A's down-stream activity from competition and thus keeps prices for the product as a whole too high. It further argues that the costs of X establishing its own up-stream facility as an alternative to that of firm A would be prohibitive and would cancel out the potential advantages it is able to offer to consumers.

— The defendant (firm A) typically argues that there are intrinsic efficiency advantages in keeping both the up-stream and down-stream activities in-house ('economies of scope'); that the 'benefits' firm X claims to be able to deliver to consumers if only it could gain access to A's up-stream facility belong to firm A as a reward for having built up a sought-after up-stream facility in the first place; and that competition and consumer interests are adequately protected by the fact that firm A faces (actual or potential) competition from firms B, C, and D (not shown in Figure 1) who supply alternative 'bundles' of the up-stream and down-stream activities to consumers.

Without investigating the facts of the case, the merits of these opposing arguments cannot safely be prejudged. The inherent conflict between static and dynamic incentives for competition can clearly be seen in the above characterisation of the arguments. It will invariably be the case that denying supply to the complainant will stifle a potential short-term gain to consumers (in price, quality and/or choice terms). Equally, however, requiring the defendant to share its assets with a down-stream competitor will invariably affect the incentives and rewards in the market, and will thus to some extent dull the motivation for others to undertake similar investments in the future.'

NOTE: *Oscar Bronner* is seen by many as being the European Court's attempt to strike that balance by setting out the limited circumstances in which a dominant undertaking will be required to open up its 'facility' to competitors. Even though *Oscar Bronner* settles a number of important issues it still leaves a number of important issues unanswered as Bergman explains.

Bergman, M.A., 'The Bronner Case—A Turning Point for the Essential Facilities Doctrine'
[2000] 21(2) ECLR 59, p. 61 [footnotes omitted]

A more restrictive view
If the new criterion set out in the *Bronner* case were to be used in other cases, without consideration of the specific circumstances, a Catch-22 situation may result. The criterion does not explicitly take into consideration that it may be impossible for the competitor to attain a market share of 50 per cent, even if in principle it would be possible to create and operate the required facility once that market share is reached. Furthermore, if this new criterion is applied generally, this will severely restrict the applicability of the essential facilities doctrine, i.e. to markets where only one firm has the possibility to be viable.

With such an interpretation, the essential facilities doctrine cannot be used to facilitate entry into markets with limited competition, as entry is only possible if more than one firm is expected to be economically viable in the long run. Instead, the doctrine will only be applicable to markets in which two or more firms can never be economically viable on their own unless the essential facilities doctrine is applied. Such markets are sometimes referred to as natural monopolies, although a more correct denomination may be 'inevitable monopolies'. In such markets, a second firm can only thrive on an artificial habitat created by the application of the doctrine. The effect of the doctrine is hence to serve as an instrument for indirect price regulation of markets that are 'inevitable monopolies'. In particular, the doctrine cannot create or preserve a market structure that will in turn stimulate competition and efficiency. The price-regulatory effect will follow because competitors will be granted access to the facility at non-discriminatory terms, which in turn will limit the dominant firm's ability to exploit customers on the related market. To favour the method of indirect price regulation over the method of creating structural conditions for competition stands in stark contrast to pre-dominant views on competition policy. Normally, measures that prevent a firm from strengthening its dominance, e.g. by eliminating its rivals with predatory measures, are preferred over measures that prevent a firm from exploiting its customers, e.g. by abusively high prices.

That the essential facilities doctrine can only be applied towards 'inevitable monopolies' is not in accordance with earlier cases that are seen as applications of the doctrine, e.g. Commercial Solvents, and cases concerning airlines' computerised booking systems (so-called CRSs), e.g. *Sabena*. When it comes to CRSs, there do indeed exist a number of such systems. It appears unlikely that the chemical compound that Commercial Solvents produced could not even theoretically be profitably produced by more than one firm. When the doctrine has been applied and analysed earlier, it has been stressed that the prerequisite must not be that it is physically impossible for a competing firm to duplicate the facility, but that it should be economically unfeasible for competing firms. The *Bronner* case must also be interpreted along these lines. The statements of the Court could be read to imply that it must be economically impossible for every firm to duplicate the facility starting from any market share—unless it could simply replace the incumbent firm. In earlier cases, in contrast, it appears sometimes to have been sufficient that it was impossible for the concerned firm. A more reasonable interpretation is that the former condition was relevant in this particular case, although not necessarily in every case that concerns the essential facilities doctrine. Even so, the (preliminary) ruling has to some extent made the conditions for applying the doctrine stricter.

FURTHER READING

Gyselen, L., and Kyriazis, N., 'Article 86 EEC: The Monopoly Power Measurement Issue Revisited' (1986) 11 ELRev 134.

Jebsen, P., and Stevens, R., 'Assumptions, Goals and Dominant Undertakings: The Regulation of Competition under Article 86 of the European Union' (1995–6) 64 Antitrust L.J., 143.

Baker, S., and Wu, L., 'Applying the Market Definition Guidelines of the European Commission' [1998] ECLR 273.

9

UK merger control

SECTION 1: **Introduction: FTA 1973**

Merger policy is probably the most politically sensitive aspect of UK competition policy. The question of the appropriate degree of merger control and the form it should take have been widely debated, most recently in relation to the reform of UK merger control introduced by Part III of the Enterprise Act.

Rodger, B.J., 'Reinforcing the Scottish "Ring-fence": A Critique of UK Mergers Policy vis-à-vis the Scottish Economy'
[1996] ECLR 104

Two views predominate on the exercise of control that may be deemed to be most appropriate. On the one hand, some argue that such intervention can only be justified if the merger is likely to have an adverse effect on the competitive formation of the industry, otherwise decisions ought to be left in the capable hands of the entrepreneurs. Protagonists of the second view would argue that a more interventionist stance is required, since mergers have generally been found not to produce the expected benefits, and 'so that various socio-political considerations, such as the effect of mergers upon unemployment and regional policy, can also be taken into account'.

Of all the arguments raised against mergers, that of the reduction in competition which may arise is viewed as the most prominent. The controversial issue is whether any other detrimental effects of mergers ought to be within the competition authorities' remit. It is widely believed that the effect on competition ought to be the sole consideration to be excluded from the market's determination as to the desirability of a particular merger. However the valid assumption may also be drawn that the interests of shareholders do not, at least necessarily, coincide with the public interest. This, in itself, may be viewed as the greatest justification for the existence of a control system which incorporates extraneous issues.

Various other specific detriments connected with mergers include objections as to the size and power of the merged firm, the possible detrimental effect on the balance of payments and transfer of control of a UK company into foreign hands, thus negating any economic advantages to be gained by the merger.

NOTE: The arguments that mergers are driven by efficiency gains and are beneficial for the economy in terms of enhanced R & D and innovation are not supported by any conclusive empirical data.

Sharpe, T., 'Merger Control in the United Kingdom'
[1983] ECLR 171

The most striking feature of merger policy in the United Kingdom has been its failure. The growth of concentration in manufacturing industry has continued unabated, and most of this increase can be attributed to mergers. There is little or no evidence to suggest any corresponding increase in efficiency associated with the increase in concentration. This is predictable because it is funda-mental to this article that there is a clear connection between industrial *structure* and *behaviour* in the market. The more concentrated the market, the more opportunity exists for exploiting market power. Exploitation can take many forms. Traditionally, market power is regarded as the capacity to control price and output, to extract significant profits and thereby to reduce the real incomes of consumers. But market power can be enjoyed as well as exploited. Inefficiencies can be tolerated, there is less need to be responsive to consumers' wishes. Managers working in such an environ-ment would be less than human if they did not award each other generous salaries and agreeable benefits, all of which could be justified to the inquisitive shareholder by reference to past growth and profits.

Moreover, the more concentrated a market becomes the greater is the capacity, if not for *express* collusion, at least for *tacit* collusion. There are so few players in the market. Their behaviour becomes interdependent: prices change in unison, new products are introduced in an orderly way, quality changes take place across an industry and mutually high levels of advertising expenditure maintain market shares. Technology, for some writers the source of violent discontinuities and dislocation, is, in fact, managed and directed. The stasis is confirmed and the textbook promiscuity of the market disappears. In short, mergers lead to increased market power, lower efficiency, lower real incomes and a diminishing of the sense of rivalry necessary for the market to work. The market becomes sclerotic.

NOTE: Sharpe was sceptical as to the merits of mergers and any gains for the economy. However, one should be aware of the different context in which his article was published in 1984, when perhaps a more *laisser-faire* attitude to mergers had been adopted. A number of recently pro-posed mergers, for instance *BskyB/Man Utd* (Cm 4305, 1999) and *Lloyds TSB/Abbey National* (Cm 5208, 2001) have been blocked under the FTA 1973 demonstrating the ongoing significance of the merger control provisions in the UK.

Merger controls were first introduced into UK competition law in the Monopolies and Mergers Act 1965, based on the Board of Trade White Paper of 1964, *Monopolies, Mergers and Restrictive Practices* (Cmnd 2299, London, HMSO, March 1964).

Board of Trade White Paper of 1964, Monopolies, Mergers and Restrictive Practices
paras 21–27

21. The Government recognise and welcome the contribution which mergers can make to the well-being of the economy. Mergers often enable better use to be made of resources, and result in units large enough both to finance desirable research and development and to produce economies of scale. Where this is so, mergers are clearly advantageous. They contribute to the strength of the economy, and put British industry in a better position to compete in international trade.

22. There is, however, a small minority of mergers which may have harmful results. The Govern-ment think it desirable that it should be made possible to have such cases investigated.

23. For this purpose, the Government propose that the new Monopolies Commission should be empowered at the direction of the Board of Trade, to inquire into any proposed or recently completed merger which would result in a monopoly or would increase the power of an existing monopoly. It is expected that in practice an inquiry would seldom be necessary. It would always be

possible for firms contemplating a merger to consult the Board of Trade about the proposals. The Board would welcome such consultations.

24. The Government contemplate directing the Commission's attention to certain considerations to which it should have regard in particular cases in assessing where the public interest lay. They have in mind such considerations as efficiency, technical and technological advance, industrial growth and competitive power in international trade.

25. The Government do not intend to seek powers to hold up a proposed merger while it is being investigated. This could well frustrate desirable mergers.

26. When the Commission had completed an inquiry, its function would be, as in the case of monopolies, to report on whether the merger was against the public interest, and if so in what respects. It would have to evaluate the evidence available on such questions as the extent to which competition would be reduced and the benefits to be expected from the larger scale of operation which the merger would permit.

27. In the light of the Commission's Report it would then be for the Government to take such action as they believed to be necessary. In a situation requiring such action a completed merger would be treated as a monopoly and the proposed powers for dealing with monopolies would be appropriate. Where a merger had not been completed, power would be required to prohibit it or to attach conditions to its completion. The exercise of this power would in each case be subject to Parliamentary approval.

NOTE: Tightening one area of competition law may lead to different forms of anti-competitive response by industry. It has been noted that the introduction of the Restrictive Trade Practices Act 1956, which laid down a registration system for restrictive practices, reduced the scope for British industry to employ price-fixing and market-sharing cartels which had become common-place. (See Mercer, H., *Constructing a Competitive Order, The Hidden History of British Antitrust Policies*, Cambridge, CUP, 1995.) The introduction of the 1956 legislation resulted in a 'merger boom' as industry sought alternative ways to forming cartels as a means of maximising their profits. The 1965 legislation can be viewed, at least partially, as a response to the wave of mergers which could threaten competition in the UK.

Wilks, S., *In The Public Interest, Competition Policy and the Monopolies and Mergers Commission*
Manchester, MUP, 1999, pp. 204–208

The debates over the introduction of merger control in the UK were largely about detail and emphasis, they were not marked by fundamental disagreements and were bi-partisan (indeed, tri-partisan, with Liberal support). This allowed an incremental development of policy with much of the running being made by officials in the BoT. It follows that the principles and the core arguments about merger control were not fully exposed and debated. The outcome was, first, that merger control squeezed into competition policy largely unannounced; and second, that the model of control adopted was based on the methods of monopoly control. Charles Rowley was able to observe that 'perhaps the most important post-war extension of the power of the executive in the affairs of the private sector was legislated with scarce a suspicion of public anxiety'. Rowley's view seems initially to smack of hyperbole but, in historical perspective, the interventionist preoccupations of the Labour Government have melted like early morning mist, leaving intact an apparatus of merger control that has become a more and more dominant feature of the regulatory landscape.

This low key series of policy innovations incorporated a series of principles which have continued to influence merger policy. There are six principles to be emphasised:

- mergers are regarded with favour
- merger control is administrative, not judicial

- the American model of prohibition is rejected
- the economic impact of mergers is subject to a 'monopoly' test
- the procedures and the ultimate criteria are politically controlled
- the main discipline is business self-regulation.

These principles are explored later in the chapter and surface regularly throughout the book. Nevertheless, they deserve a little further elaboration here. They emerged in the 1960s, form part of the genetic code of British merger control, and have exerted continued influence over the thirty plus years of merger experience.

Mergers are regarded with favour

A slightly surreal tone is imparted to the debate over merger control by the repeated protestations that mergers are desirable. This surfaces again and again in official papers, in parliamentary debates and in lobbying. In his opening of the second reading debate, Jay observed that 'greater size and further amalgamations may be desirable in the public interest; and the Government may be justified in actually promoting amalgamations'. The official papers are even more adamant. In their response to the Cabinet Economic Development Committee's approval of the Bill, which defined the planned contents, the BoT officials note the need to avoid 'putting obstacles in the way of the larger number of desirable or neutral mergers. Mergers . . . may be positively beneficial.' This position echoes down the decades. In 1983 the Deputy Director of Fair Trading (herself one of the originators of the Act) can be found observing to a business audience that, 'We frequently point out to firms that British law is basically *favourable* to mergers'. This encouraging stance rested on an unholy alliance of Labour rationalisers who wanted strategic mergers; industrialists who wanted freedom; early libertarians defending property rights; and the City in pursuit of freedom to transact. Even the TUC General Council expressed concern to the BoT in July 1965 that 'the Government's proposals may "discourage desirable mergers"'. Merger control was therefore created as a system of exceptional intervention to pick up cases of extraordinary harm. It was not seen as a policy systematically pursuing economic or social goals.

Merger control is administrative, not judicial

It is striking that the courts have been kept out of merger control. The choice of an administrative procedure, emphasising discretion and based on a broad public interest test, has moulded the development of policy. This may have been a choice congenial to officials but it also accorded well with the views of industry. As we have seen, the FBI had come to detest the workings of the Restrictive Practices Court. It had proved severe, the burden of proof was against the practice, and appearances before the Court could be quite terrifying. Hence, in their summary of the FBI submission to the BoT, officials noted that, 'if there is to be machinery for inquiry into mergers, the FBI consider that this should be administrative not legal, because the principal matter for consideration in the field of mergers, namely the economic effect of monopoly, cannot in their view be subjected to the rules of judicial procedure'. It therefore proved very convenient to turn to the administrative procedures of the MC and to the case-by-case approach. Later debates about the lack of precedents and guidelines generate criticisms which simply follow logically from this early choice.

Rejection of the American model

At this point the only operational merger regime was to be found in the United States (the German system required reporting of mergers but no control until 1973). Officials spent relatively little energy studying American practice and there is little evidence of US lobbying, although during the passage of the Bill the Foreign Office became agitated about extra-territoriality. Both the Poole and the Bow Group reports examined American experience more systematically but could see little merit in the Clayton Act approach, which involved a prohibition based upon the effect on competition. They and the BoT also reviewed the embryonic mechanisms of EEC competition policy but noted the absence of any system of merger control. The preference was for an indigenous regime and was deep seated.

The Bow Group observed, disapprovingly, that competition 'is taken as part of the American way of life and it is almost true to say that competition would be preferred to efficiency'—shades of Keith Joseph! Ellis also saw a basic philosophical divide between an American 'structural' approach concerned to apply general principles, and a British 'performance' approach concerned with a carefully pragmatic analysis of individual cases.

The application of a 'monopoly' test
The stimulus to the creation of merger control was a popular and political concern with industrial giganticism, with the tactics of hostile takeovers, and with foreign takeovers of major British companies. But the policy and the administrative response was to place merger control in the context of monopoly control and in the hands of the MC. The test for judging a merger was therefore, 'is it likely to create a monopoly that would operate against the public interest?', *not* whether it restricted competition, whether the takeover was fair, or whether politically undesirable economic concentration would result.

These early choices meant that the long and elaborate MMC investigation process was also applied to mergers. It also meant that the MMC did not concern itself with the fairness and the dynamics of the merger process itself (that was sub-contracted to the Takeover Panel). It was concerned with predicted outcomes, not mechanisms, although it did become concerned with the managerial aspects of what became known in the 1980s as 'the market for corporate control'. The calibre and likely strategy of management teams featured quite prominently in several early reports and were factors which seemed to incline MMC groups to be more sceptical of hostile takeovers. The logic of linking the merger criteria to prospective monopoly abuses was that size and industrial structure were important in the MMC evaluation. Franks and Harris pointed out that the average value of a rejected bid (1965–85) was five times higher than that of an accepted bid; and observers have consistently pointed out a rough correlation between post-merger market share and rejection. This would have lent itself to a structural guideline as used by the Department of Justice in the US except that the MMC doctrine of case-by-case examination, and the DTI's affection for the public interest test, made such a regularisation of policy impossible. The 1965 Act, therefore, arguably set up a structural test for merger control; but then set up administrative machinery unable to codify structural rules.

The maintenance of ultimate political control
Built into the merger control mechanism is the classic pragmatism of the British civil service. References and the choice of remedies were placed under ministerial control. The only exception (and it is a substantial one) is that if the MMC finds no public interest detriment the matter ends there and the merger is allowed. Later observers stressed the extraordinary politicisation of the process of merger control and, as we have seen with monopolies, the referral process is of central importance. The MMC can only investigate what is referred to it, and it is interesting that the 1963 Cabinet Sub-committee on Monopolies had recommended that 'the initiative for making an investigation into a merger would rest with the Commission'. The White Paper had transferred the initiative to the Registrar and, when that idea was shelved, the referral process was kept within the BoT. Some guidance on the public interest had been canvassed in the White Paper. This stressed 'efficiency, technical and technological advance, industrial growth and competitive power in international trade', which were essentially industrial policy criteria and would have changed the nature of merger control. But the attempt to define the public interest in mergers was abandoned and the 1965 Act defined the public interest in merger cases even more widely than for monopolies (it was aligned to the monopolies definition in the 1973 Act). This emphasis on executive discretion was always built into the system but O'Brien actually identified the resort to administrative and discretionary solutions as growing throughout the 1970s.

Control through business self-regulation
The record of merger control exhibits a tolerant attitude towards industry and a basic belief that

industry will behave reasonably. This is in the tradition of the post-war settlement and the 1948 Act but it contrasts with the prohibition approach of the 1956 Restrictive Practices Act and the resale price maintenance prohibitions. This posture reflects, of course, the essentially benign view of mergers, but it also reflects two strong traditions in relations between government and industry (see chapter 1). The first is the respect for property rights, the second a faith in industry's ability to police itself. The respect for property rights is second nature. It rests partly on the fact that the pre-eminent legal responsibility of the company director is to the shareholders and on the norm that companies should have the freedom to contract in pursuit of shareholder interests. This position was re-stated in the DTI's 1988 Consultation Paper, which affirms that 'intervention by public authorities in lawful commercial transactions should be kept to a minimum' and that 'a decision to prevent a merger entails a considerable limitation of property owners' ordinary rights to sell their assets as they choose, and should not be taken lightly'. From this perspective mergers are mainly a concern for shareholders, not a matter of public policy. And even then, both the shareholder interests and the public interest can be defended by self-regulation. The resort to self-regulation, supported by reasonable administrative action rather than legal powers, is entirely characteristic of British relations with industry. In this arena it is seen graphically in the City Panel on Takeovers and Mergers and its associated Code, created in 1967 and so much a part of merger scrutiny that in its evidence to the TIC in 1991 the DTI observes that takeovers 'are subject to both the merger control system and Takeover Code, the two systems running in parallel'.

The idea of working co-operatively and reasonably with the subject community is basic to any system of successful regulation and is equally important in competition policy. Nonetheless, the emphasis on property rights and shareholders, on trust in self-regulation, and trust in the candour and good faith of companies has sometimes been the subject of criticism. As we saw in chapter 4, trust is very much part of the culture of the MMC.

NOTE: Wilks, *In the Public Interest*, is a thought-provoking analysis of the history of the MMC, the precursor to the Competition Commission, and the parallel development of British competition policy. The introduction of merger control in 1965 he notes, regenerated the Commission although this crucial development 'sneaked in with little debate'. For further reading, see Pickering, J.F., 'The Implementation of British Competition Policy on Mergers' [1980] ECLR 177.

The CA 1998, outlined in earlier chapters, did not affect the existing system of merger control in the UK, set out in Part V of the FTA 1973, involving the traditional tripartite system of enforcement, with the DGFT, Secretary of State for Trade and Industry and the Competition Commission each playing a key role. It should be noted that the reforms introduced by the Enterprise Act will not affect the existing scheme for newspaper mergers, although neither that special scheme nor statutory provisions applying to specific sectors such as water and sewerage will be considered in this chapter. This chapter will look at the three broad stages in a merger inquiry: referral, Commission inquiry and report, subsequent enforcement action under the FTA 1973 and thereafter under the Enterprise Act, Part 3. It is important to understand the development of policy and practice under the FTA 1973 in order to appreciate the similarities with and differences from the new system to be introduced by the Enterprise Act.

SECTION 2: **Referral**

A: Qualification for investigation

There are a number of stages in determining whether a merger qualifies for referral. First, if a merger is a Community dimension merger, thereby falling within the scope of Merger Regulation 4064/89, as discussed in Chapter 10, the European Commission has sole competence under Article 21(2) to assess the merger. The UK authorities are precluded from using national merger controls unless they seek resort to Articles 9 or 21(3) of the Regulation. Second, a merger situation must be established.

Fair Trading Act 1973 [s. 64(1)]

64—(1) A merger reference may be made to the Commission by the Secretary of State where it appears to him that it is or may be the fact that two or more enterprises (in this section referred to as 'the relevant enterprises'), of which one at least was carried on in the United Kingdom or by or under the control of a body corporate incorporated in the United Kingdom, have, at a time or in circumstances falling within subsection (4) of this section, ceased to be distinct enterprises, and that either—

(a) as a result, the condition specified in subsection (2) or in subsection (3) of this section prevails, or does so to a greater extent, with respect to the supply of goods or services of any description, or

(b) the value of the assets taken over exceeds £70 million provided that this variation shall not have effect in relation to any merger reference which was made to the Monopolies and Mergers Commission before 10.4.1980.

NOTE: The key issue under this provision is when enterprises 'cease to be distinct'.

Fair Trading Act 1973 [s. 65(1)]

65—(1) For the purposes of this Part of this Act any two enterprises shall be regarded as ceasing to be distinct enterprises if either—

(a) they are brought under common ownership or common control (whether or not the business to which either of them formerly belonged continues to be carried on under the same or different ownership or control), or

(b) either of the enterprises ceases to be carried on at all and does so in consequence of any arrangements or transaction entered into to prevent competition between the enterprises.

NOTE: The merger control provisions are resorted to more commonly in the former situation and the FTA 1973 makes further provision for when common ownership or control results from a merger in s. 65(3) and 65(4). It is important to understand that common ownership or control does not only arise where 100 per cent of a company's shares are acquired. Effective control may be derived from the acquisition of a lesser shareholding, even where this does not include a majority of the shares and voting rights, partly dependent on the spread of ownership of the remainder of the shares. It should be noted that there is additional provision extending common control to situations involving interconnected bodies (s. 65(2)) and also in respect of 'creeping mergers' where the thresholds are cumulatively satisfied by a series of transactions over a period of time. (Section 66A as inserted by s. 150(1) of the Companies Act 1989.)

Third, in order to qualify for investigation, the merger has to satisfy either of two alternative tests. The test most commonly resorted to is the assets value test based on the gross, worldwide assets of the acquired enterprise, and the required figure is currently £70 million. (Section 64(1)(b) as amended by Merger References (Increase in Value of Assets) Order 1994 SI 1994/72.) The other test, the market-share test, reflecting the competition concern regarding increased concentration in the market following the merger, is satisfied where, as a result of the merger:

Fair Trading Act 1973, [s. 64 (2)]

64—(2) The condition referred to in subsection (1)(a) of this section, in relation to the supply of goods of any description, is that at least one-quarter of all the goods of that description which are supplied in the United Kingdom, or in a substantial part of the United Kingdom, either—
- (a) are supplied by one and the same person or are supplied to one and the same person, or
- (b) are supplied by the persons by whom the relevant enterprises (so far as they continue to be carried on) are carried on, or are supplied to those persons.

NOTE: Section 64(3) makes parallel provision in respect of services. Given that the relevant market is defined as goods or services of any description, this test is fairly flexible, in situations where the assets value criterion is not satisfied. It also extends to mergers where the market share is increased beyond an existing level of 25 per cent or more.

The Act requires the 25 per cent market share to be held in the UK, or in a substantial part of the UK. In R v Monopolies and Mergers Commission, ex parte South Yorkshire Transport Ltd [1993] 1 All ER 289 it was noted that 'the reference area must be ... of such size, character and importance as to make it worth consideration for the purposes of the Act' (at p. 297). This test was subsequently applied in Stagecoach Holdings plc v Secretary of State for Trade and Industry (1997 SLT 940 (OH)).

B: Making a merger reference

A distinctive feature of the FTA 1973 is that only the Secretary of State may make a merger reference to the Competition Commission (under s. 64(1)). The DGFT has no formal statutory role although he is required to remain informed about actual and prospective mergers, (s. 76(1)(a)) and make appropriate recommendations to the Secretary of State (s. 76(2)(b)). In practice, merger references are normally made on the advice of the DGFT although the Secretary of State is not bound by the DGFT's advice. If a merger is not referred within a statutory four-month period it is effectively cleared. (See s. 64(4) as amended by the Deregulation (Fair Trading Act 1973) (Amendment) (Merger Reference Time Limits) Order 1996 SI 1996/345.)

C: Policy on referrals

Given the limited number of qualifying mergers which have been actually referred to the Competition Commission, ascertaining the policy on referrals is important. The following passage suggests that the referral process lacks transparency:

Rodger, B.J., 'Reinforcing the Scottish "Ring-fence": A Critique of UK
Mergers Policy vis-à-vis the Scottish Economy'
[1996] ECLR 104, pp. 111–112

The failure of current merger policy[56]

This section seeks to examine the nature and effect of prevailing government policy on the administration of the merger provisions. This will be investigated together with an insight into their practical
effect in relation to the recent 'takeovers' of Distillers, Britoil and William Low.

The decision to refer is effectively taken by the Director General and the internal Merger Panel,
whose discussions and reasoning need not be made public. The Office of Fair Trading has pointed
out that although the section 84 guidelines were not addressed to the Director General they were
factors taken into account by him in his advice to the Secretary of State.[57] This randomness of
selection for referral has been one of the main criticisms of the operation of the Act. It was generally
believed both that the referral process needed to be more visible and that the reasons for referral
ought to be more easily discernible. One view is that UK merger policy had failed because of the
wide-ranging public interest criteria and 'the authorities ceased to be interested in competition',[58]
and most observers thought that non-competition issues ought to be left to the market or taken
from the Commission and 'given to the Secretary of State in a more politically responsible way'.[59] It is
considered that this separation of competition and non-competition issues would render the whole
process more consistent. This indicates a belief that the law in these areas was initiated with the
concern solely for the promotion of competition.[60]

The Liesner Report in May 1978 recognised that 'Governments have not adopted the promotion of
competition in all circumstances as an overriding objective'.[61] To this end, they recommended the
retention of the 'case by case' basis of merger control, and no alterations were made to the law as a
result of the Report.[62] This issue of any prospective changes to the merger controls was dealt with
admirably in a prophetic article by David Simpson early in 1983.[63] A change in the set of public
interest guidelines was considered appropriate, although his concern was that such a move to
redefine the public interest would be instituted by a government committed to free market forces.
Simpson also harboured fears that the Government's tactics may result in policy changes being
introduced by a 'quiet backdoor method'.

The dominant influence on merger control policy of recent years is undoubtedly the statement by
Mr Norman Tebbit, the then Secretary of State for Trade and Industry, issued in July 1984 and often
referred to as the 'Tebbit Doctrine'.[64] This confirmed that, save for the two tests in section 64, there
were no statutory criteria for referral to the Commission. The 'Tebbit Doctrine' was spelled out as a

---

56 See Ashcroft and Love, Note 10 above, Chapters 6 and 7.

57 See, for example, Office of Fair Trading booklet, *Mergers: A Guide to Procedures under the Fair Trading
Act 1973*.

58 Sharpe, 'Merger Control in the United Kingdom' [1983] FCLR 171, at 171.

59 *The Economist*, 5 February 1983. See also Hall, 'Merger Control: The Persistence of an Illusion'
[1982] ECLR 347. For parallel views at the European Community level, see Ehlermann, 'Reflections on a
European Cartel Office' [1995] CMLR 471.

60 See Ellis, 'A Survey of the Government Control of Mergers in the United Kingdom' [1971] NILQ
Volume 22, 251. This issue is particularly topical given the recent comments of Sir Bryan Carlsberg in the
OFT Annual Report 1994 and the House of Commons Trade and Industry Select Committee Report on
Competition Policy which will be considered below.

61 'A Review of Monopolies and Mergers Policy', Cmnd 7198 (1978), at paragraph 2.1.

62 The Report recommended that a more critical stance together with a neutral stance ought to be
adopted, in contrast with the existing presumption that mergers are beneficial.

63 Simpson, 'Be it Marriage or Merger, Any Change in the Ceremony Calls for Deep Thought',
Financial Guardian, 8 February 1983.

64 DTI Press Notice, 5 July 1984.

means of bridging this inherent gap in the legislation, or perhaps as a 'backdoor method' to amend the public interest. 'I regard mergers policy as an important part of the Government's general policy of promoting competition . . . Accordingly my policy has been and will continue to be to make references primarily on competition grounds.'

The justification to designate this statement as an underhand method of restricting the public interest derives from the all-important position which the referral process occupies within the UK system. Under present arrangements, merger policy is made at least as much at the referral stage as by the Commission itself. With such a small percentage of mergers being selected for investigation by the Commission in accordance with the public interest, the chosen few will inevitably depend to a great extent on the prevalence, if any, of a particular government priority. This approach is consistent with the Conservative ethos that consumers' best interests are served by ensuring maximum competition and choice. There is no fault in this purest strand of theory, namely that the promotion of competition is to be ensured to the ultimate advantage of the consumer. Thus, mergers resulting in excessive concentration within a particular market should be considered sceptically. However, the underlying rationale to merger control may be neglected as a result of the non-interventionist stance adopted in tandem with the promotion of competition. It is, considered that mergers raising non-competition issues should generally be left to the adjudication of the free market, considering it to be a better arbiter of what constitutes a good merger than the Government. It is, though, decidedly unlikely for the decision-makers in the market to forego an intended takeover of a competitive Scottish company for what would be deemed as parochial concerns over the loss of control and resultant effects on the Scottish economy.

The justification which the Secretary of State obviously had in mind was 'the desire of companies for stability and predictability in this field of policy'. However, in areas where the law and economic policy coincide, greater consistency may be achieved at the expense of an even more important principle or policy goals.[65]

NOTE: This critique of the merger referral process is set in the context of a discussion on merger control and regional policy. In the article the author noted that a previous series of reports on the public interest implications of takeovers of strategically important Scottish companies could effectively be ignored by the Secretary of State. Indeed, the FTA 1973 provided no legal basis upon which references are to be made and does not even require the Secretary of State to refer to the public interest test in s. 84 of the Act. See also Soames, T., 'Merger Policy: As Clear as Mud' [1991] ECLR 53. The Tebbitt doctrine on referral policy will in effect be given statutory effect when the Enterprise Act is enacted, and indeed a key cornerstone of the new regime is to remove ministerial involvement, and hence politics, from the merger control process.

Upon making a reference, a press release is issued which highlights the issues of concern which have prompted the Secretary of State to refer the merger.

DTI Press Release P/2001/100
23 February 2001

Stephen Byers refers proposed acquisition of Abbey National by Lloyds TSB to the competition commission
Stephen Byers, Secretary of State for Trade and Industry, today referred to the Competition Commission the proposed acquisition of Abbey National plc by Lloyds TSB Bank plc. Mr Byers made his decision in accordance with the advice of the Director General of Fair Trading (DGFT).

Mr Byers said:

---

65 See Brent and Lever, Note 8 above. For the debate at the EC level, see for instance, Frazer, 'Competition Policy after 1992: The Next Step' [1990] MLR 609 and Ehlermann, Note 59 above.

The DGFT has advised me that this proposed acquisition raises competition concerns which warrant reference to the Competition Commission. The proposed merger would lead to the elimination from the market of one of the most significant branch-based competitors to the UK's four largest banks. This might result in a substantial lessening of competition, particularly in the market for current accounts. The merger would also remove a potential competitor in the provision of banking services to small to medium-sized companies. I have carefully considered the DGFT's advice and agree with his conclusions. I am therefore referring the proposed merger to the Competition Commission so that it can be fully investigated.

The decision to make a reference does not in any way prejudge the question of whether or not the merger would be against the public interest. It is for the Competition Commission to report on this after investigation. The Commission is to make its report by 12 June 2001.

Notes for editors

1. The Fair Trading Act 1973 empowers the Secretary of State to refer to the Competition Commission actual or proposed mergers which create or increase a market share of 25 per cent of the supply of particular goods or services in the UK or a substantial part of the UK, or involve the takeover of assets exceeding £70 million. Once a reference has been made, the Competition Commission investigates the merger and delivers a report to the Secretary of State on whether or not the merger operates, or may operate against the public interest. If the Competition Commission finds that the merger will or may operate against the public interest, it may recommend possible remedies.

NOTE: In most cases, competition is the key issue in deciding whether to refer a merger. The time limit for consideration by the Competition Commission may subsequently be extended, as it was in this instance.

D: Avoiding a reference

There is a statutory procedure in the FTA 1973 which allows parties to avoid a merger reference and the Competition Commission inquiry process by offering undertakings to alleviate the Secretary of State's/DGFT's concerns about the merger. These can be structural undertakings (as provided for by ss. 75G–75K), such as to divest assets or brands from the merged enterprise, or they can be behavioural undertakings (as provided for by s. 75H) entailing a commitment to modify behaviour post-merger regarding issues such as pricing and service levels.

DTI Press Release, P/2001/296
8 May 2001

Proposed acquisition by BSkyB of control of BIB

Kim Howells, Minister for Consumers and Corporate Affairs, announced today that he has accepted undertakings from British Sky Broadcasting Group plc (BSkyB) to remedy competition concerns arising from its proposed acquisition of control of British Interactive Broadcasting Holdings Limited (BIB). His decision is in accordance with the advice of the Director General of Fair Trading (DGFT).

Dr Howells said:

This proposed acquisition raises concerns in the market for pay TV. There is the potential for BSkyB to provide premium pay TV channels to rival distributors in a form that contains interactive elements which do not work properly on other platforms. This could harm the commercial interests of rival distributors and thereby reduce consumer choice.

For this reason, I announced on 12 October that I had asked the DGFT to seek undertakings from BSkyB to provide 'clean feed' of premium TV channels to rival distributors—i.e. a version of the channel which lacks the interactive elements. On 20 March 2001, I published the draft undertakings for consultation so that third parties would have an opportunity to comment on them.

The DGFT has now submitted to me undertakings offered by BSkyB, having taken account of the comments made during the consultation period. The DGFT has advised me that, in his view, undertakings in the form proposed should remedy or prevent the adverse effects that might result from the merger. I agree with the DGFT's advice and, accordingly, have decided to accept the undertakings from BSkyB in lieu of a reference to the Competition Commission. I am publishing the undertakings and the DGFT's advice as I am required to do.

Notes to editors

1. Section 75G of the Fair Trading Act 1973 (inserted by Section 147 of the Companies Act 1989 and amended by the Deregulation and Contracting Out Act 1994) enables the Secretary of State to accept undertakings as an alternative to making a merger reference to the Competition Commission. The Secretary of State must consider whether such undertakings remedy or prevent adverse effects of the merger specified by the DGFT.

NOTE: The FTA 1973 allows for references of mergers which have already taken place and for proposed mergers. In respect of the latter, although there is no compulsory pre-notification, there is the possibility for parties to seek confidential guidance as to whether their proposed merger is likely to be referred although the guidance is not binding. In addition there exists the more formal mechanism of statutory pre-notification of the merger under ss. 75A–75F of the Act where a final, formal decision is guaranteed within 35 days, failing which the merger cannot be referred to the Competition Commission. (See Fair Trading Act (Amendment) (Merger Pre-Notification) Regulations 1994 SI 1994/1934.)

SECTION 3: **The inquiry and Competition Commission Report**

The reporting panel of the Competition Commission undertakes the following tasks:

The Fair Trading Act 1973 [s. 69]

69 Different kinds of merger references

(1) Subject to the following provisions of this Part of this Act, on a merger reference the Commission shall investigate and report on the questions—

(a) whether a merger situation qualifying for investigation has been created, and

(b) if so, whether the creation of that situation operates, or may be expected to operate, against the public interest.

(2) A merger reference may be so framed as to require the Commission, in relation to the question whether a merger situation qualifying for investigation has been created, to exclude from consideration *paragraph (a) of subsection (1) of section 64* of this Act, or to exclude from consideration *paragraph (b)* of that subsection, or to exclude one of those paragraphs if the Commission find the other satisfied.

(3) In relation to the question whether any such result as is mentioned in section 64(1)(a) of this Act has arisen, a merger reference may be so framed as to require the Commission to confine their investigation to the supply of goods or services in a specified part of the United Kingdom.

(4) A merger reference may require the Commission, if they find that a merger situation qualifying for investigation has been created, to limit their consideration thereafter to such elements in, or possible consequences of, the creation of that situation as may be specified in the reference, and to consider whether, in respect only of those elements or possible consequences, the situation operates, or may be expected to operate, against the public interest.

NOTE: Accordingly, the Commission is first required to be satisfied that the statutory criteria for investigating the merger are met. *Stagecoach Holdings plc v Secretary of State for Trade and Industry* (1997 SLT 940 (OH)) highlighted that there is little scope for successful judicial review of the Commission's determination.

In order to discharge both of these functions under s. 69, the Competition Commission has developed a set of procedures in the investigation of a merger situation. At the beginning of an inquiry the Competition Commission identifies parties which are likely to have an interest in the matter, such as the companies most directly involved, customers and consumer bodies and it will approach these parties for evidence. In addition, press advertisements are used to invite other interested persons to give their views. Questionnaires are often sent to the companies involved in a merger. The Commission has power to require parties to attend hearings and also to provide documentary evidence. After it has collected this initial evidence and information the Commission will identify the public interest issues raised. Before an oral hearing takes place, the Commission will forward an issues letter giving the parties advance notice of the issues likely to be raised. In addition, in merger inquiries, parties are also advised, most commonly in a combined issues and remedies statement, of the hypothetical remedies proposed by the Commission in order to alleviate the public interest issues raised.

Competition Commission Issues and Remedies Statement, Interbrew/Bass
55/00, 24 October 2000

Competition commission inquiry into the acquisition by Interbrew SA of Bass PLC's brewing interests

The Competition Commission has sent an issues and remedies letter to Interbrew SA in its inquiry into the acquisition by Interbrew of Bass PLC's brewing interests.

An issues letter is always sent before the Competition Commission has reached any conclusions and is designed to highlight those matters which have been identified by the investigating group for further consideration, and to ensure nothing has been missed. The statement of issues and remedies is being made public to inform all interested parties should there be any further points they wish to raise with the Competition Commission within two weeks. No conclusions have yet been reached by the Competition Commission about whether any matters operate or may be expected to operate against the public interest. Conclusions will not be reached until the issues have been discussed with Interbrew.

The issues the Commission intend to consider are as follows:

1. The effects of the merger on brewing

   (a) Whether the merger will reduce competition in the brewing of beer as a result of Interbrew having control of the brewing operations of Bass and Whitbread;

   (b) Whether the merger will have the effect of making market conditions more conducive to a reduction in price competition, escalation in non-price competition and reduction in product innovation on the part of Interbrew and Scottish & Newcastle (S&N); and, if so, in what way such behaviour might manifest itself and with what effects;

   (c) Whether the merger will increase barriers to entry or expansion in brewing;

(d) Whether the merger will create a position of market dominance for Interbrew based on leading brands;

(e) Whether S&N and Carlsberg-Tetley have brand portfolios and the necessary financial resources to support them, that will enable them to compete effectively with Interbrew;

(f) Whether other competitors, including Anheuser-Busch, Guinness, Heineken and the regional and local brewers, have brand portfolios and the necessary financial resources to support them, that will enable them to compete effectively with Interbrew;

(g) Whether there will be scope for competitors to respond to price increases by increasing output or by importing beer;

(h) Whether the merger will lead to higher levels of overall market spending; whether this will be in the interests of consumers; and whether this will raise barriers to the entry of new brands or new firms into the market;

(i) Whether Interbrew will have an incentive to rationalise the Whitbread and Bass portfolios;

(j) What will be the effect of the merger on exports of beer from the UK;

(k) Whether, in the light of the fact that Interbrew has acknowledged that in prior years it has taken actions which are incompatible with the competition rules of the EU; and has also stated that it is now compliant with the competition rules prohibiting restrictive agreements and concerted practices and is committed to ensuring that its business practices are now fully compliant with the regulations in the markets where it operates, it would nonetheless be reasonable to infer an expectation that such conduct will occur following the merger;

(l) Whether Interbrew has a financial incentive to increase wholesale prices as a result of the price it paid to acquire Bass.

2. The effect of the merger on the wholesaling and distribution of beer

(a) Whether the merger will reduce competition in the wholesaling and distribution of beer as a result of Interbrew having control of the wholesaling and distribution operations of Bass and Whitbread;

(b) Whether the merger will increase barriers to entry or expansion in wholesaling and distribution;

(c) Whether the merger will have any impact on Carlsberg-Tetley's position in the wholesaling and distribution of beer;

(d) Whether Interbrew will be able to use its expanded brand portfolio to deny leading brands to competing brewers and wholesalers on terms that would enable them to compete effectively for the business of retail outlets;

(e) Whether Interbrew will be in a position to require wholesalers or retailers to take its complete product range (full-line forcing);

(f) Whether the differences in the net prices charged to different buyers by Bass and Whitbread are cost-justified; and what effect would the merger have on these net price differentials;

(g) Whether Interbrew's increased portfolio will enable it to spread distribution costs across multiple brands, cross-subsidise prices and offer high promotional support or discounts on specific brands within its portfolio, to the disadvantage of its competitors;

(h) Whether Interbrew will have a financial incentive to promote brands from its enhanced portfolio at the expense of competing brands;

(i) Whether Interbrew will be able to lower the price of its own brands, or artificially increase the price of competing brands, in order to encourage sales of its own brands to retail outlets and disadvantage its competitors;

(j) Whether Interbrew will have greater access to information about its competitors' sales to retail outlets, and whether this will give Interbrew the ability to compete selectively to secure sales to those outlets;

(k) Whether Interbrew will be able to control the route to market, especially to the on-trade, for competing brewers, or potential entrants to the market who lack their own wholesaling and distribution functions, thereby placing them at a competitive disadvantage;

(l) Whether the merger will have any adverse effects on the wholesaling and distribution of beer to the off-trade;

(m) Whether synergies will justify the purchase price for the merger; and what percentage of those synergies would be passed to consumers of beer.

3. The effect of the merger on the retailing of beer

(a) Whether the long-term supply agreements which Interbrew has entered into with the retained estates of Bass and Whitbread effectively foreclose the estates to competitors for the duration of the agreements and beyond; and if so, by what means;

(b) Whether these agreements will enable Interbrew to compete more aggressively for other business;

(c) Whether the pub companies have sufficient buyer power to enable them to withstand the increased market power of Interbrew;

(d) Whether the merger will have an adverse effect on the free trade.

4. Possible adverse effects on the public interest

The Competition Commission invites views on the following possible adverse effects of the merger on the public interest:

(a) Higher wholesale prices and, eventually, higher retail prices in the on-trade than otherwise would be the case;

(b) Increased price discrimination between buyers leading to adverse effects on the structure of the retail market and on independent wholesalers;

(c) Reduced choice of brands for retailers and consumers and a reduced rate of new product innovation;

(d) Escalation of marketing expenditure leading to increases in entry barriers into brewing.

5. Possible remedies

The Competition Commission invites views on the following possible remedies, in the hypothetical situation that the merger is found to be against the public interest:

(a) Divestment of the Bass business in its entirety; or possibly without its activities in Scotland and Northern Ireland;

(b) Divestment of the Whitbread brewing business, either with or without the rights to the Stella Artois brand;

(c) Divestment of such brands and associated brewing and wholesaling capacity as would enable the creation of a competitive fourth brewer-wholesaler;

(d) Divestment of the wholesaling and distribution businesses of Bass and/or Whitbread;

(e) Divestment of the Interbrew/Bass interest in Tradeteam and re-negotiation of the supply contract with Tradeteam on an arm's-length and non-preferential basis;

(f) Termination of the supply agreements with the retained estates of Bass and/or Whitbread;

(g) Requirement not to discriminate in pricing at the brewing level, that is, to avoid differentials not justified by cost differences between sales to wholesalers and direct sales to retailers;

(h) Requirement not to discriminate in pricing at the wholesaling level, that is, to avoid differentials not justified by cost differences between sales of Interbrew beers and sales of competitors' beers;

(i) Requirement not to engage in line forcing at both brewing and wholesaling levels, that is, not to require, or induce through differential terms, the purchase of a full range of Interbrew products.

Notes to editors

1. This reference was made under the Fair Trading Act 1973 on 6 September 2000 (see DTI Press Notice P/2000/701).

2. Stephen Byers, Secretary of State for Trade and Industry, requested the EC Commission to refer the Interbrew/Bass merger to the UK authorities on 1 August 2000 because he considered that it raised competition concerns in distinct markets within the UK (DTI Press Notice P/2000/553). The EC Commission announced on 22 August 2000 their decision to refer the case to the UK authorities.

3. No conclusions will be reached about whether any matters operate or may be expected to operate against the public interest until the Competition Commission submits its report to the Secretary of State, on 6 December 2000.

4. The inquiry is being chaired by Professor Paul Geroski, one of the Commission's members. The other members of the group are Timothy Richmond, Dame Helena Shovelton and David Stark.

5. Further information can be obtained from the Commission website http://www.competition-commission.org.uk/ref.htm

NOTE: It is clear that the Commission group dealing with a merger inquiry requires to gain an understanding of the position in the relevant industry in a relatively short period of time. Although the merger control provisions have been criticised in the past for the delays they produce in commercial and strategic business planning, given the complexity of many of the industries under investigation, such as brewing and banking, a maximum period of six months does not appear to be particularly long. It should be noted that Interbrew were subsequently successful in seeking judicial review of the Commission report into this merger and the Secretary of State's decision to follow their recommendation to block it, due to the flaws in the Commission procedure on consulting on their proposed remedies.

The key issue for the Commission is to report on whether the merger is expected to operate against the public interest. The public interest test is set out in s. 84 of the Act.

The Fair Trading Act 1973 [s. 84]

84 Public interest

(1) In determining for any purposes to which this section applies whether any particular matter operates, or may be expected to operate, against the public interest, the Commission shall take into account all matters which appear to them in the particular circumstances to be relevant and, among other things, shall have regard to the desirability—

(a) of maintaining and promoting effective competition between persons supplying goods and services in the United Kingdom;

(b) of promoting the interests of consumers, purchasers and other users of goods and services in the United Kingdom in respect of the prices charged for them and in respect of their quality and the variety of goods and services supplied;

(c) of promoting, through competition, the reduction of costs and the development and use of new techniques and new products, and of facilitating the entry of new competitors into existing markets;

(d) of maintaining and promoting the balanced distribution of industry and employment in the United Kingdom; and

(e) of maintaining and promoting competitive activity in markets outside the United Kingdom on the part of producers of goods, and of suppliers of goods and services, in the United Kingdom.

(2) This section applies to the purposes of any functions of the Commission under this Act other than functions to which section 59(3) of this Act applies.

NOTE: The first point to note is the balance of proof in merger cases. Section 72(2) of the Act requires the Commission to establish that the merger 'operates or may be expected to operate against the public interest' and it has been noted that this is a high standard of proof. (See *S&W Berisford/British Sugar Corporation* 1980–1981 HC 241 at para. 9.40.) In addition they are required to 'specify in their report, the particular effects, adverse to the public interest'. (Sections 54(3) and 72(2).) The Liesner Report in 1978 recommended that a more critical stance should be adopted towards mergers but no alterations were made to the FTA 1973 as a result. (*A Review of Monopolies and Mergers Policy*, Cmnd 7198, 1978, para. 2.1.)

The public interest test is notable for its breadth. 'Competition' is a key issue but paras (a) to (e) are guidelines to be taken into account, together with any other relevant considerations. There is no presumption that promoting competition is the sole test as this would be incompat-ible with the other guidelines in the section, for instance the reference to 'regional policy' in subsection (d). See Sharpe, T., 'Merger Control in the UK' [1983] ECLR 171, and Rodger, B.J., 'Reinforcing the Scottish "Ring-fence": A Critique of UK Mergers Policy vis-à-vis the Scottish Economy' [1996] ECLR 104. Given the wide scope of the public interest test, it is inevitable that there have been criticisms of the Commission for its lack of consistency and predictability, see for instance Franks, J.R., and Harris, R.S., 'The Role of the Mergers and Monopolies Com-mission in Merger Policy: Costs and Alternatives', *Oxford Review of Economic Policy, Vol. 2 No. 4* 58. The following passage discusses the extent to which the Commission's reports can be based on precedent.

Wilks, S., *In The Public Interest, Competition Policy and the Monopolies and Mergers Commission*
Manchester, MUP, 1999, pp. 220–221

The third aspect is the question of precedents. This is a general issue running through all MMC cases and is discussed in chapter 5. It has been a constant source of criticism in merger cases and has been a matter of sustained concern for the Commission. From Sutherland's study in 1969 to the TIC investigation in 1991, analysts have searched for consistency across the various merger cases and complained that it was not to be found. Different critics stress different aspects of consistency. Certainly the procedures are consistent but what about the reasoning, the economic analysis and the findings? Fairburn's influential discussion is fairly typical. He concludes that 'it is hard to trace the Commission's reasoning from report to report, or even to perceive that it regards such continuity as an important matter'. This may reflect a difference of perception between economists and lawyers. While lawyers are concerned with regularity and precedent they are less concerned with universal economic principles. They tend to understand that legally precedent does not bind the Commission and that each case is different. Economists might accept that the cases are different but insist that the principles are the same. Curiously it has therefore been the economists who have been most agitated about precedent, lawyers have been more forgiving.

The Commission's concern about precedent in the late 1980s was fuelled by Peter Lilley's speech in June 1991 in which he declared, 'I welcome the emphasis Sir Sydney Lipworth . . . has given to maintaining consistency and developing the greater use of precedent in the MMC's work'. A *Prece-dents Handbook* was prepared in 1988 and is regularly updated and circulated to team managers and Chairmen. Similarly when Graeme Odgers was appointed in 1993 his creation of the Deputy Chairman's group was explicitly orientated towards maintaining consistency over time and between cases. Every meeting included briefings on current cases. But, despite all this attention, the fact remains that each case is different; the public interest test cannot be reduced to a formula. More-over, each group is different. Chairmen have different mixes of skills and priorities and a group considering a particular precedent might well feel that it would not have come to the same conclu-sion. In honesty most members would concede this reality. One recently retired member observed in his valedictory note to the Chairman that, 'I am suspicious of resort to precedents in looking at cases. The facts of every case are different, and the application of similar principles might well lead to different conclusions in cases which might look similar on superficial investigation . . . I look upon the MMC very much as an economic jury, making individual judgements'. The precedents issue also has a temporal dimension. A case from 1976 may provide poor precedent in 1999, where industrial context, the stress on competition and evolution of economic theory would all bring new perspectives to bear. With the Commission constituted on its present basis it has put its emphasis on consistency of approach. Not only would binding precedents be of doubtful legality, they would contradict the whole essence of the Commission concept.

NOTE: Wilks correctly emphasises that Commission merger reports cannot be precedent based. Each merger should be looked at on its own facts, given the particular characteristics of the parties and the industrial sector involved. Nonetheless, it is also clear that in recent years, in line with the Tebbit doctrine, the Commission has most frequently been concerned with competition-related issues arising from a merger or proposed merger.

The following excerpts from recent, high-profile Commission reports demonstrate the focus on competition issues in merger inquiries.

Competition Commission Summary of Ladbroke/Coral Report
Cm 4030, 1998

The Secretary of State for Trade and Industry asked us to investigate the implications for the public interest of the acquisition by Ladbroke Group PLC (Ladbroke) on 31 December 1997 of the Coral betting business from Bass PLC (Bass) (see Appendix 1.1 for our terms of reference).

Ladbroke is the largest firm in the UK off-course betting industry with a chain of some 1,900 licensed betting offices (LBOs). Its total turnover from LBOs and from its telephone betting business in 1997 was some £1.75 billion. Coral was number three in the industry, with a UK chain of 833 LBOs and a total turnover in 1996/97 of nearly £900 million. The only other national chain of LBOs is that of the William Hill Organization Limited (William Hill).

There are a number of distinctive features to the off-course betting market. Regulation of the industry on public policy grounds plays an important role, and has taken a form which has restrained competition. Moreover most bets are placed at prices (odds) which are not set in the off-course market but are determined in the on-course market at horse and greyhound race meetings in the form of board prices and starting prices.

We received submissions from about 90 third parties and held a larger than usual number of hearings. Many (but not all) of the third party submissions were, to a greater or lesser degree, hostile to the merger in its entirety or to major aspects of it.

For its part, Ladbroke argued that its acquisition of Coral did not present problems for the public interest for the following reasons:

- In keeping with the main thrust of our predecessors' report in 1989 on the Mecca/William Hill merger, competition among LBO operators was essentially a local matter; in this fundamental respect, the market had not changed;
- Since most racing betting was at prices determined by the operation of on-course markets, there was little scope for price variation in off-course LBOs;
- Punters' choice of LBOs was determined primarily by convenience of location, but secondarily by the quality of outlet and the service provided;
- Possession of a well-known brand name brought little competitive advantage; and
- Independent firms were fully capable of providing effective competition to outlets of the national chains.

Ladbroke said that in order to address the situation where, in local markets defined in terms of a 400 metre radius as used in our predecessors' report, the merger would eliminate competition, it had entered into a conditional agreement to sell 134 LBOs to Tote Bookmakers Limited (Tote

Bookmakers). During the course of the inquiry, Ladbroke also proposed to dispose of two more tranches, of 98 and 69 LBOs respectively, the two Coral greyhound race tracks, and the Coral telephone betting business together with the Coral brand.

In our view there is an important national component to competition in the provision of off-course betting services through pricing and through branding and quality of outlet. We believe this could be enhanced in an appropriate competitive environment. In particular, there is scope for price competition in the provision of early prices for racing bets, in the odds offered on other sports and numbers betting and in the terms of betting offered by different firms and outlets. The steps taken since 1989 to deregulate some aspects of the industry and its relations with customers, together with the effect of the National Lottery on public attitudes to gambling, have led us to the view that the further development of competition is both practicable and to be encouraged.

The merger increases Ladbroke's share of LBOs from 21 to 30 per cent and its share of off-course betting turnover from 26 to 38 per cent (these figures do not take account of the—relatively small—effect of the conditional sale of LBOs to Tote Bookmakers). As a consequence, Ladbroke has markedly increased its lead in the national retail betting market and its size in that market relative to William Hill. The merger also has the effect of removing Coral, which we consider to have been an important third national competitive force in this market. The structural effects of the merger are therefore quite different from those addressed in the 1989 report. That report, moreover, warned of the future risks of growing concentration of the market at national level.

The effect of this merger would, in our view, be to lead to a weakening of price competition, actual and potential, at national level to the detriment of punters. We also believe the merger would have a dampening effect on innovation and reduce punters' choice of major LBO chains. Prices and standards of service in telephone betting may be expected to be less favourable to punters.

As in much of retailing, the preservation of consumer choice at the local level is important. As national chains become more influential and market concentration increases in the provision of LBO services, so competition for sites in individual localities becomes an important element of the search for market share. In our view this merger will have significant adverse effects in reducing local choice and these effects go beyond the 134 local markets where Ladbroke has entered into a conditional agreement to dispose of outlets to Tote Bookmakers.

There are a number of other aspects on which the merger has consequences which, to a greater or lesser extent, we regard as undesirable, although as a Group we have made no formal findings with respect to them. These concern Satellite Information Services (Holdings) Limited, which supplies a televised information service to LBOs; Bookmakers' Afternoon Greyhound Services Limited (BAGS), which arranges for greyhound meetings to be held at times suitable for LBO punters to bet on; the betting industry's relationship with horse racing; and employment. However, two of us believe that the strengthening of Ladbroke's position in BAGS and in the ownership of greyhound tracks would have adverse effects on the public interest, additional to those described in paragraphs 1.8 to 1.10.

The adverse effects of the merger described in paragraphs 1.8 to 1.10 are not, in our view, offset by benefits and we conclude that the merger is against the public interest. We consider that the adverse effects can only effectively be remedied by restoring an industry structure which is conducive to the development of competition. This would best be achieved by Ladbroke divesting, as a single business, the entirety of Coral's UK business which it acquired from Bass, including those Coral LBOs which are part of Ladbroke's conditional agreement with Tote Bookmakers. We would not, however, rule out the possibility of its sale in more than one part if that seemed likely to lead to a more robust competitive environment. We therefore recommend that Ladbroke be required to divest the Coral business in a manner approved by the Director General of Fair Trading within six months of the publication of our report.

Competition Commission Summary of BskyB/Man Utd Report
Cm 4305, 1999

On 29 October 1998 the Secretary of State referred to us the proposed acquisition by British Sky Broadcasting Group plc (BSkyB) of Manchester United PLC (Manchester United). Our terms of reference are in Appendix 1.1. We have concluded that arrangements are in progress or in contemplation which, if carried into effect, will result in the creation of a merger situation qualifying for investigation.

BSkyB is a vertically integrated broadcaster which buys TV rights, including those for sporting events, makes some of its own programmes, packages programmes from a range of sources into various channels, and distributes and retails these channels to its subscribers using its direct-to-home satellite platform as well as selling them wholesale to other retailers using different distribution platforms.

On all relevant measures, Manchester United is the strongest English football club. Its football-related activities include the supply of TV rights for its matches. At present the rights to Manchester United's Premier League matches, together with those of other Premier League clubs, are sold collectively by the Premier League itself. This arrangement is currently the subject of a Restrictive Practices Court (RPC) case brought by the Director General of Fair Trading.

We have concluded that the relevant football market in which Manchester United operates is no wider than the matches of Premier League clubs. We considered whether the broadcasting market in which BSkyB operates ought to compromise both pay TV and free-to-air TV and concluded that it was more appropriate to treat pay TV as a separate market. Based primarily on considerations of substitutability, we concluded that the relevant market for our purposes was for sports premium TV channels.

Except for small niche channels, BSkyB is currently the only provider of sports premium channels. Entry into this market depends crucially upon the ability of a channel provider to obtain the appropriate live sports rights. We think it unlikely that there are enough such rights to sustain many sports premium channels and BSkyB currently provides three. BSkyB's very high market share together with the difficulties of entry lead us to conclude that BSkyB has market power in the sports premium channel market.

In considering the public interest consequences of the merger, we looked primarily at its effect on competition among broadcasters for live Premier League rights. Because of uncertainties about the outcome of the RPC case on the collective selling of Premier League rights, we considered four scenarios, one or other of which may be expected to occur.

Our first scenario involved the continuation of existing collective selling arrangements and no other mergers between broadcasters and Premier League clubs. We have concluded that under this scenario, BSkyB would, as a result of the merger, gain influence over and information about the Premier League's selling of rights that would not be available to its competitors. It would also benefit from its ownership stake in Premier League rights, providing a further advantage in the bidding process.

Taken together, these factors would significantly improve BSkyB's chances of securing the Premier League's rights. We would expect this to influence the behaviour of BSkyB's competitors causing them to bid more cautiously than would otherwise be the case and, in some cases, even not to bid at all. This would enhance BSkyB's already strong position arising from its market power as a sports premium channel provider and from being the incumbent broadcaster of Premier League football. The effect would be to reduce competition for Premier League rights leading to less choice for the Premier League and less scope for innovation in the broadcasting of Premier League football.

Under our other scenarios we have concluded that:

(a) If the live rights of Premier League clubs were to be sold on an individual basis and there were no other mergers between broadcasters and clubs, BSkyB would, as a result of the merger, have substantial advantages over other broadcasters competing for the rights. This would have adverse effects for competition similar to those we identified under our first scenario.

(b) If existing selling arrangements continued and the BSkyB/Manchester United merger were to precipitate a further merger between a broadcaster and a Premier League club, the effects would be broadly similar to those of our first scenario. If there were several mergers between broadcasters and Premier League clubs precipitated by the BSkyB/Manchester United merger, then we believe that collective selling would continue only if broadcasters agreed among themselves to share the rights, which would have at least as adverse an effect on competition as our first scenario.

If rights were sold on an individual basis and there were several mergers between broadcasters and Premier League clubs precipitated by the BSkyB/Manchester United merger, all of the feasible outcomes would be less competitive than the situation in which rights were individually sold and no broadcaster/Premier League club mergers had occurred.

In most of the situations described in paragraphs 1.7 to 1.9, the merger would enhance BSkyB's ability to secure the Premier League rights in the future. We would expect this further to restrict entry into the sports premium channel market by new channel providers, causing the prices of BSkyB's sports channels to be higher and choice and innovation less than they otherwise would be. Reduced entry by sports premium channel providers would feed through into reduced competition in the wider pay TV market.

We conclude that, under all of the scenarios described in paragraphs 1.7 to 1.9, the merger may be expected to reduce competition for Premier League rights with the consequential adverse effects we have identified.

We have based our public interest conclusions mainly on the effects of the merger on competition among broadcasters. However, we also think that the merger would adversely affect football in two ways. Firstly, it would reinforce the existing trend towards greater inequality of wealth between clubs, thus weakening the smaller ones. Second, it would give BSkyB additional influence over Premier League decisions relating to the organisation of football, leading to some decisions which did not reflect the long-term interests of football. On both counts the merger may be expected to have the adverse effect of damaging the quality of British football. This adverse effect would be more pronounced if the merger precipitated other mergers between broadcasters and Premier League clubs.

We were unable to identify any public interest benefits from the proposed merger. We therefore conclude that the proposed merger between BSkyB and Manchester United may be expected to operate against the public interest.

We considered whether the adverse effects we have identified could be remedied by undertakings by BSkyB. We did not find any that we regarded as effective. We think that the adverse effects are sufficiently serious that prohibiting the merger is both an appropriate and a proportionate remedy. Accordingly, we recommend that the acquisition of Manchester United by BSkyB should be prohibited.

NOTE: These reports demonstrate the vitality of the UK merger control rules and that the merger control provisions may impact upon many aspects of our lives. For instance, if Ladbroke had been allowed to proceed with their merger with Coral, there would have been one fewer 'big' bookmaker in the market and it was likely that competition would have been reduced, resulting in lower odds, and less winnings for 'punters'. The Commission report on the competition consequences of the BskyB/Man Utd merger, perhaps the most contentious merger in recent years, was not favourable. In addition, the Commission highlighted the problems stemming from exacerbating inequality between football clubs and demonstrated its concern over the long-term effects on English football. Both of these mergers were blocked on the basis of the Commission's report.

Prior to the Tebbitt doctrine, there were a number of merger reports in which the Commission relied strongly on the regional policy guideline in s. 84(d).

Rodger, B.J., 'Reinforcing the Scottish "Ring-fence": A Critique of UK Mergers Policy vis-à-vis the Scottish Economy'

[1996] ECLR 104, pp. 109–110

The Commission and the magic ring around Scotland

'It is not the function of the Commission merely to promote competition; it is there to ensure market forces do not operate against the public interest'.[35] This section seeks to recount the passing of an era in which considerable weight was given to the regional policy issue as expressed within section 84(d) Fair Trading Act 1973 ('FTA'). There will be an examination of the series of important Commission reports on Scottish takeovers in which the consideration of singularly Scottish effects inherent in the aftermath of such takeovers brought issues such as the loss of employment and autonomous decision-making to the forefront of public debate. Sceptics believed the Commission in particular, and the referring agencies, to be constructing an artificial 'ring-fence' around Scottish companies, thus preventing predator takeovers. This belief was ultimately confounded, although this section will seek to analyse the reasons for the creation of this perception, its veracity and possible consequences.

Most commentators perceive the Highland Distilleries Report by the Commission as the starting point for discussion on this topic.[36] In August 1980 the Commission reported on the proposed merger between Hiram Walker, a Canadian company with an existing Scottish subsidiary (Hiram Walker Scotland), and Highland Distilleries, a Scottish whisky distilling company employing 1,600 people. Fears were expressed over the possibility of reduced investment in the Scottish company following a merger, especially since it was 'inherently unlikely that investment decisions, taken in the Canadian Head Office of a worldwide group with most of its assets and interests outside the United Kingdom, would favour Scotland'.[37] The Commission appreciated the concern of the SDA as to the removal of decision-making centres and, in particular, in this case the loss of marketing functions. They concluded, despite Hiram Walker's avowed intention of maintaining Highland Distilleries' autonomy, that 'the merger is likely to have an adverse effect on career opportunities in Scotland since Highland's top management will be deprived of the opportunity to take strategic decisions'. This admittedly limited effect on career opportunities was important in the Commission's ultimate refusal to allow the merger to proceed, although they indicated that their major concern was the increasing concentration of distillery ownership which would have resulted.[38]

The Royal Bank of Scotland's Board considered in the early 1980s that a merger with a suitable partner was required to enable the group to expand internationally. The Royal Bank's preferred means of expansion was with Standard Chartered, in defiance of a hostile bid by the Hong Kong and Shanghai Banking Corp., registered in Hong Kong. However, both bids were referred together to the Commission by the Secretary of State amidst a strong Scottish lobby in opposition to any merger or takeover. Evidence was submitted by such organisations as the SDA, Strathclyde University's Fraser of Allander Institute, the Edinburgh Chamber of Commerce and the Bank of Scotland pointing to the possible damage to the Scottish industrial and financial communities if the Royal Bank lost its independence.

The Commission accepted the general arguments that the process of external control via

---

35 MacQueen, 'The Monopolies Commission and the Scottish Factor' [1982] JBL 316.

36 Hiram Walker/Highland Distilleries HCP (1979/80) 743. Although the issue was earlier recognised in Lonrho/Suits/House of Fraser HCP (1978/79) 261.

37 Hiram Walker/Highland Distilleries HCP, Note 36 above, at paragraph 6.14.

38 See Ashcroft and Love, Note 10 above, Chapter 5.

acquisitions had accentuated 'the economic difficulties of regions such as Scotland'.[39] In depicting Scotland as becoming a 'branch economy',[40] they recognised that this could reduce the responsiveness of the local business to local needs. They also realised, importantly, the wider implications of the resulting reduction in local career opportunities.

> Functions such as marketing or product development may be removed from Scotland. Bright young Scots have less opportunity to develop their talents, or realise their potential by leaving. The harm done by such loss or failure to develop their skills goes wider than the direct effect on them and their businesses and to the vigour of a local economy affected by the general level of professional and business skills available there . . . and the effect of losing good people from Scotland or failing to develop their talents adequately, is fundamental.[41]

It was indicated that the impact of these general arguments would vary with each merger, depending 'on the nature of the company and its importance for the economy of Scotland'.[42]

In the instant case, the Commission foresaw 'a detriment to the public interest in Scotland arising from the removal of ultimate control from Edinburgh'[43] owing to the size of the company, the degree of control exercised from Edinburgh and the importance of it and its industry in Scotland. They upheld this objection in the face of assurances from both bidders that control would remain in Edinburgh as it was thought that in practice these were unlikely to be complied with in the long run.[44] The lower priority attached to the decision-making in Scotland would also result in reduced career opportunities and in many able Scots leaving the country. Loss of Scottish control of the Royal Bank of Scotland would be seen as a significant step in the long process of centralisation and of weakening local control over economic affairs. It would reinforce the impression of a 'branch economy' and diminish confidence and morale in Scottish business.[45]

MacQueen recognises this report as simultaneously the high and low point of the supremacy of regional considerations over purely commercial ones. Following this report, as Baur indicated, a theory was emerging that Scottish companies were becoming almost bid-proof and that 'a magic political ring-fence [had] been erected to protect them from predators'.[46] The present writer believes neither view to be a proper analysis, nor for that matter can either of the two extremes be of benefit to the Scottish economy. An absolute and artificial 'ring-fence' would inhibit takeovers of ailing Scottish companies in need of a boost for various reasons,[47] yet an exceptional protection would appear rather haphazard in the light of the literature on the expectation of detrimental effects from takeovers on the Scottish economy.

These reports created neither a 'ring-fence' nor an exceptional circumstance.[48] It highlighted at the time, and in the circumstances, the precedence attached by the Commission to 'regional policy'

---

39 The Hong Kong and Shanghai Banking Corp./Standard Chartered Bank/The Royal Bank of Scotland Group, Cmnd 8472 (1982), at paragraph 12.7. See also the earlier report, Lonrho/House of Fraser HCP (1981/82) 73.

40 Ibid., at paragraph 12.8.

41 Ibid., at paragraph 12.9.

42 Ibid., at paragraph 12.11.

43 Ibid., at paragraph 12.16.

44 Compare later events in the Guinness/Distillers and BP/Britoil takeovers.

45 The report contained two dissentient speeches by Mr Smethurst and Sir Alan Neale. See the views of MacQueen, Note 35 above, particularly at 318. It is interesting to note that there have been recent reports of further purported hostile bids for the Royal Bank.

46 Baur, Note 34 above.

47 See for instance Ashcroft and Love, Note 10 above, and the findings in their study that many of the acquisitions were actively sought after by the acquiree.

48 On the one hand, owing to the recognised significance of such a major Scottish company as the Royal Bank, and on the other, owing to the awareness by the Commission of wider external effects of such takeovers.

implications under section 84(d), albeit in the case of an exceptionally significant Scottish company. However, the mythical existence of an artificial 'ring-fence' around Scottish companies displeased both the City and 'free-marketeers', who were keen on restricting the grounds on which mergers could be declared against the public interest.

NOTE: This article demonstrates the importance of a particular non-competition-related issue in a series of Commission inquiries prior to the application of the Tebbitt doctrine in referral policy. The non-referral of the Guinness plc takeover of the Scottish company, Distillers plc in the late 1980s confirmed the primacy given to competition considerations in merger policy, and the Enterprise Act reforms seek to give this statutory effect.

Where the Commission considers that a merger can be expected to operate against the public interest, it is required to consider what action should be taken in order to remedy or prevent the adverse effects (s. 72(2)(a)). In addition, the Commission may, and routinely does, make recommendations as to the appropriate action to be taken (s. 72(2)(b)).

Competition Commission Summary of Bass/Carlsberg/Tetley Report
Cm 3662, 1997, pp. 1–2

This inquiry concerns a complex transaction which is intended to lead to a merger between Bass PLC (Bass) and Carlsberg-Tetley PLC (CT). Our terms of reference are set out in Appendix 1.1.

Bass is the UK's second largest brewer, having 23 per cent of the beer market and owning about 4,400 tied houses. CT is the third largest, with 14 per cent of the market but no tied estate. The merged business would become the UK's largest brewer, ahead of Scottish Courage, the beer division of Scottish & Newcastle PLC (S&N). Scottish Courage has 28 per cent of the market. S&N owns about 2,700 tied houses. The fourth largest brewer is Whitbread PLC (Whitbread) with 13 per cent of the market and about 4,400 tied houses.

Under agreements entered into on 25 August 1996 Bass acquired a 50 per cent stake in CT from Allied Domecq PLC (AD). The other 50 per cent is owned by Carlsberg A/S (Carlsberg). Subject to regulatory approval on terms satisfactory to Bass, Bass has agreed to merge its brewing interests with CT and acquire a further 30 per cent stake in the merged enterprise, which we have termed Bass Carlsberg-Tetley (BCT). If such regulatory approval is not forthcoming there are fallback arrangements under which Bass may require Carlsberg to buy its 50 per cent stake in CT.

The beer market has changed radically since the introduction of the Beer Orders in 1989 following an MMC monopoly inquiry into the supply of beer, and continues in flux. Consumption of domestically-produced beer has been declining. The off-trade has grown relative to the on-trade and now accounts for some 28 per cent of beer sales, compared with some 17 per cent in 1985. About one-third of all pubs are now owned by brewers, compared with over half in 1991. Large retail pub chains with significant buying power have emerged, and these now own about one-third of all pubs.

At the brewing and wholesaling level, the market has become steadily more concentrated. Competition is keen. The wholesale price of beer, net of duty, has fallen in real terms by 8 per cent over the last four years, while retail prices in the on-trade, net of duty, have risen in real terms by around 10 per cent.

The proposed merger would lead to a reduction in the number of major brewers and would give Bass a significant increase in market power, as a result of which we expect wholesale and on-trade retail prices of beer to be higher in the longer term than would otherwise be the case. On-trade retailers and the consumer would suffer. In the short term, regional brewers and independent wholesalers could also be adversely affected because BCT might choose to lower its prices to target their markets selectively.

The proposed merger would lead to some net efficiency gains which would not be achieved in the absence of the merger. But in our judgment these benefits would not be sufficient to outweigh the adverse effects we have identified.

The majority of us believe that it is possible to remedy the adverse effects of the proposed merger with measures designed to counteract the increase in Bass's market power resulting from the merger. To that end we recommend a package of remedies involving a reduction in the number of Bass's tied houses to a maximum of 2,500. If satisfactory undertakings to implement these remedies cannot be obtained, we recommend that the merger should be prohibited.

Professor Newbery was not persuaded that these remedies would sufficiently alleviate the adverse effects. He concluded that the merger should not be allowed to proceed.

NOTE: The Secretary of State is not bound to accept the Commission's conclusions or recommendations. In this instance, the Secretary of State was not convinced that the proposed structural undertakings would remedy the public interest detriments and effectively blocked the proposed merger. It has also been fairly common for there to be a dissenting member of the group charged with carrying out the Commission inquiry and for a separate dissenting conclusion to be published with the report. It should be noted that no action can be taken on a conclusion in a Competition Commission report unless it is the conclusion of two-thirds of the members of the group. (Sch. 3, para. 16(2) to the FTA 1973.) In the Lloyds TSB/Abbey National Report, (Cm 5208, 2001) the Commission looked in some detail at the issue of appropriate remedies.

Excerpt from Competition Commission Summary of Lloyds TSB/Abbey National Report
Cm 5208, 2001, pp. 4–5

As well as outright prohibition of the merger, we considered several possible types of remedy for the adverse effects which we identified:

(a) We reviewed the possibility that Lloyds TSB might be required to divest Cheltenham & Gloucester or cahoot, Abbey National's standalone Internet bank. Cheltenham & Gloucester operates to a very small extent in the PCA market and not at all in the SME market, and anyone acquiring it would do so primarily for its mortgages and savings businesses. We think it unlikely, given the absence of PCA and SME customers, that the Cheltenham & Gloucester branch network would be seen as an attractive platform for entry or expansion into those markets. Cahoot has only about 0.1 per cent of the PCA market: its divestment would be wholly inadequate as a remedy for the loss of Abbey National, particularly as it would not affect the reduction in branch-based competition which would result from the merger. We concluded that there are no Lloyds TSB or Abbey National businesses which could be divested in order to remedy the adverse effects of the merger.

(b) We considered the possible divestment of branches. Any such divestment would have to include the customer base if it was to affect competition. Both Lloyds TSB and Abbey National saw considerable difficulties about such action though Lloyds TSB was prepared to contemplate it on a modest scale. However, in order to address adequately the adverse effects of the merger, the number of branches to be divested would have to be substantial. The process would be difficult, slow, and unpredictable. Even if it could be done, there could be no guarantee that the transferred customers would stay and it would be uncertain whether the acquirer would provide effective competition to compensate for the loss of Abbey National. We concluded that divestment of branches and customers would not be a suitable remedy.

(c) We considered the possibility of requiring Lloyds TSB to give undertakings regarding the terms of individual products to be offered by the merged group, and Lloyds TSB put forward specific proposals on these lines. However, we see difficulties both of principle and practice:

(i) Undertakings of this type would represent an interference in the operation of market forces. In our view such regulatory intervention is second best to the play of competitive forces which allows markets to develop in ways which reflect consumers' observed preferences.

(ii) We see considerable difficulties in the drawing up and monitoring of suitable undertakings.

We therefore do not consider that proposals on these lines would be an appropriate or effective remedy.

(d) We contemplated steps to improve the awareness of customers of the enlarged group concerning the terms of the products they were buying and how they compared with those from competing suppliers. Such a remedy would itself be a weak step, however, and would be useful only alongside other action which safeguarded the competitiveness of the market. Since we have not identified remedies which would achieve that end, an information-based remedy would not be effective.

We have therefore concluded that the possible remedies short of prohibiting the merger would not adequately address the adverse effects. The importance of Abbey National is that it has developed a successful business model which is based on a national network of branches. Its PCA and SME businesses are built on that foundation and cannot be separated from it. It may become possible in due course for non-branch-based suppliers to compete effectively and win a substantial share of the PCA and SME markets but we do not expect that to happen for a considerable period.

Having reviewed all possibilities, and considering the nature and extent of the adverse effects that we identified, we have concluded that prohibiting the merger is the only remedy capable of fully addressing those adverse effects. Accordingly, we recommend that the merger be prohibited.

SECTION 4: Enforcement following a report

The Secretary of State is required to publish the report and lay it before Parliament. If the report is not adverse, or less than two-thirds of the group support any adverse findings, no formal enforcement action can be taken. Otherwise, the Secretary of State is empowered, under s. 73 of the Act, to make Orders under Sch. 8 to the Act, and can additionally make interim orders in accordance with s. 74 of the Act. In particular, Part II, para. 14 of Sch. 8 provides:

The Fair Trading Act 1973 [para. 14 of Sch. 8]

An order may provide for the division of any business by the sale of any part of the undertaking or assets or otherwise (for which purpose all the activities carried on by way of business by any one person or by any two or more interconnected bodies corporate may be treated as a single business), or for the division of any group of interconnected bodies corporate, and for all such matters as may be necessary to effect or take account of the division, including—

    (a) the transfer or vesting of property, rights, liabilities or obligations;

    (b) the adjustment of contracts, whether by discharge or reduction of any liability or obligation or otherwise;

    (c) the creation, allotment, surrender or cancellation of any shares, stock or securities;

    (d) the formation or winding up of a company or other association, corporate or unincorporate, or the amendment of the memorandum and articles or other instruments regulating any company or association;

    (e) the extent to which, and the circumstances in which, provisions of the order affecting a company or association in its share capital, constitution or other matters may be altered by the company or association, and the registration under any enactment of the other by companies or associations so affected;

    (f) the continuation, with any necessary change of parties, of any legal proceedings.

NOTE: This remedy is more commonly known as divestiture. Although it is a particularly controversial remedy in 'monopoly' cases, it is the logical conclusion to the finding that a merger can be expected to operate against the public interest. Given that the UK merger controls apply equally to proposed mergers and mergers which have already been effected, i.e. there is no compulsory pre-notification, it is most apposite in relation to the latter. However, it should be noted that para. 14 does not cover only the full divestiture remedy but can also be used to introduce Orders requiring, for instance, the sale of certain assets or brands, particularly where this remedy has been recommended by the Commission. Most frequently the Secretary of State does not resort to his Order-making powers but requests the DGFT to negotiate undertakings with the relevant parties in order to alleviate the public interest concerns raised.

DTI Press Release P/98/713
23 September 1998 *re Ladbroke/Coral*

Peter Mandelson, Secretary of State for Trade and Industry, announced today that he has decided not to permit the acquisition by Ladbroke of the Coral betting business. Mr Mandelson accepted the findings and recommendations of the Monopolies and Mergers Commission (MMC), and the advice of the Director General of Fair Trading (DGFT), that the merger may be expected to operate against the public interest and that it should be prohibited.

Publishing the MMC's report today, Mr Mandelson said:

'I accept the MMC's unanimous conclusions that the merger would lead to a weakening of price competition at national level to the detriment of punters, have a dampening effect on innovation and reduce punters' choice of major chains of betting shops, as well as reducing their local choice of betting shops in many areas. I also accept their conclusion that as a result of the merger, prices and standards of service in telephone betting would be less favourable to punters.

'I agree with the MMC's recommendation that these adverse effects could only effectively be remedied by requiring Ladbroke to divest the whole of Coral's UK business in order to restore an industry structure conducive to the development of competition.

'Before the merger, Ladbroke was already the largest firm in the UK off-course betting industry with a chain of some 1,900 licensed betting offices (LBOs). With its acquisition of the Coral business, Ladbroke increased its share of all LBOs from 21 to 30 per cent, and its share of off-course betting turnover rose from 26 to 38 per cent. The only other national chain is that of the William Hill Organisation, which has around 1,500 LBOs.

'I accept the MMC's view that there is an important national component to competition in off-course betting services through pricing (particularly in early prices for racing bets, in the odds offered on other sports and numbers betting, and in the terms of betting) and through branding and quality of outlet. The MMC believe this could be enhanced in an appropriate competitive environment and that further development of competition is both practicable and to be encouraged. They noted that as a result of the merger Ladbroke had markedly increased its lead in the national retail betting market and its size relative to William Hill, and that the merger also had the effect of removing Coral, which they consider to have been an important third national competitive force.

'Taking all these factors into account, I have decided to prohibit this merger, and to ask the DGFT to seek undertakings from Ladbroke that within a period of six months they will divest the whole of Coral's UK betting business in a manner approved by the DGFT and which he considers will restore an industry structure which is conducive to the development of competition.

'If satisfactory undertakings cannot be obtained by 23 December 1998 I would then have to consider using my powers to make an Order to enforce these remedies.'

NOTE: The earlier inquiry into the Mecca/William Hill merger was distinguishable as the market circumstances facing the merging parties here were different, as were the general market conditions. Similarly, the proposed merger between Halifax plc and the Bank of Scotland plc was not referred to the Competition Commission by the Secretary of State (P/2001/385, 19 July 2001) as, unlike the Lloyds TSB/Abbey National proposed merger, which was blocked following the Commission report, (Cm 5208, 2001) it did not involve one of the Big Four banks.

The Secretary of State is not required to act upon any Competition Commission conclusion and recommendation. In Bass/Carlsberg/Tetley (Cm 3662, 1997) he disregarded the recommendation that a sale of assets would be a sufficient remedy and effectively blocked the merger. Conversely, following an earlier report, *Charter Consolidated/Anderson Strathclyde* (Cmnd 8711, 1982) the Secretary of State allowed a takeover bid to proceed although the Commission had concluded, by a 4–2 majority, that it should be blocked as against the public interest. Judicial review of the Secretary of State's decision was subsequently unsuccessful in *R* v *Secretary of State for Trade and Industry, ex parte Anderson Strathclyde plc* [1983] 2 All ER 233.

R v *Secretary of State for Trade and Industry, ex parte Anderson Strathclyde plc*
[1983] 2 All ER 233 *per* Dunn LJ at pp. 241–242 and 243

The submission of leading counsel for Anderson was that on the true construction of the Act, if the commission or the majority of the commission conclude, as they did in this case, that a merger situation may be expected to operate against the public interest, and if they specify in their report, as they did, the particular effects adverse to the public interest which in their opinion the creation of the merger situation may be expected to have, then the Secretary of State is bound by that conclusion and his discretion is limited to a choice of which order may be made under Sch. 8.

I cannot accept that submission. The words 'the Secretary of State may by order' in s. 73(2), and the words 'in determining whether, or to what extent or in what manner' in s. 73(3) indicate that the Secretary of State has a complete discretion whether to make any order or whether to make no order at all. Counsel's construction would have required quite different words in sub-ss.(2) and (3) to the words that we find.

His construction would also give power to the majority of the commission to decide whether a merger situation was adverse to the public interest, and is inconsistent with the provision in s. 82(3) that a statement of dissent should be included in the report, indicating that the Secretary of State is entitled to take into account the whole report including the statement of dissent. It is also inconsistent with the duty placed on the Secretary of State, under s. 86(1), to take account of the advice of the Director General and with his duty, under s. 91(2), to consider representations made after notice and before making his order. As counsel for the Secretary of State and the minister said, if leading counsel for Anderson is right the Secretary of State would be unable to take action if there were a change of circumstances after publication of the report.

In my judgment, the Act read as a whole shows that the Secretary of State is not bound by the conclusions of the majority of the commission, that he has a wide discretion in deciding whether to make any order at all, and in exercising that discretion he is entitled to take into account all the relevant circumstances, and to consider the opinion of the minority of the commission, and also representations and advice from persons other than members of the commission.

The second ground on which it is said that he took into account a matter which he should not have taken into account was to be inferred from the statement, 'it is no more than speculative to conclude that the merger might harm the public interest'.

Leading counsel for Anderson referred us to passages in their report in which the majority specifically refer to the evidence in support of their conclusions, and he said in those circumstances the minister was wrong to say that their conclusion was 'no more than speculative'. But on the basis which I have held to be the true basis, that the Secretary of State was entitled to have regard to the note of dissent, it is necessary to look at that. The two dissenting members of the commission said, in effect, that the evidence was insufficient to support the conclusion to which the majority had come.

In my view, it was a matter for the minister, in his unfettered discretion, to choose between those two views, taking into account any other relevant matters including the advice which he received from the Director General. He preferred the view of the minority. Whether he was right or wrong about that is a matter of political judgment, and not a matter of law.

No reason has been shown which would entitle this court, on well-established principles, to interfere with his decision on a matter of that kind. We have not gone into, and it is no part of the function of this court to go into, the merits of whether or not this proposed merger should be allowed. Our sole function is to consider whether the minister, in refusing to stop the merger, acted lawfully. That involves answering two questions and two questions only. (1) Did the minister have the power under the Fair Trading Act 1973 to take the course he did? He did have that power. (2) In exercising the power, did he take into consideration any matter which he should not have taken into consideration? He did not. Accordingly, this application, in my view, must fail and be dismissed.

NOTE: This case highlights the reluctance of the judiciary to interfere in what is perceived as essentially a political decision-making process by the Secretary of State under the FTA 1973. In relation to merger control, parties can seek the limited remedy of judicial review of the decision making of the competition authorities. The court does not act as a court of appeal by substituting its own assessment of a decision. Judicial review seeks to quash the decision based on its unfairness or unreasonableness and the broad grounds for seeking judicial review are illegality, irrationality and procedural impropriety.

There was a successful judicial review under the merger control provisions of the 1973 Act in 2001 in *Interbrew SA/Interbrew Holdings UK Ltd* v *Competition Commission/Secretary of State for Trade and Industry* (CO/402/2001, 25 May 2001, QBD, Moses J.). The Competition Commission report into the acquisition by Interbrew SA of the brewing interests of Bass plc ('Bass Brewing') (Cmnd 5014) concluded that the merger may be expected to operate against the public interest as it would reduce competition in the market, lead to higher prices for end consumers, and reduce consumer choice. It would effectively create a duopoly between Interbrew and Scottish & Newcastle as the two largest brewers/distributors. The Commission concluded that the only adequate remedy in respect of the adverse effects was for Interbrew to divest itself of Bass Brewers in the UK. This was endorsed by the DGFT and the Secretary of State confirmed that he would decide in accordance with the Commission's conclusions and requested the DGFT to seek undertakings from Interbrew requiring them to divest Bass Brewers to a buyer approved by the DGFT (DTI P/2001/11, 3 January 2001).

Interbrew SA/Interbrew Holdings UK Ltd v *Competition Commission/Secretary of State for Trade and Industry*
(CO/402/2001, 25 May 2001, QBD, Moses J [2001] UKCLR 964), paras 69–72 and 88–90.

Unfairness
69 There can be no doubt but that the Commission owed a duty of fairness in conducting its investigation as to the merger. The content of the duty will vary from case to case but generally it will require the decision-maker to identify in advance areas which are causing him concern in reaching

the decision in question.[20] Where Convention rights are at stake those adversely affected should be involved in the decision-making process to a degree sufficient to provide them with the 'requisite protection of their interests'. Absent such participation the interference will not be regarded as necessary.[21] The jurisprudence of the European Court of Justice is to like effect[22]:

Any person who may be adversely affected by a decision should be placed in a position in which he may effectively make his views known, at least as regards the matters taken into account by the Commission as the basis for its decision.

70 The flexibility of the requirement of fairness in the context of an investigation by the Monopolies and Mergers Commission has been the subject of judicial comment in the United Kingdom. In *Hoffmann-La Roche & Co. Ag* v *Secretary of State for Trade and Industry*[23] Lord Diplock said:

The Commission makes its own investigation into facts. It does not adjudicate upon a lis between contending parties. The adversarial procedure followed in a court of law is not appropriate in its investigations. It has a wide discretion as to how they should be conducted. Nevertheless, I would accept it is the duty of the Commissioners to observe the rules of natural justice in the course of their investigation—which means no more than they must act fairly in giving to the person whose activities are being investigated reasonable opportunity to put forward facts and arguments in justification of his conduct of those activities before they reach a conclusion which may affect him adversely.

71 In *R* v *Monopolies and Mergers Commission, ex parte Elders Ixl Ltd*[24] Mann J referred to the flexibility of the demands of fairness:

There is thus no set of rules of fairness which is applicable to all investigative procedures. . . . What is fair in relation to a particular process, and a particular situation which is subject to that process, is for determination by the Court.

72 In *R* v *Monopolies and Mergers Commission, ex parte Matthew Brown plc* [FN25] Macpherson J appeared to take the view that the test of whether the procedure followed was fair was simply one of *Wednesbury* unreasonableness. The Commission do not, rightly, adopt that approach but draw attention to the views of Collins J in *R* v *Monopolies and Mergers Commission, ex parte Stagecoach Holdings plc* [FN26] in which he said:

I entirely accept that the Court will be slow to intervene (in procedural matters). This is because regard must be had to the nature of the MMC and the knowledge that having directed itself properly on the requirements of fairness it will be unlikely that nonetheless it will be unfair. As Lloyd LJ said at page 184D (of *R* v *Panel on Take-Overs and Mergers ex parte Guinness* [FN27] the Court will give great weight to the tribunal's own view of what is fair. No doubt, this will mean that in the vast majority of cases the Court will be unlikely to regard what the MMC has reasonably believed to be fair as unfair so that in practice the adoption of the *Wednesbury* test will make little difference.

. . .

88 The Secretary of State, in supporting the Commission's submissions, referred to the fact that the decision already taken by the Secretary of State is far from being the final word. There will be further opportunities for comments when the DGFT seeks to secure appropriate undertakings or by way of representations before the laying of any draft order or during the Parliamentary affirmative

20 See, *e.g. R* v *Secretary of State for the Home Department, ex parte Fayed (No. 1)* [1998] 1 W.L.R. 763, at pp. 773H to 774A.
21 See *Mcmichael* v *United Kingdom (A/308)*: (1995) 20 E.H.R.R. 205 (a case concerning Art. 8).
22 *Case T-42/96 Eyckeler & Malt Ag* v *E.C. Commission, 19 February 1998*: [1998] E.C.R. II-401: [1998] 3 C.M.L.R. 1077, para. [78].
23 [1975] A.C. 295, at p. 368.
24 [1987] 1 W.L.R. 1221.

resolution procedure. But none of those stages can cure the defect in failing to give a fair opportunity to Interbrew at a stage before the Commission had made up its mind on the issue which compelled its recommendation. It is plain from its reasoning, that absent its concerns as to the effect of Interbrew's dual capacity, it would have recommended divestment of Whitbread with Stella Artois.

89 Nor do I think this case is analogous to *Hoffmann-La Roche*. In that case *Hoffmann-La Roche* chose not to deal with any alternative remedy. In the instant case the stance taken by Interbrew does not reveal that it had made a tactical decision not to deal with the Commission's concerns as to the lack of viability and independence of Whitbread with Stella Artois. The basis for that concern had never been raised.

90 In those circumstances, despite the skill and expertise of the Commission and the care with which its report was prepared, I am driven to the conclusion that there was such unfairness that its decision cannot stand. It must follow that the Secretary of State's decision must also be set aside. I am far from saying that the Commission would not be entitled to reach the same view or that the Secretary of State would not be entitled to follow any recommendation made by the Commission based on the conclusion that Whitbread with Stella Artois would not be a viable and independent third force in the market. But, as I have said, fairness demands that Interbrew be given a proper opportunity to deal with the effect on Whitbread with Stella Artois of Interbrew's capacity as owner of Bass and licensor of Stella Artois. For that reason this application is allowed. Neither the Commission nor the Secretary of State has sought to argue that even if there was a want of fair procedure I should exercise my discretion to dismiss the application on the grounds that any representation by Interbrew would make no difference.

NOTE: Moses J rejected the challenges to the substance of the Commission's decision, in particular regarding the proportionality of the recommended remedy of divestiture of Bass Brewers. Nonetheless, the application for judicial review was allowed on the basis that the Commission procedure in reaching its conclusion was unfair. Accordingly, both the Commission's recommendation and the Secretary of State's decision to accept that recommendation on remedies were quashed. The Secretary of State was ordered to reconsider the question of remedies with assistance by the DGFT. It should be noted that this was a merger investigation following a referral to the UK authorities under Article 9 of the EC Merger Regulation 4064/89.

SECTION 5: **Reform of merger control**

The CA 1998 beckoned a new era in UK competition law with a new institutional and regulatory framework and substantive competition law principles, introducing a dramatic change from the traditional public interest test under the FTA 1973. For a fuller discussion on the matter arising under the CA 1998, see Rodger, B.J., and MacCulloch, A. (eds), *The UK Competition Act: A New Era for UK Competition Law*, Hart Publishing, Oxford, 2000. However, the Act did not set out to reform merger control in any way and, indeed, agreements which give rise to a merger situation within Part V of the FTA 1973 are excluded from the Chapter I and II prohibitions. (Schedule 1, para. 3. See also OFT 416, Exclusion for Mergers and Ancillary Restrictions.) However, although earlier recommendations for reform of merger control had not been acted upon (for example, Trade and Industry Committee, *Takeovers and Mergers*, First Report, (1991–92) HCP 90, DTI, *Blue Paper on Mergers Policy*,

London: HMSO, 1988) the DTI made proposals for reform of the system not long after the enactment of the CA 1998. In August 1999 the DTI published *Mergers: A Consultation Document on Proposals for Reform* and this was followed by *Mergers: The Response to the Consultation on Proposals for Reform* in October 2000. (Available at *www.dti.gov.uk*)

Rodger, B.J., 'UK Merger Control: Politics, the Public Interest and Reform'
[2000] ECLR 24 at p. 25 and pp. 28–29 [footnotes omitted]

Aims of the reform
Although the DTI document stresses the 'overarching aim' of reform as promoting competitiveness, the consumer interest, effectiveness and efficiency, the key principles reflect the main underlying concerns:

— clarity, transparency and consistency, which in turn promote predictability, fairness and accountability;
— responsiveness to the needs of business and other users of the system, imposing only the minimum necessary burdens;
— effective and proportionate control of mergers which have harmful effects.

These clearly prioritise the interests of business as 'consumers' of competition law and resembles the European Merger Regulation intention to facilitate mergers by reducing regulatory burdens.
  The two main tenets of the proposals which seek to achieve these aims are to:

— focus decisions more clearly on competition; and
— minimise Ministerial involvement in decision-making.

These two tenets are, however, untenable if one considers competition policy, especially mergers policy, to be particularly politically sensitive. One can legitimately argue that competition law should serve the public interest which should therefore form the cornerstone of competition policy. The document indeed reflects the fairly empty debate on aims and goals of competition law undertaken during the passage of the Competition Bill, with the limited exceptions of the Parliamentary debates on resale price maintenance ('RPM') for over-the-counter medicines and newspaper pricing. The key issue of stakeholders in merger policy, it is suggested, has been skewered in favour of potentially merging companies.
  Although understated in the DTI document, it is clear that the international dimension and the Community merger regime form an important aspect of the reform proposals. The Document notes the increasing extent of cross-border and global mergers and the concerns over duplication and multiplication of regulatory requirements. It is accepted that there is scope for procedural harmonisation, including notification forms, timetables, etc., but it is not clear that substantive harmonisation is necessary: this would proceed on the basis that facilitating international mergers is a goal of merger policy. Indeed, as the DTI notes, the arguments for harmonisation with the EC Merger Regulation are weak given the exclusive competence of the Commission where the Regulation applies and the lack of jurisdiction overlap.

Conclusions
The United Kingdom's distinctive merger control tradition with the public interest as its cornerstone has been under attack for a number of years and this Document is a culmination of that informal process. It is submitted that merger policy reform should be based on the promotion of the broad interests of the economy and it must be sceptical of the perceived benefits of mergers, given the lack of any compelling evidence of general benefits derived from them. The reforms are driven by the relentless pressure by practitioners and business for greater certainty and predictability in the law.

There has been within that community growing unease over public interest competition enquiries and pejorative allegations of 'intervention on non-competition grounds'. This pressure is at the expense of a proper debate on the goals of merger policy, and the inevitable element of uncertainty in prediction involved in merger control has been ignored. The system of UK merger control has, in any event, already been informally altered to resemble the focus of the present proposals, notably by the Tebbit doctrine. Despite this, Stephen Byers, the Trade and Industry Secretary, has stressed that 'business is entitled to know that important merger decisions will not be influenced by short-term political considerations'. For instance, there were concerns expressed over the potential influence of certain Ministers in relation to the proposed BSkyB/Manchester United merger. However, 'political' and 'non-competition' considerations will inevitably be involved in some mergers and if we accept the need for a broad-based stakeholder basis for competition policy where business is not the 'consumer', then concerns regarding resort to short-term politics could be alleviated by the imposition of a duty on the Secretary of State, or alternatively the Director General, to comply with the public interest criteria in section 84 in their decision-making. It is submitted that reform of the assessment of merger situations should not focus purely on competition and that the wider public interest must be recognised. A competition and economic analysis is crucial but there are many other factors which should not be ignored. Geoffrey Howe, as the Minister for Trade Affairs, in the aftermath of the passing of the 1973 Act, summed up accurately the value of a public interest test in merger control:

> If a merger seemed likely to cause significant redundancies or to be incompatible with the Government's regional policies, the case for full investigation would be fully strengthened . . . What I have deliberately not attempted to do is to say what weight is to be attributed, for all time, to any particular aspects. Our national priorities change. The Government's powers must be sufficiently flexible to reflect these changing priorities.

The writer has a particular interest in regional policy and the public interest, and the concern over migration of company headquarters from Scotland following external takeovers. Interestingly, in the week following the DTI proposals there was speculation concerning the proposed takeover of Highland Distillers, a major Scottish whisky producing company, by another Glasgow-based company. As the *Herald* noted:

> Bids for large Scottish companies invariably mean a raider from south of the Border or overseas taking control. However many new jobs are created at the lower end of the scale, corporate Scotland is invariably left the poorer as the centre of decision making shifts elsewhere. Happily this is not the case with Highland Distillers.

In response to the DTI Document, similar sentiments were expressed by Unison in urging the retention of community and social interests within UK merger policy. The CBI has commented that there is little pressure for change—no doubt based on familiarity with the post-Tebbit doctrine system. In any event, it is thought that legislation is unlikely before the next General Election as the Government is likely to consider how the Competition Act 1998 'beds in', but there is the possibility that stricter time-tabling for the merger control process may be introduced in the interim.

NOTE: This critique is aimed at the initial proposals in the DTI 1999 proposals but these were largely confirmed in the October 2000 Document subject to minor modifications. For instance the October 2000 Document proposed that the new focused competition test should be that of a 'substantial lessening of competition' in order to avoid some of the difficulties encountered under the EC Merger Regulation 4064/89 with its dominance-based test, particularly in relation to collective dominance. The 'modernising' of the UK merger regime based on these proposals was taken forward in the DTI White Paper, 'A World Class Competition Regime' in July 2001. (Cm 5233, 2001.)

DTI White Paper, A World Class Competition Regime, July 2001
(Cm 5233, 2001) at pp. 23–25

- The Government is committed to introducing a new merger regime—with final decisions taken by independent competition authorities on the basis of a competition test.
- There will also be procedural and other improvements, building greater transparency into the process.
- The Government has now finalised the few remaining areas of policy—the conclusions are set out in this chapter.

5.1 The Government announced in 1999 its intention to reform the merger regime by taking most decisions out of the political arena. In October 2000, following a wide ranging consultation exercise, the Government announced its main conclusions on the way ahead. It also triggered further consultation on certain points of detail. This covered such matters as the treatment of consumer benefits in a competition-focused regime, and the development of the Competition Commission's procedures for identifying remedies. Following this consultation, the Government has taken a number of further decisions—set out below.

5.2 Government policy in recent years has been to take merger decisions primarily on competition grounds. Practice has also been for the Government to follow the advice of the competition authorities in most cases. The reform proposals build on these developments. They have two central elements. Firstly, decisions on the vast majority of mergers will be transferred from Ministers to the OFT and the Competition Commission. Secondly, the test against which mergers are assessed will be changed from a broad-based 'public interest' test to a new competition-based test. The Government is also committed to procedural and other improvements, such as the introduction of maximum statutory timetables for investigations, and building more transparency into the process.

Removing Ministers from the decision-making process
5.3 Removing Ministers from most decisions will bring the UK's merger regime into line with best practice in other countries. Decisions will be taken by those best qualified to make them—namely the expert competition authorities—in line with one of the Government's principles for competition policy.

5.4 This change will clarify arrangements and make decision-making more predictable. Business will no longer need to factor in the possibility that decisions will be influenced by political considerations.

Exceptional public interest cases
5.5 The new regime will, however, allow Ministers to continue to take final decisions on the small minority of mergers raising defined exceptional public interest issues. National security, covering essential defence interests and other public security concerns, will be defined as an exceptional public interest from the outset. Ministers will be able to define further criteria subsequently, but only by statutory instrument subject to the affirmative resolution procedure in both Houses of Parliament.

Box 5.1: How will the new merger regime work?

- Final decisions on most mergers will be taken by independent competition authorities rather than Ministers.
- The test they will apply will be to determine whether the merger results in a substantial lessening of competition rather than the current public interest test.
- Exceptionally, where competition considerations point the other way, it will be possible for the authorities to clear a merger or allow it to proceed with less stringent competition remedies where they believe it will bring overall consumer benefits.

- The Secretary of State for Trade and Industry will continue to decide the small minority of mergers which raise defined exceptional public interest issues.
- National security will be defined at the outset as an exceptional public interest issue. It will be possible to define further exceptional public interest issues by statutory instrument using the affirmative resolution procedure.
- The new regime will retain a two-stage approach to merger investigations. The OFT will carry out first stage investigations which will be sufficient to decide most cases. The Competition Commission will continue to carry out second stage, in depth investigations where necessary.
- There will be statutory maximum timetables for both first and second stage investigations by the competition authorities. There will also continue to be the option of an administrative timetable at stage one.
- The criteria used to determine which mergers qualify for investigation will be modernised to focus more efficiently on cases that may raise concerns.
- The UK's system of voluntary rather than compulsory pre-notification of mergers will be retained.

Interim measures in advance of legislation

5.6 The reforms announced last October require legislative change. At the time, the then Secretary of State for Trade and Industry announced that he would take steps in advance of legislation to reduce Ministerial involvement in current merger decisions. His policy would, save in exceptional circumstances, be to accept the advice received from the OFT on whether or not to refer merger cases to the Competition Commission. The interim policy has worked well. Since October, the Secretary of State has taken more than 150 decisions on whether or not to refer mergers to the Competition Commission. On each occasion, the Secretary of State has accepted the Director General of Fair Trading's advice on reference.

5.7 The Government announced last autumn that it would consider whether it is appropriate to take an additional interim step so that Ministers follow the recommendations of the Competition Commission on remedies in all but exceptional circumstances. Since then, the Government has announced that it will introduce an Enterprise Bill in the current Parliamentary session. Given this, the Government believes there is no need to take this additional interim step.

The competition test and the treatment of consumer benefits

5.8 In the new regime, mergers will be assessed against a test of whether they will result in a substantial lessening of competition. Making competition the focus of the assessment will ensure that the underlying economic arguments can be brought to bear on the analysis of a merger in a clear and straightforward manner.

5.9 The Government recognises, however, that there will occasionally be circumstances where a merger which results in a substantial lessening of competition can, nonetheless, bring overall benefits to consumers. The challenge is to identify a framework which allows such benefits—which will arise only infrequently—to be taken into account without undermining the central importance of the competition analysis.

5.10 In October, the Government sought views on how to take this issue forward. In the light of comments received, the Government has decided to proceed as follows:

- The competition test will be at the heart of the assessment carried out by the competition authorities. The authorities will be required to reach a clear view on the competition aspects of each case. A merger will be cleared unless the authorities expect it would result in a substantial lessening of competition in any UK market.

- Where a merger fails the competition test, the authorities will have to take steps to remedy the competition problem.
- However, the authorities will—exceptionally—be able to clear a merger or allow it to proceed with less stringent competition remedies than would otherwise be the case where they believe that the merger will bring overall benefits to UK consumers affected by the merger.
- The authorities will be able to take account of consumer benefits which take the form of lower prices, or greater innovation, choice or quality of products or services. They must expect such benefits to materialise within a reasonable period and be satisfied they would be unlikely to happen without the merger.
- Consumer benefits will cover benefits to end-consumers, but will also extend to customer benefits in upstream markets where the immediate beneficiaries of a merger are other businesses.

NOTE: These proposals will effectively depoliticise merger control law by removing ministerial involvement and the public interest test, although there will remain scope for the introduction of exceptional public interest criteria. The insertion of a new consumer interest test in relation to merger control is notable. Other ancillary reforms include a new turnover-based test for quali-fication for investigation and strictly enforced time limits for merger investigations, and the types of Order available under Sch. 8 following an adverse report will be extended. However, notification of mergers will remain non-compulsory.

SECTION 6: **Enterprise Act, Part 3**

This part of the Act is immensely complicated and the key features will be outlined in this section. We shall focus on the key differences between the new approach and the old system.

A: Political involvement

The new system seeks to remove politicians from the merger control process, except in certain defined cases, both at the stage of referral and subsequent enforcement.

DTI, *Government Response to Consultation*
December 2001, p. 5

Removing Ministers from merger decisions [paragraphs 5.3–5.7]

10. The White Paper re-iterated the Government's decision to remove Ministers from all merger decisions, other than those raising defined exceptional public interest issues.

11. There continues to be almost unanimous support for the principle of removing Ministers from the vast majority of merger decisions. Some respondents said that if the Competition Commission (CC) was to be given the final decision-making role on remedies both here and following market investigations, its procedures and composition needed to be improved and its accountability enhanced.

Government's response
The Government intends to press ahead with the removal of all but a tiny minority of merger decisions from Ministers. Decisions will be taken by those best qualified to make them—namely the expert competition authorities.

The Government intends to enhance the accountability of the competition authorities. There will be greater transparency in the operation of the new regime, and a new statutory right of appeal against certain decisions. The OFT and CC will be required to publish reasons for their important decisions, building on recent trends towards greater transparency. The CC Chairman will be required to set procedural rules for CC reporting groups so there will be greater certainty about how enquiries will be handled. The Government is also inviting Parliament through its Select Committees to play an active role in the scrutiny of the competition regime.

NOTE: This aspect was keenly debated in Parliament, and, although there were some concerns regarding the lack of democratic accountability in relation to mergers which may have serious repercussions on the economy, the greater independence of the competition authorities was generally supported, in line with UK monetary policy developments. There are particular provisions for public interest mergers and special public interest mergers which we shall discuss briefly below.

B: Referral

There are several differences in approach introduced at this stage. First, references are to be made by the OFT and not the Secretary of State. In addition the OFT is to be placed under an obligation to refer mergers.

Enterprise Act [s. 22(1–2)]

22 Duty to make references in relation to completed mergers
(1) The OFT shall, subject to subsections (2) and (3), make a reference to the Commission if the OFT believes that it is or may be the case that—
    (a) a relevant merger situation has been created; and
    (b) the creation of that situation has resulted, or may be expected to result, in a substantial lessening of competition within any market or markets in the United Kingdom for goods or services.
(2) The OFT may decide not to make a reference under this section if it believes that—
    (a) the market concerned is not, or the markets concerned are not, of sufficient importance to justify the making of a reference to the Commission; or
    (b) any relevant customer benefits in relation to the creation of the relevant merger situation concerned outweigh the substantial lessening of competition concerned and any adverse effects of the substantial lessening of competition concerned.

NOTE: There are similar provisions in relation to anticipated mergers (s. 33). The obligation to refer is subject to two provisos. First, that a relevant merger situation has been created:

Enterprise Act [s. 23]

23 Relevant merger situations
(1) For the purposes of this Part, a relevant merger situation has been created if—
    (a) two or more enterprises have ceased to be distinct enterprises at a time or in circumstances falling within section 24; and
    (b) the value of the turnover in the United Kingdom of the enterprise being taken over exceeds £45 million.

(2) For the purposes of this Part, a relevant merger situation has also been created if—

   (a) two or more enterprises have ceased to be distinct enterprises at a time or in circumstances falling within section 24; and

   (b) as a result, one or both of the conditions mentioned in subsections (3) and (4) below prevails or prevails to a greater extent.

(3) The condition mentioned in this subsection is that, in relation to the supply of goods of any description, at least one-quarter of all the goods of that description which are supplied in the United Kingdom, or in a substantial part of the United Kingdom—

   (a) are supplied by one and the same person or are supplied to one and the same person; or

   (b) are supplied by the persons by whom the enterprises concerned are carried on, or are supplied to those persons.

(4) The condition mentioned in this subsection is that, in relation to the supply of services of any description, the supply of services of that description in the United Kingdom, or in a substantial part of the United Kingdom, is to the extent of at least one-quarter—

   (a) supply by one and the same person, or supply for one and the same person; or

   (b) supply by the persons by whom the enterprises concerned are carried on, or supply for those persons.

(5) For the purpose of deciding whether the proportion of one-quarter mentioned in subsection (3) or (4) is fulfilled with respect to goods or (as the case may be) services of any description, the decision-making authority shall apply such criterion (whether value, cost, price, quantity, capacity, number of workers employed or some other criterion, of whatever nature), or such combination of criteria, as the decision-making authority considers appropriate.

(6) References in subsections (3) and (4) to the supply of goods or (as the case may be) services shall, in relation to goods or services of any description which are the subject of different forms of supply, be construed in whichever of the following ways the decision-making authority considers appropriate—

   (a) as references to any of those forms of supply taken separately;

   (b) as references to all those forms of supply taken together; or

   (c) as references to any of those forms of supply taken in groups.

(7) For the purposes of subsection (6) the decision-making authority may treat goods or services as being the subject of different forms of supply whenever—

   (a) the transactions concerned differ as to their nature, their parties, their terms or their surrounding circumstances; and

   (b) the difference is one which, in the opinion of the decision-making authority, ought for the purposes of that subsection to be treated as a material difference.

(8) The criteria for deciding when goods or services can be treated, for the purposes of this section, as goods or services of a separate description shall be such as in any particular case the decision-making authority considers appropriate in the circumstances of that case.

(9) For the purposes of this Chapter, the question whether a relevant merger situation has been created shall be determined as at—

   (a) in the case of a reference which is treated as having been made under section 22 by virtue of section 37(2), such time as the Commission may determine; and

   (b) in any other case, immediately before the time when the reference has been, or is to be, made.

NOTE: As under the FTA 1973, this requires that the enterprises have ceased to be distinct, and this is determined by sections 26 and 27 (and section 29 re obtaining control by stages), similar in nature to the FTA 1973 provisions. In addition, the merger must satisfy one of two additional tests. The key change here is the replacement of the assets value test with a turnover test, calculated in accordance with section 28.

The second proviso is the introduction of formal referral criteria, the principal reform introduced by section 22 the OFT must believe that the merger will result in a substantial lessening of competition. Section 22(2) introduces a *de minimis* provision and allows the OFT not to refer a merger where the consumer benefits outweigh the adverse competition consequences of the merger. This will be a difficult balancing exercise for the OFT at the referral stage. (See section 30 re relevant customer benefits below.) Note also that the Enterprise Act contains provisions, similar to those under the FTA 1973, for avoiding references by giving undertakings to the OFT.

C: The Competition Commission inquiry

The two main differences from the FTA 1973 are the introduction of a competition test at the core of the inquiry, and the role for the Commission in deciding upon remedies.

(a) *The competition test*

How would the competition test be framed? This was the subject of considerable debate following the White Paper, 'World Class Competition Regime', 2001.

DTI Government Response to Consultation
December 2001, p. 6, paras 5.8–5.10

The competition test and treatment of consumer benefits [paragraphs 5.8–5.10]

12. The White Paper re-iterated the Government's intention to replace the current public interest test for assessing mergers with a test based on whether mergers will result in a substantial lessening of competition. The White Paper set out the circumstances in which the authorities will be able to take account of consumer benefits in deciding what remedies to apply to a merger that has failed the competition test.

13. Responses to the White Paper showed continuing strong support for the decision to adopt a test focused on a substantial lessening of competition. A small minority of respondents continued to prefer the 'dominance' test that is applied under the European Community Merger Regulation. They felt that this would avoid creating a divergence with EU arrangements, and that the proposed domestic test represented a more stringent standard for assessing mergers. A number of respondents said that there would need to be a clear understanding of how the authorities would apply the new test.

14. There was strong support, particularly from business, for the Government's decision announced in the White Paper, that the competition authorities should be able to take account of customer benefits in upstream markets where the immediate beneficiaries were other businesses, as well as benefits to end-consumers.

15. Three respondents objected to the narrow competition focus of the new test. These respondents considered that other issues such as employment, the environment and the impact on local communities should be capable of being taken into account.

16. Two respondents connected with the water sector asked about the Government's plans regarding the future of the special regime for assessing water company mergers.

Government's response

The Government intends to replace the current public interest test with a substantial lessening of competition test. This will allow the competition authorities to take action whenever there is an increase of sole, joint or collective market power as a result of a merger. The competition authorities will publish guidance on the way the competition test will be applied in referring and assessing mergers.

NOTE: Ultimately, the American model of 'substantial lessening of competition' has been adopted in preference to the Community Merger Regulation dominance-style test. Although in most cases their application would lead to the same result, the SLC test should avoid the difficulties evidenced by the application of the collective dominance model under the Merger Regulation. (See e.g. *Airtours* detail, Motta, M., 'EC Merger policy and the Airtours case' [2000] ECLR 199.) Sections 35 and 36 use the term 'anti-competitive outcome' as shorthand for satisfaction of the SLC test. If that is the case, the Commission has to decide what action to remedy the anti-competitive outcome or any adverse effects arising from it. (Sections 35(3–4) and 36(2–3) respectively.) In carrying out this task, the Competition Commission's task is more demanding than under the 1973 Act, as it requires to 'have regard to the need to achieve as comprehensive a solution as is reasonable and practicable'. (Sections 35(4) and 36(3) respectively.)

Perhaps of greater significance is the requirement on the Commission, in line with the OFT at referral stage, to consider 'the effect of any action on any relevant consumer benefits in relation to the creation of the relevant merger situation concerned'. (Sections 35(5) and 36(4).) Consumer benefits, for OFT and Commission purposes, are defined in section 30 as follows:

Enterprise Act [s. 30]

30 Relevant customer benefits

(1) For the purposes of this Part a benefit is a relevant customer benefit if—

    (a) it is a benefit to relevant customers in the form of—

        (i) lower prices, higher quality or greater choice of goods or services in any market in the United Kingdom (whether or not the market or markets in which the substantial lessening of competition concerned has, or may have, occurred or (as the case may be) may occur); or

        (ii) greater innovation in relation to such goods or services; and

    (b) the decision-making authority believes—

        (i) in the case of a reference or possible reference under section 22 or 45(2), as mentioned in subsection (2); and

        (ii) in the case of a reference or possible reference under section 33 or 45(2), as mentioned in subsection (3).

(2) The belief, in the case of a reference or possible reference under section 22 or section 45(2), is that—

    (a) the benefit has accrued as a result of the creation of the relevant merger situation concerned or may be expected to accrue within a reasonable period as a result of the creation of that situation; and

    (b) the benefit was, or is, unlikely to accrue without the creation of that situation or a similar lessening of competition.

(3) The belief, in the case of a reference or possible reference under section 33 or 45(4) is that—

    (a) the benefit may be expected to accrue within a reasonable period as a result of the creation of the relevant merger situation concerned; and

    (b) the benefit is unlikely to accrue without the creation of that situation or a similar lessening of competition.

(4) In subsection (1) 'relevant customers' means—

(a) customers of any person carrying on an enterprise which, in the creation of the relevant merger situation concerned, has ceased to be, or (as the case may be) will cease to be, a distinct enterprise;

(b) customers of such customers; and

(c) any other customers in a chain of customers beginning with the customers mentioned in paragraph (a);

and in this subsection 'customers' includes future customers.

NOTE: Consumer benefits are defined fairly narrowly for both referral and remedial purposes and are restricted to the creation of merger-specific efficiencies.

D: Enforcement

Enforcement is set out in Chapter 4 of Part III of the Act. The Secretary of State has no general role in relation to enforcement and the OFT has various powers to accept undertakings and make orders prior to or in lieu of references. (Sections 70–75.) However, the main reform has been to enhance the role of the Commission, which will no longer merely recommend remedial action following a negative report, but the Commission is under a duty to remedy the negative consequences of completed or anticipated mergers.

Enterprise Act [s. 41]

41 Duty to remedy effects of completed or anticipated mergers

(1) Subsection (2) applies where a report of the Commission has been prepared and published under section 38 within the period permitted by section 39 and contains the decision that there is an anti-competitive outcome.

(2) The Commission shall take such action under section 82 or 84 as it considers to be reasonable and practicable—

(a) to remedy, mitigate or prevent the substantial lessening of competition concerned; and

(b) to remedy, mitigate or prevent any adverse effects which have resulted from, or may be expected to result from, the substantial lessening of competition.

(3) The decision of the Commission under subsection (2) shall be consistent with its decisions as included in its report by virtue of section 35(3) or (as the case may be) 36(2) unless there has been a material change of circumstances since the preparation of the report or the Commission otherwise has a special reason for deciding differently.

(4) In making a decision under subsection (2), the Commission shall, in particular, have regard to the need to achieve as comprehensive a solution as is reasonable and practicable to the substantial lessening of competition and any adverse effects resulting from it.

(5) In making a decision under subsection (2), the Commission may, in particular, have regard to the effect of any action on any relevant customer benefits in relation to the creation of the relevant merger situation concerned.

NOTE: The Competition Commission has been given power to accept final undertakings (section 82) and make such orders (sections 83 and 84) as are permitted by Sch. 8 to the Act. This includes the new remedy of divestment whereby the parties require to find an 'up-front buyer'. Monitoring and enforcement of undertakings and orders is to be undertaken by the OFT. There is provision in section 120 for review of decisions under Part III by the CAT.

E: Public interest cases

The public interest has not disappeared altogether from UK merger control but has been retained in very restricted format. There are two exceptional types of mergers in which there are modifications to the general merger control scheme and in relation to which the Secretary of State will continue to play a role, albeit limited. The provisions in Chapter 2 are complex, even by the Enterprise Act standards. In the first place, the Secretary of State may make an intervention notice, under section 42, to the OFT where there is a relevant merger situation involving a public interest consideration. Following an OFT report, the merger may be referred under section 45 to the Competition Commission directly by the Secretary of State. Following a Competition Commission report (section 50), the Secretary of State can decide whether to make an adverse public interest finding (section 54) and thereafter exercise the enforcement powers available to him under Sch. 7 to the Act. (Section 55.) Public interest considerations are specified in section 58 as follows:

Enterprise Act [section 58]

58 Specified considerations

(1) The interests of national security are specified in this section.

(2) In subsection (1) 'national security' includes public security; and in this subsection 'public security' has the same meaning as in article 21(3) of the European Merger Regulations.

(3) The Secretary of State may by order modify this section for the purpose of specifying in this section a new consideration or removing or amending any consideration which is for the time being specified in this section.

(4) An order under this section may, in particular—

(a) provide for a consideration to be specified in this section for a particular purpose or purposes or for all purposes;

(b) apply in relation to cases under consideration by the OFT, the Commission or the Secretary of State before the making of the order as well as cases under consideration on or after the making of the order.

NOTE: Public interest considerations are currently restricted to national security issues. This section was vigorously debated in Parliament. Some viewed the range of public interest considerations as too restricted. Others were concerned at the scope for extension by the order-making power available, although the government stressed, during the passage of the Bill, that it did not envisage any circumstances in which the range of public interest considerations would be extended. However, it should be noted that there is additional provision, in Chapter 3 of this Part of the Act, in relation to 'special public interest cases' where an enterprise involved in a merger is a relevant government contractor, due to concerns over the UK's essential national security interests. There is also specific provision, in sections 67–68, for intervention to protect legitimate interests as permitted by Article 21(3) of the European Merger Regulation.

QUESTIONS

1. To what extent is the substantive analysis of the effects of mergers by the Competition Commission likely to be affected by the introduction of the new competition-based test?

2. Do you agree that ministerial involvement in the merger control process should be removed? To what extent does the retention of a more limited role support the view that merger control raises important issues concerning democratic accountability?

FURTHER READING

Finbow, R., and Parr, N., *UK Merger Control, Law and Practice*, Sweet & Maxwell, London, 1995.

Wilks, S., *In the Public Interest, Competition Policy and the Monopolies and Mergers Commission*, MUP: Manchester, 1999.

10

EC merger control

SECTION 1: **Introduction**

Merger Control in the EC is one of the most politicised areas of competition law. The political importance of decisions taken by the Commission in the merger field is one of the reasons that no proper merger control was adopted in the EC until 1990. Prior to 1990 the Community's competition rules provided some means of control but were generally regarded as inadequate. Once the political deadlock was broken, the EC adopted the Merger Control Regulation which came into force in 1990.

SECTION 2: **The EC Merger Regulation**

Council Regulation 4064/89/EEC on the Control of Concentrations between Undertakings, OJ, 1990, L257/13 as amended by Council Regulation 1310/97/EC, OJ, 1997, L180/1

Article 1 Scope
[1. Without prejudice to Article 22, this Regulation shall apply to all concentrations with a Community dimension as defined in paragraphs 2 and 3.]
    2. For the purposes of this Regulation, a concentration has a Community dimension where:
        (a) the combined aggregate worldwide turnover of all the undertakings concerned is more than ECU 5,000 million; and
        (b) the aggregate Community-wide turnover of each of at least two of the undertakings concerned is more than ECU 250 million, unless each of the undertakings concerned achieves more than two-thirds of its aggregate Community-wide turnover within one and the same Member State.
[3. For the purposes of this Regulation, a concentration that does not meet the thresholds laid down in paragraph 2 has a Community dimension where:
        (a) the combined aggregate worldwide turnover of all the undertakings concerned is more than ECU 2,500 million;
        (b) in each of at least three Member States, the combined aggregate turnover of all the undertakings concerned is more than ECU 100 million;

(c) in each of at least three Member States included for the purpose of point (b), the aggregate turnover of each of at least two of the undertakings concerned is more than ECU 25 million; and

(d) the aggregate Community-wide turnover of each of at least two of the undertakings concerned is more than ECU 100 million; unless each of the undertakings concerned achieves more than two-thirds of its aggregate Community-wide turnover within one and the same Member State.

4. Before 1 July 2000 the Commission shall report to the Council on the operation of the thresholds and criteria set out in paragraphs 2 and 3.

5. Following the report referred to in paragraph 4 and on a proposal from the Commission, the Council, acting by a qualified majority, may revise the thresholds and criteria mentioned in paragraph 3.]

Article 2 Appraisal of concentrations

1. Concentrations within the scope of this Regulation shall be appraised in accordance with the following provisions with a view to establishing whether or not they are compatible with the common market.

In making this appraisal, the Commission shall take into account:

(a) the need to maintain and develop effective competition within the common market in view of, among other things, the structure of all the markets concerned and the actual or potential competition from undertakings located either within or outwith the Community;

(b) the market position of the undertakings concerned and their economic and financial power, the alternatives available to suppliers and users, their access to supplies or markets, any legal or other barriers to entry, supply and demand trends for the relevant goods and services, the interests of the intermediate and ultimate consumers, and the development of technical and economic progress provided that it is to consumers' advantage and does not form an obstacle to competition.

2. A concentration which does not create or strengthen a dominant position as a result of which effective competition would be significantly impeded in the common market or in a substantial part of it shall be declared compatible with the common market.

3. A concentration which creates or strengthens a dominant position as a result of which effective competition would be significantly impeded in the common market or in a substantial part of it shall be declared incompatible with the common market.

[4. To the extent that the creation of a joint venture constituting a concentration pursuant to Article 3 has as its object or effect the coordination of the competitive behaviour of undertakings that remain independent, such coordination shall be appraised in accordance with the criteria of Article 85(1) and (3) of the Treaty, with a view to establishing whether or not the operation is compatible with the common market.

In making this appraisal, the Commission shall take into account in particular:

— whether two or more parent companies retain to a significant extent activities in the same market as the joint venture or in a market which is downstream or upstream from that of the joint venture or in a neighbouring market closely related to this market,

— whether the coordination which is the direct consequence of the creation of the joint venture affords the undertakings concerned the possibility of eliminating competition in respect of a substantial part of the products or services in question.]

Article 3 Definition of concentration

1. A concentration shall be deemed to arise where:

(a) two or more previously independent undertakings merge, or

(b) — one or more persons already controlling at least one undertaking, or

— one or more undertakings

acquire, whether by purchase of securities or assets, by contract or by any other means, direct or indirect control of the whole or parts of one or more other undertakings.

2. The creation of a joint venture performing on a lasting basis all the functions of an autonomous economic entity [. . .] shall constitute a concentration within the meaning of paragraph 1(b).

3. For the purposes of this Regulation, control shall be constituted by rights, contracts or any other means which, either separately or in combination and having regard to the considerations of fact or law involved, confer the possibility of exercising decisive influence on an undertaking, in particular by:

(a) ownership or the right to use all or part of the assets of an undertaking;

(b) rights or contracts which confer decisive influence on the composition, voting or decisions of the organs of an undertaking.

4. Control is acquired by persons or undertakings which:

(a) are holders of the rights or entitled to rights under the contracts concerned; or

(b) while not being holders of such rights or entitled to rights under such contracts, have the power to exercise the rights deriving therefrom.

5. A concentration shall not be deemed to arise where:

(a) credit institutions or other financial institutions or insurance companies, the normal activities of which include transactions and dealing in securities for their own account or for the account of others, hold on a temporary basis securities which they have acquired in an undertaking with a view to reselling them, provided that they do not exercise voting rights in respect of those securities with a view to determining the competitive behaviour of that undertaking or provided that they exercise such voting rights only with a view to preparing the disposal of all or part of that undertaking or of its assets or the disposal of those securities and that any such disposal takes place within one year of the date of acquisition; that period may be extended by the Commission on request where such institutions or companies can show that the disposal was not reasonably possible within the period set;

(b) control is acquired by an office-holder according to the law of a Member State relating to liquidation, winding up, insolvency, cessation of payments, compositions or analogous proceedings;

(c) the operations referred to in paragraph 1(b) are carried out by the financial holding companies referred to in Article 5(3) of the Fourth Council Directive 78/660/EEC of 25 July 1978 on the annual accounts of certain types of companies, as last amended by Directive 84/569/EEC, provided however that the voting rights in respect of the holding are exercised, in particular in relation to the appointment of members of the management and supervisory bodies of the undertakings in which they have holdings, only to maintain the full value of those investments and not to determine directly or indirectly the competitive conduct of those undertakings.

Article 4 Prior notification of concentrations

1. Concentrations with a Community dimension defined in this Regulation shall be notified to the Commission not more than one week after the conclusion of the agreement, or the announcement of the public bid, or the acquisition of a controlling interest. That week shall begin when the first of those events occurs.

2. A concentration which consists of a merger within the meaning of Article 3(1)(a) or in the acquisition of joint control within the meaning of Article 3(1)(b) shall be notified jointly by the

parties to the merger or by those acquiring joint control as the case may be. In all other cases, the notification shall be effected by the person or undertaking acquiring control of the whole or parts of one or more undertakings.

3. Where the Commission finds that a notified concentration falls within the scope of this Regulation, it shall publish the fact of the notification, at the same time indicating the names of the parties, the nature of the concentration and the economic sectors involved. The Commission shall take account of the legitimate interest of undertakings in the protection of their business secrets.

Article 5 Calculation of turnover

1. Aggregate turnover within the meaning of Article 1(2) shall comprise the amounts derived by the undertakings concerned in the preceding financial year from the sale of products and the provision of services falling within the undertakings' ordinary activities after deduction of sales rebates and of value added tax and other taxes directly related to turnover. The aggregate turnover of an undertaking concerned shall not include the sale of products or the provision of services between any of the undertakings referred to in paragraph 4.

Turnover, in the Community or in a Member State, shall comprise products sold and services provided to undertakings or consumers, in the Community or in that Member State as the case may be.

2. By way of derogation from paragraph 1, where the concentration consists in the acquisition of parts, whether or not constituted as legal entities, of one or more undertakings, only the turnover relating to the parts which are the subject of the transaction shall be taken into account with regard to the seller or sellers.

However, two or more transactions within the meaning of the first subparagraph which take place within a two-year period between the same persons or undertakings shall be treated as one and the same concentration arising on the date of the last transaction.

[3. In place of turnover the following shall be used:
  (a) for credit institutions and other financial institutions, as regards Article 1(2) and (3), the sum of the following income items as defined in Council Directive 86/635/EEC of 8 December 1986 on the annual accounts and consolidated accounts of banks and other financial institutions, after deduction of value added tax and other taxes directly related to those items, where appropriate:
     (i) interest income and similar income;
     (ii) income from securities:
          — income from shares and other variable yield securities,
          — income from participating interests,
          — income from shares in affiliated undertakings;
     (iii) commissions receivable;
     (iv) net profit on financial operations;
     (v) other operating income.
The turnover of a credit or financial institution in the Community or in a Member State shall comprise the income items, as defined above, which are received by the branch or division of that institution established in the Community or in the Member State in question, as the case may be;
  (b) for insurance undertakings, the value of gross premiums written which shall comprise all amounts received and receivable in respect of insurance contracts issued by or on behalf of the insurance undertakings, including also outgoing reinsurance premiums, and after deduction of taxes and parafiscal contributions or levies charged by reference to the amounts of individual premiums or the total volume of premiums; as regards Article 1(2)(b) and (3)(b), (c) and (d) and the final part of Article 1(2) and (3), gross

premiums received from Community residents and from residents of one Member State respectively shall be taken into account.]

[4. Without prejudice to paragraph 2, the aggregate turnover of an undertaking concerned within the meaning of Article 1(2) and (3) shall be calculated by adding together the respective turnovers of the following:]

(a) the undertaking concerned;

(b) those undertakings in which the undertaking concerned, directly or indirectly:

— owns more than half the capital or business assets, or

— has the power to exercise more than half the voting rights, or

— has the power to appoint more than half the members of the supervisory board, the administrative board or bodies legally representing the undertakings, or

— has the right to manage the undertakings' affairs;

(c) those undertakings which have in the undertaking concerned the rights or powers listed in (b);

(d) those undertakings in which an undertaking as referred to in (c) has the rights or powers listed in (b);

(e) those undertakings in which two or more undertakings as referred to in (a) to (d) jointly have the rights or powers listed in (b).

[5. Where undertakings concerned by the concentration jointly have the rights or powers listed in paragraph 4(b), in calculating the aggregate turnover of the undertakings concerned for the purposes of Article 1(2) and (3):]

(a) no account shall be taken of the turnover resulting from the sale of products or the provision of services between the joint undertaking and each of the undertakings concerned or any other undertaking connected with any one of them, as set out in paragraph 4(b) to (e);

(b) account shall be taken of the turnover resulting from the sale of products and the provision of services between the joint undertaking and any third undertakings. This turnover shall be apportioned equally amongst the undertakings concerned.

Article 6 Examination of the notification and initiation of proceedings

1. The Commission shall examine the notification as soon as it is received.

(a) Where it concludes that the concentration notified does not fall within the scope of this Regulation, it shall record that finding by means of a decision.

(b) Where it finds that the concentration notified, although falling within the scope of this Regulation, does not raise serious doubts as to its compatibility with the common market, it shall decide not to oppose it and shall declare that it is compatible with the common market.

[The decision declaring the concentration compatible shall also cover restrictions directly related and necessary to the implementation of the concentration.]

[(c) Without prejudice to paragraph 1(a), where the Commission finds that the concentration notified falls within the scope of this Regulation and raises serious doubts as to its compatibility with the common market, it shall decide to initiate proceedings.]

[1a. Where the Commission finds that, following modification by the undertakings concerned, a notified concentration no longer raises serious doubts within the meaning of paragraph 1(c), it may decide to declare the concentration compatible with the common market pursuant to paragraph 1(b).

The Commission may attach to its decision under paragraph 1(b) conditions and obligations intended to ensure that the undertakings concerned comply with the commitments they have entered into vis-à-vis the Commission with a view to rendering the concentration compatible with the common market.]

[1b. The Commission may revoke the decision it has taken pursuant to paragraph 1(a) or (b) where:

(a) the decision is based on incorrect information for which one of the undertakings is responsible or where it has been obtained by deceit, or

(b) the undertakings concerned commit a breach of an obligation attached to the decision.]

[1c. In the cases referred to in paragraph 1(b), the Commission may take a decision under paragraph 1, without being bound by the deadlines referred to in Article 10(1).]

2. The Commission shall notify its decision to the undertakings concerned and the competent authorities of the Member States without delay.

Article 7 Suspension of concentrations

[1. A concentration as defined in Article I shall not be put into effect either before its notification or until it has been declared compatible with the common market pursuant to a decision under Article 6(1)(b) or Article 8(2) or on the basis of a presumption according to Article 10(6).]

2. [. . .]

3. [Paragraph 1] shall not prevent the implementation of a public bid which has been notified to the Commission in accordance with Article 4(1), provided that the acquirer does not exercise the voting rights attached to the securities in question or does so only to maintain the full value of those investments and on the basis of a derogation granted by the Commission under paragraph 4.

[4. The Commission may, on request, grant a derogation from the obligations imposed in paragraph 1 or 3. The request to grant a derogation must be reasoned. In deciding on the request, the Commission shall take into account inter alia the effects of the suspension on one or more undertakings concerned by a concentration or on a third party and the threat to competition posed by the concentration. That derogation may be made subject to conditions and obligations in order to ensure conditions of effective competition. A derogation may be applied for and granted at any time, even before notification or after the transaction.]

[5. The validity of any transaction carried out in contravention of paragraph 1 shall be dependent on a decision pursuant to Article 6(1)(b) or Article 8(2) or (3) or on a presumption pursuant to Article 10(6).

This Article shall, however, have no effect on the validity of transactions in securities including those convertible into other securities admitted to trading on a market which is regulated and supervised by authorities recognised by public bodies, operates regularly and is accessible directly or indirectly to the public, unless the buyer and seller knew or ought to have known that the transaction was carried out in contravention of paragraph 1.]

Article 8 Powers of decision of the Commission

1. Without prejudice to Article 9, all proceedings initiated pursuant to Article 6(1)(c) shall be closed by means of a decision as provided for in paragraphs 2 to 5.

[2. Where the Commission finds that, following modification by the undertakings concerned if necessary, a notified concentration fulfils the criterion laid down in Article 2(2) and, in the cases referred to in Article 2(4), the criteria laid down in Article 85(3) of the Treaty, it shall issue a decision declaring the concentration compatible with the common market.

It may attach to its decision conditions and obligations intended to ensure that the undertakings concerned comply with the commitments they have entered into vis-à-vis the Commission with a view to rendering the concentration compatible with the common market. The decision declaring the concentration compatible with the common market shall also cover restrictions directly related and necessary to the implementation of the concentration.]

[3. Where the Commission finds that a concentration fulfils the criterion defined in Article

2(3) or, in the cases referred to in Article 2(4), does not fulfil the criteria laid down in Article 85(3) of the Treaty, it shall issue a decision declaring that the concentration is incompatible with the common market.]

4. Where a concentration has already been implemented, the Commission may, in a decision pursuant to paragraph 3 or by separate decision, require the undertakings or assets brought together to be separated or the cessation of joint control or any other action that may be appropriate in order to restore conditions of effective competition.

5. The Commission may revoke the decision it has taken pursuant to paragraph 2 where:

(a) the declaration of compatibility is based on incorrect information for which one of the undertakings is responsible or where it has been obtained by deceit; or

(b) the undertakings concerned commit a breach of an obligation attached to the decision.

6. In the cases referred to in paragraph 5, the Commission may take a decision under paragraph 3, without being bound by the deadline referred to in Article 10(3).

Article 9 Referral to the competent authorities of the Member States

1. The Commission may, by means of a decision notified without delay to the undertakings concerned and the competent authorities of the other Member States, refer a notified concentration to the competent authorities of the Member State concerned in the following circumstances.

[2. Within three weeks of the date of receipt of the copy of the notification a Member State may inform the Commission, which shall inform the undertakings concerned, that:

(a) a concentration threatens to create or to strengthen a dominant position as a result of which effective competition will be significantly impeded on a market within that Member State, which presents all the characteristics of a distinct market, or

(b) a concentration affects competition on a market within that Member State, which presents all the characteristics of a distinct market and which does not constitute a substantial part of the common market.]

3. If the Commission considers that, having regard to the market for the products or services in question and the geographical reference market within the meaning of paragraph 7, there is such a distinct market and that such a threat exists, either:

(a) it shall itself deal with the case in order to maintain or restore effective competition on the market concerned; or

[(b) it shall refer the whole or part of the case to the competent authorities of the Member State concerned with a view to the application of that State's national competition law.

In cases where a Member State informs the Commission that a concentration affects competition in a distinct market within its territory that does not form a substantial part of the common market, the Commission shall refer the whole or part of the case relating to the distinct market concerned, if it considers that such a distinct market is affected.]

If, however, the Commission considers that such a distinct market or threat does not exist it shall adopt a decision to that effect which it shall address to the Member State concerned.

4. A decision to refer or not to refer pursuant to paragraph 3 shall be taken:

(a) as a general rule within the six-week period provided for in Article 10(1), second subparagraph, where the Commission, pursuant to Article 6(1)(b), has not initiated proceedings; or

(b) within three months at most of the notification of the concentration concerned where the Commission has initiated proceedings under Article 6(1)(c), without taking the preparatory steps in order to adopt the necessary measures under Article 8(2), second subparagraph, (3) or (4) to maintain or restore effective competition on the market concerned.

5. If within the three months referred to in paragraph 4(b) the Commission, despite a reminder from the Member State concerned, has not taken a decision on referral in accordance with paragraph 3 nor has taken the preparatory steps referred to in paragraph 4(b), it shall be deemed to have taken a decision to refer the case to the Member State concerned in accordance with paragraph 3(b).

6. The publication of any report or the announcement of the findings of the examination of the concentration by the competent authority of the Member State concerned shall be effected not more than four months after the Commission's referral.

7. The geographical reference market shall consist of the area in which the undertakings concerned are involved in the supply and demand of products or services, in which the conditions of competition are sufficiently homogeneous and which can be distinguished from neighbouring areas because, in particular, conditions of competition are appreciably different in those areas. This assessment should take account in particular of the nature and characteristics of the products or services concerned, of the existence of entry barriers or of consumer preferences, of appreciable differences of the undertakings' market shares between the area concerned and neighbouring areas or of substantial price differences.

8. In applying the provisions of this Article, the Member State concerned may take only the measures strictly necessary to safeguard or restore effective competition on the market concerned.

9. In accordance with the relevant provisions of the Treaty, any Member State may appeal to the Court of Justice, and in particular request the application of Article 186, for the purpose of applying its national competition law.

[10. This Article may be re-examined at the same time as the thresholds referred to in Article 1.]

Article 10 Time limits for initiating proceedings and for decisions

1. The decisions referred to in Article 6(1) must be taken within one month at most. That period shall begin on the day following that of the receipt of a notification or, if the information to be supplied with the notification is incomplete, on the day following that of the receipt of the complete information.

That period shall be increased to six weeks if the Commission receives a request from a Member State in accordance with Article 9(2) [or where, after notification of a concentration, the undertakings concerned submit commitments pursuant to Article 6(1a), which are intended by the parties to form the basis for a decision pursuant to Article 6(1)(b).]

2. Decisions taken pursuant to Article 8(2) concerning notified concentrations must be taken as soon as it appears that the serious doubts referred to in Article 6(1)(c) have been removed, particularly as a result of modifications made by the undertakings concerned, and at the latest by the deadline laid down in paragraph 3.

3. Without prejudice to Article 8(6), decisions taken pursuant to Article 8(3) concerning notified concentrations must be taken within not more than four months of the date on which proceedings are initiated.

4. The periods set by paragraphs 1 and 3 shall exceptionally be suspended where, owing to circumstances for which one of the undertakings involved in the concentration is responsible, the Commission has had to request information by decision pursuant to Article 11 or to order an investigation by decision pursuant to Article 13.

5. Where the Court of Justice gives a Judgment which annuls the whole or part of a Commission decision taken under this Regulation, the periods laid down in this Regulation shall start again from the date of the Judgment.

6. Where the Commission has not taken a decision in accordance with Article 6(1)(b) or (c) or Article 8(2) or (3) within the deadlines set in paragraphs 1 and 3 respectively, the concentration shall be deemed to have been declared compatible with the common market, without prejudice to Article 9.

Article 11 Requests for information

1. In carrying out the duties assigned to it by this Regulation, the Commission may obtain all necessary information from the Governments and competent authorities of the Member States, from the persons referred to in Article 3(1)(b), and from undertakings and associations of undertakings.

2. When sending a request for information to a person, an undertaking or an association of undertakings, the Commission shall at the same time send a copy of the request to the competent authority of the Member State within the territory of which the residence of the person or the seat of the undertaking or association of undertakings is situated.

3. In its request the Commission shall state the legal basis and the purpose of the request and also the penalties provided for in Article 14(1)(c) for supplying incorrect information.

4. The information requested shall be provided, in the case of undertakings, by their owners or their representatives and, in the case of legal persons, companies or firms, or of associations having no legal personality, by the persons authorised to represent them by law or by their statutes.

5. Where a person, an undertaking or an association of undertakings does not provide the information requested within the period fixed by the Commission or provides incomplete information, the Commission shall by decision require the information to be provided. The decision shall specify what information is required, fix an appropriate period within which it is to be supplied and state the penalties provided for in Articles 14(1)(c) and 15(1)(a) and the right to have the decision reviewed by the Court of Justice.

6. The Commission shall at the same time send a copy of its decision to the competent authority of the Member State within the territory of which the residence of the person or the seat of the undertaking or association of undertakings is situated.

Article 12 Investigations by the authorities of the Member States

1. At the request of the Commission, the competent authorities of the Member States shall undertake the investigations which the Commission considers to be necessary under Article 13(1), or which it has ordered by decision pursuant to Article 13(3). The officials of the competent authorities of the Member States responsible for conducting those investigations shall exercise their powers upon production of an authorisation in writing issued by the competent authority of the Member State within the territory of which the investigation is to be carried out. Such authorisation shall specify the subject matter and purpose of the investigation.

2. If so requested by the Commission or by the competent authority of the Member State within the territory of which the investigation is to be carried out, officials of the Commission may assist the officials of that authority in carrying out their duties.

Article 13 Investigative powers of the Commission

1. In carrying out the duties assigned to it by this Regulation, the Commission may undertake all necessary investigations into undertakings and associations of undertakings.
   To that end the officials authorised by the Commission shall be empowered:
   - (a) to examine the books and other business records;
   - (b) to take or demand copies of or extracts from the books and business records;
   - (c) to ask for oral explanations on the spot;
   - (d) to enter any premises, land and means of transport of undertakings.

2. The officials of the Commission authorised to carry out the investigations shall exercise their powers on production of an authorisation in writing specifying the subject matter and purpose of the investigation and the penalties provided for in Article 14(1)(d) in cases where production of the required books or other business records is incomplete. In good time before the investigation, the Commission shall inform, in writing, the competent authority of the Member State within the territory of which the investigation is to be carried out of the investigation and of the identities of the authorised officials.

3. Undertakings and associations of undertakings shall submit to investigations ordered by decision of the Commission. The decision shall specify the subject matter and purpose of the investigation, appoint the date on which it shall begin and state the penalties provided for in Articles 14(1)(d) and 15(1)(b) and the right to have the decision reviewed by the Court of Justice.

4. The Commission shall in good time and in writing inform the competent authority of the Member State within the territory of which the investigation is to be carried out of its intention of taking a decision pursuant to paragraph 3. It shall hear the competent authority before taking its decision.

5. Officials of the competent authority of the Member State within the territory of which the investigation is to be carried out may, at the request of that authority or of the Commission, assist the officials of the Commission in carrying out their duties.

6. Where an undertaking or association of undertakings opposes an investigation ordered pursuant to this Article, the Member State concerned shall afford the necessary assistance to the officials authorised by the Commission to enable them to carry out their investigation. To this end the Member States shall, after consulting the Commission, take the necessary measures within one year of the entry into force of this Regulation.

Article 14 Fines

1. The Commission may by decision impose on the persons referred to in Article 3(1)(b), undertakings or associations of undertakings fines of from ECU 1,000 to 50,000 where intentionally or negligently:
   (a) they fail to notify a concentration in accordance with Article 4;
   (b) they supply incorrect or misleading information in a notification pursuant to Article 4;
   (c) they supply incorrect information in response to a request made pursuant to Article 11 or fail to supply information within the period fixed by a decision taken pursuant to Article 11;
   (d) they produce the required books or other business records in incomplete form during investigations under Article 12 or 13, or refuse to submit to an investigation ordered by decision taken pursuant to Article 13.

2. The Commission may by decision impose fines not exceeding 10% of the aggregate turnover of the undertakings concerned within the meaning of Article 5 on the persons or undertakings concerned where, either intentionally or negligently, they:
   (a) fail to comply with an obligation imposed by decision pursuant to Article 7(4) or 8(2), second subparagraph;
   (b) put into effect a concentration in breach of Article 7(1) or disregard a decision taken pursuant to Article 7(2);
   (c) put into effect a concentration declared incompatible with the common market by decision pursuant to Article 8(3) or do not take the measures ordered by decision pursuant to Article 8(4).

3. In setting the amount of a fine, regard shall be had to the nature and gravity of the infringement.

4. Decisions taken pursuant to paragraphs 1 and 2 shall not be of criminal law nature.

Article 15 Periodic penalty payments

1. The Commission may by decision impose on the persons referred to in Article 3(1)(b), undertakings or associations of undertakings concerned periodic penalty payments of up to ECU 25,000 for each day of delay calculated from the date set in the decision, in order to compel them:

(a) to supply complete and correct information which it has requested by decision pursuant to Article 11;

(b) to submit to an investigation which it has ordered by decision pursuant to Article 13.

2. The Commission may by decision impose on the persons referred to in Article 3(1)(b) or on undertakings periodic penalty payments of up to ECU 100,000 for each day of delay calculated from the date set in the decision in order to compel them:

(a) to comply with an obligation imposed by decision, pursuant to Article 7(4) or Article 8(2), second subparagraph, or

(b) to apply the measures ordered by decision pursuant to Article 8(4).

3. Where the persons referred to in Article 3(1)(b), undertakings or associations of undertakings have satisfied the obligation which it was the purpose of the periodic penalty payment to enforce, the Commission may set the total amount of the periodic penalty payments at a lower figure than that which would arise under the original decision.

Article 16 Review by the Court of Justice

The Court of Justice shall have unlimited jurisdiction within the meaning of Article 172 of the Treaty to review decisions whereby the Commission has fixed a fine or periodic penalty payments; it may cancel, reduce or increase the fine or periodic penalty payments imposed.

Article 17 Professional secrecy

1. Information acquired as a result of the application of Articles 11, 12, 13 and 18 shall be used only for the purposes of the relevant request, investigation or hearing.

2. Without prejudice to Articles 4(3), 18 and 20, the Commission and the competent authorities of the Member States, their officials and other servants shall not disclose information they have acquired through the application of this Regulation of the kind covered by the obligation of professional secrecy.

3. Paragraphs 1 and 2 shall not prevent publication of general information or of surveys which do not contain information relating to particular undertakings or associations of undertakings.

Article 18 Hearing of the parties and of third persons

1. Before taking any decision provided for in [Article 7(4)], Article 8(2), second subparagraph, and (3) to (5) and Articles 14 and 15, the Commission shall give the persons, undertakings and associations of undertakings concerned the opportunity, at every stage of the procedure up to the consultation of the Advisory Committee, of making known their views on the objections against them.

[2. By way of derogation from paragraph 1, a decision to grant a derogation from suspension as referred to in Article 7(4) may be taken provisionally, without the persons, undertakings or associations of undertakings concerned being given the opportunity to make known their views beforehand, provided that the Commission gives them that opportunity as soon as possible after having taken its decision.]

3. The Commission shall base its decision only on objections on which the parties have been able to submit their observations. The rights of the defence shall be fully respected in the proceedings. Access to the file shall be open at least to the parties directly involved, subject to the legitimate interest of undertakings in the protection of their business secrets.

4. In so far as the Commission or the competent authorities of the Member States deem it necessary, they may also hear other natural or legal persons. Natural or legal persons showing a sufficient interest and especially members of the administrative or management bodies of the undertakings concerned or the recognised representatives of their employees shall be entitled, upon application, to be heard.

Article 19 Liaison with the authorities of the Member States

1. The Commission shall transmit to the competent authorities of the Member States copies of notifications within three working days and, as soon as possible, copies of the most important documents lodged with or issued by the Commission pursuant to this Regulation.

[Such documents shall include commitments which are intended by the parties to form the basis for a decision pursuant to Articles 6(1)(b) or 8(2).]

2. The Commission shall carry out the procedures set out in this Regulation in close and constant liaison with the competent authorities of the Member States, which may express their views upon those procedures. For the purposes of Article 9 it shall obtain information from the competent authority of the Member State as referred to in paragraph 2 of that Article and give it the opportunity to make known its views at every stage of the procedure up to the adoption of a decision pursuant to paragraph 3 of that Article; to that end it shall give it access to the file.

3. An Advisory Committee on concentrations shall be consulted before any decision is taken pursuant to Article 8(2) to (5), 14 or 15, or any provisions are adopted pursuant to Article 23.

4. The Advisory Committee shall consist of representatives of the authorities of the Member States. Each Member State shall appoint one or two representatives; if unable to attend, they may be replaced by other representatives. At least one of the representatives of a Member State shall be competent in matters of restrictive practices and dominant positions.

5. Consultation shall take place at a joint meeting convened at the invitation of and chaired by the Commission. A summary of the case, together with an indication of the most important documents and a preliminary draft of the decision to be taken for each case considered, shall be sent with the invitation. The meeting shall take place not less than 14 days after the invitation has been sent. The Commission may in exceptional cases shorten that period as appropriate in order to avoid serious harm to one or more of the undertakings concerned by a concentration.

6. The Advisory Committee shall deliver an opinion on the Commission's draft decision, if necessary by taking a vote. The Advisory Committee may deliver an opinion even if some members are absent and unrepresented. The opinion shall be delivered in writing and appended to the draft decision. The Commission shall take the utmost account of the opinion delivered by the Committee. It shall inform the Committee of the manner in which its opinion has been taken into account.

7. The Advisory Committee may recommend publication of the opinion. The Commission may carry out such publication. The decision to publish shall take due account of the legitimate interest of undertakings in the protection of their business secrets and of the interest of the undertakings concerned in such publication's taking place.

Article 20 Publication of decisions

1. The Commission shall publish the decisions which it takes pursuant to Article 8(2) to (5) in the *Official Journal of the European Communities*.

2. The publication shall state the names of the parties and the main content of the decision; it shall have regard to the legitimate interest of undertakings in the protection of their business secrets.

Article 21 Jurisdiction

1. Subject to review by the Court of Justice, the Commission shall have sole jurisdiction to take the decisions provided for in this Regulation.

2. No Member State shall apply its national legislation on competition to any concentration that has a Community dimension.

The first subparagraph shall be without prejudice to any Member State's power to carry out any enquiries necessary for the application of Article 9(2) or after referral, pursuant to Article 9(3), first subparagraph, indent (b), or (5), to take the measures strictly necessary for the application of Article 9(8).

3. Notwithstanding paragraphs 1 and 2, Member States may take appropriate measures to protect legitimate interests other than those taken into consideration by this Regulation and compatible with the general principles and other provisions of Community law.

Public security, plurality of the media and prudential rules shall be regarded as legitimate interests within the meaning of the first subparagraph.

Any other public interest must be communicated to the Commission by the Member State concerned and shall be recognised by the Commission after an assessment of its compatibility with the general principles and other provisions of Community law before the measures referred to above may be taken. The Commission shall inform the Member State concerned of its decision within one month of that communication.

Article 22 Application of the Regulation

[1. This Regulation alone shall apply to 'concentrations as defined in Article 3, and Regulations No 17, (EEC) No 1017/68, (EEC) No 4056/86 and (EEC) No 3975/87 shall not apply, except in relation to joint ventures that do not have a Community dimension and which have their object or effect the coordination of the competitive behaviour of undertakings that remain independent.]

2. [. . .]

[3. If the Commission finds, at the request of a Member State or at the joint request of two or more Member States, that a concentration as defined in Article 3 that has no Community dimension within the meaning of Article 1 creates or strengthens a dominant position as a result of which effective competition would be significantly impeded within the territory of the Member State or States making the joint request, it may, insofar as that concentration affects trade between Member States, adopt the decisions provided for in Article 8(2), second subparagraph, (3) and (4).]

[4. Articles 2(1)(a) and (b), 5, 6, 8 and 10 to 20 shall apply to a request made pursuant to paragraph 3. Article 7 shall apply to the extent that the concentration has not been put into effect on the date on which the Commission informs the parties that a request has been made.

The period within which proceedings may be initiated pursuant to Article 10(1) shall begin on the day following that of the receipt of the request from the Member State or States concerned. The request must be made within one month at most of the date on which the concentration was made known to the Member State or to all Member States making a joint request or effected. This period shall begin on the date of the first of those events.]

5. Pursuant to paragraph 3 the Commission shall take only the measures strictly necessary to maintain or restore effective competition within the territory of the Member State [or States] at the request of which it intervenes.

6. [. . .]

Article 23 Implementing provisions

The Commission shall have the power to adopt implementing provisions concerning the form, content and other details of notifications pursuant to Article 4, [time limits pursuant to Articles 7, 9, 10 and 22], and hearings pursuant to Article 18.

[The Commission shall have the power to lay down the procedure and time limits for the submission of commitments pursuant to Articles 6(1a) and 8(2).]

Article 24 Relations with non-member countries

1. The Member States shall inform the Commission of any general difficulties encountered by their undertakings with concentrations as defined in Article 3 in a non-member country.

2. Initially not more than one year after the entry into force of this Regulation and thereafter periodically the Commission shall draw up a report examining the treatment accorded to Community undertakings, in the terms referred to in paragraphs 3 and 4, as regards concentrations in non-member countries. The Commission shall submit those reports to the Council, together with any recommendations.

3. Whenever it appears to the Commission, either on the basis of the reports referred to in paragraph 2 or on the basis of other information, that a non-member country does not grant Community undertakings treatment comparable to that granted by the Community to undertakings from that non-member country, the Commission may submit proposals to the Council for an appropriate mandate for negotiation with a view to obtaining comparable treatment for Community undertakings.

4. Measures taken under this Article shall comply with the obligations of the Community or of the Member States, without prejudice to Article 234 of the Treaty, under international agreements, whether bilateral or multilateral.

Article 25 Entry into force

1. This Regulation shall enter into force on 21 September 1990.

2. This Regulation shall not apply to any concentration which was the subject of an agreement or announcement or where control was acquired within the meaning of Article 4(1) before the date of this Regulation's entry into force and it shall not in any circumstances apply to any concentration in respect of which proceedings were initiated before that date by a Member State's authority with responsibility for competition.

[3. As regards concentrations to which this Regulation applies by virtue of accession, the date of accession shall be substituted for the date of entry into force of this Regulation. The provision of paragraph 2, second alternative, applies in the same way to proceedings initiated by a competition authority of the new Member States, or by the EFTA Surveillance Authority.]

NOTE: One of the most controversial issues surrounding merger control in the EC is the point at which merger control moves from the control of Member States to the Community institutions. This is controversial because a merger decision, either to allow a merger or to prohibit it, may well have major political consequences for individual Member States. By letting control move to the Community, the Member States effectively accepted that they could no longer successfully control major pan-European mergers at state level. Even though the Member States had accepted there was a need for EC merger control, the division of responsibility between the EC and the Member States has proved to be a bone of contention throughout the process before the adoption of the Regulation, and its subsequent reform in 1997. The thresholds adopted under the Regulation, are based on the turnover of the merging undertakings. This has the benefit of being relatively easy to establish for those involved in a concentration, as it is termed in the Regulation but it does not, in itself, indicate whether the concentration raises any competition concerns. The main aim of the adoption of the Community system was to avoid situations in which undertakings would have to notify a concentration in several Member States and therefore undergo a highly complex series of different procedures. Guidance is given on the calculation of turnover in Article 5 of the Regulation and a Commission Notice on the Calculation of Turnover, OJ, 1998, C66/25. Concentrations which fall within the thresholds must be notified to the Commission within one week, under Article 4, and is suspended via Article 7. This means that a concentration should not be carried out until it has received Commission approval. This is vitally important as it is very difficult to undo a concentration once it has taken place.

Because of the sensitive nature of most concentrations, the time limits within the Merger Regulation are very important. The initial stage of the investigation must take place within one month of the day after the notification, under Article 10(1). If a second-stage procedure is initiated it must be completed within four months, under Article 10(3).

SECTION 3: **The nature of a concentration**

Commission Notice on the Concept of Concentration
OJ, 1998, C66/5, paras 1–12

1. Introduction

1. The purpose of this Notice is to provide guidance as to how the Commission interprets the term 'concentration' used in Article 3 of Council Regulation (EEC) No 4064/89[1] as last amended by Regulation (EC) No 1310/97[2] (hereinafter referred to as 'the Merger Regulation'). This formal guidance on the interpretation of Article 3 should enable firms to establish more quickly, in advance of any contact with the Commission, whether and to what extent their operations may be covered by Community merger control.

This Notice replaces the Notice on the notion of a concentration[3].

This Notice deals with paragraphs (1), (3), (4) and (5) of Article 3. The interpretation of Article 3 in relation to joint ventures, dealt with in particular under Article 3(2), is set out in the Commission's Notice on the concept of full-function joint ventures.

2. The guidance set out in this Notice reflects the Commission's experience in applying the Merger Regulation since it entered into force on 21 December 1990. The principles contained here will be applied and further developed by the Commission in individual cases.

3. According to recital 23 to Regulation (EEC) No 4064/89, the concept of concentration is defined as covering only operations which bring about a lasting change in the structure of the undertakings concerned. Article 3(1) provides that such a structural change is brought about either by a merger between two previously independent undertakings or by the acquisition of control over the whole or part of another undertaking.

4. The determination of the existence of a concentration under the Merger Regulation is based upon qualitative rather than quantitative criteria, focusing on the concept of control. These criteria include considerations of both law and fact. It follows, therefore, that a concentration may occur on a legal or a *de facto* basis.

5. Article 3(1) of the Merger Regulation defines two categories of concentration:

— those arising from a merger between previously independent undertakings (point (a));
— those arising from an acquisition of control (point (b)).

These are treated respectively in Sections II and III below.

II. Mergers between previously independent undertakings

6. A merger within the meaning of Article 3(1)(a) of the Merger Regulation occurs when two or

---

1 OJ L 395, 30.12.1989, p. 1, corrected version OJ L 257, 21.9.1990, p. 13.
2 OJ L 180, 9.7.1997, p. 1.
3 OJ C 385, 31.12.1994, p. 5.

more independent undertakings amalgamate into a new undertaking and cease to exist as separate legal entities. A merger may also occur when an undertaking is absorbed by another, the latter retaining its legal identity while the former ceases to exist as a legal entity.

7. A merger within the meaning of Article 3(1)(a) may also occur where, in the absence of a legal merger, the combining of the activities of previously independent undertakings results in the creation of a single economic unit[4]. This may arise in particular where two or more undertakings, while retaining their individual legal personalities, establish contractually a common economic management[5]. If this leads to a *de facto* amalgamation of the undertakings concerned into a genuine common economic unit, the operation is considered to be a merger. A prerequisite for the determination of a common economic unit is the existence of a permanent, single economic management. Other relevant factors may include internal profit and loss compensation as between the various undertakings within the group, and their joint liability externally. The *de facto* amalgamation may be reinforced by cross-shareholdings between the undertakings forming the economic unit.

III. Acquisition of control

8. Article 3(1)(b) provides that a concentration occurs in the case of an acquisition of control. Such control may be acquired by one undertaking acting alone or by two or more undertakings acting jointly.

Control may also be acquired by a person in circumstances where that person already controls (whether solely or jointly) at least one other undertaking or, alternatively, by a combination of persons (which controls another undertaking) and/or undertakings. The term 'person' in this context extends to public bodies[6] and private entities, as well as individuals.

As defined, a concentration within the meaning of the Merger Regulation is limited to changes in control. Internal restructuring within a group of companies, therefore, cannot constitute a concentration.

An exceptional situation exists where both the acquiring and acquired undertakings are public companies owned by the same State (or by the same public body). In this case, whether the operation is to be regarded as an internal restructuring depends in turn on the question whether both undertakings were formerly part of the same economic unit within the meaning of recital 12 to Regulation (EEC) No 4064/89. Where the undertakings were formerly part of different economic units having an independent power of decision, the operation will be deemed to constitute a concentration and not an internal restructuring[7]. Such independent power of decision does not normally exist, however, where the undertakings are within the same holding company[8].

9. Whether an operation gives rise to an acquisition of control depends on a number of legal and/or factual elements. The acquisition of property rights and shareholders' agreements are important, but are not the only elements involved: purely economic relationships may also play a decisive role. Therefore, in exceptional circumstances, a situation of economic dependence may lead to control on a *de facto* basis where, for example, very important long-term supply

4 In determining the previous independence of undertakings, the issue of control may be relevant. Control is considered generally in paragraphs 12 *et seq.* below. For this specific issue, minority shareholders are deemed to have control if they have previously obtained a majority of votes on major decisions at shareholders' meetings. The reference period in this context is normally three years.

5 This could apply for example, in the case of a *'Gleichordnungskonzern'* in German law, certain *'Groupements d'Intérêt Economique'* in French law, and certain partnerships.

6 Including the State itself, e.g. Case IV/M.157—*Air France/Sabena*, of 5 October 1992 in relation to the Belgian State, or other public bodies such as the Treuhand in Case IV/M.308—*Kali und Salz/MDK/Treuhand*, of 14 December 1993.

7 Case IV/M.097—*Péchiney/Usinor*, of 24 June 1991; Case IV/M.216—*CEA Industrie/France Telecom/SGS-Thomson*, of 22 February 1993.

8 See paragraph 55 of the Notice on the concept of undertakings concerned.

agreements or credits provided by suppliers or customers, coupled with structural links, confer decisive influence[9].

There may also be acquisition of control even if it is not the declared intention of the parties[10]. Moreover, the Merger Regulation clearly defines control as having 'the possibility of exercising decisive influence' rather than the actual exercise of such influence.

10. Control is nevertheless normally acquired by persons or undertakings which are the holders of the rights or are entitled to rights conferring control (Article 3(4)(a)). There may be exceptional situations where the formal holder of a controlling interest differs from the person or undertaking having in fact the real power to exercise the rights resulting from this interest. This may be the case, for example, where an undertaking uses another person or undertaking for the acquisition of a controlling interest and exercises the rights through this person or undertaking, even though the latter is formally the holder of the rights. In such a situation, control is acquired by the undertaking which in reality is behind the operation and in fact enjoys the power to control the target undertaking (Article 3(4)(b)). The evidence needed to establish this type of indirect control may include factors such as the source of financing or family links.

11. The object of control can be one or more undertakings which constitute legal entities, or the assets of such entities, or only some of these assets[11]. The assets in question, which could be brands or licences, must constitute a business to which a market turnover can be clearly attributed.

12. The acquisition of control may be in the form of sole or joint control. In both cases, control is defined as the possibility of exercising decisive influence on an undertaking on the basis of rights, contracts or any other means (Article 3(3)).

NOTE: The number of ways in which the management and relationships between undertakings can change is infinite, but the Notice attempts to put some concepts at the fore of the merger Regulation. Where entirely new undertakings are created from others the position is generally clear, but it is much more difficult to pick up on situations in which there is a gradual shift of control. In that situation the attainment of a 'decisive influence' is key. It should also be borne in mind that such influence does not have to be formal, but must be able to be exercised in practice. See, for instance, Case IV/M764, *St Gobain/Poliet*, OJ, 1996, C225/08 and Case IV/M025, *Arjomari/ Wiggins Teape Appleton*, OJ, 1990, C321/16, [1991] 4 CMLR 854. That influence can be achieved either solely, by one undertaking, or jointly, by more than one undertaking working together.

Commission Notice on the Concept of Full Function Joint Ventures
OJ, 1998, C66/1

I. Introduction
1. The purpose of this notice is to provide guidance as to how the Commission interprets Article 3 of Council Regulation (EEC) No 4064/89[1] as last amended by Regulation (EC) No 1310/97[2] (hereinafter referred to as the Merger Regulation) in relation to joint ventures[3].

---

9 For example, in the *Usinor/Bamesa* decision adopted by the Commission under the ECSC Treaty. See also Case IV/M.258—*CCIE/GTE*, of 25 September 1992, and Case IV/M.697—*Lockheed Martin Corporation/Loral Corporation*, of 27 March 1996.

10 Case IV/M.157—*Air France/Sabena*, of 5 October 1992.

11 Case IV/M.286—*Zürich/MMI*, of 2 April 1993.

1 OJ L 395, 30.12.1989, p. 1, corrected version No L 257, 21.9.1990, p. 13.

2 OJ L 180, 9.7.1997, p. 1.

3 The Commission intends, in due course, to provide guidance on the application of Article 2(4) of the Merger Regulation. Pending the adoption of such guidance, interested parties are referred to the principles set out in paragraphs 17 to 20 of the Commission Notice on the distinction between concentrative and cooperative joint ventures, OJ C 385, 31.12.1994, p. 1.

2. This Notice replaces the Notice on the distinction between concentrative and cooperative joint ventures. Changes made in this Notice reflect the amendments made to the Merger Regulation as well as the experience gained by the Commission in applying the Merger Regulation since its entry into force on 21 September 1990. The principles set out in this Notice will be followed and further developed by the Commission's practice in individual cases.

3. Under the Community competition rules, joint ventures are undertakings which are jointly controlled by two or more other undertakings[4]. In practice joint ventures encompass a broad range of operations, from merger-like operations to cooperation for particular functions such as R & D, production or distribution.

4. Joint ventures fall within the scope of the Merger Regulation if they meet the requirements of a concentration set out in Article 3 thereof.

5. According to recital 23 to Council Regulation (EEC) No 4064/89 it is appropriate to define the concept of concentration in such a manner as to cover only operations bringing about a lasting change in the structure of the undertakings concerned.

6. The structural changes brought about by concentrations frequently reflect a dynamic process of restructuring in the markets concerned. They are permitted under the Merger Regulation unless they result in serious damage to the structure of competition by creating or strengthening a dominant position.

7. The Merger Regulation deals with the concept of full-function joint ventures in Article 3(2) as follows:

> 'The creation of a joint venture performing on a lasting basis all the functions of an autonomous economic entity shall constitute a concentration within the meaning of paragraph 1(b).'

II. Joint ventures under Article 3 of the Merger Regulation

8. In order to be a concentration within the meaning of Article 3 of the Merger Regulation, an operation must fulfil the following requirements:

1. Joint control

9. A joint venture may fall within the scope of the Merger Regulation where there is an acquisition of joint control by two or more undertakings, that is, its parent companies (Article 3(1)(b)). The concept of control is set out in Article 3(3). This provides that control is based on the possibility of exercising decisive influence over an undertaking, which is determined by both legal and factual considerations.

10. The principles for determining joint control are set out in detail in the Commission's Notice on the concept of concentration[5].

2. Structural change of the undertakings

11. Article 3(2) provides that the joint venture must perform, on a lasting basis, all the functions of an autonomous economic entity. Joint ventures which satisfy this requirement bring about a lasting change in the structure of the undertakings concerned. They are referred to in this Notice as 'full-function' joint ventures.

12. Essentially this means that a joint venture must operate on a market, performing the functions normally carried out by undertakings operating on the same market. In order to do so the joint venture must have a management dedicated to its day-to-day operations and access to

---

4 The concept of joint control is set out in the Notice on the concept of concentration.
5 Paragraphs 18 to 39.

sufficient resources including finance, staff, and assets (tangible and intangible) in order to conduct on a lasting basis its business activities within the area provided for in the joint-venture agreement[6].

13. A joint venture is not full-function if it only takes over one specific function within the parent companies' business activities without access to the market. This is the case, for example, for joint ventures limited to R & D or production. Such joint ventures are auxiliary to their parent companies' business activities. This is also the case where a joint venture is essentially limited to the distribution or sales of its parent companies' products and, therefore, acts principally as a sales agency. However, the fact that a joint venture makes use of the distribution network or outlet of one or more of its parent companies normally will not disqualify it as 'full-function' as long as the parent companies are acting only as agents of the joint venture[7].

14. The strong presence of the parent companies in upstream or downstream markets is a factor to be taken into consideration in assessing the full-function character of a joint venture where this presence leads to substantial sales or purchases between the parent companies and the joint venture. The fact that the joint venture relies almost entirely on sales to its parent companies or purchases from them only for an initial start-up period does not normally affect the full-function character of the joint venture. Such a start-up period may be necessary in order to establish the joint venture on a market. It will normally not exceed a period of three years, depending on the specific conditions of the market in question[8].

Where sales from the joint venture to the parent companies are intended to be made on a lasting basis, the essential question is whether, regardless of these sales, the joint venture is geared to play an active role on the market. In this respect the relative proportion of these sales compared with the total production of the joint venture is an important factor. Another factor is whether sales to the parent companies are made on the basis of normal commercial conditions[9].

In relation to purchases made by the joint venture from its parent companies, the full-function character of the joint venture is questionable in particular where little value is added to the products or services concerned at the level of the joint venture itself. In such a situation, the joint venture may be closer to a joint sales agency. However, in contrast to this situation where a joint venture is active in a trade market and performs the normal functions of a trading company in such a market, it normally will not be an auxiliary sales agency but a full-function joint venture. A trade market is characterised by the existence of companies which specialise in the selling and distribution of products without being vertically integrated in addition to those which are integrated, and where different sources of supply are available for the products in question. In addition, many trade

---

6 Case IV/M.527—*Thomson CSF/Deutsche Aerospace* of 2 December 1994 (paragraph 10)—intellectual rights, Case IV/M.560—*EDS/Lufthansa* of 11 May 1995 (paragraph 11)—outsourcing, Case IV/M.585—*Voest Alpine Industrieanlagenbau GmbH/Davy International Ltd* of 7 September 1995 (paragraph 8)—joint venture's right to demand additional expertise and staff from its parent companies, Case IV/M.686—*Nokia/Autoliv* of 5 February 1996 (paragraph 7), joint venture able to terminate 'service agreements' with parent company and to move from site retained by parent company, Case IV/M.791—*British Gas Trading Ltd/Group 4 Utility Services Ltd*, of 7 October 1996, (paragraph 9) joint venture's intended assets will be transferred to leasing company and leased by joint venture.

7 Case IV/M.102—*TNT/Canada Post* etc. of 2 December 1991 (paragraph 14).

8 Case IV/M.560—*EDS/Lufthansa* of 11 May 1995 (paragraph 11); Case IV/M.686—*Nokia/Autoliv* of 5 February 1996 (paragraph 6); to be contrasted with Case IV/M.904—*RSB/Tenex/Fuel Logistics* of 2 April 1997 (paragraphs 15–17) and Case IV/M.979—*Preussag/Voest-Alpine* of 1 October 1997 (paragraphs 9–12). A special case exists where sales by the joint venture to its parent are caused by a legal monopoly downstream of the joint venture, Case IV/M.468—*Siemens/Italtel* of 17 February 1995 (paragraph 12), or where the sales to a parent company consist of by-products, which are of minor importance to the joint venture, Case IV/M.550—*Union Carbide/Enichem* of 13 March 1995 (paragraph 14).

9 Case IV/M.556—*Zeneca/Vanderhave* of 9 April 1996 (paragraph 8); Case IV/M.751—*Bayer/Hüls* of 3 July 1996 (paragraph 10).

markets may require operators to invest in specific facilities such as outlets, stockholding, warehouses, depots, transport fleets and sales personnel. In order to constitute a full-function joint venture in a trade market, an undertaking must have the necessary facilities and be likely to obtain a substantial proportion of its supplies not only from its parent companies but also from other competing sources[10].

15. Furthermore, the joint venture must be intended to operate on a lasting basis. The fact that the parent companies commit to the joint venture the resources described above normally demonstrates that this is the case. In addition, agreements setting up a joint venture often provide for certain contingencies, for example, the failure of the joint venture or fundamental disagreement as between the parent companies[11]. This may be achieved by the incorporation of provisions for the eventual dissolution of the joint venture itself or the possibility for one or more parent companies to withdraw from the joint venture. This kind of provision does not prevent the joint venture from being considered as operating on a lasting basis. The same is normally true where the agreement specifies a period for the duration of the joint venture where this period is sufficiently long in order to bring about a lasting change in the structure of the undertakings concerned[12], or where the agreement provides for the possible continuation of the joint venture beyond this period. By contrast, the joint venture will not be considered to operate on a lasting basis where it is established for a short finite duration. This would be the case, for example, where a joint venture is established in order to construct a specific project such as a power plant, but it will not be involved in the operation of the plant once its construction has been completed.

III. Final

16. The creation of a full-function joint venture constitutes a concentration within the meaning of Article 3 of the Merger Regulation. Restrictions accepted by the parent companies of the joint venture that are directly related and necessary for the implementation of the concentration ('ancillary restrictions'), will be assessed together with the concentration itself[13].

Further, the creation of a full-function joint venture may as a direct consequence lead to the coordination of the competitive behaviour of undertakings that remain independent. In such cases Article 2(4) of the Merger Regulation provides that those cooperative effects will be assessed within the same procedure as the concentration. This assessment will be made in accordance with the criteria of Article 85(1) and (3) of the Treaty with a view to establishing whether or not the operation is compatible with the common market.

The applicability of Article 85 of the Treaty to other restrictions of competition, that are neither ancillary to the concentration, nor a direct consequence of the creation of the joint venture, will normally have to be examined by means of Regulation No 17.

17. The Commission's interpretation of Article 3 of the Merger Regulation with respect to joint ventures is without prejudice to the interpretation which may be given by the Court of Justice or the Court of First Instance of the European Communities.

NOTE: The position of joint ventures within the merger regime was dramatically altered following the 1997 amendments to bring more joint ventures within the system. Under the previous version of the regime, more joint ventures were dealt with under Article 81 EC, but this meant that the usually beneficial arrangements did not benefit from the strict time limits under the

---

10 Case IV/M.788—*AgrEVO/Marubeni* of 3 September 1996 (paragraphs 9 and 10).

11 Case IV/M.891—*Deutsche Bank/Commerzbank/JM. Voith* of 23 April 1997 (paragraph 7).

12 Case IV/M.791—*British Gas Trading Ltd/Group 4 Utility Services Ltd* of 7 October 1996 (paragraph 10); to be contrasted with Case IV/M.722—*Teneo/Merill Lynch/Bankers Trust* of 15 April 1996 (paragraph 15).

13 See Commission Notice regarding restrictions ancillary to concentrations, OJ No C 203, 14.8.1990, p. 5.

Merger Regulation. Full function joint ventures will now fall within the Merger Regulation because the entity created has the character of a new self-contained business entity and will operate without reliance on its parent undertakings. This concentration on self-reliance assures that the joint venture is not being used as a vehicle for the parents to cooperate in the future, which would better be controlled by Article 81 EC, but to form a new business. The joint venture must have the financial and management resources to operate on a lasting basis. It may still deal with the parent undertakings but must do so on an arm's-length basis. See *Texaco/Norsk Hydro* (Case IV/M511) OJ, 1995, C23/3. If the parent undertakings continue to have significant activities in the same market as the joint venture, it is still possible for the concentration to be considered under Article 81 EC but within the Merger Control system, under Article 2(4) of the Regulation.

SECTION 4: **Procedure under the Regulation**

Commission Notice on a simplified procedure for treatment of certain concentrations
OJ, 2000, C217/32, paras 1–9

1. This Notice sets out a simplified procedure under which the Commission intends to treat certain concentrations that do not raise competition concerns. The Notice is based on experience gained by the Commission in applying Council Regulation (EEC) No 4064/89 of 21 December 1989 on the control of concentrations between undertakings, as amended by Regulation (EC) No 1310/97 (the 'Merger Regulation') to date, which has shown that certain categories of notified concentrations are normally cleared without having raised any substantive doubts, provided that there were no special circumstances.

2. By following the procedure outlined in the following sections, the Commission aims to make Community merger control more focused and effective.

I. Overview of the simplified procedure
3. This Notice sets out the conditions under which the simplified procedure will be applied, together with the procedure itself. Pre-notification contact between the notifying parties and the Commission in such cases is encouraged. When all necessary conditions are met, and provided there are no special circumstances, the Commission will adopt a short-form clearance decision within one month from the date of notification, pursuant to Article 6(1)(b) of the Merger Regulation. Where it considers it appropriate in any particular case, the Commission may, naturally, launch an investigation and/or adopt a full decision within the time-limits laid down in Article 10(1) of the Merger Regulation.

II. Categories of concentrations suitable for treatment under the simplified procedure

Eligible concentrations
4. The simplified procedure will apply to the following categories of concentrations:

(a) two or more undertakings acquire joint control of a joint venture, provided that the joint venture has no, or negligible, actual or foreseen activities within the territory of the European Economic Area (EEA). Such cases occur where:
   (i) the turnover of the joint venture and/or the turnover of the contributed activities is less than EUR 100 million in the EEA territory; and

   (ii) the total value of assets transferred to the joint venture is less than EUR 100 million in the EEA territory;

(b) two or more undertakings merge, or one or more undertakings acquire sole or joint control of another undertaking, provided that none of the parties to the concentration are engaged in business activities in the same product and geographical market, or in a product market which is upstream or downstream of a product market in which any other party to the concentration is engaged;

(c) two or more undertakings merge, or one or more undertakings acquire sole or joint control of another undertaking:

   (i) and two or more of the parties to the concentration are engaged in business activities in the same product and geographical market (horizontal relationships); or

   (ii) one or more of the parties to the concentration are engaged in business activities in a product market which is upstream or downstream of a product market in which any other party to the concentration is engaged (vertical relationships), provided that their combined market share is not 15 per cent or more for horizontal and 25 per cent or more for vertical relationships.

5. The Commission's experience in applying the Merger Regulation to date has shown that, except in exceptional circumstances, concentrations falling into the above categories do not combine market positions in a way that would give rise to competition concerns.

Safeguards and exclusions

6. In assessing whether a concentration falls into one of the above categories, the Commission will ensure that all relevant circumstances are established with sufficient clarity. Given that market definitions may be a key element in this assessment, the parties are invited to provide information on possible alternative market definitions during the pre-notification phase (see point 10). Notifying parties are responsible for describing all alternative relevant product and geographic markets on which the notified concentration could have an impact and for providing data and information relating to the definition of such markets. The Commission retains the discretion to take the ultimate decision on market definition, basing its decision on an analysis of the facts of the case. Where it is difficult to define the relevant markets or to determine the parties' market shares, the Commission will not apply the simplified procedure.

7. While it can normally be assumed that concentrations falling into the above categories will not raise serious doubts as to their compatibility with the common market, there may none the less be certain situations, which exceptionally require a closer investigation and/or a full decision. In such cases, the Commission may refrain from applying the simplified procedure.

8. The following are indicative examples of types of cases which may be excluded from the simplified procedure. Certain types of concentrations may increase the parties' market power, for instance by combining technological, financial or other resources, even if the parties to the concentration do not operate in the same market. Concentrations involving conglomerate aspects may also be unsuitable for the simplified procedure, in particular, where one or more of the parties to the concentration holds individually a market share of 25 per cent or more in any product market in which there is no horizontal or vertical relationship between the parties. In other cases, it may not be possible to determine the parties' precise market shares. This is often the case when the parties operate in new or little developed markets. Concentrations in markets with high entry barriers, with a high degree of concentration or other known competition problems may also be unsuitable. Finally, the Commission may not apply the simplified procedure where an issue of coordination as referred to in Article 2(4) of the Merger Regulation arises.

9. If a Member State expresses substantiated concerns about the notified concentration within three weeks of receipt of the copy of the notification, or if a third party expresses substantiated

concerns within the time-limit laid down for such comments, the Commission will adopt a full decision. The time-limits set out in Article 10(1) of the Merger Regulation apply. The simplified procedure will not be applied if a Member State requests the referral of a notified concentration pursuant to Article 9 of the Merger Regulation.

NOTE: The adoption of this procedure allows the Commission to dispose of several well-known categories of case without needing to go through the full procedure. This obviously reduces the administrative burden on the Commission and will allow it to focus on more important cases. It also gives a degree of certainty to undertakings involved in such a concentration that the concentration is very likely to be approved.

Vodafone Airtouch
(Case IV/M1430) OJ, 1999, C295/2

Two large communications companies, who both provided mobile telecom packages, announced their intention to merge. Vodafone was based in the UK but had interests across Europe while Airtouch was based in the US, but also had interests across Europe.

Competition concerns
26. There are currently four operators on the German market for mobile telecommunications. The merged entity would have joint control in two of the four operators in the German market, D2 and E-Plus, which together command a 50–60 per cent share of the market. The only other large player in the market is T-Mobil, a subsidiary of Deutsche Telekom, with a market share of 35–45 per cent on the basis of figures provided by the parties. The fourth German operator, VIAG Interkom, is a fledgling operator which only launched its service in October 1998 and commands a market share of just 5 per cent.

27. The market for provision of mobile telecoms services in Germany is—as in other Member States—regulated at national level. This necessarily restricts entry to the market, since all operators must first gain a licence from the national regulator. The national regulator's ability to award new licences is in itself restricted by the limited amount of available radio frequencies.

28. The presence of T-Mobil makes it unlikely that the newly combined entity would be able to achieve single dominance in the market. Nevertheless, it would have decisive influence and joint control within the meaning of the ECMR over two of the main three players, who together enjoy a combined share of 50–60 per cent of the market. In addition, the proposed operation, by creating a structural link between two of the three main market operators in Germany would create a duopolistic market situation, accounting for almost 100 per cent of a market which has considerable barriers to entry and in which information is readily available to customers and competitors who wish to make pricing comparisons. It cannot be ruled out at this stage that these factors could lead to anti-competitive parallel behaviour.

29. In the absence of the modifications to the proposal offered by the parties (see below), the operation would have raised doubts serious enough to warrant the opening of proceedings in accordance with Article 6(1)(c) of the ECMR.

Sweden
30. In Sweden, Airtouch and Vodafone have holdings of 51.1 per cent and 20.0 per cent respectively in Europolitan, which has a 14.6 per cent share of the Swedish market. According to figures provided by the parties, this shareholding overlap, which does not lead to any increase in market share, and to any modification in the nature of control over this company, leaves the combined entity

in third place behind the two leading players, Telia Mobitel and Comviq, and hence does not give rise to any competition concerns.

V. Modifications to the proposal

31. In order to remove the concerns raised by the operation, Vodafone submitted a divestment undertaking in the form of a proposal for modification of the operation in accordance with the terms of Article 6(2) of the ECMR. This undertaking involves the divestment of Vodafone's entire 17.2 per cent stake in E-Plus.

32. Under the terms of the undertaking the parties have a period of . . . within which to complete the Divestment. An independent Trustee will be appointed to monitor the viability and saleability of the divestment assets in accordance with the undertaking, and ensure that the rights Vodafone has as a shareholder in E-Plus are exercised on an arm's length basis until completion of the sale.

Provisions are included for the Trustee to provide written reports on progress with the discharge of the Trustee's mandate. Vodafone will, in addition, ensure that confidential information relating to E-Plus is not divulged to Mannesmann Mobilfunk and vice-versa. If Vodafone has not effected a sale within . . . of this Decision, the Trustee will acquire powers to step in and take control of the sale process in order to ensure the divestment takes place within the agreed period.

33. Text of divestment undertaking removed for reasons of commercial confidentiality.

34. The Commission will:

(a) use its best endeavours to inform the Seller, as soon as reasonably practicable and within 14 working days of the Seller contacting the Commission (i) as regards the suitability of any proposed purchaser(s) (ii) if it agrees with a representation made by the Seller that discharging a certain Additional Function is unnecessary or not in accordance with the Mandate and (iii) if and to what extent the Trustee has found the Seller, in one of the Trustee reports or otherwise, not to be able to discharge its mandate;

(b) in determining whether any proposed purchaser is suitable, take into account whether the prospective purchaser concerned (i) appears to it to possess the status and resources necessary to acquire the Divestment Assets, (ii) is independent of the Seller, (iii) can be shown not to have relevant and significant connection with the Seller and (iv) has, or reasonably can obtain, all necessary approvals for the purchase from the relevant competition and regulatory authorities in the European Community and elsewhere.

35. The divestment would have the effect of removing any competition concerns which might otherwise have resulted from the overlap on the German market between the activities of E-Plus and D2. In a subsequent market test conducted by the Commission, none of the third parties consulted voiced significant objections to the substance of the planned divestment.

VI. Conclusion

36. The Commission has concluded that the undertakings are sufficient to address the competition concerns raised by this concentration. Accordingly, it has decided not to oppose the notified operation and to declare it compatible with the common market and with the EEA Agreement. This decision is adopted in application of Article 6(1)(b) of Council Regulation (EEC) No 4064/89.

NOTE: The *Vodafone/Airtouch* decision illustrates an important part of the Commission's administrative armoury under the Merger Regulation. It will often try to reach an agreement with the parties to allow a merger to go ahead, while dealing with any competition concerns that have arisen. In order to increase the awareness of the ability to negotiate a settlement in this manner, the Commission has also published a Notice on what they term as remedies, Commission Notice on Remedies, OJ, 2001, C68/3. To facilitate such a discussion, and to increase the possibility of a quick settlement, the Commission also encourages pre-notification communications from undertakings to identify the potential issues of concern as soon as possible. The remedies procedure is very important, as demonstrated by a large number of high-profile cases. See, for instance, Case IV/M623 *Kimberley-Clark/Scott Paper* OJ, 1996, L183/1, and Case IV/M1845 *AOL/Time Warner* OJ, 2001, L268/28.

A: Appraisal

The appraisal of merger cases is based on the 'creation or strengthening of a dominant position' test found in Article 2 of the Regulation. The jurisprudence of the Court under Article 82 EC is obviously instructive in what constitutes a dominant position. The Merger Task Force has to go through the same tests as under Article 82 EC to identify the relevant markets and establish the potential for the combined undertakings to create or strengthen a dominant position. See Chapter 8. As these steps are very similar to those already discussed, we will not deal with them further here, but there are a number of issues which are peculiar to merger control and need to be highlighted.

Gencor Limited v *Commission*
(Case T-102/96) [1999] ECR II-753, [1999] 4 CMLR 971

The Commission had declared a merger between two South African-based platinum producers as incompatible with the Common Market.

[106] As regards the argument that the Community cannot claim to have jurisdiction in respect of a concentration on the basis of future and hypothetical behaviour, namely parallel conduct on the part of the undertakings operating in the relevant market where that conduct might or might not fall within the competence of the Community under the Treaty, it must be stated, as pointed out above in connection with the question whether the concentration has an immediate effect, that, while the elimination of the risk of future abuses may be a legitimate concern of any competent competition authority, the main objective in exercising control over concentrations at Community level is to ensure that the restructuring of undertakings does not result in the creation of positions of economic power which may significantly impede effective competition in the common market. Community jurisdiction is therefore founded, first and foremost, on the need to avoid the establishment of market structures which may create or strengthen a dominant position, and not on the need to control directly possible abuses of a dominant position.

NOTE: While Article 82 EC dominance focuses on structure leading to abuse, the Merger Regulation focuses on the future structure of a market alone, and the potential for competition continuing to operate effectively on the market following the concentration. That focus is indicated in the test which has two parts: (1) creates or strengthens dominant position; (2) as a result of which effective competition would be significantly impeded in the common market or in a substantial part of it.

Mercedes-Benz/Kässbohrer
(Case IV/M477) OJ, 1995, L211/1

This decision concerns the proposed acquisition of Karl Kässbohrer Fahrzeugwerke GmbH by Mercedes-Benz AG. Both companies produce buses and coaches for the German market. After initiating a second-stage investigation and receiving some undertakings from the parties, the Commission eventually approved the merger as being compatible with the common market. Initial concerns were raised as the market shares of the combined undertakings on several different bus markets would be as follows: city buses—45.5 per cent (Mercedes-Benz 42.9 per cent and Kässbohrer 1.6 per cent), intercity buses—73.7 per cent (Mercedes-Benz 34.6 per cent and Kässbohrer 39.1 per cent), and touring coaches—54 per cent. While those market shares were high, the Commission also took a number of other factors into account.

[65] High market shares do not in themselves justify the assumption of a dominant position. At any rate, they do not allow a dominant position to be assumed if other structural factors are detectable which, in the foreseeable future, may alter the conditions of competition and justify a more relative view of the significance of the market share of the merged companies (see the precedents of the Commission Decisions in *Alcatel/Telettra*, Decision of 12 April 1991, IV/M.042 (5), and *Mannesmann/ Hoesch*, Decision of 12 November 1992, IV/M.222 (6)). Such structural factors could, for example, be the ability of actual competitors to constrain the action of the new entity, the expectation of a significant increase in potential competition from powerful competitors, the possibility of a quick market entry or the buying power of important customers. In the present case, the market shares of the merged companies are relativized by the fact that it may be expected that there will be substantial actual and in particular potential competition, as explained in the following sections.

[66] (e) The proposed merger would allow Mercedes-Benz and Kässbohrer to achieve certain synergy effects. This applies in particular to research and development, production and administration. Kässbohrer will in future benefit from the size of Mercedes-Benz in joint purchasing. The further advantage of component standardization is limited, since Mercedes-Benz and Kässbohrer already to a large extent use common components. Furthermore, it is not possible to apply further standardization in customer-sensitive and labour-intensive areas like design and equipment. The parties point out that the variety of types is often greatest in the case of smaller manufacturers such as Van Hool or Neoplan. In sales and service too, the merged companies will achieve only limited synergies (in logistics), since they will pursue a two-brand strategy in the market, and this presupposes separate sales and service. Lastly, competitors have questioned whether the expected synergy effects are enough to offset the existing cost disadvantages of Mercedes-Benz in comparison to its competitors. According to the information given by the parties at the hearing, such cost disadvantages are substantial: they amount per bus to between DM . . . (= . . . %) compared with Neoplan and DM . . . (= . . . %) compared with Ikarus.

[67] In the touring coach market, Mercedes-Benz will achieve an advantage through the acquisition of Kässbohrer in that Kässbohrer has a good brand image here, while Mercedes-Benz has a comparatively weaker position in this area. According to Mercedes-Benz's own data, the merger will lead to an extension in its product range, particularly as regards double-decker and triple-axle buses. Kässbohrer also has production flexibility and a recognized potential in the development of new bus types. However, in view of the variety of types and equipment in touring coaches, as explained above, the importance of the synergy effects achieved through the merger will be only limited.

[68] In addition to the potential effects of the merger, the size of the new entity Mercedes-Benz/ Kässbohrer has to be considered. Mercedes-Benz is the leading European bus producer in the world market. According to the press, in 1992 it produced 30,000 buses worldwide, whereas Volvo, the second largest producer, produced less than 6,000. Just under 19,000 Mercedes-Benz buses are produced in Brazil, though 90 per cent of these are only in chassis form. These buses are being sold exclusively in South America. The fact remains, however, that through Mercedes-Benz the new entity would have a worldwide sales network which would facilitate trade in second-hand buses. This, plus the fact that Mercedes-Benz is also the largest truck manufacturer in Germany and the EEA, coupled

with the financial strength of the Daimler-Benz Group, would stand the new entity in good stead. For many years Mercedes-Benz was able to finance its loss-making bus business out of the profits earned from its other activities. The total amount of DM 3.2 billion over 20 years mentioned by a competitor has, however, simply been deduced from the notional operating result, which can be explained by Mercedes-Benz's balance-sheet policy, and is disputed by Mercedes-Benz.

NOTE: Paragraph 65 gives an indication of some of the reasons that the Commission or Court would allow a merger to go ahead even though the combined undertaking would have a high market share. In this case the Commission was of the view that there would still be effective competition on the market. Another point to note is that in the city bus market the merger itself did not lead to a substantial lessening of competition as the 1.6 per cent market share that Kassbohrer would bring to the combined undertaking would result in little change from the previous position. There should be a causal link between the merger itself, and the impediment to future competition. See *France* v *Commission* Cases C-68/94 & C-30/95 [1998] ECR I-1375, [1998] 4 CMLR 829, discussed below.

Another important issued raised by the Commission is the possibility of the Commission accepting an 'efficiency defence'. It may be the case that when two undertakings combine they create a dominant position which might impede competition, but at the same time the merger may result in the undertaking making considerable efficiencies in production that may produce costs savings. The US Merger Guidelines have specific reference to an efficiency defence but the position is less clear under the Merger Regulation, the Regulation itself only refers to 'technical or economic progress' in Article 2(1)(b). In para. 66 the Commission appears to accept that the merger would achieve certain 'synergy' or efficiencies. Although it is not clear how important those synergies were to the Commission's decision, it is obvious that they were a factor. While there is no efficiency defence in the EC system, improved efficiencies alone will not negate a prohibition, improved efficiencies will play a part alongside other factors in encouraging the Commission to approve a merger. For recent discussion of the place of efficiencies in the Merger Regulation see the Green Paper on the Review of Council Regulation (EEC) No 4064/89, COM(2001) 745/6 final, paras 170–172.

Camesasca, P.D., 'The Explicit Efficiency Defence In Merger Control: Does It Make The Difference?'
[1999] ECLR 14, pp. 25–26 [footnotes omitted]

Alcatel/Telettra, *Mannesmann/Valourec/Ilva*, *Mercedes-Benz/Kässbohrer*, *ABB/Daimler-Benz* and *Agfa-Gevaert/DuPont* show, however, that the Commission is ready to rely on efficiencies to clear a merger. The public dispute accompanying these mergers also exemplified the main problem with the Commission's approach—by handling efficiencies in between lines, the Commission has no fall-back line to defend itself against accusations of industrial policy considerations, or paying attention to the competition from undertakings located outside the Community. To avoid this criticism, the Commission seems to insert efficiencies during the evaluative process of the merger at hand and in doing so, avoids a final finding of dominance. Market shares thus represent an important factor of evidence of a dominant position 'provided they not only reflect current conditions but are also a reliable indicator of future conditions'. The dynamic aspects of a market, as indicated by entry and exit, fluctuations of market share, and the pace of technological change and innovation, clearly have come to play a prominent part in the Commission's approach, pointing towards the necessity to make some sort of prediction about future developments when assessing mergers. This is probably what the Commission implied when it stated that 'the test of dominance is to be understood as an appreciable freedom of action uncontrolled by actual or potential competition'. Quite instructive for the Commission's willingness to take efficiencies into account implicitly while shaping its decision is the principle formulated in *Cyanamid/Shell*, where a finding of dominance was avoided as '[a]n analysis focusing on market share alone is not particularly probative in a dynamic and R&D-intensive industry'. As a result, the Commission has been prepared to approve very high market shares, especially in innovative markets. Most indicative, efficiencies move to the centre of the stage in *ABB/Daimler-Benz*, leading the Commission to conclude after assessing the purported synergies, that on the competitive conditions in general, the transaction will not worsen the situation; structurally speaking it will tend to improve it.

France v Commission
(Cases C-68/94 & C-30/95), [1998] ECR I-1375, [1998] 4 CMLR 829

In 1993, the Commission approved a merger between the German potash producers K + S and MdK. The merger was approved as the Commission was of the view that MdK would have gone out of business in any event and K + S would have acquired their market share as they were no other competitors on the market. There was also no prospect of any other undertaking acquiring MdK. The utilisation of such a 'failing firm defence' was, *inter alia,* challenged.

[90] The French Government criticises the Commission for applying the Regulation incorrectly by authorising, through the use of the 'failing company defence' and without imposing any conditions, a concentration leading to the creation of a monopoly on the German potash market.

[91] As regards the incorrect use of the 'failing company defence', the French Government notes that this defence is derived from United States antitrust legislation, under which a concentration may not be regarded as causing a dominant position to come into being or strengthening it if the following conditions are met:

(a) one of the parties to the concentration is in a position such that it will be unable to meet its obligations in the near future;
(b) it is unable to reorganise successfully under Chapter 11 of the Bankruptcy Act;
(c) there are no other solutions which are less anti-competitive than the concentration; and
(d) the failing undertaking would be forced out of the market if the concentration were not implemented.

[92] The Commission, it is submitted, referred to the 'failing company defence' without taking into account all the criteria used in the United States antitrust legislation, in particular those mentioned at (a) and (b), whereas only application of the United States criteria in full ensures that a derogating mechanism is established whose application does not have the effect of aggravating a competitive situation already in decline.

[93] The French Government submits that the Commission, which considered that K + S would take over MdK's market share in Germany in any case, arbitrarily introduced the criterion of the absorption of market shares.

[94] It submits that the absorption by K + S of MdK's market share if MdK is forced out proves that the German market is impermeable to competition, but does not mean that the anti-competitive nature of the concentration can be dismissed.

[95] In addition, it submits that the Commission did not show that the criteria it adopted concerning the undertaking's elimination from the market and the absence of a less anti-competitive alternative were in fact satisfied in this case.

[96] As regards the allegation that MdK would be forced out if the concentration did not take place, the French Government states that the Commission completely ignored the possibility that MdK might become viable again following an autonomous restructuring operation carried out with financial assistance from Treuhand compatible with Articles 92 and 93 EC.

[97] Finally, it considers that the Commission has not shown that there was no other way of carrying out the acquisition which was less harmful to competition. It observes in this respect that the MdK trade unions had stated that there was a lack of transparency in the tendering procedure.

[98] As regards the absence of conditions for authorisation of the concentration on the German market, the French Government submits that in any event the contested decision is vitiated by a manifest error of assessment, inasmuch as it authorises without any conditions the concentration on the German market where the joint undertaking will have a market share of 98 per cent, and is contrary to Article 2(3) of the Regulation. The concentration will clearly strengthen K + S's dominant position in Germany, with the result that competition will be significantly impeded in a substantial part of the Common Market.

[99] On this point, the Government observes that while the objective of economic and social cohesion mentioned in Articles 2 and 3(j) EC and also referred to in the thirteenth recital in the preamble to the Regulation, which the Commission referred to in its decision, must be taken into account in assessing concentrations, it cannot in any case justify an authorisation which frustrates the essential aim of Community control of concentrations, namely the protection of competition. Ultimately, the Commission could authorise the concentration by reference to the objective of economic and social cohesion only if the notifying undertakings had entered into precise and adequate commitments to open the relevant market to competition, as Nestlé did in Commission Decision 92/553 relating to a proceeding under Council Regulation 4064/89 (Case No IV/M.190—*Nestlé/Perrier*) (hereinafter 'the *Nestlé/Perrier* decision' [[1992] OJ L356/1]).

[100] The Commission concedes that in the contested decision it did not adopt the American 'failing company defence' in its entirety. However, it fails to see how that could affect the lawfulness of its decision.

[101] It considers, moreover, that it has shown to the necessary legal standard that the criteria it used for the application of the 'failing company defence' were indeed satisfied in the present case.

[102] With respect to the likelihood that MdK would soon be forced out unless it was acquired by another operator, the Commission observes that in points 76 and 77 of the contested decision it stated that Treuhand could not be expected to use public funds to cover the long-term debts of an undertaking which was no longer economically viable, and that even if it does not happen immediately, for social, regional and general policy reasons, it is very probable that MdK will close down in the near future.

[103] It is also not disputed that MdK's share of the market in Germany will in all probability be absorbed by K + S.

[104] As regards the condition that there should be no less anti-competitive alternative to the acquisition of MdK, the Commission refers to points 81 to 90 of the contested decision. It considers, moreover, that the French Government has not shown how the criticisms of the MdK trade unions could call into question its assessment. After all, the Commission was not satisfied with the finding that the tendering procedure had not permitted another purchaser to be found, but had itself carried out a further inquiry.

[105] With respect to the absence of conditions for authorisation of the concentration on the German market, the Commission observes that the French Government does not specify what commitments K + S and MdK could have entered into in order to open the German market to competition. The argument which the French Government attempts to base on the *Nestlé/Perrier* decision is immaterial. In that decision, according to the Commission, it was possible to authorise the concentration in view of certain commitments relating to the structure of competition in the relevant product market. In the present case, however, in order to open the German market to competition, it would be necessary to attack not the structure of competition but the behaviour of buyers. In the Commission's opinion, even if the means to open the German market could have been structural, no solution to the acquisition of MdK with a lesser effect on competition was available.

[106] The German Government submits that, under Article 2(3) of the Regulation, a concentration may be prohibited only if it will worsen conditions of competition. There is no causal link between the concentration and its effect on competition where the identical worsening of conditions of competition is to be expected even without the concentration. That will be the case when the three conditions applied by the Commission are satisfied.

[107] The German Government submits that, contrary to the French Government's contention, the Commission has shown to the necessary legal standard that the conditions it laid down were satisfied. First, MdK is not viable on its own, that is to say, it is not possible to restructure the undertaking while preserving its autonomy in the market. In point 76 of the contested decision, the Commission gave solid reasons for considering that with Treuhand's 100 per cent ownership being maintained MdK was not likely to be rescued in the long term. Second, there is no doubt that MdK's market share would automatically be absorbed by K + S, since K + S would be alone on the relevant market after MdK had been forced out, and that is an essential condition in this context. Third, the German Government submits that the Commission gave exhaustive reasons as to why no alternative means of acquiring MdK was available.

[108] As to the approval of the concentration on the German market without conditions or obligations, the German Government observes that in the absence of a causal link between the concentration and the strengthening of a dominant position, one of the conditions for imposing a prohibition under Article 2(3) of the Regulation was not fulfilled. The concentration therefore had to be authorised without obligations or conditions.

[109] The Court observes at the outset that under Article 2(2) of the Regulation, a 'concentration which does not create or strengthen a dominant position as a result of which effective competition would be significantly impeded in the Common Market or in a substantial part of it shall be declared compatible with the Common Market'.

[110] Thus if a concentration is not the cause of the creation or strengthening of a dominant position which has a significant impact on the competitive situation on the relevant market, it must be declared compatible with the Common Market.

[111] It appears from point 71 of the contested decision that, in the Commission's opinion, a concentration which would normally be considered as leading to the creation or reinforcement of a dominant position on the part of the acquiring undertaking may be regarded as not being the cause of it if, even in the event of the concentration being prohibited, that undertaking would inevitably achieve or reinforce a dominant position. Point 71 goes on to state that, as a general matter, a concentration is not the cause of the deterioration of the competitive structure if it is clear that:

— the acquired undertaking would in the near future be forced out of the market if not taken over by another undertaking,

— the acquiring undertaking would gain the market share of the acquired undertaking if it were forced out of the market,

— there is no less anti-competitive alternative purchase.

[112] It must be observed, first of all, that the fact that the conditions set by the Commission for concluding that there was no causal link between the concentration and the deterioration of the competitive structure do not entirely coincide with the conditions applied in connection with the United States 'failing company defence' is not in itself a ground of invalidity of the contested decision. Solely the fact that the conditions set by the Commission were not capable of excluding the possibility that a concentration might be the cause of the deterioration in the competitive structure of the market could constitute a ground of invalidity of the decision.

[113] In the present case, the French Government disputes the relevance of the criterion that it must be verified that the acquiring undertaking would in any event obtain the acquired undertaking's share of the market if the latter were to be forced out of the market.

[114] However, in the absence of that criterion, a concentration could, provided the other criteria were satisfied, be considered as not being the cause of the deterioration of the competitive structure of the market even though it appeared that, in the event of the concentration not proceeding, the acquiring undertaking would not gain the entire market share of the acquired undertaking. Thus, it would be possible to deny the existence of a causal link between the concentration and the deterioration of the competitive structure of the market even though the competitive structure of the market would deteriorate to a lesser extent if the concentration did not proceed.

[115] The introduction of that criterion is intended to ensure that the existence of a causal link between the concentration and the deterioration of the competitive structure of the market can be excluded only if the competitive structure resulting from the concentration would deteriorate in similar fashion even if the concentration did not proceed.

[116] The criterion of absorption of market shares, although not considered by the Commission as sufficient in itself to preclude any adverse effect of the concentration on competition, therefore helps to ensure the neutral effects of the concentration as regards the deterioration of the competitive structure of the market. This is consistent with the concept of causal connection set out in Article 2(2) of the Regulation.

NOTE: The argument in this case was not so much about the existence of a 'failing firm defence' under the Merger Regulation, but more about the exact nature and extent of the defence. In this case the merger was allowed to go ahead even though K + S would effectively gain a 98 per cent market share in Germany. While that was the case the Commission, and the Court, were of the view that K + S would have gained that share without the merger going ahead. Thus the necessary causal connection between the merger and the significant impediment to competition is not present. For a merger to benefit from the defence, it must meet the three conditions approved by the Court: (1) the acquired undertaking would in the near future be forced out of the market if not taken over by another undertaking, (2) the acquiring undertaking would gain the market share of the acquired undertaking if it were forced out of the market, and (3) there is no less anti-competitive alternative purchase. Although the interveners in the above case argued for a stricter application of the failing firm defence, the Commission and Court have not utilised it in many subsequent cases, even though it has been strongly argued by the parties.

Comité Central d'Enterprise de la Société Anonyme Vittel v *Commission*
(Case T-12/93) [1995] ECR II-1247

In 1992 the Commission approved the *Nestlé /Perrier* merger as being compatible with the Common Market, subject to certain undertakings (*Nestlé/Perrier* (Case IV/M190) OJ, 1992, L536/1). Part of those undertakings required the divestment of certain mineral water brands and sources to allow a viable competitor on to the market. One of those sources was the Pierval source which was operated by Vittel SA. That Decision was challenged by the Comité, the works council for the Pierval plant. Many of the issues discussed by the Court concerned the standing of the parties, but it also considered the factors which could be taken into account when taking decisions under the Merger Regulation.

[37] In the present case, it must therefore be ascertained whether the contested decision affects the applicants by virtue of attributes which are peculiar to them or by reason of circumstances in which they are differentiated from all other persons and which thereby distinguish them individually just as in the case of the person addressed.

[38] For that purpose it must be noted to begin with that in the scheme of Regulation No 4064/89, the primacy given to the establishment of a system of free competition may in certain cases be reconciled, in the context of the assessment of whether a concentration is compatible with the common market, with the taking into consideration of the social effects of that operation if they are liable to affect adversely the social objectives referred to in Article 2 of the Treaty. The Commission may therefore have to ascertain whether the concentration is liable to have consequences, even if only indirectly, for the position of the employees in the undertakings in question, such as to affect the level or conditions of employment in the Community or a substantial part of it.

[39] Article 2(1)(b) of Regulation No 4064/89 requires the Commission to draw up an economic balance for the concentration in question, which may, in some circumstances, entail considerations of a social nature, as is confirmed by the thirteenth recital in the preamble to the regulation, which states that 'the Commission must place its appraisal within the general framework of the achievement of the fundamental objectives referred to in Article 2 of the Treaty, including that of strengthening the Community's economic and social cohesion, referred to in Article 130a'. In that legal context, the express provision in Article 18(4) of the regulation, giving specific expression to the principle stated in the nineteenth recital that the representatives of the employees of the undertakings concerned are entitled, upon application, to be heard, manifests an intention to ensure that the collective interests of those employees are taken into consideration in the administrative procedure.

[40] In those circumstances, the Court considers that, in the scheme of Regulation No 4064/89, the position of the employees of the undertakings which are the subject of the concentration may in certain cases be taken into consideration by the Commission when adopting its decision. That is why the regulation makes individual mention of the recognized representatives of the employees of those undertakings, who constitute a closed category clearly defined at the time of adoption of the decision, by expressly and specifically giving them the right to submit their observations in the administrative procedure. Those organizations, who are responsible for upholding the collective interests of the employees they represent, have a relevant interest with respect to the social considerations which may in appropriate cases be taken into account by the Commission in the context of its appraisal of whether the concentration is lawful from the point of view of Community law.

NOTE: This case indicates that individual decisions taken under the Merger Regulation will not only be based on competition concerns. The decision-making process plays a part in the wider goals of the Community. This is also apparent from the decision-making process within the Commission. Decisions are initially drafted by the DG Competition but are finally taken by the whole College of Commissioners. This means that Commissioners with responsibility for other parts of Commission policy have an input into decision making. It is a matter of debate how far those non-competition concerns influence decisions, but they certainly play a role. See Banks, D., 'Non-Competition Factors And Their Future Relevance Under European Merger Law' [1997] ECLR 182.

B: Collective dominance

France v *Commission*
(Cases C-68/94 & C-30/95) [1998] ECR I-1375, [1998] 4 CMLR 829

The Commission argued that the combined undertaking would have a collective dominant position with the French undertaking SCPA as the undertakings had long-standing commercial links and the remaining competition was too fragmented to be effective competition to their combined market share of 60 per cent. The use of the Merger Regulation to prohibit the creation or strengthening of a collective dominant position was challenged before the Court.

[165] The Court finds, first of all, that the applicants' submission, to the effect that the choice of legal bases in itself militates in favour of the argument that the Regulation does not apply to collective dominant positions, cannot be accepted. As the Advocate General observes in point 83 of the Opinion, Articles 87 and 235 of the Treaty can in principle be used as the legal bases of a regulation permitting preventive action with respect to concentrations which create or strengthen a collective dominant position liable to have a significant effect on competition.

[166] Second, it cannot be deduced from the wording of Article 2 of the Regulation that only concentrations which create or strengthen an individual dominant position, that is, a dominant position held by the parties to the concentration, come within the scope of the Regulation. Article 2, in referring to 'a concentration which creates or strengthens a dominant position', does not in itself exclude the possibility of applying the Regulation to cases where concentrations lead to the creation or strengthening of a collective dominant position, that is, a dominant position held by the parties to the concentration together with an entity not a party thereto.

[167] Third, with respect to the *travaux preparatoires*, it appears from the documents in the case that they cannot be regarded as expressing clearly the intention of the authors of the Regulation as to the scope of the term 'dominant position'. In those circumstances, the *travaux preparatoires* provide no assistance for the interpretation of the disputed concept (see, to that effect, Case 15/60, *Simon* v *Court of Justice* [[1961] ECR 115]).

[168] Since the textual and historical interpretations of the Regulation, and in particular Article 2 thereof, do not permit its precise scope to be assessed as regards the type of dominant position concerned, the provision in question must be interpreted by reference to its purpose and general structure (see, to that effect, Case 11/76, *Netherlands* v *EC Commission* [[1979] ECR 245, para. [6]]).

[169] As may be seen from the 1st and 2nd recitals in its preamble, the Regulation is founded on the premiss that the objective of instituting a system to ensure that competition in the Common Market is not distorted is essential for the achievement of the internal market by 1992 and for its future development.

[170] It follows from the 6th, 7th, 10th and 11th recitals in the preamble that the Regulation, unlike Articles 85 and 86 of the Treaty, is intended to apply to all concentrations with a Community dimension in so far as they are likely, because of their effect on the structure of competition within the Community, to prove incompatible with the system of undistorted competition envisaged by the Treaty.

[171] A concentration which creates or strengthens a dominant position on the part of the parties concerned with an entity not involved in the concentration is liable to prove incompatible with the system of undistorted competition which the Treaty seeks to secure. Consequently, if it were accepted that only concentrations creating or strengthening a dominant position on the part of the parties to the concentration were covered by the Regulation, its purpose as indicated in particular by the above mentioned recitals would be partially frustrated. The Regulation would thus be deprived of a not insignificant aspect of its effectiveness, without that being necessary from the perspective of the general structure of the Community system of control of concentrations.

[172] Neither the argument based on the lack of procedural safeguards nor the argument based on the 15th recital in the preamble to the Regulation can cast doubt on its applicability to cases where a collective dominant position is the result of a concentration.

[173] As to the first argument, it is true that the Regulation does not expressly provide that undertakings, not involved in the concentration, which are regarded as the external members of the dominant oligopoly must be given an opportunity to make their views known effectively where the Commission intends to attach to the 'authorisation' of the concentration conditions or obligations specifically affecting them. The same applies in a situation where the Commission intends to attach conditions or obligations affecting third parties to a concentration which will lead simply to the creation or strengthening of an individual dominant position.

[174] In any event, even on the assumption that a finding by the Commission that the proposed concentration creates or strengthens a collective dominant position involving the undertakings concerned on the one hand and a third party on the other may in itself adversely affect that third party, it must be borne in mind that observance of the right to be heard is, in all proceedings liable to culminate in a measure adversely affecting a particular person, a fundamental principle of Community law which must be guaranteed even in the absence of any rules governing the procedure (see, to that effect, Case 85/76, *Hoffmann-La Roche* v *EC Commission* [[1979] ECR 461; [1979] 3 CMLR 211]] and Case C-32/95 P, *EC Commission* v *Lisrestal and Others* [[1996] ECR I-5373; [1997] 2 CMLR 1, para. [21]]).

[175] Given the existence of that principle, and the purpose of the Regulation as explained above, the fact that the Community legislature did not expressly provide in the Regulation for a procedure safeguarding the right to be heard of third party undertakings alleged to hold a collective dominant position together with the undertakings involved in the concentration cannot be regarded as decisive evidence of the Regulation's inapplicability to collective dominant positions.

[176] As to the second argument, the presumption that concentrations are compatible with the Common Market if the undertakings concerned have a combined market share of less than 25 per cent, as stated in the 15th recital in the preamble, is not developed in any way in the operative part of the Regulation.

[177] The 15th recital in the preamble to the Regulation must, having regard in particular to the realities of the market underlying this recital, be interpreted as meaning that a concentration which does not give the undertakings concerned a combined share of at least 25 per cent of the reference market is presumed not to create or strengthen an anti-competitive dominant position on the part of those undertakings.

[178] It follows from the foregoing that collective dominant positions do not fall outside the scope of the Regulation.

NOTE: It is not entirely surprising the Court confirmed that the concept of dominance found under Article 82 EC is the same as the concept used in the Merger Regulation, and therefore the Regulation can be used to prevent the creation or strengthening of a collective dominant position. The inclusion of the concept means that the Commission has an important structural tool to prevent the concentration of a market into a potentially uncompetitive oligopoly. This is important as the collective dominance cases under Article 82 EC have shown the problems that the Commission and Court have faced when dealing with the behaviour of existing oligopolies. The Merger Regulation's ability to deal with their creation should be a useful addition to the Commission's armoury in maintaining competitive markets within the Community.

Gencor Limited v *Commission*
(Case T-102/96) [1999] ECR II-753, [1999] 4 CMLR 971

[163] In assessing whether there is a collective dominant position, the Commission is therefore obliged to establish, using a prospective analysis of the relevant market, whether the concentration in question would lead to a situation in which effective competition in the relevant market would be significantly impeded by the undertakings involved in the concentration and one or more other undertakings which together, in particular because of factors giving rise to a connection between them, are able to adopt a common policy on the market and act to a considerable extent independently of their competitors, their customers and, ultimately, of consumers. [*France and Others* v *EC Commission*, para. (221)]

. . .

[276] Furthermore, there is no reason whatsoever in legal or economic terms to exclude from the notion of economic links the relationship of interdependence existing between the parties to a tight oligopoly within which, in a market with the appropriate characteristics, in particular in terms of market concentration, transparency and product homogeneity, those parties are in a position to anticipate one another's behaviour and are therefore strongly encouraged to align their conduct in the market, in particular in such a way as to maximise their joint profits by restricting production with a view to increasing prices. In such a context, each trader is aware that highly competitive action on its part designed to increase its market share (for example a price cut) would provoke identical action by the others, so that it would derive no benefit from its initiative. All the traders would thus be affected by the reduction in price levels.

[277] That conclusion is all the more pertinent with regard to the control of concentrations, whose objective is to prevent anti-competitive market structures from arising or being strengthened. Those structures may result from the existence of economic links in the strict sense argued by the applicant or from market structures of an oligopolistic kind where each undertaking may become aware of common interests and, in particular, cause prices to increase without having to enter into an agreement or resort to a concerted practice.

[278] In the [present] case, therefore, the applicant's ground of challenge alleging that the Commission failed to establish the existence of structural links is misplaced.

[279] The Commission was entitled to conclude, relying on the envisaged alteration in the structure of the market and on the similarity of the costs of Amplats and Implats/LPD, that the proposed transaction would create a collective dominant position and lead in actual fact to a duopoly constituted by those two undertakings.

NOTE: The *Gencor* judgment was important for the development of the doctrine of collective dominance in both merger control and under Article 82 EC. The importance of economic links between the combined undertaking and the other potential members of the collective dominant undertaking is an important part of the doctrine but will, in many cases, prove to be difficult. An example of the difficulties faced by the Commission in that regard can be seen in *Airtours plc* v *Commission* (Case T-342/99), judgment of 6 June 2002. The Commission had originally prohibited the merger between Airtours and First Choice, two UK-based tour operators, as the merger would have created three similarly sized tour operators in the UK in a collective dominant position. In its examination of the case, the CFI rejected the Commission's argument on practically every point on the basis that the evidence did not support the Commission's findings. The CFI therefore annulled the Commission Decision (*Airtours/First Choice*, Case IV/M1524, OJ, 2000, L93/1). The Commission did not produce sufficient economic evidence to support its finding that the market would operate in an uncompetitive manner following the merger.

SECTION 5: **International application of the Merger Regulation**

Gencor Limited v *Commission*
(Case T-102/96) [1999] ECR II-753, [1999] 4 CMLR 971

The Commission's decision was also challenged on the basis that the Merger Regulation could not control a merger where both parties were established outside the EC.

[78] The Regulation, in accordance with Article 1 thereof, applies to all concentrations with a

Community dimension, that is to say to all concentrations between undertakings which do not each achieve more than two-thirds of their aggregate Community-wide turnover within one and the same Member State, where the combined aggregate worldwide turnover of those undertakings is more than 5,000 million ECUs and the aggregate Community-wide turnover of at least two of them is more than 250 million ECUs.

[79] Article 1 does not require that, in order for a concentration to be regarded as having a Community dimension, the undertakings in question must be established in the Community or that the production activities covered by the concentration must be carried out within Community territory.

[80] With regard to the criterion of turnover, it must be stated that, as set out in paragraph (13) of the contested Decision, the concentration at issue has a Community dimension within the meaning of Article 1(2) of the Regulation. The undertakings concerned have an aggregate worldwide turnover of more than 10,000 million ECUs, above the 5,000 million ECUs threshold laid down by the Regulation. Gencor and Lonrho each had a Community-wide turnover of more than 250 million ECUs in the last financial year. Finally, they do not each achieve more than two-thirds of their aggregate Community-wide turnover within one and the same Member State.

[81] The applicant's arguments to the effect that the legal bases for the Regulation and the wording of its preamble and substantive provisions preclude its application to the concentration at issue cannot be accepted.

[82] The legal bases for the Regulation, namely Articles 87 and 235 of the Treaty, and more particularly the provisions to which they are intended to give effect, that is to say Articles 3(g) and 85 and 86 of the Treaty, as well as paragraphs (1) to (5) and (9) to (11) in the preamble to the Regulation, merely point to the need to ensure that competition is not distorted in the Common Market, in particular by concentrations which result in the creation or strengthening of a dominant position. They in no way exclude from the Regulation's field of application concentrations which, while relating to mining and/or production activities outside the Community, have the effect of creating or strengthening a dominant position as a result of which effective competition in the Common Market is significantly impeded.

[83] In particular, the applicant's view cannot be founded on the closing words of paragraph (11) in the preamble to the Regulation.

[84] That paragraph states that:

> a concentration with a Community dimension exists . . . where the concentrations are effected by undertakings which do not have their principal fields of activities in the Community but which have substantial operations there.

[85] By that reference, in general terms, to the concept of substantial operations, the Regulation does not, for the purpose of defining its territorial scope, ascribe greater importance to production operations than to sales operations. On the contrary, by setting quantitative thresholds in Article 1 which are based on the worldwide and Community turnover of the undertakings concerned, it rather ascribes greater importance to sales operations within the Common Market as a factor linking the concentration to the Community. It is common ground that Gencor and Lonrho each carry out significant sales in the Community (valued in excess of 250 million ECUs).

[86] Nor is it borne out by either paragraph (30) in the preamble to the Regulation or Article 24 thereof that the criterion based on the location of production activities is well founded. Far from laying down a criterion for defining the territorial scope of the Regulation, Article 24 merely regulates the procedures to be followed in order to deal with situations in which non-member countries do not grant Community undertakings treatment comparable to that accorded by the Community to undertakings from those non-member countries in relation to the control of concentrations.

[87] The applicant cannot, by reference to the judgment in *Wood Pulp*, rely on the criterion as to the

implementation of an agreement to support its interpretation of the territorial scope of the Regulation. Far from supporting the applicant's view, that criterion for assessing the link between an agreement and Community territory in fact precludes it. According to *Wood Pulp*, the criterion as to the implementation of an agreement is satisfied by mere sale within the Community, irrespective of the location of the sources of supply and the production plant. It is not disputed that Gencor and Lonrho carried out sales in the Community before the concentration and would have continued to do so thereafter.

[88] Accordingly, the Commission did not err in its assessment of the territorial scope of the Regulation by applying it in this case to a proposed concentration notified by undertakings whose registered offices and mining and production operations are outside the Community.

B Compatibility of the contested decision with public international law

[89] Following the concentration agreement, the previously existing competitive relationship between Implats and LPD, in particular so far as concerns their sales in the Community, would have come to an end. That would have altered the competitive structure within the Common Market since, instead of three South African PGM suppliers, there would have remained only two. The implementation of the proposed concentration would have led to the merger not only of the parties' PGM mining and production operations in South Africa but also of their marketing operations throughout the world, particularly in the Community where Implats and LPD achieved significant sales.

[90] Application of the Regulation is justified under public international law when it is foreseeable that a proposed concentration will have an immediate and substantial effect in the Community.

[91] In that regard, the concentration would, according to the contested Decision, have led to the creation of a dominant duopoly on the part of Amplats and Implats/LPD in the platinum and rhodium markets, as a result of which effective competition would have been significantly impeded in the Common Market within the meaning of Article 2(3) of the Regulation.

[92] It is therefore necessary to verify the three criteria of immediate, substantial and foreseeable effect are satisfied in this case.

NOTE: In *Gencor*, the CFI followed the position adopted by the European Court under Articles 81 and 82 and gave the Merger Regulation extraterritorial effect. The Court affirmed the 'implementation' test set out in *Wood Pulp* (Cases C-89/85, C-104/85, C-114/85, C-116/85, C-117/85, C-125/85, & C-129/85) [1998] ECR 5193, [1988] 4 CMLR 901, but goes somewhat further and refers to what is known as the 'effects' doctrine in paragraph 90. This means that the Merger Regulation may be utilised even if there was no direct trading inside the EC, but the merger would in some way disturb the Community market. See Fox, E.M., 'The Merger Regulation and its Territorial Reach: *Gencor Ltd* v *Commission*' [1999] ECLR 334. Because of the increasing number of globally important mergers, the necessity for extraterritorial application of the Merger Regulation is increasingly important, but it also raises the potential for increasing conflict between different competition authorities that seek to deal with a global merger under several different regulatory systems at the same time. See e.g. Case IV/M877 *Boeing/McDonnel Douglas* OJ, 1997, L336/16 and Case IV/M1845 *AOL/Time Warner* OJ, 2001, L268/28 and Chapter 12 generally.

SECTION 6: **Reform of the Merger Regulation**

Green Paper on the Review of Council Regulation
(EEC) No 4064/89, COM(2001) 745/6 final, paras 22–28, 66–68 & 159–169

Jurisdictional thresholds
22. In the course of its review, the Commission has re-assessed the continued appropriateness of the turnover thresholds in Article 1 in the light, not only of their effectiveness, but also of their predictability and transparency. It should be pointed out that failure to attain the jurisdictional criteria in Article 1 normally means that the transaction will be subject to mandatory notification requirements in one or more Member States.

23. As to the functioning of the current thresholds, the review has not, as set out in further detail in Annex 1, indicated any urgent need to amend Article 1(2). This Article continues to provide results that are generally in line with subsidiarity, and a revision of the threshold levels set out therein would not be well suited to dealing with the multiple filing problem. Nor has the review brought to light any urgent need to modify the level of the two-thirds rule. The rule, which adopts a centre of gravity approach to the division of competence, appears to provide results that are generally in line with subsidiarity. Furthermore, to the limited extent that the two-thirds rule leads to multiple filings, it is very rare for this to go beyond notifications to two national authorities.

24. On the other hand, it must be concluded that Article 1(3) has fallen short of achieving its underlying objective. At the time of its adoption in 1997, this provision was intended to confer Commission competence over cases that affect three or more Member States. While the review broadly supports the validity of this objective on the grounds that these are generally cases with a Community interest, the provision has not lived up to expectations. Only a small proportion of such cases have fallen within the Merger Regulation. In 2000, only 20 cases were notified under Article 1(3), compared to 75 multiple notifications to three or more Member States. The failure of Article 1(3) is also shown by the fact that in 2000 only some 5 per cent of all notifications were made under this Article, representing a significant decrease from the already low level in 1999.

25. The review has provided indications that many of those multiple filing cases involved cross-border interests. One such indication in itself is the fact that three or more national notifications were required. Furthermore, in a majority of these cases, some or all of the Member States involved assessed and/or defined the relevant geographic market as wider than national. It is also notable that the majority of these cases satisfied the jurisdictional test in so far as it relates to the Community level, while remaining far from having a national centre of gravity (i.e. the two-thirds rule). The fact that many of these concentrations involved cross-border interests beyond the countries where notification took place is also supported by the fact that many of these cases involved business activities in several Member States where the concentration was not notified.

26. From the viewpoint of the companies involved, the review has also provided indications that multiple filings in three or more Member States give rise to a number of additional difficulties, in terms of length of process, costs and legal certainty (see Annex 1 for details of the results of the studies).

27. This conclusion is further strengthened by two additional factors. First, a trend may be observed according to which multiple notifications involving three or more Member States are steadily increasing, both in absolute terms and in relation to the number of cases notified under the Merger Regulation. This shows that this problem is growing, even within the current EU15. The approaching enlargement of the Community as from 2004 is likely to further accentuate the negative effects of multiple filings involving a significant number of Member States.

28. The Commission is aware of, and fully supports, the recent initiative by the competition authorities of the Member States for closer cooperation in dealing, inter alia, with merger cases that are notified in more than one country. Such cooperation should certainly have a beneficial impact in terms of strengthening the level of protection of competition, while at the same time increasing procedural efficiency. It nevertheless appears doubtful whether such cooperation, even if significantly developed, could be seen as an equivalent substitute for one-stop shop control of mergers with cross-border effects.

. . .

66. Despite having provided results generally in line with subsidiarity, the jurisdictional criteria of the Merger Regulation could, in principle, be amended so as to provide a more direct and case-related test for establishing the cross-border nature of any concentration.

67. One possibility would be to create a system where the turnover thresholds are removed from the ECMR, and where the triggering event for a Commission notification would be the fact that the case is subject to multiple filing requirements in the EU. In this way, the determination of which cases can be assumed to have a Community interest would be directly connected to the fact that the case will have an impact in several Member States. One of the key conditions necessary for such a system to function would, however, be that further harmonisation of national merger control thresholds could be achieved. The Commission's surveys indicate that the currently non-harmonised notification requirements in Member States do not permit reliable identification of the Member States in which a particular concentration will have a significant impact. A more systematic approach to the setting of notification thresholds in national merger laws could, however, allow these thresholds to serve as direct measurements of the cross-border impact of individual concentrations.

68. In order to develop a network approach to merger control in Europe it would also be useful to strengthen the existing degree of de facto alignment of merger control rules within the Community. This applies in particular to certain key-issues such as the concept of a concentration and important parts of the procedural framework. Another topic for consideration would be the extent to which further harmonisation of the applicable competition test would be beneficial to effective and transparent protection of competition and the maintenance of a level playing field. Such a harmonised environment would also be beneficial to the creation of a more seamless network of competition authorities, where ultimately the Commission and one or more national authority could share the task of assessing the totality of impacts from a concentration on anything from global to local markets.

NOTE: After consulting on the Green Paper, the Commission published a Proposal for a new Regulation, COM(2002) 711 final, on 11 December 2002. The Proposed Regulation does not follow the "3 + " referral system suggested in the Green Paper, adopting a system based on streamlined referrals under Articles 9 and 22 of the Merger Regulation. A case may be referred to the Community if three Member States agree to such a referral, and the Commission may also invite Member States to make referrals under Article 9 or 22 of the Regulation. The criteria for referrals under those articles will also be improved and may be utilized at a pre-notification stage.

Substantive test

159. The substantive test according to which notified concentrations are appraised is set out in Article 2 of the Merger Regulation. In the course of this review it has been suggested that the Commission should use this opportunity to discuss the merits of the dominance test contained therein. Both procedural and substantive reasons have been advanced for a re-evaluation of the appropriateness of this test.

160. From a procedural viewpoint, the main reason proposed in favour of such a re-evaluation is that it could allow an alignment of the Merger Regulation's appraisal criteria with those applied in

other major jurisdictions, such as the US, Canada and Australia, which rely on a concept of substantial lessening of competition ('the SLC-test'). Such an alignment towards a global standard for merger assessment holds certain attractions. It would, for example, facilitate merging parties' global assessment of possible competition issues arising from contemplated transactions, by obviating the current need to argue their case according to differently formulated tests. This would in turn provide competition agencies with a better basis on which to build effective cooperation in cases that are notified in several jurisdictions. Moreover, as a common test would tend to highlight the actual application of the test, rather than the test itself, it would provide for better bench-marking of the activities of competition authorities and courts, as well as facilitating the development of competition-oriented research and modelling.

161. It should nevertheless be pointed out that an amendment of the test in the Merger Regulation could also involve some drawbacks. Although this effect should not be exaggerated, interested parties may, at least for an initial period following such a reform, face greater difficulties in forecasting the likely outcome of merger control proceedings in Europe. The reason for this would be that the existing body of case-law (emanating from both the Commission and the courts) has been built up under the Regulation's dominance test. Another possible complication relates to the fact that most Member States (as well as the Candidate Countries) have aligned their merger control provisions to the current dominance test. Thus, unless national rules were also amended, changing the Merger Regulation's competition test could have the awkward effect of creating greater alignment internationally, while leading to greater disparity within the Community.

162. From a substantive viewpoint it should be noted that there are many similarities between the dominance test and the SLC-test. Both types of test, will, for example, involve an investigation into the scope of the relevant market as well as an assessment of how the market(s) will be affected by the proposed concentration and which competitive constraints would be faced by the merged entity. It should also be noted that, despite the current difference in legal tests, the vast majority of cases dealt with by the Commission and other major jurisdictions using the SLC-test have revealed a significant degree of convergence in the approach to merger analysis.

163. Since the adoption of the Merger Regulation in 1989, the application of the notion of dominance has evolved, allowing it to be adapted both to developments in economic theory and to refinements of the now available econometric tools to measure market power. This implies that merger assessment today can be less reliant on the rather blunt and imprecise market share test than it was ten years ago. The fact that the dominance test has undergone such an evolution is natural, and Article 2 has so far proved sufficiently flexible to accommodate an effects analysis made on the basis of more sophisticated micro-economic tools, instruments and models developed by econometric and industrial organisation research.

164. The perhaps most well-known example of this evolution is the European courts' interpretation of the Merger Regulation's competition test as applying to situations of collective dominance, in the judgments of the Court of Justice and the Court of First Instance in the *Kali und Salz* and *Gencor* cases.

165. It has nevertheless been suggested that the SLC-test might be closer to the spirit of the economically-based analysis undertaken in merger control and less (legally) rigid than the dominance test. As such, some consider it better adapted to an effective merger control, in particular in the context of growing industrial concentration. At the same time, it has also been suggested that adopting the more open-ended SLC-test would lead to a greater degree of legal uncertainty.

166. One of the more specific hypothetical questions that has occasionally been raised about the reach of the dominance test in the Merger Regulation is the extent to which it would allow for effective control in some specific situations where firms unilaterally may be able to raise price and

thus exercise market power. The type of example that tends to be cited is of a merger between the second and third largest players in a market, where these firms are the closest substitutes. In such a scenario the merging firms may remain smaller than the existing market leader. The argument goes that the SLC-test would be better adapted to addressing such a situation, in particular if the market characteristics would not be conducive to a finding of collective dominance. While interesting as a hypothetical discussion, the Commission has so far not encountered a situation of this kind.

167. In conclusion, experience in applying the dominance test has not revealed major loopholes in the scope of the test. Nor has it frequently led to different results from SLC-test approaches in other jurisdictions. Still, in view in particular of the increasingly international scope of merger activity, the Commission believes that the time is right to initiate a thorough debate on the respective merits of the two tests for merger control.

168. In order to open up a full debate on these important issues, interested parties are invited to submit their substantiated views on any perceived advantages or disadvantages resulting from the current wording of Article 2 of the Merger Regulation, and to also assess the effectiveness of the test by contrast with the SLC-test.

169. As this discussion touches on principles of fundamental importance to competition law, not only at the Community level, but also at Member State level, it is recognized that it may not be possible to reach definitive conclusions within the timeframe available for this review exercise.

NOTE: The Proposed Regulation, COM(2002) 711 final, decided that while the 'SLC' test had some advantages those advantages could be achieved by reinterpreting the existing 'dominance' test. It therefore suggests amendment of Article 2 of the Merger Regulation to bring oligopoly control more clearly within the test by including undertakings that 'hold the economic power to influence appreciably and sustainably the parameters of competition'. This has the additional advantage of decoupling the dominance test in mergers from Article 82 EC. A Notice on Horizontal Mergers will also be published to support the amended test.

Ysewyn, J., 'The New World Of The Merger Task Force'
[2002] ECLR 207, pp. 208–209

Finally, the Commission has put forward for debate the substantive test that it applies for clearing— or blocking—mergers. Today, this test is based on 'dominance', but as the Green Paper suggests, it may be replaced by the US-inspired 'substantial lessening of competition' test (SLC for short). In addition, the Commission is also exploring ways of considering the efficiencies generated by the merger in its review process.

This debate could determine the future of EC merger control. Will the introduction of SLC alter the Commission's appraisal procedure, improving the outcome of its merger control review? In particular, will SLC align the European and US procedures in a way that really addresses the issue? And, to use an oversimplification, would *GE/Honeywell* have been decided differently, had the Commission toiled away with SLC?

One cannot get away from the simple truth: the underlying test in merger control is one of single-firm and multi-firm market power. In Europe, this led to a test based on 'dominance'. In the United States, the same test was baptised as reviewing the 'substantial lessening of competition'. Both tests wield the familiar instruments of market definition, the calculation of market shares, and the determination of concentration ratios. More sophisticated economics may increase the strength of the reasoning (especially in the United States) but why then does the Green Paper hide behind a semantic discussion of whether 'dominance' or 'substantial lessening of competition' is the better test? On both sides of the Atlantic the issue should be market power to the detriment of consumers. Once the dust settles and the contributions are counted, the Commission should acknowledge that introducing SLC would merely be a 'subtle language confusion'.

It has been suggested that the dominance test does not allow for a proper consideration of efficiencies that may result from mergers. It is true that, to date, the issue of efficiencies has only been raised in a limited number of decisions under the ECMR and, as the Commission acknowledges, the precise scope for taking such considerations into account may not have been fully developed. The US system, by contrast, expressly provides for an efficiency defence to rebut a finding of anticompetitive effects. The Green Paper indicates that the Commission is willing to debate how, and the extent to which, efficiencies should be taken into account in the merger analysis, but has not taken any sides.

NOTE: Interestingly, the UK Merger regime is moving towards an SLC test in the Enterprise Bill. See Chapter 9.

QUESTION

Should the EC Merger Regulation explicitly recognise an 'efficiency defence' in the same way as the US system?

FURTHER READING

Cook and Kerse, *EC Merger Control*, 3rd edn, London, Sweet & Maxwell, 2000.

11

State aid

SECTION 1: **Introduction**

One of the principal objectives of the Community competition law rules is to introduce a level playing field throughout the Community. However, this could be distorted if Member States were able to influence the competitive process in the Community by providing their companies with financial assistance in order for them to 'beat competition' from other Member States. The state aid rules seek to limit the extent to which this is possible.

European Commission, Eighth Survey on State Aid in the European Union
Brussels, 1 April 2000, COM (2000) 205 final, Introduction, p. 5, para. 1

The need to maintain free and undistorted competition is recognised as being one of the basic principles upon which the European Union is built. By way of Community Competition policy the Commission aims to help strengthen the competitiveness of European industry, ensure effective competition in the internal market and create the conditions for markets to function well whilst accounting for Europe's particular social market economy. A key element of Competition policy is Community State aid control, the benefits of which are clear. State aid can frustrate free competition by preventing the most efficient allocation of resources and pose a threat to the unity of the single market. In many cases the grant of State aid reduces economic welfare and weakens the incentives for firms to improve their efficiency. Aid also enables the less efficient to survive at the expense of the more efficient. The resulting distortions of the market can lead to frictions between governments and sometimes to retaliatory measures by third countries, which may be a source of further inefficiency. The unique system of control that exists throughout the European Union and indeed the European Economic Area is aimed at attenuating these inefficiencies. Based on an agreed set of fundamental principles firmly anchored in the European Treaties, this system of control makes an important contribution towards fully realising the benefits of the internal market and single currency.

NOTE: The system is 'unique' because domestic competition systems do not require an equivalent protection against 'beggar thy neighbour' governmental subsidies. The application of the state aid rules is the most contentious area of EU competition policy and has led to political tensions in the past, notably where state aid has been granted to national flag-carrying airlines where they have been uncompetitive and under threat of going out of business. See Soames, T., and Ryan, A., 'State Aid and Air Transport' [1995] ECLR 290. It is clear that a 'neutral referee' is required to supervise the state aid rules and that this role has to be carried out centrally by the Commission. Unlike Articles 81 and 82, there is very limited scope for decentralised enforcement of the state aid rules. See further, Ross, M., 'State Aids and National Courts: Definitions and other problems—A case of Premature Emancipation?' (2000) 37 CMLRev, pp. 401–423, below.

SECTION 2: **The prohibition**

The basic prohibition is contained in Article 87(1) EC. Articles 87(2) EC and 87(3) EC provide for exemptions from the prohibition.

Article 87(1) EC

1. Save as otherwise provided in this Treaty, any aid granted by a Member State or through State resources in any form whatsoever which distorts or threatens to distort competition by favouring certain undertakings or the production of certain goods shall, insofar as it affects trade between Member States, be incompatible with the common market.

NOTE: The terms of this prohibition can be broken down into the following constituent elements: advantage; state resources; selectivity; affect trade and distortion of competition. This should allow parties to ascertain whether a measure constitutes state aid under Article 87(1) EC which would thereby require notification to the Commission under Article 88(3) EC. It should be noted that the introduction of a Regulation on State Aid procedures in 1999 (Council Regulation (EC) No 659/1999 of 22 March 1999 laying down detailed rules for the application of Article 93 EC of the EC Treaty, OJ L 83/1, 1999) did not further clarify the scope of Article 87(1) EC, and it is the case-law of the Court which sheds light on each of these issues.

A: Advantage

Article 87(1) EC refers to aid in any form whatsoever and therefore the Commission and Court have sought to ascertain how wide this phrase ought to be interpreted. The first point to note is that the concept of aid is objective, irrespective of its purpose.

France v *Commission*
(Case C-241/94) [1996] ECR I–4551

> French legislation provided for contributions by the French Government through the *Fonds National d'Emploi* ('FNE'), a state body, to redundancy and redeployment costs involved in a social plan required to be drawn up by the undertaking following a restructuring. Did this amount to aid within Article 87(1)?

[19] It must be borne in mind that Article 92(1) of the Treaty provides that any aid granted by a Member State, or through State resources in any form whatsoever, which distorts or threatens to distort competition by favouring certain undertakings or the production of certain goods is incompatible with the common market.

[20] According to settled case-law, Article 92(1) does not distinguish between measures of State

intervention by reference to their causes or aims but defines them in relation to their effects (Case 173/73 *Italy* v *Commission* [1974] ECR 709, paragraph 13).

[21] The social character of the FNE assistance is not therefore sufficient to exclude it outright from being categorized as aid for the purposes of Article 92 of the Treaty.

[22] It must also be noted that FNE intervention is not limited sectorially or territorially or by reference to a restricted category of undertakings.

[23] However, as the Commission has rightly pointed out, the FNE enjoys a degree of latitude which enables it to adjust its financial assistance having regard to a number of considerations such as, in particular, the choice of beneficiaries, the amount of the financial assistance and the conditions under which it is provided. The French Government itself concedes that the administration may depart from its own guidelines where particular circumstances justify that course of action.

[24] In those circumstances, it must be held that, by virtue of its aim and general scheme, the system under which the FNE contributes to measures accompanying social plans is liable to place certain undertakings in a more favourable situation than others and thus to meet the conditions for classification as aid within the meaning of Article 92(1) of the Treaty.

NOTE: There may be scope in some situations for parties to argue that the state was not the source of funding. See Cases C-52–54/97 *Viscido and others* v *Ente Poste Italiane* [1998] ECR I-2629.

More recently the Court has been required to consider the extent to which a party has been favoured by a state measure.

Demenagements-Manutention Transport SA (DMT)
(Case C-256/97) [1999] ECR I–3913, [1999] All ER (EC) 601

A Belgian undertaking facing insolvency was found to have been granted an exceptionally long period of grace for payment of mandatory employees' contributions by the national security office. By sustaining artificially the business of an insolvent undertaking did this constitute state aid?

[17] In order to reply to the first question, it is necessary to determine whether the various components of the definition of State aid in Article 92(1) of the Treaty are present.

[18] It is common ground that in the case in the main proceedings the payment facilities which the ONSS granted DMT were granted through State resources for the purposes of Article 92(1) of the Treaty, inasmuch as the ONSS is a public body established by the Belgian State which has been made responsible, under State supervision, for collecting mandatory employers' and workers' social security contributions and managing the social security system (see, to that effect, Joined Cases C-72/91 and C-73/91 *Sloman Neptun* [1993] ECR I-887, paragraph 19).

[19] As regards the concept of aid, it is settled case-law that that concept is wider than that of a subsidy because it embraces not only positive benefits, such as subsidies themselves, but also measures which, in various forms, mitigate the charges which are normally included in the budget of an undertaking (see Case C-387/92 *Banco Exterior de España* v *Ayuntamiento de Valencia* [1994] ECR I-877, paragraph 13). Where a public body with responsibility for collecting social security contributions tolerates late payment of such contributions, its conduct undoubtedly gives the recipient undertaking a significant commercial advantage by mitigating, for that undertaking, the burden associated with normal application of the social security system.

[20] However, DMT and the Belgian, French and Spanish Governments essentially argue that, where payment facilities are granted for a limited period, the advantage gained is offset in economic terms

by the increase in the amounts payable in the form of interest and penalties for late payment, and it is therefore not possible to conclude that there is State aid.

[21] However, it should be noted that any interest or penalties for late payment which an undertaking experiencing very serious financial difficulties might have to pay in return for generous payment facilities, such as those which, according to the order for reference, the ONSS granted to DMT over a period of eight years, cannot wholly undo the advantage gained by that undertaking.

[22] Secondly, it is settled case-law that in order to determine whether a State measure constitutes aid for the purposes of Article 92 of the Treaty, it is necessary to establish whether the recipient undertaking receives an economic advantage which it would not have obtained under normal market conditions (Case C-342/96 *Spain* v *Commission* [1999] ECR I-2459, paragraph 41).

[23] The Commission contends that the payment facilities accorded to DNT amount to a contributions credit and that, in the light of the economic information provided in the order for reference, it seems highly unlikely that, having regard to its situation, DMT would have been able to finance itself on the market by obtaining a loan from a private investor.

[24] It should be noted in that connection that the ONSS did not, in granting the payment facilities in question, act as a public investor whose conduct must, in accordance with settled case-law (see, in particular, Case C-42/93 *Spain* v *Commission* [1994] ECR I-4175, paragraph 14), be compared to the conduct of a private investor pursuing a structural policy—whether general or sectoral—guided by the longer term prospects of profitability of the capital invested. Indeed, as the Advocate General has pointed out in points 34 to 36 of his Opinion, the ONSS must be held to have acted, *vis-à-vis* DMT, as a public creditor which, like a private creditor, is seeking to obtain payment of sums owed to it by a debtor in financial difficulties (see, to that effect, the judgment in *Spain* v *Commission*, cited above, paragraph 46).

[25] It is for the national court to determine whether the payment facilities granted by the ONSS to DMT are manifestly more generous than those which a private creditor would have granted. To that end, the ONSS must be compared with a hypothetical private creditor which, so far as possible, is in the same position *vis-à-vis* its debtor as the ONSS and is seeking to recover the sums owed to it.

[26] The French Government argues that payment facilities in relation to social security contributions do not constitute State aid if they are granted in identical circumstances to any undertaking experiencing financial difficulties. That would seem to be the case under the regime established by the Belgian legislation. The Commission, however, claims that the ONSS has a discretionary power in regard to the grant of payment facilities.

[27] It follows from the wording of Article 92(1) of the Treaty that general measures which do not favour only certain undertakings or the production of only certain goods do not fall within that provision. By contrast, where the body granting financial assistance enjoys a degree of latitude which enables it to choose the beneficiaries or the conditions under which the financial assistance is provided, that assistance cannot be considered to be general in nature (see, to that effect, Case C-241/94 *France* v *Commission* [1996] ECR I-4551, paragraphs 23 and 24).

[28] It is for the national court in the main proceedings to determine whether the ONSS's power to grant payment facilities is discretionary or not and, if it is not, to establish whether the payment facilities granted by the ONSS are general in nature or whether they favour certain undertakings.

[29] It should also be pointed out that, if payment facilities such as those in the case in the main proceedings constitute aid, they may distort or threaten to distort competition under Article 92(1) of the Treaty by favouring certain undertakings and affecting trade between Member States, especially where the recipient undertaking will, as in DMT's case, be carrying on a cross-border activity.

[30] Consequently, the answer to the first question must be that payment facilities in respect of social security contributions granted in a discretionary manner to an undertaking by the body

responsible for collecting such contributions constitute State aid for the purposes of Article 92(1) of the Treaty if, having regard to the size of the economic advantage so conferred, the undertaking would manifestly have been unable to obtain comparable facilities from a private creditor in the same situation *vis-à-vis* that undertaking as the collecting body.

NOTE: This case is a clear application of the various aspects of Article 87(1) EC to the problem. The reference to the term 'manifest' is new and appears similar to the appreciability requirement under Article 81(1) EC. See Ross, M., pp. 439–440, above.

B: State source of funding

The rationale behind the state aid rules is to prevent companies being subsidised by the state. The first difficulty lies in determining what constitutes an organ of the state for these purposes. It is clear that it extends to local authorities but to what extent does it cover the activity of private bodies acting with state authority?

Compagnie Nationale Air France v *Commission (Air France)*
(Case T-358/94) [1996] ECR II-2112, [1997] 1 CMLR 492

Air France had been in severe financial difficulties for a number of years and in October 1992 drew up a second restructuring plan aimed at reducing costs. It approached the CDC-P, a wholly owned subsidiary of the Caisse, a special public body established by statute to assist it in certain financing transactions. These proceeded and subsequently the Commission adopted a decision declaring that the assistance constituted state aid and was incompatible with the Treaty.

[55] The issue to be examined is whether the investment in question by the CDC-P could properly be regarded by the Commission as arising from conduct imputable to the French State (Case C-303/88 *Italy* v *Commission*, cited above, paragraph 11).

[56] Article 92(1) of the Treaty and Article 61(1) of the EEA Agreement refer to aid granted by the States or through State resources 'in any form whatsoever'. Consequently, those provisions must be interpreted not on the basis of formal criteria but rather by reference to their purpose, which, according to Article 3(g) of the Treaty, is to ensure that competition is not distorted. It follows that all subsidies from the public sector threatening the play of competition are caught by the abovementioned provisions, it being unnecessary for those subsidies to be granted by the government or by a central administrative authority of a Member State (see, to that effect, Case C-305/89 *Italy* v *Commission* [1991] ECR I-1603, paragraph 13, and *Sloman Neptun*, cited above, paragraph 19).

[57] In the present case, the Court may restrict its examination to the statute of the Caisse. Even though the subscription to the securities in question was formally carried out by the CDC-P, a limited company governed by private law, the applicant has expressly accepted (reply, paragraph 12) that this 'investment was carried out at the decisive instigation of its majority shareholder [the Caisse] and with the funds which the Caisse placed at its disposal'. It follows that, on any view, the subscription in question is imputable to the Caisse. Consequently, the applicant's argument that the CDC-P is independent is irrelevant.

[58] The Caisse was established by the Finance Law of 1816 as an *'établissement spécial'* placed 'under the supervision and guarantee of the legislature'. Its tasks—including in particular the administration of public and private funds composed of compulsory deposits—are governed by

statutory and regulatory rules and its Director-General is appointed by the President of the Republic, the appointment of its other directors being a matter for the government.

[59] Those factors are sufficient for it to be held that the Caisse belongs to the public sector. Although it is subject only to the 'legislature', the legislative power is one of the constitutional powers of a State, and thus conduct of the legislature is necessarily imputable to the State.

[60] This reasoning is confirmed by the case-law of the Court of Justice concerning Member States' failure to fulfil their obligations under Article 169 of the Treaty. Under that case-law, a Member State incurs liability whatever the agency of the State whose action or inaction caused the failure to fulfil its obligations, 'even in the case of a constitutionally independent institution' (Case 77/69 *Commission* v *Belgium* [1970] ECR 237, paragraph 15). That assessment also applies in relation to control of State aid, since the Court of Justice has held that the means of redress provided for by the second subparagraph of Article 93(2) of the Treaty is merely a variant of the action for a declaration of failure to fulfil Treaty obligations, specifically adapted to the special problems which State aid poses for competition within the common market (Case C-301/87 *France* v *Commission* [1990] ECR I-307, paragraph 23).

[61] The Commission was accordingly entitled to treat the Caisse as a public-sector body whose conduct is attributable to the French State.

[62] That conclusion is not undermined by the arguments to the effect that the Caisse enjoys legal autonomy from the political authorities of the State, that the appointment of its Director-General, who is subject solely to supervision by an independent supervisory commission, is irrevocable, that the Caisse has a special statute in relation to the *Cour des Comptes*, and that it has a particular accounting and fiscal regime. Those arrangements are part of the internal organization of the public sector, and the existence of rules for ensuring that a public body remains independent of other authorities does not call into question the principle itself of the public nature of that body. Community law cannot permit the rules on State aid to be circumvented merely through the creation of autonomous institutions charged with allocating aid.

[63] In so far as the applicant then contests the characterization of the investment in question as State aid by pointing to the private source of the funds managed by the Caisse and to the fact that the depositors of those funds may require their repayment at any time, the Court of Justice has held (*Van Tiggele*, cited above, paragraph 25, and Joined Cases 213/81, 214/81 and 215/81 *Norddeutsches Vieh-und Fleischkontor* v *BALM* [1982] ECR 3583, paragraph 22) that in order for the investment in question to be regarded as State aid, it must amount to an advantage granted directly or indirectly through State resources, which presupposes that 'the resources from which the aid is granted come from the Member State'.

[64] The applicant claims that, because they are reimbursable, the funds deposited with the Caisse are not identical to the 'compulsory contributions' considered in Case 173/73 *Italy* v *Commission*, cited above, because it is only the latter contributions which are permanently at the State's disposal. In that regard, it should be observed that in that judgment (paragraphs 15 and 16) the Court of Justice held that the partial reduction of social charges on undertakings in a particular industrial sector was aid within the meaning of Article 92 of the Treaty, since the loss of revenue resulting from it was made good by resources accruing from obligations made compulsory by the State's legislation.

[65] It is true that the present case differs from Case 173/73 *Italy* v *Commission* in that the sums deposited with the Caisse are not non-repayable but may be withdrawn by depositors. Consequently, unlike revenue from taxation or compulsory contributions, those sums are not permanently at the disposal of the public sector. Nevertheless, it is necessary to consider the extent to which the legal status of the funds managed by the Caisse is reflected by economic reality, having

regard in particular to the fact that Community law applies to aid granted through State resources 'in any form whatsoever'.

[66] It is to be observed here that deposits with, and withdrawals from, the Caisse produce a constant balance which the Caisse is able to use as if the funds represented by that balance were permanently at its disposal. In that regard, the Caisse may therefore, as the applicant itself observed, 'act as an investor responding to developments on the markets' (application, paragraph 11) by using that available balance, at its own risk.

[67] The Court considers that the investment in question, financed by the balance available to the Caisse, is liable to distort competition within the meaning of Article 92(1) of the Treaty in the same way as if that investment had been financed by means of revenue from taxation or compulsory contributions. That provision therefore covers all the financial means by which the public sector may actually support undertakings, irrespective of whether or not those means are permanent assets of the public sector. Consequently, it is irrelevant that the funds used by the Caisse were repayable. Moreover, there is nothing in the documents before the Court to suggest that the realization of the investment in question was hampered by the refundability of the funds used.

[68] Finally, this conclusion is not undermined by the judgment of the Court of Justice in Case 290/83 *Commission* v *France* [1985] ECR 439, paragraph 15, in which it held that 'Article 92 of the Treaty covers aid which . . . was decided and financed by a public body and the implementation of which is subject to the approval of the public authorities . . .'. That judgment is not to be interpreted as meaning that a finding of State aid always presupposes the existence of approval of the public authorities, even where the financial transaction in question was decided upon and financed by a body which is itself part of the public sector. The Court was merely listing all the factors actually existing in the case before it and went on to conclude from them that, on any view, those factors, taken together, were caught by Article 92(1) of the Treaty. Consequently, even if the investment made by the Caisse in this case was not the subject of approval by the French Government, the fact that the Caisse, belonging to the public sector, used for that investment funds which were at its disposal is sufficient, as explained above, to characterize the investment as State action which may constitute aid within the meaning of Article 92(1) of the Treaty.

NOTE: The Court adopted a wide interpretation of what constitute state action and therefore was not required to distinguish the apparent requirement set out by the Court in *Commission* v *France* Case 290/83, [1985] ECR 439, for the existence of approval by a public authority.

The second difficulty is in ascertaining whether the advantage is granted from state resources.

Sloman Neptun Schiffahrts AG v *Seebetriebstraat Bodo Ziesmer der Sloman Neptun Schiffahrts AG*
(Cases C-72 and 73/91) [1993] ECR I-887

National shipping legislation in the Federal Republic of Germany provided for the employment of foreign seafarers without a permanent abode or residence in the FRG on working conditions and rates of pay less favourable than those of German seafarers.

[18] It is important to note that, under Article 92(1) of the EEC Treaty, any aid granted by a Member State or through State resources in any form whatsoever which distorts or threatens to distort competition by favouring certain undertakings or the production of certain goods is, in so far as it affects trade between Member States, incompatible with the Common Market.

[19] As the Court held in its judgment in Case 82/77 *Openbaar Ministerie of the Netherlands* v *Van Tiggele* ([1978] ECR 25, paragraphs 23–25), only advantages which are granted directly or indirectly through State resources are to be regarded as State aid within the meaning of Article 92(1) of

the EEC Treaty. The wording of this provision itself and the procedural rules laid down in Article 93 of the EEC Treaty show that advantages granted from resources other than those of the State do not fall within the scope of the provisions in question. The distinction between aid granted by the State and aid granted through State resources serves to bring within the definition of aid not only aid granted directly by the State, but also aid granted by public or private bodies designated or established by the State.

[20] Therefore it is necessary to determine whether or not the advantages arising from a system such as that applicable to the ISR are to be viewed as being granted through State resources.

[21] The system at issue does not seek, through its object and general structure, to create an advantage which would constitute an additional burden for the State or the abovementioned bodies, but only to alter in favour of shipping undertakings the framework within which contractual relations are formed between those undertakings and their employees. The consequences arising from this, in so far as they relate to the difference in the basis for the calculation of social security contributions, mentioned by the national court, and to the potential loss of tax revenue because of the low rates of pay, referred to by the Commission, are inherent in the system and are not a means of granting a particular advantage to the undertakings concerned.

[22] It follows that a system such as that applicable to the ISR is not a State aid within the meaning of Article 92(1) of the EEC Treaty.

NOTE: The Court here placed significance on the need for a measure to involve charges on public funds in order to constitute state aid. See Slotboom, M., 'State Aid in Community Law: A broad or narrow definition?' [1998] ELRev 289. The Court is obviously concerned to limit the application of state aid where national legal regimes are involved.

More recently, the Court confirmed, in Cases C-52–54/97 *Viscido and others* v *Ente Poste Italiane* [1998] ECR I-2629 that national labour law regimes are excluded from the prohibition as they do not involve any direct or indirect transfer of state resources.

Rodger, B.J., 'State Aid—A Fully Level Playing Field?'
[1999] ECLR 251 at 254–255

Conclusions
The wider significance of this case concerns the coverage and extent of the state aid rules and Community competition law in general. This case merely highlights the problems faced in competition law enforcement by the lack of any clear dividing line between competition law and 'non-competition' law. For instance, industrial policy, environmental policy and other policy sectors have a role in competition policy assessment and, looking specifically at state aid, the goal of the level competitive playing field across the Community would appear to intersect with a whole range of policies at the Community and national level. In response to the earlier cases, *Sloman Neptun Schiffahrts* and *Kirsammer-Hack*, Davies, an eminent labour lawyer, discussed the difficulties involved in the interplay between the state aid rules and labour law in the context of the relationship generally between market integration and social policy.[21] That article noted the different position taken by A.G. Darmon from that adopted by the ECJ in both cases,[22] but its general theme was that in the areas, including state aid policy, where Community law conflicted with national labour policies either any attempt at balancing was avoided by the Court or the reasoning of the Court was hidden.

21 P. Davies, 'Market Integration and Social Policy in the Court of Justice', [1995] I.L.J., Vol. 24, 49.
22 He noted for instance that 'The Court was from the outset in favour of the solution which involved no further broadening of Article 92 and thus the exclusion of the labour law provisions *in limine*. The Advocate General . . . , by contrast, was in favour of bringing the labour law provisions into the net and subjecting them to Community law evaluation' (at pp. 59–60) .

It was suggested that subsidiarity considerations as provided for in Article 3b of the Treaty would be more clearly articulated by the Court.[23]

This acceptance of the broadened potential scope for competition law inevitably has significant effects on the relationship between competition policies and other Community policies and also as between national and Community policies and law. In competition law generally, and particularly under Article 85, the problem of diagonal conflicts arising between the application of Community competition law and national policies such as cultural policy has been evidenced, for instance in the treatment by the ECJ of national systems of resale price maintenance for books.[24] Perhaps it might have been anticipated, given the Advocate General's opinion in the two earlier cases and the developing notions both of what may constitute state aid and of the role of subsidiarity, that the European Court may have revised its earlier pronouncements. However, it appears that at least national labour and social policies will not be subject to state aid scrutiny. This exclusion itself may reflect subsidiarity concerns or more likely the acceptance that Community state aid control has practical limitations, as was noted by A.G. Jacobs in the present case: 'The answer is perhaps essentially a pragmatic one: to investigate all such regimes would entail an enquiry on the basis of the Treaty alone into the entire social and economic life of a member state'.[25]

NOTE: The Advocate General's comments are self-explanatory as to the perceived limits of the state aid prohibition.

C: Selectivity

This aspect requires one to differentiate between general economic measures and those measures which are more selective and benefit certain industries or undertakings therein. This provides similar difficulties to those encountered in ascertaining what constitutes state resources. General tax measures would not constitute state aid but specific and targeted tax reductions and differential rates of taxation may. See *R* v *Customs and Excise Commissioners, ex parte Lunn Poly and another* [1999] EuLr 653 and Bacon, K., 'Differential Taxes, State Aids and the *Lunn Poly* Case' [1999] ECLR 384. Cf. Case 173/73, *Italy* v *Commission* [1974] ECR 709, [1974] 2 CMLR 593.

Industrie Aeronautiche E Meccaniche Rinaldo Piaggio SpA v *International Factors Italia SpA (Ifitalia), Dornier Luftfahrt GmbH and Ministero della Difesa*
(Case C-295/97) [2000] 3 CMLR 825, [1999] ECR I-3735

Piaggio bought three aircraft for the Italian armed forces from the German company Dornier. In 1994, Piaggio was placed under special administration under Italian legislation for large companies in difficulties. In these circumstances the legislation provided, *inter alia,* for payments by insolvent undertakings in the two years prior to the decree of insolvency to be set aside for the benefit of the body of creditors and for the state to guarantee certain debts. On the basis of these provisions, Piaggio sought to recover the sums paid to Dornier, which

23 See generally Joerges, for instance, 'The Impact of European Integration on Private Law: Reductionist Perceptions, True Conflicts and a New Constitutionalist Perspective', 1997 3 ELJ 378.

24 Schmid, 'Diagonal Conflicts: Europeanised Competition Law with National Law', paper presented at Private Law Adjudication in the European Multi-level System, a workshop at the EUI, Florence, October 2–3, 1998, as yet unpublished.

25 at para. 16.

claimed in its defence that the provisions in question were contrary to the Community rules on state aid.

[34] As the Court has already held, the concept of aid is wider than that of a subsidy because it embraces not only positive benefits, such as subsidies themselves, but also measures which, in various forms, mitigate the charges which are normally included in the budget of an undertaking and which, without therefore being subsidies in the strict meaning of the word, are similar in character and have the same effect (Case C-387/92 *Banco Exterior de España* v *Ayuntamiento de Valencia* [1994] ECR I-877, paragraph 13; *Ecotrade*, paragraph 34).

[35] The expression 'aid', within the meaning of Article 92(1) of the Treaty, necessarily implies advantages granted directly or indirectly through State resources or constituting an additional charge for the State or for bodies designated or established by the State for that purpose (see, in particular, Joined Cases C-52/97 to C-54/97 *Viscido and Others* v *Ente Poste Italiane* [1998] ECR I-2629, paragraph 13).

[36] By analogy with what the Court held in *Ecotrade* concerning Article 4c of the ECSC Treaty, several characteristics of the system established by Law No 95/79, particularly in the light of the facts in the main proceedings, might, if the significance attributed to them below were to be confirmed by the national court, make it possible to establish the existence of aid within the meaning of Article 92(1) of the Treaty.

[37] First, it is apparent from the documents before the Court that Law No 95/79 is intended to apply selectively for the benefit of large industrial undertakings in difficulties which owe particularly large debts to certain, mainly public, classes of creditors. As the Court held in paragraph 38 of its judgment in *Ecotrade*, it is even highly probable that the State or public bodies will be among the principal creditors of the undertaking in question.

[38] It is also important to note that, even if the decisions of the Minister for Industry to place the undertaking in difficulties under special administration and to allow it to continue trading are taken with regard, as far as possible, to the interests of the creditors and, in particular, to the prospects for increasing the value of the undertaking's assets, they are also influenced, as the Court held in paragraph 39 of its judgment in *Ecotrade* and as the national court has confirmed, by the concern to maintain the undertaking's economic activity in the light of national industrial policy considerations.

[39] In those circumstances, having regard to the class of undertakings covered by the legislation in issue and the scope of the discretion enjoyed by the minister when authorising, in particular, an insolvent undertaking under special administration to continue trading, that legislation meets the condition that it should relate to a specific undertaking, which is one of the defining features of State aid (see, to that effect, Case C-241/94 *France* v *Commission* [1996] ECR I-4551, paragraphs 23 and 24).

[40] Next, whatever the objective pursued by the national legislature, it would seem that the legislation in question is liable to place the undertakings to which it applies in a more favourable situation than others, inasmuch as it allows them to continue trading in circumstances in which that would not be allowed if the ordinary insolvency rules were applied, since under those rules protection of creditors' interests is the determining factor. In view of the priority accorded to debts connected with the pursuit of economic activity, authorisation to continue to pursue that activity might, in those circumstances, involve an additional burden for the public authorities if it were in fact established that the State or public bodies were among the principal creditors of the undertaking in difficulties, all the more so because, by definition, that undertaking owes debts of considerable value.

[41] Furthermore, apart from the grant of a State guarantee under Article 2a of Law No 95/79 which the Italian authorities agreed to notify to the Commission in advance, placing an undertaking under special administration entails extension of the prohibition and suspension of all individual actions for

enforcement to tax debts and penalties, interest and increases for belated payment of corporation tax, release from the obligation to pay fines and pecuniary penalties in the case of failure to pay social security contributions, and application of a preferential rate where all or part of the undertaking is transferred, the transfer being subject to a flat-rate registration duty of ITL 1 million, whereas the ordinary rate of registration duty is 3 per cent of the value of the property sold.

[42] Those advantages, conferred by the national legislature, could also entail an additional burden for the public authorities in the form of a State guarantee, a *de facto* waiver of public debts, exemption from the obligation to pay fines or other pecuniary penalties, or a reduced rate of tax. It could be otherwise only if it were established that placing the undertaking under special administration and allowing it to continue trading did not in fact entail or should not entail an additional burden for the State, compared to the situation that would have arisen had the ordinary insolvency provisions been applied. It is for the national court to verify those matters, after seeking clarification from the Commission if need be.

[43] In the light of the foregoing, it must be concluded that application to an undertaking of a system of the kind introduced by Law No 95/79, and derogating from the rules of ordinary law relating to insolvency, is to be regarded as giving rise to the grant of State aid, within the meaning of Article 92(1) of the Treaty, where it is established that the undertaking

— has been permitted to continue trading in circumstances in which it would not have been permitted to do so if the rules of ordinary law relating to insolvency had been applied, or

— has enjoyed one or more advantages, such as a State guarantee, a reduced rate of tax, exemption from the obligation to pay fines and other pecuniary penalties or *de facto* waiver of public debts wholly or in part, which could not have been claimed by another insolvent undertaking under the application of the rules of ordinary law relating to insolvency.

NOTE: Despite the underlying problems in ascertaining what constitutes state aid, this case suggests that it is becoming more difficult to argue that a state measure is general rather than selective. In particular, even where measures are of general application, they are more likely to constitute state aid where there exists some discretion in their application. To a great extent this confirms the earlier dicta in Case 290/83 *Commission* v *France* [1985] ECR 439.

D: Affect Intra-Community Trade/Distortion of Competition

The first aspect is fairly straightforward to satisfy as the granting of state aid will almost inevitably strengthen the competitive position of the aided undertaking(s) in relation to undertakings from other Member States, and thereby affect the flow of trade in the Community. See Case C–173/73 *Italy* v *Commission* [1974] ECR 709, [1974] 2 CMLR 593. Similarly the Court has confirmed that it is sufficient for the Commission to demonstrate the existence of the state aid as indicative of a distortion or potential distortion of competition. *Phillip Morris Holland BV* v *Commission* (Case 730/79) [1980] ECR 2671, [1981] 2 CMLR 321. The mere strengthening of the competitive position of the aided undertaking distorts competition. See Case 173/73 *Italy* v *Commission (Textiles)* [1974] ECR 709, [1974] 2 CMLR 593.

Phillip Morris Holland BV v *Commission*
(Case 730/79) [1980] ECR 2671, [1981] 2 CMLR 321

The applicant was the Dutch subsidiary of a major tobacco manufacturer. It requested the Court to annul a Commission decision in respect of proposed government assistance to increase its production capacity. The aim of the aid in question was to help the applicant to concentrate and develop its production of cigarettes by closing one of the two factories which it owned in the Netherlands and by raising the annual production capacity of the second.

[9] The applicant maintains, that, in order to decide to what extent specific aid is incompatible with the Common Market, it is appropriate to apply first of all the criteria for deciding whether there are any restrictions on competition under Articles 85 and 86 of the Treaty. The Commission must therefore first determine the 'relevant market' and in order to do so must take account of the product, the territory and the period of time in question. It must then consider the pattern of the market in question in order to be able to assess how far the aid in question in a given case affects relations between competitors. But these essential aspects of the matter are not found in the disputed decision. The decision does not define the relevant market either from the standpoint of the product or in point of time. The market pattern and moreover for that matter, the relations between competitors resulting therefrom which might in a given case be distorted by the disputed aid, have not been specified at all.

[10] It is common ground that when the applicant has completed its planned investment it will account for nearly 50 per cent of cigarette production in the Netherlands and that it expects to export over 80 per cent of its production to other Member States. The 'additional premium for major schemes' which the Dutch Government proposed to grant the applicant amounted to Hfl 6.2 million (2.3 million EUA) which is 3.8 per cent of the capital invested.

[11] When State financial aid strengthens the position of an undertaking compared with other undertakings competing in intra-Community trade the latter must be regarded as affected by that aid. In this case the aid which the Dutch Government proposed to grant was for an undertaking organised for international trade and this is proved by the high percentage of its production which it intends to export to other Member States. The aid in question was to help to enlarge its production capacity and consequently to increase its capacity to maintain the flow of trade including that between Member States. On the other hand the aid is said to have reduced the cost of converting the production facilities and has thereby given the applicant a competitive advantage over manufacturers who have completed or intend to complete at their own expense a similar increase in the production capacity of their plant.

[12] These circumstances, which have been mentioned in the recitals in the preamble to the disputed decision and which the applicant has not challenged, justify the Commission's deciding that the proposed aid would be likely to affect trade between Member States and would threaten to distort competition between undertakings established in different Member States.

NOTE: This demonstrates that both of these requirements for a measure to constitute state aid are easily satisfied. The Commission does not have to quantify any actual advantage gained and the Court is unlikely to interfere with the Commission's discretion in making complex economic and social assessment of the issues. See Cases T-132/96 & T-143/96 *Freistaat Sachsen & Others* v *Commission* [1999] ECR II-3663.

However, what is the position if the aid granted is minimal? In this case, the state aid may be regarded as *de minimis*, in a similar way to agreements which are not appreciable under Article 81(1) EC, where it satisfies the following test.

Regulation 69/2001
OJ L10/30, 2001, Article 2

De minimis aid
1. Aid measures shall be deemed not to meet all the criteria of Article 87(1) of the Treaty and shall therefore not fall under the notification requirement of Article 88(3) of the Treaty, if they fulfil the conditions laid down in paragraphs 2 and 3.

2. The total *de minimis* aid granted to any one enterprise shall not exceed EUR 100,000 over any period of three years. This ceiling shall apply irrespective of the form of the aid or the objective pursued.

3. The ceiling in paragraph 2 shall be expressed as a cash grant. All figures used shall be gross, that is, before any deduction for direct taxation. Where aid is awarded in a form other than a grant, the aid amount shall be the gross grant equivalent of the aid.

Aid payable in several instalments shall be discounted to its value at the moment of its being granted. The interest rate to be used for discounting purposes and to calculate the aid amount in a soft loan shall be the reference rate applicable at the time of grant.

NOTE: The Commission was empowered to introduce a Regulation on *de minimis* by Article 2 of Regulation 944/98. Regulation 69/2001 adopts the earlier Commission policy set out in the 1996 Commission Notice on the *de minimis* rules for state aid, OJ C68/06, 1996.

(a) The Market Economy Investor Principle (MEIP)

Throughout the European Community there exists great disparity in the extent to which Member States are involved in public ownership or control of undertakings and the extent to which they also invest in private undertakings. This poses the difficulty that any investment by a Member State in an undertaking would prima facie appear to constitute state aid. The state aid rules seek to avoid this problem by applying the market economy investor principle to distinguish between investment which would also have been acceptable to a private investor, which is not state aid, and conversely aid which would not have been acceptable to a private investor in a market economy, which is state aid. The following passage indicates the rationale and application of the MEIP.

Abbamonte, G.B., 'Market Economy Investor Principles: A Legal Analysis of an Economic Problem'
[1996] ECLR 258 at pp. 258–260

The Treaty of Rome does not prohibit Member States from running a mixed economy. Article 222 establishes the principle of neutrality of property ownership by stating that 'This Treaty shall in no way prejudice the rules in the Member States governing the system of property ownership'. Member States are, therefore, free to create public undertakings, acquire shareholdings and nationalise existing undertakings operating in all sectors of the economy. However, Member States do not enjoy unlimited freedom of action under Article 222 because they must comply with all the other provisions of the Treaty, including those on competition. Unlimited freedom under Article 222 could translate into the Member States having unrestricted power to grant financial support to the national industry. This would certainly be at odds with the institution of a system of undistorted competition in the Common Market, which according to Article 3(g) of the Treaty is one of the activities of the Community.

In particular, notwithstanding the current trend towards privatisation, it is unquestionable that certain segments of the market are characterised by a significant presence of state-owned undertakings. In different economic sectors public and private undertakings coexist and compete with each other. However, public and private undertakings do not always compete on a similar footing. Private undertakings are mainly driven by profit, while public undertakings may be driven by reasons other than economic ones. Public undertakings may be used by the public authorities which exert an influence over them as instruments of economic policy to maintain employment levels or carry out burdensome public service obligations.

The pursuit of public duties leads to the creation of special financial relations between public undertakings and public authorities which are different from the normal commercial relations existing between private firms and their owners. In their financial relations with the State, public undertakings may benefit from favourable financing opportunities which are not available to their private competitors. Such inequality of access to public funding, namely either tax revenues or public borrowings, may be state aid and thus involve discrimination against the private sector. If this state aid went unchecked it would, *inter alia*, harm the principle of equal treatment as between public and private undertakings, which is principally enshrined in Article 90 of the Treaty.

As a general rule state aid, if certain conditions are fulfilled, is incompatible with the Common Market and is thus *prima facie* prohibited. Article 92(1) states that 'any aid granted by a Member State or through State resources in any form whatsoever which distorts or threatens to distort competition by favouring certain undertakings or the production of certain goods shall, in so far as it affects trade between Member States, be incompatible with the common market'.

For the purpose of establishing whether a financial transaction between a Member State and an undertaking involves state aid the Commission applies the market economy investor principle ('MEIP'). According to the MEIP the transaction involves state aid if it takes place in circumstances that would not be acceptable to a private investor operating under normal market economy conditions. The MEIP is also used by the Commission to determine the amount of aid involved in the transaction (see below).

Application of the MEIP safeguards the principle of neutrality of the Treaty with regard to the system of property ownership and the principle of equal treatment as between public and private undertakings. The MEIP strikes a balance between the Member States' interest in owning and running individual firms or entire economic sectors and the common interest in safeguarding a system of undistorted competition. The MEIP is a very blunt test; political, social or philanthropic considerations are extraneous to the principle. In treating the State as a venture capital investor and assessing the aid element as the difference between the preferential conditions and market ones, public and private firms are put on an equal footing.

The MEIP has been devised by the Commission and endorsed by the Council. On several occasions the Court of Justice has confirmed the validity of the principle, by stating that in order to determine if the public investment amounts to state aid the criterion is that of the possibility for the undertaking 'of raising finance on the private capital market'. In its first judgments the Court appeared to compare the behaviour of the State to that of an ordinary private investor who normally seeks to maximise profits. According to the Court, 'the test is, in particular, whether in similar circumstances a private shareholder, having regard to the foreseeability of obtaining a return and leaving aside all social, regional-policy and sectoral considerations, would have subscribed to the capital in question'.

However, the Court's case law did not consider whether another category of investor, such as a financial holding company which owns or aims at acquiring a strategic stake in a company, was the appropriate benchmark. The size of the investor and the importance of his shareholding in the company play an important role in investment decisions. An investor which does not hold a controlling stake and does not seek to acquire control of a company will normally be guided by short-term profitability prospects. On the other hand a holding company pursues a group strategy and will not necessarily seek profit in the short term.

The Court refined its position in two cases involving Italy. In the *Alfa Romeo* case the Court stated that

> In order to determine whether such measures are in the nature of State aid, it is necessary to consider whether in similar circumstances a private investor of a size comparable to that of the bodies administering the public sector might have provided capital of such an amount.
>
> It should be added that although the conduct of a private investor with which the intervention of the public investor pursuing economic policy aims must be compared need not be the conduct of an ordinary investor laying out capital with a view to realizing a profit in the relatively short term, it must at least be the conduct of a private holding company or group of undertakings pursuing a structural policy—whether general or sectoral—and guided by profitability prospects in the longer term.

In the *ENI-Lanerossi* case the Court noted that:

> a parent company may also, for a limited period, bear the losses of one of its subsidiaries in order to enable the latter to close down its operations under the best possible conditions. Such decisions may be motivated not solely by the likelihood of an indirect material profit but also by other considerations, such as a desire to protect the group's image or to redirect its activities.
>
> However, when injections of capital by a public investor disregard any prospect of profitability, even in the long term, such provision of capital must be regarded as aid within the meaning of Article 92 of the Treaty . . .

These decisions represent a considerable widening of the scope of application of the MEIP. First, it follows from these judgments that the public investor need not choose always the most profitable investment. A holding company which has the option to invest in a telecommunication company or an oil company will not be obliged to invest in the telecommunication company because, as an illustration, this venture has a higher return than the other. The holding company may provide financial support to the less profitable company without the capital investment being aid, provided that an adequate return on the investment is foreseeable at the time the investment decision was taken.

Second, the public parent company may invest money in a loss-making subsidiary to prevent it from going bankrupt, because this event would affect the image of the whole group. By way of example, the group 'White' produces cosmetics and toiletries, which are both marketed under the trade mark *White*. The group consists of a financial holding company and two operating subsidiaries: A, which produces and sells cosmetics, and B, which deals with toiletries. A is loss-making and nearly bankrupt, while B is profitable. The holding company may decide to restructure and recapitalise A because its disappearance from the market could create a public perception that the group is not doing well, which could adversely affect the value of the brand to the immediate detriment of B. Therefore, the holding company's decision to fund the less profitable investment can be justified.

NOTE: As Abbamonte notes, this is a particularly difficult exercise for the Commission. The task has been facilitated to an extent by Commission Directive 2000/52/EC of 26 July 2000 amending Directive 80/723/EEC on the transparency of financial relations between Member States and public undertakings OJ L193/75, 2000. The comparison with a private investor must take into account the future prospects of profitability, even if this is not necessary in the short term. The next case demonstrates how the Commission applies the market economy investor principle.

Neue Maxhutte Stahlwerke v *Commission*

(Cases T-129/95, T-2/95 and T-97/96) [1999] ECR II-17, [1999] 3 CMLR 366 at
paras 104–109 and 116

NMS, a German steel production company sought annulment of a decision by
the Commission that state aid had been granted to it by German authorities.

[104] It is common ground that the financial contributions provided for in the context of the privatisation of NMS and the loans granted by Bavaria constitute a transfer of public resources to a steel
undertaking. In order to determine whether such a transfer constitutes state aid within the meaning
of Article 4(c) of the ECSC Treaty, it is necessary to consider whether in similar circumstances a
private investor of a size comparable to that of the bodies administering the public sector might have
provided capital of such an amount (see the judgments in *Alfa Romeo*, cited in paragraph 75 above,
paragraph 19, and in *Hytasa*, cited in paragraph 75 above, paragraph 21).

[105] The private investor test emanates from the principle that the public and private sectors are to
be treated equally. Pursuant to that principle, capital placed directly or indirectly at the disposal of an
undertaking by the State in circumstances which correspond to normal market conditions cannot be
regarded as state aid (judgments in *ENI-Lanerossi*, cited in paragraph 76 above, paragraph 20, and in
Case T-358/94 *Air France* v *Commission* [1996] ECR II-2109, paragraph 70).

[106] The Court of Justice has held, in the context of the application of Article 92(1) of the EC Treaty,
that the consideration by the Commission of the question whether a particular measure may be
regarded as aid, where the State had allegedly not acted 'as an ordinary economic agent', involves
a complex economic appraisal (see the judgment in Case C-56/93 *Belgium* v *Commission* [1996]
ECR I-723, paragraphs 10 and 11; see also the judgment in *Air France*, cited in the preceding
paragraph, paragraph 71). The consideration of this same question in the context of the application
of Article 4(c) of the ECSC Treaty requires equally complex appraisals of the same kind.

[107] It is in the light of the above considerations that the arguments put forward in the case must
be assessed.

[108] While acknowledging that the private investor test is the essential point of reference, the
applicants strive to demonstrate that the defendant's interpretation of this criterion is too narrow in
the present case and consequently incorrect.

[109] In this regard, it is clear that although the conduct of a private investor with which that of a
public investor pursuing economic policy aims must be compared need not be the conduct of an
ordinary investor laying out capital with a view to realising a profit in the relatively short term, it must
at least be the conduct of a private holding company or a private group of undertakings pursuing a
structural policy—whether general or sectoral—and guided by prospects of profitability in the
longer term (judgment in *Alfa Romeo*, cited in paragraph 75 above, paragraph 20).

[116] Contrary to what is maintained by the applicants in Case T-129/95, when injections of capital
by a public investor disregard any prospect of profitability, even in the long term, such provision of
capital constitutes state aid (judgment in *ENI-Lanerossi*, cited in paragraph 76 above, paragraph 22).
A redirection of the activities of the recipient undertaking can justify an injection of capital only if
there is a reasonable likelihood that the assisted undertaking will become profitable again.

NOTE: This issue arose under the relevant provisions of the ECSC Treaty but the Court noted
that the principles were the same as those under the EC Treaty. There are a wide range of
scenarios in which the MEIP will be applied to ascertain whether state aid has been granted. The
most obvious are by direct capital and equity injections by the state and in these circumstances
the Commission will normally require the existence of a viable restructuring plan as the basis for
investment in a loss-making undertaking. See for example Commission Decision (94/118/EC)

Aer Lingus OJ L54/30, 1994. The Court has confirmed that review of the Commission's assessment of the MEIP would be limited to the grounds of procedural irregularity, manifest error or misuse of powers. See *Air France* v *Commission* (Case T-358/94) [1996] ECR II-2109, [1997] 1 CMLR 492 and Slocock, B., 'The Market Economy Investor Principle', June 2002, Commission Competition Policy Newsletter, p. 23. State aid comprises more than mere cash subsidies or loans and also extends, *inter alia*, to loan guarantees, where the undertaking would not have been given a loan, or would have faced a higher interest repayment rate, without the guarantee of repayment by the state in the event of default. See Commission Notice on the application of Articles 87 and 88 of the EC Treaty to State Aids in the form of Guarantees, OJ C71/7, 2000.

QUESTION

Do you consider the application of the MEIP to be justified or too restrictive of state investment in industry?

SECTION 3: **Exemptions**

There are two types of exemption in respect of the state aid prohibition, mandatory and discretionary.

A: Mandatory exemptions

Article 87(2) EC sets out the mandatory exemptions:

> (2) The following shall be compatible with the common market:
> - (a) aid having a social character, granted to individual consumers, provided that such aid is granted without discrimination related to the origin of the products concerned;
> - (b) aid to make good the damage caused by natural disasters or exceptional occurrences;
> - (c) aid granted to the economy of certain areas of the Federal Republic of Germany affected by the division of Germany, insofar as such aid is required in order to compensate for the economic disadvantages caused by that division.

B: Discretionary exemptions

Article 87(3) sets out the range of discretionary exemptions from the state aid prohibition on the basis that the state aid may contribute to the achievement of Community objectives:

> 3. The following may be considered to be compatible with the common market:
> - (a) aid to promote the economic development of areas where the standard of living is abnormally low or where there is serious underemployment;
> - (b) aid to promote the execution of an important project of common European interest or to remedy a serious disturbance in the economy of a Member State;
> - (c) aid to facilitate the development of certain economic activities or of certain economic areas, where such aid does not adversely affect trading conditions to an extent contrary to the common interest;

(d) aid to promote culture and heritage conservation where such aid does not affect trading conditions and competition in the Community to an extent that is contrary to the common interest;

(e) such other categories of aid as may be specified by decision of the Council acting by a qualified majority on a proposal from the Commission.

NOTE: Aid falling within Article 87(3) EC requires to be notified for approval by the Commission. In order to increase transparency in its application of the discretionary rules, the Commission has adopted a range of frameworks and guidelines clarifying how it will assess certain types of aid. This guidance exists in relation to forms of 'horizontal aid' (such as employment aid and regional aid), aid for restructuring of undertakings in difficulty, and also for particular industries e.g. shipbuilding, transport etc. These are available at the Commission website (http://europa.eu.int/comm/competition/index en.html). The following are two particular types of horizontal aid for which the Commission has developed a particular approach.

(a) *Regional aid*

Regional aid can fall within Article 87(3)(a) EC and 87(3)(c) EC. The Commission has set out its policy on when national regional aid is exemptible in guidelines.

Guidelines on National Regional Aids
OJ C74/6, 1998, paras 3.5–3.10

3.5. Article 92(3)(a) provides that aid to promote the economic development of areas where the standard of living is abnormally low or where there is serious underemployment may be considered compatible with the common market. As the Court of Justice of the European Communities has held, 'the use of the words "abnormally" and "serious" in the exemption contained in Article 92(3)(a) shows that it concerns only areas where the economic situation is extremely unfavourable in relation to the Community as a whole'[12].

The Commission accordingly considers, following a tried and tested approach, that the conditions laid down are fulfilled if the region, being a NUTS[13] level II geographical unit, has a per capita gross domestic product (GDP), measured in purchasing power standards (PPS), of less than 75.0% of the Community average[14]. The GDP/PPS of each region and the Community average to be used in the analysis must relate to the average of the last three years for which statistics are available. These amounts are calculated on the basis of data furnished by the Statistical Office for the European Communities.

The derogation in Article 92(3)(c)
3.6. In contrast to Article 92(3)(a), where the situation in view is identified precisely and formally, Article 92(3)(c) allows greater latitude when it comes to defining the difficulties of a region that can be alleviated with the help of aid measures. The relevant indicators do not therefore necessarily boil down in this case to standards of living and underemployment. In any case, the appropriate framework for evaluating these difficulties may be provided not only by the Community as a whole but also by the relevant Member State in particular.

The Court of Justice, in Case 248/84 (see footnote 12), has expressed its views on these two matters (range of problems covered and reference framework for the analysis), as follows: 'The exemption in Article 92(3)(c), on the other hand, is wider in scope inasmuch as it permits the

---

12 Case 248/84 *Germany* v *Commission* [1987] ECR 4013, at paragraph 19.

13 Nomenclature of Statistical Territorial Units.

14 The underlying assumption being that the GDP indicator is capable of reflecting synthetically both the phenomena mentioned.

development of certain areas without being restricted by the economic conditions laid down in Article 92(3)(a), provided such aid "does not adversely affect trading conditions to an extent contrary to the common interest". That provision gives the Commission power to authorise aid intended to further the economic development of areas of a Member State which are disadvantaged in relation to the national average'.

3.7. The regional aid covered by the derogation in point (c) must, however, form part of a coherent regional policy of the Member State and adhere to the principles of geographical concentration set out above. Inasmuch as it is intended for regions which are less disadvantaged than those to which point (a) relates, such aid is, to a greater extent than the latter, exceptional and can be allowed only to a very limited degree. This being so, only a small part of the national territory of a Member State may *prima facie* qualify for the aid in question. This is why the population coverage of regions falling under Article 92(3)(c) must not exceed 50 per cent of the national population not covered by the derogation under Article 92(3)(a)[15].

On the other hand, the fact that the nature of such aid makes it possible to take account of the national peculiarities of a Member State does not exempt the aid from the need for scrutiny from the viewpoint of Community interests. The determination of the regions eligible in each Member State must therefore fit into a framework guaranteeing the overall coherence of such determination at Community level[16].

3.8. So as to afford national authorities sufficient latitude when it comes to choosing eligible regions without jeopardising the effectiveness of the system of checks operated by the Commission in respect of this type of aid and the equal treatment of all Member States, the determination of the regions eligible under the derogation in question consists of two parts:

— the fixing by the Commission, for each country, of a ceiling on the coverage of such aid,
— the selection of eligible regions.

The latter part will obey transparent rules but will also be sufficiently flexible to allow for the diversity of situations potentially justifying the application of the derogation. The aid coverage ceiling is designed to be conducive to the above-mentioned flexibility in the choice of eligible regions whilst ensuring the uniform treatment required by acceptance of such aid from the Community point of view.

3.9. To guarantee effective control of regional aid while contributing to the achievement of the objectives set out in Article 3 of the Treaty, in particular under points (g) and (j), the Commission sets an overall ceiling for the coverage of regional aid in the Community in terms of population. The overall ceiling covers all the regions eligible under the 92(3)(c) and 92(3)(a) derogations. Since the regions eligible for regional aid under the Article 92(3)(a) derogation and their global coverage at Community level are determined exogenously and automatically by applying the criterion of 75 per cent of per capita GDP/PPS, it follows that the Commission decision on the overall ceiling defines, simultaneously, the ceiling on coverage under the Article 92(3)(c) derogation, at Community level. The Article 92(3)(c) ceiling is obtained by deducting from the overall ceiling the population of the regions eligible under the 92(3)(a) derogation. It is then distributed among the different Member States in the light of the relative socio-economic situation of the regions within each Member State, assessed in the context of the Community. The method of determining this percentage in each Member State is described in Annex III.

3.10. The Member States notify to the Commission, under Article 93(3), the methodology and the

15 Barring a transitional exception arising from the application of point 8 of Annex III to these Guidelines.
16 See, in this connection, the judgments of the Court of Justice in Cases 730/79 *Philip Morris*, at paragraph 26, and 310/85 *Deufil* [1987] ECR 901, at paragraph 18.

quantitative indicators which they wish to use to determine the eligible regions, and the list of regions they propose for the (c) derogation and the relative intensities[17]. The percentage for the population of the regions concerned may not exceed the said ceiling on coverage for the purposes of the 92(3)(c) derogation.

NOTE: These guidelines replaced the earlier Commission Communication on regional aid in 1988, OJ C212/02, 1988. The Guidelines demonstrate the possibility of seeking exemption under either Article 87(3)(a) EC or 87(3)(c) EC. There are maps of regions available for aid and the Commission has set appropriate aid ceilings for different regions according to the relative weakness of their economies, OJ C165/5, 2000. Exemption will not be granted if the assistance is directed at one undertaking. See Commission Decision (94/696/EC) *Olympic Airways*, OJ l273/22, 1994. The state aid exemption for regional aid demonstrates the cohesion between the state aid rules and the broader objective of the Community in reducing economic disparities between the regions of the Community.

(b) *Sectoral aid—rescue and restructuring aid*

Assistance from government is often sought and granted on the basis that there are circumstances in which state aid for rescuing firms in difficulty and helping them to restructure may be justified. The Commission has issued the following guidelines:

Community Guidelines on State aid for rescuing and restructuring firms in difficulty
OJ C288/02, 1999, paras 22–48

(22) This chapter deals exclusively with aid measures that are notified individually to the Commission. Under certain conditions, the Commission may authorise rescue or restructuring aid schemes: those conditions are set out in Chapter 4.

3.1. Rescue aid
(23) In order to be approved by the Commission, rescue aid as defined in point 12 must:

(a) consist of liquidity support in the form of loan guarantees or loans[17]. In both cases, the loan must be granted at an interest rate at least comparable to those observed for loans to healthy firms, and in particular the reference rates adopted by the Commission;
(b) be linked to loans that are to be reimbursed over a period of not more than twelve months after disbursement of the last instalment to the firm[18];
(c) be warranted on the grounds of serious social difficulties and have no unduly adverse spillover effects on other Member States;
(d) be accompanied on notification by an undertaking on the part of the Member State concerned to communicate to the Commission, not later than six months after the rescue aid measure

---

17 See points 4.8 and 4.9.
17 An exception may be made in the case of rescue aid in the banking sector, in order to enable the credit institution in question to continue temporarily carrying on its banking business in accordance with the prudential legislation in force (Council Directive 89/647/EEC of 18 December 1989 on a solvency ratio for credit institutions, OJ L 386, 30.12.1989, p. 14). Any aid granted in a form other than that described in subparagraph (b), for example a capital injection or a subordinated loan, will be taken into account when any compensatory measures under a restructuring plan are examined in accordance with points 35 to 39.
· 18 Reimbursement of the loan linked to the rescue aid may possibly be covered by the restructuring aid subsequently approved by the Commission.

has been authorised, a restructuring plan or a liquidation plan or proof that the loan has been reimbursed in full and/or that the guarantee has been terminated;

(e) be restricted to the amount needed to keep the firm in business for the period during which the aid is authorised (for example, covering wage and salary costs or routine supplies).

(24) The rescue aid will initially be authorised for not more than six months or, where the Member State concerned has submitted a restructuring plan within that period, until the Commission reaches its decision on the plan. In duly substantiated exceptional circumstances and at the request of the Member State concerned, the Commission may extend the initial six-month period.

(25) Rescue aid is a one-off operation designed to keep a company in business for a limited period, during which its future can be assessed. On the other hand, repeated rescues that would merely maintain the status quo, postpone the inevitable and in the meantime shift the attendant economic and social problems on to other, more efficient producers or other Member States cannot be allowed.

(26) If the Member State fails to communicate the information stipulated in (d) of point 23 before the six-month deadline expires and does not make a duly substantiated request for the deadline to be extended, the Commission will initiate proceedings under Article 88(2).

(27) The approval of rescue aid does not necessarily mean that aid under a restructuring plan will subsequently be approved; such aid will have to be assessed on its own merits.

3.2. Restructuring aid

3.2.1. Basic principle

(28) Aid for restructuring raises particular competition concerns as it can shift an unfair share of the burden of structural adjustment and the attendant social and economic problems onto other producers who are managing without aid and to other Member States. The general principle should therefore be to allow the grant of restructuring aid only in circumstances in which it can be demonstrated that it does not run counter to the Community interest. This will only be possible if strict criteria are met, and if it is certain that any distortions of competition will be offset by the benefits flowing from the firm's survival (in particular, where it is clear that the net effect of redundancies resulting from the firm going out of business, combined with the effects on its suppliers, would exacerbate local, regional or national employment problems or, exceptionally, where the firm's disappearance would result in a monopoly or tight oligopolistic situation) and, where appropriate, there are adequate compensatory measures in favour of competitors.

3.2.2. Conditions for the authorisation of aid

(29) Subject to the special provisions for assisted areas, SMEs and the agricultural sector (see points 53, 54 and 55 and Chapter 5), the Commission will approve aid only under the following conditions:

(a) Eligibility of the firm

(30) The firm must qualify as a firm in difficulty within the meaning of these Guidelines (see points 4 to 8).

(b) Restoration of viability

(31) The grant of the aid is conditional on implementation of the restructuring plan which must be endorsed by the Commission in the case of all individual aid measures.

(32) The restructuring plan, the duration of which must be as short as possible, must restore the long-term viability of the firm within a reasonable timescale and on the basis of realistic assumptions as to future operating conditions. Restructuring aid must therefore be linked to a viable restructuring plan to which the Member State concerned commits itself. The plan must be submitted in all relevant

detail to the Commission and include, in particular, a market survey[19]. The improvement in viability must derive mainly from internal measures contained in the restructuring plan and may be based on external factors such as variations in prices and demand over which the company has no great influence if the market assumptions made are generally acknowledged. Restructuring must involve the abandonment of activities which would remain structurally loss-making even after restructuring.

(33) The restructuring plan should describe the circumstances that led to the company's difficulties, thereby providing a basis for assessing whether the proposed measures are appropriate. It should take account, *inter alia*, of the present state of and future prospects for supply and demand on the relevant product market, with scenarios reflecting best-case, worst-case and intermediate assumptions and the firm's specific strengths and weaknesses. It should enable the firm to progress towards a new structure that offers it prospects for long-term viability and enables it to stand on its own feet.

(34) The plan should provide for a turnaround that will enable the company, after completing its restructuring, to cover all its costs including depreciation and financial charges. The expected return on capital should be enough to enable the restructured firm to compete in the marketplace on its own merits.

(c) Avoidance of undue distortions of competition

(35) Measures must be taken to mitigate as far as possible any adverse effects of the aid on competitors. Otherwise, the aid should be regarded as 'contrary to the common interest' and therefore incompatible with the common market.

(36) This condition usually takes the form of a limitation on the presence which the company can enjoy on its market or markets after the end of the restructuring period.

Where the size of the relevant market(s)[20] is negligible at Community and at EEA level, or the firm's share of the relevant market(s) is negligible it should be considered that there is no undue distortion of competition. This condition should accordingly be regarded as not normally applying to small or medium-sized enterprises, except where otherwise provided by rules on State aid in a particular sector.

(37) The compulsory limitation or reduction of the company's presence on the relevant market(s) represents a compensatory factor in favour of its competitors. It should be in proportion to the distortive effects of the aid and, in particular, to the relative importance of the firm on its market or markets. The Commission will determine the extent of the limitation or reduction on the basis of the market survey attached to their structuring plan and, where the procedure has been initiated, on the basis of information supplied by interested parties. The reduction in the firm's presence is to be put into effect through the restructuring plan and any conditions attached thereto.

(38) A relaxation of the need for compensatory measures may be contemplated if such a reduction or limitation is likely to cause a manifest deterioration in the structure of the market, for example by having the indirect effect of creating a monopoly or a tight oligopolistic situation.

19 The items of information which the Commission needs in order to examine the aid satisfactorily are listed in Annex I.

20 As defined in point 7.6 of the multisectoral framework on regional aid for large investment projects (OJ C 107, 7.4.1998, p. 7): 'The relevant product market(s) for determining market share comprises the products envisaged by the investment project and, where appropriate, its substitutes considered by the consumer (by reason of the products' characteristics, their prices and their intended use) or by the producer (through flexibility of the production installations). The relevant geographic market comprises usually the EEA or, alternatively, any significant part of it if the conditions of competition in that area can be sufficiently distinguished from other areas of the EEA. Where appropriate the relevant market(s) may be considered to be global'. A footnote states that, where the investment concerns the production of intermediate goods, the relevant market may be the market for the final product if most of the production is not sold on the open market.

(39) Compensatory measures can take different forms according to whether or not the firm is operating in a market where there is excess capacity. In assessing whether or not there is excess capacity on a given market, the Commission can take into account all the relevant data in its possession:

(i)   where there is a Community-wide or EEA-wide structural excess of production capacity in a market served by the recipient, the restructuring plan must make a contribution, in proportion to the amount of aid received and its impact on that market, to the improvement of market conditions by irreversibly reducing production capacity. A capacity reduction is irreversible when the relevant assets are rendered permanently incapable of achieving the previous rate of output, or are permanently converted to another use. The sale of capacity to competitors is not sufficient in this case, except if the plant is sold for use in a geographic market in which its continued operation is unlikely to have significant effects on the competitive situation in the Community. The capacity reduction requirements must contribute to a reduction in the recipient's firm's presence on its market or markets;

(ii) where, on the other hand, there is no Community-wide or EEA-wide structural excess of production capacity in a market served by the recipient, the Commission will nevertheless examine whether compensatory measures should be required. Where any such compensatory measures involve a reduction in the capacity of the firm concerned, the necessary reduction could be achieved through the hiving-off of assets or subsidiaries. The Commission will have to examine the compensatory measures proposed by the Member State concerned, whatever form they take, and determine whether they are sufficient in scope to mitigate the potentially distortive effects of the aid on competition. In examining the necessary compensatory measures, the Commission will take account of the state of the market, and in particular its level of growth and the extent to which demand is met.

(d) Aid limited to the minimum

(40) The amount and intensity of the aid must be limited to the strict minimum needed to enable restructuring to be undertaken in the light of the existing financial resources of the company, its shareholders or the business group to which it belongs. Aid beneficiaries will be expected to make a significant contribution to the restructuring plan from their own resources, including through the sale of assets that are not essential to the firm's survival, or from external financing at market conditions. To limit the distortive effect, the amount of the aid or the form in which the aid is granted must be such as to avoid providing the company with surplus cash which could be used for aggressive, market-distorting activities not linked to the restructuring process. The Commission will accordingly examine the level of the firm's liabilities after restructuring, including the situation after any postponement or reduction of its debts, particularly in the context of its continuation in business following collective insolvency proceedings brought against it under national law[21]. Neither should any of the aid go to finance new investment that is not essential for restoring the firm's viability.

(41) In any event, it must be demonstrated to the Commission that the aid will be used only for the purpose of restoring the firm's viability and that it will not enable the recipient during the implementation of the restructuring plan to expand production capacity, except in so far as this is essential for restoring viability without unduly distorting competition.

(e) Specific conditions attached to the authorisation of aid

(42) In addition to the compensatory measures described in points 35 to 39, and in the event that such provisions have not been adopted by the Member State concerned, the Commission may impose any conditions and obligations it considers necessary in order to ensure that the aid does not distort competition to an extent contrary to the common interest. For example, it may require the Member State:

21 See the third paragraph of point 6.

(i)   to take certain measures itself (e.g. to open up certain markets to other Community operators);

(ii) to impose certain obligations on the recipient firm (e.g. to refrain from acting as price leader on certain markets);

(iii) to refrain from granting other types of aid to the recipient firm during the restructuring period.

(f) Full implementation of restructuring plan and observance of conditions

(43) The company must fully implement the restructuring plan that has been accepted by the Commission and must discharge any other obligations laid down in the Commission Decision. The Commission will regard any failure to implement the plan or to fulfil the other obligations as misuse of the aid.

(44) Where restructuring operations cover several years and involve substantial amounts of aid, the Commission may require payment of the restructuring aid to be split into instalments and may make payment of each instalment, subject to:

(i)   confirmation, prior to each payment, of the satisfactory implementation of each stage in the restructuring plan, in accordance with the planned timetable; or

(ii) its approval, prior to each payment, after verification that the plan is being satisfactorily implemented.

(g) Monitoring and annual report

(45) The Commission must be put in a position to make certain that the restructuring plan is being implemented properly, through detailed regular reports communicated by the Member State concerned.

(46) In the case of aid to large firms, the first of these reports will normally have to be submitted to the Commission not later than six months after approval of the aid. Reports will subsequently have to be sent to the Commission at least once a year, at a fixed date, until the objectives of the restructuring plan can be deemed to have been achieved. They must contain all the information the Commission needs in order to be able to monitor the implementation of the restructuring pro-gramme, the timetable for payments to the company and its financial position and the observance of any conditions or obligations laid down in the decision approving the aid. They must in particular include all relevant information on any aid for any purpose which the company has received, either on an individual basis or under a general scheme, during the restructuring period (see points 90 to 93). Where the Commission needs timely confirmation of certain key items of information, e.g. on closures or capacity reductions, it may require more frequent reports.

(47) In the case of aid to small or medium-sized enterprises, transmission each year of a copy of the recipient firm's balance sheet and profit and loss account will normally be sufficient, except where stricter conditions have been laid down in the decision approving the aid.

3.2.3. 'One time, last time' condition

(48) In order to prevent firms from being unfairly assisted, restructuring aid should be granted once only. When planned restructuring aid is notified to the Commission, the Member State must specify whether the firm concerned has in the past already received restructuring aid, including aid granted before entry into force of these Guidelines and any unnotified aid[22]. If so, and where less than 10 years has elapsed since the restructuring period came to an end[23] or implementation of the

---

22 With regard to unnotified aid, the Commission will take account in its analysis of the possibility that the aid could have been declared compatible with the common market other than as restructuring aid.

23 Unless otherwise specified, the restructuring period will normally come to an end when the deadline for implementation of the various measures provided for in the restructuring plan expires (see the sixth indent in point IV of Annex I).

plan has been halted, the Commission will normally[24] allow further restructuring aid only in exceptional and unforeseeable circumstances for which the company is not responsible[25]. An unforeseeable circumstance is one which could in no way be anticipated when the restructuring plan was drawn up.

NOTE: Rescue aid is intended to provide temporary respite from financial problems in order for a longer-term solution to be determined. Restructuring is intended to restore the long-term viability of the undertaking. These guidelines revised the earlier 1994 guidelines, OJ C368/05, 1994 but it should be noted that there are specific policies for certain sectors including agriculture, fisheries and steel.

The following is an example of a decision taken by the Commission in respect of proposed restructuring aid.

Sabena Commission Decision
(91/555/EC) OJ L300/49, 1991

THE COMMISSION OF THE EUROPEAN COMMUNITIES,

Having regard to the Treaty establishing the European Economic Community, and in particular the first subparagraph of Article 93(2) thereof,

Having given notice to the parties concerned to submit their comments as provided for in Article 93,

Whereas,

I

By letter of 5 April 1991 the Belgian Government, in conformity with Article 93(3) of the EEC Treaty, notified the Commission of its intention to grant aid to Sabena.

According to this notification the Belgian Government intends to support the restructuring of the Belgian air carrier Sabena with a package of measures including:

— a transfer of Bfrs 16.2 billion into Sabena's capital which had been granted by the State over the period 1949 to 1981,
— a capital increase of Bfrs 10 billion by subscription of shares and immediate payment,
— a capital reduction with cancellation of ordinary shares held by the Belgian State amounting to Bfrs 30.2 billion and made up of:

— wiping out losses of Bfrs 22.6 billion,
— provision for restructuring Bfrs 7.6 billion.

Furthermore, the Belgian Government intends to inject an additional amount of Bfrs 9 billion in the context of a second stage of recapitalization. It is foreseen that new industrial partners and private Belgian shareholders will contribute with an amount of Bfrs 10 billion to the completion of the

---

24 Given the degree of liberalisation and specific features of each sector, two situations should be noted:
— in the air transport sector, entirely liberalised since 1997, the Commission will apply the 'one time, last time' principle within the limits and conditions of the guidelines on State aid in the aviation sector.
— in other sectors, if the effects of the liberalisation of Community markets that were previously closed to competition have created new economic conditions, derogations may be considered.

25 For the purposes of this paragraph, aid granted before 1 January 1996 to enterprises in the former GDR and declared compatible with the common market by the Commission is not taken into account. In addition, the paragraph does not apply to cases of aid to such enterprises notified before 31 December 2000. However, the Commission considers that restructuring aid should normally only need to be granted once and will examine such cases in the light of this principle.

recapitalization programme. After the completion of this recapitalization programme, it is foreseen that Sabena will have the following ownership structure:

— Belgian State:	26.7 %
— Belgian shareholders:	26.7 %
— Industrial partners:	40.0 %
— Staff:	6.0 %

The Belgian Government has also announced its intention to base its participation in restructuring Sabena on the double condition that the company:

— is commercially viable in future,
— finds a reliable industrial partner (airline) for future cooperation.

The Belgian Government has furthermore informed the Commission of Sabena's intention to reduce its permanent staff from 12,180 in 1991 to about 9,000 towards the end of 1993.

II

On the basis of the information in the notification, the Commission carried out an assessment of the compatibility of these measures with Article 92 of the EEC Treaty. This led to the conclusion that, at that stage, the aid measures were not compatible with the common market and could not, on the basis of the available information, qualify for one of the exceptions set out in Article 92(2) and (3).

This preliminary conclusion of the Commission was mainly based on a lack of sufficient guarantees with regard to the one-off character of this operation, doubts on the commercial viability of the restructuring concept, a lack of clarity regarding the conditions to be accepted by the companies concerned and the substance of new company statutes. Finally, the Commission felt that the Belgian Government had not given sufficient assurances that no other measure would be established or maintained in order to favour Sabena in relation to other companies established in or being active to and from Belgium.

Accordingly, the Commission decided on 8 May 1991 to initiate the Article 93(2) procedure. The Belgian Government was informed by letter dated 13 May 1991. The notice was published in the *Official Journal of the European Communities*[1]. Interested parties were invited to present their observations within one month of the publication date.

III

By letter dated 5 June 1991 the Belgian Government presented its observations on the Commission's decision to initiate the official examination procedure as laid down in Article 93(2) of the EEC Treaty.

In this letter the Belgian Government specifically confirmed the one-off character of the proposed measures and confirmed its intention to abstain from granting any further aid in favour of Sabena. The Belgian Government reiterated its two-step approach aiming, during the first phase, at deleting debts and other commitments accumulated during the past and, during the second phase, at improving the financial structure of the company. The Belgian Government explicitly confirmed that the Belgian State will not participate in any capital increase for the second phase if Sabena fails to find an industrial partner (i.e. another airline) willing to take a financial share.

In this letter the Belgian Government reiterated its intention to establish a new company statute based on private commercial law. However, details of this new statute were not given. In addition, the Belgian Government, in its initial reaction, failed to outline in full detail the financial arrangements with other existing shareholders and the proposed new shareholders including an airline partner, and to give precise information on the latest economic and financial developments which is essential to carrying out a realistic assessment of the company's current financial standing. Furthermore, the Belgian Government did not comment explicitly on the Commission's request not to maintain or to

1 OJ No C 138, 29. 5. 1991, p. 3.

introduce other new measures with the effect of favouring Sabena in relation to other carriers operating to and from Belgium. Finally, the Belgian Government announced its intention to provide more detailed confidential information.

In view of these outstanding questions, a meeting with representatives of the Belgian authorities took place on 4 July 1991.

At this meeting, clarifying a number of questions related to the financial arrangements, it became evident that arrangements with new private partners, including an airline partner have not yet been finally concluded.

In the context of negotiations with potential investors the substance of a new company statute does play a major role. The Belgian authorities committed themselves to make the full text available to the Commission immediately after the completion of these negotiations.

The representatives also confirmed that the State-held shares (*actions privilégiées*) will be transformed into normal capital during the first phase of the restructuring programme. The other shares, however, will continue to enjoy a special status (*actions préférentielles*) including a guaranteed dividend until the end of 1995. Until that date, these shareholders will have the option to return the shares to the State or to accept their conversion into normal risk capital.

Existing shareholders agreed to accept a reduction of the level of the guaranteed dividend from 10 to 8 per cent, i.e. from Bfrs 50 per share to Bfrs 40. This will in practice mean that the company will, irrespective of its financial situation, have to pay guaranteed dividends totalling Bfrs 1.3 billion during the restructuring programme, i.e. between 1992 and 1995. Other existing financial guarantees will, however, be phased out immediately.

The Belgian authorities stressed their view that no other measures apart from the proposed State aid, which favour Sabena in relation to other air carriers operating to and from Belgium, exist nor are envisaged. They specifically contested the view that exclusive rights in the area of ground handling at Zaventem airport and catering represent a privileged treatment.

The Belgian authorities also underlined that the aeronautical authorities are already going beyond Community requirements when designating other air carriers to scheduled flights inside the Community.

By letter dated 9 July 1991 the Belgian Government gave written explanations and clarifications on these points, including an update of the latest financial development and the most recent operational results.

Following the publication in the Official Journal, two other air carriers, an airline association, a consumer organization and two Member States presented their observations.

IV

In view of the accumulated debts and the costs of the restructuring programme, no investor apart from the State would at present be prepared to take part in the restructuring programme of Sabena. Therefore, the proposals notified by the Belgian Government have to be considered as State aid within the meaning of Article 92(1) of the EEC Treaty.

The setting up of a common aviation market by gradually phasing out bilateral restrictions on market access and capacity sharing and by relaxing rules on air fares has increased potential competition on many of the routes incorporated in Sabena's network. This trend should continue in the years to come. Consequently the aid to Sabena distorts or threatens to distort competition between this airline and other air carriers in the Community.

Article 92(3) of the Treaty specifies the types of aid which may be considered to be compatible with the common market. Such compatibility must be determined in the context of the Community and not of a single Member State. Article 92(3) provides for exceptions from the principle set out in Article 92(1): but in order to ensure that the common market functions properly, and in the light of Article 3(f) of the Treaty, those exceptions must be strictly construed when an aid scheme or a particular application of such exceptions is being examined.

In particular, those exceptions are applicable only in cases where the Commission is able to establish that, without the aid, market forces alone would not be sufficient to persuade the future recipient of aid to act in such a way as to help achieve one of the objectives of those exceptions.

Article 92(3)(a) and (c) provides for exceptions in respect of aid to promote or facilitate the development of certain regions. The proposed aid scheme, however, does not qualify for the exceptions provided for in Article 92(3)(a) since, in Belgium, the standard of living is not abnormally low nor is there serious underemployment. Nor can the aid scheme be described as intended 'to facilitate the development . . . of certain economic areas' (Article 92(3)(c)), since it does not serve the purposes of any earlier investment or of job creation as is stipulated in the Commission's 1979 communication on regional aid systems[1]. In any case, the Belgian Government has put forward no regional arguments in support of the proposed aid.

As for Article 92(3)(b), the evidence suggests that the aid in question was not intended to promote the execution of an important project of common European interest nor to remedy a serious disturbance in the Belgian economy. Moreover, the Belgian Government has not invoked this.

With regard to the exception under Article 92(3)(c) for 'aid to facilitate the development of certain economic activitites', the Commission may consider some restructuring aid as compatible with the common market if it meets a number of conditions[2]. These conditions must be seen in the context of the two principles enunciated in Article 92(3)(c)—i.e. that the aid must be required for developing the activity from the standpoint of the Community and that the aid may not adversely affect trading conditions to an extent contrary to the common interest[3].

These criteria have been interpreted in a sectoral (aviation) context in Memorandum No 2 which stipulates that the Commission may in certain cases decide in accordance with Article 92 that aid may be granted to individual airlines which have serious financial difficulties, provided certain conditions are met:

(a) The aid must form part of a programme, to be approved by the Commission, to restore the airline's health, so that it can, within a reasonably short period, be expected to operate viably without further aid. Thus the aid must be of limited duration. If the restoration of financial viability requires capacity reductions, this would be included in the programme. Any alterations in the programme would also have to be approved by the Commission. Naturally any proposed changes to the aid would also have to be notified to the Commission.

(b) The aid in question must not transfer the difficulties from that Member State to the rest of the Community.

(c) Any such aid must be structured so that it is transparent and can be verified.

In the case of Sabena it must at first be concluded that the company is, if assessed by normal commercial standards, in a difficult financial position. On the basis of the latest figures submitted on 9 July 1991 by the Belgian Government, the debt-equity ratio of about 4:1 is, against normal standards of the airline industry, very poor. The operations of the airline (Sabena World Airlines) led in 1990 to a net loss of Bfrs 7,462 billion on a total turnover of Bfrs 42,055 billion. Additional losses totalling Bfrs 259 million have been suffered by the subsidiaries Sabena Catering and Sabena Technics.

This weak financial situation results from various reasons among which low labour productivity and high personnel costs have played a major role.

In the short run the crucial point for Sabena will be, on the one hand, to make full use of the market potential Brussels offers and, on the other hand, to keep cost factors under control.

---

1 OJ No C 31, 3. 2. 1979, p. 9.

2 Eighth report on competition policy, point 176.

3 See the Judgment of the Court of Justice of 17 September 1980 in Case No 730/79—*Philip Morris*—[1980] ECR, p. 2671.

The intention of the air carrier Sabena to reduce the staff by 29 per cent and the willingness of the Belgian State to compensate for the cost of these lay-offs can be seen, under these circumstances, as important steps for regaining commercial viability.

In addition, the Government's request to develop a new commercially-oriented company statute and to increase substantially the share of private risk capital suggests a political willingness to restrict the role of the State to that of a normal shareholder and to abstain from (potentially cost-increasing) interventions for other than commercial reasons.

However, the contents of Sabena's new company statute must be clarified.

The fact that the decisions on the company's new statutes have yet to be taken has to be considered as an uncertainty in relation to the company's and the Belgian State's effective commitment to put the company on a genuine commercial footing and to solve, thereby, one of the most important underlying reasons for the developments during the past. Any decision of the Commission approving the measures must, therefore, be linked to the modification of the company statutes of Sabena.

It is also essential to ensure that new shareholders do not enjoy privileges and guarantees. Such guarantees could only be taken as a lack of confidence on behalf of private investors in the possibility of re-establishing long-term viability. Since arrangements with new shareholders have yet to be concluded, approval by the Commission would necessitate checking the Belgian State's commitment in this field. Only the provision of genuine risk capital sufficiently indicates the commercial viability of the restructuring concept. It is, therefore, necessary to oblige the Belgian Government to report regularly on the substance of decisions taken in this context.

The aid in question must be granted degressively and be clearly linked to the restructuring process.

The two-step approach envisaged by the Belgian Government can be seen as some form of degressive support. The Belgian Government has committed itself in a sufficiently clear way not to go ahead with the second capital injection of Bfrs 9 billion if an airline partner has not been found and if private shareholders will not contribute at least Bfrs 10 billion to Sabena's restructuring process. Major private investments following a massive 'clean-up' of the burden resulting from the past can be seen as ensuring the degressive nature of the whole operation.

The intensity of the aid must be reasonably related to the size of the underlying problems in order to keep possible distortions of competition to a minimum.

The question whether the proposed support for Sabena will go beyond the level required for the purpose of restoring the company, needs to be assessed in a broader context taking into account the aeropolitical environment.

The Belgian Government has, in the past, taken cautious steps to open up the Belgian market and to grant, to a limited extent and only on an individual case-by-case basis, licences for scheduled air transport to other carriers, namely to TEA.

The question whether the proposed aid amounts exceed the level required for achieving the objectives of the restructuring process also depends on the use of the additional funds.

The business plans presented by the company concerned indicate that these resources will largely be used for two purposes.

Firstly for writing off accumulated debts. Between 1984 and 1990 financial debt had increased from Bfrs 17 to 43 billion. The corresponding poor debt-equity ratio will be improved in order to re-establish commercial viability.

Secondly, resources will be used to fulfil modernization needs. The fleet modernization will require investments amounting to Bfrs 46,250 billion until 1995. The new equipment is required in order to lower operating costs and to comply with stricter noise emission rules as established by Community legislation.

These investments will not increase the capacities offered by Sabena. The restructuring of Sabena's network towards profitable routes will initially lead to a reduction of the capacities measured as available ton-kilometres (ATK) from nearly 2,000 million in 1990 to about 1,300 million ATKs in 1993. Afterwards an increase in line with the overall development of traffic volume is expected.

However, the aid could at the end of the restructuring process eventually lead to improving Sabena's financial standing (i.e. debts-equity ratios) above levels actually achievable by some of Sabena's competitors.

Information made available to the Commission suggests that the Belgian authorities and the company concerned envisage a debt-equity ratio of about 1:25 as an objective to be achieved by the end of the recapitalization process.

In a normal micro-economic and sectorial environment this level can be considered as indicating a well-balanced financial situation in line with standards of the industry.

At present however, certain Community air carriers have, due to the general difficult situation of the aviation industry, a less sound financial structure.

Under these circumstances the financial support is justifiable only under the condition that the Belgian Government commits itself to avoid all forms of privileged treatment in areas determining the competitiveness of companies operating to and from Belgium.

V

In the light of the foregoing, the Commission considers that the exception laid down in Article 92(3) (c) of the EEC Treaty can be applied to the aid measures proposed by the Belgian Government for supporting the restructuring programme of the air carrier Sabena if a number of conditions are fulfilled in order to ensure that the aid does not adversely affect trading conditions to an extent contrary to the common interest.

NOTE: This emphasises the requirement for a viable restructuring plan. The need for submission of a credible restructuring plan, particularly regarding the recipient's long-term profitability, was emphasised by the Court in Case C-17/99 *France* v *Commission*, 22 March 2001. There had been criticism in the past that the Commission had approved aid on this basis to the same company on more than one occasion, for instance in relation to financial assistance given to Air France. See e.g. Commission Decision (94/653/EC) OJ L254/73, 1994. The new guidelines are tighter and seek to restrict the amount of aid given for these purposes. In particular the 'one time, last time' rule is stricter and the rules on eligibility as firms in difficulty excludes new firms.

(c) *Procedure and remedies*

The state aid rules are principally enforced by the Commission but the enforcement mechanisms are different from those under Articles 81 and 82 EC. Until recently there was no equivalent of Regulation 17/62 in relation to the state aid rules. In order to enhance transparency and legal certainty, the Commission has used its powers under Article 89 EC to introduce Regulation 659/99 to codify and modify existing practice in relation to the enforcement of the state aid rules, Council Regulation 659/99/EC laying down detailed rules for the application of Article 93 of the EC Treaty, OJ L83/1, 1999.

Sinnaeve, A., and Slot, P.J., 'The New Regulation on State Aid Procedures'
36 (1999) CMLRev, 1153 at 1153–1157

1. Introduction: the context and objectives of the procedural regulation
On 22 March 1999, the Council adopted a 'Regulation laying down detailed rules for the application of Article 93 of the Treaty'. This Regulation is long overdue as, in 40 years of State aid policy, the procedural rules had never been codified. While in the anti-trust field, the implementation of Articles

81 and 82 (ex 85 and 86) of the EC Treaty, had taken place very early with Regulation no 17/62 and subsequent rules, Articles 87 and 88 (ex 92 and 93) had, until recently, not been properly implemented by means of a regulation adopted by the Council on the basis of Article 89 (ex 94) EC.

The Commission's past reluctance to use Article 89 was mainly due to the experiences which it had had at the end of the 1960s and the beginning of the 1970s. At that time, two proposals for regulations based on Article 89 were made, but neither of them led to a regulation. This negative experience left the Commission with a profound scepticism about the expediency of making proposals on the basis of Article 89. There was indeed a risk that once a proposal was submitted to the Council it would be out of the Commission's control, and the very wide powers which the Treaty conferred upon the Commission would be reduced. Apart from the risks involved, the Commission considered that there was no direct need for regulations, since the necessary rules for State aid law could be developed and clarified through soft law and case law.

The turning point in the unsuccessful history of Article 89 EC came in the middle of the 1990s, when the Commission launched a broad reform project for the modernization of State aid control. The reform proposed by the Commission aimed to increase transparency and legal certainty in the State aid field and to make the control system more efficient, in particular, by the introduction of block exemptions and the codification of procedural rules. For the implementation of the Commission's reform plans, regulations on the basis of Article 89 were no longer excluded since they appeared to be the most appropriate instrument to achieve the objectives. Moreover, the Commission's previous hesitancy regarding Article 89 had diminished over the years, as the circumstances and the general environment had changed since the first proposals were made. The Commission, supported by the Court, had meanwhile fully established its State aid policy and felt more confident about the general acceptance of its powers by Member States. If the reform was to be carried out, there had to be recourse to Article 89. Finally, some developments in the case law of the Court, and in particular the *Sytraval* judgment of the CFI seem to have given a direct impulse to the Commission's plans regarding a procedural regulation. Rather than waiting until the Courts changed the procedural framework, the Commission preferred to take the initiative itself. This set of reasons explains the change in the Commission's policy with regard to Article 89.

The Regulation was formally adopted by the Council on 22 March 1999, and entered into force on 16 April 1999.

The first objective of the Regulation was to integrate the procedural rules into one coherent and binding legal text. In the absence of a regulation, those rules had been developed over the years through the case law of the Court of Justice and the Commission's practice. Where important procedural issues had arisen or needed to be clarified, the Commission had also issued notices and communications, normally published in the Official Journal. These had provided some clarification, but from a legal point of view, they had contained no more than an interpretation by the Commission of certain procedural questions and did not provide legal certainty. Moreover, the piecemeal fashion in which procedures developed gradually resulted in a fragmentation of rules, which had reduced the clarity of the system provided for in the Treaty. A codification was necessary.

The second and equally important objective of the procedural Regulation was to strengthen the control of aid. Where aspects of the existing system could be considered as hampering the proper functioning and effective enforcement of the rules, the efficiency of the procedural system had to be reinforced, in particular with regard to unlawful aid and its recovery, and in relation to the monitoring of Commission decisions. The Regulation thus also sought to expand the system with some new instruments and to tighten the rules on those points where the current system was not entirely satisfactory.

2. The structure of the regulation and the basic concepts of State aid procedures

2.1. *The structure of the procedural Regulation: four different procedures*
The Regulation provides for four different procedures (chapters II–IV, Regulation) according to the

type of State aid involved: a procedure for notified aid . . . , for unlawful aid . . . for misuse of aid . . . and for existing aid schemes. . . . A definition of these concepts can be found in chapter I of the Regulation. The qualification of aid as notified, unlawful, misused or existing is of utmost importance, since it determines which chapter of the Regulation applies. Each procedure is only subject to the rules of the relevant chapter, except where cross-references to other chapters are made. The number of cross-references increases the complexity of the Regulation, but it avoids unnecessary repetitions and ensures coherence. In view of the basic obligation to notify every new aid to the Commission, the main procedure is that regarding notified aid. It sets out a two-phase procedure for the examination of notified aid, based on Article 88(2) and (3) EC as developed by the Court and reinforced by new rules. The procedure for unlawful aid only defines those rules which differ from the rules for notified aid and adds a cross-reference to the applicable articles contained in the chapter on notified aid. The content of most of the provisions in this chapter is derived from the case law of the Courts. Some new provisions are designed to increase the efficiency of State aid control. Chapter IV of the Regulation on misuse of aid is limited to one article since it is largely based on the chapter regarding unlawful aid. Chapter V mainly codifies the procedure for existing aid as it is foreseen by Article 87(1) EC and has been applied by the Commission for a long time.

NOTE: The main aspect of the legislation concerns the requirement to notify new aid and the subsequent procedure involved. The Regulation gives the Commission powers to monitor and supervise the state aid rules and also introduces a new power under Article 22 to undertake site inspections in relation to its state aid duties. For a fuller discussion of the impact of the Regulation see Sinnaeve and Slot *op. cit.*

(d) *Notification of new aid*

Article 88(3) EC of the Treaty provides:

Article 88(3) EC

3. The Commission shall be informed, in sufficient time to enable it to submit its comments, of any plans to grant or alter aid. If it considers that any such plan is not compatible with the common market having regard to Article 87, it shall without delay initiate the procedure provided for in paragraph 2. The Member State concerned shall not put its proposed measures into effect until this procedure has resulted in a final decision.

NOTE: This is known as the 'standstill' provision and provides that aid cannot be paid until notified and approved by the Commission under Article 88(2) EC. The notification requirement has been codified in Article 2(1) of Regulation 659/99. The Regulation provides no definition of state aid and one is referred back to Article 87(1) EC and the existing body of Court jurisprudence. Notification is not required where the aid is *de minimis* or if it is existing aid already authorised and not exceeded by 20 per cent. The Regulation codifies existing Commission practice in relation to its decision making by providing for a preliminary examination phase and a formal investigation procedure in accordance with Article 88(2) EC of the Treaty (*per* Article 6). See Sinnaeve and Slot *op. cit.* for a fuller discussion. The recipient of state aid which is subject to a Commission decision has standing to bring an action under Article 230 EC challenging the Commission decision. See Case 332/82 *Intermills* v *Commission* [1984] ECR 3809, [1986] 1 CMLR 614.

Aid which has been implemented prior to notification and approval by the Commission is known as unlawful or illegal aid. What are the consequences of the grant of unlawful legal aid? This question was examined in the following case:

France v *Commission ('Boussac')*
(Case C-301/87) [1990] ECR I-307, paras 9–19

The French Government sought annulment of a Commission decision on aid granted to a producer of textiles, clothing and paper products—Boussac Saint Freres. The financial assistance was provided without prior notification to and approval by the Commission. The Commission found that it had not been notified in advance of plans to grant the aid and for that reason considered it to be unlawful.

[9] It is necessary, as a preliminary point, to consider a problem raised by the Commission. It takes the view that, since the Court has already recognized the direct effect of the final sentence of Article 93(3) of the Treaty, a clear, binding provision involving public policy, failure to comply with that provision is in itself sufficient to render that aid unlawful. Such illegality, it contends, makes it unnecessary to examine the matter in detail and entitles the Commission to order recovery of the aid. For that reason, the Commission believes that the Court should refuse to entertain the objections raised by the French Government against that part of the contested decision in which the Commission concludes that the aid in question is incompatible with Article 92 of the Treaty.

[10] The French Government contends that a possible failure to comply with the procedural rules in Article 93(3) of the Treaty cannot by itself render the financial assistance illegal and justify recovery of the aid. The Commission ought, in any case, to have carried out a detailed examination of the disputed contributions.

[11] It must be observed that each of these two arguments is liable to give rise to major practical difficulties. On the one hand, the argument put forward by the Commission implies that aid which is compatible with the common market may be declared unlawful because of procedural irregularities. On the other hand, it is not possible to accept the French Government's argument to the effect that the Commission, when faced with aid which has been granted or altered by a Member State in breach of the procedure laid down in Article 93(3) of the Treaty, has only the same rights and obligations as those which it has in the case of aid duly notified at the planning stage. Such an interpretation would in effect encourage the Member State concerned not to comply with Article 93(3) and would deprive that paragraph of its effectiveness.

[12] In the light of those arguments, it is necessary to examine the problem by analysing the powers and responsibilities which the Commission and the Member States have in cases where aid has been granted or altered.

[13] In the first place, it should be noted that Articles 92, 93 and 94, which form part of Section 3 of the Treaty entitled 'Aids granted by States', lay down procedures which imply that the Commission is in a position to determine, on the basis of the material at its disposal, whether the disputed financial assistance constitutes aid within the meaning of those articles.

[14] Secondly, it should be noted that the Council has not as yet adopted any recommendation under Article 94 of the Treaty for the application of Articles 92 and 93 thereof.

[15] Furthermore, it is necessary to bear in mind the established case-law of the Court. In its judgment of 22 March 1977 in Case 78/76 *Steinike und Weinlig* v *Germany* [1977] ECR 595, the Court held that the prohibition contained in Article 92(1) of the Treaty is neither absolute nor unconditional, since paragraph (3) in particular of that article confers on the Commission a wide discretion to admit aid by way of derogation from the general prohibition in Article 92(1). The assessment in such cases of whether a State aid is or is not compatible with the common market raises problems which presuppose the examination and appraisal of economic facts and conditions which may be both complex and liable to change rapidly.

[16] That was the reason for which the Treaty provided in Article 93 for a special procedure under which the Commission would monitor aid schemes and keep them under constant review. With regard to new aid which Member States might be intending to grant, a preliminary procedure was established; if this procedure was not followed, the aid could not be regarded as having been properly granted. By providing under Article 93 for the Commission to monitor and keep under constant review all aid schemes, the Treaty intended that any finding that aid might be incompatible with the common market should, subject to review by the Court, be the outcome of an appropriate procedure for the implementation of which the Commission was responsible.

[17] The Court has also held (see the judgment of 9 October 1984 in Joined Cases 91/83 and 127/83 *Heineken Brouwerijen BV v Inspecteurs der Vennootschapsbelasting, Amsterdam and Utrecht* [1984] ECR 3435) that the purpose of the first sentence of Article 93(3) of the Treaty is to provide the Commission with the opportunity to review, in sufficient time and in the general interest of the Communities, any plan to grant or alter aid. The final sentence of Article 93(3) of the Treaty constitutes the means of safeguarding the machinery for review laid down by that article, which, in turn, is essential for ensuring the proper functioning of the common market. The prohibition laid down in that article on putting any proposed measures into effect is designed to ensure that a system of aid cannot become operational before the Commission has had a reasonable period in which to study the proposed measures in detail and, if necessary, to initiate the procedure provided for in Article 93(2).

[18] In order for it to be effective, the system analysed above presupposes that measures may be taken to counteract any infringement of the rules laid down in Article 93(3) of the Treaty and that such measures may, with a view to protecting the legitimate interests of the Member States, form the subject of an action. With regard to this system, there can be no dispute as to the need to introduce conservatory measures in cases where the effect of practices engaged in by certain Member States with regard to aid is to render nugatory the system established by Articles 92 and 93 of the Treaty.

[19] Once it has established that aid has been granted or altered without notification, the Commission therefore has the power, after giving the Member State in question an opportunity to submit its comments on the matter, to issue an interim decision requiring it to suspend immediately the payment of such aid pending the outcome of the examination of the aid and to provide the Commission, within such period as it may specify, with all such documentation, information and data as are necessary in order that it may examine the compatibility of the aid with the common market.

NOTE: This emphasises the importance of notification of any proposed new aid schemes. The Regulation codifies existing powers to require information (Article 10(3)), order suspension of unlawful aid (Article 11(1)) and take provisional action (Article 11(2)). Article 14 confirms the Commission's powers to order recovery of aid except where it is contrary to a general principle of Community law, or recovery is beyond a ten-year limitation period. Earlier Court jurisprudence confirmed that recovery is only limited where it is impossible or would contravene the recipients' legitimate expectations.

Belgium v *Commission*
(Case 142/87) [1990] ECR I-959, [1991] 3 CMLR 213, paras 61–63

This was an application for annulment of a Commission decision that aid granted, in various forms, by the Belgian State to a steel pipe and tube manufacturer was illegal, and incompatible with the common market and ordering its recovery.

[61] In principle the recovery of aid unlawfully paid must take place in accordance with the relevant

procedural provisions of national law, subject however to the proviso that those provisions are to be applied in such a way that the recovery required by Community law is not rendered practically impossible (see the judgment of 2 February 1989 in Case 94/87 *Commission* v *Federal Republic of Germany* [1989] ECR 175).

[62] Moreover, that is the reason why the Commission stated at the hearing that the Belgian Government had fulfilled its obligations under the contested measure in regard to the recovery of the aid since, after the dismissal of its application for interim measures by the President of the Court, the Belgian Government sought to have its debt registered as one of Tubemeuse's unsecured liabilities and lodged an appeal against the judgment rejecting that application.

[63] It should be added that any procedural or other difficulties in regard to the implementation of the contested measure cannot have any influence on the lawfulness of the measure.

NOTE: This issue was confirmed again more recently in Case C–261/99 *France* v *Commission* [2001] ECR I-6557. The limitation based on 'legitimate expectations' is interpreted very strictly and is likely to be available only when the Commission was responsible for the recipient's 'legitimate expectations'. See Case 5/89 *Commission* v *Germany* [1990] ECR I-3437, [1992] 1 CMLR 117. Article 88(3) EC has direct effect and therefore an action may be raised before a national court which is required to take appropriate measures to ensure suspension and recovery of any unlawful/illegal aid. For an example in the UK, see *R* v *Customs and Excise Commissioners, ex parte Lunn Poly* [1998] 2 CMLR 560 (DC) in which judicial review of a Finance Act imposing differential taxes was successful.

(e) *Competitor remedies*

Regulation 659/99 gives competitors, who were aggrieved at the granting of state aid, certain rights in relation to the Commission investigation procedure.

Regulation 659/99, Article 20

Article 20: Rights of interested parties

1. Any interested party may submit comments pursuant to Article 6 following a Commission decision to initiate the formal investigation procedure. Any interested party which has submitted such comments and any beneficiary of individual aid shall be sent a copy of the decision taken by the Commission pursuant to Article 7.

2. Any interested party may inform the Commission of any alleged unlawful aid and any alleged misuse of aid. Where the Commission considers that on the basis of the information in its possession there are insufficient grounds for taking a view on the case, it shall inform the interested party thereof. Where the Commission takes a decision on a case concerning the subject matter of the information supplied, it shall send a copy of that decision to the interested party.

3. At its request, any interested party shall obtain a copy of any decision pursuant to Articles 4 and 7, Article 10(3) and Article 11.

NOTE: This provision largely codifies existing practice, see e.g. *Sytraval* v *Commission* (Case T-95/94) [1995] ECR II-2651, although it does not afford the same rights as aggrieved competitors in relation to Articles 81 EC and 82 EC.

Competitors can also take proceedings to the Court under Articles 230 EC and 232 EC in order to challenge a Commission decision approving a state aid measure or a failure to act upon a complaint. One potential problem under Article 230 EC is in determining whether a contested decision is of 'direct and individual concern' to the party. This was discussed by the Court of First Instance in:

British Airways and Others v *Commission*
(Joined Cases T-371/94 and T-394/94) [1998] ECR II-2405, para. 83

British Airways and others challenged a Commission decision to approve a plan by the French authorities to inject FF 20 billion into Air France on the basis that the plan could restore the economic and financial viability of Air France and a genuine restructuring would enhance the competitiveness of the European air industry.

[83] In these contentions, the applicants and the interveners supporting them claim that the Commission authorised aid in an amount exceeding the restructuring requirements of Air France. These contentions are based essentially on the judgment in *Philip Morris* v *Commission* (paragraph 17, cited above in paragraph 79), in which the Court of Justice ruled that Member States could not be permitted to make payments which would improve the financial situation of the recipient undertaking 'although they were not necessary for the attainment of the objectives specified in Article 92(3)'.

NOTE: The Court annulled the Commission decision on the basis of inadequate legal reasoning for approving Air France's purchase of 17 new aircraft, and for failing to analyse the competitive effect the subsidy would have on business on routes outside the EEA in satisfying the conditions of Article 87(3)(c) EC. In relation to the question of admissibility, redress under Article 232 EC is similarly not restricted to potential addressees of a decision. In *Gestevision Telecino SA* v *Commission* (Case T-95/96) [1998] ECR II-3407, the Court of First Instance noted, at para. 65, that redress could be sought by those 'whose interests might be affected by the grant of the aid, in particular competing undertakings and trade associations'. See also Case 323/82 *Intermills* v *Commission* [1984] ECR 3809, para. 16. Nonetheless, a works council and trade union representing the sector were not held to be individually concerned in Case C-106/98 *Comité d'entreprise de la Société française de production* v *Commission* [2000] ECR I-833.

As noted above, the notification obligation and standstill clause of Article 88(3) EC have direct effect and competitors may seek a decision in the national courts to prohibit the grant of illegal aid. In addition, where state aid is granted illegally, the Court has confirmed that individuals can seek redress in the national courts.

Syndicat Francais de l'Express International v *La Poste ('La Poste')*
(Case C-39/94) [1996] ECR I-3547, [1996] 3 CMLR 369, paras 72–76

SFEI and other companies brought an action before the Tribunal de Commerce, Paris, on 16 June 1993 against the Post Office and other parties. They sought a declaration that the logistical and commercial assistance afforded by the Post Office to other parties constituted state aid and had been implemented without prior notification to the Commission. They sought an order *inter alia* seeking repayment of state aids and also claimed damages of FF 216 million from the defendants.

[72] By its third and fourth questions, the national court asks in essence whether the recipient of aid who does not verify that the aid has been notified to the Commission in accordance with Article 93(3) of the Treaty may incur liability on the basis of Community law.

[73] The machinery for reviewing and examining State aids established by Article 93 of the Treaty does not impose any specific obligation on the recipient of aid. First, the notification requirement and the prior prohibition on implementing planned aid laid down in Article 93(3) are directed to the Member State. Second, the Member State is also the addressee of the decision by which the

Commission finds that aid is incompatible with the common market and requests the Member State to abolish the aid within the period determined by the Commission.

[74] That being so, Community law does not provide a sufficient basis for the recipient to incur liability where he has failed to verify that the aid received was duly notified to the Commission.

[75] That does not, however, prejudice the possible application of national law concerning non-contractual liability. If, according to national law, the acceptance by an economic operator of unlawful assistance of a nature such as to occasion damage to other economic operators may in certain circumstances cause him to incur liability, the principle of non-discrimination may lead the national court to find the recipient of aid paid in breach of Article 93(3) of the Treaty liable.

[76] In the light of the foregoing considerations, the answer to the third and fourth questions must be that a recipient of aid who does not verify that the aid has been notified to the Commission in accordance with Article 93(3) of the Treaty cannot incur liability solely on the basis of Community law.

NOTE: This case confirmed that damages may be sought from the relevant State on the basis of the non-contractual liability of Member States for breaches of Community law. See, for example, Case 46/93 *Brasserie du Pêcheur SA-Factortame III* [1996] ECR I-1029, [1996] 1 CMLR 889 and Hernandez, A.G., 'The Principle of Non-contractual liability for Breaches of EC law and its Application to State Aids' [1996] ECLR 355. The Court also pointed out that remedies may be sought from the recipient of the aid where provided by the rules of national law. In the legal systems of the UK, this may be possible under the rules on unjust enrichment, although there has been no case-law to date. For a fuller discussion, see Rodger, B.J., 'The Interface between State Aid, Unjust Enrichment and Private International Law', in Schrage, (ed.), *Unjust Enrichment and the Law of Contract*, Kluwer, The Hague, 2001. In order to assist the national courts in their limited role in relation to the state aid rules, the Commission issued a Notice on Co-operation between the National Courts and the Commission in the state aid field in 1995 OJ C312/7, 1995.

QUESTION

To what extent is there scope for decentralisation of state aid enforcement in line with the modernisation of enforcement of Articles 81 and 82 EC?

SECTION 4: **Recent and future developments**

In the late 1990s the Commission decided that the system of enforcement of the state aid rules required modernisation. It introduced Regulation 994/98 which enables the Commission to introduce Regulations for categories of horizontal aid, thereby exempting them from the requirement of notification.

Council Regulation (EC) No 994/98 on the application of Articles 92 and 93 of the Treaty establishing the European Community to certain categories of horizontal state aid
OJ L142/1, 1998, Article 1(a)

Article 1: Group exemptions

1. The Commission may, by means of regulations adopted in accordance with the procedures laid down in Article 8 of this Regulation and in accordance with Article 92 of the Treaty, declare that the following categories of aid should be compatible with the common market and

shall not be subject to the notification requirements of Article 93(3) of the Treaty:

(a) aid in favour of:

    (i) small and medium-sized enterprises;

    (ii) research and development;

    (iii) environmental protection;

    (iv) employment and training.

NOTE: The Commission indicated, in the Eighth and Ninth Surveys on State Aids, its shift away from supporting individual companies and that state aid policy in the future will be more focused on exempting aid where it contributes to Community objectives. The Commission has already introduced Regulations in relation to small and medium-sized enterprises, Regulation 70/2001 L10/30, 2001, and training aid, Regulation 68/2001, L10/30 2001, under these provisions. Regulations on R & D are anticipated and, as noted above, a Regulation on *de minimis* aid has already been introduced under Article 2 of Regulation 994/98.

QUESTION

Is state aid a necessary element of the Community competition law framework?

FURTHER READING

Hancher L. et al, *EC State Aids* (2nd edn) London: Sweet and Maxwell, 1999.

Quigley, C., and Collins, A., *EC State Aids: Law and Policy*, Oxford, Hart Publishing, 2001.

12

Competition law and policy in global markets

SECTION 1: **Introduction**

There has been a significant increase in the number of countries which have introduced competition laws in recent years. At the beginning of the 1990s, there were only ten or so antitrust regimes in the world; today that figure stands at more than 80, including countries as diverse as China, Zimbabwe and Romania and many more countries are in the process of establishing competition laws. The risk of substantial disharmony between legal systems is obvious. The increase in domestic competition law regimes also comes at a time of enhanced market globalisation. The position is aptly described by the US First Circuit Court of Appeals as follows: 'We live in an age of international commerce, where decisions reached in one corner of the world can reverberate around the globe in less time than it takes to tell the tale' (*United States* v *Nippon Paper Industries Co.* 109 F, 3d (1st Cir. 1997)). Competition policy is no exception to this trend. International cartels, large-scale mergers and abuses of dominant positions transcend national borders and present challenges for all competition authorities in a globalised economy. The growth of national regimes also demands a rethink among antitrust authorities as to how to address multijurisdictional antitrust enforcement. There are three key issues for discussion.

1. The first is the controversial practice of extraterritoriality, whereby one state unilaterally extends the application of its competition laws to the conduct of one or more undertakings situated overseas.

2. The second is bilateral cooperation as a response to the practice of extraterritoriality, for example, between the US and the European Community, making it possible to investigate cases jointly, or at least to exchange information and investigatory assistance.

3. Finally, arguably the most ambitious and often presented as a solution to the problems caused by the practice of extraterritoriality and the limitations of bilateral cooperation—the construction of a multilateral code.

We shall consider each of these in turn.

SECTION 2: **Extraterritoriality**

Extraterritoriality is controversial because it implies an infringement of a state's territorial sovereignty. The US developed the notion of extraterritorial application of antitrust at a period in time where few countries had competition rules. The discussion begins with Judge Learned Hand's famous exposition of the 'effects doctrine' in *Alcoa*.

United States v *Aluminium Co. of America*
148 F, 2d 416 (2d Cir. 1945)

> The US Department of Justice brought an action against a Canadian corporation that allegedly conspired with Alcoa in 1931 and 1936 to restrain commerce in the manufacture and sale of virgin aluminium ingot. The alleged conspiracy was effected entirely outside the United States. The court had to consider whether the conduct complained of violated s. 1 of the Sherman Act. The key passage is highlighted in italic.

The answer does not depend upon whether we shall recognize as a source of liability a liability imposed by another state. On the contrary we are concerned only with whether Congress chose to attach liability to the conduct outside the United States of persons not in allegiance to it. That being so, the only question open is whether Congress intended to impose the liability, and whether our own Constitution permitted it to do so: as a court of the United States, we cannot look beyond our own law. Nevertheless, it is quite true that we are not to read general words, such as those in this Act, without regard to the limitations customarily observed by nations upon the exercise of their powers; limitations which generally correspond to those fixed by the 'Conflict of Laws'. We should not impute to Congress an intent to punish all whom its courts can catch, for conduct which has no consequences within the United States. *American Banana Co.* v *United Fruit Co.*, 213 US 347, 357, 29 S. Ct. 511, 53 L. Ed. 826, 16 Ann. Cas. 1047; *United States* v *Bowman*, 260 US 94, 98, 43 S. Ct. 39, 67 L. Ed. 149; *Blackmer* v *United States*, 284 US 421, 437, 52 S. Ct. 252, 76 L. Ed. 375. *On the other hand, it is settled law . . . that any state may impose liabilities, even upon persons not within its allegiance, for conduct outside its borders that has consequences within its borders which the state reprehends; and these liabilities other states will ordinarily recognize.* Strassheim *v* Daily, 221 US 280, 284, 285, 31 S. Ct. 558, 55 L. Ed. 735; *Lamar* v *United States*, 240 US 60, 65, 66, 36 S. Ct. 255, 60 L. Ed. 526, *Ford* v *United States*, 273 US 593, 620, 621, 47 S. Ct. 531, 71 L. Ed. 793; Restatement of Conflict of Laws Sec. 65. It may be argued that this Act extends further. Two situations are possible. There may be agreements made beyond our borders not intended to affect imports, which do affect them, or which affect exports. Almost any limitation of the supply of goods in Europe, for example, or in South America, may have repercussions in the United States if there is trade between the two. Yet when one considers the international complications likely to arise from an effort in this country to treat such agreements as unlawful, it is safe to assume that Congress certainly did not intend the Act to cover them. Such agreements may on the other hand intend to include imports into the United States, and yet it may appear that they had no effect upon them. That situation might be thought to fall within the doctrine that intent may be a substitute for performance in the case of a contract made within the United States; or it might be thought to fall within the doctrine that a statute should not be interpreted to cover acts abroad which have no consequence here. We shall not choose between these alternatives; but for argument we shall assume that the Act does not cover agreements, even though intended to affect imports or exports, unless its performance is shown actually to have had some effect upon them. Where both conditions are satisfied, the situation certainly falls within such decisions as *United States* v *Pacific & Artic R. & Navigation Co.*, 228 US 87, 33 S. Ct. 443, 57 L. Ed. 742; *Thomsen* v *Cayser*, 243 US 66, 37 S. Ct. 353, 61 L. Ed. 597, Ann. Cas. 1917D, 322 and *United States* v *Sisal Sales Corporation*, 274 US, 268, 47 S. Ct. 592, 71 L. Ed. 1042. (*United States* v *Nord Deutcher Lloyd*, 223 US, 512, 32 S. Ct. 244, 56 L. Ed. 531, illustrates the same conception in another field.) It is true that in those cases the persons held liable had sent agents into the United States to perform part of the agreement; but an agent is merely an animate means of executing his principal's purposes, and, for the purposes of this case, he does not differ from an inanimate means; besides, only human agents can import and sell ingot.

Both agreements would clearly have been unlawful, had they been made within the United States; and it follows from what we have just said that both were unlawful, though made abroad, if they were intended to affect imports and did affect them. Since the shareholders almost at once agreed that the agreement of 1931 should not cover imports, we may ignore it and confine our discussion to that of 1936: indeed that we should have to do anyway, since it superseded the earlier agreement. The judge found that it was not the purpose of the agreement to 'suppress or restrain the exportation of aluminum to the United States for sale in competition with '*Alcoa*'. By that we understand that he meant that the agreement was not specifically directed to '*Alcoa*', because it only applied generally to the production of the shareholders. If he meant that it was not expected that the general restriction upon production would have an effect upon imports, we cannot agree, for the change made in 1936 was deliberate and was expressly made to accomplish just that. It would have been an idle gesture, unless the shareholders had supposed that it would, or at least might, have that effect. The first of the conditions which we mentioned was therefore satisfied; the intent was to set up a quota system for imports.

NOTE: Not surprisingly, the legal basis for this doctrine is contentious and traditional public international law principles of jurisdiction based on nationality or territorial grounds have limited value. Moreover, in *Timberlane Lumber Co.* v *Bank of America* 549 F 2d 597 (9th Cir. 1976) the Ninth Circuit Court of Appeals declared that the effects doctrine did not afford sufficient weight to the interests of other governments and that it failed to 'expressly take into account the full nature of the relationship between the actors and this country'. This so-called 'jurisdictional rule of reason' rests on the premise that the United States has jurisdiction but should choose not to exercise it in certain circumstances. It is questionable as Durack asserts, whether the courts are best placed to assess the diplomatic political and economic issues in cases involving a conflict of laws.

Durack, P., QC, Attorney General of Australia, 'Extraterritorial Application of US Law and US Foreign Policy'
Remarks before the ABA Section of International Law (August 12 1981)

[I]t is not merely that the courts lack the expertise. It is not part of the judicial function to decide whether a law or policy is necessary and justified by what it conceives to be the national interest. That is the political function. It is even more difficult if a court were to attempt that task in relation to the law or policy of a foreign country. In large measure what a State conceives to be important depends upon the values of that society, as for example, whether and to what extent it wishes to protect its environment. Even where the law is based upon ostensibly objective considerations as, for example, the trading law of a country, it is not procedurally practicable to establish the significance of that law to the national interest in a court of law. Consider only the mass of facts of an economic character which in such a case would need to be proved.

There is this further consideration. In the case of this kind of conflict an important matter is the question of its impact upon foreign relations. That this is important is recognised by United States authority. But such a matter is not, I think, justiciable. It is the stuff of diplomatic negotiations. However, the Supreme Court's bullish decision in *Hartford Insurance* in which it stated that principles of international comity do not prevent the United States from exercising jurisdiction over conduct by British reinsurance companies based in London indicates a retreat from *Timberlane*'s conflict of laws analysis.

Hartford Fire Ins. Co. v *California*
509 US 764 (1993)

> Nineteen states and numerous private plaintiffs brought actions under s. 1 of the Sherman Act 1890 against domestic insurers and domestic and foreign reinsurers of general commercial liability. The plaintiffs alleged that the insurance companies, acting in the UK, had collaborated in refusing commercial liability reinsurance coverage for US lawyers except on terms agreed amongst themselves. The London defendants denied they had entered into any anti-competitive agreements and further that they acted in accordance with UK law and moved to dismiss. The Court responded as follows:

Noted by Lowenfield, A.F., 'Conflict, Balancing of Interests, and the Exercise of Jurisdiction to Prescribe: Reflections on the *Insurance Antitrust* Case'
(1995) 89 AJIL 42

The English defendants did not deny that their actions had effects in the United States—indeed, direct and substantial effects. They argued, however, that their conduct was legal in the state where it took place; that they had operated in full compliance with a regime of regulation and self-regulation as prescribed by the British Parliament; and that under principles of international law and comity, as spelled out particularly in two major decisions of US courts of appeals—*Timberlane Lumber Co.* v *Bank of America* and *Mannington Mills, Inc.* v *Congoleum Corp*—as well as two generations of the Restatement of the Foreign Relations Law of the United States, jurisdiction to apply US law should not be exercised in this case.

In the much-discussed *Timberlane* case, it will be recalled, Judge Choy had written that the 'effects doctrine' as formulated by Judge Learned Hand in *Alcoa* is incomplete, because it fails to consider the interests of other nations in the application or nonapplication of United States law. Judge Choy had proposed a three-part test: first, to see if the challenged conduct had had some effect on the commerce of the United States—the mininum contact to support application of US law; second, to see if a greater showing could be made that the conduct in question imposed a burden or restraint on US commerce—i.e., whether the complaint stated a claim under the antitrust laws; and third, to consider 'the additional question which is unique to the international setting of whether the interests of, and links to, the United States . . . are sufficiently strong, vis-à-vis those of other nations, to justify an assertion of extraterritorial authority.

Judge Choy then proceeded to set out seven factors by which to judge the third or 'ought to' question, based on a list of factors proposed some years earlier by Professor Kingman Brewster. Other courts and the Restatement (Third) modified the criteria somewhat, but for the most part adopted the approach of the *Timberlane* case.

In *Insurance Antitrust*, the federal district court in San Francisco and the US Court of Appeals for the Ninth Circuit both considered the international aspect of the case in the light of *Timberlane*, and in particular in the light of the list of factors set out in that case by Judge Choy. Judge Schwarzer in the district court dismissed the action, on the basis that the conflict with English law and policy which would result from the extra-territorial application of the [US] antitrust laws in this case is not outweighed by other factors'. Judge Noonan, for the court of appeals, going through the same factors, acknowledged the 'significant conflict' with English law and policy, but held that the conflict was outweighed by the 'significance of the effects on American commerce, their foreseeability and their purposefulness'. Accordingly, the court of appeals reinstated the action. Thus, when the Supreme Court granted review, much of the argument on the international aspect of the case focused on the relative importance under *Timberlane* of conduct—clearly in England—versus effect—largely in the United States. Since both lower courts had accepted that there was a conflict between US and English law, not much argument focused on defining the conflict. In the Supreme Court, however, it was precisely the existence or nonexistence of conflict that divided the majority and the dissent . . .

Justice David Souter, for the majority of five, wrote: 'The only substantial question in this case is whether there is in fact a true conflict between domestic and foreign law'.

Justice Souter went on to acknowledge the argument of the London reinsurers, supported by the British Government, that applying the Sherman Act to their conduct would conflict significantly with British law. But British law did not require the agreements that were the basis of the challenge under the Sherman Act. All that British law did was to establish a regulatory—and largely self-regulatory— regime with which the challenged conduct was consistent. '[T]his,' said Justice Souter, citing the Restatement, 'is not to state a conflict. . . . No conflict exists, for these purposes, where a person subject to regulation by two states can comply with the laws of both'.

. . . For the moment, I want to point out only that Justice Souter's opinion seems to equate 'conflict' with 'foreign compulsion'. For conflict, that is for inconsistent interests of states, *Timberlane* taught that one should evaluate or balance; for foreign compulsion, in contrast, we had understood since the *Nylon* and *Light Bulb* cartel cases of the early 1950s that no person would be required to do an act in another state that is prohibited by the law of that state or would be prohibited from doing an act in another state that is required by the law of that state; in other words, that the territorial preference would make balancing unnecessary. But Justice Souter said nothing about the controversial subject of balancing—either for or against—and barely mentioned *Timberlane*. 'We have no need in this case,' he concluded, 'to address other considerations that might inform a decision to refrain from the exercise of jurisdiction on grounds of international comity'.

To Justice Scalia and the four-person minority, the case looked entirely different. Justice Scalia started with two presumptions: first, that legislation of Congress, unless a contrary intent appears, 'is meant to apply only within the territorial jurisdiction of the United States'; and second, that 'an act of congress ought never to be construed to violate the law of nations if any other possible construction remains', a quotation going back to Chief Justice Marshall, and that customary international law includes limitations on a nation's exercise of its jurisdiction to prescribe. The first point, of course, begs the question about whether one looks at conduct—here in London—or effect—here in the United States. If one looks at effect, then application of the Sherman Act would not be extraterritorial. In any event, Justice Scalia conceded that there were numerous precedents for application of the Sherman Act to conduct outside the United States. The second point, about customary international law, led Justice Scalia right to the series of court of appeals decisions from *Alcoa* to *Timberlane* and *Mannington Mills*, plus decisions by the US Supreme Court in a series of seamen's cases cited to the Court by the English defendants, as well as the Restatement. 'Whether the Restatement precisely reflects international law in every detail matters little here,' he wrote, 'as I believe this case would be resolved the same way under virtually any conceivable test that takes account of foreign regulatory interests'. Justice Scalia went through the approach of the Restatement, including the factors set out in section 403(2). 'Rarely,' he concluded, perhaps exaggerating in order to emphasize his difference from the majority, 'would these factors point more clearly against application of United States law'.

Further, on the conclusion by the majority that a true conflict would exist only if compliance with US law would constitute violation of the other state's law, Justice Scalia wrote: 'That breathtakingly broad proposition, which contradicts the many cases discussed earlier, will bring the Sherman Act and other laws into sharp and unnecessary conflict with the legitimate interests of other countries—particularly our closest trading partners'.

NOTE: In *United States* v *Nippon Paper Industries Co.*, 109 F 3d (1st Cir. 1997) the Supreme Court established that antitrust actions predicated on foreign conduct which has an intended and substantial effect in the US fall within the jurisdictional ambit of the Sherman Act, thereby exposing foreign nationals and companies to significant fines and imprisonment. An indictment served on Nippon Paper alleged that its predecessor met with various co-conspirators on a number of occasions in 1990 to discuss increasing prices of jumbo roll thermal fax paper to be sold in the United States and Canada. Although the meetings took place in Japan, the effects of the agreement to increase prices had a substantial adverse effect on commerce in the United States and unreasonably restrained trade in violation of s. 1 of the Sherman Act. Nippon Paper argued in its defence that 'if the alleged conduct occurred at all, it took place entirely in Japan, and thus the indictment failed to limit an offense under Section One of the Sherman Act'. The Court concluded that s. 1 of the Sherman Act used precisely the same language to identify criminal conduct as it used to delineate conduct violative of civil law, provided the conduct produced substantial and intended effects within the United States. The Court then rejected arguments that it should refrain from exercising jurisdiction on the basis of international comity on the basis that a nation's decision to prosecute wholly foreign conduct is discretionary.

> [W]e see no tenable reason why principles of comity should shield [the defendant] from prosecution. We live in an age of international commerce, where decisions reached in one corner of the world can reverberate around the globe in less time than it takes to tell the tale. Thus, a ruling in [the defendant's] favor would create perverse incentives for those who would use nefarious means to influence markets in the United States, rewarding them for enacting as many territorial firewalls as possibility between cause and effect.

NOTE: The decision has been widely criticised. For a particularly critical account see Fox, E.M., 'National Law, Global Markets, and *Hartford*: Eyes Wide Shut' (2000) Antitrust L.J. Vol. 68/1, 73. However, an article by Harry First in the same symposium, 'The Vitamins Case: Cartel Prosecutions and the Coming of International Competition Laws, Antitrust at the Millenium', Antitrust Law Journal, Part III, Vol. 68/3 711 suggests that the once controversial issue of extraterritoriality has now faded as a matter of concern as states cooperate on international cartel enforcement.

In 1982 Congress approved an amendment to the Sherman Act entitled the Foreign Trade Antitrust Improvements Act of 1982. The Sherman Act no longer applies to conduct involving trade or commerce (other than import trade or commerce) unless it has a 'direct, substantial and reasonably foreseeable effect on domestic trade or commerce'. However, this test is widely construed and the amendment is virtually meaningless. See e.g. *Hartford Fire Insurance* discussed above. Note the return to the *Alcoa* jurisdictional test with the additional requirement that the effects are foreseeable. What purpose, if any, does this requirement serve?

In 1995, the Department of Justice and Federal Trade Commission (the Agencies) jointly issued Antitrust Enforcement Guidelines for International Operations. The Guidelines indicate that the Agencies will evaluate the laws and policies of foreign nations before they take any action, but where the United States antitrust enforcement mechanism is in a 'better position' to address the 'competitive problem', the DOJ and FTC will handle the situation (s. 3.2). The Guidelines clearly reflect the expansionist approach adopted by Congress and the Supreme Court in *Hartford Fire*. See Brockbank, D., 'The 1995 International Antitrust Guidelines: The Reach of US Antitrust Law Continues to Expand', 2 Journal of Int'l Legal Studies 1.

Not surprisingly, foreign governments have protested strongly against US assertions of extra-territorial jurisdiction. For an account see e.g. Griffin, J.P., 'Foreign Governmental Reactions to US Assertions of Extraterritorial Jurisdiction' [1998] ECLR 64. Besides the usual diplomatic exchanges, some countries have enacted 'blocking' statutes to impede discovery outside the United States or render certain types of US antitrust judgment unenforceable in foreign courts. The UK Government has always protested against US antitrust enforcement abroad, preferring a more traditional view of jurisdiction based on the territorial and nationality principles of public international law. The British Secretary of State for Trade, in introducing the Protection of Trading Interests Bill in 1979, stated that the objective of the law was 'to reassert and reinforce the defences of the United Kingdom against attempts by other countries to enforce their economic and commercial policies unilaterally on us'. Thus, the legislation applies to any activity that may harm the commercial interests of the UK and is not confined to competition matters.

Protection of Trading Interests Act 1980
Reprinted in 21 ILM 834 (1982)

1. Overseas measures affecting United Kingdom trading interests
(1) If it appears to the Secretary of State—
(a) that measures have been or are proposed to be taken by or under the law of any overseas country for regulating or controlling international trade; and
(b) that those measures, in so far as they apply or would apply to things done or to be done outside the territorial jurisdiction of that country by persons carrying on business in the United Kingdom, are damaging or threaten to damage the trading interests of the United Kingdom, the Secretary of State may by order direct that this section shall apply to those measures either generally or in their application to such cases as may be specified in the order.

(2) The Secretary of State may by order make provision for requiring, or enabling the Secretary of State to require, a person in the United Kingdom who carries on business there to give notice to the Secretary of State of any requirement or prohibition imposed or threatened to be imposed on that person pursuant to any measures in so far as this section applies to them by virtue of an order under subsection (1) above.

(3) The Secretary of State may give to any person in the United Kingdom who carries on business there such directions for prohibiting compliance with any such requirement or prohibition as aforesaid as he considers appropriate for avoiding damage to the trading interests of the United Kingdom.

(4) The power of the Secretary of State to make orders under subsection (1) or (2) above shall be exercisable by statutory instrument subject to annulment in pursuance of a resolution of either House of Parliament.

(5) Directions under subsection (3) above may be either general or special and may prohibit compliance with any requirement or prohibition either absolutely or in such cases or subject to such conditions as to consent or otherwise as may be specified in the directions; and general directions under that subsection shall be published in such manner as appears to the Secretary of State to be appropriate.

(6) In this section 'trade' includes any activity carried on in the course of a business of any description and 'trading interests' shall be construed accordingly.

2. Documents and information required by overseas courts and authorities
(1) If it appears to the Secretary of State—
(a) that a requirement has been or may be imposed on a person or persons in the United

Kingdom to produce to any court, tribunal or authority of an overseas country any commercial document which is not within the territorial jurisdiction of that country or to furnish any commercial information to any such court, tribunal or authority; or

(b) that any such authority has imposed or may impose a requirement on a person or persons in the United Kingdom to publish any such document or information, the Secretary of State may, if it appears to him that the requirement is inadmissible by virtue of subsection (2) or (3) below, give directions for prohibiting compliance with the requirement.

(2) A requirement such as is mentioned in subsection (1)(a) or (b) above is inadmissible—

(a) if it infringes the jurisdiction of the United Kingdom or is otherwise prejudicial to the sovereignty of the United Kingdom; or

(b) if compliance with the requirement would be prejudicial to the security of the United Kingdom or to the relations of the government of the United Kingdom with the government of any other country.

(3) A requirement such as is mentioned in subsection (1)(a) above is also inadmissible—

(a) if it is made otherwise than for the purposes of civil or criminal proceedings which have been instituted in the overseas country; or

(b) if it requires a person to state what documents relevant to any such proceedings are or have been in his possession, custody or power or to produce for the purposes of any such proceedings any documents other than particular documents specified in the requirement.

(4) Directions under subsection (1) above may be either general or special and may prohibit compliance with any requirement either absolutely or in such cases or subject to such conditions as to consent or otherwise as may be specified in the directions; and general directions under that subsection shall be published in such manner as appears to the Secretary of State to be appropriate.

(5) For the purposes of this section the making of a request or demand shall be treated as the imposition of a requirement if it is made in circumstances in which a requirement to the same effect could be or could have been imposed; and

(a) any request or demand for the supply of a document or information which, pursuant to the requirement of any court, tribunal or authority of an overseas country, is addressed to a person in the United Kingdom; or

(b) any requirement imposed by such a court, tribunal or authority to produce or furnish any document or information to a person specified in the requirement, shall be treated as a requirement to produce or furnish that document or information to that court, tribunal or authority.

(6) In this section 'commercial document' and 'commercial information' mean respectively a document or information relating to a business of any description and 'document' includes any record or device by means of which material is recorded or stored.

3. Offences under ss. 1 and 2

(1) Subject to subsection (2) below, any person who without reasonable excuse fails to comply with any requirement imposed under subsection (2) of section 1 above or knowingly contravenes any directions given under subsection (3) of that section or section 2(1) above shall be guilty of an offence and liable—

(a) on conviction on indictment, to a fine;

(b) on summary conviction, to a fine not exceeding the statutory maximum.

(2) A person who is neither a citizen of the United Kingdom and Colonies nor a body corporate incorporated in the United Kingdom shall not be guilty of an offence under subsection

(1) above by reason of anything done or omitted outside the United Kingdom in contravention of directions under section 1(3) or 2(1) above.

(3) No proceedings for an offence under subsection (1) above shall be instituted in England, Wales or Northern Ireland except by the Secretary of State or with the consent of the Attorney General or, as the case may be, the Attorney General for Northern Ireland.

(4) Proceedings against any person for an offence under this section may be taken before the appropriate court in the United Kingdom having jurisdiction in the place where that person is for the time being.

4. Restriction of Evidence (Proceedings in Other Jurisdictions) Act 1975

A court in the United Kingdom shall not make an order under section 2 of the Evidence (Proceedings in Other Jurisdictions) Act 1975 for giving effect to a request issued by or on behalf of a court or tribunal of an overseas country if it is shown that the request infringes the jurisdiction of the United Kingdom or is otherwise prejudicial to the sovereignty of the United Kingdom; and a certificate signed by or on behalf of the Secretary of State to the effect that it infringes that jurisdiction or is so prejudicial shall be conclusive evidence of that fact.

5. Restriction on enforcement of certain overseas judgments

(1) A judgment to which this section applies shall not be registered under Part II of the Administration of Justice Act 1920 or Part I of the Foreign Judgments (Reciprocal Enforcement) Act 1933 and no court in the United Kingdom shall entertain proceedings at common law for the recovery of any sum payable under such a judgment.

(2) This section applies to any judgment given by a court of an overseas country, being—
  (a) a judgment for multiple damages within the meaning of subsection (3) below;
  (b) a judgment based on a provision or rule of law specified or described in an order under subsection (4) below and given after the coming into force of the order; or
  (c) a judgment on a claim for contribution in respect of damages awarded by a judgment falling within paragraph (a) or (b) above.

(3) In subsection (2)(a) above a judgment for multiple damages means a judgment for an amount arrived at by doubling, trebling or otherwise multiplying a sum assessed as compensation for the loss or damage sustained by the person in whose favour the judgment is given.

(4) The Secretary of State may for the purposes of subsection (2)(b) above make an order in respect of any provision or rule of law which appears to him to be concerned with the prohibition or regulation of agreements, arrangements or practices designed to restrain, distort or restrict competition in the carrying on of business of any description or to be otherwise concerned with the promotion of such competition as aforesaid.

(5) The power of the Secretary of State to make orders under subsection (4) above shall be exercisable by statutory instrument subject to annulment in pursuance of a resolution of either House of Parliament.

(6) Subsection (2)(a) above applies to a judgment given before the date of the passing of this Act as well as to a judgment given on or after that date but this section does not affect any judgment which has been registered before that date under the provisions mentioned in subsection (1) above or in respect of which such proceedings as are there mentioned have been finally determined before that date.

6. Recovery of awards of multiple damages

(1) This section applies where a court of an overseas country has given a judgment for multiple damages within the meaning of section 5(3) above against—
  (a) a citizen of the United Kingdom and Colonies; or
  (b) a body corporate incorporated in the United Kingdom or in a territory outside the

United Kingdom for whose international relations Her Majesty's Government in the United Kingdom are responsible; or

(c) a person carrying on business in the United Kingdom, (in this section referred to as a 'qualifying defendant') and an amount on account of the damages has been paid by the qualifying defendant either to the party in whose favour the judgment was given or to another party who is entitled as against the qualifying defendant to contribution in respect of the damages.

(2) Subject to subsections (3) and (4) below, the qualifying defendant shall be entitled to recover from the party in whose favour the judgment was given so much of the amount referred to in subsection (1) above as exceeds the part attributable to compensation; and that part shall be taken to be such part of the amount as bears to the whole of it the same proportion as the sum assessed by the court that gave the judgment as compensation for the loss or damage sustained by that party bears to the whole of the damages awarded to that party.

(3) Subsection (2) above does not apply where the qualifying defendant is an individual who was ordinarily resident in the overseas country at the time when the proceedings in which the judgment was given were instituted or a body corporate which had its principal place of business there at that time.

(4) Subsection (2) above does not apply where the qualifying defendant carried on business in the overseas country and the proceedings in which the judgment was given were concerned with activities exclusively carried on in that country.

(5) A court in the United Kingdom may entertain proceedings on a claim under this section notwithstanding that the person against whom the proceedings are brought is not within the jurisdiction of the court.

(6) The reference in subsection (1) above to an amount paid by the qualifying defendant includes a reference to an amount obtained by execution against his property or against the property of a company which (directly or indirectly) is wholly owned by him; and references in that subsection and subsection (2) above to the party in whose favour the judgment was given or to a party entitled to contribution include references to any person in whom the rights of any such party have become vested by succession or assignment or otherwise.

(7) This section shall, with the necessary modifications, apply also in relation to any order which is made by a tribunal or authority of an overseas country and would, if that tribunal or authority were a court, be a judgment for multiple damages within the meaning of section 5(3) above.

(8) This section does not apply to any judgment given or order made before the passing of this Act.

In the *Dyestuffs* case (discussed below) the UK Government submitted an *aide-mémoire* which set out the government's objections to the jurisdiction claimed by the Commission.

Aide-mémoire submitted by the UK government to the European Court in the *Dyestuffs* case [1972] ECR 619, in Lowe, A.V., *Extraterritorial Jurisdiction: An Annotated Collection of Legal Materials*

(Grotius Publications Ltd, 1983) pp. 144–146

Aide-mémoire

The United Kingdom Government have noted, in the *Journal Officiel* of the European Communities dated 7 August 1969, the publication of a decision of the Commission of 24 July 1969 (No IV/26267) concerning proceedings pursuant to Article 85 of the Treaty establishing the European Economic Community in the matter of dyestuffs. Article 1 of this decision declares that 'the concerted practices of fixing the rate of price increases and the conditions of application of these increases in the dyestuffs sector . . . constitute violations of the provisions of Article 85 of the EEC Treaty'. Article 2 of the decision inflicts or purports to inflict certain fines upon the commercial undertakings who are alleged to have participated in these concerted practices. Among the undertakings specified in Articles 1 and 2 of the decision are Imperial Chemical Industries Limited (hereinafter referred to as 'I.C.I.'), which is a company incorporated and carrying on business in the United Kingdom. Article 4 of the decision declares that the present decision is directed to the undertakings mentioned in Article 1; it then goes on to state that as far as I.C.I. and certain Swiss undertakings are concerned, '[the decision] may likewise be notified to them at the seat of one of their subsidiaries established in the Common Market'.

The United Kingdom Government neither wish nor intend to take issue with the Commission about the merits of this particular case. They accept that it is for the undertakings to whom the decision is directed to pursue whatever remedies are available to them under the EEC Treaty if they desire for their part to challenge the legality or correctness of this measure taken by the Commission. It is in any event their understanding that certain of the undertakings to whom the decision is directed have already indicated their intention to institute proceedings before the European Court of Justice challenging the decision on various grounds.

The concern of the United Kingdom Government in this matter is rather directed towards the more fundamental point concerning the reach and extent of the jurisdiction exercisable by the Commission *vis-à-vis* undertakings which are neither incorporated in the territory of a Member-State of the European Economic Community, nor carrying on business nor resident therein.

The Commission will be aware that certain claims to exercise extra-territorial jurisdiction in antitrust proceedings have given rise to serious and continuing disputes between Western European Governments (including the Governments of some EEC Member-States) and the United States Government, inasmuch as these claims have been based on grounds which the Western European Governments consider to be unsupported by public international law.

In particular, the United Kingdom Government have for their part consistently objected to the assumption of extra-territorial jurisdiction in antitrust matters by the courts or authorities of a foreign state when that jurisdiction is based upon what is termed the 'effects doctrine'—that is to say, the doctrine that territorial jurisdiction over conduct which has occurred wholly outside the territory of the State claiming jurisdiction may be justified because of the resulting economic 'effects' of such conduct within the territory of that State. This doctrine becomes even more open to objection when, on the basis of the alleged 'effects' within the State claiming jurisdiction of the conduct of foreign corporations abroad (that is to say, conduct pursued outside the territory of that State), such corporations are actually made subject to penal sanctions.

The United Kingdom Government are of the view that certain of the 'considerations' advanced in the decision of the Commission of 24 July 1969 conflict with the principles of public international law concerning the basis upon which personal and substantive jurisdiction may be exercised over foreign corporations in antitrust matters. A summary statement of these principles as seen by the United Kingdom Government, is annexed to this *aide-mémoire* for ease of reference.

In particular, it will be noted that the method by which the decision of the Commission was purportedly notified to I.C.I. (Article 4 of the decision) ignores the clear legal distinction between a parent company and its subsidiaries and the separate legal personalities of the latter. The United Kingdom Government consider that this attempted 'notification' of a parent company through its subsidiary is designed to support a doctrine of substantive jurisdiction which is itself open to objection as going beyond the limits imposed by the accepted principles of international law.

So far as substantive jurisdiction is concerned, the United Kingdom Government are of the view that the decision of the Commission incorporates an interpretation of the relevant provisions of the EEC. Treaty which is not justified by the accepted principles of international law governing the exercise of extra-territorial jurisdiction over foreigners in respect of acts committed abroad.

The United Kingdom Government deem it necessary to bring these considerations to the attention of the Commission lest there be any misunderstanding as to their position in the matter.

Statement of Principles According to which in the view of the UK government jurisdiction may be exercised over foreign corporations in antitrust matters, in Lowe, A.V., *Extraterritorial Jurisdiction: An Annotated Collection of Legal Materials*

(Grotius Publications Ltd, 1983), pp 146–147

The basis on which personal jurisdiction may be exercised over foreign corporations

(1) Personal jurisdiction should be assumed only if the foreign company 'carries on business' or 'resides' within the territorial jurisdiction.

(2) A foreign company may be considered to 'carry on business' within the jurisdiction by an agent only if the agent has legal power to enter into contracts on behalf of the principal.

(3) A foreign parent company may not be considered to 'carry on business' within the jurisdiction by a subsidiary company, unless it can be shown that the subsidiary is the agent for the parent in the sense of carrying on the parent's business within the jurisdiction.

(4) The separate legal personalities of a parent company and its subsidiary should be respected. Such concepts as 'enterprise entity' and 'reciprocating partnership' when applied for the purpose of asserting personal jurisdiction over a foreign parent company by reason of the presence within the jurisdiction of a subsidiary (and a foreign subsidiary by reason of the presence of its parent company) are contrary to sound legal principle in that they disregard the distinction of personality between parent and subsidiary.

(5) The normal rules governing the exercise of personal jurisdiction should not be extended in such a manner as to extend beyond proper limits the exercise of substantive jurisdiction in respect of the activities of foreigners abroad. Nor can the assertion of extended personal jurisdiction be justified on the basis that it is necessary for the enforcement of legislation which in itself exceeds the proper limits of substantive jurisdiction.

(6) There is no justification for applying a looser test to methods of personal service in antitrust matters than is permissible in relation to other matters.

The basis on which substantive jurisdiction may be exercised in antitrust matters

(1) On general principles, substantive jurisdiction in antitrust matters should only be taken on the basis of either

(a) the territorial principle, or
(b) the nationality principle.

There is nothing in the nature of antitrust proceedings which justifies a wider application of these principles than is generally accepted in other matters: on the contrary there is much which calls for a narrower application.

(2) The territorial principle justifies proceedings against foreigners and foreign companies only in respect of conduct which consists in whole or in part of some activity by them in the territory of the State claiming jurisdiction. A State should not exercise jurisdiction against a foreigner who or a foreign company which has committed no act within its territory. In the case of conspiracies the assumption of jurisdiction is justified:

(a) if the entire conspiracy takes place within the territory of the State claiming jurisdiction; or
(b) if the formation of the conspiracy takes place within the territory of the State claiming jurisdiction even if things are done in pursuance of it outside its territory; or

(c) if the formation of the conspiracy takes place outside the territory of the State claiming jurisdiction, but the person against whom the proceedings are brought has done things within its territory in pursuance of the conspiracy.

(3) The nationality principle justifies proceedings against nationals of the State claiming jurisdiction in respect of their activities abroad only provided that this does not involve interference with the legitimate affairs of other States or cause such nationals to act in a manner which is contrary to the laws of the State in which the activities in question are conducted.

FURTHER READING

Lowe, A.V., 'Blocking Extraterritorial Jurisdiction', 75 AJIL 1981.

A: Position in the Community

The European Court has exercised a cautionary approach to the extraterritorial application of Articles 81 and 82 EC and cases have been resolved without reference to the controversial 'effects' doctrine. Instead the Court has relied on the 'single economic entity' doctrine.

ICI v *Commission* (*Dyestuffs*)
(Case 48/69) [1972] ECR 619, [1972] CMLR 557, paras 130–142

> The Commission found that ten undertakings, including ICI, were guilty of concerted practices, which infringed Article 81(1) EC, on the grounds that they had participated in illegal price-fixing agreements through subsidiaries which were under their control and which were located within the EEC. ICI appealed on the basis, that as it was outside the territory of the EEC, the Commission lacked jurisdiction and could not impose fines on it merely on the basis of effects produced in the territory of the EEC by actions alleged to have taken place outside the EEC. Note the UK was not in the EEC at the time the alleged conduct was meant to have occurred.

[130] By making use of its power to control its subsidiaries established in the Community, the applicant was able to ensure that its decision was implemented on that market.

[131] The applicant objects that this conduct is to be imputed to its subsidiaries and not to itself.

[132] The fact that a subsidiary has separate legal personality is not sufficient to exclude the possibility of imputing its conduct to the parent company.

[133] Such may be the case in particular where the subsidiary, although having separate legal personality, does not decide independently upon its own conduct on the market, but carries out, in all material respects, the instructions given to it by the parent company.

[134] Where a subsidiary does not enjoy real autonomy in determining its course of action in the market, the prohibitions set out in Article 85(1) may be considered inapplicable in the relationship between it and the parent company with which it forms one economic unit.

[135] In view of the unity of the group thus formed, the actions of the subsidiaries may in certain circumstances be attributed to the parent company.

[136] It is well-known that at the time the applicant held all or at any rate the majority of the shares in those subsidiaries.

[137] The applicant was able to exercise decisive influence over the policy of the subsidiaries as regards selling prices in the Common Market and in fact used this power upon the occasion of the three price increases in question.

[138] In effect the Telex messages relating to the 1964 increase, which the applicant sent to its subsidiaries in the Common Market, gave the addressees orders as to the prices which they were to charge and the other conditions of sale which they were to apply in dealing with their customers.

[139] In the absence of evidence to the contrary, it must be assumed that on the occasion of the increases of 1965 and 1967 the applicant acted in a similar fashion in its relations with its subsidiaries established in the Common Market.

[140] In the circumstances the formal separation between these companies, resulting from their separate legal personality, cannot outweigh the unity of their conduct on the market for the purposes of applying the rules on competition.

[141] It was in fact the applicant undertaking which brought the concerted practice into being within the Common Market.

[142] The submission as to lack of jurisdiction raised by the applicant must therefore be declared to be unfounded.

The Commission's application of the effects doctrine was supported by Advocate General Mayras.

C—I have stated, in reviewing national legislation, that the principal criterion for the applicability of laws on competition is the territorial effect. But I do not myself believe that this criterion should be accepted unless its *conditions* and *limits* are specified in relation to international law.

1. **The conditions for the application of the criterion of territorial effect**
   (a) I think that the first condition lies in the fact that the agreement or the concerted practice must create a *direct and immediate* restriction on competition on the national market or, as here, on the Community market. In other words, an agreement only having effects at one stage removed by way of economic mechanisms themselves taking place abroad could not justify jurisdiction over participating undertakings whose registered offices are also situated abroad. I would suggest that the American Restatement of Foreign Relations Law should be interpreted in this way in so far as it states that jurisdiction over conduct occurring abroad may be admitted when the effect occurs as a *direct result of that conduct*.
   (b) Secondly, the effect of the conduct must be *reasonably foreseeable*, although there is no need to show that the effect was intended.
   (c) Thirdly and lastly, the effect produced on the territory must be *substantial*.

It should also be noted that the main intention of the counter-legislation adopted in France, as in the Netherlands and in other countries, is to forbid their own nationals to submit to inquiries, supervision and orders emanating from foreign authorities. These facts lead me to adopt the distinction made in international law by the Commission and by academic writers between 'prescriptive jurisdiction' and 'enforcement jurisdiction', or between *jurisdictio* and *imperium*.

Whether it be criminal law or, as in the present cases, administrative proceedings that are involved, the courts or administrative authorities of a State—and, *mutatis mutandis*, of the Community—are certainly not justified under international law in taking coercive measures or indeed any measure of inquiry, investigation or supervision outside their territorial jurisdiction where execution would inevitably infringe the internal sovereignty of the State on the territory of which they claimed to act.

On the other hand, it must be recognized that those same authorities are competent to prohibit an agreement or practice which produces direct, foreseeable and substantial effects inimical to competition on their own territory and thus, in this case, in the Common Market, and that they are even competent to impose sanctions, even pecuniary ones, by judicial or administrative decisions.

Although the Court did not support the Advocate General's endorsement of the effects doctrine it upheld the Commission's decision on the basis of the single economic entity doctrine

The decision has been criticised because it disregarded the separate legal personality of the companies. See the UK Government's *aide-mémoire* discussed above. Griffin explains the US practice:

Griffin, J.P., 'Foreign Governmental Reactions to US Assertions of Extraterritorial Jurisdiction'
[1998] ECLR, pp. 69–70 [footnotes omitted]

Jurisdiction based on nationality
Nearly all nations agree that nationality can be a valid basis for asserting extraterritorial jurisdiction. However, US assertions of jurisdiction based upon the control exercised by an American parent over a subsidiary incorporated and operating abroad are not accepted as valid under international law by a number of nations. These nations contend that despite the American parent's majority ownership or its possession of effective working control, under international law nationality is properly determined by the place of incorporation. Moreover, according to one knowledgeable British official, 'even where nationality is a legitimate basis for extraterritorial jurisdiction it must remain subject to the primacy of the laws and policies of the territorial state'. US officials typically respond to these contentions with the assertion that they cannot permit 'technicalities' such as the place of incorporation and inconsistent policies of host states to be used by American companies to evade their obligations under US law.

The Court has employed the single economic entity doctrine in other contexts. See Chapter 5 and Cases 6 and 7 *Commercial Solvents* [1974] ECR 223, para. 37.

In *Wood Pulp* the Commission decided that there was a concerted practice between undertakings situated in non-EC countries and that jurisdiction could be based on the *effects* of that concerted practice on competition in the Community (OJ, 1985, L85/1). Although the Court did not endorse the effects doctrine, it confirmed that jurisdiction could be exercised extraterritorially where the agreement or concerted practice was *implemented* in the Community.

A Ahlström Oy v *Commission*
(Cases 89, 104, 11, 116, 117 and 125–129/85) (*Re Wood Pulp*) [1988] 5 ECR 5193,
[1988] 4 CMLR 901

[11] In so far as the submission concerning the infringement of Article 85 of the Treaty itself is concerned, it should be recalled that that provision prohibits all agreements between undertakings and concerted practices which may affect trade between Member States and which have as their object or effect the restriction of competition within the common market.

[12] It should be noted that the main sources of supply of wood pulp are outside the Community, in Canada, the United States, Sweden and Finland and that the market therefore has global dimensions. Where wood pulp producers established in those countries sell directly to purchasers established in the Community and engage in price competition in order to win orders from those customers, that constitutes competition within the common market.

[13] It follows that where those producers concert on the prices to be charged to their customers in the Community and put that concertation into effect by selling at prices which are actually coordinated, they are taking part in concertation which has the object and effect of restricting competition within the common market within the meaning of Article 85 of the Treaty.

[14] Accordingly, it must be concluded that by applying the competition rules in the Treaty in the circumstances of this case to undertakings whose registered offices are situated outside the Community, the Commission has not made an incorrect assessment of the territorial scope of Article 85.

[15] The applicants have submitted that the decision is incompatible with public international law on the grounds that the application of the competition rules in this case was founded exclusively on the economic repercussions within the common market of conduct restricting competition which was adopted outside the Community.

[16] It should be observed that an infringement of Article 85, such as the conclusion of an agreement which has had the effect of restricting competition within the common market, consists of conduct made up of two elements, the formation of the agreement, decision or concerted practice and the implementation thereof. If the applicability of prohibitions laid down under competition law were made to depend on the place where the agreement, decision or concerted practice was formed, the result would obviously be to give undertakings an easy means of evading those prohibitions. The decisive factor is therefore the place where it is implemented.

[17] The producers in this case implemented their pricing agreement within the common market. It is immaterial in that respect whether or not they had recourse to subsidiaries, agents, sub-agents, or branches within the Community in order to make their contacts with purchasers within the Community.

[18] Accordingly the Community's jurisdiction to apply its competition rules to such conduct is covered by the territoriality principle as universally recognized in public international law.

[19] As regards the argument based on the infringement of the principle of non-interference, it should be pointed out that the applicants who are members of KEA have referred to a rule according to which where two States have jurisdiction to lay down and enforce rules and the effect of those rules is that a person finds himself subject to contradictory orders as to the conduct he must adopt, each State is obliged to exercise its jurisdiction with moderation. The applicants have concluded that by disregarding that rule in applying its competition rules the Community has infringed the principle of non-interference.

[20] There is no need to enquire into the existence in international law of such a rule since it suffices to observe that the conditions for its application are in any event not satisfied. There is not, in this case, any contradiction between the conduct required by the United States and that required by the Community since the Webb Pomerene Act merely exempts the conclusion of export cartels from the application of United States anti-trust laws but does not require such cartels to be concluded.

[21] It should further be pointed out that the United States authorities raised no objections regarding any conflict of jurisdiction when consulted by the Commission pursuant to the OECD Council Recommendation of 25 October 1979 concerning cooperation between member countries on restrictive business practices affecting international trade (*Acts of the organization*, Vol. 19, p. 376).

[22] As regards the argument relating to disregard of international comity, it suffices to observe that it amounts to calling in question the Community's jurisdiction to apply its competition rules to conduct such as that found to exist in this case and that, as such, that argument has already been rejected.

[23] Accordingly it must be concluded that the Commission's decision is not contrary to Article 85 of the Treaty or to the rules of public international law relied on by the applicants.

NOTE: Compare the practice followed by some Member States (as amended) e.g. Germany. The German Act Against Restraints of Competition, explicitly states that 'this act shall apply to all restrictions of competition occurring in the territory of the application of the act itself, even if they result from restraints conducted outside such territory' (s. 130(2)).

Note also the distinction between effects and implementation remains unclear although Griffin suggests that in practice the EC and US tests often produce similar outcomes, with the exception of a narrow, but significant group of cases.

Griffin, J.P., 'Foreign Governmental Reactions to US Assertions of Extraterritorial Jurisdiction'
[1998] ECLR, p. 68

For example, if a cartel of American purchasers declined to purchase goods from European sellers, it is doubtful that the purchasers would be deemed to have 'implemented' their conduct within the European Union. Similarly, an agreement by a group of American companies who refuse to sell to firms in the European Union would not likely be viewed as 'implemented' in the Union. Thus, in a narrow class of cases, i.e. situations where the United States would assert jurisdiction over wholly foreign conduct that satisfies the jurisdictional test of the FTAIA, the ECJ has not yet asserted jurisdiction.

In an implicit acceptance of the ABA's criticism, the footnote in the International Guidelines was changed to read, '*in the context of import trade*, the "implementation" test adopted in the European Court of Justice usually produces the same outcome as the "effects" test employed in the United States'.

NOTE: The UK Government's position on extraterritoriality is more recently articulated in the CA 1998. Section 2(3) provides that the prohibition set out in subsection (1) shall only apply 'if the agreement, decision or practice is, or intended to be, *implemented* in the United Kingdom'. The italicised phrase is an explicit reference to the Court's decision in *Wood Pulp*. Following the reasoning of the Court in that case, it is possible that the Chapter I prohibition could be applied extraterritorially, where the agreement, having its origins outside the UK is implemented within it. Although this is a much wider view of jurisdiction than UK practice has followed, the government made it clear that it does not wish to follow the Community position on the 'effects' doctrine. Lord Simon explained:

> by copying out the test in *Wood Pulp* on the face of the Bill, we are also ensuring that in the event that EC jurisprudence develops and creates a pure effects-doctrine, the application of the UK prohibitions will not follow suit. (Hansard, HL, 13 November 1997, col. 261.)

The Enterprise Act

The territorial reach of the Enterprise Act will not be confined to the domestic arena. The DTI White Paper (2001) confirms that in relation to global cartels action can be taken separately against individuals as the agreement will be caught by the new offence where it is implemented or intended to be implemented in the UK (p. 44, point 7.44). The Under-Secretary of State for Trade and Industry, Melanie Johnson, remarked in Parliament that 'the agreement does not need to have been implemented to be caught. The making of the agreement is the offence. That is what matters, not whether it was implemented'. When pressed further on the issue she states 'subsection 3 [of section 190—the cartel offence: penalty and prosecution] requires that in those circumstances some subsequent action must have been taken to implement the agreement in the UK. That action could be no more than a clear instruction by telephone or e-mail into the UK to implement the agreement and it would be for the courts to determine whether such action had been taken'. Whilst this is not a strict US-style effects doctrine, the suggestion that e-mails and faxes could amount to implementation lowers the threshold of what constitutes implementation under UK law. This is a long way from traditional notions of territorial jurisdiction based on some nexus with the UK, for example, a subsidiary operating on UK soil. It is unclear how rigorously the UK Government will pursue individuals implementing anti-competitive behaviour from abroad in the UK, although the suggestion from Ms Johnson that 'this sends a message that nobody should escape justice simply by crossing a national border' would seem to suggest a firm approach at least in principle. Realpolitik dictates perhaps that the government will be less inclined to pursue extraterritorial jurisdiction in practice. Extraterritoriality also raises the possibility of extradition. Given the requirement of 'double criminality' in extradition treaties, it is unlikely that Member States will extradite those suspected of participating in hardcore cartels to the UK where the alleged offence is not a crime in the extraditing country. Hardcore cartel activity is a crime under s. 1 of the Sherman Act 1890 but it is difficult to imagine top-level US executives being extradited to stand trial in the UK.

NOTE: Extraterritoriality has particular relevance in the context of mergers which often transcend international borders. The Merger Regulation 4064/89 applies to all mergers with a Community dimension.

Gencor Ltd v *Commission*
(Case T-102/96) [1999] ECR II-753, [1999] 4 CMLR 971

> Gencor Ltd was a metals company incorporated under South African law and whose platinum group metals activities were performed by Implats, a company controlled by Gencor and also incorporated under South African law. Lonhro plc was a metals company incorporated under English law. Gencor and Lonrho sought to acquire joint control of Implats which would then acquire sole control of LPD and combine their platinum group metals business. The South African Competition Board approved the proposed concentration, but the Commission prohibited the merger on the basis that it would lead to a situation of oligopolistic dominance. On appeal, Gencor contended that the Merger Regulation did not give the Commission jurisdiction to assess whether the proposed concentration was compatible with the common market as the activities forming the subject matter of the concentration were conducted outside the Community. The CFI responded as follows.

[78] The Regulation, in accordance with Article I thereof, applies to all concentrations with a Community dimension, that is to say to all concentrations between undertakings which do not each achieve more than two-thirds of their aggregate Community-wide turnover within one and the same Member State, where the combined aggregate worldwide turnover of those undertakings is more than ECU 5,000 million and the aggregate Community-wide turnover of at least two of them is more than ECU 250 million.

[79] Article I does not require that, in order for a concentration to be regarded as having a Community dimension, the undertakings in question must be established in the Community or that the production activities covered by the concentration must be carried out within Community territory.

[80] With regard to the criterion of turnover, it must be stated that, as set out in paragraph 13 of the contested decision, the concentration at issue has a Community dimension within the meaning of Article 1(2) of the Regulation. The undertakings concerned have an aggregate worldwide turnover of more than ECU 10,000 million, above the ECU 5,000 million threshold laid down by the Regulation.

Gencor and Lonrho each had a Community-wide turnover of more than ECU 250 million in the latest financial year. Finally, they do not each achieve more than two-thirds of their aggregate Community-wide turnover within one and the same Member State.

[81] The applicant's arguments to the effect that the legal bases for the Regulation and the wording of its preamble and substantive provisions preclude its application to the concentration at issue cannot be accepted.

[82] The legal bases for the Regulation, namely Articles 87 and 235 of the Treaty, and more particularly the provisions to which they are intended to give effect, that is to say Articles 3(g) and 85 and 86 of the Treaty, as well as the first to fifth, ninth and eleventh recitals in the preamble to the Regulation, merely point to the need to ensure that competition is not distorted in the common market, in particular by concentrations which result in the creation or strengthening of a dominant position. They in no way exclude from the Regulation's field of application concentrations which, while relating to mining and/or production activities outside the Community, have the effect of creating or strengthening a dominant position as a result of which effective competition in the common market is significantly impeded.

[83] In particular, the applicant's view cannot be founded on the closing words of the 11th recital in the preamble to the Regulation.

[84] That recital states that 'a concentration with a Community dimension exists . . . where the concentrations are effected by undertakings which do not have their principal fields of activities in the Community but which have substantial operations there'.

[85] By that reference, in general terms, to the concept of substantial operations, the Regulation does not, for the purpose of defining its territorial scope, ascribe greater importance to production operations than to sales operations. On the contrary, by setting quantitative thresholds in Article 1 which are based on the worldwide and Community turnover of the undertakings concerned, it rather ascribes greater importance to sales operations within the common market as a factor linking the concentration to the Community. It is common ground that Gencor and Lonrho each carry out significant sales in the Community (valued in excess of ECU 250 million).

[86] Nor is it borne out by either the 30th recital in the preamble to the Regulation or Article 24 thereof that the criterion based on the location of production activities is well founded. Far from laying down a criterion for defining the territorial scope of the Regulation, Article 24 merely regulates the procedures to be followed in order to deal with situations in which non-member countries do not grant Community undertakings treatment comparable to that accorded by the Community to undertakings from those non-member countries in relation to the control of concentrations.

[87] The applicant cannot, by reference to the judgment in *Wood Pulp*, rely on the criterion as to the implementation of an agreement to support its interpretation of the territorial scope of the Regulation. Far from supporting the applicant's view, that criterion for assessing the link between an agreement and Community territory in fact precludes it. According to *Wood Pulp*, the criterion as to the implementation of an agreement is satisfied by mere sale within the Community, irrespective of the location of the sources of supply and the production plant. It is not disputed that Gencor and Lonrho carried out sales in the Community before the concentration and would have continued to do so thereafter.

[88] Accordingly, the Commission did not err in its assessment of the territorial scope of the Regulation by applying it in this case to a proposed concentration notified by undertakings whose registered offices and mining and production operations are outside the Community.

2. Compatibility of the contested decision with public international law

[89] Following the concentration agreement, the previously existing competitive relationship between Implats and LPD, in particular so far as concerns their sales in the Community, would have

come to an end. That would have altered the competitive structure within the common market since, instead of three South African PGM suppliers, there would have remained only two. The implementation of the proposed concentration would have led to the merger not only of the parties' PGM mining and production operations in South Africa but also of their marketing operations throughout the world, particularly in the Community where Implats and LPD achieved significant sales.

[90] Application of the Regulation is justified under public international law when it is foreseeable that a proposed concentration will have an immediate and substantial effect in the Community.

[91] In that regard, the concentration would, according to the contested decision, have led to the creation of a dominant duopoly on the part of Amplats and Implats/LPD in the platinum and rhodium markets, as a result of which effective competition would have been significantly impeded in the common market within the meaning of Article 2(3) of the Regulation.

[92] It is therefore necessary to verify whether the three criteria of immediate, substantial and foreseeable effect are satisfied in this case.

[93] With regard, specifically, to the criterion of immediate effect, the words 'medium term' used in paragraphs 206 and 210 of the contested decision in relation to the creation of a dominant duopoly position are, contrary to the applicant's assertion, entirely unambiguous. They clearly refer to the time when it is envisaged that Russian stocks will be exhausted, enabling a dominant duopoly on the part of Amplats and Implats/LPD to be created on the world platinum and rhodium markets and, by the same token, in the Community as a substantial part of those world markets.

[94] That dominant position would not be dependent, as the applicant asserts, on the future conduct of the undertaking arising from the concentration and of Amplats but would result, in particular, from the very characteristics of the market and the alteration of its structure. In referring to the future conduct of the parties to the duopoly, the applicant fails to distinguish between abuses of dominant position which those parties might commit in the near or more distant future, which might or might not be controlled by means of Articles 85 and/or 86 of the Treaty, and the alteration to the structure of the undertakings and of the market to which the concentration would give rise. It is true that the concentration would not necessarily lead to abuses immediately, since that depends on decisions which the parties to the duopoly may or may not take in the future. However, the concentration would have had the direct and immediate effect of creating the conditions in which abuses were not only possible but economically rational, given that the concentration would have significantly impeded effective competition in the market by giving rise to a lasting alteration to the structure of the markets concerned.

[95] Accordingly, the concentration would have had an immediate effect in the Community.

[96] So far as concerns the criterion of substantial effect, it should be noted that, as held in paragraph 297 below, the Commission established to the requisite legal standard that the concentration would have created a lasting dominant duopoly position in the world platinum and rhodium markets.

[97] The applicant cannot maintain that the concentration would not have a substantial effect in the Community in view of the low sales and small market share of the parties to the concentration in the EEA. While the level of sales in western Europe (20 per cent of world demand) and the Community market share of the entity arising from the concentration ((. . .) per cent in respect of platinum) were already sufficient grounds for the Community to have jurisdiction in respect of the concentration, the potential impact of the concentration proved even higher than those figures suggested. Given that the concentration would have had the effect of creating a dominant duopoly position in the world platinum and rhodium markets, it is clear that the sales in the Community potentially affected by the concentration would have included not only those of the Implats/LPD undertaking but also those of Amplats (approximately 35 per cent to 50 per cent), which would have represented a more than substantial proportion of platinum and rhodium sales in western Europe and a much higher combined market share held by Implats/LPD and Amplats (approximately (. . .) per cent to 65 per cent).

[98] Finally, it is not possible to accept the applicant's argument that the creation of the dominant position referred to by the Commission in the contested decision is not of greater concern to the Community than to any other competent body and is even of less concern to it than to others. The fact that, in a world market, other parts of the world are affected by the concentration cannot prevent the Community from exercising its control over a concentration which substantially affects competition within the common market by creating a dominant position.

[99] The arguments by which the applicant denies that the concentration would have a substantial effect in the Community must therefore be rejected.

[100] As for the criterion of foreseeable effect, it follows from all of the foregoing that it was in fact foreseeable that the effect of creating a dominant duopoly position in a world market would also be to impede competition significantly in the Community, an integral part of that market.

[101] It follows that the application of the Regulation to the proposed concentration was consistent with public international law.

[102] It is necessary to examine next whether the Community violated a principle of non-interference or the principle of proportionality in exercising that jurisdiction.

[103] The applicant's argument that, by virtue of a principle of non-interference, the Commission should have refrained from prohibiting the concentration in order to avoid a conflict of jurisdiction with the South African authorities must be rejected, without it being necessary to consider whether such a rule exists in international law. Suffice it to note that there was no conflict between the course of action required by the South African Government and that required by the Community given that, in their letter of 22 August 1995, the South African competition authorities simply concluded that the concentration agreement did not give rise to any competition policy concerns, without requiring that such an agreement be entered into (see, to that effect, *Wood Pulp*, paragraph 20).

[104] In its letter of 19 April 1996 the South African Government, far from calling into question the Community's jurisdiction to rule on the concentration at issue, first simply expressed a general preference, having regard to the strategic importance of mineral exploitation in South Africa, for intervention in specific cases of collusion when they arose and did not specifically comment on the industrial or other merits of the concentration proposed by Gencor and Lonrho. It then merely expressed the view that the proposed concentration might not impede competition, having regard to the economic power of Amplats, the existence of other sources of supply of PGMs and the opportunities for other producers to enter the South African market through the grant of new mining concessions.

[105] Finally, neither the applicant nor, indeed, the South African Government in its letter of 19 April 1996 have shown, beyond making mere statements of principle, in what way the proposed concentration would affect the vital economic and/or commercial interests of the Republic of South Africa.

[106] As regards the argument that the Community cannot claim to have jurisdiction in respect of a concentration on the basis of future and hypothetical behaviour, namely parallel conduct on the part of the undertakings operating in the relevant market where that conduct might or might not fall within the competence of the Community under the Treaty, it must be stated, as pointed out above in connection with the question whether the concentration has an immediate effect, that, while the elimination of the risk of future abuses may be a legitimate concern of any competent competition authority, the main objective in exercising control over concentrations at Community level is to ensure that the restructuring of undertakings does not result in the creation of positions of economic power which may significantly impede effective competition in the common market. Community jurisdiction is therefore founded, first and foremost, on the need to avoid the establishment of market structures which may create or strengthen a dominant position, and not on the need to control directly possible abuses of a dominant position.

[107] Consequently, it is unnecessary to rule on the question whether the letter of 22 August 1995 from the South African Competition Board constituted a definitive position on the concentration, on whether or not the South African Government was an authority responsible for competition matters and, finally, on the scope of South African competition law. There is accordingly no need to grant the application for measures of organisation of procedure or of inquiry made by the applicant in its letter of 3 December 1996.

[108] In those circumstances, the contested decision is not inconsistent with either the Regulation or the rules of public international law relied on by the applicant.

[109] For the same reasons, the objection, based on Article 184 of the Treaty, that the Regulation is unlawful because it confers upon the Commission competence in respect of the concentration between Gencor and Lonrho must be rejected.

[110] As regards the reasoning in the contested decision justifying Community jurisdiction to apply the Regulation to the concentration, it must be held that the explanations contained in paragraphs 4, 13 to 18, 204 to 206, 210 and 213 of the contested decision satisfy the obligations incumbent on the Commission under Article 190 of the Treaty to give reasons for its decisions so as to enable the Community judicature to exercise its power of review, the parties to defend their rights and any interested party to ascertain the conditions in which the Commission applied the Treaty and its implementing legislation.

[111] Accordingly, both pleas of annulment which have been examined must be rejected, without it being necessary to grant the application for measures of organisation of procedure or of inquiry made by the applicant in its letter of 3 December 1996.

NOTE: The parallels with the US effects doctrine are obvious. Given the European Court's reluctance to embrace the effects doctrine, the judgment in *Gencor* is significant, particularly since the Court did not consider the fact that LPD's parent company, Lonrho, was established in the United Kingdom as an alternative ground for jurisdiction. It is not yet clear whether the judgment will be restricted to merger control. Fox has suggested that 'in matters of antitrust, the most prohibitory nation wins', Fox, E.M., 'National Law, Global Matters, and *Hartford*. Eyes Wide Shut' 68(1) Antitrust L.J. (2000) 81. For example, what would have happened if the South African competition authorities had taken a more proactive stance in favour of their 'national champion'?

FURTHER READING

Fox, E.M., 'The Merger Regulation and its Territorial Reach: *Gencor Ltd* v *Commission*' [1999] ECLR 334.

Fiebig, A., 'International Law Limits on the Extraterritorial Application of the European Merger Control Regulation and Suggestions for Reform' [1998] ECLR 323.

SECTION 3: **Cooperation**

Multijurisdictional competition law enforcement is clearly a complex issue and presents national competition authorities with many challenges. However, as Karl Van Miert explains:

Commission's 28th Report on Competition Policy (1998)
p. 8

National or regional competition authorities are ill-equipped to grapple with the problems posed by commercial behaviour occurring beyond their borders. Information may be difficult to obtain, and decisions—once taken—may be impossible to enforce. Although new competition legislation has been introduced in many countries in recent years, some behaviour might not be unlawful in the country where it is being carried out, or the authorities there may be unwilling to condemn it. Alternatively, incoherent or even directly contradictory conclusions might be reached by different enforcement authorities, both of which may claim jurisdiction over the same subject-matter. Such divergent treatment not only entails the risk of precipitating a dispute between countries or trading blocks, as was illustrated by the initial disagreement between the US and the EU over the proposed Boeing/MDD merger last year, but is also a source of considerable uncertainty and cost for companies engaging in global transactions.

Cooperation among the national competition authorities is vital to deal with anti-competitive practices with transnational characteristics. Cooperation among the Member States' national competition authorities is common and likely to increase following implementation of the White Paper programme. See Chapter 3. The UK Government has also indicated that it will legislate to allow increased sharing of competition and consumer information between the UK authorities and overseas authorities for the purpose of criminal and civil investigations following enactment of the Enterprise Bill. Cooperation in the global arena however, is only a recent phenomenon. Faull makes some suggestions as to why this is the case:

Faull, J., 'Why Do We Need More Cooperation in the Field of Competition Policy?'
Speech delivered in Tokyo, Japan Competition Policy Seminar, 22 November 1995

One reason may be that countries do not always agree on the purposes of competition policy. Even if the details of tax law differ from one country to another, most countries would agree that tax fraud is an offence. More generally, democratic countries share basically the same approach on the scope of the criminal law, although rules differ from jurisdiction to jurisdiction. Perhaps this sort of broad consensus has not yet been achieved in some areas of competition policy.

Within the same country, policy emphasis may vary over time. Competition policy is influenced by political change and our developing understanding of economics. Above all, policy must change and adapt to the rapid evolution of the industries and markets which are its focus of attention. I am sure that no-one pretends that our policies in the EU and in Japan must remain static and impervious to changes in the world around us. Our friends in the USA have lived through such changes recently: US competition policy today is somewhat different from the one conducted by the Reagan administration, which was itself different from the policy implemented by previous administrations.

We must also acknowledge that competition policies focus on domestic markets. A good illustration of this approach is the fact that export cartels, which have harmful effects on foreign markets, are, in most instances, not subjected to competition rules. However, in Europe I think it is fair to recognize that our active competition policy in support of the completion of the Single Market has helped third country firms establish themselves on an equal footing.

A second obstacle to cooperation among competition authorities stems from the very nature of competition policy. This can be better understood if we compare competition policy with trade policy.

Trade policy deals with measures adopted by countries, which in most cases, are publicly known and easily identifiable. It has therefore been possible under the GATT (and now under the WTO) to set up dispute settlement mechanisms in order to ensure that measures adopted by national authorities are consistent with internationally agreed principles and rules. Assuming that comparable sets of common rules could be negotiated among competition authorities, we would still have a specific difficulty with fact-finding, which is after all an essential part of competition policy. Restrictive practices are often concealed and are certainly not readily identifiable. Even if all the contracting parties to a possible international agreement on competition rules undertook to put an end to certain restrictive practices, it would be far from easy to make sure that these commitments were fully complied with.

Despite these difficulties the competition authorities of the world have devised a number of ways to cooperate on competition matters. The EC Competition Commissioner outlines the merits of cooperation in the next extract.

Commission's 30th Report on Competition Policy (2000)
Foreword extract, Mario Monti

The rapid globalisation of the world economy brings major limitations—both legal and practical—to our ability to apply our own rules extraterritorially. Even when this possibility is not prevented, there are many drawbacks in doing so: it can give rise to conflicts, or to incoherence, with the rulings of foreign agencies or courts, and even to conflicts with foreign laws. As a result, undertakings operating on a global environment may be able to escape those rules that are essential to govern economic and social processes.

The main policy response available to competition authorities is one that calls upon them to establish networks and instruments of global governance ensuring that the international integration of markets leads to maintained competitive outcomes, thus making the globalisation process both economically more efficient and socially more acceptable. In this context, competition policy—and specifically international cooperation on competition policy—has an important role to play, if we are to avoid resentment against globalisation and a protectionist backlash.

A: Bilateral cooperation

The European Community has been at the forefront of developments in bilateral cooperation with its main trading partners. The first, and probably best example of a bilateral cooperation agreement, is provided by the agreements entered into between the European Communities and the United States in the past decade. The first agreement, concluded in 1991, represented an important advancement in transatlantic competition relations. The 1991 Agreement provides for notification, consultation, information sharing and cooperation and coordination on enforcement matters. It came into force in 1995.

Agreement between the European Communities and the United States
23 September 1991 [1991] 30 ILM 1487

THE GOVERNMENT OF THE UNITED STATES OF AMERICA AND THE COMMISSION OF
THE EUROPEAN COMMUNITIES,

Recognizing that the world's economies are becoming increasingly interrelated, and in particular that this is true of the economies of the United States of America and the European Communities;

Noting that the Government of the United States of America and the Commission of the European Communities share the view that the sound and effective enforcement of competition law is a matter of importance to the efficient operation of their respective markets and to trade between them;

Noting that the sound and effective enforcement of the Parties' competition laws would be enhanced by cooperation and, in appropriate cases, coordination between them in the application of those laws;

Noting further that from time to time differences may arise between the Parties concerning the application of their competition laws to conduct or transactions that implicate significant interests of both Parties;

Having regard to the Recommendation of the Council of the Organization for Economic Cooperation and Development Concerning Cooperation Between Member Countries on Restrictive Business Practices Affecting International Trade, adopted on June 5, 1986;

and

Having regard to the Declaration on US–EC Relations adopted on November 23, 1990,

HAVE AGREED AS FOLLOWS:

Article I: Purpose and definitions

1. The purpose of this Agreement is to promote cooperation and coordination and lessen the possibility or impact of differences between the Parties in the application of their competition laws.

2. For the purpose of this Agreement, the following terms shall have the following definitions:

A. 'competition law(s)' shall mean

(i) for the European Communities, Articles 85, 86, 89 and 90 of the Treaty establishing the European Economic Community, Regulation (EEC) No 4064/89 on the control of concentrations between undertakings, Articles 65 and 66 of the Treaty establishing the European Coal and Steel Community (ECSC), and their implementing Regulations including High Authority Decision No 24-54, and

(ii) for the United States of America, the Sherman Act (15 USC paras 1–7), the Clayton Act (15 USC paras 12–27), the Wilson Tariff Act (15 USC paras 8–11), and the Federal Trade Commission Act (15 USC paras 41–68, except as these sections relate to consumer protection functions),

as well as such other laws or regulations as the Parties shall jointly agree in writing to be a 'competition law' for purposes of this Agreement;

B. 'competition authorities' shall mean (i) for the European Communities, the Commission of the European Communities, as to its responsibilities pursuant to the competition laws of the European Communities, and (ii) for the United States, the Antitrust Division of the United Stated Department of Justice and the Federal Trade Commission;

C. 'enforcement activities' shall mean any application of competition law by way of investigation or proceeding conducted by the competition authorities of a Party; and

D. 'anticompetitive activities' shall mean any conduct or transaction that is impermissible under the competition laws of a Party.

Article II: Notification

1. Each Party shall notify the other whenever its competition authorities become aware that their enforcement activities may affect important interests of the other Party.

2. Enforcement activities as to which notification ordinarily will be appropriate include those that:

(a) are relevant to enforcement activities of the other Party;

(b) involve anticompetitive activities (other than a merger or acquisition) carried out in significant part in the other Party's territory;

(c) involve a merger or acquisition in which one or more of the parties to the transaction, or a company controlling one or more of the Parties to the transaction, is a company incorporated or organized under the laws of the other Party or one of its States or Member States;

(d) involve conduct believed to have been required, encouraged or approved by the other Party; or

(e) involve remedies that would, in significant respects, require or prohibit conduct in the other Party's territory.

3. With respect to mergers or acquisitions required by law to be reported to the competition authorities, notification under this Article shall be made:

(a) in the case of the Government of the United States of America,
   (i) not later than the time its competition authorities request, pursuant to 15 USC para 18 a(e), additional information or documentary material concerning the proposed transaction,
   (ii) when its competition authorities decide to file a complaint challenging the transaction, and
   (iii) where this is possible, far enough in advance of the entry of a consent decree to enable the other Party's views to be taken into account; and

(b) in the case of the Commission of the European Communities,
   (i) when notice of the transaction is published in the Official Journal, pursuant to Article 4 (3) of Council Regulation No 4064/89, or when notice of the transaction is received under Article 66 of the ECSC Treaty and a prior authorization from the Commission is required under that provision,
   (ii) when its competition authorities decide to initiate proceedings with respect to the proposed transaction, pursuant to Article 6(1)(c) of Council Regulation (EEC) No 4064/89, and
   (iii) far enough in advance of the adoption of a decision in the case to enable the other Party's views to be taken into account.

4. With respect to other matters, notification shall ordinarily be provided at the stage in an investigation when it becomes evident that notifiable circumstances are present, and in any event far enough in advance of:

(a) the issuance of a statement of objections in the case of the Commission of the European Communities, or a complaint or indictment in the case of the Government of the United States of America; and

(b) the adoption of a decision or settlement in the case of the Commission of the European Communities, or the entry of a consent decree in the case of the Government of the United States of America;

to enable the other Party's views to be taken into account.

5. Each Party shall also notify the other whenever its competition authorities intervene or otherwise participate in a regulatory or judicial proceeding that does not arise from its enforcement activities, if the issues addressed in the intervention or participation may affect the other Party's important interests. Notification under this paragraph shall apply only to:

(a) regulatory or judicial proceedings that are public;

(b) intervention or participation that is public and pursuant to formal procedures; and

(c) in the case of regulatory proceedings in the United States, only proceedings before federal agencies.

Notification shall be made at the time of the intervention or participation or as soon thereafter as possible.

6. Notifications under this Article shall include sufficient information to permit an initial evaluation by the recipient Party of any effects on its interests.

Article III: Exchange of information

1. The Parties agree that it is in their common interest to share information that will (a) facilitate effective application of their respective competition laws, or (b) promote better understanding by them of economic conditions and theories relevant to their competition authorities' enforcement activities and interventions or participation of the kind described in Article 11(5).

2. In furtherance of this common interest, appropriate officials from the competition authorities of each Party shall meet at least twice each year, unless otherwise agreed, to (a) exchange information on their current enforcement activities and priorities, (b) exchange information on economic sectors of common interest, (c) discuss policy changes which they are considering, and (d) discuss other matters of mutual interest relating to the application of competition laws.

3. Each Party will provide the other Party with any significant information that comes to the attention of its competition authorities about anti-competitive activities that its competition authorities believe is relevant to, or may warrant, enforcement activity by the other Party's competition authorities.

4. Upon receiving a request from the other Party, and within the limits of Articles VIII and IX, a Party will provide to the requesting Party such information within its possession as the requesting Party may describe that is relevant to an enforcement activity being considered or conducted by the requesting Party's competition authorities.

Article IV: Cooperation and coordination in enforcement activities

1. The competition authorities of each Party will render assistance to the competition authorities of the other Party in their enforcement activities, to the extent compatible with the assisting Party's laws and important interests, and within its reasonably available resources.

2. In cases where both Parties have an interest in pursuing enforcement activities with regard to related situations, they may agree that it is in their mutual interest to coordinate their enforcement activities. In considering whether particular enforcement activities should be coordinated, the Parties shall take account of the following factors, among others:

  (a) the opportunity to make more efficient use of their resources devoted to the enforcement activities;
  (b) the relative abilities of the Parties' competition authorities to obtain information necessary to conduct the enforcement activities;
  (c) the effect of such coordination on the ability of both Parties to achieve the objectives of their enforcement activities; and
  (d) the possibility of reducing costs incurred by persons subject to the enforcement activities.

3. In any coordination arrangement, each Party shall conduct its enforcement activities expeditiously and, insofar as possible, consistently with the enforcement objectives of the other Party.

4. Subject to appropriate notice to the other Party, the competition authorities of either Party may limit or terminate their participation in a coordination arrangement and pursue their enforcement activities independently.

Article V: Cooperation regarding anti-competitive activities in the territory of one Party that adversely affect the interests of the other Party

1. The Parties note that anti-competitive activities may occur within the territory of one Party that, in addition to violating that Party's competition laws, adversely affect important interests of the

other Party. The Parties agree that it is in both their interests to address anti-competitive activities of this nature.

2. If a Party believes that anti-competitive activities carried out on the territory of the other Party are adversely affecting its important interests, the first Party may notify the other Party and may request that the other Party's competition authorities initiate appropriate enforcement activities. The notification shall be as specific as possible about the nature of the anti-competitive activities and their effects on the interests of the notifying Party, and shall include an offer of such further information and other cooperation as the notifying Party is able to provide.

3. Upon receipt of a notification under paragraph 2, and after such other discussion between the Parties as may be appropriate and useful in the circumstances, the competition authorities of the notified Party will consider whether or not to initiate enforcement activities, or to expand ongoing enforcement activities, with respect to the anti-competitive activities identified in the notification. The notified Party will advise the notifying Party of its decision. If enforcement activities are initiated, the notified Party will advise the notifying Party of their outcome and, to the extent possible, of significant interim developments.

4. Nothing in this Article limits the discretion of the notified Party under its competition laws and enforcement policies as to whether or not to undertake enforcement activities with respect to the notified anti-competitive activities, or precludes the notifying Party from undertaking enforcement activities with respect to such anti-competitive activities.

Article VI: Avoidance of conflicts over enforcement activities

Within the framework of its own laws and to the extent compatible with its important interests, each Party will seek, at all stages in its enforcement activities, to take into account the important interests of the other Party. Each Party shall consider important interests of the other Party in decisions as to whether or not to initiate an investigation or proceeding, the scope of an investigation or proceeding, the nature of the remedies or penalties sought, and in other ways, as appropriate. In considering one another's important interests in the course of their enforcement activities, the Parties will take account of, but will not be limited to, the following principles:

1. While an important interest of a Party may exist in the absence of official involvement by the Party with the activity in question, it is recognized that such interests would normally be reflected in antecedent laws, decisions or statements of policy by its competent authorities.
2. A Party's important interests may be affected at any stage of enforcement activity by the other Party. The Parties recognize, however, that as a general matter the potential for adverse impact on one Party's important interests arising from enforcement activity by the other Party is less at the investigative stage and greater at the stage at which conduct is prohibited or penalized, or at which other forms of remedial orders are imposed.
3. Where it appears that one Party's enforcement activities may adversely affect important interests of the other Party, the Parties will consider the following factors, in addition to any other factors that appear relevant in the circumstances, in seeking an appropriate accommodation of the competing interests:

   (a) the relative significance to the anti-competitive activities involved of conduct within the enforcing Party's territory as compared to conduct within the other Party's territory;
   (b) the presence or absence of a purpose on the part of those engaged in the anti-competitive activities to affect consumers, suppliers or competitors within the enforcing Party's territory;
   (c) the relative significance of the effects of the anti-competitive activities on the enforcing Party's interests as compared to the effects on the other Party's interests;

(d) the existence or absence of reasonable expectations that would be furthered or defeated by the enforcement activities;

(e) the degree of conflict or consistency between the enforcement activities and the other Party's laws or articulated economic policies; and

(f) the extent to which enforcement activities of the other Party with respect to the same persons, including judgments or undertakings resulting from such activities, may be affected.

Article VII: Consultation

1. Each Party agrees to consult promptly with the other Party in response to a request by the other Party for consultations regarding any matter related to this Agreement and to attempt to conclude consultations expeditiously with a view to reaching mutually satisfactory conclusions. Any request for consultations shall include the reasons therefor and shall state whether procedural time limits or other considerations require the consultations to be expedited.

These consultations shall take place at the appropriate level, which may include consultations between the heads of the competition authorities concerned.

2. In each consultation under paragraph 1, each Party shall take into account the principles of cooperation set forth in this Agreement and shall be prepared to explain to the other Party the specific results of its application of those principles to the issue that is the subject of consultation.

Article VIII: Confidentiality of information

1. Notwithstanding any other provision of this Agreement, neither Party is required to provide information to the other Party if disclosure of that information to the requesting Party (a) is prohibited by the law of the Party possessing the information, or (b) would be incompatible with important interests of the Party possessing the information.

2. Each Party agrees to maintain, to the fullest extent possible, the confidentiality of any information provided to it in confidence by the other Party under this Agreement and to oppose, to the fullest extent possible, any application for disclosure of such information by a third party that is not authorized by the Party that supplied the information.

Article IX: Existing law

Nothing in this Agreement shall be interpreted in a manner inconsistent with the existing laws, or as requiring any change in the laws, of the United States of America or the European Communities or of their respective States or Member States.

Article X: Communications under this Agreement

Communications under this Agreement, including notifications under Articles II and V, may be carried out by direct oral, telephonic, written or facsimile communication from one Party's competition authority to the other Party's authority. Notifications under Articles II, V and XI, and requests under Article VII, shall be confirmed promptly in writing through diplomatic channels.

Article XI: Entry into force, termination and review

1. This Agreement shall enter into force upon signature.

2. This Agreement shall remain in force until 60 days after the date on which either Party notifies the other Party in writing that it wishes to terminate the Agreement.

3. The Parties shall review the operation of this Agreement not more than 24 months from the date of its entry into force, with a view to assessing their cooperative activities, identifying additional areas in which they could usefully cooperate and identifying any other ways in which the Agreement could be improved.

The Parties agree that this review will include, among other things, an analysis of actual or potential cases to determine whether their interests could be better served through closer cooperation.

It was supplemented by a second cooperation agreement in 1998 which reinforces the principle of positive comity in Article V of the first Agreement.

Article III Positive comity
The competition authorities of a Requesting Party may request the competition authorities of a Requested Party to investigate and, if warranted, to remedy anti-competitive activities in accordance with the Requested Party's competition laws. Such a request may be made regardless of whether the activities also violate the Requesting Party's competition laws, and regardless of whether the competition authorities of the Requesting Party have commenced or contemplate taking enforcement activities under their own competition laws.

Article IV Deferral or suspension of investigations in reliance on enforcement activity by the Requested Party
1. The competition authorities of the Parties may agree that the competition authorities of the Requesting Party will defer or suspend pending or contemplated enforcement activities during the pendency of enforcement activities of the Requested Party.

2. The competition authorities of a Requesting Party will normally defer or suspend their own enforcement activities in favor of enforcement activities by the competition authorities of the Requested Party when the following conditions are satisfied:

(a) The anti-competitive activities at issue:
   (i)   do not have a direct, substantial and reasonably foreseeable impact on consumers in the Requesting Party's territory, or
   (ii) where the anti-competitive activities do have such an impact on the Requesting Party's consumers, they occur principally in and are directed principally towards the other Party's territory;

(b) The adverse effects on the interests of the Requesting Party can be and are likely to be fully and adequately investigated and, as appropriate, eliminated or adequately remedied pursuant to the laws, procedures, and available remedies of the Requested Party. The Parties recognize that it may be appropriate to pursue separate enforcement activities where anti-competitive activities affecting both territories justify the imposition of penalties within both jurisdictions; and

(c) The competition authorities of the Requested Party agree that in conducting their own enforcement activities, they will:
   (i)   devote adequate resources to investigate the anti-competitive activities and, where appropriate, promptly pursue adequate enforcement activities;
   (ii) use their best efforts to pursue all reasonably available sources of information, including such sources of information as may be suggested by the competition authorities of the Requesting Party;
   (iii) inform the competition authorities of the Requesting Party, on request or at reasonable intervals, of the status of their enforcement activities and intentions, and where appropriate provide to the competition authorities of the Requesting Party relevant confidential information if consent has been obtained from the source concerned. The use and disclosure of such information shall be governed by Article V;
   (iv) promptly notify the competition authorities of the Requesting Party of any change in their intentions with respect to investigation or enforcement;
   (v)   use their best efforts to complete their investigation and to obtain a remedy or initiate

proceedings within six months, or such other time as agreed to by the competition authorities of the Parties, of the deferral or suspension of enforcement activities by the competition authorities of the Requesting Party;

(vi) fully inform the competition authorities of the Requesting Party of the results of their investigation, and take into account the views of the competition authorities of the Requesting Party, prior to any settlement, initiation of proceedings, adoption of remedies, or termination of the investigation; and

(vii) comply with any reasonable request that may be made by the competition authorities of the Requesting Party.

When the above conditions are satisfied, a Requesting Party which chooses not to defer or suspend its enforcement activities shall inform the competition authorities of the Requested Party of its reasons.

3. The competition authorities of the Requesting Party may defer or suspend their own enforcement activities if fewer than all of the conditions set out in paragraph 2 are satisfied.

4. Nothing in this Agreement precludes the competition authorities of a Requesting Party that choose to defer or suspend independent enforcement activities from later initiating or reinstituting such activities. In such circumstances, the competition authorities of the Requesting Party will promptly inform the competition authorities of the Requested Party of their intentions and reasons. If the competition authorities of the Requested Party continue with their own investigation, the competition authorities of the two Parties shall, where appropriate, coordinate their respective investigations under the criteria and procedures of Article IV of the 1991 Agreement.

NOTE: Mergers do not fall within the scope of the Agreement as both EC and US merger legislation provides for a deferral or suspension of action as envisaged by the Agreement. It is worth noting that other countries have concluded similar bilateral cooperation agreements, e.g. US and Canada, and Australia and New Zealand. There is no doubting that such cooperation can be highly effective and substantially reduce the risk of a protectionist backlash or resentment against globalisation against which the EC Competition Commissioner has warned (ibid.). Bilateral cooperation between the EC and the US has proved highly effective over the years, and has facilitated a convergent approach towards the analysis of markets and appropriate sanctions. However, the limitations of this case-specific cooperation were exposed in the *Boeing/McDonnell Douglas* case.

Boeing and McDonnell Douglas (MDC) notified the US and EC competition authorities of a decision to merge in February 1997. In July the US Federal Trade Commission concluded that the transaction would not substantially lessen competition.

In the Matter of The Boeing Company/McDonnell Douglas Corporation File No 971–0051

Statement of Chairman Robert Pitofsky and Commissioners Janet D. Steiger, Roscoe B. Starek III and Christine A. Varney

After an extensive and exhaustive investigation, the Federal Trade Commission has decided to close the investigation of The Boeing Company's proposed acquisition of McDonnell Douglas Corporation. For reasons discussed below, we have concluded that the acquisition would not substantially lessen competition or tend to create a monopoly in either defense or commercial aircraft markets.

There has been speculation in the press and elsewhere that the United States antitrust authorities might allow this transaction to go forward—particularly the portion of the transaction dealing with the manufacture of commercial aircraft—because aircraft manufacturing occurs in a global market, and the United States, in order to compete in that market, needs a single powerful firm to serve as its 'national champion'. A powerful United States firm is all the more important, the argument proceeds, because that firm's success contributes much to improving the United States' balance of trade and to providing jobs for US workers.

The national champion argument does not explain today's decision. Our task as enforcers, conferred in clear terms by Congress in enacting the antitrust statutes, is to ensure the vitality of the free market by preventing private actions that may substantially lessen competition or tend to create a monopoly. In the Boeing-McDonnell Douglas matter, the Commission's task was to review a merger between two direct competitors.

We do not have the discretion to authorize competitive but 'good' mergers because they may be thought to advance the United States' trade interests. If that were thought to be a wise approach, only Congress could implement it. In any event, the 'national champion' argument is almost certainly a delusion. In reality, the best way to boost the United States' exports, address concerns about the balance of trade, and create jobs is to require United States' firms to compete vigorously at home and abroad. Judge Learned Hand put the matter well a half century ago in describing the reasons for the commitment in the United States to the protection of the free market:

> Many people believe that possession of unchallenged economic power deadens initiative, discourages thrift and depresses energy; that immunity from competition is a narcotic, and rivalry is a stimulant, to industrial progress; that the spur of constant stress is necessary to counteract inevitable disposition to let well enough alone.[1]

On its face, the proposed merger appears to raise serious antitrust concerns. The transaction involves the acquisition by Boeing, a company that accounts for roughly 60 per cent of the sales of large commercial aircraft, of a non-failing direct competitor in a market in which there is only one other significant rival, Airbus Industrie, and extremely high barriers to entry. The merger would also combine two firms in the US defense industry that develop fighter aircraft and other defense products. Nevertheless, for reasons we will now discuss, we do not find that this merger will substantially lessen competition in any relevant market.

The Commission reached its decision not to oppose the merger following a lengthy and detailed investigation into the acquisition's potential effects on competition by a large team of FTC attorneys, economists and accountants. The Commission staff interviewed over 40 airlines (including almost every US carrier, large and small, and many foreign carriers), as well as other industry participants, such as regional aircraft producers and foreign aerospace companies. Staff deposed McDonnell Douglas and Boeing officials responsible for marketing commercial aircraft, assessing their firms' financial conditions, and negotiating the proposed acquisition. Finally, the Commission staff reviewed hundreds of boxes of documents submitted by the merging companies and third parties, such as airlines and aircraft manufacturers.

With respect to the commercial aircraft sector, our decision not to challenge the proposed merger was a result of evidence that (1) McDonnell Douglas, looking to the future, no longer constitutes a meaningful competitive force in the commercial aircraft market and (2) there is no economically plausible strategy that McDonnell Douglas could follow, either as a standalone concern or as part of another concern, that would change that grim prospect.

The evidence collected during the staff investigation, including the virtually unanimous testimony of 40 airlines that staff interviewed, revealed that McDonnell Douglas's commercial aircraft division,

---

1. *United States* v *Aluminum Company of America*, 148 F.2d 416, 427 (2d Cir. 1945).

Douglas Aircraft Company, can no longer exert a competitive influence in the worldwide market for commercial aircraft. Over the past several decades, McDonnell Douglas has not invested at nearly the rate of its competitors in new product lines, production facilities, company infrastructure, or research and development. As a result, Douglas Aircraft's product line is not only very limited, but lacks the state of the art technology and performance characteristics that Boeing and Airbus have developed.[2] Moreover, Douglas Aircraft's line of aircraft do not have common features such as cockpit design or engine type, and thus cannot generate valuable efficiencies in interchangeable spare parts and pilot training that an airline may obtain from a family of aircraft, such as Boeing's 737 family or Airbus's A-320 family.

In short, the staff investigation revealed that the failure to improve the technology and efficiency of its commercial aircraft products has led to a deterioration of Douglas Aircraft's product line to the point that the vast majority of airlines will no longer consider purchasing Douglas aircraft and that the company is no longer in a position to influence significantly the competitive dynamics of the commercial aircraft market.

Our decision not to challenge the proposed merger does not reflect a conclusion that McDonnell Douglas is a failing company or that Douglas Aircraft is a failing division. Nor does our decision not to challenge the proposed merger reflect a conclusion that Douglas Aircraft could maintain competitively significant sales, but has simply decided to redeploy or retire its assets. While McDonnell Douglas's prospects for future commercial aircraft sales are virtually non-existent, its commercial aircraft production assets are likely to remain in the market for the near future as a result of a modest backlog of aircraft orders. As a result, it is unlikely that the aircraft division would have been liquidated quickly. Moreover, the failing company defense comes into play only where the Commission first finds that the transaction is likely to be anti-competitive. Here, the absence of any prospect of significant commercial sales, combined with a dismal financial forecast, indicate that Douglas Aircraft is no longer an effective competitor, and there is no prospect that position could be reversed.

The merger also does not threaten competition in military programs. Though both Boeing and McDonnell Douglas develop fighter aircraft, there are no current or future procurements of fighter aircraft by the Department of Defense in which the two firms would likely compete. Finally, there are no other domestic military markets in which the products offered by the companies are substitutes for each other. The Department of Defense, in a letter to the Commission dated July 1, 1997, indicated that competition would remain in the defense industry post-merger.

While the merger seems to pose no threat to the competitive landscape in either the commercial aircraft or in various defense markets, we find the 20 year exclusive contracts Boeing recently entered with three major airlines potentially troubling. Boeing is the largest player in the global commercial aircraft market and though the contracts now foreclose only about 11 per cent of that market, the airlines involved are prestigious. They represent a sizeable portion of airlines that can serve as 'launch' customers for aircraft manufacturers, that is, airlines that can place orders large enough and have sufficient market prestige to serve as the first customer for a new airplane. We intend to monitor the potential anti-competitive effects of these, and any future, long term exclusive contracts.

Federal Trade Commissioner Mary Azcuerga dissented

Statement of Commissioner Mary L. Azcuenaga

The Commission today announces that it will not challenge the proposed merger of The Boeing Company and McDonnell Douglas Corporation. I agree that no action is warranted against the

---

2. Our colleague Commissioner Azcuenaga seems to speculate that these problems may be the result of 'strategic behavior' to avoid government challenge, and that others in the future may pursue a similar strategy. Speculation is easy, but there is absolutely no evidence that any such behavior occurred here.

combination of assets in the defense and space lines of business, which constitutes the greater portion of the proposed transaction, although I do not join the discussion of the other commissioners[1] on this point.

I also agree with my colleagues that no action is warranted concerning the 20-year exclusive arrangements for commercial aircraft that Boeing recently reached with three major US airlines. The arrangements account for an estimated 11 per cent of the market, well below any level that should be of concern under the laws enforced by the Commission. Given the state of the law and the fact that the exclusive arrangements apparently are unrelated to the proposed transaction, what is curious is that my colleagues choose to mention them at all.

Another aspect of the proposed transaction is the combination of two of the three remaining manufacturers of commercial aircraft in the world. Boeing is the largest commercial aircraft firm in the world; McDonnell Douglas, through Douglas Aircraft Company ('Douglas'), is number three in the industry. This horizontal combination of two of the three firms in the market appears to present a rather straightforward case for a challenge by the Commission. Absent action by the Commission, the merger will eliminate one of three firms in a highly concentrated market in which entry is difficult and unlikely.

My colleagues conclude that most airlines will not buy planes from Douglas, a factual conclusion with a surprising reach for a simple announcement of failure to prosecute and a conclusion and implication of competitive insignificance with which I disagree after having reviewed the available information. It is true that Douglas has a small share of the commercial aircraft market, but that does not mean that it exercises no competitive constraint.[2] The evidence shows that Douglas has added an element of competition at the stage at which commercial aircraft producers bid for the business of airlines, and it has continued to win some business.

My colleagues rely in their statement on the so-called *General Dynamics*[3] defense, that is, that market shares based on past performance may overstate a firm's future competitive significance. In *General Dynamics*, the government's statistical case based on historical production of coal was deemed an inadequate predictor of anti-competitive effects in light of the acquired firm's inability to obtain additional coal reserves. The company could not compete for future sales, because its coal reserves already were committed and it could not acquire additional reserves. No such definitive impediment is present here. Douglas may need more customers for its products, but having won fewer customers than it might want does not make Douglas unable to compete for future sales.[4] One problem with accepting a 'flailing firm' or 'exiting assets' claim is that it creates an incentive for strategic action to avoid competitive overlaps and government challenge under s. 7 of the Clayton Act.[5] This is a dangerous precedent when we move from the realm of finite reserves of natural

---

1. See Statement of Chairman Robert Pitofsky and Commissioners Janet D. Steiger, Roscoe B. Starek, III, and Christine A. Varney in The Boeing Company, File No. 971-0051 (1 July, 1997).

2. In 1996, Douglas obtained orders amounting to '4 per cent of the total narrow-body and wide-body orders received in the commercial aircraft industry', and its backlog of commercial aircraft orders was $7 billion at the end of 1996, down from $7.2 billion at the end of 1995. 1996 McDonnell Douglas Corporation Annual Report 30 and 34 (Jan. 1977). Although the six months since the December 1996 announcement of the merger with Boeing may not be representative (because one would expect customers to be chary of placing orders for future delivery given the uncertainty about the business), Douglas has continued to seek aircraft business. See, e.g., 'Customer Interest Is Renewed as First MD-95 Takes Shape', *Flight International*, 18 June, 1997; 'Jet Leasing Takes Off in Taiwan; McDonnell To Hold 20% Stake in Venture', *Int'l Herald Tribune*, 20 June, 1997.

3. *United States* v *General Dynamics Corp.*, 415 US. 486 (1974).

4. The stringent requirements of the failing firm defense apply to test whether a firm's imminent failure would, absent the proposed transaction, cause the firm to exit the relevant market. See 1992 Horizontal Merger Guidelines 5. As I understand it, the parties to the transaction do not claim that the failing firm defense applies to this proposed transaction.

5. 15 USC 18 (barring acquisitions the effect of which 'may be substantially to lessen competition, or to tend to create a monopoly').

resources to the more indeterminate realm of managerial discretion, because of the susceptibility of the defense to self-serving statements, manipulation and strategic behavior.[6]

After reviewing the available information, I conclude that the combination in the commercial aircraft market creates a classic case for challenge in accordance with the merger guidelines, and I find reason to believe that it would violate s. 7 of the Clayton Act. What is less clear on the existing information is the availability of an adequate remedy. On that issue, it seems to me that reasonable people can disagree but, on balance, I would pursue the matter further.

NOTE: By contrast the European Commission concluded that the transaction would significantly strengthen an already dominant position in the global market for large commercial jet aircraft and should be prohibited unless significant remedies were agreed.

Commission press release IP/97/729

The Commission clears the merger between Boeing and McDonnell Douglas under conditions and obligations

Brussels, 30th July 1997

The European Commission has decided to declare the acquisition by The Boeing Company (Boeing) of the McDonnell Douglas Corporation (MDC) compatible with the common market subject to full compliance by Boeing with commitments submitted to the Commission. The Commission has found that the proposed merger leads to a significant strengthening of Boeing's already existing dominant position in the worldwide market for large commercial jet aircraft. The Commission considers that this strengthening arises from MDC's own competitive potential in large commercial jet aircraft, from the enhanced opportunity for Boeing to enter into long-term exclusive supply deals with airlines (already exemplified by those with American, Continental and Delta), and from the acquisition of MDC's defence and space activities, which latter confer advantages in the commercial aircraft sector through 'spill-over' effects in the form of R&D benefits and technology transfer.

Boeing, in the course of intensive negotiations with the Commission, has offered commitments to resolve the competition problems identified by the Commission.

These include:

— the cessation of existing and future exclusive supply deals,
— the 'ring-fencing' of MDC's commercial aircraft activities,
— the licensing of patents to other jet aircraft manufacturers,
— commitments not to abuse relationships with customers and suppliers and—a commitment to report annually to the Commission on military and civil aeronautics R&D projects benefiting from public funding.

These commitments are considered adequate to resolve the identified competition problems, and the Commission has therefore decided to declare the operation compatible with the common market subject to conditions and obligations. The Commission has reached its decision after a rigorous analysis based on EU merger control law, and in accordance with its own past practice and the jurisprudence of the European Court. The Commission expects Boeing to comply fully with its decision, in particular as regards the commitments made by Boeing to resolve the competition problems identified by the Commission. The Commission will strictly monitor Boeing's compliance with these commitments. The EU Merger Regulation allows for appropriate measures to be taken by the Commission in the event of non-compliance by Boeing.

The market for large commercial jet aircraft is world-wide and the EU is an integral and important

6. See Azcuenaga, 'New Directions in Antitrust Enforcement', remarks before NERA 12th Annual Antitrust & Trade Regulation Seminar 11–15 (4 July, 1991).

part of this world market, with a similar competitive structure. European airlines are forecast to account for almost a third of future demand over the next ten years, and Boeing and MDC's combined market share is about two thirds of the EU market.

In arriving at this decision the Commission has taken into account concerns expressed by the US Government relating to important US defence interests. The Commission took the US Government's concerns into consideration to the extent consistent with EU law, and has limited the scope of its action to the civil side of the operation, including the effects of the merger on the commercial jet aircraft market resulting from the combination of Boeing's and MDC's large defence and space interests.

After an intensive five-month investigation, the Commission has found that Boeing, a fully integrated civil and military aerospace company, already has a dominant position in the world-wide market for large commercial jet aircraft. Boeing's existing dominance stems from its very high market share (64 per cent world-wide), the size of its fleet in service (60 per cent world-wide), and the fact that it is the only manufacturer that offers a complete family of aircraft. This position cannot be challenged by potential new entrants, given the extremely high barriers to entry in this hugely capital intensive market. Boeing's dominance is further demonstrated by the recent conclusion of long-term exclusive supply deals with three of the world's leading carriers, American, Delta and Continental Airlines, who would have been unlikely to lock themselves into twenty year agreements with a supplier who did not already dominate, and seem likely to continue to dominate, the large jet aircraft market.

The most immediate reinforcement of Boeing's dominance in large commercial jet aircraft would arise through Boeing's increase in overall market share (in terms of current order backlog) from 64 per cent to 70 per cent. Moreover, Boeing could add to its already existing monopoly in the largest wide-body aircraft segment (the segment of the Boeing 747) a further monopoly in the smallest narrow-body segment.

The Commission recognises that Douglas Aircraft Company (DAC, the commercial aircraft division of MDC) has suffered a decline in its business performance in recent years (although the potential success of the MD95 has not yet been tested). This decline has been due to a level of investment which has been low relative to that of Boeing and Airbus, and seems likely to have been exacerbated by a fall in customer and investor confidence following MDC's abandonment of the MDXX program, and indeed the announcement of the proposed Boeing take-over. Nevertheless, Boeing itself has declared since that announcement that it would be able to benefit from DAC's remaining competitive potential. The acquisition of such an advantage constitutes a strengthening of a dominant position under EU law.

Another vital element in the strengthening of Boeing's dominance would result from the large increase of Boeing's customer base, from 60 per cent to 84 per cent of the current world-wide fleet in service. By ensuring preferential access to this customer base, Boeing would increase opportunities for future sales through significant leverage over existing MDC aircraft users (through customer support services for example). Closer ties with those airlines that currently use MDC aircraft would give Boeing the opportunity to better identify and influence customer needs, or to induce them to change their current MDC aircraft for Boeing models. In particular, Boeing could use this leverage to induce airlines to enter into long term exclusive deals. Boeing has already entered into exclusive agreements with airlines which are currently the first, third and fourth largest operators of MDC aircraft. Prior to these agreements, exclusivity deals of this kind had never been used in this industry. The proposed merger would further enhance Boeing's capability to enter into similar exclusive agreements in the future, and could create a knock-on effect on other large airlines which could be induced to enter into similar deals.

Although the Commission's investigation did not lead it to conclude that the proposed merger would create or strengthen dominance in the defence or space sectors, the Commission considers that Boeing's dominant position on the civil aircraft market would be significantly strengthened as a result of the addition of MDC's defence and space business. The acquisition of the world's number two defence manufacturer and leading manufacturer of military aircraft would considerably enhance Boeing's access to publicly-funded R&D and intellectual property. The large increase in Boeing's defence-related R&D would confer an increase in know-how and other general advantages as well as an increase in the benefits obtained from the transfer of military technology to commercial aircraft. The combination of Boeing's and MDC's know-how and patent portfolio would be a further element for the strengthening of Boeing's dominance. Moreover, the overall combination of both the civil and defence and space activities of the two companies would increase Boeing's bargaining power vis-à-vis suppliers, enabling Boeing to leverage its relationships with suppliers to the detriment of its competitors.

Boeing has proposed remedies, with a view to resolving the reinforcement of the dominant position resulting from the combination of the competitive potential of DAC with Boeing's dominant position, from the increased opportunity for exclusive contracts, which have a foreclosure effect on the market, and from the overall effects ('spillover') arising from military operations, in particular research and development, on large commercial jet aircraft activities. As far as the first point is concerned, the Commission's investigations revealed that no existing aircraft manufacturer was interested in acquiring DAC from Boeing, nor was it possible to find a potential entrant to the commercial jet aircraft market who might achieve entry through the acquisition of DAC. In view of the impossibility of a divestment of DAC, Boeing commits itself to maintain DAC as a separate legal entity for a period of ten years and to supply to the Commission reports, publicly available and certified by an independent auditor, on DAC's results. Moreover, Boeing proposes to limit the lever-age effect created by MDC's existing fleet, by committing itself not to link the sale of Boeing aircraft to its access to the DAC fleet in service. As far as exclusive deals are concerned, Boeing commits itself to refrain from further such deals until 2007, and not to enforce the exclusivity rights in the existing contracts.

On the overall effects, Boeing has offered to concede to competitors non-exclusive licenses for patents, together with underlying know-how, held by Boeing arising from publicly-financed R&D. Moreover, Boeing commits itself to provide to the Commission, for a period of 10 years, an annual report on 'non-classified' aeronautical projects in which it participates, and which benefit from public financing. These commitments will increase transparency of links between civil and military activities. Finally Boeing commits itself not to profit from its relationships with suppliers in order to obtain preferential treatment. This package of remedies, taken as a whole, addresses the competition problems identified by the Commission, and the Commission has therefore decided to declare the operation compatible with the common market.

In accordance with the Agreement between the European Communities and the Government of the United States of America regarding the application of their competition laws, the European Commission and the Federal Trade Commission have carried out consultations. The Commission has taken into account concerns expressed by the US Government relating to important US defence interests. The Commission took the US Government's concerns into consideration to the extent consistent with EU law, and has limited the scope of its action to the civil side of the opera-tion, including the effects of the merger on the commercial jet aircraft market resulting from the combination of Boeing's and MDC's large defence and space interests.

NOTE: Although the parties had formal recourse to the framework set out in the 1991 Agree-ment, Schaub, writing in the Competition Policy Newsletter after the affair noted that '[p]rocedures of notification and consultation and the principles of traditional and positive comity allow us to bring our respective approaches closer in cases of common interest but there exist no mechanisms for resolving conflicts in cases of substantial divergence of analysis'. Indeed the general impression in the US was that 'naked economic nationalism' predicated the EC's decision to prohibit the merger. Certainly Boeing's European rival, Airbus, enjoyed a prominent role in proceedings courtesy of the Commission—the company was allowed to question Boeing's witnesses and was even permitted to review Boeing's proposed remedial obligations before the Commission accepted them. The FTC's tolerance of the merger suggested to Commission officials that political motivations were the main concern. However, Kovacic cautions against assuming that national champion considerations shaped the decisions of the competition officials on both sides of the Atlantic and suggests that competition policy scrutiny formed the substance of the final outcome.

Kovacic, W.E., 68/3, Antitrust L. J.805 'Transatlantic Turbulence: The Boeing-McDonnell Douglas Merger and International Competition Policy'

(2001) *Antitrust Law Journal* Vol. 68 Issue 3 2001 at p. 842 (footnotes omitted)

The author advised McDonnell Douglas on the merger, which offers us a unique insight into the transaction and the issues at stake.

The competition agency leaders know that if they accept the national champion argument in one case, they will invite similar pleas in other matters and will lose their ability to resist them. Competition agencies also make a number of contentious, high-stakes enforcement decisions that contradict the interests of home country champions.

Without more revelations by insiders, we cannot confidently say why the policy officials acted as they did. Perhaps the best we can do is to evaluate the decisions by their consistency with past enforcement practice. A decision severely at odds with previous decisions of the tribunal or reviewing courts might provide a rough, initial basis for suspecting that the competition officials have embraced new decision-making criteria. An abrupt departure from a mainstream of analysis, undertaken in a politically charged environment, could suggest that the competition body bent its judgment to account for factors alien to routine antitrust analysis.

Even this is admittedly a modest test of political influence. Applying 'mainstream' antitrust principles often involves the exercise of discretion. Deciding, for example, whether a firm lacks capability to compete for future sales under the *General Dynamics* standard can require problematic assessments of the acquired firm's business prospects. In close cases, a host of unexpressed or inexpressible motives or intuitions could shape the exercise of discretion. Nevertheless, if we use obvious departures from analytical orthodoxy as a measure of motive, it is hard to find evidence of economic nationalism in the FTC or EC decisions in the *Boeing-MDC* case.

NOTE: This view is not widely shared e.g. Bishop argues that 'the actual result was a compromise making little economic sense since customers were not protected by it at all' and 'by the light of international politics it was all too easy to understand the result', Editorial [1997] ECLR 417. Another controversial EU/US dispute in the context of international mergers was GE/Honeywell. On 31 July 2001, the Commission declared the proposed merger between the US companies General Electric (GE) and Honeywell incompatible with the common market (see [2001] OJ CO74/06), despite receiving clearance from the US authorities. The decision followed a lengthy investigation, which found that the combination of the leading aircraft make with the leading avionics/engine manufacturer would create a dominant position in the relevant markets in which the companies were active. The Commission could not agree remedies with the parties and the merger was not implemented. The decision was received with horror in US political circles, including President Bush. See Burnside, A., 'Gee, Honey, I Sunk the Merger' [2002] ECLR 107 and Pflanz, M., and Caffarra, C., 'The Economics of GE/Honeywell' [2002] ECLR 115. What lessons can we draw from *Boeing/MDC* and *GE Honeywell/General Electric*? If there is no mechanism for resolving conflicts in cases of substantial divergence of analysis as noted by Schaub, what purpose do the 1991/1998 cooperation agreements serve?

B: Multilateral cooperation

Although the promotion of deeper bilateral cooperation is widely supported, bilateral agreements are limited both in scope and effect—few countries have actually concluded such agreements and those that have lack substantive rules or principles. Moreover, *Boeing/MDC* demonstrates the limitations of bilateral cooperation where key political or economic interests are at stake. Many commentators believe that the promulgation of a multilateral code is now required. See e.g. Fox, E.M., 'Toward World Antitrust and Market Access', 1997 AJIL. Assuming a code could be constructed which fora would house it? Once again the EC has been at the forefront of efforts:

Communication submitted by Sir Leon Brittan and Karl Van Miert, 'Towards an international framework of competition rules', Communication to the Council COM (96) 284

There are four alternative fora to house an international framework: the OECD, UNCTAD, the negotiation of a separate, standalone agreement, or the WTO.

The OECD has been involved in the area of international competition rules for a long time and is serviced by an independent Secretariat. It has the organisational capacity to cater for the negotiation of an agreement on international competition rules. However the OECD has three disadvantages: it does not have a track record of dealing with binding commitments and dispute settlement, it does not provide the disciplines on competition-related trade measures (which are dealt with in the WTO), and, importantly, it has a limited membership.

UNCTAD developed a full Competition Code in the 1970s which has been regularly revised. However, many of the same objections that apply to the OECD also apply to UNCTAD, i.e. the absence of a tradition of dealing with binding commitments and the lack of an overlap with competition-related trade disciplines (which are dealt with in WTO).

It may be difficult to gather the necessary political momentum in different countries for an independent, standalone agreement, and its functioning would likely have higher overhead costs.

The WTO is the prime candidate for a framework of competition rules: it has a near universal membership. The WTO can provide a balanced response sensitive to the varying interests and concerns of both developed and developing countries.

The WTO is the recognised institution for trade-related international economic rules. Many of its present rules are closely related to competition issues (especially those on subsidies, state enterprises and intellectual property). Some of its Agreements already have a number of specific provisions to address anticompetitive practices.

The institutional infrastructure of the WTO includes a system of transparency and surveillance through notification requirements and monitoring provisions. These are common to many WTO/GATT Agreements. The WTO also provides a forum for continuous negotiation and consultation, where its Members could bring their trade-related competition concerns. Furthermore, the Organisation has a reinforced and legalised dispute settlement system between governments. This can backup agreed rules and provide means for conflict resolution.

The WTO also caters for the possibility of negotiating an Agreement with specific disciplines between a limited number of signatories (thereby creating a so-called Plurilateral Agreement under Annex IV of the WTO Agreement).

III. An international framework of rules on competition—issues for consideration

A premise of this Communication is that the creation of an International Competition Authority, with its own powers of investigation and enforcement, is not a feasible option for the medium term. Countries would at this stage be unwilling to accept the constraints on national sovereignty and policies that such a structure would impose. The proposals set out below and in the annex therefore reflect a more modest approach, built on commitments binding governments and providing inter-governmental procedures. This is also the model on which the international trading system has been built since the Second World War.

Work on a framework of international competition rules is most likely to make headway if a progressive approach is adopted.

The objective would be to strengthen competition policy coordination in steps (building-blocks approach). This could be achieved through the creation of a working group in WTO, whereby initial work might be limited to those areas where consensus can be mustered at an early stage, and more ambitious objectives would be tackled later. The main steps can be identified as follows:

(a) Adoption of domestic competition structures
A first step could be taken by WTO Members committing themselves individually to assuring the existence of domestic competition structures. The core elements of such a structure would be:

— having basic competition rules in domestic laws to address anti-competitive practices, covering restrictive agreements of companies, abuse of dominant position, and mergers;
— having or creating domestic enforcement structures to guarantee an effective implementation of those rules, including proper investigatory instruments and appropriate sanctions;
— ensuring access for private parties to the domestic enforcement authorities, including national courts, on equitable, transparent and non-discriminatory terms.

(b) Adoption of common rules
In parallel WTO Members could seek to identify a core of common principles, and work towards their adoption at international level. This would:

— promote equal conditions of competition world-wide;
— facilitate closer cooperation between competition authorities and pave the way for the coordination of international enforcement activity;
— promote a gradual convergence of competition laws.

Common principles or rules can be developed progressively and step by step. It may be opportune, in a first stage, to concentrate on horizontal restraints (price or output fixing or market sharing cartels, bid-rigging, group boycotts, export cartels). Work on other practices (abuse of a dominant position, certain vertical restraints such as exclusive distribution or supply agreements) could start in parallel, but may take more time.

(c) Establishment of an instrument of cooperation between competition authorities
Transparency is an essential element of a framework of competition. Provisions could be developed on notification, information exchange and cooperation between competition authorities. These could include provisions regarding cooperation procedures, for example when agencies are launching parallel investigations into the same practice. Negative and positive comity instruments could also be developed further.

(d) Dispute settlement
Apart from its natural role as a permanent forum for negotiation adapting or strengthening agreed rules and obligations, the WTO also provides a compliance mechanism to help settle disputes between governments when a country claims that agreed WTO rules have been breached. Private parties do not have access to the WTO's dispute settlement system. The WTO mechanisms could be applied if a country for example fails to set up a domestic competition structure or if it fails to react in a specific case to a request for enforcement action lodged by another WTO Member. The relevant rules could be adapted, if necessary, to the specificities of competition law and policy, and could be applied in a progressive way.

IV. Related issues

(a) Who should participate?

An international agreement on competition rules would bring benefits to all nations of the trading community. All countries could participate in an agreement to incorporate competition law provisions in their domestic laws.

At the same time the application of the cooperation and enforcement provisions would require, of participating countries, that they have a sophisticated administration capable of handling sensitive information and of assessing commercial practices in a dynamic context. Many developing countries do not yet have this administrative machinery.

It is therefore realistic to expect that, if adopted, cooperation provisions of a competition agreement would, in a first stage, apply only between a limited number of signatories with mature antitrust agencies. Provisions could group together developed and advanced developing countries to start with, and gradually come to include more countries. Any country able to shoulder the obligations of the agreement could be eligible to participate. A different intensity of cooperation, for example in the field of information exchange, could apply between different countries.

(b) The interest of developing countries

Private anticompetitive practices have long been a concern for developing countries. As the turnover of many multinationals has come to surpass the GDP of middle size developing countries, developing countries have seen a growing need for a minimum of discipline on private conduct in their markets. It was in response to this that UNCTAD developed its competition Code in 1980. It would certainly be consistent with this stance for developing countries to support a further strengthening of international rules, certainly if these would come to cover practices, such as export cartels, that today escape effective control.

Even if developing countries might not, in a first stage, participate in the provisions on cooperation between competition authorities (see under IIIa, above), they would be beneficiaries of enhanced control over anticompetitive practices with an international dimension. They would also, like other WTO Members, have access to the dispute settlement provisions if agreed basic rules and enforcement structures had not been properly implemented by other countries. Moreover, they would benefit from the acceptance by developed or newly industrialised countries of MFN obligations in the competition field, even if their own obligations were lighter (e.g. in respect of transitional periods). Finally, all WTO Members, including developing countries, would benefit from possible dispute settlement judgments which might create new market access opportunities.

Insofar as competition rules can ensure that investments are made under sound and fair conditions, effective competition structures can support liberal investment regimes.

The establishment of appropriate competition structures is a complex task and requires substantial resources and training. A framework on competition should include provisions on technical assistance for those countries requesting it.

(c) The relation to trade defence instruments

The relation between the elaboration of a competition framework and the functioning of existing trade instruments is a key issue in the trade-competition debate. It is true that the incorporation of competition provisions into trade law and/or more comprehensive and effective enforcement of competition policies through increased international cooperation, would lessen the need to have recourse to instruments of commercial defence. However, competition instruments cannot be seen as substitutes for trade instruments. The latter only lose their raison d'être in the context of fully integrated markets. A framework of competition rules would, therefore, complement present trade law and create a new instrument to tackle anticompetitive behaviour in markets which are not integrated. Thus the development of new instruments would complement, not supplant, present instruments.

NOTE: The reference to trade and competition policy in the last paragraph. There is a plethora of literature which discusses the interaction between trade and competition norms and the issue is worthy of a book in its own right. See e.g. Tarullo, D.K., 'Norms and Institutions in Global Competition Policy', 3 AJIL 478. In an earlier article Tarullo discusses the merits of a competition code housed under the auspices of the WTO.

Tarullo, D., 'Competition Policy for Global Markets'
(1999) *Journal of International Economic Law* Vol. 2 number 3, 445

In deciding how to proceed, two questions are key: first, to what degree will international competition be treated as a trade policy issue and negotiated within the WTO? Second, should international competition issues be addressed through creation of a new code or arrangement, as opposed to through successive initiatives that build on existing arrangements?

The importance of the first question arises from the fact that trade and competition authorities have different, often very different, perspectives on the same economic activities. Trade negotiators tend to pursue the interests of companies from their countries, rather than the competitive markets and consumer interests generally pursued by competition enforcers. While these goals are frequently complementary, they can sometimes conflict. Moreover, the trade policy approach tends to pit nation against nation, with one complaining on behalf of its producers and the other defending on behalf of its own producers. There is, of course, nothing wrong with this approach in and of itself. But the trade agreements approach that has evolved in the WTO does not create frameworks for governments to achieve their shared interest in regulating private international economic activities.

An alternative approach, already pursued by competition authorities to some degree, is for nations to undertake collective efforts to protect their consumers from private anti-competitive conduct that crosses national boundaries. Rather than acting as surrogates for private market actors, national regulatory officials organize themselves to achieve the shared end of controlling anti-competitive activities by private market actors. This strategy of regulatory coordination has its own limitations, including inaction on market access problems whose competition implications are not agreed among national antitrust authorities. An instinct to preserve cooperation with their counterparts on key enforcement issues may lead national authorities to avoid pushing too hard on what they regard as peripheral market access concerns.

An important consideration in answering this question is that conflict between trade and competition aims and processes may be inevitable in practice, even if it can be avoided in theory. As a result, governments and their constituencies may need to choose between these priorities in fashioning international responses to competition problems.

FURTHER READING

Volume 2, Number 3 of the Journal of International Economic Law, 1999 contains a symposium of articles on competition policy in a global economy.

See also Nicolaides, P., 'Competition Policy in the Process of Economic Integration' (1997) World Competition, Vol. 21/1, 117.

NOTE: A further potential, although controversial, way of improving international cooperation in antitrust matters is to conclude 'second generation' agreements which make it possible to share confidential information and use compulsory process on behalf of the other party.

The US, traditionally a staunch opponent of multilateral cooperation, has finally accepted that the time has come for a multilateral initiative to complement bilateral cooperation and facilitate convergence. Again developments in this area of international competition policy are too lengthy to speak of in any detail here, but mention must be made of a recent initiative launched in October 2001 which is the focus of current attention. Officials from the world's leading antitrust authorities announced the formation of the International Competition Network (ICN) in New York. The ICN is the first international body to have the full support of the antitrust agencies and will be devoted exclusively to competition law enforcement. According to the Memorandum on the Establishment and Operation of the International Competition Network, the ICN will be 'a project-orientated, consensus-based informal network of antitrust agencies from developed and developing countries'. This is a welcome development in international antitrust cooperation and will enhance convergence between competition authorities although regrettably the ICN will not exercise any rule-making function. Moreover, where the ICN reaches consensus on recommendations arising from the various projects, it will be left to the individual antitrust agencies to decide whether and how to implement the recommendations, which suggests that it is little more than a 'talking-shop'. For a fuller discussion of this initiative see e.g. Murphy, G., 'Responding to the Challenges of a Globalised Marketplace' [2002] ECLR 227. The ICN's first project will focus on substantive and procedural issues arising from the proliferation of merger regimes.

QUESTION

While markets are increasingly global, competition law is national or regional.

Discuss.

FURTHER READING

Reynolds, R., Sicilian, J., and Wellman, P., 'The Extraterritorial Application of the US Antitrust Laws to Criminal Conspiracies', [1998] ECLR 151.

INDEX